The Long March

The Long March
Xenophon and the Ten Thousand

EDITED BY
ROBIN LANE FOX

Yale University Press
NEW HAVEN AND LONDON

Copyright © 2004 by Yale University

All rights reserved. This book may not be reproduced in whole or in part, in any form (beyond that copying permitted by Sections 107 and 108 of the U.S. Copyright Law and except by reviewers for the public press), without written permission from the publishers.

For information about this and other Yale University Press publications, please contact:
U.S. Office: sales.press@yale.edu   yalebooks.com
Europe Office: sales@yaleup.co.uk   www.yalebooks.co.uk

Set in Minion by SNP Best-set Typesetter Ltd, Hong Kong
Printed in Great Britain by CPI, Bath

Library of Congress Cataloging-in-Publication Data
   The long march: Xenophon and the ten thousand/edited by Robin Lane Fox.—1st ed.
     p. cm.
   Includes bibliographical references and index.
   ISBN 0-300-10403-0 (alk. paper)
   1. Xenophon. Anabasis. 2. Greece—History—Expedition of Cyrus, 401 B.C.—Historiography. 3. Iran—History—To 640—Historiography. 4. Cyrus, the Younger, d. 401 B.C. I. Lane Fox, Robin, 1946–
    PA4494.A7L66 2004   935′.05′092—dc22   2004012259

A catalogue record for this book is available from the British Library

Fessus ut exsultat miles qui rursus ab alto
Lucida ridentis conspicit ora maris,
Sic oculis lustrans laeteris, amice, libellum,
Quo breviter longum nos renovamus iter.

L. V. P.

Contents

	List of Illustrations	ix
	Preface	x
	Introduction ROBIN LANE FOX	1
1.	When, How and Why did Xenophon Write the Anabasis? GEORGE CAWKWELL	47
2.	One Anabasis or Two? P. J. STYLIANOU	68
3.	Xenophon's Dangerous Liaisons THOMAS BRAUN	97
4.	One Man's Piety: The Religious Dimension of the Anabasis ROBERT PARKER	131
5.	The Persian Empire CHRISTOPHER TUPLIN	154
6.	Sex, Gender and the Other in Xenophon's Anabasis ROBIN LANE FOX	184
7.	Xenophon's Ten Thousand as a Fighting Force MICHAEL WHITBY	215
8.	'This was Decided' (edoxe tauta): The Army as polis in Xenophon's Anabasis – and Elsewhere SIMON HORNBLOWER	243

9.	*The Ambitions of a Mercenary* JAMES ROY	264
10.	*Exchange as Entrapment: Mercenary Xenophon?* V. AZOULAY	289
11.	*Panhellenism and Self-Presentation: Xenophon's Speeches* TIM ROOD	305
12.	*You Can't Go Home Again: Displacement and Identity in Xenophon's* Anabasis JOHN MA	330

Contributors   346
Index   348

Illustrations

Maps

1. The itinerary of Cyrus and the Ten Thousand   *page xii*
2. Map of Northern Pontius (*Anab.* 4.6.4–4.8.22)   25

Plates

1. The springs of the Marsyas River. Courtesy of Valerio Manfredi
2. The Cilician Gates. Courtesy of Valerio Manfredi
3. A tell near the River Chalus. Courtesy of Valerio Manfredi
4. 'A big settlement named Corsote', near Bashirie. Courtesy of Valerio Manfredi
5. The probable site of the Battle of Cunaxa. Courtesy of Valerio Manfredi
6. Ancient Nimrud. Courtesy of Valerio Manfredi
7. The ford at the Centrites River. Courtesy of Valerio Manfredi
8. The 'villages of the bonfires'. Courtesy of Valerio Manfredi
9. The Black Sea, seen above Boztepe. Courtesy of Tim Mitford
10. The peninsula of Calpe. Courtesy of Valerio Manfredi
11. Rhododendron luteum. Courtesy of Patricia Daunt
12. The Great Bustard (*Otis tarda*). Courtesy of rspb-images.com. Photograph by Carlos Sanchez
13. An Athenian red-figure lekythos, with a female pyrrhic dancer. Courtesy of the Iziko Museums of Cape Town. Photograph by Cecil Kortjie
14. A rolling from a cylinder seal of the Greco-Persian class. Rosen Collection, New York

Preface

Xenophon's *Anabasis* is the story of his 'long march' with fellow Greek mercenary soldiers through parts of the western Persian Empire and Thrace between spring 401 BC and spring 399 BC. It is a classic account of an army in action and on the move, but it is also full of incidental interest for anyone who is curious about the ancient Greeks and about Xenophon's artful way of writing. It has been well described as both a 'mine and a minefield'.[1]

The essays in this book originate from a seminar which I organized at Oxford University during October and November 2001. Seven of them were delivered to audiences on Tuesday afternoons in New College and three others (by Braun, Stylianou and myself) were then volunteered by participants. Two (Whitby and Azoulay) were added at my request by non-participants. The eighth contribution to our seminar was a topographic study, excellently illustrated, by Valerio Manfredi. It is represented here by a selection of his personal photographs of Xenophon's route, by frequent references to his published topographical study (copies of which he donated to Oxford), and by my introduction's engagement with his important theory of an identifiable gap in Xenophon's chronology of the march.

If a set of silver bowls and cups had been found in 2001 in, say, Eastern Turkey, decorated with captioned scenes of Xenophon and his officers in action, there would have been newspaper features, a televised documentary ('Discovering the Ten Thousand') and big crowds to see the objects, 'of uncertain provenance', on display in a major American museum. The Anabasis would for a while have been the talk of the town, and yet when the shock of the new subsided, litigation ceased, and the objects returned as 'heritage' to a new museum in Erzerum, they would have taught us only a fraction of what the slumbering Greek text of the *Anabasis* had already been offering us for cen-

---

1. F. M. Fales, in Pierre Briant (ed.), *Dans les pas des Dix-Mille: peuples et pays du Proche-Orient vus par un grec, Pallas* 43 (Toulouse, 1995), p. 289.

turies. Xenophon's story has thousands of scenes, linked into intelligible action, but as texts become too hard to read or require a theoretical square-dance before anyone can dare to 'read' them head-on, the evidence of mute objects is exalted instead. Historians need both kinds of evidence, and have to interpret both, but the *Anabasis* has a human range, variety and cheapness (£12.99 in Greek and English) which a silver cup ($1.5 million) does not.

Readers with little or no Greek can enjoy the *Anabasis* in two excellent recent translations, the Loeb Library edition of Carleton Brownson's English and an accompanying Greek text (revised by the expert John Dillery, with a helpful introduction and notes, in 1998) or Rex Warner's *The Persian Expedition*, published in the Penguin Classics, with an excellent introductory essay and notes by George Cawkwell, in 1972. It was a particular pleasure for our seminar in 2001 that Cawkwell gave the first paper in such a personal, and penetrating, style.

As editor, I have not harmonized the opposing views which are expressed in several of the essays. The authors were aware of each other's differences, and it is for their readers to judge, if possible, between competing views on Xenophon's sources or method of work, Hellas' family tree, or the value of Diodorus' account. One underlying debt is unarguable. Without the care and scholarly vigilance of my Oxford colleague Luke Pitcher, our diverse texts would never have been harmonized into a consistent style. His accuracy, knowledge and good humour have been unfailing and essential, particularly to me. A word of thanks is also due to Dorjana Sirola, for her tireless labours at a key stage in the volume's production.

Robin Lane Fox

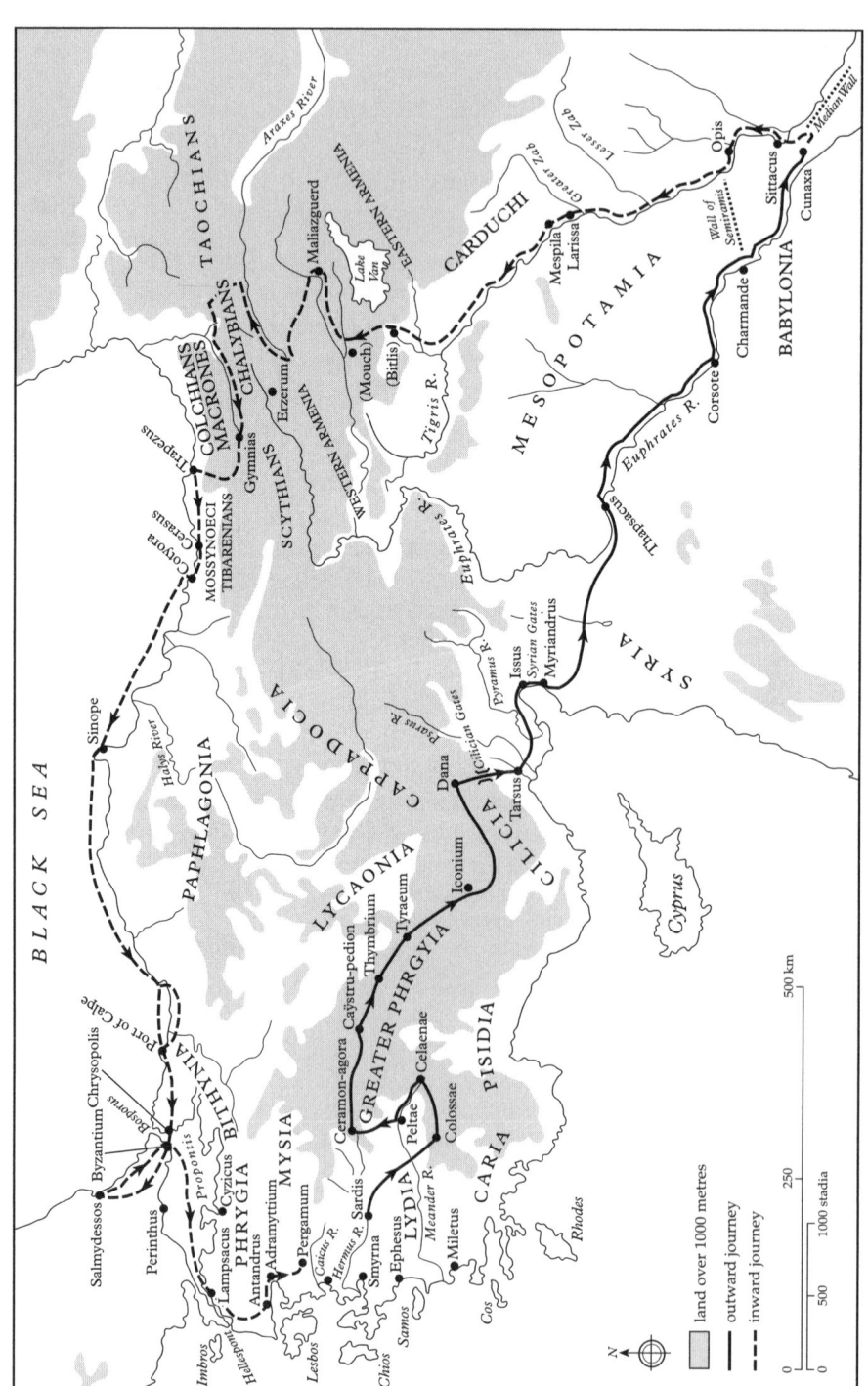

Map 1. The itinerary of Cyrus and the Ten Thousand

Introduction

ROBIN LANE FOX

I

In spring 401, Xenophon the Athenian and 'Ten Thousand' Greek mercenaries set off through western Asia on a campaign for their paymaster, the Persian prince Cyrus. The aim, as they came to realize, was to defeat Cyrus' elder brother, the ruling Persian king Artaxerxes II, and to make Cyrus the king of Persia. The purpose was fratricide, but the outcome was disaster. In Mesopotamia (modern Iraq), Cyrus the Younger was killed in September during the battle of Cunaxa. The 'Ten Thousand' Greeks then had to negotiate their return with the Persian King's generals and to make it a reality, in a very hard march northwards into Armenia and beyond, through deep snow and steep mountains during winter 401/400. In May 400, the survivors (about three-quarters of those who set out) saw the coast again near Trapezus on the southern shore of the Black Sea. Their cry of joy, 'Thalatta, Thalatta' (the Sea! the Sea!), has echoed down the ages, but another year of adventures followed, along the southern coast of the Black Sea, over into south-eastern Thrace and then back again into north-west Asia for yet more raids.

Thanks to Xenophon's book, this Greek long march has remained extremely famous. In antiquity, Alexander the Great was said (perhaps correctly) to have reminded his troops of the Ten Thousand's exploits in order to encourage them before the battle of Issus, the battle they ought to have lost in November 333.[1] Without Xenophon, it was later said (wrongly), there would have been no Alexander the Great.[2] Alexander's most useful surviving historian, Arrian, actually identified with Xenophon and wished to be known as the 'new Xenophon', sharing Xenophon's interests in hunting, war, and an Asian

---

1. Arr. *Anab.* 2.7.8, with the problem of an introductory *legetai* (which does not exclude Ptolemy or Aristobulus). 2.4.3 is surely an 'Anabasis echo' at the time, at the Cilician Gates.
2. Eunapius *V.S.* 1.1.

expedition.³ Before him, in 36 BC, Mark Antony was said to have exclaimed 'O, Ten Thousand' when he led his own suffering troops through similar terrain after a catastrophic march against the Parthians in Armenia.⁴ In 131 or 132, Arrian himself travelled overland by Xenophon's general route northwards and then went along the south coast of the Black Sea, Xenophon territory, on a voyage of inspection as a Roman provincial governor. He cited Xenophon no fewer than eight times in the little text about his journey which he dedicated to the Emperor Hadrian. He visited Trapezus (now Trebizond) where the Ten Thousand (he believed) had first seen the sea and shouted 'Thalatta'. A statue of Hadrian had been specially erected on the site.⁵

More recently, Xenophon and his story have intrigued great men of letters. In 1780, Samuel Johnson was holding forth on them most interestingly: 'he apprehended', Boswell tells us, 'that the delineation of characters in the end of the first book of the Retreat of the Ten Thousand was the first instance of the kind known' (whatever we make of the chronology, we would cite the end of the second book for most of these character sketches, not the first where the praise of Cyrus is not actually at the end).⁶

The year 1821 was of particular interest. Out in Italy, during foul January weather, Byron was detained in Bologna and took to reading Xenophon's story of the Ten Thousand, interspersing it with forays of his own. On 5 January, 'Clock struck – going out to make love. Somewhat perilous, but not disagreeable.'⁷ And then, back to finish off Xenophon's story. In April, in London, William Hazlitt had a more bland approach. He published his *Table Talk*, in which he complained that 'we have not that union in modern times of the heroic and literary character which was common among the ancients. Julius Caesar and Xenophon recorded their own acts with equal clearness of style and modesty of temper . . .'⁸ The year 1821 was also to be the final year of

---

3. P. A. Stadter, *Arrian of Nicomedia* (Chapel Hill, 1980), pp. 2–3 and index; A. B. Bosworth, *Commentary on Arrian's History of Alexander I* (Oxford, 1980), pp. 6–7; A. B. Bosworth, *Alexander and the East* (Oxford, 1996), pp. 55–6.
4. Plut. *Ant*. 45.
5. Arr. *Periplus* 1.1; 2.3; 11.1; 12.5; 13.6; 14.4; 16.3; 25.1.
6. J. Boswell, *Life of Johnson* (Oxford Standard Edition, 1969), p. 1088: followed by 'Supposing [said he] a wife to be of a studious or argumentative turn, it would be very troublesome: for instance, if a woman should continually dwell on the subject of the Arian heresy.'
7. *Works of Lord Byron, Volume V: Letters and Journals*, ed. R. E. Prothero (London 1901), pp. 152–3.
8. *The Selected Writings of William Hazlitt, Volume 6: Table Talk*, ed. Duncan Wu (London 1998), p. 96.

Introduction

the young John Keats, who had previously been sharing rooms in London with the up and coming man of affairs Charles Dilke. Dilke was extremely keen to give his son a good education, and would duly send the boy to Westminster School. In 1819 Keats had written that 'we lead very quiet lives here – Dilke is at present into Greek histories and antiquities – and talks of nothing but the electors of Westminster and the retreat of the Ten Thousand . . .'.[9] In fact, the first topographic study of Xenophon's route in Asia had appeared in the previous year. John Macdonald Kinneir, an officer of the East India Company, had diverted from his main purpose, to check India's vulnerability to western invasion, and had gone instead on his *Journey through Asia Minor, Armenia and Koordistan*. His inquiring mind and exact eye left an invaluable record, by the first of Xenophon's many British explorers on the ground, although his ideas of the route are not always ours nowadays.

The greatest of the book's admirers is Tolstoy. In 1870, having finished *War and Peace*, he turned his restless mind to learning ancient Greek and, proceeding without a formal grammar, was soon able to take on the *Anabasis*, claiming that he read the entire work (in December–January) within a week. Twenty years later, in 1891, he still remembered it and looked back on the 'very great impression' which it had left with him.[10] Tolstoy, too, had known military service near the Black Sea, and it is in times of war that the *Anabasis* comes most powerfully to mind. In spring 1941, the poet Louis MacNeice was busy in Oxford writing a radio script on the Ten Thousand, which was then broadcast by the BBC in mid April. Its story of a brave return to the sea had a special appeal to the 'Dunkirk spirit' of the British public at the time.[11] For MacNeice the text had associations from his youth: he recalls how in September 1927, on holiday from Oxford,

> I drove with my family to Connemara: my father had not been back there . . . so that all the time my reactions to the West were half my father's. That is, I was not seeing the West for the first time; I had been born there sixty years before and this was my homecoming. When we drove over a hill-top and there was the Atlantic gnashing its teeth in the distance, my father rose in his seat and shouted, 'The Sea!' And something rose inside me and shouted "The Sea! *Thalatta! Thalatta!* To hell with all the bivouacs

---

9. *The Letters of John Keats, Volume 2*, ed. Hyder E. Rollins (Harvard, 1958), p. 64.
10. C. J. G. Turner, *A Karenina Companion* (Waterloo, 1993), p. 103.
11. Jon Stallworthy, *Louis MacNeice* (London, 1995), p. 293: 'perhaps under Dodds' influence'. Compare p. 454.

in the desert: Persia can keep our dead but the endless parasangs have ended.'[12]

Recently, the text has acquired new resonances. The outline of its story was used as a framework by the New York author Sol Yurick, and was then brought to a worldwide public by the Hollywood film-maker Walter Hill. His 1979 film, *The Warriors*, was one of a cluster of 'punk' gang movies set in American big cities but it has established itself as the most lasting, with a cult status and a continuing list of revivals. In it, the *Anabasis* becomes the explicit cue for a story of brutal fighting among the gangs who operate in the five boroughs of New York. At a joint meeting of the gangs in the South Bronx, their supremo, the deliberately named Cyrus, is shot by a member of the audience after explaining that the city is there for the taking ('60,000 gang members and 20,000 cops: you dig it?'). Blame is pinned on the gang from Coney Island, the Warriors of the film's title. They have to escape the rival gangs' attempts to kill them and prevent them from forcing a safe return to the sea (Thalatta!) and their base on Coney Island. Their opponents on their journey home include face-painted Baseball Furies (whereas Xenophon met body-painted Mossynoecians) and seductive females (the Lizzies), a temptation the real Ten Thousand never encountered, except as submissive courtesans. Like Xenophon's men, the Warriors quarrel among themselves, survive their hazards, and use a high level of violence, which in their case provoked fights in cinemas when the film was first screened in 1979. Eventually, they reach the sea-shore ('when we see the Ocean, we figure we're home, we're safe') and are excused by their pursuers. This film is now the Ten Thousand's best-known legacy, and its ethics are not so far removed from behaviour discussed in this volume.

Even since 1979, the text has acquired yet another range of associations. Its account of the tough Spartan warrior Clearchus has caused him to be analysed recently as an early example of post-traumatic stress disorder, the condition that he shares (on this view) with modern combatants and allows his state of mind to be compared with the mentality of soldiers during the Vietnam War.[13] Other fighters, meanwhile, have been serving as mercenary warriors in Asia: will one of the Afghan Arabs eventually write a memoir of the 'long march' to and from Tora Bora? The Ten Thousand's march in Mesopotamia has also been overlaid by others' recent marching in Iraq. According to some

12. L. MacNeice, *The Strings are False* (London, 1965), ch. 20.
13. L. A. Tritle, *From Melos to My Lai* (London, 2000), pp. 56–79, esp. pp. 73–6.

topographers, the battle of Cunaxa occurred precisely on the site of Baghdad's Saddam Hussein airport.

For students of the classics, the *Anabasis* has one special association: it is so often the prose text from which beginners first learn to read long passages of Greek. Tolstoy was not deterred, but Xenophon has certainly suffered. If the *Anabasis* is fit for beginners, it is surely too simple for fully fledged historians. Besides, the author has been seen as rather simple too; he was much too right-wing for a generation of political historians in the 1950s and 1960s who prized a different 'long march', the road to Athenian democracy which empowered the ordinary man (as socialism, they thought, had empowered him again in their lifetime) and had thrown out the likes of Xenophon into a long and well-deserved exile. In Latin, beginners began with the works of Julius Caesar, and in Greek, they began with Xenophon's *Anabasis*. If they went on to the heights of the subject in a university, they left these foothills of their youth behind them. Cicero's letters, Thucydides, and Tacitus took over, and almost nobody would dare to crawl down to Xenophon for really serious research.

The 'clearness of style and modesty of temper' which Hazlitt naively admired continued to be questioned too. Caesar, their Latin exponent, was manifestly too self-congratulating to be convincing, even to schoolboys. Those who looked harder found downright dishonesty. One British scholar, C. E. Stevens, returned from a wartime training in propaganda, and during the 1950s and 1960s his articles and teaching combined the lessons of this experience with a fine unwillingness to give Caesar the benefit of any doubt. In the same spirit, the most recent collection of essays on the *Gallic Wars* is entitled *Julius Caesar as Artful Reporter*, and even his 'clearness of style' is now seen to be part of his artful spin.[14] On the Greek side, Xenophon the 'artful reporter' has been most familiar from his *Hellenica*, or 'Greek affairs', whose narrative went down to 362. This work's favour for Sparta and its willingness to omit large and unpleasant facts have long been notorious. A similar tendency has been suspected in the *Anabasis*: our book amplifies it and presents an artful Xenophon, not a simple Xenophon.

How do we best expose the artfulness of an artful reporter? One way is to try to expose him from the evidence of his own text, as if he has not consistently covered his own tracks. The fourth section of my introduction is an example of this approach. Another way is to set other evidence against his own.

---

14. Kathryn Welch and Anton Powell (eds), *Julius Caesar as Artful Reporter* (Swansea, 1998), especially the essays by Lindsay Hall, pp. 11–44, and B. M. Levick, pp. 61–84.

In antiquity, two other Greeks were credited with histories which touched on events described in the *Anabasis*: Ctesias, the Persian King's court doctor, a Greek from Cnidus, and the enigmatic Sophaenetus from Arcadia. Ctesias's *Persica* is known to us only in a few quotations and abridgements, and Sophaenetus and his work are even less known than that. Instead, the main surviving narrative which we can set beside Xenophon's is given by Diodorus, the incompetent author of a 'universal history' in the late first century BC.[15] The value and sources of this narrative have been variously estimated. Essays in this volume revisit these questions again, from widely differing angles.

As the study of Greek has declined, the effect of learning it through the *Anabasis* has receded. The text now deserves to return to the centre of cultural histories of the Greeks. There is still plenty of space for it. The exploits of the Ten Thousand have escaped burial in that capacious historical sarcophagus, the revised *Cambridge Ancient History*. Its 1,077-page volume on the fourth century BC gives them only three passing mentions, and the volume on the fifth century BC omits the story of their exploits altogether. There are advantages in landing on a chronological borderline (401–399 BC). There are particular advantages, too, in living on spatial borderlines, those fascinating points of contact between different cultures. For two years, the 'Ten Thousand' met all sorts of foreign 'others', and so Xenophon presents us with impressions of many non-Greeks, whether Persians, Thracians, or strange Mossynoecians. His story also involves a wide range of Greeks, not just Greeks from Athens and Sparta, the usual 'big two' of modern historians. Xenophon presents us with a rare range of speakers (using his own words) and agents (in his own selective narrative) from the 'third Greece' elsewhere. He introduces us to people like the odious Heraclides from Maronea, the amiable Leon from Thurii, the pederastic Episthenes from Olynthus, or smooth-speaking Hecatonymus from Sinope. No other classical text has such space for Greeks 'from the margin'. In Xenophon's text, these people do not show much local and regional idiosyncrasy: refreshingly, they seem like Greeks the world over. But there is also the hand of Xenophon himself behind their presentation. He was born and bred an Athenian, though the distinctive 'Athenian-ness' of Xenophon, and its social niche, if any, remain fascinating questions. Ultimately the *Anabasis* is his.

His story of a great adventure is packed with unexpected details of life. In print and in the field, the details of its exact location are the details which continue to attract the most attention. During the 1980s, Valerio Manfredi engaged

---

15. Ctesias *FGH* 688 FF16–28; Sophaenetus *FGH* 109 FF1–4; Diod. Sic. 14.19–31.

Introduction 7

in three separate *anabaseis* to try to narrow the uncertainties about Xenophon's entire route in Asia. His book, published in 1986, is the best one-volume survey of the problems of topography and their possible solutions.[16] In 1995 a conference was held in Toulouse, 'Dans les pas des Dix Mille', and here too, questions of topography and logistics were prominent. The best of the published papers studied the army's route through Mesopotamia, not least in the light of earlier Mesopotamian evidence.[17] Since then, there have been further advances, a new candidate for the Persians' Royal Road in western Asia, a new study of Xenophon's route through the Taurus mountains, a new candidate for the site of Thapsacus where he crossed the Euphrates and above all, renewed study of the probable siting of the famous trophy which the Ten Thousand erected on first seeing the Black Sea.[18] In 2000, Tim Mitford published findings which claim to have located it exactly.

One way to exploit a text with so much latent detail is to write a commentary on it line by line. The fullest recent commentary on a particular section of the march is Jan Stronk's on the expedition's adventures in Thrace.[19] It is especially strong on places and objects, on the topography of Seuthes' Thracian sites or on the details of known 'drinking-horns', or *rhyta*, to set beside Xenophon's mentions of them. The most recent commentary on the entire text is by O. Lendle, in 1995, which also aimed to cite supporting evidence outside the text, to discuss its topography stage by stage, and to be helpful to non-academic readers too.[20]

Increasingly, commentaries remind historians that they must always check carefully on one fundamental detail: the words printed by editors as Xenophon's Greek text. Like its author, this favourite school-book is no longer a simple specimen. Its older editors usually preferred the readings found in its Paris manuscript (dating to the ninth–tenth century AD) and printed them instead of alternatives found in later, and supposedly inferior, manuscripts.

---

16. V. Manfredi, *La Strada dei Diecimila* (Milan, 1986).
17. Pierre Briant (ed.), *Dans les pas des Dix-Mille. Peuples et pays du Proche-Orient vus par un grec* [*Pallas* 43] (Toulouse, 1995); note especially F. Joannès, 'L'Itineraire des Dix-Mille en Mésopotamie et l'apport des sources cunéiformes', pp. 173–200.
18. F. Williams, 'Xenophon's Dana and the passage of Cyrus' army over the Taurus mountains', *Historia* 45 (1996), pp. 284–314; D. French, et al., 'Thapsacus and Zeugma', *Iraq* 58 (1996), pp. 123–33. A. Comfort and R. Ergec, 'Following the Euphrates in antiquity: north south routes around Zeugma', *AS* 51 (2001), pp. 19–50; T. Mitford, 'Thalatta, Thalatta: Xenophon's view of the Black Sea', *AS* 50 (2000), pp. 127–31.
19. Jan P. Stronk, *The Ten Thousand in Thrace: An Archaeological and Historical Commentary on Xenophon's Anabasis VI iii–VII* (Amsterdam, 1995).
20. O. Lendle, *Kommentar zu Xenophons Anabasis (Bücher 1–7)* (Darmstadt, 1995).

Since the 1960s, this preference has been abandoned, not least because of the increased evidence of bits of *Anabasis* text which have been preserved on much earlier papyrus.[21] They justify an eclectic approach, which judges between all readings without giving priority to the Paris manuscript which others at times contradict. This change of perspective can have major consequences. At *Anabasis* 7.8.1. we meet Euclides, a man from Phlius in the Peloponnese. He is a 'diviner', a *mantis*, whose father Cleagoras either 'painted the murals [reading *entoichia*] in the Lyceum', the well-known gymnasium in Athens, or else (as I prefer) 'wrote up the dreams [reading *enhypnia*, with more manuscripts] in the Lyceum', a more natural family origin for a seer or diviner. Where does Cleagoras belong: in a history of wall-painting and immigrant Greek artisans in late fifth-century Athens (where he would be welcome evidence) or in the history of specialized texts and 'oneiromancy', or divination by dreams, in the Athens of the sceptical Thucydides? On a fine textual question, such big choices depend.

With such details of wording come hundreds of details which serve as springboards into evidence from other sources and into unimagined snapshots of people's lives. Even when you know the main story, there are scores of such details to fasten on and enlarge during a rereading of the text. Quite suddenly, it is the last book of the *Anabasis* which gives us our single most important evidence for the circulation of books in the classical Greek world. On the Black Sea coast of eastern Thrace, beyond the so-called Delta, Xenophon describes the local Thracian shipwreckers who would plunder ships which were going up to the Black Sea and became grounded by the shallows. Among their cargo goods there were found 'many written book-rolls', evidently being carried up to Black Sea ports. This one reference lights up a whole literate world of export and import: the ships came aground at a really bleak and faraway spot, the Salmydessus which the poet Archilochus had once execrated. If texts were shipped past here in quantity, the 'literate habit' was surely widespread in the Greek world.[22]

When I first read the *Anabasis* as a historian in 1969–70, I was looking for evidence on the Persians and their empire which could be brought to bear on

---

21. A. H. R. E. Paap, *The Xenophon Papyri*, Pap. Lugd. Bat. 18 (Leiden, 1970) p. 11; J. Dillery and T. Gagos, 'P.Mich.Inv.4922: Xenophon and an unknown Christian text with an appendix of all Xenophon papyri', *ZPE* 93 (1982), pp. 87–9, with *ZPE* 99 (1993), p. 19.
22. The context tells against the view of G. L. Cawkwell, notes to *The Persian Expedition*, trans. Rex Warner (London, 1972), p. 328 n. 7: 'of course, such cargoes are likely to have been rare'.

Introduction

the context of Alexander the Great's later conquests. On the whole Xenophon disappointed me: there was so much more that he could have described but did not. But, as these essays try to show, the gains so often lie in small details which are mentioned in passing. Already in 1969 I was drawn into closer study of the 'villages of Parysatis', the Persian queen and mother of Cyrus, which the Ten Thousand found both in Syria and in Mesopotamia.[23] There was a textual problem with the first such villages: were they 'given to her for her livelihood' (reading *zōē*, with most manuscripts) or 'for her girdle' (reading *zōnē*, with overtones of underwear)? It was fascinating to discover that evidence in Babylonian cuneiform texts had been assembled to prove the existence of other properties related to Parysatis, a line of study which has now been advanced by G. Cardascia.[24] In Syria and Babylonia Queen Parysatis had villages for her personal upkeep, just as Imelda Marcos might have had them for the costs of her innumerable shoes.

Beyond the Euphrates Xenophon encountered ostriches and fat birds called '*otides*' which I learned to identify as bustards and to follow, together with the ostriches, into the late antique letters of Synesius, the hunting Christian in Libya, before encountering them myself on horseback many years later in Kenya and verifying Xenophon's perceptions of their movements.[25] In the hills just south of Trapezus there was the infamous narcotic honey, but like Xenophon's text I did not yet connect it with the region's azaleas, a fact which my Oxford history teachers had not picked up, even in the years of 'flower power'. It was first brought to my notice in 1971 by the artist Derek Hill and his memories of his travels in north Turkey with the great plantsman Patrick Synge. But the azaleas, like everything else, turned out to have a much older bibliography. In part IV, I will return to show how they are of extreme importance in catching 'artful Xenophon' about his business.

At the end of the march we then meet the émigré Iranian Asidates, who is preserved in the text with the 'towers' of his fortified residence and a remarkable quantity of slaves. This rare glimpse of social realities in the countryside

23. *Anab.* 1.4.9 (with *zoēn* in MSS C, B, A. E.); 2.4.27: compare Hdt. 2.98 and, less securely, Plat. *1Alcib.* 123B.
24. G. Cardascia, 'La Ceinture de Parysatis: une Morgengabe chez les Achéménides', in D. Charpin and F. Joannès (eds), *Marchands, diplomates et empereurs. Études sur la civilisation mésopotamienne offerts à P. Garelli* (Paris, 1991), pp. 363–9: I reject his explanation of them as 'Morgengabe'.
25. *Anab.* 1.5.2–3: Synes. *Epist.* 5; on Arabian ostrich meat for the Great King, Heraclides *FGH* 689 F2 and in Chinese travellers, P. Bernard, 'Une Statue d'Héraclès à Séleucie de Tigre', *JS* (1990), p. 49 nn. 67–9; on bustards, www.greatbustard.com, especially as an emblem in Wiltshire, England.

of Persian Asia Minor had not escaped the sharp economic eye of Rostovtzeff. It had remained, so I found, a prominent item in Russian scholarship of the 1960s on Achaemenid exploitation and economic structures.[26] Near to Asidates' seat there were even some Hyrcanian cavalry, a rare glimpse of a Persian-appointed military colony which had a direct parallel in the vulgate accounts of Alexander the Great and his first Persian battle.[27] But there were also less faraway Greeks in the story: Socrates the philosopher, and a direct echo (I later found out) of Themistocles and also descendants of the medizing Spartan Demaratus, the king who had been immortalized by Herodotus.[28] 'Does the *Anabasis* show that Xenophon was a faithful pupil of Socrates?' my Oxford colleague George Forrest liked to ask, while equally disliking both of them as anti-democratic nuisances. The lady Hellas, in *Anabasis* book 7, turned out to be a daughter (or granddaughter) of Themistocles whose Asian exile she had outlived. A cluster of medizing Greek blood-lines confronts us in books 2 and 7: there are descendants of the very Gongylus who was said to have carried the Spartan Pausanias' letter to King Xerxes, at least according to history's first 'dirty dossier'; there are also descendants of the aforementioned Demaratus, whose expatriate hymn of honour has been brilliantly identified recently by Michael Whitby.[29] Did Herodotus hear this song being sung by his fellow guests when he visited the Demaratid family in exile, some fifty years before Xenophon would meet Demaratus' descendants?

There are dozens of such thought-provoking individuals. In this volume, John Ma fastens on the déraciné Macronian peltast, and Robert Parker on the Boeotian Coiratadas, the man who kept travelling round, trying to have himself appointed to be a general. Ever since my first reading, I have tried to conjure up the horses. They include the mounts for the fifty improvised cavalrymen who were equipped with leather breastplates beyond the Greater Zab river; or the equine recipients of clever snow-boots to help them through wintry Armenia; or the horses to whom Cyrus would specially send food

---

26. M. I. Rostovtzeff, *Studien zur Geschichte des römischen Kolonates* (Leipzig, 1910), pp. 240–6; the inspiring article of Muhammed Dandamayev, 'Achaemenid Babylonia', in I. M. Diakanoff (ed.), *Ancient Mesopotamia: Socio-economic History* (Moscow, 1969), pp. 296–311, esp. pp. 301–2, is now most accessible in the volume's 1982 reprint from Schaan/Liechtenstein.
27. *Anab.* 7.8.15; Diod. Sic. 17.19.4.
28. *Anab.* 3.1.5; 7.8.8; 2.1.3; and 7.8.17.
29. M. Whitby, 'An international symposium? Ion of Chios fr. 27 and the margins of the Delian League', in E. Dabrowa (ed.), *Ancient Iran and the Mediterranean World* (Krakow, 1998), pp. 207–24.

because they carried his friends; or the Persians' horses with their protective armour on their faces and chests, many of whom withdrew to hold a hill at Cunaxa before scattering as the Greeks approached them. There is the hard-mouthed Pasakas, Cyrus' own 'rampageous horse', or Xenophon's two successive horses, the 'rather old', damaged one which he gave to the Armenian chieftain to take care of and then sacrifice to the sun god (for whom horses in Armenia were sacred), and the colt which he took in exchange, one of the spirited, small Armenian horses being reared by the thousand as tribute for the Persian king.[30]

It would be fun to experience the *Anabasis* through the eyes of the 'warrior' who knew the horses best, Lycius the Athenian, who was put in charge of the fifty improvised cavalrymen when the army passed beyond the Greater Zab. Once they were over the River Centrites, it was Lycius who led the horsemen in pursuit of the fugitive Carduchi, and who broke into their straggling baggage train and captured 'fine clothing and cups', two particularly precious types of spoil in the eyes of Greeks who plundered oriental camps. When the men at the front of the column saw the sea and started to shout 'Thalatta', it was Lycius who galloped forwards with Xenophon to see what was going on.[31] Xenophon introduces him resoundingly into the narrative by placing his name at the end of a sentence: 'Lycius son of Polystratus, an Athenian'.[32] And yet, as so often, there is more to be said. Lycius was one of three brothers, all of whom were horsemen in the later fifth century; two of them are known to us from funerary inscriptions in Attica. Their father, Polystratus, was the infamous oligarch who was twice tried in court during the political upheavals of 411 and was defended by one of his sons in our 'Lysias' Speech 20.[33] This son, a horseman, was in my view Lycius himself; he was no natural democrat; he had served in Sicily and survived, he said, to fight and plunder there after 413; he returned home, but he presumably had had to leave Athens in 404/3 for participating too keenly in the months of rule by the Thirty Tyrants.[34] Xenophon,

---

30. Ctesias *FGH* 688 F19; *Anab*. 4.5.35–6.
31. *Anab*. 3.3.20; *Anab*. 4.3.22–5 with W. K. Pritchett, *The Greek State at War: Part V* (California, 1991), pp. 174–9, and R. Lane Fox, 'Theophrastus's characters and the historian', *PCPhS* 42 (1996), pp. 127–71 at p. 145 nn. 182–4; *Anab*. 4.7.24.
32. *Anab*. 3.3.20.
33. *IG* ii^2 12499, 12658, 12969 with J. K. Davies, *Athenian Propertied Families* (Oxford, 1971), pp. 467–8; Lys. 20.4, 24–8.
34. I identify Lycius and the speaker of Lys. 20.11ff.; I confess to a darker suspicion too. Lys. 20.24–6 connects the speaker with military service for Catana in and after 413, and implies that he was an opponent of Syracuse. I doubt if anything said here is honest. At *Anab*. 1.10.14, Xenophon refers to an important cavalryman at Cunaxa, 'Lycius the

his fellow horseman, had had to leave too: the two of them, mounted warriors, had many an undemocratic memory which they could have shared, two partners in prejudice on the winter march north to the sea.

II

The Ten Thousand's march belongs in time between the great masterpiece of the elderly Sophocles (when over eighty), his *Oedipus at Colonus*, and the trial and death of Socrates. Xenophon's narrative was written long afterwards, but it is a very good read and is usually intelligible on its own terms. But it begins abruptly (not unlike his *Hellenica*) and some of the turns in the story need more explanation.

First, the Persian side of things. King Darius II had died in 405/4, probably later rather than earlier in a year running from spring to spring. His son Cyrus then went up to the court in Persia (probably in summer 404) and was said to have tried to plot against the new King, his elder brother Artaxerxes II. He was forgiven, allegedly through the pleading of his mother, Parysatis, and he then returned to his governorship in western Asia (by summer 403).[35] Here, as at court, his main rival was the more experienced satrap Tissaphernes. Their respective roles have long been a problem for historians.

Back in 413, Tissaphernes had been despatched by the then Persian King to be 'General of those "down there"' in western Asia Minor. Tissaphernes used this position, under orders, to pressurize the Greek cities of Ionia and elsewhere along the Asian coast. His exact responsibilities remain disputed, but in my view he was satrap at Sardis over Lydia, Ionia, and neighbouring territories (we do not know how many).[36] By spring 407, we do know that he had been eclipsed by Cyrus, who was still only sixteen years old but was benefiting from his mother's favour at court. Cyrus was to govern Lydia (from Sardis), Greater Phrygia, and Cappadocia, and to have a military command over 'those

Syracusan'. Could there really have been two such prominent horsemen here with the same Greek name? Is not the 'Syracusan' Xenophon's allusion (witty, perhaps, or actually true) to one and the same Lycius and his wicked western Greek escapades? *Anab.* 3.3.20 is then his formal reintroduction, now as an Athenian with his patronymic.

35. P. Briant, *From Cyrus to Alexander* (Indiana, 2002), pp. 615–27, for a general survey of evidence, D. M. Lewis, *Sparta and Persia* (Leiden, 1977), pp. 120 and 136–7; A. Andrewes, 'Two notes on Lysander', *Phoenix* 25 (1971), pp. 206–26, at pp. 206–16.
36. Thuc. 8.5.4.

who gather in the plain of Castolus'. Possibly Tissaphernes had had the same general command, but after Cyrus' appointment he was reduced to governing Caria, where he had a big property and, probably, family roots. At most, he may have governed Lycia too.[37] There was obvious scope for rivalry and jealousy, the besetting vices of Persian satraps in previous history.

After Darius II's death, some three years later, Cyrus went up to court for the accession ceremony. He was suspected of plotting at once against the new King, his brother, and it is a highly plausible story that Tissaphernes had been denouncing him.[38] But in due course, he was reinstated to his governorship at Sardis, evidently with power still over Greater Phrygia and Cappadocia. The date of his return to Sardis is disputed, but the strongest case is for summer 403. It is also disputed whether or not he had a specific governorship of Ionia along the coast of Asia Minor, with its various Greek cities. On any view, he was less burdensome to most of these Greek cities than Tissaphernes had been during the years from 413 to 408. At first, it is true, Cyrus had liaised closely with the Spartan Lysander and had gone along with Lysander's practice of installing small cliques of oligarchic supporters, the hated 'decarchies', in Greek cities along the coast between 407 and 405/4. But soon after Cyrus' return, perhaps in autumn 403, the Spartans abandoned Lysander's unpopular tactic and abolished all the decarchies: on one view, the Ionian Greek cities were then left with a pact, or treaty, agreed in 408/7 by a Spartan envoy with the Persian King.[39] If so, they were to be 'autonomous' and, arguably, exempt from unwanted garrisons.

From mid 403 onwards, Cyrus began artfully to send funds to individual Greeks who applied to him. In Thessaly, at the Hellespont, and elsewhere he developed secret links with Greek mercenary commanders who could one day be asked to repay their obligations by sending him troops for his own ends. Satraps did sometimes maintain small troops of Greek mercenaries in their satrapy, but a big mercenary army of their own was certainly frowned on by their King.[40] So Cyrus built up a foreign network on which he could call in

37. P. Debord, *L'Asie Mineure en IVème siècle 412–323 a.c.* (Paris, 1999), p. 123.
38. Plut. *Artax.* 3.
39. S. Ruzicka, 'Cyrus and Tissaphernes, 407–401 BC', *CJ* 80 (1985), pp. 204–11, sets out the evidence helpfully. Andrewes, 'Two notes on Lysander' and Lewis, *Sparta and Persia*, pp. 120–38, esp. 120–1, 122–5 and 131 n. 136, for the postulated 'treaty'; against, P. A. Cartledge, *Agesilaos* (London, 1987), pp. 189–90, with further bibliography.
40. Schol. on Demosth. 4.19; for Alexander, Diod. Sic. 17.106.2–3; Briant, *From Cyrus to Alexander*, pp. 791–2, however, is doubtful.

due course. He also knew that he had a very strong claim to official military support from the Spartans after all he had done to help them to defeat the Athenians in 405/4.

Cyrus also pursued local quarrels with his two adjoining satraps. To the north, his Lydian satrapy adjoined the satrapy of Hellespontine Phrygia, the seat of the experienced Pharnabazus. Back in spring–summer 404, according to Ephorus and Diodorus, Pharnabazus had already suspected Cyrus' intentions towards his brother, the new King.[41] There are then hints that after his return in 403 Cyrus started to dispute control of Aeolis, in the south-west sector of Pharnabazus' satrapy.[42] In the south, Cyrus' Lydia marched with Caria, the satrapy of his suspicious rival Tissaphernes. When Xenophon's story begins, the two of them are at odds over 'the Ionic cities' (*Ionikai poleis*), which had been 'given of old' to Tissaphernes. 'All of them' except Miletus had 'revolted' to Cyrus. The scope, rights, and meaning of this dispute have been much discussed.[43]

The general view is that these cities are the Ionian cities up and down the coast of Asia Minor and that they had been 'given' to Tissaphernes back in 413 when he started to harass them for tribute. But the difficulties in this view have been pointed out and when Xenophon says that they had now 'revolted' to Cyrus he appears to be meaning that until 403/2, the cities in question had been in Tissaphernes' domain. A satrapy of all Ionia and Caria, combined into one, would be odd in Persian arrangements: I have a different solution to this classic problem.

In my view, the dispute was much more localized. As in the north with Pharnabazus, so in the south with Tissaphernes, the friction was over border territory, in this case on the borders of Tissaphernes' Caria. The boundaries of his satrapy were not, in fact, defined by the River Maeander, the 'natural' frontier to us when we look at our modern maps. In reality Caria extended north beyond the river, to the Messogis hills, potentially including Magnesia and Tralles.[44] As the River Maeander hooked southwards to the coast, the border question resurfaced here too. Was Ionian Miletus in Caria? What about Ionian

---

41. Diod. Sic. 14.11.1–2.
42. Diod. Sic. 14.19.6: the appointment of Tamos to Aeolis in 401; Debord *L'Asie Mineure en IVème siècle*, pp. 123–4; on Aeolis' status, N. Sekunda, 'Itabelis and the satrapy of Mysia', (1989) *AJAH* 14 (1998), pp. 73–102, at 92–4.
43. *Anab.* 1.1.6–7; Lewis, *Sparta and Persia*, pp. 119–23.
44. L. Robert, *Documents d'Asie Mineure* (Paris, 1987), p. 44, and P. Bernard, 'Aornos bactrien et Aornos indien', *Topoi* 6 (1996), pp. 490–6.

Myus or, across the river, Priene? There is a stretch of territory here which is later specified precisely as 'Ionopolitis'.[45] When Xenophon writes of 'all the cities except Miletus', is he perhaps referring only to the Ionian cities in this border region? He uses the adjective *Ionikai* (a ktetic form, not an ethnic): strictly, we could expect it to assert their Ionic 'identity', from an outsider's viewpoint, as has been well shown for the similar ktetic *Pontikos*.[46] But as a use of the word in the *Hellenica* shows, there are other senses of 'identity' which can be relevant; they might be 'Ionic' cities, in the sense of not being Aeolic or Dorian in the totality of Greek cities in Asia Minor.[47] By itself, *Ionikos* does not require the local sense (non-Carian), but there remains the improbability that Tissaphernes had lost all Ionia to Cyrus because it 'revolted' to him. In my view, the main Ionian cities may indeed have been autonomous since 407, with the exception only of those cities in or adjoining Caria. We know that Cyrus and Tissaphernes were certainly quarrelling over Miletus, which is precisely in this border area, and here it was Cyrus (as Braun's chapter reminds us) who was supporting undemocratic exiles, whereas Tissaphernes was supporting Milesian democrats. Xenophon goes on to tell us that four thousand Greek mercenaries came to his help under Xenias the Arcadian (a proven loyalist) from 'the cities' under dispute.[48] In my view, they too were troops from the Ionic borderlands which were at risk to Tissaphernes, the 'Ionopolitis', therefore, but not all of Ionia: the rest of Ionia (on one analysis) was still protected by a pact from being garrisoned by Persian governors.

If the two satraps' quarrel was a localized friction, we can see why the King (according to Xenophon) was 'not vexed' at the expense and the troops being put into it all by his younger brother Cyrus.[49] What Xenophon does not explain is that the new King, Artaxerxes, also had bigger problems further south. From local non-Greek sources, we can deduce that there had been a revolt in the Egyptian Delta from at least 404 onwards. Xenophon does mention that Abrocomas, a Persian commander, marched up from Phoenicia while Cyrus was marching into Syria in summer 401. Abrocomas had a large army and it is an attractive guess that he had initially been sent to Phoenicia to conduct an

---

45. *SIG*[3] 633 and Milet 1.350 lines 84ff., 100–5, 149 (all *c.* 182 BC). I owe this to P. Thonemann.
46. S. Mitchell, 'In search of the Pontic community', in Alan K. Bowman et al. (eds), *Representations of Empire* (Oxford, 2002), pp. 35–64, esp. pp. 38–9.
47. *Hell.* 3.1.3–5.
48. *Anab.* 1.2.1.
49. *Anab.* 1.1.8.

invasion of the rebellious parts of Egypt.[50] When Cyrus planned his departure from Sardis in spring 401, he had, then, picked a time when the forces at his royal brother's disposal would be most conveniently split. Besides Egypt, there may also (such is our ignorance) have been other rebellions in the Empire, whose eastern history is lost to us.

Cyrus' forces included a majority of non-Greeks, troops from the western satrapies whom the fame of Xenophon and his fellow Greek marchers has rather obscured. At their peak, the Greek 'Ten Thousand' numbered 12,900, but the non-Greeks numbered at least another 17,000 (ancient Greek sources, however, alleged Cyrus had as many as 70–100,000 non-Greek troops in all). His Greeks were a varied bunch. A Spartan contingent met him in Cilicia (via Ephesus), although Xenophon obscures its official Spartan backing.[51] Spartans were particularly open to requests from proven friends of theirs, and Cyrus' recent help to them made his case to them irresistible. In the light of it, his restrained behaviour to most of the Greek cities on the Asian coast would not have been a serious factor in Sparta's decision to help him.

Others with debts in his 'favour box' included Aristippus and Clearchus. Xenophon is not explicit, but in each case we can give them more of a context. Aristippus the Thessalian was the bigger investment. In September 404, as the Peloponnesian War ended, we can trace the increasing turmoil in Thessaly which focused on the emergence of the military leader Lycophron at Pherae. The pattern would persist well into the following century: basically, Lycophron and his Pheran supporters were no friends of the established nobles elsewhere. Aristippus, suitably named, was one such noble, an Aleuad from Larissa. After Lycophron's bloody victory over Larissans and others on 3 September 404, Aristippus must have travelled off to his friend Cyrus and asked him for help, 'being hard pressed by members of the opposite faction', Larissan non-nobles, therefore, who were emboldened by Lycophron's victory. In 403/2, Cyrus gave this nobleman enough money to support four thousand mercenaries for six months. It was a big gift, with future strings.[52]

---

50. *Anab.* 1.6.5 with E. Kraeling (ed.), *The Brooklyn Museum Aramaic Papyri: New Documents of the Fifth Century BCE* (New Haven, 1953), no. 12, followed by A. E. Cowley (ed.), *Aramaic Papyri of the Fifth Century BC* (Oxford, 1957), no. 35; Briant, *From Cyrus to Alexander*, pp. 619–20.
51. *Anab.* 1.2.21, 1.4.2; Diod. Sic. 14.21.1–2; note Plut. *Moral.* 173E–F.
52. J. S. Morrison, 'Meno of Pharsalus, Polycrates, and Ismenias', *CQ* 36 (1942), pp. 57–78, is the brilliant study, still, esp. pp. 66–8; *Hell.* 2.3.4: *Anab.* 1.1.10; Diod. Sic. 14.82.5 Plat. *Men.* 70B; T. S. Brown, 'Menon of Thessaly', *Historia* 35 (1986), pp. 387–404.

In fact, the troops he funded had a rough time, as evidence outside Xenophon implies. In winter 403/2, another Thessalian nobleman, the young Menon from Pharsalus, was also down in Athens, presumably seeking help against Pherae on the grounds of his family's long-running Athenian connections. To us, Menon is immortalized at Athens in Plato's dialogue about him, with a dramatic date, therefore, of early 402. It was soon afterwards that a third noble, the Larissan Medeius (possibly an Aleuad too), was to be found holding the key point of Pharsalus with a garrison. Presumably this garrison too was being afforced by Cyrus' newly financed mercenaries.[53] Cyrus had told Aristippus not to reconcile himself with his enemies, but he can hardly have expected that such a big Thessalian conflict would pin his men down. It was so big that when he called in his debts in Thessaly in 401, only one thousand of the four thousand troops went off to him. Their leader was now Menon, not Aristippus with whom, then, Menon had been cooperating. The remaining three thousand mercenaries stayed behind, presumably to hold on to Pharsalus and other key points. They were then massacred there in such a gory battle that 'all the crows in the Peloponnese and Attica flocked to the feast'.[54] Three-quarters of Cyrus' investment was wasted.

If Thessaly was one pool muddied by Cyrus, the Hellespont was certainly another. As Braun's essay reminds us, Clearchus the Spartan had a long and unsavoury career behind him. The 'enigma' of it has also been excellently explored recently by S. R. Bassett.[55] In 408, Clearchus had alienated the Byzantines by denying supplies to their women and children, but in 403/2 he was back in the city again, before being forced to withdraw before a Spartan-led army. He actually attacked this army in the field near Selymbria. He then took refuge in Ionia, made contact with Cyrus and received funding for a mercenary army with which to fight against the 'Thracians who dwelt beyond the Chersonese and Perinthus'. Braun stresses the value of anecdotes preserved for us in Polyaenus (using Ephorus) about Clearchus' extremely dirty tricks here. No doubt Cyrus had told Clearchus, too, to keep a war going, until he himself would have need of the mercenaries. As Bassett has well emphasized, Xenophon is evasive about these manoeuvrings.

In Thrace, then, and in Thessaly, Cyrus had been promoting mercenary warriors simply for his own long-term ends. In Thessaly, they were fighting an

---

53. Morrison, 'Meno of Pharsalus, Polycrates, and Ismenias', pp. 76–7: Diod. Sic. 14.82.5.
54. Aristot. *Hist. Anim.* 618B15.
55. S. R. Bassett, 'The enigma of Clearchus', *AHB* 15 (2001), pp. 1–13, who cites the evidence, esp. Diod. Sic. 14.12.2–7.

enemy favoured by Sparta: in Thrace, the war was being led by a man whom the Spartans had exiled. Even if the Spartans knew of Cyrus' involvement with these people, it did not stop them sending help of their own to him. But the prelude to the Greek mercenaries' arrival in Cyrus' Sardis had certainly been scrappy.

For how long had Cyrus been considering a rebellion and a bid for the throne? According to Ephorus, Alcibiades had already heard through informants of Cyrus' intended rebellion and had told Pharnabazus in Hellespontine Phrygia. He had then set out personally for the Persian King in order to tell him the news. But Pharnabazus wished to break the news himself and so he sent men ahead to kill Alcibiades on his route. They surrounded him and killed him in 'a village in Phrygia', the place which other sources name as Melissa, and whose Phrygian location (far inland) is now fixed.[56] Alcibiades' murder occurred in 404 (unfortunately the timing is unclear) and if Ephorus is right, Cyrus had already had in mind a coup against his brother. It was soon after his father's death, but it is entirely likely; even Xenophon lets us know that King Artaxerxes had appointed the important person Orontas to be in Lydia beside Cyrus. At one point, Orontas had even taken over the acropolis at Sardis on Artaxerxes' orders, before Cyrus forced him back into loyal surrender. Here, too, there are early signs of tension.[57]

In spring 401, Cyrus and his assembled mercenaries set off. Gabrielli has pointed out that in the next six months or so, only 85 days out of some 180 are specified as given over to marching. The average rate was about thirty kilometres on these days and Dalby, Descat, and Gabrielli have studied the accompanying logistics.[58] On crossing the Euphrates, Cyrus chose a hard, sparse route down the far bank (in French, the 'rive gauche'): the topography has been very well discussed here by Joannès, while referring back to the precedent of the Assyrian king Tukulti Ninurta II's march in 884 BC.[59] Cyrus was now hurrying, not so much because he feared yet more revolts among his Greek troops as because he was aware that Abrocomas was on the way with a large army (presumably, the one intended originally for the attack on Egypt)

---

56. Diod. Sic. 4.11: Plat. *Alcib.* 38, and the fine study by L. Robert, *A travers l'Asie Mineure* (Paris, 1980), pp. 257–79.
57. *Anab.* 1.6.6–7.
58. A. Dalby, 'Social organization and food among the Ten Thousand', *JHS* 102 (1992), pp. 16–30; R. Descat, 'Marché et tribut: l'approvisionnement des Dix-Mille', and M. Gabrielli, 'Transport et logistique militaire dans l'Anabase', both in Briant, *Dans les pas des Dix-Mille*.
59. Joannès, 'L'Itineraire des Dix-Mille'.

and that he must try to attack his brother's forces before he and Abrocomas could unite.

Why ever did Cyrus think he could win, Cawkwell asked acutely in 1972? He had only three thousand cavalry and he was sure to be heavily outnumbered. So, later, was Alexander at Gaugamela, but unlike Cyrus he had a balanced, long-practised force with years of victory behind them. Cawkwell suggested that Cyrus had put his trust in his heavily armoured Greek mercenaries, his real ace card.[60] This analysis is very attractive. At Cunaxa, in about mid September, Xenophon describes his hero Cyrus as a warrior without any fear: he even stresses that he went into battle without a helmet, a style which the artist of the Alexander Mosaic later applied to Alexander, in that case symbolically, rather than historically.[61] 'I see the man,' Xenophon's Cyrus exclaims on spotting his brother, the King, and charges at him impetuously on the hard-mouthed horse Pasakas, but 'somebody' hit him violently under the eye with a javelin. Nonetheless, 'Cyrus and the King and their attendants' fought together and in Xenophon, Cyrus simply 'died'.[62] However, the details of his death, and the identity of his assailant became another historical battleground. Xenophon does not name anyone as responsible for it or say anything other than the one remark about the physical wound.

The variants have been studied again recently, and the most telling are those given by Ctesias, the Persian King's attending doctor.[63] Cyrus (Ctesias says) wounded the King with a spear throw which penetrated his chest and knocked him from his horse; Cyrus then shouted 'Out of the way, you wretches!' at his surrounding enemies, in Persian (the words, though, are a hexameter ending in Greek); but his head-covering, his tiara, fell off and a young Persian called Mithridates struck him with his spear on the side of his forehead beside the eye. Blood gushed out, Cyrus fell off, his horse ran off, and the bloodstained horse-blanket (the *ephippeios pilos*) fell off and was picked up by Mithridates' attendant. It then transpires that Artaxerxes sent gifts to Mithridates as his reward 'for finding and bringing to me Cyrus' horse-blanket'. A fellow Persian teased Mithridates for this noble exploit and Mithridates crossly objected to

---

60. G. L. Cawkwell, introduction to *The Persian Expedition*, p. 40.
61. One of the reasons for rejecting E. Badian, 'A note on the Alexander Mosaic', in F. B. Titchener and R. F. Morton (eds), *The Eye Expanded . . . A Festschrift for Peter Green* (Berkeley, 1999), pp. 77–92.
62. *Anab.* 1.8.26–9.
63. S. R. Bassett, 'The death of Cyrus the Younger', *CQ* 49 (1999), pp. 473–83, although pp. 480–3 are not convincing, as I will argue elsewhere.

this 'nonsense'.[64] The point here is that King Artaxerxes himself wanted to claim the credit for killing Cyrus with his own hand. By Deinon, later, he is actually said to have done so, at the third attempt.[65] In Ctesias, however, Mithridates is named for the vital wound, while an unnamed Caunian then follows up with a strike at the back of Cyrus' knee, causing him to knock his wounded head on a stone. Xenophon knew Ctesias' version but, as Bassett has brought out, shies away yet again from giving an equally detailed account of his hero's full demise. In fact, Artaxerxes' insistence on claiming the credit and cutting out Mithridates' role is a classic instance of royal 'truth' telling, exemplified in the Bisitun royal inscriptions and saying much about the humiliations of life at the Persian court for any self-respecting person.

With Cyrus dead, negotiations began over the future of his Greek mercenaries. An oath was eventually exchanged between Tissaphernes and the Greek leaders, but suspicions persisted, and there was plenty of scope for misinterpreting the Persian side's intentions.[66] Meanwhile, the great 'Wall of Media', built by Nebuchadnezzar II, was passed on the Greeks' march, and so was Opis and yet more 'villages of Parysatis'.[67] Then a treacherous slaughter of the Greek generals followed. Xenophon's text conveys the preceding atmosphere of mutual suspicion very well, but it is for us to infer the likely role of Menon the Thessalian in the outcome. He was the intimate friend of the Persian Ariaeus who had rejoined the King's side; he went regularly to talk with Tissaphernes and his associates – Xenophon is explicit about Menon's jealousy of Clearchus and when he also tells us that Menon was the one detainee to be spared, we are surely right to give him a crucial role in setting up the plot. Ctesias was explicit on the point. But Menon's immunity did not last, and this noble young Thessalian, once the impatient sparring partner with Socrates, was soon put to death on the Persian King's orders.[68]

---

64. Ctesias *FGH* 688 F20, F16, F26 with Bassett, 'The death of Cyrus the Younger', pp. 480–1.
65. Deinon *FGH* 690 F17, with R. B. Stevenson, 'Lies and invention in Deinon's *Persica*', in H. Sancisi-Weerdenburg and A. Kuhrt (eds), *Achaemenid History II* . . . (Leiden, 1987), pp. 27–35.
66. S. R. Bassett, 'Innocent victims or perjurers betrayed? The arrest of the generals in Xenophon's Anabasis', *CQ* 52 (2002), pp. 447–61.
67. R. D. Barnett, 'Xenophon and the Wall of Media', *JHS* 83 (1963), pp. 1–26, is still basic, now with H. Gasche, 'Autour des Dix-Mille: vestiges archéologiques dans les environs du "Mur de Médié"', in Briant, *Dans les pas des Dix-Mille*, pp. 201–16, esp. pp. 203–4 on possible relics of the Ten Thousand.
68. *Anab.* 2.5.31, 2.6.29: Ctesias *FGH* 688 F27, with a 'burial miracle', not unlike Sophocles' Antigone's, for Clearchus.

III

The march from Sardis to Cunaxa is the true Anabasis (the 'march up-country'): it took from spring to early September 401.[69] The march from Cunaxa up to Armenia and then on to the Black Sea coast at Trapezus is the Katabasis (the march 'down' to the coast although it was a march northwards): it took from September 401 to late May 400. At first, the murder of the Greeks' generals was followed by harassing from Tissaphernes' army, which was heading eventually back to Asia Minor. When the Greeks reached the lands of the hostile Carduchians (northern Iraq), Tissaphernes left them alone and went his own way home. No doubt he was never expecting to see these Greeks again. They would surely never survive the coming winter, the mountains, and a hostile country ahead of them.

They did survive ('Thalatta!'), and from Trapezus they began their Parabasis (a journey 'along' the southern coastline of the Black Sea). It was peppered with debates and quarrels and was partly achieved on board ship. Some of the contingent went by sea from Trapezus to Cotyora; then they all went by ship from Cotyora to Sinope and Sinope to Heraclea. From Heraclea, they went on by sea to Calpe and then crossed by sea to Chrysopolis, which was still in Asia. They then crossed over to Byzantium in Europe (autumn 400) and began a long detour overland in south-eastern Thrace. They first went to the coast just beyond Perinthus: then they looped all the way back to the 'Thracian Delta' in the most south-westerly corner of the Black Sea. They marched up its coastline to rough Salmydessus and then all the way down, overland, to Selymbria, which was once more on Thrace's coastline with the Propontis. This toing and froing in Seuthes' company spanned winter 400/399 until spring 399. They then crossed the Propontis south-westwards and re-entered Asia at Lampsacus. They hurried south through the Troad, had a good raid near Pergamum, and were finally recruited into a newly arrived Spartan army, which was now active in Aeolis and led by Thibron.

The Katabasis is the section which poses the most difficult questions of topography and an intriguing question of chronology. But the Parabasis, from book 5.3 onwards, is to my mind the most fascinating part of the entire work. Several of the essays which follow emphasize the question of Xenophon's

---

69. G. Cousin, *Kyros le Jeune en Asie Mineure* (Paris-Nancy, 1905), pp. 213 and 219, posited 6 March as the departure date from Sardis, but the Arcadian festival, forty-six days later, at *Anab.* 1.2.10 cannot be dated exactly.

apology in it; the quantity of direct speeches increases here, especially those given by Xenophon himself; the glimpses of the Mossynoecians, Seuthes and his Thracians, the various articulate 'Greeks from the margin' in Thrace or southern Pontus and expatriate Greeks near Pergamum are all extremely rewarding. Cunaxa and the cry 'Thalatta!' have dominated modern memories of Xenophon's text, but book 7, especially, is richer and more diverse.

The 'warriors' did not lose their war skills on the way back. In his recent judgemental study of Alexander and the East, Brian Bosworth has compared the pattern of fighting of the Ten Thousand with the 'dramatic contrast' of Alexander's reign. In Xenophon, he suggests, there is 'precious little record of actual fighting' and 'the campaign in Thrace was notable for its lack of military action'.[70] If 'military action' is defined only as big pitched battles, this reading is sustainable. But the Ten Thousand were constantly risking lives on dangerous raiding and on plundering parties in search of supplies. There was certainly hand-to-hand combat, though the text does not focus it on Xenophon himself.[71] In the Thracian section, these actions are still a running theme. Whereas Alexander was aiming to conquer Asia, the Ten Thousand were simply trying to survive and escape from it. Hence a difference in the scale of their fighting. But the Greeks took part, nonetheless, in a campaign in Thrace whose strategy exceeds much of Alexander's own. On it, their leader Seuthes burned villages whose main crime had been to be prosperous and not in his alliance: he burned them 'completely', not because they had resisted him, but because they would be a demonstrative lesson in terror and would make 'the others' more ready to obey him. A thousand or so captives were taken on the spot; more villages were threatened with burning; and on news of Seuthes' successes, even more Thracians came down to join his army, just as Indians poured in to serve with Alexander against other Indians who were their enemies.[72] In the narrative, Xenophon describes the burning, the raiding, and the terror tactics in sentences with Seuthes as their grammatical subject. But in a speech, he lets himself talk of how 'we', the Greeks, 'were marching wherever we wished through this land [Thrace], sacking whatever of it we wished and burning whatever we wished'.[73] By contrast, Alexander's initial entry into India was not narrated as a march of such indiscriminate devastation.

70. Bosworth, *Alexander in the East*, p. 26.
71. Anab. 7.4.14–18.
72. Anab. 7.4.1: compare 7.3.11, 7.3.48: 7.5.15; Arr. Anab. 5.20.3–6, 6.3.5.
73. Anab. 7.7.5–6.

Raiding kept the 'warriors' constantly alert, but here I only wish to touch on a few problems which puzzle unwary readers. I also aim to show once, in detail, how problems may lurk behind the text's apparently simple surface. I have chosen four types of problem: Xenophon's reticence, the accuracy (or otherwise) of his description of his route (his 'chorography'), the context of Seuthes, and lastly, the toing and froing in various Spartans' decisions about what to do with the survivors of this march. I have reserved the Katabasis' major problem of chronology until the next section, although it is crucial in recognizing what Xenophon leaves out.

First, an example of reticence or perhaps plain ignorance. In book 4.7.18 to 19, Xenophon describes how the army left the ferocious (eastern) Chalybes.

The Greeks came to the Harpasus river, which was four plethra wide [just over 120 metres]. Then they marched through the Scytheni for four stages, twenty parasangs across a plain to villages: in them, they remained for three days and acquired provisions. From there they travelled four stages, twenty parasangs to a great and prosperous inhabited city which was called Gymnias. From Gymnias, a guide promised to show them the sea within five days.

This sort of bare journey-record seems so dull that readers easily pass it over. However, it can be given an exceptional topographic interest thanks to a brilliant recent study by Paul Bernard on a parallel series of Greek explorations in this area, those conducted subsequently under Alexander the Great.[74] Typically, Xenophon's dull record of the march at this point has not been unanimously located by topographers: where exactly is this River Harpasus? Already in 1816, the acute John Macdonald Kinneir was aware of a River 'Harpa su' in this very region, to the north of the River Araxes. The similarity of name attracted him, as it later attracted Boucher, who tried to support it with further arguments.[75] This equation is not entirely impossible, because the surrounding stretch of the Ten Thousand's route remains, as we shall see, the most enigmatic. However, even the few supporters of this 'Harpa su' then accept that the troops went on northwards and came very close to the south bank of the next

---

74. P. Bernard, 'Alexandre, Menon et les mines d'or d'Armenie', in M. Amandry and S. Huster (eds), *Travaux de numismatique grecque offerts à Georges Le Rider* (London, 1999), pp. 37 64.
75. J. M. Kinneir, *Journey through Asia Minor, Armenia and Koordistan* (London, 1818), p. 491.

major river, the Coruh. This river is known in later Greek texts as the Acampsis ('unbending', from the straightness of its lower course into the Black Sea) or once, even, as the Boas (from its noisy gorges, perhaps, and also from a local Armenian name, 'Voh').[76] All recent scholars since Boucher simply identify the River Coruh itself as Xenophon's Harpasus. In my view, they are right (despite the tempting 'Harpa su'). Xenophon and the troops probably approached the Coruh up the fertile Tortum valley (the 'plain') as O. Blau first urged in 1862.[77]

The next minor uncertainty is where the army first reached the Harpasus-Coruh. To travellers going up this river's course, the first significant scatter of villages is at Ispir, but the river here is in a narrow gorge, not 'four plethra wide' and hence it must be right to make Xenophon meet it further on up its course.[78] Again, the question is not crucial, because the army evidently marched back down the Coruh's course (probably on the north bank, the 'rive gauche') in order to reach their destination, Gymnias. In view of the sequel, Gymnias is now widely (in my view, rightly) identified with the site of the important modern town of Bayburt (or if not, with sites only a shortish way to the west of it).[79] To reach Bayburt-Gymnias, the army had to go westwards on the general line of the Coruh, as every topographer agrees. What, then, Xenophon does not describe for us is the much narrower and much more cramped nature of the routes here. Above all, he says nothing of a major fact which was shown to one of Alexander the Great's officers in exactly this area, the existence of productive mines, especially the gold-mines worked near modern Ispir.[80]

Whatever season (between February and April) we assign to this march, the silence is notable. In antiquity the region around Ispir was called 'Hysparitis' or 'Sysparitis'. Unarguably, the troops were aware of this place name. At the end of the *Anabasis*, the concluding 'appendix' lists the 'rulers' through whose

---

76. Arr. *Periplus* 7.4–5; Procop. *Bell. Goth.* 8.2.6–9; Procop. *Bell. Pers.* 2.29.14; Bernard, 'Alexandre, Menon et les mines d'or', p. 86 n. 39, pointing out H. Hübschmann, 'Die altarmenischen Ortsnamen, mit Beiträge zur historischen Topographie Armeniens und einer Karte', *Indogermanische Forschungen* 16 (1904), pp. 357–9.
77. O. Blau, 'Miszellen zur alten Geographie', *Zeitschr. für allgemeine Erdkunde* n. s. 12 (1862), pp. 296–9; A. Bryer and D. Winfield, *The Byzantine Monuments and Topography of the Pontos, I* (Washington, 1985), p. 38.
78. G. Stratil-Sauer, 'From Baiburt via Ispir to Lazistan', *Geograph. Jour.* 86 (1935), pp. 402–10.
79. Lendle, *Kommentar zu Xenophons Anabasis*, pp. 272–3 with bibliography: Bryer and Winfield, *The Byzantine Monuments*, p. 35 and p. 38 n. 26 for local alternatives.
80. Bernard, 'Alexandre, Menon et les mines d'or', esp. pp. 45–6.

Map 2. Northern Pontius (Anab. 4.6.4–4.8.22)

territories the 'Ten Thousand' passed: Tiribazus (whom the main text presents as the satrap of Armenia) is listed as ruler of the Phasians and 'Hesperitae'.[81] These Phasians are not the Phasians who are known in other texts up on the further, south-eastern coast of the Black Sea: they are the Phasians in Armenia, people around the river which Xenophon and the men had called the 'Phasis', although it was later (correctly) known as the Araxes. As we shall see, this point in the march is particularly interesting for Xenophon's reticence: the 'Phasians' earn only a passing mention in his actual text. But as Bernard's study has helped us to see, the 'Hesperitae' are also extremely interesting, although the spelling of this name is a textual corruption (or an author's mistake). They are the 'Hysparitidai', or Herodotus' 'Saspares', the people who were located in exactly this section of the Harpasus (Coruh) river country where Xenophon passed through the Scytheni's plain.[82]

Topographers nowadays bring Xenophon's army to modern Ispir on the Coruh (Harpasu-Acampsis) river: there is a small burst of fertility here in the surrounding hills and a clustering of 'villages' on the strength of it. In May 1925, Stratil-Sauer penetrated the river-related route from Bayburt up to Ispir and referred to the locals' accounts of their 'fifty villages' around Ispir and also to the 'villages' on the northern bank of the Coruh river, where a 'broad open landscape' begins beyond the cramped river gorge by Ispir itself.[83] Here, indeed, could be the very 'villages' that Xenophon cites and where the troops took provisions during three days. From there, they marched in 'four days' to Gymnias. The route from Ispir west to Bayburt took Stratil-Sauer three days; in 1836, Hamilton (on horseback) took eighteen hours, although he was alone (he was following a route on the Coruh's southern bank).[84] Directly down the river valley the distance to Gymnias-Bayburt is about eighty kilometres. The Greek troops would probably keep above the narrower parts of the Coruh valley and, mostly lacking horses, they would indeed need four days for their straggling march.

In 330 (on my dating), Menon the Thessalian was 'led up' to precisely this valley at Ispir, after leaving Alexander's expedition and penetrating to this point (as Bernard has established) which was so wonderfully far from

---

81. *Anab.* 7.8.25.
82. Hdt. 7.79 with 1.104, 1.110, 3.94, 4.37, 4.40; Bernard, 'Alexandre, Menon et les mines d'or', p. 46 and nn. 75–6 (in n. 75, the reference, which he does not elaborate, should be *Anab.* 7.8.25, a text which is surely not from Sophaenetus, as he suggests).
83. Stratil-Sauer, 'From Baiburt via Ispir to Lazistan', p. 406.
84. W. J. Hamilton, *Researches in Asia Minor, Pontus and Armenia . . . I* (1842), pp. 219–32.

Alexander's own route.[85] Surely Menon had entered Armenia with his fellow Thessalian Medeius, the noble Aleuad from Larissa, the soldier, the aristocrat, the host to Alexander at the great man's final dinner party in late May in Babylon seven years later, and the co-author with Cyrsilus the Pharsalian of the book in which he, Medeius, advanced one of antiquity's most dazzling theories, that the Armenians were kinsmen of the Thessalians and direct descendants of a Thessalian ancestor.[86] Perhaps Menon began by visiting the lower Araxes with Medeius, but there were also people around who knew that inland, the gold-mines of Hysparitis at Ispir needed exploration too. Had Alexander's staff already known of these mines, or was Menon acting only on the spur of local Armenian information? Prior knowledge is not improbable. In 400, there had been Thessalians with Xenophon and his troops in this very region, Magnesians and Aenianian survivors or men like Boiscus, the Thessalian boxer.[87] Had they seen the local gold-mines in 400, talked of them to friends and family at home and kept them alive in Thessalians' minds? As Menon the Thessalian was deliberately escorted up to see them, the mines were certainly being worked in the years of the Achaemenids: here indeed was something for Xenophon's men to see and investigate.

Xenophon has recently been commended for his keen eye for local resources during his march: 'dans les pays qu'il traverse, Xenophon voit tout de suite les resources.'[88] These 'resources', admittedly, were envisaged as agricultural resources and while elaborating on them Suzanne Amigues has also credited him with a huntsman's sense, 'l'odorat du chasseur', and the detailed observations of a good naturalist.[89] But even these types of rural details are patchy in his narrative and when the 'resources' concern mineral resources, Xenophon says nothing about them. He says nothing about the local asset which later deserved such a remote detour from a member of the next Greek conquering army to march near Armenia. Why is he silent? Did Xenophon and the troops

---

85. Arr. *Anab.* 3.23.1–25.1, with the Thessalian volunteers at 3.25.4 (they must include Menon, Cyrsilus, and Medeius), is surely the correct context for the 'Délégation thessalienne en Arménie', via the mouth of the Araxes at the Caspian Sea; I cannot accept Bernard, 'Alexandre, Menon et les mines d'or', pp. 48–51, proposing a mission from Babylon in autumn 331.
86. The brilliant study of P. Bernard, 'Les Origines thessaliennes de l'Arménie vues par deux historiens thessaliens de la génération d'Alexandre', *Topoi* supp. 1 (ed. P. Briant) (1997), pp. 131–216, illumines Strabo 11.14.12–4.
87. *Anab.* 6.1.7, 5.8.23; note the Aenianians' supposed Asian connection in Strabo 11.14.14.
88. M.-C. Amouretti, *Le Pain et l'huile dans la Grèce antique* (Paris, 1986), p. 233.
89. S. Amigues, 'Végétation et cultures du Proche-Orient dans l'Anabase', in Briant, *Dans les pas des Dix-Mille*, pp. 61–78, at p. 76.

keep to the north of the River Coruh on the uplands and simply miss the goldmine in winter, along with a nearby copper mine and a silver mine further upstream?[90] It is a conspicuous silence, because in most scholars' views, the army actually paused at Ispir among the 'Saspares' and took provisions for three days. Was there something to hide: did the troops so distress the locals there that Xenophon says not a word about these people's local asset, an asset which was almost as valuable as food? For the mine-workings at Ispir are major workings when we know them in late antiquity.[91] Seventy years after Xenophon, they were a long-distance magnet for Menon: did Xenophon simply miss them (a tribute to his myopia) or were there facts here which he wished to omit (Azoulay in chapter 10 of this volume suggests that a 'mercenary' ethic of financial gain was problematic for his narrative)?

From Trapezus, in June–July 400, the army then set out on its Parabasis westwards. For many of them the first stages were spent on board ships to Cerasus, although others, Xenophon states, went by land, 'a journey of three days'. The doubts which many have expressed here are as old as modern attempts at a topography of his route. In 1818 Kinneir already wrote, 'From Cerasunt direct by sea to Trebizond it is about ninety miles and surely the road distance must be greater through so rugged a country – so that the army must have marched upwards of thirty miles a day, although the roads, to Xenophon's own account, were regarded as impassable. Can this be credited?'[92] In fact, the site of Xenophon's Cerasus was much nearer to Trapezus. The answer to this long-running 'problem' is that it was not at Gireson ('new Cerasus'), but, as Boucher first realized, just to the east of Vakfikebir, at Kireşon (Kerason) Dere. As Bryer and Winfield observe, 'this name may still reflect one of the most curious survivals on this coast', the very town where Xenophon's troops were counted in summer 400.[93]

From this Cerasus to Cotyora, from Cotyora to Sinope and Sinope to Heraclea the journey was mainly conducted by ship. Twice only Xenophon mentions a colourful 'historical' detail, though each is a mythical one to us: he refers to Cape Jason where the Argo 'is said' to have beached, and at

---

90. Stratil-Sauer, 'From Baiburt via Ispir to Lazistan', p. 406, for the northern route.
91. Procop. *Bell. Pers.* 1.15.18–19, 26–32, with Jo. Malalas, ed. Dindorf (*Corpus Scriptorum Historiae Byzantinae*, 1831), pp. 455–6, and Bernard, 'Alexandre, Menon et les mines d'or', pp. 41, 45–6, and esp. p. 59 n. 78, all fundamental now, on mines at and near Pharangion.
92. Kinneir, *Journey through Asia Minor, Armenia and Koordistan*, p. 495.
93. Bryer and Winfield, *The Byzantine Monuments*, p. 154.

Heraclea he mentions the 'Acherusian Chersonnese where Heracles is said to have descended after the dog Cerberus'.[94] In both cases, other sources confirm him. At Heraclea, the local River Acheron and the 'descent' have been located and carefully studied, although the water-pools at the bottom of the modern 'descent' prevent us from verifying Xenophon's depth of 'more than two stades'.[95] At Cape Jason, pseudo-Scylax mentions a 'Jasonion' and again, Bryer and Winfield discuss the cape's topography.[96] Neither at Heraclea nor at this cape does any surviving source mention these mythical details before Xenophon. Indeed, even after him, the 'Cape of Jason' is conspicuously absent from Apollonius' learned *Argonautica*. Xenophon's remark reads, then, like a truly local tradition, with its own non-literary genesis. In 1985, in their excellent topographic study of the region, Bryer and Winfield wondered, 'Is it perhaps possible that Cape Jason is no more than a classical rationalization of an earlier and unconnected name?', while also observing that 'the Cape itself was a religious centre of some significance'.[97] There is now an answer to this question, too. While discussing the theory of a 'Thessalian' Armenia, Paul Bernard explained the country's reported possession of 'Jasonia', or 'Jason cult-sites'; they are a Greek misunderstanding of the West Iranian word for a religious site, *ayadana/ayazana*.[98] This excellent observation can solve Bryer and Winfield's question: on the Cape, too, there had surely been an *ayazana*, a word which was misunderstood as 'Iasonia' by local Greeks. Xenophon is thus reporting a bit of mythical geography which had grown up locally and orally: surely (Greeks would infer), the Argo had also beached on the side of Jason's Cape, a place with a good natural harbour. This point too, I assume, was a local, oral tale.

But we have only to read the great modern connoisseurs of this region, Bryer and Winfield and Louis Robert, to realize how much else Xenophon has left out. On board ship, he makes no allusion to the 'land of the Amazons', which was located by the Thermodon river.[99] Instead, he cites this river and three

---

94. *Anab.* 6.2.1–2: on the force of *legetai*, T. C. W. Stinton, 'Si credere dignum est', *PCPS* 202 (1976), pp. 60–89, at p. 65 n. 15.
95. W. Hoepfner, 'Topographische Forschungen: das Acherontale bei Herakleia Pontike', *Denkschriften Akad. Wien.* 106 (1972), pp. 40–6.
96. Ps. Scylax, *Perip.* 88.
97. Bryer and Winfield, *The Byzantine Monuments*, p. 119.
98. Bernard, 'Les Origines thessaliènes', pp. 143–8, with J. Markwart, *Südarmenien und die Tigrisquellen nach griechischen und arabischen Geographen* (Vienna, 1930), pp. 531–45.
99. Robert, *A travers l'Asie Mineure*, pp. 191–201, on the Amazon country; Strabo 12.3.15–16 (from Theophanes, with Pompey); Bryer, and Winfield, *The Byzantine Monuments*, pp. 69–137.

others and Jason's Cape at a point in his narrative when the cape and three of these rivers had already been left behind by the troops on board ship. As Louis Robert has very well shown, Xenophon is roughly correct about the widths and the accessibility of three of these rivers when he mentions them in a separate context in his story.[100] Yet he had never seen them personally on land: is he, then, drawing on his notes at the time, based on details of local knowledge which he has muddled here in the wrong context? He can hardly be giving such precise details as river widths from memory, many years later. As no author is previously known to have mentioned Jason's Cape, any literary source which Xenophon used would have to be one now lost to us. In my view, his remark is all based on an item found, and misplaced, among his own notes which he had kept at the time.

For these Greek cities on the Black Sea, Xenophon's Parabasis is our best surviving source at this date. Our next glimpses of them are clustered in the siege manual of a fellow military man, the enigmatic Aeneas. Like Xenophon, this Aeneas uses a very rare word for wooden towers, *mossynes*, the key word of Xenophon's Mossynoecians.[101] Aeneas's anecdotes about Propontid and Pontic cities derive, I suggest, from his own experience in this region. It was there that he picked up this rare word first-hand (he did not cull it in isolation from Xenophon's narrative). Many consider Aeneas to be an Arcadian, a man of Stymphalus, like the Aeneas of Stymphalus who had served, and died, among the Ten Thousand on the route to the Black Sea coast.[102] But even if our later Aeneas was an Arcadian, he had (like his namesake) a real personal knowledge of this general area. Either as an Arcadian émigré or as a man from north-west Asia, he had served and travelled there in 'Parabasis country' like Xenophon's men before him.

In this area, Xenophon's story confirms the major importance of Sinope, the rapid passage of news along the network of coastal cities and the robust civic life in the region.[103] But as Tuplin's paper observes, 'a direct Persian presence is elusive' and Xenophon gives not a hint that much of this coastline and Paphlagonia might have had important relations with officers of the Persian

---

100. Robert, *A travers l'Asie Mineure*, pp. 192 and 198 on *Anab.* 5.6.9.
101. Aen. Tact. 33.3.
102. Aen. Tact. 11.10,12; 15.8; 24.3; 27.7; 28.6; 31.33–5; 40.4; on possible origins, still see L. Hunter, *Aeneas on Siegecraft* (Oxford, 1927), pp. xiv–xxvii, and H. Sauppe, *Ausgewählte Schriften* (Berlin, 1896), pp. 631–45.
103. *Anab.* 5.5.7; 5.6.21–2; 6.1.15; Christian Marek, *Pontus et Bithynia. Die römische Provinz* (Maine, 2003), p. 30, summarizes a very important inscription, not published, in which Sinope and Heraclea swear to help each other if attacked, except by the Persian king.

King. To Tuplin's argument, we can add two others which imply the potential importance of a 'Persian dimension'. In the mid fifth-century people in Heraclea are said (by Justin) to have been friendly with the Persians and hence to have refused to pay tribute to the Athenians; in 424, a small Athenian naval force was sent against them and failed.[104] From Xenophon's narrative, we would never guess that Persians had anything to do with Heracleots. In a most ingenious study, Bosworth and Wheatley have now proposed that estates, granted to Iranian nobles, also existed near the coastline of the southern Black Sea coast, perhaps near the very hinterland of Heraclea. Here, they formed the original heartland of what became the royal dynasty of Mithridates.[105] If their conjecture is right, an Iranian presence was also more important here than the passing Xenophon suggests. It did not impinge on his journey, and so he ignores it.

Similarly, he ignores the interesting past of his Thracian host, Seuthes. In due course, we learn about Seuthes' father, the diminution of his kingdom, and the relations with the Odrysian kingdom further inland. But we have to look beyond the story to infer that this greater Odrysian kingdom had fragmented with the death of its important king in about 408, and we have to look outside the *Anabasis* to recall the dealings of Xenophon's Seuthes with a highly significant figure, the Athenian Alcibiades, in the years of the kingdom's fragmentation.[106] Seuthes had already 'given' Alcibiades the very forts which, in 400/399, he then promises all over again to Xenophon. The *Anabasis* draws no connection (was Alcibiades too controversial a precedent?) but the fact would be relevant to Seuthes' Athenophile outlook.[107] Late in the Peloponnesian War, Seuthes had even offered an army to help the Athenians against the Spartans. As Braun's chapter reminds us, this offer is part of the context for Clearchus the Spartan's campaigning against Thracian enemies during 402/1. As the anecdotes preserved in Polyaenus (from Ephorus, Braun suggests) remind us all too clearly, there would be no fond memories of Spartans among Seuthes' subjects and neighbours.[108] However, Xenophon does not give us this background,

---

104. Justin 16.3.3 and Thuc. 4.75.2, with Mitchell, 'In search of the Pontic community', p. 54 n. 129.
105. A. B. Bosworth and P. V. Wheatley, 'The origins of the Pontic house', *JHS* 118 (1998), pp. 155–64.
106. Stronk, *The Ten Thousand in Thrace*, pp. 48–58 with evidence.
107. Plut. *Alcib.* 36.3; Nepos *Alcib.* 7.4; Stronk, *The Ten Thousand In Thrace*, p. 197; *Anab.* 7.5.8.
108. Polyaen. 2.2.8; compare 2.2.6.

although it could have lent force to Seuthes' exploitation of the Greeks (including Spartans) for his own ends.

Lastly, there are the perplexing roles of the various official Spartan commanders who had served up in the Hellespont since the Spartan victory over Athens in 404. To begin at the end: in spring 399 the Greek survivors crossed the Hellespont to Lampsacus, marched through the Troad, and after crossing Mount Ida, became involved in local raiding with the encouragement of the egregious Hellas, who was based at Pergamum. This part of the story has recently been praised for its 'renseignements très vivants' on the political geography of the Troad and Aeolis and its 'tableau assez précis de la Troade'.[109] In fact, Xenophon hurried the troops through the Troad to Mount Ida without any detail at all. The liveliness comes from the descriptions of the raid on Asidates' property, Hellas' involvement, and the participation of the Spartan Demaratus' descendants (which was not lukewarm: when Asidates' troops appeared to be winning, they pitched in to help the faltering Greek raiders, rather than counting the risks and joining the enemy).[110] What we can also gain from Xenophon in this area is the outline of a list of towns which were held by exiled Greek families after being granted by the King: Pergamum, Gambreium, Palaigambreium, Myrina, and Gryneium had passed to the descendants of the medizing Gongylus from Eretria, and Teuthrania and Halisarna to the descendants of medizing Demaratus.[111]

The remainder of the "Cyreans", Cyrus' Greeks, are then recruited by the Spartan commander Thibron for further action in Asia Minor. This recruitment is the final twist in a tangle of Spartan actions that need to be understood in sequence. In 401, the Spartans had sent help officially to Cyrus. In May/June 400, at Trapezus, the Spartan Chirisophus told the surviving Greeks that he was confident he could fetch ships to transport them home by appealing personally to his friend Anaxibius, the Spartan admiral. In fact, Chirisophus returned with no more than a commendation for the troops from Anaxibius and an offer of pay if they would come out of the Black Sea area.[112] It then transpired that Cleander the Spartan governor (harmost) at Byzantium might come across to meet them with triremes at Calpe on the coast of Bithynia. But when this harmost met them, he became involved in quarrels

---

109. Debord, *L'Asie Mineure au IVème siècle*, p. 238.
110. *Anab.* 7.8.18, where I disagree with Debord, *L'Asie Mineure au IVème siècle*, p. 239.
111. Debord, *L'Asie Mineure au IVème siècle*, p. 238, for this list.
112. *Anab.* 5.1.4; 6.1.16.

and slanders among the soldiers and began by threatening not just to ban them from Byzantium, but to see that they would be banned from every other Greek city, the Spartans being the dominant power now in Greece.

He then calmed down and agreed to welcome them in Byzantium, his city.[113] The army moved on to Chrysopolis (still in Asia) and once again was ordered by the top Spartan, still the admiral Anaxibius, to come promptly out of Asia and to cross to Byzantium. Anaxibius is said explicitly to be acting at this point on the demands of Pharnabazus, the Persian satrap of north-western Asia Minor, who had previously been the enemy of Cyrus. When the army did reach Byzantium, Anaxibius still wanted them to leave it as soon as possible.[114] He wanted them to go on to Cyniscus, evidently a fellow Spartan, who was in the Chersonese (also outside Asia) and who would pay them. There was then an awful skirmish and Anaxibius' suspicions were not overcome. On leaving his job, he even told Cleander's successor as Spartan harmost to sell off as slaves any of Cyrus's Greeks who were left in Byzantium. The incoming harmost, Aristarchus, actually did sell four hundred of them into slavery: Pharnabazus was still urging Aristarchus to keep the Greek troops out of Asia, with promises of reciprocal aid.[115]

There was now a major volte-face by a Spartan. The retiring admiral, the same Anaxibius, changed tack and told Xenophon to take the army across into Asia nonetheless. Xenophon does not explain why, but there is a hint that Anaxibius had felt slighted by Pharnabazus (who was dealing only with his successor) and wished to take revenge. In my view, his reasons were indeed personal, out of pique at this local event. But his successor, Aristarchus, was having none of it. When Xenophon cited Anaxibius' order, Aristarchus told him it was no longer valid and that he personally would sink anyone he might find on the sea. Instead, the Greek troops should go off to the Chersonese.[116] In fact, they went off to Seuthes, but in early spring 399, two Spartiates arrived as envoys in Thrace at Selymbria and invited the Greeks over into Asia after all. Thibron the Spartan was now campaigning officially in Asia against Tissaphernes and would like their help.[117]

Whatever was going on among the Spartans to account for these shifting loyalties and contradicting orders? Some of it was certainly driven by events

113. *Anab.* 6.2.13; 6.6.5–9.
114. *Anab.* 7.1.1–14.
115. *Anab.* 7.2.6–7; 7.2.12–13.
116. *Anab.* 7.2.7–8 and 12–13.
117. *Anab.* 7.6.1.

on the spot. They account for Cleander's hostility, for Anaxibius' increasing hostility to troops whom he had initially invited into Byzantium, and then for his departing suggestion that they should defy Pharnabazus and cross into Asia after all. Anaxibius' parting rivalry with Aristarchus is worthy of the rivalry of Persian satraps at their most touchy. But were official changes of Spartan policy also at issue, decisions voted in Sparta itself? In spring 401, the Spartans had certainly sent their help to Cyrus after an official vote. The defeat at Cunaxa made that decision look like a disaster, but how soon would the Spartans know of it at home? Questions of news and information in Greek states have been raised recently by S. Lewis, but this particular case is not one she chooses.[118] The events of mid September would surely not have reached Spartan ears before November 401, at the very earliest: by then, the navarch for the year 401/0 would already have been sent out. That navarch was Anaxibius.

On hearing from the returning Greek troops at the Black Sea, Anaxibius maintained a constant position, at least until his parting act of pique: they must come out of the Black Sea area altogether, the 'Pontos' in Xenophon's designation, and they must stay out of Asia, making themselves useful in Europe somewhere (Thrace or the Chersonese).[119] A clear division between Europe and Asia has old roots in Spartan thinking; was Anaxibius acting here on specific orders from the Spartans at home?[120] Since the news of Cunaxa, had the Spartans voted to cut links with their troops (and the rest of the Ten Thousand) while the troops were still in Asia, the King's land? Certainly they would not wish to provoke the King any more. But had official messages gone off from Sparta to Anaxibius to tell him of a new decision? It is more likely, surely, that the Spartans, like anyone else in Greece, gave the Ten Thousand no real chance of returning ever into the Greek world. Rather than acting on a new vote in his home assembly, Anaxibius may only have been sizing up the local realities when the 'Ten Thousand' turned up. He wanted to stay well in with Pharnabazus, the important Hellespontine satrap with power over the Bithynians and others along the south Pontic coast. In the light of these realities, he was well able to tell the Ten Thousand where to go without the guidance of a Spartan vote at home.

118. S. Lewis, *News and Society in the Greek Polis* (London, 1996).
119. *Anab.* 6.1.16, with Strabo 1.2.10 and S. West, '"The most marvellous of all seas": the Greek encounter with the Euxine', *G&R* 50 (2003), pp. 151–66, at pp. 157–8.
120. Cawkwell, introduction to *The Persian Expedition*, p. 46: 'When [Cyrus] failed, Sparta had to atone, which we see her doing in keeping the Ten Thousand out of the satrapy of Pharnabazus.' This 'her' and this doctrine of 'atonement' are what I am doubting.

Introduction

In spring/summer 400, however, Tissaphernes arrived back in western Asia and, as in 413, he was starting to harass the Ionic cities, this time all of them, probably all along the coast. So the Ionic cities sent envoys to Sparta and extended the threat, as if it was to all the Greek cities in Asia (*Hellanides poleis*); the Spartans voted to send help – Thibron went out and arrived up in Aeolis in spring 399 (perhaps as early as March).[121] Here, indeed, was a policy with a significant emphasis. By helping Cyrus in 401, Spartans had opposed Tissaphernes, with Asian Greek approval: in 400/399, they continued, even without Cyrus, to oppose Tissaphernes and please the Asian Greeks. In this policy, the remainder of Cyrus' Greeks could be very useful to them. Hence the two Spartan envoys were sent to Thrace to invite the Greek troops across into Asia after all.

There had not, in my view, been a double shift in Spartan policy, of which the first, after sending troops to Cyrus (401), lay in refusing to back them anywhere in Asia (summer 400 onwards), and the second (with Thibron) in welcoming them back against Tissaphernes in Asia (spring 399). Rather, the decisions of Anaxibius and Aristarchus were local decisions, interesting episodes in the grim history of Spartan governors abroad. Back home, however, there was only one big decision, the assembly's decision to send out Thibron. It has been judged 'the greatest error of policy ever made by Sparta'. In my view, it was not a volte-face, but a step further on the road which Sparta had first taken when helping Cyrus in 401. It 'saved the Ten Thousand and in due course destroyed the Spartan empire', but it was not a complete change of course.[122]

IV

After sighting the Black Sea and shouting 'Thalatta', the expedition advanced into the land of the Macronians. They then had two of their strangest encounters, one linguistic, the other narcotic. A light-armed peltast stood forward from the ranks and explained to Xenophon that he had once been a slave at Athens. 'I think', he said, 'that this is my home country: I recognize these people's language.' Restored to his roots, he spoke to the Macronians in their own tongue and helped to win their pledge of friendship.[123] The Greek troops

121. *Hell.* 3.1.3–4.
122. Cawkwell, introduction to *The Persian Expedition*, p. 46.
123. *Anab.* 4.8.4.

were then led safely against the Macronians' enemies, the neighbouring Colchians. Like Alexander the Great in India, the Ten Thousand made progress by helping peoples with their existing local enmities.

On the Colchians' boundary there was a 'big mountain', but the Greeks fought their way to the top. Then they encamped in numerous villages which had many supplies for them. 'There were many beehives there', but all who ate the honeycombs 'went out of their minds' (*aphrones*), vomited, had diarrhoea, and 'could not stand up straight'. Those who 'ate only a little were like people who were exceedingly drunk, whereas those who ate a lot were like madmen, or people dying'. There was 'great despondency', as so many people lay about the place, but 'on the next day they began to recover their wits at about the same hour' as when they had fallen sick.[124]

Contrary to modern champions of the mature product, honey has a long history of poisoning its consumers. The effect hits them if they eat it when it is in a 'green' and over-toxic state. Near to the site of this outbreak, the Mossynoecians' descendants would later leave combs of wild honey to tempt Pompey's invading soldiers. The soldiers ate it, became delirious and were easy game for their enemies.[125] Similar tactics continued to be used in later Black Sea wars, most notably against invading Russians in AD 946. This honey is so intoxicating because it is made from particular wild flowers in full fresh bloom. Although Xenophon does not specify them (did he even know?), the sources of it among the Colchian villages were bushes of wild rhododendrons, as travellers and field botanists have established. The first surviving author to name this type of plant as the culprit is the elder Pliny. By 'rhododendron' he did not, on this occasion, mean the oleander, or Nerium oleander, as even the authoritative handbook of Victor Hehn still inferred in 1912.[126] 'Mad honey' has been traced all along the Black Sea coast, on into Bithynia and across the Bosphorus into the mountain ranges of south-eastern Thrace: Pliny mentions the rhododendron while discussing the honey near Heraclea, a site which was also on Xenophon's Black Sea Parabasis. The oleander is not at all common in nature in any of these areas. Conversely, 'mad honey' is not attested in areas where the oleander is widely cultivated or naturalized. By 'rhododendron', Pliny really meant our rhododendron. The mauve-flowered Rhododendron

---

124. *Anab.* 4.8.20.
125. Strabo 12.3.18; John T. Ambrose, 'Insects in warfare', *Army* 14 (1974), pp. 33–8.
126. Plin. *H. N.* 21.77 (with 21.74's aigolethron too); S. Amigues, 'Sur l'arbre sinistre de Théophraste et de Pline', *J.S.* (1983), pp. 33–43, at p. 36; V. Hehn, *Kulturpflanzen und Haustiere in ihren Übergang aus Asien nach Griechenland*, 3rd edn (Berlin, 1911).

Introduction 37

ponticum has therefore been proposed as one source of this honey, a very vigorous plant which has overrun whole woodlands when planted in Britain. However, there is no real danger from its honey when it is worked by the bees of Surrey or Scotland. The real culprit is the yellow-flowered Rhododendron luteum. Its alternative, but botanically incorrect, name is Azalea pontica, a nickname which has contributed to confusion among non-botanical outsiders and to a belief that the mauve 'ponticum' is the culprit. The credit belongs to the yellow form: travellers have noticed that even the gusts of scent from dense natural groupings of this rhododendron have a mildly intoxicating effect. In modern Greece, they grow wild now only in mountainous areas of Lesbos.

As late as 1926, inquirers found that local residents of Xenophon's 'mad honey' zone were often unsure of its true origin. Chestnut trees or tobacco fields were still being proposed as its source, although others, when questioned, did know that rhododendrons were the culprits. In fact, the toxicologist P. C. Plugge had made a scientific analysis of the 'Trebizond honey' back in 1891 and had correctly identified its active element as what we now call 'acetyl-andromedol', a type of graynotoxin.[127] Classical scholars, meanwhile, had collected lore about this honey, most notably C. F. Lehmann-Haupt, a tradition which has continued to Adrienne Mayor and her accessible general article published in 1995. Fresh honey from flowers of the yellow rhododendron is 'green' or 'maddening'; popularly in English it has been called 'azalea honey', though azaleas are actually rhododendrons. In Turkish it is known as *deli bal*. In Turkish culture it has been used to gain a mild 'high' when mixed into alcohol. *Deli bal* has been identified as 'a major Black Sea export in the eighteenth century: 25 tons of toxic honey, known to Westerners as *miel fou*, were shipped to Europe each year to be added to drinks sold in taverns.'[128]

The Ten Thousand's encounter is not only of great botanical interest. As the botanist Georg Gassner first emphasized in 1953, it is an extremely important marker for the chronology of Xenophon's march north from Armenia to the hinterland of Trapezus and the first prospect of the sea. His arguments have since been refined and developed with force by Manfredi, but first there is neglected, comparative evidence which bears more precisely on the proposed dating.

---

127. A. Mayor, 'Mad honey', *Archaeology* 48 (1999), pp. 32–40, at p. 34.
128. C. F. Lehmann-Haupt, *Armenien Einst und Jetzt II* (Berlin, 1926), pp. 816–22; Mayor, 'Mad honey'.

In 1930, the great plant-hunter Frank Kingdon Ward travelled into northern Burma with his companion, Lord Cranbrook.[129] 'Exploration means days of boredom,' he later wrote, 'punctuated with moments of ecstasy.' For Kingdon Ward, the aim was to collect new plants in the wild, but for Cranbrook it was to kill and collect birds and wildlife. 'Cranbrook shot squirrels daily,' Kingdon Ward records, 'the ordinary squirrels . . . were not difficult to get, but the striped squirrels and the black were less easy.' Cranbrook also shot jungle fowl, deer, and monkeys; he 'collected' ninety-two species of birds and forty-five species of mammals; he trapped rats, mice, and shrews; he shot rare gorals (animals like antelopes); in February 1931, 'it was Cranbrook's busy season . . . we were trapping small nocturnal animals as well as shooting birds and he had to skin them all.' On 19 June, Kingdon Ward noted, 'I returned to camp early . . . Cranbrook had shot a blood pheasant and seemed very pleased with himself . . .' But 'nothing ruffled him. Cranbrook had the sweetest temper imaginable . . .' In November, however, 'a large family of blood-pheasants stalked into the firing line one morning and five of them were casualties in as many minutes. It seemed unkind to shoot them; they took no notice of us and Cranbrook knocked them over one after another like coconuts at a fair while they took little squawking runs this way and that, trying to disperse but not connecting their discomfiture in any way with us . . . they were distraught.'

In early May 1931, across the Burmese border with Tibet, Cranbrook had had a dose of nature's own medicine. A Tibetan headman brought 'real honey' into camp and later in the day Cranbrook set off up-river as usual with his gun. Suddenly, he collapsed, fell into the river and was only revived by the coldness of its water. He crawled back to bed, but recovered that evening, whereupon another companion fell ill, having eaten the honey too.

On the Tibetan border, rhododendrons abound and are a rich source of honey, but as Kingdon Ward verified, it was only the very fresh 'real honey' which had intoxicating properties. In 1926, K. Krause and the entomologist Dr H. Bischoff were told of a similar variation by their local Turkish informants around Trapezus and Cerasus. At some times of year the local honey is innocuous, but at others, very potent. Bees are not responsible for this variation and although the health of the consumer is a relevant factor, Krause emphasized the importance of the quantity and the age of the honey

---

129. F. Kingdon Ward, *A Plant Hunter's Paradise*, reprint (London, 1985), p. 51; pp. 46, 123, 257 for Cranbrook; pp. 110–11 for the honey.

consumed.[130] After eating fresh 'mad honey', Cranbrook suffered exactly the 'Ten Thousand syndrome' of twenty-four hours of delirious sickness. Xenophon notes that some people ate a lot, others less, and the inference is that those who ate most recovered at just about the hour when they had first fallen sick on the previous day. Like Cranbrook, therefore, they had eaten fresh honey, not a stored supply. With due allowance for the differing regions and differing varieties of rhododendron, Cranbrook and Xenophon are both witnesses to the effect of 'mad honey' if it is eaten when absolutely fresh.

In Manfredi's view, refining Gassner's, the Ten Thousand encountered beehives which were well stocked with honeycombs. As bees live through the winter on their stores of honey from the previous year, the encounter (he argues) must have occurred when new honey was being laid down and when spring, therefore, was well advanced. Manfredi combines this inference with others about the seasonal accessibility of the Zigana Pass (his preferred site in 1986 for Xenophon's 'big mountain') and the building of a trophy without accompanying problems from snowfalls. He therefore proposes that the Ten Thousand drew near to Trapezus in early May.[131] If we now add the fact that the offending 'mad honey' can only have come from absolutely fresh combs and flowers, the dating becomes even more circumscribed. But first, the topography and its problems need to be considered.

In Manfredi's view, in 1986, the highest spur of the Zigana Pass is the 'big mountain' which the Greeks climbed before camping further on in 'many villages' among the Colchians and encountering the honey.[132] The pass itself is at a height of 6,645 feet and on it, remark Bryer and Winfield, 'one is struck by the two quite distinct cultural and geographic worlds which it divides ... the endless ranges of Chaldia stretching into Armenia to the south and the dark Pontic rainlands (but never the sea itself) to the north. Small wonder that 19th century travellers ... identified it with Xenophon's Theches and dutifully added their stone to the cairns of the pass.'[133]

For the chronology, it is not too important that this identification of Mount Theches with the Zigana is disputed, being 'unjustifiable' (Bryer and Winfield) or plainly wrong (Mitford). Mitford's recent researches prefer to place the

130. K. Krause, 'Über dem giftigen Honig des Pontischen Kleinasien', *Die Naturwiss* 14 (1926), pp. 976–8.
131. Manfredi, *La Strada dei Diecimila*, pp. 211–15.
132. Ibid., pp. 225–7 with photos 35–6.
133. Bryer and Winfield, *The Byzantine Monuments*, p. 265.

Greeks' trophy and their first glimpse of the sea further east, about a mile north-west of Kalat. The choice, in fact, is between the route of the Roman Antonine Itinerary (which named Zigana as one of its stages) or the Peutinger Table's route, the route of the Hadrianic road which has now been rediscovered by Mitford (Kalat being the Peutinger Table's Bylae). For if Mitford is correct, the 'trophy' was in land of an even higher altitude, up to 8,200 feet, and yet snow was no longer a big problem to the Greek soldiers.[134] After building the trophy they passed on to the territory of the Macronians, which they traversed in either three or five to six days. For Manfredi, this territory lay on the west of their route from the Zigana, but led to the 'big mountain' which was also in the same Zigana complex. For Mitford, however, the Macronian territory began at Maçka (later known to the ancients as Dikasimon, twenty miles from Trapezus). His arguments are very attractive, even though they require that the Greeks then took five whole days over the last twenty miles to Trapezus itself. It was, on Mitford's view, after Maçka and across the Degirmendere river (known as the Pyxites to Greeks after Xenophon) that the Greeks reached the 'big mountain', perhaps after only twelve miles' advance. On the top, in Colchian territory, they encountered the villages and the mad honey, whereas Manfredi in 1986 (and the Antonine Itinerary) would locate the episode further inland and to the south-west. Certainly, the honey was found two days' marching away from Trapezus, after a steep mountainous climb, although Manfredi and Mitford disagree on the exact location.

Here, an earlier traveller (neglected by both of them) is indispensable. In 1836, William J. Hamilton reached Trebizond, only to set off again on travels into the hill ranges behind the city. On 25 May he records with his usual meticulous care how 'we started at 9 am, ascending the steep hills to the S and SSE of the town, the view of which, as we looked back, was highly picturesque. On reaching the summit of the ridge I found the yellow Azalea pontica and the purple Rhododendron in full flower, growing wild with great luxuriance, the former scenting the air with its sweet perfume...'[135] By early afternoon they left 'Jivislik' and then 'for three miles we ascended the hills, partly cultivated and partly wooded until we reached the summit of the ridge which separates the two valleys mentioned, of which that to the west is called Matchka and that to the east Moromana.' 'Matchka', the valley's destination, is

---

134. Mitford, 'Thalatta, Thalatta'.
135. Hamilton, *Researches in Asia Minor*, p. 162.

exactly Mitford's Maçka, the ancient Dikasimon where the Macronian territory began; Hamilton was just to the east of the ancient route which Xenophon most probably took, but he was certainly very close to it and on the same latitude.

Then, the world smiled on him.

> For nearly three miles our road led along the crest, through the most beautiful scenery that can be imagined and between thick woods of beech and fir, under which azaleas and rhododendrons covered with a profusion of fragrant flowers formed an impenetrable and luxuriant underwood, while the eye wandered over extensive hills and deep secluded valleys to the left, the summits of which were covered with woods while their sides were cultivated wherever it was possible. Nature appeared in one of her most fascinating garbs. As we advanced, the azaleas increased in number and in size and the whole scene rather resembled a garden or beautiful shrubbery than a mountain in its native wildness.[136]

Here, exactly on the borders of Macronian country, is one of the blossom deposits to which Colchian bees would have strayed in the year 400. Hamilton never made the point, but he was travelling right through the heartland of Xenophon's narcotic honey. On climbing higher, however, he had the impression that the

> azaleas and rhododendrons suddenly disappeared, a forest of gigantic beech-trees continuing still higher. But all vegetation had ceased, except for a few stunted sycamores before we reached the wretched hovel of Karakaban, a cold and dreary spot . . . the calculated distance being 9 hours or 21 miles from Trebizond, while the real distance is only about 20 miles SSW.

But Karakaban is exactly a place where Tim Mitford has now rediscovered 'the ancient road-bed remarkably preserved' (he does not discuss Hamilton, a predecessor).[137] Karakaban, then, is also in Macronian country, probably where the Ten Thousand passed through, with the azalea paradise just ahead of them.

---

136. Ibid., p. 164.
137. Mitford, 'Thalatta, Thalatta', p. 130.

Hamilton noted with his usual sharpness that the azaleas were to be seen on the north side of the mountains behind Trapezus, but not on the south: in 400, Xenophon had ascended his 'big mountain' from the south, before dropping down the north-facing descent and the final stages into the town. But the crucial fact is Hamilton's carefully recorded date: 25 May, when Rhododendron luteum was in full yellow bloom. In 1962, the expert Patrick Synge noted it likewise behind Cerasus in flower in the third week in May. At a greater height (where Hamilton wrongly believed it to disappear) Dr Martyn Rix recorded it in the last stages of flowering during the first week of July 1965, up on the slopes of the Zigana Pass at 5–6,000 feet.[138] Across a hundred and thirty years, the azalea's flowering season has been consistent: it is not March or April, but mid May to mid June in Colchian territory, with flowers as late as July at the higher altitudes which the Ten Thousand had attained only shortly before.[139] As Kinneir had already correctly noted, the climate of Trapezus is not a mild and early one. It has a late spring which is

138. I am very grateful to Dr Martyn Rix for this information, based on his own field notes; for the 'north slope' observation too, Hamilton, *Researches in Asia Minor*, pp. 166–7.
139. Patricia Daunt has just made me aware of her valuable study, 'The Country Houses That Ride In Storm', *Cornucopia* 12 (1997), pp. 54–73, which describes her journey to the Firtina river-valley in the Pontic region, inland through what was formerly known as the Makredin district (now Konak Lar), over the Kalkar range, past Çamli Hemçin and on down east of the two river-valleys into which the Firtina river forks, before uniting with the Coruh river, Xenophon's Harpasus (the ancient Acampsis). One river-valley leads to Yusefeli, the other to Ispir, just to the north, then, of a stage on the Ten Thousand's route. On both valleys, she observed Rhododendron luteum in full flower from 6 June, 1993 onwards, at heights between 1,500 metres and 2,000 metres.

Further west, above Inebolu (the ancient Ionopolis, or Abonouteichos of oracular fame), she had found luteum in full flower among mauve ponticum under beech and pine trees, at heights of 1,200 metres, just short of Kure 'where the lignite mines begin, west of Sinop'. There, the flowering date was 11 June, 1992. Above Inebolu, she notes, the climate is colder and drier than the hotter and wetter regions leading back to Çamli Hemçin and so the slightly later flowering season here is not surprising.

Up in the valleys of the Makredin district, the rhododendrons have established themselves freely on screes created by landslips which have destroyed the indigenous beech forests. Here, as Hamilton noticed at Makça, the yellow luteum prefers the north (east) facing scree, leaving the south (west) face to ponticum. 'The huge splashes of mauve and yellow are the sight nobody ever forgets,' she assures me, 'nor the intoxication of the scent of luteum on the wind. And when it comes to bees, they are everywhere...'

I am very grateful for these acute botanical notes whose calendar-dates confirm my argument about the march's chronology, implying dates from about 20 May to 10 June for the major flowering of yellow azaleas in Xenophon's Macronian territory, sited between her two recently observed stands of this very plant.

chilled by winds between the sea and the high hinterland. Bees on those hills' north-facing slopes would not be laying down fresh 'mad honey' from azaleas before mid to late May.[140]

The notion, previously widespread, that the Ten Thousand reached Trapezus in February–March 400 is therefore wrong. It founders on the absence of snows, which would have blocked the passes at that date, but above all it founders on the exact azalea season below Maçka. As Manfredi also observes, a later arrival date in Trapezus in late spring fits a subsequent event, the Greeks' discovery of newly harvested grain among the Mossynoecians. They encountered it after leaving Trapezus, but such grain would probably not exist before July.[141]

Among the Colchians, the fresh 'mad honey' is a mid May to early June phenomenon. If we then work backwards down Xenophon's route, we find the Greeks encountering their first snowfalls by the River Centrites as they entered into Armenia in late 401.[142] Here, snow regularly begins in late November, or at most, early December. From the encounter with this snow until the meeting with 'mad honey', Xenophon specifies 'stages' along the route, and if we assume each is a day's march and add more for the sporadic fighting and resting in the narrative, we end up with about seventy stages, or ten weeks.[143] On the evidence, then, of the narrative and nothing else, the Greeks should have reached the honey and the Colchian villages by mid February. In fact, they did not reach them until mid May or early June. At least three months of the story have therefore dropped out of Xenophon's account.

In Manfredi's view, there were probably awkward facts in these months which Xenophon, with hindsight, preferred to omit. He points to problems which have been much discussed in connection with the troops' arrival at the River Phasis: where did they then go and for how long? In 1818, the first 'Xenophon topographer', Kinneir, had also suspected a gap in what Xenophon

---

140. G. Gassner, 'Der Zug der Zehntausend nach Trapezus', *Abh. der Braunschweig. Wiss. Gesell.* 5 (1953), pp. 1–35, esp. pp. 6–7 showing Rhododendron luteum in flower south of Trapezus at a height of only 200 metres on 1 May 1935. At 1,190 metres, H. Grothe, *Auf Türkischer Erde* (Berlin, 1903), found it full out in early June.
141. Manfredi, *La Strada dei Diecimila*, pp. 233–4 and n. 453; Amigues, 'Sur l'arbre sinistre de Théophraste', p. 73, on this *zeia* wheat, 'blé amidonnier'.
142. *Anab.* 4.4.8.
143. Between *Anab.* 4.4.8 and 4.8.20, Xenophon allows us to count about sixty days/stages; arguably, 4.6.1 shows that the narrative of 4.5.23–4.6 only occupies this one week. I have allowed another ten days, in all, to be generous, to cover bits like 4.7. But we hardly need more.

describes in this area of the march: for him, the gap happens on the way up to the Phasis and is proved by Xenophon's discrepant markers of distance: 'quite irreconcilable unless we suppose that they were properly misled by the guide and that in consequence they wandered about for many days without making any progress towards their journey's end, a conjecture rendered more probable by the bailiff having escaped'.[144]

For Manfredi, the error arose from the naming of the 'Phasis', a river which was actually the River Araxes. There were Greeks, he suggests, who had an idea of a real Phasis much further north which would indeed take them up on to the Black Sea, so they persuaded the troops to follow this apparent 'Phasis' (really, the Araxes), although it actually ran east, not north.[145] When their mistake eventually became clearer, they had to loop back, before eventually marching on to the River Harpasus (the northerly River Coruh).

Mistaken ideas about river names and river courses are eminently credible among Greeks without local maps: we need only cite the errors about rivers which occurred to Alexander and his officers in Asia. It may seem problematic that in antiquity nobody called the Araxes the 'Phasis' again, and when it was next visited by a Greek, by Alexander's noble Thessalian, Medeius, it was clearly known as the Araxes. Kinneir, however, gives a clue to support Xenophon: the name 'Araxes' is certainly based on an Armenian name, but Kinneir noticed in 1815 how 'some of the Armenians' locally still called the river 'Phasin Su'.[146] The Ten Thousand's error is then eminently understandable. They misunderstood what the locals said.

On this view, the Great Lacuna, three months or so of it, occurs in *Anabasis* 4.6, perhaps precisely at 4.6.4–5. Manfredi has also suggested that the proposed eastward detour down the Araxes would have caused heavy casualties in the severe winter weather and if Xenophon felt any responsibility for it, he would prefer to leave the whole story out. Without external evidence, a silence remains a silence and we can only suspect this one's whereabouts and try to penetrate it by guessing. Whether casualties lie behind it is entirely uncertain. What is certain, however, is that by the 360s (a favoured date for the composition of the *Anabasis*) Xenophon could omit a three-month chunk of the story without too much concern for the criticisms of fellow survivors. In my view, the lacuna is indeed likely to occur in the winter phase, between 4.4

---

144. Kinneir, *Journey through Asia Minor, Armenia and Koordistan*, p. 490.
145. Manfredi, *La strada dei Diecimila*, pp. 210–11 and 215–19.
146. Kinneir, *Journey through Asia Minor, Armenia and Koordistan*, p. 489.

Introduction

and 4.7 (the arrival among the Taochians), because the subsequent narrative is sufficiently precise for topographers to believe that they can still fix it on the ground. Moreover, the terrain (and weather) from the Taochians on was no longer snowy and wintry. A chunk has gone missing in winter, and only since 1985 has its absence begun to become evident. Some might connect this artful silence with Xenophon's supposed lack of written notes. In my view, it fits neatly with the Xenophon of the essays in this volume: evasive, apologetic, and a master of leaving unwelcome things out.

What we have, then, is a Snow Lacuna, which is cleverly concealed, like a crevasse, by our author's smooth narrative. It took azaleas and 'mad honey' to expose it again, and nowadays it can only be filled by our guesses and imagination. On the tracks of Xenophon and his honey, no imagination has been more fertile than Rose Macaulay's, who allowed this part of the *Anabasis* to wind as a subtheme through the middle chapters of her *Towers of Trebizond*, first published in 1956.[147] At Rize, east of Trapezus, where the Ten Thousand camped, she introduces her own latter-day Xenophon, the student Xenophon Paraclydes, a Greek who (she claims) was visiting his maternal grandfather and had been named 'Xenophon' by his father, 'so as to vex his mother who wanted to call him Mehmet'. With Xenophon as their driver and guide, her female narrator (Laurie) and the travellers set off uphill, 'among the rhododendrons and the azaleas which had supplied the madding honey to the Ten Thousand, and the May breezes blew about, sweet with the tangs of lemon trees and fig trees and aromatic shrubs'. In a hotel and a restaurant, they ate azalea blossoms with sugar and honey ('spécialité maison in these hotels around Trebizond') but they never ate mad honey themselves. Instead, the narrator lets her fancy fly, enhanced (she says) by a green potion, given to her (supposedly) by a sorcerer in Trebizond. 'I lay in a swoon, pretending to be dead, because the barbarous Pontic nations, the Mossynoici, were all about and I saw the boys they kept, fattened up on boiled chestnuts and tattooed all over with bright flowers, just as Xenophon had said . . .' The rest of her dream is printed as the epigraph to my chapter later in this book: then 'the days and nights went by, and I got them rather mixed up . . . and this was partly the potion, which made the world melt away into a hazy dream and the far past become mixed with the present, so that I got confused about when and who I was and what I was doing . . .' When Xenophon sat down to write up his *Anabasis*, perhaps as much as forty

147. Rose Macaulay, *Towers of Trebizond* (London, 1956), ch. 15.

years after the event, I do not think that he, too, was 'confused'. He left a gap but he knew exactly what he was doing. The reasons for this Snow Lacuna are topics over which our imaginations can range, provoked by the various studies in this book.

1   *When, How and Why did Xenophon Write the* Anabasis?

GEORGE CAWKWELL

I

I have had a love affair with Xenophon which dates from an evening in New College, Oxford, fifty years ago. On that occasion, the great Greek historian H. T. Wade-Gery remarked to the company in the course of conversation, 'Of course, the man who doesn't like Xenophon has lost his soul.' As a young man I privately hero-worshipped Wade-Gery (and indeed, as an old man, I still do). But at that time I was rather neutral about Xenophon. I had read some, but not much, of the *Hellenica* and the *Anabasis*, but that very evening, I went back to my own Oxford college and began to read more. Since then I have been a fairly acute case of what might be termed 'Xeno-Philia'. Indeed I have almost attained the arrogant feeling that I am a reincarnation of Xenophon and almost know him as I know myself, too well to admire unreservedly but still with sufficient sympathy to wish to write about him again. Thirty years ago I wrote an introduction to a reprint of Rex Warner's translation in the Penguin Classics.[1] I still want to uphold the views there expressed and defend them here in more detail.

First of all, I cling to the widely held view that the *Anabasis* was written in the 360s, to my mind probably in the early part of that decade. When in the third chapter of book 5 Xenophon recounts how at Cerasus the spoils were divided and what he did with his share, he paints a picture of his life at Skillous, where he was settled by the Spartans, probably in 392, and he tells how his sons would go hunting wild boar. To judge by a remark he made in his speech to the army justifying his dealing with the Thracian king Seuthes, he had had no sons by winter 400/399, and he had no time for marriage while serving with the Spartans in Asia. So his two sons would hardly be old enough

---

1. G. L. Cawkwell, introduction to *Xenophon: The Persian Expedition* (Harmondsworth, 1972).

to go out hunting boars before the later 370s, and since he describes life at Skillous entirely in imperfect tenses, it seems reasonable to suppose that he was not writing until, in the aftermath of the battle of Leuctra, he had left his estate at Skillous and taken up residence in Corinth.[2]

Further precision is not possible. For me the study of his language and his style with the aid of the computer is a light that failed. Perhaps not too many will quarrel with the view that he began his literary activity at Skillous with his philosophical works, in which he would have included his picture of ideal kingship, the *Cyropaedia*, to which was added in the late 360s the disillusioned and embittered postscript to that work which is the eighth chapter of book 8. In between may be set the *Anabasis*, in which his Cyrus is a prince in shining armour. There is no knowing when precisely he wrote the *Cyropaedia*. It was presumably before 367, when Persia ceased to support Sparta and declared itself in favour of Messenian independence,[3] the great betrayal which prompted Xenophon's disillusion and embitterment evident in the postscript. To that earlier mood in which Persia and the Great King could conceivably be admirable, the *Anabasis* would seem to belong. The laudation of Cyrus in the ninth chapter of book 1, in which, as Fortinbras said of Hamlet, 'he was likely, had he been put on, to have proved most royally', seems in tune with the laudation of Cyrus the Great. If one thinks of the *Anabasis* being written between 370 and 367, one is probably not far wrong.

This argument presumes that the *Anabasis* was written, as it were, in one piece. There seems nothing to be said for the idea that Xenophon ever contemplated concluding his account when the army reached Cerasus. There had indeed been at that moment a review of the army and a division of the proceeds of the sale of captives, and when the army moved on westwards the sick, the over-forties, the women and children did not rejoin the march.[4] In

---

2. H. R. Breitenbach, 'Xenophon', *RE* IX A2 (1967), cols 1579–1656, reviews the indications of date. P. Masqueray, *Xénophon: Anabasis* (Paris, 1930), pp. 7–10, places the *Anabasis* before Isocrates' *Panegyricus* of 380, following the argument of A. Kappelmacher, 'Zur Abfassungszeit von Xenophons *Anabasis*', *Anzeiger der Akademie der Wissenschaften in Wien* 60 (1924), pp. 15–24, and treating *Anab.* 5.3.4–13 as a later insertion. J. Dillery, *Xenophon and the History of his Times* (London, 1995), accepts a date post-Leuctra, following A. Körte, 'Die Tendenz von Xenophons *Anabasis*', *Neue Jahrbücher für das klassisches Altertum* 49 (1922), pp. 15–24, at p. 16, and others. J. Mesk, 'Die Tendenz der Xenophontischen *Anabasis*', *Wiener Studien* 43 (1922–3), pp. 136–46, at p. 137, adequately dealt with Xenophon's use of the imperfect tense in *Anab.* 5.3.10. For dating pre-367, ibid., p. 140. The remark to the army: *Anab.* 7.6.34.
3. *Hell.* 7.1.36.
4. É. Delebecque, *Essai sur la vie de Xénophon* (Paris, 1957), at pp. 98, 199, 288–99, supposes that the Parabasis (i.e. the march along the Black Sea coast, from Cerasus onwards) was added later. The arrival at Cerasus: *Anab.* 5.3.3. Those who were left behind: *Anab.* 5.3.1.

no sense, however, was Cerasus the end for the Ten Thousand, and there is no reason whatsoever for Xenophon ever to have thought of it as the end of his story. He could possibly have considered the reaching of Chrysopolis at the end of book 6 as a terminal point. But why would he have cut short the good story? The seven books are a unity.

There are minor difficulties undeniably. In the fourth chapter of book 6 Xenophon describes in glowing terms the charms of Calpe as a site suitable for development. If the Ten Thousand had been minded to found a city, they could not, he implies, have chosen better; it had everything, including easily accessible timber for shipbuilding, cereals, fruits, vines (the grapes of which made a sweet wine), everything indeed except olives and olive oil, which could have been obtained only by a roaring trade with Greece itself. It was, in short, a land fit for heroes. And, lo and behold, the Ten Thousand were, he asserts, heroes. Most of them had not come because they were looking for a job; they had been attracted to service under Cyrus by report of his excellent qualities; some had brought followers and some had spent money on getting there; they had left their homes and families intending to return enriched.

All this reads very oddly in a book which recounts the undisciplined behaviour of the Arcadians and the Achaeans, and in the previous book Xenophon is found giving a serious warning to the army as to what would result if they continued to behave with the bad faith and the violence they had displayed at Cerasus. Later in that same book it emerges that in the Armenian snows one man had tried to get over the problem of transporting a sick man by burying him alive in the snow.[5] There was, in short, no shortage of roughs on the long march, and one cannot help wondering whether Xenophon had at some time written up this passage of apologia for his plan to found a colony and his laudation of the men who might have filled it, and then later inserted it in his narrative somewhat incongruously.

Similar suspicions are excited by the laudation of Cyrus, which is encomium indeed. It goes far beyond what is likely to have been Xenophon's direct experience, though he may have been retailing largely what his friend Proxenus had told him. One detail is striking. Xenophon asserts that although no one went over from Cyrus to the King, many left the King for Cyrus, and in the *Oeconomicus* he says 'many myriads' deserted the King for Cyrus. The same sort of thing is found in Ctesias: 'many deserted from Artaxerxes to Cyrus, but from Cyrus to Artaxerxes not one.' No such desertions are mentioned in Xenophon's narrative in the *Anabasis* save for the four hundred Greek

---

5. Warning to the army: *Anab.* 5.7.12–26. The snow burial in Armenia: *Anab.* 5.8.9–11.

mercenaries of Abrocomas just before the army went through the Syrian Gates and that hardly justifies the comment in this laudation.[6] There seems to be some detachment between narrative and obituary. The latter may well have been written at a somewhat different time from the rest of book 1.

The suspicions aroused by these two passages do not, however, suffice to justify the notion that the work was written in two portions. There may have been additions and corrections, but the work is a unity, composed in the period immediately following his moving to Corinth, between say 370 and 367.

Certainly he wrote after the publication of Ctesias' *Persica*, to which he refers in his account of the battle – fortunately, for there is no other indication of which book was published first. Whether Xenophon wrote after the publication of an *Anabasis* by Sophaenetus of Stymphalus in Arcadia is a teasing speculation. What there is of an *Anabasis* written by a Sophaenetus is contained in four entries in Stephanus of Byzantium. Nothing in them could prove or disprove that Sophaenetus derived his *Anabasis* from Xenophon's and the relation between the two works is a matter of hypothesis. However, since the oldest general on the long march back was Sophaenetus of Stymphalus in Arcadia and Xenophon was one of the two youngest, and since it is credible enough to suppose that someone else who had been on the march wrote up his experiences, and since the account of the fourth-century historian Ephorus of Cyme reflected in the extant history of Diodorus Siculus gave a detailed version which differed from that of Xenophon, the hypothesis that the shadowy and uncertain Sophaenetus of Stephanus was indeed none other than the general has had respectable advocates and is here accepted.[7] It is true that Xenophon mentions his fellow general six times only and never in a way that could suggest that Xenophon knew of him as author of another *Anabasis*. But Xenophon is a far from candid historian and keeps his cards uncommonly

---

6. The laudation of Cyrus: *Anab.* 1.9.1–31. Assertions of desertion from Artaxerxes: *Anab.* 1.9.29; *Oec.* 4.18; Ctesias Frag. 16.58. The mercenaries of Abrocomas: *Anab.* 1.4.3.
7. Reference to the *Persica*: *Anab.* 1.8.26. Jacoby, *RE* XI 2 (1922), col. 2036, argued that Ctesias probably wrote the *Persica* in the 390s. An allusion to that work is perhaps to be found in *Anab.* 2.1.7, where 'a single Greek' Phalinus is among the messengers sent by Artaxerxes and Tissaphernes to the Greeks after the battle. Ctesias had included himself (Plut. *Artax* 13.5). For an account of Ctesias, cf. R. Drews, *The Greek Accounts of Eastern History* (Cambridge, Mass., 1973), pp. 103–16. Sophaenetus as the oldest general: *Anab.* 6.5.13. Xenophon as one of the two youngest: *Anab.* 3.2.37. The fragments of Sophaenetus are to be found in *FGH* 109. Cf. E. Bux, 'Sophaenetus', *RE* III A1 (1927), cols 1008–13, and W. W. Tarn, 'Persia, from Xerxes to Alexander', in *Cambridge Ancient History* VI, 1st edn (Cambridge, 1927), pp. 1–24, at p. 8. It is to be noted that Sophaenetus (frag. 4) sited Charmande opposite 'the Babylonian Gates', differently from Xenophon (*Anab.* 1.5.10). For further discussion of the relation between the two authors, see p. 61.

close to his chest, notable often for what he chooses not to say. Silence can be his severest censure. If there was an *Anabasis* of Sophaenetus, Xenophon could be saying what he thought of it by saying nothing.

Above all, Xenophon is a gifted writer. He had been on the long march from Sardis to the battlefield of Cunaxa and back to Chrysopolis. He had seen and done much and, like many a veteran of war, he remembered vividly. His especial talent was to be able to write it all up as if it had happened only recently. No one should be misled by the freshness of the *Anabasis* into thinking that so much time as three decades could not have elapsed since the events he describes.[8]

II

But how did he write it? Obviously he would not have been present at every event he relates. For instance, the scene where at Cyrus' bidding the Persian grandees, heedless of their fine raiment, dashed down into the mud to help push wagons that were stuck was probably heard about rather than witnessed. Much he could have heard from his friend, the general Proxenus, who was privy to all that Clearchus had to say, including small details like the villages known as 'the girdle of Parysatis' or 'the villages of Cyrus' mother'. Possibly the interpreter who spoke Persian could have given, directly or indirectly, a good deal of information, such snippets as, for instance, Tiribazus' function of getting the King mounted on his horse. In general it is not difficult to imagine how Xenophon could have heard tell of many parts of his story which he had not himself witnessed.[9]

Not all, however, can be satisfactorily accounted for in this way. As the Ten Thousand march up the Tigris, they come to a deserted city called Larisa,

---

8. Similarly lively, much of the *Hellenica* was written three decades and more after the events it records. Cf. G. L. Cawkwell, introduction to *Xenophon: A History of My Times* (Harmondsworth, 1979), pp. 17–22. It is hardly possible here to present a full picture of Xenophon's development. I share the view that he did not take up his pen until he had laid down the weapons of war, i.e. until he had settled at Skillous. His great resource, so amply to be displayed in the *Hellenica*, was his lively memory. He commenced by recording what he remembered of Socrates.
9. The wagons in the mud: *Anab.* 1.5.8. 'The girdle of Parysatis': *Anab.* 1.4.9. 'The villages of Cyrus' mother': *Anab.* 2.4.7. The 'Persian' interpreter: *Anab.* 4.5.34; he presumably spoke Aramaic, the language of the administration of the Empire (cf. J. C. Greenfield, 'Aramaic in the Achaemenian Empire', in *Cambridge History of Iran* II (Cambridge, 1985), pp. 698–708). Tiribazus' function: *Anab.* 4.4.4.

which is generally thought to be Assyrian Calah, modern Nimrud. Xenophon declares that it had once been inhabited by Medes. He gives the width of its walls and their height and says that the circuit of the walls was two parasangs. 'This city,' he adds, 'the king of the Persians besieged when he took over the empire from the Medes but could in no way take, but a cloud covered the sun and caused it to disappear until the inhabitants left, and so the city was captured. Beside this city was a stone pyramid, one plethron in width and two plethra high. On it many of the barbarians from the nearby villages had taken refuge.'[10]

How did he gather this information (and misinformation)? The army was being harried. There was no time for Xenophon, or anyone else, to stand guessing at the dimensions of the walls, let alone to pace out their circuit, and the measurements appear to be accurate enough.[11] Nor is this the sort of information sought through an interpreter. The Ten Thousand were not tourists. Xenophon could see for himself the refugees on the Ziggurat. But how did he get the rest of the information?

Having dealt with Larisa, Xenophon proceeds immediately to deal with Mespila, generally agreed to be the site of famous, proud Nineveh.[12] The information he provides here is remarkably similar in method to what he said of Larisa. He describes it as a large, deserted city, once inhabited by Medes; the basis of polished stone (in which there are many shells), fifty feet wide and fifty feet high; and on top of it had been built a brick wall, fifty feet wide and one hundred feet high, the circuit of the wall being six parasangs. Then, as with Larisa, he rounds off his account with a historical note about the wife of the Median king taking refuge there when the Medes lost their empire to the Persians and the King of the Persians laid siege to it but could not capture it either by wearing them out or by assault until Zeus cowed the inhabitants with a thunderbolt and thus the city was captured.

Some of this Xenophon could have observed for himself, but he would hardly have had the time to measure this circuit of the wall (a circuit of six parasangs would have taken six hours to walk) or the opportunity to measure its thickness. One cannot help suspecting that both these notes derived from

10. *Anab.* 3.4.7.
11. Cf. M. E. L. Mallowan, *Nimrud and its Remains* (London, 1966), p. 81. However, Xenophon's assertion that the city was abandoned is not accurate, ibid., p. 230.
12. *Anab.* 3.4.10. The text is uncertain. Xenophon appears to say that 'a large, abandoned fortification lay beside the city', but he goes on to say that the city was called Mespila and that the Medes once inhabited it, which suggests that Mespila was part of Nineveh.

some sort of literary source. Who or what that could have been one can only conjecture. It was probably not Ctesias, whose *Persica* was hardly a geographical guide and who placed Nineveh on the Euphrates.[13] (Indeed Xenophon is unlikely to have got the names Larisa and Mespila from him if they are correctly identified with Calah and Nineveh. Ctesias gave a fairly ample history of the Medes, as the second book of Diodorus shows, and he would hardly have called these great Assyrian cities by the names Xenophon uses without making plain what they had once been.)

One is inclined to look for some not very ample guidebook for Xenophon to have drawn on and in the paucity of our knowledge one is inevitably drawn to Hecataeus' *Asia* (to use the title constantly used by Stephanus of Byzantium).[14] This geographical description appears to have gone beyond mere geography. Perhaps it furnished brief historical notes of a sort which Xenophon could have used. Certainly anyone who had been on that long march might have read parts of Hecataeus with interest.

Elsewhere Xenophon makes geographical assertions for which his own personal experience would not have sufficed. For instance, he says that they journeyed for seven stages at five parasangs a day along the River Phasis, which was a plethron wide. How did he know it was the Phasis? The name was familiar to the Greeks, but how was this river identified by Xenophon? Or again they came to a river which Xenophon declared was the boundary between the Macrones and the Scytheni. How did he find that out? One cannot help suspecting that he would have had to have recourse to Hecataeus or some other Periegetic writer. Of course it is possible that the Persian-speaking interpreter was able to discover such details, but although Aramaic was the language of Persian administration, one doubts whether the odd native rounded up for interrogation would have been much use.[15]

---

13. Diod. 2.3.2.
14. For Hecataeus (*FGH* 1), Drews, *The Greek Accounts of Eastern History*, pp. 11–19. E. Herzfeld, *The Persian Empire* (Wiesbaden, 1968), confidently attributed to Hecataeus various bits of Herodotus, e.g. the list of satrapies at 3.88–97 (p. 288), the note on the Eretrians at Ardericca at 6.119 (p. 13), the sacred horse drowning in the River Gyndes at 1.189 (p. 7), and, most relevant here, the Royal Road of 5.52 (p. 100). These attributions may be correct. Cf. Breitenbach, 'Xenophon', cols 1650–5, for the similarities between the *Anabasis* and Periegetic literature.
15. The journey beside the Phasis: *Anab.* 4.6.4. Hdt. 6.84.2 referred to the river as if no elaboration was needed. But was the river that Xenophon called the Phasis the river that Herodotus alluded to? This part of the long march is very uncertain (cf. O. Lendle, *Kommentar zu Xenophons Anabasis* [Darmstadt, 1995], ad *Anab.* 4.6.4). The boundary between the Macrones and the Scytheni: *Anab.* 4.8.1.

By whatever means Xenophon gathered such pieces of information, it has been blithely assumed that he kept a diary.[16] We who live in a world of books, including a plenitude of reference works, do not need to rely on our memories and so find it hard to believe that Xenophon could have written the *Anabasis* largely out of memory; he must have kept and used a diary. But it is even harder to believe that he did. When Xenophon answered Proxenus' invitation to join him, Xenophon could have had no suspicion of what he would shortly be engaged on.

When exactly Xenophon himself began to suspect that Cyrus had more in mind than to deal with the Pisidians and then to settle scores with Abrocomas, the satrap of Syria, is unclear. It was not until the army reached Thapsacus on the Euphrates that Cyrus declared that the journey would be 'to Babylon and against the Great King'. Proxenus and his fellow generals may have guessed what was afoot quite early, but it was not until the army reached Tarsus that suspicions hardened.[17] Perhaps at that point it might have seemed to Xenophon that he was on no common campaign and that he might with profit write it up. But he could not have foreseen that Cyrus would die in battle and that the Greeks would have an arduous and dangerous march through unknown lands. It seems unlikely that he would have been ready both psychologically and with ink and papyrus for the keeping of a diary.

Even if he had been able to find and carry an adequate supply of writing materials, he must have been far too busy at times to make a record of what he had seen and done, and often the physical conditions would have made it impossible. When the Ten Thousand began on their long march on their own, they burnt their tents at the same time as they rid themselves of unnecessary bits of baggage[18] and Xenophon, had he been keeping a diary, would at all times have found it difficult to write. In the bitter winter of the Armenian highlands it would have been impossible. Any heavy downpour would have had the same effect and in general the picture of Xenophon keeping a diary in such circumstances is absurd.

There were persons in the army of Alexander the Great who kept an official diary, the *Ephemerides*. That was their whole job and doubtless they went well

---

16. Cf. Breitenbach, 'Xenophon', cols 1649–50. The presumption that Xenophon kept some sort of record is universal. Cf. Lendle, *Kommentar zu Xenophons Anabasis*, ad *Anab.* 5.5.4.
17. Dealing with the Pisidians: *Anab.* 3.1.9. Settling scores with Abrocomas: *Anab.* 1.3.20. The declaration at Thapsacus: *Anab.* 1.4.11. Suspicion at Tarsus: *Anab.* 1.3.1–21.
18. Burning the tents: *Anab.* 3.3.1. Abandoning baggage: cf. *Anab.* 3.2.27–8.

prepared. The term, however, is never heard of in any army before that time, and in general there appears to have been no word for 'diary' in Greek in the age of Xenophon. We hear of *hypomnēmata*, which might remind one of how, for instance, the great Socrates had argued. Plato mentions such an activity,[19] and Xenophon's *apomnēmeumata*, the so-called *Memorabilia*, is a prime example. But, as far as we know, people did not keep diaries in the late fifth century.

And what sort of diary would it have been that Xenophon is supposed to have kept? At one point, for example, he says the army was halted 'more than twenty days'. If he was writing his *Anabasis* from a diary, he might have been more precise, just as elsewhere he says that Chirisophus was deprived of the sole command 'on the sixth or seventh day after he was elected'.[20]

Moreover, if Xenophon was a diarist, he was uncommonly fitful. He failed to mention the Lesser Zab. The Greater Zab was a big river, four plethra wide. One might in memory fuse the two, but not in a diary. The Lesser Zab is not unnoticeable. It certainly got a mention in Herodotus' description of the Royal Road and it must surely have got into the diary, if there had been one.[21] Why is it missing in the *Anabasis*?

Xenophon had a lively memory. His *Hellenica*, the major part of which was written long after the events described,[22] bears no mark of documentation. It is essentially personal, reflecting his own experience and his own range of friendships and society. He was able to write it, not because he had been consciously accumulating material over four decades but because his memory furnished him with a sort of history of his times. Similarly with the *Anabasis*. The various incidents in which he played a part he saw as clearly as he saw them long ago, and his speeches play so large a part because they were so plain in his memory, material for embellishment.

But, it will be objected, without a diary how could Xenophon remember all those numbers of stages (stathmoi) and parasangs? That is the real difficulty.

19. Pl. *Tht.* 143a.
20. 'More than twenty days': *Anab.* 2.4.1. 'On the sixth or seventh day': *Anab.* 6.2.12.
21. The Greater Zab: *Anab.* 2.5.1. No doubt much may have changed in the last sixty years but in the Geographical Handbook Series published (for official use only) during the War of 1939–45 the average discharge of the Lesser Zab in September 'is calculated at 1,340 cubic feet per second', and though it rises to 16,140 cubic feet by March it was at no time unnoticeable. Admittedly in September it is only half as large as the Greater Zab but it is one of the four main rivers draining the mountain borderland of Iraq into the Tigris (cf. Hdt. 5.52).
22. i.e. everything from *Hell.* 2.3.10 onwards. Cf. Cawkwell, introduction to *Xenophon: A History of my Times*, pp. 17–22.

No matter how good his memory was he could not have remembered all that, and, as a general rule, remembered accurately.

An answer is suggested by the fragments of Ctesias. Book 23 of the *Persica*, according to Photius' epitome, provided not only a list of the kings from Ninus to Artaxerxes, but also the 'number of stathmoi, days, and parasangs from Ephesus to Bactria and India'. Was this a bald statement of total time and distance like the various interpolations in the text of the *Anabasis*? Or was it part of a description of the main roads of the empire of a sort of which we hear later?[23]

The most notable example of what may be called Periegetic is furnished by the *Parthian Stages* (*Stathmoi Parthikoi*) of Isidore of Charax, a writer of the Augustan period. Fragment 2 gives a flavour of what his description of Parthia was like, a detailed account of locations of cities (though not of villages) and the distances between them in schoinoi, which were units of measure, one schoinos being sixty stades according to Herodotus, according to others different figures.[24]

---

23. Photius' epitome of Ctesias: *FGH* 688 F33. Interpolations in the *Anabasis*: *Anab*. 2.2.6, 5.5.4, 7.8.25. Lendle, *Kommentar zu Xenophons Anabasis*, p. 338, is persuaded that the totals given in *Anab*. 5.5.4. stem from 'das originale Tagebuch Xenophons', but on p. 486 he calls in Ctesias' list as a supplement (which in view of the gaps in the postulated Tagebuch is just as well). On p. 97 ad *Anab*. 2.2.6 he takes *ēlthon* as a first person singular and makes Xenophon himself responsible for the summation. One looks in vain for an explanation why a Greek should use the Persian measure of parasangs. As Bosworth notes ad Arr. *Anab* 1.4.4, Alexander's Bematists measured in stadioi (cf. *FGH* 119 FF2 and 3). Herodotus has parasangs as the Persian measure for land (Hdt. 6.42.2), just as on his Royal Road distances are in stathmoi and parasangs (Hdt. 5.52), translated in the following chapter into the Greek measure, stadioi.

24. Isidore of Charax: *FGH* 781. Cf. also W. W. Tarn, *The Greeks in Bactria and India* (Cambridge, 1951), pp. 53–5. M. Rostovtzeff, *The Social and Economic History of the Hellenistic World* (Oxford, 1941), p. 1038, before discussing Isidore, remarked that the stathmoi of Hellenistic monarchies 'were based on similar Persian itineraries'. (On these Hellenistic itineraries, see p. 1583 n. 3.) For schoinoi, Hdt. 2.6.2 and A. B. Lloyd, *Herodotus Book II: Commentary 1–98* (Leiden, 1976), p. 44. Robin Lane Fox has drawn my attention to two milestones from Persis of the early Hellenistic period published in *SEG* XLV (1995), nos 1879 and 1880. P. Bernard, 'Remarques additionnelles', *CRAI* (1995), pp. 73–95, at pp. 87–8, commented that probably there were no such stones in the Achaemenid period. It would not be surprising that stones recording the number of parasangs were not in place along the roads. The parasang was a measure of time, not of distance (cf. Lammert, *RE* III A col. 2177 'kein Raummass, sondern ein Zeitmass'; Becher, *RE* XVIII 4, col. 1375; A. Pretor, *The Anabasis of Xenophon* (Cambridge, 1881) ad *Anab*.1.2.5; Lendle, *Kommentar zu Xenophons Anabasis*, p. 262). No doubt Herodotus was right enough in converting Persian parasangs into Greek stades (Hdt. 5.53.1) but the actual distance per parasang would have varied with the terrain. The important point here is that there were no distance stones for Xenophon to count and record if he had been able and minded to.

When, How and Why did Xenophon Write the Anabasis? 57

How far back in time had such records been made? The so-called Bematists of Alexander the Great's army obviously had an important influence. The results of their labours, 'the trusted record of the *Stathmoi*', were used by Eratosthenes in the third century. Elsewhere they were referred to as the *Asiatic Stathmoi*, and it would seem that that work covered not just the parts of Asia traversed by Alexander, but substantially the whole of Asia; it gave, for instance, the distances northwards from Thapsacus to 'the Armenian Gates'. Was the work of the Bematists a new departure, or were they improving on and adding to previous work?[25]

The movement of royal armies over long distances was one of the great achievements of Persia. Indeed if the Persians had not been so good at it, the Empire could never have been extended so vastly and then maintained. But the movement of large armies always involves serious logistical problems, and it was essential for the King's generals to know the distances to be covered.[26]

It is therefore probable enough that there were versions of the *Stathmoi* before Alexander. Herodotus was able to describe the Royal Road from Sardis to Susa and give the number of stathmoi and parasangs. It is probably a correct guess that the *Periegesis of Asia* of Hecataeus was the source of his account, but from wherever Herodotus got his figures they show that there was some sort of description of the Empire available to him, just as from some source he derived that supposed Army List of 480.[27]

There was, it was here proposed, a resource available to Xenophon when his memory faltered. There is no need to find in his detailed and generally accurate figures proof that he kept a diary on the March Up-country and on the Long March home. Distances and times of movement in the parts of the Empire that had been reduced and kept in order could easily enough be checked. When the Ten Thousand moved into places 'beyond the Pale', notably Kurdistan, he speaks simply of the number of days the journey took. When he

25. The Bematists: *FGH* 119–23. Their use by Eratosthenes: Strabo 15.1.11. '*Asiatic Stathmoi*': Strabo 15.2.8. Distances to 'the Armenian Gates': Strabo 2.1.26.
26. The Persepolis Tablets have made plain how carefully rationing was managed in the Empire. Cf. M. A. Dandamaev and V. G. Lukonin, *The Culture and Social Institutions of Ancient Iran* (Cambridge, 1989), p. 108, '. . . stations with reserves of foodstuffs were situated at a distance of one day's travel on the main roads', and p. 107, 'Orders went out from Susa to all the provinces, while reports from the Satraps and other civil servants arrived in Susa on state business from various ends of the Empire.' In such a system properly measured itineraries were, one would have thought, indispensable.
27. The Royal Road: Hdt. 5.52–3. The Army List: Hdt. 7.61–88. Cf. also G. Nenci (ed.), *Erodoto: Le Storie – Libro V* (Milan, 1994), ad Hdt. 5.52.

gets back into Armenia he returns to stathmoi and parasangs.[28] (It is to be noted that whereas the *Asiatic Stathmoi* used by Eratosthenes gave measurements for the route from Thapsacus to 'the Armenian Gates', the route through Gordyene (i.e. the Cardouchi, the Kurds) was 'unmeasured' – which is confirmation of a sort for the hypothesis.)

After the Ten Thousand left the satrapy of Armenia, the record is somewhat fitful, and after Trapezus there is no further mention of stathmoi and parasangs (save at 5.5.1, where he speaks of their journeying eight stathmoi without mention of parasangs, by which one would suppose he means eight stops). When he is in valleys, he seems to resort to the formal terms. Off the beaten track, as it were, it is a matter of how many days. It is noteworthy however that most of the peoples through whom the march is measured in stathmoi and parasangs appear on that (alleged) Army List of 480 produced by Herodotus. It is in fact no such thing, but part of a Description of the Empire. An early listing of distances in stathmoi and parasangs could well have dealt with areas no longer under control by 400.[29]

Anyone who has a better than average memory will sympathize with Xenophon. He remembers a great deal and in detail, and every so often important matters fall into black holes. The omissions of his *Hellenica* are astonishing and scandalous. One seeks to explain them in terms of his prejudices and his interests, but some are just black holes. So perhaps it was with the Lesser Zab. He simply forgot. If the Description available to him was made

28. Kurdistan: *Anab.* 4.3.2. Armenia: *Anab.* 4.5.2–3.
29. The Description: Hdt. 7.61–88. Breitenbach, 'Xenophon', cols 1579–638, sets out in tabular form the contents of the *Anabasis*. The column giving distances and times of marching makes clear how various Xenophon's practice was. His use of the term *stathmos* is varied. As F. W. Sturz notes in his *Lexicon Xenophonteum* (Leipzig, 1801–4), s.v. *stathmos*, it can either be a stopping place, 'caravanserai' as it were, or the time of a day's journey. In general on what one supposes are regular Persian routes he gives both stathmoi and parasangs, but elsewhere he marks the passage of time simply in days. Thus, between the Euphrates and the Tigris those uncertain marches are measured only in days, while on the journey up the left bank of the Tigris he gives as well the Persian measure of parasangs. A difficult case is *Anab.* 1.5.5, where he gives the distance from Corsote to the Babylonian Gates as 'thirteen deserted stages and ninety parasangs', i.e. Persian measures for a march through the desert where there was no regular Persian route. Indeed it was for this barren passage in all probability that Cyrus had made special provision (*Anab.* 1.10.18), and his whole strategy seems to have been to dash for Babylon down the left bank of Euphrates, while he was expected to take the longer but well-supplied route taken by Abrocomas, who was therefore late for the battle (*Anab.* 1.4.18 and 7.12). It seems reasonable to suppose, however, that Cyrus would have warned the army that they had thirteen very severe days' march through desert ahead of them at an average of nearly seven parasangs a day, i.e. seven hours a day in the scorching heat of late summer. It is no wonder that Xenophon remembered it.

on the principle followed by Isidore,[30] the distances given were between cities, and rivers were mentioned only when towns situated on them were listed. In that way an itinerary might have failed to prompt his memory. In general, however, a Persian itinerary available through some Periegetic source gave his work form and backbone.

III

So much for how Xenophon composed. Now let us turn to why. He had a good story to tell. He wrote well and doubtless enjoyed writing. But what, after thirty years' silence, moved him?

Any reader of the *Anabasis* is inevitably impressed by Xenophon's conduct of the generalship according to Xenophon. When, for example, the Ten Thousand were bivouacking and snow fell during the night, the men were reluctant to leave the comparative warmth of the snow and get up and get going, but when Xenophon dared to stand up naked and start splitting wood, quickly someone else got up, took over the job from him and began to split. On an earlier occasion two young men ran up to him as he was having his breakfast. 'Everyone knew', he tells us, 'that it was possible to approach him both when he was breakfasting and when he was dining, and if he was asleep to wake him up and talk to him about any military business', generalship as commendable as he was later to pronounce the generalship of Teleutias, the Spartan commander who is prominent in his *Hellenica*.[31]

He was, of course, unfailingly attentive to religion, refusing, until he got the right omens, to lead out his troops who were suffering from lack of food

30. See n. 25 above.
31. Splitting wood: *Anab.* 4.4.12. Consultation at breakfast: *Anab.* 4.3.10. The generalship of Teleutias: *Hell.* 5.1.7. F. Dürrbach, 'L'apologie de Xénophon dans l'Anabase', *REG* 6 (1893), pp. 343–86, following Schwartz, has had considerable influence with all those who see the *Anabasis* as essentially a work of self-justification, though his conclusion on p. 385 seems harsh ('the results of this inquiry are not therefore favourable to Xenophon . . . The retreat of the Ten Thousand is the only episode in his life which has given him a place in history and one sees what one has to think of the part he was able to play in it'). Some, e.g. H. Erbse, 'Xenophons *Anabasis*', *Gymnasium* 73 (1966), pp. 485–505, at p. 399, have found in *Anab.* 6.1.20 the key to his purpose, viz. he was seeking to justify and excuse himself to the Athenians. There may have been an element of that but if the date of composition is correctly set after his removal from Corinth he seems to have waited for too long to make his defence. But the general view that the *Anabasis* is work of self-justification (Mesk, 'Die Tendenz der Xenophontischen *Anabasis*') seems correct.

supplies – so unlike Neon, who took the (religious) law into his own hands and landed his men in disaster; fortunately Xenophon was there to rescue them. Later, when he dismounts and is asked 'Why are you getting off your horse when we have to hurry?' he virtuously replies 'I'm well aware it's not just myself who is needed. The men will run the faster and more cheerfully if I lead them on foot.'[32]

Indeed he seems never to make a mistake. Both in counsel and in action, Xenophon was always right. Not so Chirisophus, the senior general who was appointed because of where he came from, Sparta. He is found securing a comfortable billet for himself in a village while those of the rest of the army who could not finish the march had to spend the night without food or the warmth of a fire, and as a result a number perished, not a good show.[33]

Xenophon, who was in command of the rearguard, showed up, it seems, very well in taking great pains to help the sick along. When the rearguard caught up with the main body of the army, they found that no guards had been posted. He found the whole army was resting and he had to bivouac without warmth or food but he established what guards he could. The difference in style between the two generals is made apparent. Later Chirisophus beat up the guide but did not have him tied up. As a consequence of this obvious mistake, the guide ran away in the course of the night. Xenophon says that 'this, namely the harming of the guide and the carelessness, was the only difference between Xenophon and Chirisophus on the march.' Fortunately an earlier refusal to do what he was told passed off equably, Xenophon proving as usual to be right. The Xenophon of the *Anabasis* always was right and righteous. The one matter that was after debate opposed, viz. the plan to found a city on the northern coast of Asia Minor, he had to give up, but his glowing picture of the great attractions of Calpes Limen, reinforced by his account of the army when short of food amply providing themselves there, showed who was right.[34]

It seems reasonable to suppose that what prompted him after thirty years to this display of virtue was that he had fared less well at the hands of someone else. It is generally agreed that the account of Diodorus was derived from

32. Refusal to lead without the right omens: *Anab.* 6.4.12. Neon's disaster and rescue: *Anab.* 6.4.23, 26. On the religion of the *Anabasis*, see also Parker, chapter 4 in this volume. Virtuous dismounting: *Anab.* 7.3.45.
33. The appointment of Chirisophus: *Anab.* 3.2.37. His selfishness: *Anab.* 4.5.11.
34. Xenophon establishes guards: *Anab.* 4.5.21. The flight of the guide: *Anab.* 4.6.3. Earlier refusal to obey: *Anab.* 3.4.9. Cf. Whitby, chapter 7 in this volume, n. 55. Calpes Limen: *Anab.* 6.4.1–8. The troops restocking: *Anab.* 6.6.1.

Ephorus who, though in places the use of Xenophon is to be suspected, in general followed some other account or accounts which were different, as on the lowest level the differing spellings of names show. Diodorus' account of the battle of Cunaxa is plainly different; he had an entirely different name for the mountain from which the Ten Thousand first sighted the sea and he declared that the original intention was to march to Paphlagonia, a land not mentioned by Xenophon until the march leads him through it. Most strikingly Diodorus' account of how the Greek generals responded to the embassy from the King after the battle differs from Xenophon's. So the view is here accepted that the account of Diodorus is substantially based on a version differing from that of Xenophon.[35] But who was this other source? Had he written in denigration of Xenophon's part in the march of the Ten Thousand?

The fashionable guess was, and is, that the missing man was none other than Xenophon's fellow general, Sophaenetus of Stymphalus in Arcadia. Objections have been, and will continue to be, made. In the *Anabasis* Sophaenetus is a very minor character who says nothing and does nothing of note.[36] One would never suspect that he had written an account that had riled Xenophon. But Xenophon's habit of passing in silence over those of whom he disapproved is familiar to us in the *Hellenica*. The Theban general Pelopidas, for instance, is not so much damned with faint praise as almost totally disregarded. It would be wholly in character for Xenophon to treat Sophaenetus as a figure of no importance. Indeed what Xenophon does not say could be his way of dealing with a critic. The real difficulty is that the only evidence that there was an *Anabasis* written by a man called Sophaenetus consists, as already remarked, of four entries in the sixth-century lexicographer Stephanus of Byzantium, none of which enables us to form the slightest idea of what the book was like. However when one considers that the very name of the author of the highly important *Hellenica Oxyrhynchia* can only be conjectured, it is hardly sensible to rule out Sophaenetus' *Anabasis* because we find no mention of it for a thousand years.

35. Diodorus on the Ten Thousand: Diod. 14.19–31. The name of the mountain: Diod. 14.29.3. Paphlagonia: Diod. 14.25.8, 27.2. The response to the embassy: Diod. 14.25; contrast *Anab.* 2.1.7–23. Here I follow, as many have done, the line taken by Bux, 'Sophaenetus'. For the contrary view, see P. J. Stylianou, chapter 2 in this volume.
36. At *Anab.* 4.4.19 Sophaenetus is left in charge of what one presumes were the non-combatants, and at 6.5.13 his caution had to be set aside by Xenophon's dashing opinion. At *Anab.* 5.8.1 he is fined ten minas for neglecting his duty, presumably the care of the over-forties, the women, the children, and superfluous baggage (5.3.1). For the view that he was the other source, cf. e.g. A. Gwynn, 'Xenophon and Sophaenetus', *CQ* 23 (1929), pp. 38–9, Lendle, *Kommentar zu Xenophons Anabasis*, pp. 12, 249.

Certainly there is nothing to be said for the idea that the source of Ephorus' differences from Xenophon was the Oxyrhynchus Historian. Of course, if that great man had indeed included an account of the expedition of Cyrus, Ephorus would surely have drawn on him, just as he had done in earlier parts of his work, but it is very doubtful indeed whether he would have included a revolt by a Persian prince supported by a band of Greek mercenaries. It was different when it came to Agesilaus' campaign of 395; that was concerned with the liberation of the Greeks of Asia. The Oxyrhynchus Historian was, as far as we can judge, a real historian in the sense that Thucydides was. Events in the faraway highlands of Anatolia were utterly beyond his ken. To write an account of the march of the Ten Thousand, one needed to have been on it, and unless Stephanus' Sophaenetus was the merest cribber, perhaps covering his tracks by spelling names differently so that Xenophon's *Taochoi* became with him *Chaoi* and by siting places slightly differently as he did with Charmande on the Euphrates, it is not at all improbable that Stephanus' man was Sophaenetus of Stymphalus whom we meet in Xenophon's book.[37]

As Ronald Syme wrote in the preface to his *Tacitus*, 'reconstruction is hazardous, but conjecture cannot be avoided, otherwise the history is not worth writing, for it does not become intelligible'. The hypothesis, now of considerable long standing, that Xenophon's Sophaenetus wrote an *Anabasis* before Xenophon wrote his, provides the answer to why Xenophon wrote when he did.

Though Xenophon did not like what Sophaenetus had, or, rather, had not to say, Ephorus did, and that is why in the pages of Diodorus Chirisophus is appointed, straight after the arrest of the generals by Tissaphernes, to supreme command, that is, to replace Clearchus in his commanding role as we see it on the battlefield of Cunaxa. This, perhaps, moved Xenophon mightily. In his account, Chirisophus held supreme command but only for six or seven days after he returned to Sinope from his mission to Anaxibius, the Spartan nauarch, and then only after Xenophon had declined to yield to pressure and stand for election himself.[38]

---

37. The Oxyrhyncus Historian as Ephorus' source: H. D. Westlake, 'Diodorus and the expedition of Cyrus', *Phoenix* 41 (1987), pp. 241–54. Xenophon (*Anab.* 1.5.10) places Charmande somewhere in the course of the thirteen-day march through the desert which ended at the Gates (*Anab.* 1.5.5). Sophaenetus (*FGH* 109 F4) set it opposite 'the Babylonian Gates'.
38. The supreme command of Chirisophus: Diod. 14.27.1. The commanding role of Clearchus: *Anab.* 1.8.12, 2.1.4, 5, etc. Chirisophus as supreme commander in Xenophon: *Anab.* 6.1.16–22.

One cannot read the *Anabasis* without getting the impression that Xenophon was the real man. It all happened because on the night after the arrest of the generals it was he who took the initiative. It was his proposals that were accepted, including his ideas of how the army should move. The only contributions of Chirisophus on that crucial night were two. First, a pat on the back for Xenophon – 'previously all I knew about you was that you are Athenian, but now I praise you for your words and your deeds, and I could wish that there were as many as possible like you.' Then, secondly, he made a brief speech saying that things were awfully bad, a mere nine lines of the Oxford Classical Text, a ponderous statement of the obvious, after which Xenophon, dressed to the nines, makes a speech covering six and a half pages of the OCT, near the end of which he says, 'Well, if anyone sees a better way, let it be so, but if not let Chirisophus lead since he is a Spartan', the ambiguity of 'lead' carefully avoiding the issue of whether Chirisophus was to be like Clearchus the leader, or merely to be at the front of the column. 'We the youngest, Timasion and I, will guard the rear, at any rate for the present.'[39]

It would be in the rear, we are left to understand, that the real fighting would happen. In Xenophon's account, Xenophon was the true hero. Let no more be said, he implies, about Chirisophus being in command. The truth perhaps slipped out at one moment when Xenophon said that Chirisophus ordered him. For the rest it was really Xenophon who was primus inter pares. But, of course, on only one occasion was there any dissent between the two generals. (Had it been suggested that things had been otherwise?) Perhaps what moved Xenophon to write when he did was desire to put the record straight on his relations with Chirisophus. With proper restraint Chirisophus' death was no more than remarked. Is Xenophon implying that he was really nothing much to write a history about?[40]

So much by way of reasserting an old hypothesis. It does at any rate explain why Xenophon waited so long before he wrote his story. But, it will be asked, does the book bear the marks of political developments of the three decades after the failure of Cyrus' expedition?[41]

---

39. Xenophon's proposals: *Anab.* 3.2.18–22. Chirisophus' praise of Xenophon: *Anab.* 3.1.45. Chirisophus' statement of the obvious: *Anab.* 3.2.2–3. 'Well, if anyone sees a better way': *Anab.* 3.2.37. The text is uncertain here, but the imperative in one manuscript seems preferable to the optative in others (cf. Pretor, *The Anabasis of Xenophon*, ad loc.).
40. Chirisophus ordering Xenophon: *Anab.* 3.4.38. 'Only' disagreement: *Anab.* 4.6.4; cf. above n. 35. The death of Chirisophus: *Anab.* 6.4.1.
41. Cf. Körte, 'Die Tendenz von Xenophons *Anabasis*'.

The expedition changed the Greek view of Persia. Before 401 men could talk about Greece attacking Persia, but they could hardly take it seriously. Herodotus, for instance, writing in the 440s or the 430s, could envisage the Scyths proposing a joint attack on Persia, themselves by way of the River Phasis while the Spartiates would set out from Ephesus, march 'up' and join up with the Scyths in Media, a wild goose chase, or rather, since it was the River Phasis, a wild pheasant chase, if ever there was one. When Herodotus pictures Xerxes presiding over a debate at the Persian court about grand strategy, he is made to say, 'I know full well that if we refrain from action they will not but will merely campaign against our land... either all of this (i.e. Persia and the Persian Empire) will be subject to the Greeks or all of their land will be subject to the Persians. There is no middle way in our enmity.' The picture is laughable. While the Greek world was split in two by the rivalry of Athens and Sparta, such talk was the wildest dreaming.[42]

Aristophanes' comic heroine Lysistrata in her great Reconciliation speech of 411 addressed to both Spartans and Athenians made this clear. 'I want to take you and give both of you a ticking-off. You deserve it. You make altars drip, pouring from a single bowl of purifying water as though you were kin, at Olympia, the Gates, Delphi . . . and you bring destruction on Greek men and Greek cities when there are barbarians out there for an army to attack.' The truth was that in the fifth century thoughts of a major war of conquest of Persia by Greeks was sentimental bunkum and they must have known it. Cimon in his famous Dictum 'Do not leave Greece lame or Athens without her yokefellow' must have been thinking of combined operations but probably of no more than the ravaging envisaged at the inception of the Delian League.[43]

The expedition of Cyrus was thought to change all that. It was thought to show that an army could march up-country and fight and defeat the King on his own home ground. There was, of course, a world of difference between a prince of the blood royal in revolt against his brother and a Greek general at the head of a Greek army making the long march. Yet undoubtedly there was a great quickening of Panhellenist blood after 401. In 380 Isocrates in his *Panegyricus* expounded the doctrine of Panhellenism – 'what oft was thought but ne'er so well expressed', as he might have said – let the Greeks stop fighting each other and join in fighting the Persians; the King's power is not as great as it seems; one has only to think of those who went on the expedition of

42. Scythian proposal for a joint attack: Hdt. 6.84. 'I know full well': Hdt. 7.11.2–3.
43. The Reconciliation Speech: Ar. *Lys.* 1114–35. Cimon's dictum: Plut. *Cim.* 16.10. The inception of the League: Thuc. 1.96.1.

Cyrus; the Persians are an effeminate lot; we must relieve the misery of the Greeks. 'Whenever we transport a force greater than the King's, which if we wanted to we could easily do, we will safely enjoy the profits of the whole of Asia', 'transferring', as he puts it, 'the prosperity of Asia to Europe'. In the Philippus of 346 he talks specifically of 'the foundation of cities', 'the settlement of the poor and landless of Greece', but his meaning in 380 is plain enough.[44]

By the time Xenophon got down to writing his *Anabasis*, the Panhellenist idea was spreading. Agesilaus, who had planned, according to Xenophon in the *Hellenica*, in the campaigning season of 394 'to march up-country as far as he could', perhaps not all that far in truth, had been addressed by Isocrates in a letter and begged to lead the Greeks in a great Panhellenic crusade, and Jason of Pherae had, according to the *Hellenica*, been talking big about making the King subject, though according to Isocrates it was all 'words, words, words'. Panhellenist sentiments were in vogue.[45]

Panhellenism has at least tinged the *Anabasis*.[46] The obvious moment is in the speech which Xenophon presents himself as having made in the assembly held at dawn of the day after the arrest of the generals. Following on proposals covering the use of cavalry, helping themselves to guides, securing supplies, river crossings, there occurs a celebrated morale-raising passage:

> If the rivers don't permit of crossing and no guide is found for us, even so we need not lose heart. We know well that against the wishes of the Great King the Mysians, who we wouldn't say are our superiors, inhabit within the King's territory many large, prosperous cities, as do the Pisidians, and we know from our own experience that the Lycaonians have taken strongpoints in low-lying areas and live off the land. As for ourselves, I would have said we should no longer be clearly setting out for home but should make preparations as if we intended to settle here. I know the King would provide even the Mysians with plenty of guides and would give plenty of hostages as a guarantee that there was no trickery in sending them away and would

---

44. Isoc. *Paneg.* 166, 187; *Philippus* 120.
45. Agesilaus' aims: *Hell.* 4.1.41. Isocrates' plea to Agesilaus: Speusippus, *Letter to Philip* 13. Jason of Pherae: *Hell.* 6.1.12; Isoc. 5.119.
46. For Xenophon and Panhellenism, cf. J. Morr, 'Xenophon und der Gedanke eines allgriechischen Eroberungszuges gegen Persien', *Wiener Studien* 45 (1926–7), pp. 186–201, and Dillery, *Xenophon and the History of his Times*, pp. 59–63. At *Anab.* 3.4.26 Xenophon has the barbarians being lashed into firing arrows. Like the lashing of Herodotus' account of Thermopylae (Hdt. 7.223.3), such treatment of barbarians did not have to be seen to be believed.

even construct roads for them if they wanted to go off in four-horse chariots. Yea, for us he would, I am sure, have done this thrice gladly, if he had seen us preparing to stay. My fear is rather that if once we learn to live in idleness and keep ourselves in abundance and sleep with the lovely big women and maidens of the Medes and the Persians, we will, like the Lotus-eaters, forget the way home. So it seems to me right and proper in the first place to try to get to Greece and to our own people and show the Greeks that they live in penury by their own choice when they could see those who are now citizens there and have a hard time of it coming here and being rich.[47]

It cannot be proved that Xenophon did not say all this in that tense dawn assembly, but it seems very improbable. The Greeks were in an extremely difficult and dangerous situation and such cheerful talk would deceive no one. Even if they were to get home, it was hardly to be thought that other Greeks would be tempted to put their heads into the lion's jaws. The speech was pure Panhellenism – the weakness of Persia and the ease with which Asia could be colonized and Greece's economic miseries alleviated. It was the Panhellenist icing on the cake. It is to be noted this uplifting passage not only comes after a string of practical proposals but also is followed by a proposal that the wagons should be burned. The passage could be an insertion, but in any case it seems likely to represent Xenophon's afterthoughts.

Elsewhere[48] Xenophon has Cyrus address the senior officers of the Greek part of his army thus:

O Greeks, it is not because I am short of barbarian manpower that I am taking you as my fellow-warriors but, since I consider you better and more powerful than a multitude of barbarians, I have for that reason added you to my army. So see that you prove yourselves worthy of the freedom which you possess and on which I congratulate you. You know full well that I would rather have freedom in place of all I have and many times more besides.

Then in reply to an interjection by Gaulites he seems to imply that, if he is victorious, all of Artaxerxes' satraps will be replaced by Cyrus' friends.

---

47. *Anab.* 3.2.23–5.
48. *Anab.* 1.7.3. On this passage see also Braun, chapter 3 in this volume.

Did Cyrus say such things? He certainly was capable, like other Persian grandees, of the fulsome phrase, as he showed in his dealings with Lysander,[49] and one would hardly claim that such a speech could not have been made. But for Cyrus, aspirant to the royal power, to be represented as having said that he preferred liberty was going improbably far. Perhaps Xenophon's Panhellenist enthusiasm has led him to overstep the bounds.

One other passage[50] strikes one similarly. The army had waited twenty days for Tissaphernes to return and lead them back to Greece. They had begun to fear that the Oriental part of Cyrus' army would go over to the King. The Greeks went to Clearchus and Xenophon represents them as saying, 'What are we waiting for? Don't we know that the King would do anything to destroy us so as to make the rest of the Greeks afraid to campaign against the Great King?' The idea of the Greeks in general launching an attack on Persia was in 401 surely anachronistic. By the time Xenophon wrote, however, such sentiments were not inapposite and here too one may suspect that Xenophon was writing under the influence of Panhellenism.

We should not, however, regard the *Anabasis* as Panhellenist apologia. Panhellenism provided the gloss, but no more than that. Xenophon had a tale to tell in which he himself had to play the leading part. Someone had told the tale differently and moved Xenophon to put the record straight. The book was in that sense apologia, personal apologia. He was by 370 warmly Panhellenist and when two or three years later Persia dropped Sparta and looked to Thebes, he became hotly Panhellenist.[51] The rising temperature is noticeable, but it would be wrong to think of the book as essentially Panhellenist propaganda.

---

49. *Hell.* 1.5.3.
50. *Anab.* 2.4.3.
51. Cf. Mesk, 'Die Tendenz der Xenophontischen *Anabasis*', p. 140.

2   *One* Anabasis *or Two?*[1]

P. J. STYLIANOU

I

We have not one account of the expedition of Cyrus, but two: Xenophon's and Diodorus'. What is the foundation of the second account? It is a truth universally acknowledged that Diodorus' account in book 14, chapters 19–31 and 37, is a summary of a longer account which once stood in the now lost *Histories* of Ephorus, a leading historian of the fourth century.[2]

What, however, were the origins of the Ephoran narrative? It is this question which has occasioned controversy. It is a common enough belief among scholars that Ephorus had scant regard for Xenophon, so much so that he completely eschewed use of his *Hellenica* and made limited use even of the famous *Anabasis*, preferring other accounts instead.[3]

As far as the *Hellenica* is concerned Ephorus made little use of it, it is true, not only because he did not share Xenophon's political views of Athens, Sparta, and Thebes, but also because the *Hellenica* was too sparse to serve the purposes of Ephorus; it was not comprehensive enough and it certainly lacked sufficient detail.[4] The *Anabasis*, on the other hand, the work of a participant, was a different case and, as I wish to argue, could hardly be avoided.

1. This paper is in memory of His Excellency Constantine Leventis.
2. For Diodorus' general reliance on Ephorus, cf. P. J. Stylianou, *A Historical Commentary on Diodorus Siculus Book* 15 (Oxford, 1998), pp. 49f. Ephorus is named twice in connection with the expedition of Cyrus, at Diod. 14.11.2 (cf. 14.22.1) and 14.22.2.
3. My own past view too: Stylianou, *A Historical Commentary*, p. 104. I was wrong to say there (n. 275) that H. D. Westlake, 'Diodorus and the expedition of Cyrus', in *Studies in Thucydides and Greek History* (Manchester, 1989), pp. 260ff., claims that the *Anabasis* was not used at all by Ephorus. For Westlake's view, see below, n. 7.
4. Use of *Hellenica*: see Stylianou, *A Historical Commentary*, p. 104. Add *Hell.* 4.2.8: Agesilaus in 394 follows *tēn autēn hodon hēnper basileus hote epi tēn Hellada estrateuen*. Cp. Diod. 14.83.3: *tēn autēn diexiōn chōran hēn kaì Xerxēs eporeuthē, kath' hon kairon estrateusen epi tous Hellēnas*. This may well have been borrowed from Xenophon. Similarly the return to Athens of Alcibiades in 407 in Diodorus seems 'coloured' by Xenophon's vivid description; cp. in particular Diod. 13.68.3 with *Hell.* 1.4.13. Cf. also C. J. Tuplin, *The*

Nonetheless, opinion in the nineteenth century mostly favoured Sophaenetus as the chief source of Ephorus. He was the Arcadian general mentioned by Xenophon in the *Anabasis*, and was alleged to have composed an account of the expedition of Cyrus with the same title. There was a reaction to this view early in the twentieth century by Ed Schwartz and A. von Mess. Schwartz stated the matter briefly. His view was that Xenophon provides the foundation for the account in Diodorus, though with small additions from the *Persica* of Ctesias. Schwartz did not argue his case further, but a close analysis of the texts was offered by von Mess.[5]

His study is still fundamental though underrated nowadays. Von Mess notices the very many points where there is factual and even verbal correspondence between Xenophon and Diodorus and draws the logical conclusion that the latter account must ultimately, through Ephorus, be based on the former. Briefly he argues that for the Katabasis, or march through Asia to the sea, Diodorus' account is founded almost exclusively on Xenophon, with traces of another source used sparingly by Ephorus as a supplement. For the Anabasis, on the other hand, for the battle of Cunaxa and for a number of places in the early part of the Katabasis Xenophon's account was combined with another source, one which saw matters from the Persian point of view, a *Persica* in other words. Our substantial fragments from Ctesias leave us in little doubt that his *Persica* was the alternative source employed by Ephorus here.[6]

Yet many commentators have remained unconvinced by Schwartz and von Mess. They have either continued to favour the priority of Sophaenetus or made alternative proposals. Schwartz had also questioned the very genuineness of an *Anabasis* by Sophaenetus, and none other than Jacoby was inclined to agree with him.[7]

Failings of Empire: A Reading of Xenophon Hellenica 2.3.11–7.5.27 (Stuttgart, 1993), p. 24 n. 41. And of course Ephorus adapted *Hell.* 3.1.1 for his own account of the expedition of Cyrus: see text below. *Hellenica* too sparse for Ephorus: cf. Stylianou, *A Historical Commentary*, pp. 127f., 602 s.v. 'Xenophon'.

5. The alleged account of Sophaenetus: cf. E. Bux, 'Sophainetos', *RE* III A1 (1927), cols 1008ff., at col. 1010. Contrast Ed Schwartz, 'Ephoros', *RE* VI (1909), col. 10; A. von Mess, 'Untersuchungen über Ephoros', *RhM* 61 (1906), pp. 360–407.
6. Von Mess, 'Untersuchungen über Ephoros', pp. 376f. Among contemporary scholars Bigwood accepts von Mess's conclusions: J. M. Bigwood, 'The ancient accounts of the battle of Cunaxa', *AJP* 104 (1983), pp. 340ff., at p. 349. In her n. 42 she points to some significant verbal affinities between the two writers.
7. Among supporters of Sophaenetus, I single out for mention Bux, 'Sophainetos', and the more recent work of G. L. Cawkwell, introduction to *Xenophon: The Persian Expedition* (Harmondsworth, 1972), pp. 9ff., and chapter 1 of the present volume. Both are positive that Xenophon was not Ephorus' chief source. While they agree that this source cannot

One can easily see why. How is it that such a work, of the first importance if it existed, is not known to anyone through all the long centuries of antiquity, with the single exception of the Byzantine drudge Stephanus? With this single, very late exception, only Xenophon was known in antiquity to have participated in the march of the Ten Thousand and to have written an account of it.[8]

By itself this general silence about Sophaenetus as writer would not be a conclusive objection, though it is rather surprising all the same: to be used by Ephorus a generation later the hypothetical *Anabasis* of Sophaenetus would have to be fairly well-known and widely distributed. But my main objection is that I find no evidence in Diodorus for the use by Ephorus of such a source. The four fragments of 'Sophaenetus' do not correspond with Diodorus at any

be definitely identified, a simple process of elimination in their arguments points to Sophaenetus as the obvious candidate. O. Lendle, *Kommentar zu Xenophons Anabasis* (Darmstadt, 1995), pp. 12, 249, thinks it possible that Diodorus, through Ephorus, goes back to Sophaenetus, in part at least. Westlake, 'Diodorus and the expedition of Cyrus', puts forward the *Hellenica Oxyrhynchia* as the main source of Ephorus, allowing only limited use of the *Anabasis*. Not only is there not a shred of evidence to connect this particular account in Diodorus with the *Hell. Oxy.*, but it is very much to be doubted that the Oxyrhynchus Historian would have included an account of the expedition of Cyrus in his work. At most he may have referred to it very briefly at the right place, as does Xenophon in his own *Hellenica* at 3.1.1–2. If Ephorus wrote in the late 330s and 320s (Stylianou, *A Historical Commentary*, pp. 110ff.), more fourth-century works were available to him than generally supposed. None of these however can have dealt with the expedition of Cyrus, or if they did, they did so in the briefest terms. Of *Persica* compositions, use of that of Deinon is probable (Stylianou, *A Historical Commentary*, pp. 108f.), but these works cannot have dealt with the expedition as a whole. Some use may also have been made of military handbooks for odd items. But with the exception of Xenophon and Ctesias, as well as snippets from Ephorus' own knowledge in the closing stages of the Katabasis (see the text below), use of any other sources cannot be detected for certain. Schwartz's scepticism about Sophaenetus: apud von Mess, 'Untersuchungen über Ephoros', p. 372 n. 3. Jacoby's view: *FGH* II D 349f.

8. See Westlake, 'Diodorus and the expedition of Cyrus', pp. 267ff., for similar arguments. Well-informed writers like Dionysius of Halicarnassus and Aelius Aristides have not heard of any other *Anabasis* but that of Xenophon, and neither has Arrian, who makes repeated reference in his own *Anabasis* to Xenophon and the Ten Thousand. Plutarch would undoubtedly have used such a work in his *Artaxerxes* had he known it (cf. also Plut. *Ant.* 45). Earlier than all these, Polybius, arguably the best, as well as keenest military historian of antiquity, was familiar with the work of the military writer Aeneas Tacticus. Yet he refers to 'the return of the Greeks under Xenophon from the upper satrapies' (Polyb. 3.6.10) and does not know of an account of the expedition by Sophaenetus, a fellow Arcadian. Nor, for what this is worth, was Sophaenetus known to the chronographic tradition. Diodorus' chronographer does not seem to know him, though he knows Xenophon and Ctesias and other writers of *Persica*, and the same is true of Eusebius: Euseb. *Chron.* Ol. 95.1 (400/399) [*FGH* 688 T 5]: 'Xenofon, filius Grylli, et Ctesias clari habentur.'

point, though there is correspondence with Xenophon. This is especially true of the fourth fragment.[9]

This fact has been variously explained. In 1927 Bux concluded that the accounts of the expedition of Cyrus by the two men must have been very similar in most respects, not only in general outline and language, but in their detail too, in the facts and names they gave. As Diodorus' short version of the story must be based, through Ephorus, on one or the other of the two accounts, and as the 'numerous divergences' Bux perceives between Diodorus and Xenophon lead him to the view that Diodorus cannot be based on Xenophon, he is left with Sophaenetus as the only serious candidate for this role. Bux stops short of actually identifying Sophaenetus as Ephorus' main source, but his arguments allow no other conclusion.[10]

On Bux's theory then we should have to assume that there existed two detailed accounts of the expedition, so close to each other that they cannot have been easy to distinguish. Apart from begging the question at issue, this is a most improbable hypothesis and the four tiny fragments of 'Sophaenetus' in Stephanus of Byzantium are hardly sufficient to sustain it.[11] To suppose that another member of the Ten Thousand also kept notes (for the necessity of such notes see below) and composed an account of the march based on those notes which turned out to be very close to that of Xenophon, and indeed in many places coincided with it, is to strain credibility somewhat.

Cawkwell asserts the priority of Sophaenetus another way, by first examining the motives of Xenophon for writing. Since he had a good story to tell, why did he not write it for more than thirty years? What moved him to write when he did? Cawkwell's thesis[12] is that Xenophon's principal motivation for

9. The anonymity of the *Hell. Oxy.* to which Cawkwell draws attention (p. 61 above) is not therefore a good parallel: it is obvious that Ephorus did not rely on Xenophon's *Hellenica*, but on other sources, especially the *Hell. Oxy.* In addition, the three separate copies of this work on papyrus discovered so far attest to its popularity and make it increasingly unlikely that we do not know the name of the Oxyrhynchus Historian; it is just that we cannot yet decide definitely between the different candidates. 'Sophaenetus': *FGH* II B 109; the fourth fragment = *Anab.* 1.5.10.
10. Bux, 'Sophainetos', cols 1012–3.
11. Bigwood, 'The ancient accounts of the battle of Cunaxa', p. 349, aptly refers to the belief that Sophaenetus was Ephorus' chief source as 'a desperate hypothesis given that ... virtually nothing is known of Sophaenetus' work'. This rather invalidates attempts such as that by Cawkwell, introduction to *Xenophon: The Persian Expedition*, pp. 17ff., to discover Sophaenetus in Diodorus, supposedly an earlier and more balanced account than Xenophon's, and to use this against Xenophon.
12. This was originally argued by F. Dürrbach, 'L'apologie de Xénophon dans l'Anabase', *REG* 6 (1893), pp. 343–86, at pp. 346ff.

writing was the publication of an account of the expedition by Sophaenetus which, in Xenophon's opinion, did less than justice to the part he played in it.

He finds proof of this in Diodorus whose account, in Cawkwell's view, is based not on Xenophon, but in all likelihood on Sophaenetus. Xenophon did not like what Sophaenetus wrote, but Ephorus did, and that is why in Diodorus it is said that though the Greeks, after the arrest of Clearchus and the others, elected a number of generals, they 'entrusted one of them, Chirisophus the Lacedaemonian, with the overall command'. 'This, perhaps, moved Xenophon mightily,' Cawkwell suggests.[13]

I cannot agree. I consider that the whole of this section of Diodorus (like most of the rest of his account) derives ultimately from Xenophon. Immediately after stating that the overall command was assigned to Chirisophus, Diodorus goes on to say that *houtoi de diataxantes to stratopedon eis tēn hodoiporían hōs pot' autois edokei kallista ktl.* Exactly as Xenophon reports, in other words: not Chirisophus alone, but the generals together (*houtoi*) arranged the army for the march 'just as it seemed to them (*autois*) best'. We have here an instance of Ephorus reading a little more in Xenophon than he should, but understandably so. Towards the end of the meeting which followed the election of new officers Xenophon proposed that Chirisophus should lead the army on the march, 'since he is also a Lacedaemonian'. That does clearly imply a position of 'first among equals' (as Clearchus had been, as all sources agree), the general who led the van of the army, a post of honour and responsibility – why else mention his nationality (as Ephorus in Diodorus does in imitation of Xenophon)? And 'lead' the army Chirisophus did; all the way to Trapezus and beyond.[14] Diodorus 14.27.1–2 (and 30.4: *ton aphēgoumenon*) is easily enough explained on the basis of what Xenophon says, and the hypothesis of an alternative source such as Sophaenetus is not necessary.

Xenophon, it is true, is not mentioned in Diodorus until 14.37, when he was elected to sole command. However, Chirisophus himself is not mentioned either after 27.1 until 30.4, while Sophaenetus is *never* mentioned.[15] So the long

---

13. Diod. 14.27.1. See p. 62 above. On the other hand Cawkwell seems correct to me about the date of writing of the *Anabasis*, the 360s, p. 48 above.
14. 'Since he is also a Lacedaemonian': *Anab.* 3.2.37. Further examples of Chirisophus' leadership: *Anab.* 4.1.6, 7, 15. Compare also *Anab.* 3.3.3, where he speaks clearly as senior general.
15. Pace G. L. Barber, *The Historian Ephorus* (Cambridge, 1935), p. 126. Repeated at Diod. 14.27.2 is the earlier statement (at Diod. 14.25.8) that the Greeks intended to head towards Paphlagonia. It is not impossible that this is an item borrowed from Ctesias. But it seems more likely to me that it represents Ephorus' inference of what Ariaeus

One Anabasis *or Two?*

silence about Xenophon cannot be used as an argument against him and in favour of Sophaenetus as a source.

It is generally agreed that there is apologia in the *Anabasis*, that Xenophon was responding to particular criticisms and differing interpretations of the facts. However, they did not have to be written accounts of the expedition; they could just as well be oral reports, of which there must have been many.[16] We have to face the probability that Xenophon's was the only written account of the famous march by a participant. If so, it was inevitable that Ephorus should rely on the *Anabasis*, whatever he may have thought of Xenophon and the *Hellenica*.

What is more, the subject-matter of the *Anabasis* is such that a Greek patriot of the Isocratean stamp like Ephorus cannot have objected to it. Nor is Plutarch counter-evidence. He speaks of many accounts of the battle of Cunaxa, but not of the expedition as a whole.[17] I assume that what Plutarch has in mind are *Persica* or general histories such as Ephorus' or perhaps even military handbooks of one sort or another.

If the *Anabasis* of Sophaenetus is a mirage, how did belief in it come about? The town of Stymphalus in Arcadia must have been awash with stories about the expedition. Agasias the captain (a friend of Xenophon), Aeneas the captain, and Sophaenetus the general, all came from there. Stories of such people will have passed into military handbooks. Incidents related in such handbooks

    proposed to the Greeks according to Xenophon (*Anab.* 2.2.11): a longer route back to the Aegean coast than the one they had followed on the Anabasis. As Ariaeus cannot have intended heading north all the way and into the mountains of the Carduchi (the route the Greeks were in the end forced to take), he must have meant a march in a north-westerly direction which *eventually* led to Paphlagonia, though presumably they would have headed west before they entered that country, probably following the royal road which ran east–west, skirting the southern boundaries of Paphlagonia. Possibly Ephorus, who fancied himself as a geographer and ethnographer, explained all this more fully and Diodorus, in his usual way, retained only the item about Paphlagonia.

16. See e.g. at *Anab.* 2.1.17. The comments in Isocrates on Clearchus and Cyrus have such an origin: Isoc. 4.145; 5.90ff., 8.98; 9.58; 12.104. Cf. Stylianou, *A Historical Commentary*, pp. 107ff. Why Xenophon should have waited for so many years before composing an account of the deeds of the Ten Thousand is not a question we can ever hope to answer satisfactorily. There was increasing criticism of Spartan policies after the King's Peace and especially after the battle of Leuctra; Xenophon himself may have found his past life and actions under the spotlight following his expulsion from his estate at Skillous after Leuctra, when living as a refugee in Corinth in the 360s. This *may* have acted as one incentive for writing. But the origins of books are rarely transparent. C. S. Lewis offers some very pertinent remarks on this in his brilliant essay generally entitled 'Fern-seed and elephants'.

17. Plut. *Artax.* 8.1; cf. 9.4, about the killing of Artagerses by Cyrus 'about which they all write'. Xenophon gives the same information, but as *legetai*: *Anab.* 1.8.24.

from the point of view of the veteran Sophaenetus, and introduced, perhaps, with something like *Sophainetos stratēgōn en Kurou anabasei ktl* may have given rise in late antiquity to a mistaken belief that there was an actual account of the expedition by Sophaenetus. This seems to me a better explanation of the fragments in Stephanus of Byzantium than the possibility of an outright forgery.[18]

II

Before turning our attention to the text of Diodorus it is well to bear in mind certain facts. First, what we have in Diodorus is an epitome of Ephorus' account, which was itself a summary and to some extent an adaptation of Ephorus' source or sources. Ephorus was no mere compiler. He could recast his sources, and even interfere with their historical causation and interpretation. This habit of his needs especially to be watched in source criticism. Secondly, all the usual provisos apply about Diodorus' own slipshod ways.[19] Nor should we overlook the possibility of errors introduced by scribes. Also, like Ephorus, Diodorus tended to impose his own language and style on his sources. All these difficulties notwithstanding, enough remains to show that Xenophon was indeed Ephorus' principal source, as von Mess contended nearly a century ago. His case can, I think, be made stronger.

Two important general observations strongly, perhaps even decisively, point to Xenophon as the basic source of Ephorus. The first observation concerns the remnants in Diodorus of a chronological framework of the march as well

---

18. For such anecdotes in the handbooks compare Polyaenus *Strat.* 1.49; 2.2. Forgery: Westlake, 'Diodorus and the expedition of Cyrus', p. 269.
19. For Ephorus' tendency to meddle with the detail of his sources on occasion, including the numbers, see R. Meiggs, *The Athenian Empire* (Oxford, 1972), pp. 447ff.; Stylianou, *A Historical Commentary*, pp. 128ff. As for historical reinterpretation, we have an excellent example in the way Ephorus in Diodorus habitually calls the soldiers of Agesilaus in Asia in 395 'Lacedaemonians' while his source, the *Hell. Oxy.*, equally habitually refers to them as 'Greeks': Stylianou, *A Historical Commentary*, pp. 119f. This can cause problems for interpreters. Westlake, for instance, states that he intends in his study to direct attention 'not to divergences on points of detail, which could have arisen through faulty transmission, as on troop numbers, which are notoriously unreliable estimates, but rather to divergences on major issues which influenced, or might have influenced, the course of events' (Westlake, 'Diodorus and the expedition of Cyrus', p. 261). In the case of a writer like Ephorus this is a principle replete with dangers which can lead one astray, as Westlake is in fact led astray by it: see nn. 42 and 51 below. For Diodorus' methods see Stylianou, *A Historical Commentary*, esp. pp. 132ff.

as of other running data, including details such as the width of rivers. This material clearly derives from Xenophon, being Xenophon's own – otherwise we would have to suppose, a most unlikely supposition, the use by both Xenophon and Ephorus of a common *written* source to explain the striking coincidences between Diodorus and Xenophon. That this material in Xenophon is indeed Xenophon's own, based on notes he made at the time, needs to be established at this point, especially because Cawkwell has mounted a strong attack against it.[20]

The chief and most obvious indication that Xenophon kept some kind of diary is the firm, though by no means perfect, chronological framework of the march which forms the backbone of the narrative all the way from Sardis to Chrysopolis and the end of book 6.[21] No matter how good his memory, Xenophon could not possibly have recollected all these figures more than thirty years later. In fact, I doubt he could have remembered them so precisely even days later. So, if he did not keep a diary, there are only two possibilities: either he borrowed them from the work of someone else, or, if they are his own, they are largely fictitious. I cannot recall anyone ever suggesting the second alternative. Cawkwell prefers the first alternative. He proposes that Xenophon used some sort of listing or itinerary of distances and the like in the Persian Empire.

20. Cawkwell, introduction to *Xenophon: The Persian Expedition*, pp. 21ff., and pp. 54–5 above. Scholars in general agree that Xenophon kept something like a diary; cf. R. D. Barnett, 'Xenophon and the Wall of Media', *JHS* 83 (1963), pp. 1ff., at p. 1; J. Roy, 'Xenophon's evidence for the *Anabasis*', *Athenaeum* 46 (1968), pp. 37–46, at p. 43. Cawkwell's arguments against it are not compelling. From the time he accepted Proxenus' invitation Xenophon knew he was in for adventure in Asia Minor, by participating in the proclaimed expedition against the Pisidians (*Anab.* 1.1.11; 3.1.9). That was incentive enough to start making notes. Orontas did not lack either the materials or the opportunity to write to the King (*Anab.* 1.6.3); and Proxenus communicated his invitation to Xenophon by means of a letter (3.1.5). Educated, upper-class Greeks like Proxenus and Xenophon must have had writing materials in their baggage when travelling as a matter of course. I see no practical difficulties for the carrying of writing materials all through the expedition. Even after the Carduchi the Greeks were far from destitute of personal belongings (see esp. *Anab.* 4.1.12–14; 3.19; 3.30). If Silanus the seer could hold on to his 3,000 darics all the way (*Anab.* 5.6.18), then so could Xenophon to his writing materials, not to mention his valuable horse (7.2.3). We might consider the case of Captain Bligh in 1789 who, in a small, cramped, open boat, over 4,000 miles of ocean, for forty-eight days, most of these wet and cold, and with writing materials not radically different from those employed by the ancient Greeks, kept up his log with daily entries. Cawkwell further finds the occasional gaps and vagueness in Xenophon strange, if Xenophon really kept a diary. Diaries, however, are rarely perfect, for all sorts of reasons, and one does not disbelieve in them because of this.
21. Book 7 is different: below n. 27.

When Xenophon wrote there may have existed the kind of listing Cawkwell suggests, and Xenophon may have consulted such a text, as he clearly consulted the work of Ctesias (to which he rightly gave little credit, as Plutarch observes).[22] But Xenophon does not just give (when he does) the stages of the march (stathmoi) and the distances in parasangs; he also regularly gives the number of days which the troops spent resting and/or gathering provisions. Are we then to suppose that Xenophon remembered the latter type of detail thirty years later, but that the stages and distances of the march he lifted from some kind of written source?

We should also note that Cyrus down to Cunaxa, and the Ten Thousand subsequently, did not keep to the beaten track. It is a mere assumption that the kind of book Cawkwell proposes would have covered such unusual routes. Distances from one well-known point to another might have been marked in this putative handbook, but occasionally Xenophon gives distances for a march from nowhere in particular to an equally unremarkable place.[23]

The figures which Xenophon gives apply uniquely to the expedition he is describing and are therefore his own and not borrowed from any written source. It is an inevitable conclusion that they were obtained, or even worked out, by Xenophon himself certainly (see below), though initially no doubt with the help of others more familiar with the Persian Empire and its ways[24] and noted down at the time. Pace Cawkwell we should not be particularly concerned about the fact that stathmoi and parasangs peter out after Trapezus. This is hardly surprising and by itself it does not prove that the figures are not Xenophon's own.

---

22. Plut. *Artax.* 13.6. I have no objection to Xenophon employing some kind of book, as Cawkwell suggests, to add local 'colour' to his account by interspersing here and there the odd geographical or ethnological item, but is it really necessary so to assume? Cawkwell cites *Anab.* 3.4.7ff. as such instances. Note, however, the *legetai* at *Anab.* 3.4.11. I think he picked up this sort of thing, and probably noted it down too, at the time, along with the measurements he gives. Cawkwell also wonders about *Anab.* 4.8.1: how did Xenophon find out about the boundary between the Macrones and the Scytheni? Most obviously, I think, from the Macrones themselves and through the means of the Hellenized peltast who came from that part of the world. Why conjure up a written source when Xenophon was there in person? See *Anab.* 3.5.14–17, an important passage in this regard: *ēlegchon . . . elegon . . . legetai . . . ephasan . . . akousantes*, the sort of verbs found in many places in the *Anabasis*. Enquiry made at the time was the chief source of information for Xenophon, much of it noted down, in my view.
23. Cf. *Anab.* 3.4.13, 23f.
24. There are lots of possible candidates here. The Greeks made regular use of Persian speakers and guides and did not in general lack informants: *Anab.* 3.5.14–17 and 4.5.10 are particularly good instances.

One Anabasis *or Two?*

The point can, I think, be demonstrated from the text. Marching through the Arabian Desert along the east side of the Euphrates (not a common route), Cyrus, as Xenophon points out, made some of the stathmoi exceptionally long. The forced marches were necessitated not only by the need to reach water or fodder before stopping, but also by Cyrus' reasoning that the sooner they came up with the King's army, the less formidable the latter would be. This is borne out by the figures given which are thus specific to the occasion, and consequently Xenophon's own. See further *Anab*. 1.8.1: it was mid-morning and marching along they had almost reached the place (stathmos) where Cyrus had intended to stop. Their marching stathmoi, therefore, were suited to their needs and took account of the time of the year – it is very hot in that region in late summer.[25]

At the end of the battle of Cunaxa, we are told that Ariaeus fled back to the stathmos they had set off from in the morning. This stathmos was 'reported' to be four parasangs away. This is an interesting observation. Xenophon clearly obtained this item of information at the time, in parasangs, and not from some book years later. Similarly, he says that the Median Wall was 'reported' to be twenty parasangs long. Shortly before, we see Xenophon himself calculating distances in parasangs: not trusting each other, Greeks and Persians would camp with a parasang or more between them. The gist of the brief speech by Ariaeus must have been reported to Xenophon, doubtless by Proxenus, but the seventeen stathmoi mentioned in it may well be Xenophon's own calculation. Ariaeus also suggested that they ought to make the first stathmoi as long as possible in order to put as much distance between themselves and the King as possible. That was the strategy, but fate intervened, as Xenophon comments, and events developed differently. Nevertheless, had they acted on the advice of Ariaeus, Xenophon would have cited the numbers of stathmoi covered, probably with the corresponding parasangs, and these would again have been his own figures. I see no reason, therefore, for denying Xenophon this sort of information. As he could not possibly have recollected it all decades later, ergo he kept a diary.[26]

---

25. Need to reach water: *Anab*. 1.5.7. Pre-empting the King's forces: *Anab*. 1.5.9. Figures for the stathmoi: *Anab*. 1.5.1, 5. Cf. Barnett, 'Xenophon and the Wall of Media', p. 6.
26. Length of the Median wall: *Anab*. 2.4.12. Camping in mutual mistrust: *Anab*. 2.4.10. The speech of Ariaeus: *Anab*. 2.2.11–12. Fate intervenes: *Anab*. 2.2.13. The individual character and true nature of these items in Xenophon is perceived by C. Høeg, '*Xenophontos Kyrou Anabasis*. Oeuvre anonyme ou pseudonyme ou orthonyme?', *C & M* 11 (1950), pp. 151ff., at p. 174. There is much else in the *Anabasis* books 1–6 that must be the result of notes made at the time. See (very much at random): *Anab*. 2.4.13 (this 'smells' strongly

Xenophon composed the *Anabasis* more than thirty years after the event, but it was constructed on a foundation of notes made at the time. Through these notes ran the framework of the chronology of the march from Sardis to Chrysopolis, which effectively marked the end of the expedition. The whole march, both the Anabasis and the Katabasis, took a year and three months, which surely means from Sardis to Chrysopolis. Interestingly Ephorus too saw the expedition as concluded with the arrival at Chrysopolis.[27]

III

Remnants of Xenophon's chronological framework are found in a number of places in Diodorus, not only in the Katabasis, and this is worth noticing, but also in the Anabasis. In a relatively brief account of the expedition Ephorus did not require all of Xenophon's chronological and other running data. Diodorus retained even less of it, but the remains are crucially significant evidence in any source-critical study of his account.

The army stayed at Tarsus for twenty days (Diod. 14.20.4 = *Anab.* 1.3.1). The twenty days it took to march to Thapsacus at Diod. 14.21.5 are a summing up of the respective figures in *Anab.* 1.4.6–11,[28] whose figure of a five-day stay at Thapsacus Diodorus also reproduces. The three-day truce at Diod. 14.26.2–3 at first sight appears to be in conflict with Xenophon, but further reflection

of a diary entry), 2.4.24 (a bridge made of thirty-seven ships tied together), 3.4.7–12, 5.4.11ff. (on the Mossynoeci), 6.2.3 (who could remember this sort of stuff thirty-odd years later?).

27. Sardis to Chrysopolis: *Anab.* 1.2.5–6.6.38. A year and three months: *Anab.* 7.8.26. Ephorus' view of Chrysopolis: Diod. 14.31.4f. Though, to judge from Diodorus, Ephorus summarized book 7 and included it in his narrative of the war of Sparta against Persia in Asia (Diod. 14.37.1–4). Book 7 of the *Anabasis* is different in several respects from the previous books. There are a number of random chronological indications, but the running chronological framework is no longer in evidence and the book in fact covers some six months in all; cf. e.g. *Anab.* 7.8.7–8: there is no chronology and the distances are not given. The narrative is very brief and vague in places (cf. e.g. *Anab.* 7.5.12–14). It would appear that this last part of the *Anabasis* did not have the benefit of notes made at the time, but was based entirely on memory. I take *Anab.* 2.2.6, 5.5.4 and 7.8.25f. to be Xenophon's own calculations and memoranda and therefore, perhaps, part of his original jottings down (thus also Lendle, *Kommentar zu Xenophons Anabasis*, pp. 97, 338): see *elegonto* (*Anab.* 2.2.6) and *epēlthomen* (7.8.25). Why P. Masqueray, *Xénophon: Anabasis* (2 vols, Paris, 1930), ad loc., should consider, without argument, *Anab.* 7.8.25f. to have been borrowed from some other *Anabasis*, perhaps that of Sophaenetus (he suggests), is mysterious to me. It should be noted that Seuthes and Thrace are mentioned in *Anab.* 7.8.25, but it is doubtful that Sophaenetus was still serving then.

28. Thus correctly von Mess, 'Untersuchungen über Ephoros', p. 381 and n. 1. I agree with him that the sum includes the seven days Cyrus spent at Myriandrus: *Anab.* 1.4.6.

shows that what we have here is Diodorus' incompetent telescoping of Ephorus' summary of *Anab.* 2.2–3, as 2.3.17 demonstrates: the initial temporary truce did indeed last for three days and therein lies Diodorus' confusion.

The march through the land of the Carduchi took up seven days (Diod. 14.27.4 = *Anab.* 4.3.2). The figure of eight days spent in the Armenian villages (Diod. 14.29.1) corresponds with *Anab.* 4.6.1, while the fifteen days passed in the lands of the Chaoi (Taochians in Xenophon: see below for the differences in names) and Phasians again appears to be the sum of the various relevant figures in Xenophon (at *Anab.* 4.6.4, 5, 22–3, and 7.1).[29] On the other hand the four days which the Greeks are said to have spent at the river Phasis (Diod. 14.29.1) find no analogy in Xenophon (*Anab.* 4.6.4).

Thereafter they took seven days to traverse the land of the Chaldaeans before arriving at the river Harpagus, which was four plethra wide. They remained for three days in the plain of the Scytini (Scytheni in Xenophon), then setting out, they arrived on the fourth day at the city of Gymnasia, 'Gymnias' in Xenophon (Diod. 14.29.2). All these figures correspond exactly with those in Xenophon (*Anab.* 4.7.15, 18–19). From Gymnasia, after a march of fifteen days, or so the text of Diodorus tells us, they reached Mount Chenion (Theches in Xenophon) and beheld the sea (Diod. 14.29.3). It seems quite evident to me that 'fifteen' is an error for the 'five' in Xenophon (*Anab.* 4.7.21).[30]

After the episode with the lethal honey of the Colchians, 'when they had regained their strength in three days', they marched to Trapezus, where they remained for thirty days. Again, this information very obviously derives from Xenophon (*Anab.* 4.8.21–2). And so does the information that they reached Cerasus on the third day: *tritaioi* (= *Anab.* 5.3.2: *tritaioi*). Likewise the statement (Diod. 14.30.7) that they traversed the country of the Mosynoeci in eight days (= *Anab.* 5.5.1: Mossynoeci) and then that known as Tibarene in three: *en trisín* (= *Anab.* 5.5.3: *poreuomenoi duo hēmeras aphikonto eis Kotuōra*, i.e. they reached the city on the third day). Finally one must consider the comment that the Greeks remained at Cotyora for fifty days (Diod. 14.31.1) whereas Xenophon says forty-five (*Anab.* 5.5.5). This is probably the result of Ephorus rounding up Xenophon's figure.[31]

---

29. As Bux, 'Sophainetos', col. 1012, fails to notice, who therefore adds this to his list of differences between Diodorus and Xenophon. He also overlooks the verbal correspondence, *gemousas agathōn* (Diod. 14.29.1) – *agathōn gemousas* (*Anab.* 4.6.27).
30. Von Mess, 'Untersuchungen über Ephoros', p. 374 n. 3, need not therefore be so surprised by the difference.
31. Thus rightly von Mess, 'Untersuchungen über Ephoros', p. 375. For this Ephoran tendency see n. 19 above.

Considering the degree of exact correspondence between the two texts one would have to be very hard to please indeed to look elsewhere than Xenophon for the source of all these numerical items. The differences by comparison are very few and, with one exception, can be explained away.

The same is true of the second general observation. This has to do with the kind of events selected for narration, the sequence in which they are so narrated, the specific details cited, any authorial comments offered, and the diction used. The instances of correspondence are many and the interested reader is referred to the comprehensive study of von Mess. Here I wish to draw attention to a few of these more impressive examples from the Katabasis which in my view leave little doubt that Xenophon was Ephorus' basic source. Similar cases from the Anabasis are looked at below (in section IV), in the more detailed treatment of this part of the expedition in Diodorus.

The brief description of the march through the mountains of the Carduchi is unmistakably a summary of Xenophon's narrative,[32] focusing on one notable feature of his account, the remarkable prowess of the Carduchi as archers. The Carduchi were excellent archers – their arrows were more than two cubits long – they pierced both shields and breastplates – the Greeks attached straps to the arrows shot at them and used them as javelins in turn. The same remarks, in exactly the same order, are observed in Xenophon, if we ignore the intervening material which naturally is disregarded in Diodorus' severe abridgement. It is hard to believe that another writer, even if he chose to comment on the archery of the Carduchi, would have done so in the same terms and following the same sequence.

Barring some minor differences, largely of a rhetorical nature,[33] Diodorus' chapter 28 gives us the essence of *Anab.* 4.4.7 to 4.5.36, the march through Armenia, concluding with a description of Armenian underground villages which, a lacuna in the text of Diodorus notwithstanding, supplies the same detail as Xenophon and in the same order. The same is true of chapter 29, the highlight of which is the sighting of the sea, given in Diodorus (14.29.3–4) in precisely the same terms and in the same sequence as in Xenophon (*Anab.* 4.7.19–27). We should note in particular the reaction of the rearguard to the shouts of the vanguard on catching sight of the sea (Diod. 14.29.3). The rearguard, of course, was commanded by Xenophon and his description of this incident is justly famous. Would a Sophaenetus, who commanded some other

32. Diod. 14.27.4–7; *Anab.* 4.1–2.
33. Such as the *chalaza* elaboration in Diodorus; cf. von Mess, 'Untersuchungen über Ephoros', pp. 370f. Pace Bux, 'Sophainetos', col. 1010.

section of the marching column, have written thus? We may compare also *tauta gar ephasan ktl* at Diod. 14.29.5 = *tauta gar ephasan ktl* at *Anab.* 4.8.7.

However, as we have seen, there are several differences from Xenophon's names in Diodorus chapter 29. They lead von Mess to suspect that at this point Ephorus employed another source in addition to Xenophon. He is right to point to Ephorus' keen interest in geography and ethnography. Two whole books of Ephorus' *Histories* dealt with these subjects, the second of the two, book 5, specifically with Asia; it included a description of the peoples of Asia Minor. A clear instance of Ephorus altering the account of Xenophon in the light of his own knowledge is that of the towers of the Mossynoeci. At Diod. 14.29.2–3, however, the differing names Gymnasia and Chenion may represent not Ephoran alternatives to Xenophon (at *Anab.* 4.7.19, 21), but textual corruptions.[34]

At Diod. 14.29.4 much has been made of Diodorus' *anastēmata megala* as opposed to Xenophon's *kolōnon megan* (*Anab.* 4.7.25). Bux indeed goes so far as to regard the respective descriptions in Diodorus and Xenophon of what the Greeks did at this moment of joy as 'ganz verschieden in den Worten'.[35] Such a conclusion is puzzling to anyone who compares the texts. Bux once again fails to consider the choice of events related and their sequence: in both Xenophon and Diodorus the story switches immediately from the erection of the monument to the reward of the guide. This similarity is mildly curious, to say the least, if two independent participants are at work here.

What about the *anastēmata megala*, though? One notes that at 14.29.3 Diodorus writes of 'guides' in the plural (*tous hodēgēsontas*) who were to conduct the Greeks to the sea. In the next section he changes the plural to the singular, in line with Xenophon (*Anab.* 4.7.19, 26–7). This is merely a 'Diodorism', of course.[36] However, if the singular at Diod. 14.29.4 had not

---

34. Von Mess's suspicions: von Mess, 'Untersuchungen über Ephoros', pp. 372ff. He cites also the numerical variations, but these are not significant in my view, as I have already indicated. Ephorus on the peoples of Asia Minor: *FGH* II A 70 FF30–53, 43, 161–2. The towers of the Mossynoeci: Diod. 14.30.6–7; *FGH* 70 F161b; *Anab.* 5.4.26. Possible textual corruption: Ephorus may have changed Xenophon's *to oros Thēkhēs* to *to Thēkh[e]ion oros*, which was then corrupted to *Khēnion oros*. One notes however that one branch of Xenophon's MSS read *khēs* instead of *Thēkhēs*. Thus *to Chēnion oros* in Diodorus may conceivably derive from this. Similarly with the name of the Mossynoeci, spelled with a single sigma in Diodorus (and *FGH* 70 F161b), but with a double sigma in Xenophon. To judge from *FGH* 70 FF43 and 161a Ephorus may have spelled the name with a double sigma too.
35. Bux, 'Sophainetos', col. 1013.
36. As von Mess recognizes: 'Untersuchungen über Ephoros', p. 374 n. 1.

survived, or if Diodorus had shown consistency by retaining the plural, this too would doubtless have been advanced by Bux and others as an important difference between Diodorus and Xenophon pointing to a different source for the former. This type of spurious variant is an important point to bear in mind. It is a fair guess that Ephorus altered Xenophon's *kolōnon megan* to *anastēma mega*, which in turn became *anastēmata megala* in Diodorus.

Last but far from least, there is the case of the honey of the Colchians.[37] This was a remarkable incident which any narrator of the adventures of the Ten Thousand might have recounted. What impresses however is that the detail in the two authors is substantially the same and given in the same order. We note in particular the comment, common to both, that the number of those affected from eating the honey was such as to resemble a military defeat, and likewise the identical concluding remark that those recovering from the honey gave every appearance of having been on medication (*ek pharmakoposias*). The possibility that two writers working independently came up with exactly the same observations and at exactly the same place in their respective descriptions is remote in the extreme.

Compared with weighty evidence of this kind, the few minor differences pointed out, mostly over the names of tribes and places, are small beer indeed which can in general be explained away in any case, as we have seen.

There is in fact a useful control on my conclusion. Scholars rightly accept that Greek affairs in Diodorus books 13 and 14 are in the main based, through Ephorus, on the *Hellenica Oxyrhynchia*. Yet here too we can observe variations between Diodorus and his ultimate source. Nobody now doubts this source's identity. The correspondences between Diodorus and Xenophon's *Anabasis* are, if anything, much closer; striking proof that Ephorus did indeed base his account on Xenophon.

IV

I turn now to consider the early stages of the expedition down to the battle of Cunaxa. These chapters in Diodorus (14.19–22) have received rather less attention from scholars and their origins are more debatable. Concerning the background of the expedition, chapters 11 (the murder of Alcibiades) and 12 (the career of Clearchus prior to his involvement with Cyrus), about which

---

37. Diod. 14.30.1–2; *Anab.* 4.8.20–1.

Xenophon is in any case perfunctory, Ephorus, to judge from Diodorus, used other sources and took a very different line. Xenophon is vague and less than candid about the extent and chronology of Sparta's involvement in the rebellion of Cyrus. He seems equally unforthcoming, he is indeed misleading, about the circumstances of Clearchus' exile: Braun, chapter 3 in this volume, traces the evidence for quite 'another' Clearchus.

There appears moreover to be a close connection between the two events which Xenophon glosses over. Something of the truth of the matter emerges from our other sources, and Xenophon's own information, so far as it goes, does not quite add up: it is difficult to believe that Sparta would have allowed one of her own citizens, an exile under sentence of death, to roam freely with a mercenary force in the strategically important area of the Chersonese for what appears to have been a considerable time. Nor, one suspects, would Cyrus, considering his close reliance on, not to say conspiracy with, Sparta (as Xenophon himself comes close to admitting in the *Hellenica*), have acted thus with regard to Clearchus – unless there was first a reconciliation between Clearchus and his home authorities, possibly following a request by Cyrus, and a lifting of the sentence of death.[38]

It is certainly easier to believe that Clearchus' presence in the Chersonese, as well as subsequent service with Cyrus, were sanctioned by Sparta. Of such official sanction speak both Isocrates and Plutarch. Xenophon therefore may be less than truthful with us, though his sources may have misled him too. When he says that none of the Greeks had known of Cyrus' true objective 'with the exception of Clearchus' he neglects to add that the Spartan authorities were also privy to the plot.[39]

In Diodorus chapter 19 the actual account of the expedition begins. The foundation of the chapter is provided by Xenophon, though there are several differences which seem to point to some other source (or sources) used in addition. Interestingly enough, Diod. 14.19.4–5 is in essence unmistakably a paraphrase of the well-known passage in Xenophon's *Hellenica* (3.1.1),[40] with account taken also of *Anab*. 1.2.21 and 1.4.2. Cyrus, Xenophon tells us, requested the Spartans to be good friends to him now in his hour of need, just as he had been to them in their war with Athens. Judging this request to be right,

---

38. Clearchus' activities in the Chersonese: *Anab*. 1.1.9; 1.3.4. Cyrus' reliance on Sparta: *Hell*. 3.1.1.
39. Official Spartan sanction: Isoc. 8.98, 12.104; Plut. *Artax*. 6.5. 'With the exception of Clearchus': *Anab*. 3.1.10.
40. As already noted by von Mess, 'Untersuchungen über Ephoros', p. 378.

the ephors ordered their admiral, Samius, to place himself at the disposal of Cyrus. The main contribution of the Spartan fleet, Xenophon explains, was to help to overcome any resistance to Cyrus in Cilicia, something Cyrus planned in advance. Significantly, not only is the thread of the story precisely the same in Diodorus, but so also is the dénouement, the role of the fleet, as we shall see.

Of differences between the two accounts we note first the different line taken by Xenophon and Ephorus about the Spartan motives for becoming involved in the revolt. For Xenophon it was purely a matter of honour: once appealed to by Cyrus, they felt themselves honour-bound to aid him. For Ephorus, on the other hand, the Spartan involvement had selfish motives: they judged the revolt to be to their advantage; hence their positive response. There is no need to assume an alternative *written* source. Such interpretations of Spartan policy were common enough in Athens, as we see in Isocrates.[41]

On the other hand, the switch to Xenophon as the main source involved Ephorus in a contradiction with what had gone before in his *Histories*. In relating the final fate of Alcibiades, Ephorus had already represented the Spartans as making secret plans with Cyrus for the war against the King. He carried forward his opinion of the close cooperation between Sparta and Cyrus to the narrative of the expedition (Diod. 14.21.1–2), except for the serious lapse here, at 14.19.4. The contradiction clearly arose from the fact that here Ephorus followed Xenophon. The inconsistency appears to have escaped his notice. Like Thucydides, Ephorus did not live to complete his work.[42]

Another difference concerns some of the numbers given. Xenophon says that the Spartan fleet consisted of thirty-five triremes and that of Cyrus himself of twenty-five. Seven hundred hoplites under Chirisophus were added to Cyrus' mercenary army by this fleet at Cilicia. The figures in Diodorus are

41. Selfish Spartan motives: Diod. 14.19.4. For Isocrates' attitude, cf. n. 16 above.
42. Secret plans with Cyrus: Diod. 14.11.2. Westlake, 'Diodorus and the expedition of Cyrus', discerns 'two important issues' in the initial phase of the expedition in Diodorus which are 'demonstrably not dependent on . . . Xenophon'. 'The first of these is the relationship between the Spartan government and Cyrus.' In Diodorus this is said to have been unofficial, but in Xenophon the implication is that it was official (p. 261). However, Diodorus is not inconsistent with Xenophon in this respect. Note Diod. 14.11.2: *lathrai*, and 21.2: *phaneron oupō*. Cyrus himself, according to both Xenophon and Diodorus, kept his real intention secret for as long as possible. What is more, Westlake overlooks Ephorus' propensity to impose his views on his sources. Both Xenophon and Ephorus agreed that the Spartan help was official, but that the fact was not advertised. The disagreement between them lies in the motive they ascribed to the Spartans for becoming involved in the revolt, as well as in the extent and chronology of this involvement. For Westlake's second important issue see n. 51 below.

rather different: the Spartans contributed twenty-five triremes to Cyrus' fleet, which numbered fifty, while Chirisophus commanded eight hundred soldiers.[43]

It is just possible that Ephorus derived these variant figures from an alternative source, but it is much more likely that they are the result of manipulation by Ephorus of the figures in Xenophon. Elsewhere Ephorus sometimes alters the numbers in his sources. 'Samos', by the way, the name of the Spartan admiral in Diodorus, as opposed to 'Samios' in Xenophon's *Hellenica*, is an insignificant variation, almost certainly due to error. Interestingly, in the *Anabasis* Xenophon names the admiral Pythagoras, but perhaps this is Xenophon being politically coy, in the same way that he hides his authorship of the *Anabasis* under a pseudonym.[44]

Where one does feel that Ephorus employed a source additional to Xenophon is in the description of Cyrus' army. Xenophon gives no figures for Cyrus' non-Greek troops at this point, but at the review of the whole force shortly before the battle, he mentions 100,000 non-Greek troops. To these we should add Cyrus' own 'companion' Persian horse of 600. Diodorus, on the other hand, specifies that the barbarian troops numbered 70,000 infantry and 3,000 cavalry. It is impossible to know if these figures have any basis in fact, but von Mess is probably right that they appear to derive from Ctesias; the figure of 400,000 for the King's army certainly comes from him.[45]

Diodorus then gives the number of the Greek mercenaries, 13,000 as in Xenophon, and proceeds to tell us that these were divided into four groups, Peloponnesians with the exception of the Achaeans, Boeotians, Achaeans, and Thessalians, led respectively by Clearchus the Spartan, Proxenus the Theban, Socrates the Achaean, and Menon the Larissaean. This detail gives the impression of being independent information, and von Mess may be right to perceive Ctesias here too. However, it is even more likely to be an extrapolation by Ephorus from data supplied by Xenophon, although the whole passage was garbled somewhat when summarized by Diodorus. From Xenophon it indeed

---

43. *Anab.* 1.4.2–3; Diod. 14.19.5, 21.1.
44. Ephoran alteration of numbers: cf. n. 19 above. 'Samios': *Hell.* 3.1.1. Pseudonymous authorship: *Hell.* 3.1.2. See further Ed Meyer, *Geschichte des Altertums*, vol. 5 (Stuttgart and Berlin, 1902), p. 185; P. Poralla, *Prosopographie der Lakedaimonier*, 2nd edn, Intr. A. S. Bradford (Chicago, 1985), pp. 111f. For Samius as a name in one of Sparta's leading families see Hdt. 3.55.2.
45. Description of Cyrus' army: Diod. 14.19.7–9. 100,000 non-Greeks: *Anab.* 1.7.10. 600 Persian horse: *Anab.* 1.8.6. 400,000 in the King's Army: Diod. 14.22.2. Origin in Ctesias: von Mess, 'Untersuchungen über Ephoros', pp. 381, 386 and n. 1; cf. Bigwood, 'The ancient accounts of the battle of Cunaxa', p. 351. Pace Jacoby, *FGH* II C, p. 97.

appears that Proxenus' troops were recruited in Boeotia and those of Menon in Thessaly, though Xenophon does not bother to spell this out. Diodorus names only four of the generals here, but Ephorus' list must have been longer, to judge from the note that 'almost all the generals, together with Clearchus' attended the meeting with Tissaphernes. 'Almost all' implies a larger number than four. The statement that Clearchus commanded the Peloponnesians with the exception of the Achaeans is contradicted by what is said elsewhere, that there were more than four generals and that Clearchus counted for more with Cyrus than the other generals and exercised an overall command in battle. The statement is probably a distortion of what Ephorus actually said.[46]

One notable difference with Xenophon, on the other hand, concerns the specific ethnics which Diodorus provides: Proxenus was a Theban and Menon was a Larissaean. In Xenophon the first is termed a Boeotian and the second a Thessalian. Are these guesses by Ephorus or snippets of information derived from a different source, whether written or oral? Whether the first or second, this is clearly an instance of Ephorus trying to improve on his sources. One notes that for Ctesias, too, Proxenus was a Boeotian and Menon a Thessalian. Xenophon must have known precisely where the two men came from, as well as much else besides about them and their family circumstances and connections; Proxenus after all was a close friend, and his silence on these points is therefore deliberate. Menon, of course, came from Pharsalus, not Larissa, and if the mistake was indeed made by Ephorus, rather than Diodorus, who is often guilty of such blunders, he may have been misled by the beginning of Plato's famous dialogue *Menon*. More distortion, clearly Diodorus' this time, follows in the next section, 14.19.9. The various barbarian contingents, we are told, were under Persian officers, Cyrus himself being in overall charge. The truth emerges when we see Ariaeus (Aridaeus in Diodorus) in command of the barbarian troops, as in Xenophon.[47]

From Xenophon one would assume that the fleet sent to aid Cyrus was as far as the Spartan authorities went in sending official help and that the 700 soldiers under Chirisophus were mercenaries who merely hitched a lift to

46. Thirteen thousand mercenaries: *Anab.* 1.2.9. Group division as data from Ctesias: von Mess, 'Untersuchungen über Ephoros', pp. 377f. Recruitment of Proxenus' and Menon's troops: *Anab.* 1.1.10–11; on the nationality of Cyrus' Greek mercenaries see J. Roy, 'The mercenaries of Cyrus', *Historia* 16 (1967), pp. 292–323, and chapter 9 in this volume. 'Almost all the generals': Diod. 14.26.6. Number of the generals and the status of Clearchus: Diod. 14.22.5, 26.6.
47. Ethnics in Ctesias: *FGH* 688 F27. The origin of Menon: cf. Thuc. 2.22.3; Pl. *Menon* 70B. 'Aridaeus' in command of barbarian troops: Diod. 14.22.5.

Cilicia on the Spartan vessels. In line with his general attitude Ephorus chose to see the soldiers, whose number he raised to 800, as Lacedaemonians, officially, albeit secretly, sent to serve the common cause they made with Cyrus. At Cunaxa he repeatedly described Cyrus' Greek troops as 'the Lacedaemonians and the mercenaries [or the other mercenaries] under Clearchus'. Again, we need not posit an alternative source. This divergence is simply Ephorus imposing his viewpoint on his source, treating Xenophon as he, for instance, treats the *Hellenica Oxyrhynchia* and the latter's account of the campaigns of Agesilaus in Asia.[48]

There remain three more points in chapter 19 to be dealt with. There is first the matter of the purpose of the expedition and of the number of people who knew the real objective from the start. The declared purpose of the expedition, Diodorus tells us, was Cilicia and the 'tyrants' there who were in rebellion against Persia. A little later, however, Pisidia is joined with Cilicia, and the rebels are certain of the inhabitants of those areas.[49]

There can be little doubt, I think, that what we have here is, once again, a 'Diodorism': Diodorus has muddled a longer statement by Ephorus which was in broad agreement with Xenophon. As for who knew the actual objective of the expedition, one notes that Xenophon is at pains to deny that any of the Greek leaders, and certainly not his friend Proxenus, knew it, with the single exception of Clearchus. The Spartan authorities too must have known from the start. He admits however that the rank and file suspected their generals of having known the ultimate destination all along, but keeping it a secret.[50]

This view is not inconsistent with what we find in Diodorus, that Cyrus kept the truth from the mass of the troops (*to plēthos*), though not from the leaders (Diod. 14.19.3, 9). Ephorus was perfectly capable of extrapolating from his sources and Diod. 14.20.5 is a fair enough summary of *Anab.* 1.3.[51] The very

---

48. Chirisophus' 700 men: *Anab.* 1.4.3. The Ephoran angle: Diod. 14.21.1–2. 'The Lacedaemonians and the mercenaries under Clearchus': Diod. 14.22.5, 23.3, 24.5. Ephorus and *Hell. Oxy*: see n. 19 above.
49. Cilicia and the 'tyrants': Diod. 14.19.3. Pisidia joined with Cilicia: Diod. 14.19.6.
50. Ignorance of the Greek leaders: *Anab.* 3.1.10. Suspicions of the soldiery: *Anab.* 1.4.12.
51. Westlake, 'Diodorus and the expedition of Cyrus', pp. 261f., dwells on what he thinks is 'substantial disagreement between the two versions [of Xenophon and Diodorus] on a more important question, namely when, where, and to whom was the truth' about the real aim of the expedition first revealed. He perceives in Diodorus a gradual revelation of the truth: at first nobody knew (Diod. 14.19.3), then the leaders were let into the secret (14.19.9), etc. Ephorus derived all this from a different source, Westlake thinks, and this version is more satisfactory than Xenophon's. Not so. Diod. 14.19.9 is a mere restatement of 14.19.3, only now we are told that Cyrus 'had disclosed' (*ededēlōkei*) the

end of Diod. 14.19 likewise, about the great care Cyrus took to maintain the good will and fighting ability of the Greeks, is an apt summary of the many statements in Xenophon to the same effect. *dapsileis agoras hetoimazōn* especially puts us in mind of *Anab.* 1.10.18. The second point, to the effect that all 13,000 mercenaries gathered together at Sardis before setting off, is an understandable consequence of compression for which Ephorus himself is probably responsible.

The third point is another example, a good one, of Ephorus adding material to his source. It is the one clear instance in this chapter. At the end of Diod. 14.19.5 we are told that Cyrus' fleet under Tamos, together with the Spartan naval squadron, set sail for Cilicia. Chronologically the narrative here has moved ahead because the fleet cannot have set off from Ionia until a couple of months or so after Cyrus set out from Sardis. (Diodorus rather than Ephorus is probably the one responsible for the dislocation in the chronology, having missed a cue in his source.) This is a point that Xenophon does not make explicit, but it emerges from his detail. With the section on the cooperation between Cyrus and Sparta concluded, Diodorus turns again to Cyrus. Before setting out from Sardis he placed relatives of his in charge of Lydia and Phrygia, but Ionia and Aeolia he entrusted to Tamos, an Egyptian from Memphis, we are told, whereas Xenophon says simply that he was an Egyptian living at Ephesus. This man of course is the same Tamos who in the previous section is in command of Cyrus' fleet. A native of Cyme in Aeolis, and a near contemporary of these events, Ephorus clearly knew a fair amount about this man and his descendants in Ionia, and he must have recorded it in his general history, as well as in his local history of Cyme. Some of this material survives in Diodorus. One notes that according to Ephorus Ionia and Aeolis appear detached from Sardis at this stage. The same information is repeated at Diod. 14.35.3, where we are told that Tamos was the greatest of the 'satraps' in western Asia Minor and was in charge of Ionia.[52] The time is after the defeat of Cyrus and the return of Tissaphernes to Ionia.

As for the march 'up' to Cunaxa (chapters 20 and 21), again, what we appear to have is a summary of Xenophon and the differences should not mislead us.

true objective of the campaign to the leaders, as opposed to the mass of the troops. The pluperfect (missed by Westlake) is significant.

52. Survival of Ephoran material: Stylianou, *A Historical Commentary*, pp. 161, 184ff., 208f. Tamos as 'satrap': D. M. Lewis, *Sparta and Persia* (Leiden, 1977), p. 118 and n. 74, thinks that this was a temporary, ad hoc arrangement.

The march through Asia Minor is not related – a mere sentence gets us to the borders of Cilicia. But Xenophon too is sparse at this stage. Diodorus then passes on to a brief description of the Cilician Gates.[53]

There are problems with this description, as well as with what he has to say about the Cilician–Syrian Gates further down (Diod. 14.21.3–4). Schwartz blames Ephorus and his propensity to duplicate narratives. I cannot agree. While the language of the description of the two gates is close, and at one point identical (though *stenē kai parakrēmnos* is used to describe the *eisbolē*, the entrance or pass, at Diod. 14.20.1, but the *phusis tou topou*, the nature of the place, at 14.21.3), the detail given is different, with one exception. The text at Diod. 14.21.4 is corrupt, but the point nevertheless stands. The one evident error in the description of the Cilician Gates is the claim that the pass was fortified, that a wall was built from mountainside to mountainside, with gates at the roadway. Arrian, *Anabasis* 2.4.3–4, and Quintus Curtius 3.4 are in agreement with Xenophon that the Cilician Gates were not fortified. This error appears to be the result of confusion in Diodorus with the Cilician–Syrian Gates. Schwartz is right about this, though I would see the hand of Diodorus here rather than Ephorus. The confusion notwithstanding, however, enough survives in Diodorus' text to show that Ephorus' basic source for the respective Gates was Xenophon: one or more items were simply added from his own knowledge or some other written source, as, for example, the length of the narrow pass at the Cilician Gates (twenty stades) and the name of the mountain involved in the case of the Cilician–Syrian Gates (Amanus: emended by Wesseling).[54]

Xenophon was greatly impressed by the Cilician plain, by its size, beauty and fertility, and his comments are very clearly reflected in Diodorus in the statement that in beauty the plain was second to none in Asia. Barber is moved by this to remark: 'It is interesting to discover from the words . . . that its ultimate authority seems to have been an eyewitness of the places he describes.'[55] True. It is difficult, however, to understand why Barber needs to credit Sophaenetus and his hypothetical *Anabasis* with this testimony, perhaps,

---

53. The march to Cunaxa: Diod. 14.20–1. One sentence to Cilicia: Diod. 14.20.1.
54. Criticism of Ephorus: Schwartz, 'Ephoros', col. 10. For a defence, cf. Stylianou, *A Historical Commentary*, p. 124. Ephorus as Xenophon's source: von Mess, 'Untersuchungen über Ephoros', p. 380. About the Cilician Gates see R. P. Harper, 'The Cilician Gates', *Anat. St.* (1970), pp. 149ff.
55. Diod. 14.20.2; Barber, *The Historian Ephorus*, p. 127.

Barber further suggests, through the intermediary account of Ctesias (the hypotheses thereby multiply), when the obvious ultimate authority is Xenophon.

What Diodorus says about the stance adopted by the Syennesis (ruler) of Cilicia is another fairly clear instance of Ephorus borrowing material from a written source other than Xenophon, and this source once again was almost certainly Ctesias: finding himself in an impossible position, the wily Cilician contrived to escape by allying himself with both Cyrus and the King.[56] The thread of the story in Diodorus is then unmistakably resumed from Xenophon: Cyrus spent twenty days at Tarsus. This coincidence of the figures, here and elsewhere, is especially noteworthy, as we have already argued.

It was while at Tarsus that the Greek soldiers broke into mutiny, suspecting they were being led against the King. They were finally placated by an increase in their pay and Cyrus' assurance that their objective was the satrap of Syria and not the King. 'Therefore the soldiers being full of fear grew vexed, and being angry with their leaders they tried to kill them regarding them as traitors to themselves.' The passage is not too inept or inaccurate a way of summarizing Xenophon. On the other hand, Diodorus says, the soldiers' anger was occasioned by fear when they pondered the distances involved in marching against the King, and the multitudes of hostile nations – for they heard that it took four months for an army to reach Bactria and that the King's forces numbered 400,000. Without forgetting Ephorus' interest in geography and ethnography, much of this, if not all of it, plainly derives from Ctesias, though equally plainly it is embedded in a framework constructed out of Xenophon.[57]

In chapter 21 we see again the truth of the matter well illustrated: to the summarized narrative of Xenophon Ephorus might every now and then insert material from another source or add from his own knowledge. He might also impose his own interpretation on the events described. In setting off from Tarsus, Xenophon relates, Cyrus traversed the rivers Psarus and Pyramus and after marching for five days reached Issus, 'the last city of Cilicia, founded on the sea'. In Diodorus the intervening information is excluded and we are simply

---

56. Diod. 14.20.2–3; cf. *FGH* 688 F16 = Phot. *Bibl.* 72.43b; von Mess, 'Untersuchungen über Ephoros', pp. 379f.; Bigwood, 'The ancient accounts of the battle of Cunaxa', pp. 349f. Westlake, 'Diodorus and the expedition of Cyrus', p. 271 n. 8, is unnecessarily sceptical. It is clear that Ephorus borrowed material from Ctesias elsewhere, so why not here?
57. Diod. 14.20.4–5 = *Anab.* 1.3. For the Ctesias element, cf. *FGH* 688 F22 = Plut. *Artax.* 13.3; F33 = Phot. *Bibl.* 72.45a.

told that 'after marching through Cilicia Cyrus arrived at the city of Issus which is situated on the sea and is the last one of Cilicia.'[58] The dependence is perfectly clear.

In what follows, however, the arrival of the fleet, Ephorus chose to emphasize again the complicity of Sparta in Cyrus' venture, which Xenophon played down. But, that point made, Diodorus is in agreement with Xenophon that Cyrus' chief purpose in directing his fleet east to Cilicia was to help him negotiate the Gates. Once through these, the dismissal of the fleet, implied in Xenophon, is unnecessarily spelled out in Diodorus. Doubtless this is the result of Ephorus once more dotting the i's and crossing the t's of Xenophon.[59]

Diod. 14.21.5–7 is a severely compressed abridgement of *Anab.* 1.4.6–7.1, concentrating on the absolutely essential: after marching for twenty days Cyrus reached Thapsacus on the Euphrates where he stayed for five days. Here he finally announced to his troops the true objective of the expedition and overcame the Greeks' displeasure by promising each man five minas of silver once they reached Babylon.

All this coincides exactly with Xenophon, including the figures. From Thapsacus, and more particularly from the River Araxes, to the borders of Babylonia, as Xenophon explains, Cyrus proceeded by forced marches without resting the troops, both because of the arid nature of the country and because he wanted to catch the King as unprepared as possible. Once in Babylonia he slowed down and the average number of parasangs covered per day fell to a mere four. All this is conveyed exactly in Diodorus in a one-sentence summary: once over the Euphrates Cyrus made haste, marching without stopping, until he reached the borders of Babylonia, at which point he rested his army.[60] Ephorus' reliance on Xenophon could not be clearer.

We then come to the battle of Cunaxa. Thanks to the studies by von Mess and Bigwood,[61] I can limit myself to points they have overlooked or over which we disagree. As they demonstrate in detail, the framework is undoubtedly Xenophontic, but there is a much higher percentage here of material from Ctesias. The resulting amalgam is served up with some typically Ephoran (and

---

58. *Anab.* 1.4.1; Diod. 14.21.1.
59. I do not see why von Mess, 'Untersuchungen über Ephoros', p. 380, considers this a borrowing from Ctesias. On the contrary, the statement seems an obvious surmise by Ephorus.
60. Forced marches: *Anab.* 1.4.19–5.9. Four parasangs a day: *Anab.* 1.7.1. Cf. Diod. 14.21.7, and von Mess, 'Untersuchungen über Ephoros', p. 381.
61. Von Mess, 'Untersuchungen über Ephoros', pp. 382ff.; Bigwood, 'The ancient accounts of the battle of Cunaxa', esp. pp. 351ff.

Diodoran) rhetorical elaboration. Ephorus clearly made careful comparison of Xenophon and Ctesias. In combining the two, indeed in seeking to reconcile them (something he often did with conflicting sources), he brought to the fore more than Xenophon the role of Tissaphernes. From Xenophon he accepted, surely correctly, that the royal troops broke through the line of battle and raided the enemy camp. Ctesias, by contrast, was quite at fault in representing a badly wounded King as being removed from the battle and the battle itself as coming to a halt as a consequence. Ephorus nevertheless conceded to Ctesias that the wounded King abandoned the fighting. Hence the enhanced role of Tissaphernes in Diodorus: he takes over command of the royal forces at this juncture and carries on the fight.

This, I think, is Ephorus himself, not Ctesias, for the simple reason that in Ctesias' account the actual battle ceased with the removal of the wounded King. Ephorus knew, above all from Xenophon, that Tissaphernes had fled to the King from Caria shortly before Cyrus set out from Sardis, that he played a prominent role in the battle, breaking through to the rear of the Greeks where he joined up with the King at the Greek camp, and that together with the King he had briefly confronted the Greek phalanx for a second time. But he also knew that much of what Xenophon wrote about the battle, especially as regarding the Persian side, had been reported to him (cf. *elegeto* at *Anab*. 1.8.9) and that Xenophon himself was inclined to accept Ctesias' information that the King had been wounded. To be fair to both versions, to combine them into a single narrative, Ephorus promoted Tissaphernes to the position we find in Diodorus.[62]

There is a change of perspective at the start of chapter 22 which signals a switch from Xenophon to Ctesias: Diod. 14.22.1–4 is related from the King's side. The opinion that it was from Pharnabazus that the King first learned that Cyrus was intending to march against him, first stated at Diod. 14.11.2, is repeated. It is well known that in book 13 Diodorus is guilty of a confusion between Pharnabazus and Tissaphernes, which has resulted in the complete disappearance of the latter from that book. Not so in book 14, except that

---

62. Ctesias is suggested by Bigwood, 'The ancient accounts of the battle of Cunaxa', pp. 354f., who further assigns to Ctesias the description of the confrontation in Diodorus between the Greeks and the Persians under Tissaphernes. The removal of the King and cessation of battle in Ctesias: Plut. *Artax.* 11.3. The behaviour of Tissaphernes: *Anab.* 1.2.4–5, 1.10.5ff. Xenophon on Ctesias: *Anab.* 1.8.26. In Stylianou, *A Historical Commentary*, p. 108, I suggested a source other than Ctesias or Xenophon for the role of Tissaphernes, perhaps a local Cumaean tradition. I am now inclined to see it as an Ephoran device for the reconciliation of the accounts of Xenophon and Ctesias.

Diodorus has neglected to mention Tissaphernes' flight to the King in 401, which occurred, as we learn from Xenophon (*Anab.* 1.2.4–5), at the point Cyrus began assembling his forces at Sardis. In Ephorus this must have been a separate item and distinguished from the role he assigned to Pharnabazus.[63]

Ephorus may have derived this idea from Ctesias, as he certainly did some of the numbers, and the same source may well be responsible for the information, likely enough in itself,[64] that the royal plan was for all the various components of the royal army to gather at Ecbatana in Media. When the contingents from India and certain other regions were delayed because of the long distances involved, the King set out to meet Cyrus with what he had, which amounted to 400,000 troops in all, 'as Ephorus says'. This is certainly from Ctesias, as we have seen.

What follows, also almost certainly from Ctesias, has been telescoped and garbled by Diodorus and makes little sense as a result. The huge defensive trench dug by the King, in which all our sources appear to have believed, has been confused with the royal camp. The dimensions of the trench given by Xenophon and Plutarch do not correspond.[65] Diodorus started on this, but then, without completing the dimensions (*bathos* is Palmer's emendation of the MSS *mēkos*), mistakenly shifted his attention to the camp. He thus made a single impossible structure of trench and camp, whereas Ephorus had doubtless differentiated the two.

Diodorus has done well, however, to retain the valuable information that on marching out to meet Cyrus the King left behind in camp his baggage and the *achreios ochlos*, the crowd of camp-followers who were of no use in a battle. These people would have included the medical staff. The royal camp did figure in Ctesias' account, as we learn from the references to it in Plutarch, the first of which specifies that the camp was some distance away from the site of the battle. All this must bear on the question of the historical worth of Ctesias' account. His own claims notwithstanding, a Persian cavalry battle was no place for a Greek doctor like himself. Rather, this is yet another instance of

---

63. Thus I disagree with A. von Mess, 'Untersuchungen über die Arbeitsweise Diodors', *RhM* 61 (1906), pp. 244ff., at p. 263; von Mess, 'Untersuchungen über Ephoros', p. 382; and Jacoby, *FGH* II C, p. 97 (ad 70 F208 = Diod. 14.22.1–2), that Pharnabazus at Diod. 14.22.1 is a mistake for Tissaphernes committed either by Diodorus (von Mess) or Ephorus (Jacoby). Ephorus was well aware of the part Tissaphernes had played in the downfall of Cyrus; cf. Diod. 14.80.6.
64. Cf. Cawkwell, introduction to *Xenophon: The Persian Expedition*, pp. 39f.
65. *Anab.* 1.7.14–15; Plut. *Artax.* 7.2.

Ctesias' known tendency to assign to himself a larger role in the events he described.[66]

With Diod. 14.22.5 the narrative is back again with Cyrus and the Greeks and the substance of it clearly is from Xenophon, though with additions from Ctesias of varying extent. With the beginning of the fighting the rhetoric increases. Much of this is due to Diodorus himself, who has turned Ephorus' account into something approaching a Homeric struggle.[67]

I would merely draw attention to one characteristic of the account which is undoubtedly due to Ephorus' own interpretation. As noted above, according to Ephorus the troops sent to Cyrus from Sparta under Chirisophus, whose number he increases to eight hundred, only pretended to be mercenaries; in reality they were Lacedaemonian soldiers. This item occurs three times in the account of the battle and leaves us in no doubt about Ephorus' attitude to Spartan involvement. We are not faced here with a confusion by Diodorus or something borrowed from Ctesias and due to his pro-Spartan bias.[68] Rather, this is an instance of Ephorus adjusting his source to suit his own viewpoint. The same explanation holds for the emphasis on Clearchus' part in the battle: Clearchus fought the battle at the head of the Lacedaemonians and the mercenaries and was thus serving his country's interests no less than those of Cyrus. If there is any truth in the Ephoran version, it is a truth Xenophon preferred to evade.

From the end of the battle until the point Tissaphernes abandoned his efforts to bring the Greeks to heel and headed west for Ionia, Ephorus, to judge from Diod. 14.24.7–27.4, based himself mostly on Xenophon, though once

66. The royal camp: Plut. *Artax.* 12.4; 13.3. Ctesias' claim: Plut. *Artax.* 11.3. Yet this claim to have been in the thick of things is generally accepted by historians; cf. Cawkwell, introduction to *Xenophon: The Persian Expedition*, pp. 17, 39. Bigwood, 'The ancient accounts of the battle of Cunaxa', pp. 347f., is more circumspect. S. R. Bassett, 'The death of Cyrus the Younger', *CQ* 49 (1999), pp. 473ff., argues for the clinical accuracy of Ctesias' description of the spear wound sustained by Cyrus near the eye, and is so impressed by this that she is inclined to credit his account of the circumstances of the death of Cyrus at the expense of that of Xenophon. But however accurate, medically speaking, the detail cited by Ctesias (he was after all a doctor!), it does not make his account factual. On the whole I would agree with Bigwood's conclusion about the relative merits of Xenophon and Ctesias.
67. Note in particular Diod. 14.23.3–7; cf. Stylianou, *A Historical Commentary*, pp. 15ff. But Ephorus' account must have been rhetorical enough and the comment at Diod. 14.23.4 about the Peloponnesian War is more likely to be Ephoran: Stylianou, *A Historical Commentary*, p. 116 n. 312, where I missed this instance. Contra Bigwood, 'The ancient accounts of the battle of Cunaxa', p. 352 n. 53.
68. Lacedaemonian soldiers: Diod. 14.22.5, 23.3, 24.5. Imputation to Ctesias: Bigwood, 'The ancient accounts of the battle of Cunaxa', p. 352 n. 51.

more with borrowings from Ctesias. Some of these were quite considerable, so that we can speak, as in the case of the battle, of a merging in places of the accounts of the two sources. As before, Ctesias enabled Ephorus to switch from the Greeks to the Persians and to look at things from their angle. By contrast with the battle, however, there does not now appear to have been any serious disagreement between Xenophon and Ctesias to tax the powers of Ephorus: both were in complete agreement that the Persians' intention had been to force the Greeks to submit, and if they refused, as they did, to destroy them; and that the treacherous proceedings of Tissaphernes against the Greeks were aimed at achieving this objective. We have a brief and not entirely satisfactory outline of the Persian plan, which inevitably involved deception, to deal with the mercenaries in Diod. 14.26.5–7, a summary of an Ephoran chapter which combined Ctesias and Xenophon: it was necessary first to separate Ariaeus and Cyrus' native troops from the Greeks, before attempting the removal of the Greek generals, in the hope that the leaderless Greeks would then surrender. All this of course is narrated at much greater length by Xenophon.[69]

There is no support, therefore, in the sources for Cawkwell's strongly expressed view that any treachery was on the Greek side, not the Persian, and that Tissaphernes made no real attempt to block the Greeks' passage, but merely harassed them, thus speeding them on their way. Bigwood deals with the first point well, though rather more can be said about the matter. Unlike Cawkwell, I see nothing suspicious in the phrase *hōs eis agoran* at *Anab.* 2.5.30, which might thus have been misconstrued by enemies of Clearchus as indicating hostile intent, even if we interpret the Greek to mean that the two hundred soldiers who followed the captains and the generals to the meeting did not really intend to buy provisions, but merely claimed that as their purpose for going. Ephorus, it would seem from Diod. 14.26.6–7, accepted the plain meaning of the words in Xenophon, but the important fact to note is that the soldiers went along *unarmed*. Also worth noticing is the apt point raised by Xenophon himself, after the obvious lies of Ariaeus (cf. Bigwood), to which the Persians made no response. Clearly they were caught out, and their silence showed the truth of the matter.[70]

69. Ctesias and the treachery of Tissaphernes: *FGH* 688 FF27–8. For a more detailed examination of this part of Diodorus, see von Mess, 'Untersuchungen über Ephoros', pp. 388ff. About the origins of Diod. 14.26.2–3 (the three-day truce) and 14.27.1–2 (the election of new generals), see the discussion above in sections I and III.
70. Cawkwell, introduction to *Xenophon: The Persian Expedition*, pp. 24ff.; Bigwood, 'The ancient accounts of the battle of Cunaxa', pp. 356f. Soldiers unarmed: *Anab.* 3.1.29: *aneu hoplōn*. Xenophon's point unanswerable: *Anab.* 2.5.38ff.

With regard to the second point, the Greeks were clearly anxious to escape, as must have been perfectly obvious to the Persians. Consider, for example, the plain reply of Chirisophus at *Anab.* 3.3.3. The statement, one assumes, is true. So why did the Persians not take it up, if they simply wanted to get rid of the Greeks? Because common sense, if nothing else, dictated that Cyrus' Greek mercenaries should not be allowed to escape scot-free. The matter cannot be discussed in detail here, but the narrative of Xenophon makes it clear that the Persians tried their best to bring the mercenaries to book, something about which Ephorus in Diodorus is emphatic too. Tissaphernes' action in occupying a strong position by the road ahead of the Greeks at one stage and his posting of cavalry on the left of the Tigris a little later show that his aim was to prevent the Greeks from escaping. He failed because the Persians simply did not have the kind of troops necessary to tackle head-on what amounted to a powerful division of battle-hardened and determined Greek hoplites.[71]

For the rest of the Katabasis, as has already been argued, Ephorus relied almost entirely on Xenophon, though with small additions of his own here and there. There is nothing in Diodorus after 14.27.2 to indicate that Ctesias was used, and in any case this part of the narrative very probably lay outside the scope of the *Persica*, as the epitome of Photius and the fragments seem to show.[72]

---

71. Persians try to stop Greeks: Diod. 14.27.3–4; *Anab.* 3.4.37, 3.5.12, 3.5.15.
72. Cf. von Mess, 'Untersuchungen über Ephoros', p. 390; Westlake, 'Diodorus and the expedition of Cyrus', p. 267.

3 Xenophon's Dangerous Liaisons
THOMAS BRAUN

Clearchus

My first Greek lessons, over half a century ago, are among my happiest memories.[1] They reached a high point with the reading of our first continuous prose text: the second book of Xenophon's *Anabasis*. We found the Ten Thousand[2] in the heartland of Iraq, having acquitted themselves well on the battlefield of Cunaxa but lost Cyrus, to enthrone whom they had travelled so far. Now came Phalinus the Greek to deliver the demand from the Great King, Artaxerxes II, for the surrender of their arms. We boys were impressed by the resolute astuteness with which the Greek generals parried it. 'We have no asset', said an Athenian, 'beyond arms and courage. If we keep the former we think we could make use of the latter.' 'Tell him', said the Spartan Clearchus, 'that if we are to be friends of the King, we shall be worth more to him with arms than without, and if we are to make war, we shall fight better with arms than without.' Phalinus gave them the King's message: 'While you stay here, there is truce; if you go forward or back, war.' Clearchus said, 'Tell him we agree.' 'What do you mean?' 'If we stay, truce; if we go forward or back, war.' 'Then shall I report back truce or war?' 'Truce if we stay, war if we go forward or back.' Clearchus would not say which they would do. That night, they moved forward.[3]

---

1. Under John Burtt, editor of the second Loeb volume of the *Minor Attic Orators*. As our classics master at Bootham, before becoming Headmaster of Whitley Bay Grammar School, he gave us not only an excellent grounding in Greek and Latin language and literature, but, in far-reaching and delightful discussions, the lasting impression of a sane and humane outlook. This essay is dedicated to him. When it reached him he was in continuing vigour, still studying poetry in ten languages. He died, shortly after his ninety-third birthday, on 21 July, 2003.
2. This traditional figure will have to serve. Actually, the muster of Greek mercenaries at Celaenae on the Maeander is said to have come to about 11,200 (*Anab.* 1.29) – and that does not quite tally with the total of Xenophon's numbers for each contingent.
3. *Anab.* 2.1.7–23.

'Narratology' had not been invented: it did not occur to us that there could be any need for books to point out Xenophon's skill as a story-teller, his 'keen feeling for the precise possibilities of words',[4] his 'firm focus on a storyline, vivid use of details, and expression marked by simplicity, directness, brevity and rapidity'.[5] The manner was irresistible; but so was the matter. Clearchus finally won our hearts when the Greek generals were waited on again by heralds from the King, this time asking for a truce himself. 'Tell him there will have to be a battle first. There is no breakfast. And no one will dare speak of truce to Greeks without providing breakfast.' Breakfast in those days was, for schoolboys in Britain, of patriotic significance. The French colleague of a friend's father, living in a farmhouse well supplied with food despite the Nazi occupation, had quietly registered his pro-British feelings by having an English breakfast every day of the war, beginning with porridge, going on to bacon and eggs, and ending with buttered toast and marmalade. 'He who would eat well in England', it was said abroad, 'must breakfast three times a day.' Since the fathers of many of us had served in the Middle East, we readily sympathized with Greeks reduced to breakfasting by the Tigris on bread, dates, palm wine, and the crapulousness-inducing 'brain' of palm trees.[6]

Clearchus continued to command our respect on the northward march. For us, as well as for Xenophon's readers, 'there was a lesson to be learned from Clearchus' supervision', as the army crossed brimming canals by means of fallen palm trunks. The fifty-year-old general would strike dawdlers with his stick, but shame the men of up to thirty into alacrity by plunging into the mud and lending a hand himself. It was present to our minds that British officers, though not allowed to strike a private soldier in two victorious world wars – swagger-sticks were for swagger only – had willingly plunged into the mud alongside their men, and in the first of those wars had often drowned in it. The principle of lending a hand had not been so clearly recognized among the enemy: it was against regulations for a German officer in uniform to carry a parcel. Next, we read Clearchus' speech to Tissaphernes, which was that of a man of honour:

> We did not join up to wage war against the King, or march against him; as you know well, Cyrus found many pretexts to bring us here. But when we saw him in trouble, we were ashamed before gods and men to betray him,

4. W. E. Higgins, *Xenophon the Athenian* (Albany, 1977), p. 3.
5. V. J. Gray, *The Character of Xenophon's Hellenica* (London, 1989), p. 73.
6. Clearchus' ultimatum: *Anab.* 2.3.5. The 'brain' of the palm trees: *Anab.* 2.3.14–16.

having allowed him to benefit us for so long. Now that Cyrus is dead, we shall not strive for power against the King and have no reason to wish to harm his land, nor would we wish to kill him, but we would march home if no one did us any harm. With the help of the gods we shall retaliate upon anyone who wrongs us, but if anyone does good to us, we do not mean to be outdone in doing good to him in turn.

Soon after, Clearchus was slow to see through the warning sent by Cyrus' Persian generals, alleging that Tissaphernes was planning to break down the Tigris Bridge; but when a young man, possibly Xenophon, pointed out its inconsistency, he took the point. When Tissaphernes lured Clearchus and his fellow generals into his fatal trap, we did not blame Clearchus' credulity. He had excellent reason to trust to solemn oaths that were binding upon Greeks and barbarians alike. 'I would not call happy anyone who is conscious of having neglected the oaths of the gods. I do not know with what swiftness or to what refuge an enemy of the gods might flee, or into what darkness he might slink, or to what stronghold withdraw; for all things everywhere are subject to the gods and they rule all equally.'[7]

So his death at the hands of the treacherous Tissaphernes evoked our sympathy; and we young readers accepted Xenophon's final assessment of Clearchus' character and career. A warrior who loved war, Clearchus had fought for his native Sparta against Athens, and when victory was won had persuaded the ephors, Sparta's five annual executive magistrates, to send him to help the Greeks of the Chersonese and Perinthus against Thracian attack. He was at the Isthmus (of Corinth) when the ephors, 'changing their minds for some reason [*metagnontes pōs*]', recalled him; but he sailed to the Hellespont all the same, and was sentenced to death in his absence for disobeying orders. As an exile he won Cyrus' confidence and collected ten thousand gold darics from him[8] to pay for the war against the Thracians, in which he won plenty of loot. Then he followed the summons to join the Asian expedition. What bellicosity, when, without disgrace, he might have lived at ease at home in peacetime! He excelled at procuring supplies for his men and persuading them to obey him. Sullen-faced and harsh-voiced, always severe and

---

7. Clearchus' plunge into the mud: *Anab.* 2.3.11. His speech to Tissaphernes and the false warning missive: *Anab.* 2.4.16–22. His speech on the validity of oaths: *Anab.* 2.5.7.
8. Thirty-three and a third talents according to the exchange rate given in *Anab.* 1.7.18. See further D. M. Lewis, *Sparta and Persia* (Leiden, 1977), pp. 131–2 n. 138. In ancient as in recent times, the ratio of gold to silver fluctuated.

ōmos, cruel, to his men, and given to occasional fits of rage, which he would regret afterwards, he held that a soldier should fear his commander more than the enemy. This method worked. In danger, his men felt implicit confidence in his command; in danger, his face brightened and he became positively genial. But out of it, his ungraciousness could be too much for his subordinates, whom he could not easily keep; and he was held not to take kindly to subordination himself.[9]

This eulogy contains some qualifications. It was never good, in Greek eyes, to be called *ōmos*, though the meaning of the word ranges from unbending obstinacy to gross savagery.[10] Xenophon's encomium of the Spartan king Agesilaus records his mildness to ordinary soldiers, which led his men to love and obey him. Nevertheless, Xenophon clearly meant his readers to hold Clearchus in high esteem. At the outset of his first book, which I was soon to read, Clearchus is introduced as a Spartan exile. Nothing is said at this point of his being under sentence of death. As a schoolboy, I assumed that this was a common hazard in Greek political life, like losing a by-election in Britain, and so was hardly worth mentioning.[11] In book 1 his war against the Thracians is said to have been in the Greek national interest; the Hellespontine cities, Xenophon writes, contributed funds to maintain his soldiers of their own free will. 'I fought together with you', Clearchus reminded them at Tarsus, 'on behalf of Greece against those who wanted to drive out the Greek inhabitants and deprive them of their land.' At Tarsus, his men were refusing to advance further, since they had already passed by the Pisidian tribesmen, to fight whom they had been told they were marching; they began to suspect that their Journey into the Interior would be against the Great King. Clearchus, attempting to force them on, narrowly escaped being stoned to death. Then, in a far from ungracious speech, he professed continuing loyalty to Cyrus, his generous

9. Clearchus' character-sketch: *Anab.* 2.6.1–15.
10. K. J. Dover, *Greek Popular Morality* (Oxford, 1974), pp. 202–3.
11. The Spartan king Pausanias (*Hell.* 3.5.25) and the Athenian statesmen Themistocles and Callistratus, whose meritorious careers led to their being sentenced to death in their absence, have had their modern successors throughout the Balkans. In 1935, Eleutherios Venizelos, Greece's pre-eminent politician, who figures today on the Greek fifty lepta coin, was as a septuagenarian sentenced to death in his absence after a failed rebellion (not his first). At lunch in Merton College I often sat next to Professor Norman Davis, who was in Albania when sentenced to death by a Bulgarian court in 1941, and was reprieved by a clause in the Anglo-Bulgarian peace treaty. His offence had been to hide the leader of the agrarian party in the boot of his car and drive him to safety in Turkey. 'They take their politics very seriously in those countries,' said Churchill on 16 August 1945 after telling how, following his election defeat, a Yugoslav lady had commented, 'Poor Mr. Churchill. I suppose now he will be shot.'

xenos (guest-friend), but told his men that his Greek loyalty was greater: whatever they decided, he would go with them. 'No one shall ever say that I betrayed Greeks and preferred the friendship of barbarians!'[12]

This profession was insincere. He was all the time in secret communication with Cyrus, and privately briefed some of the apparently spontaneous speakers in the ensuing debate. Yet there is no trace of dramatic irony in Xenophon's account of his success in persuading the Greeks to continue their march, while still withholding its true purpose. To those in the know it still seemed a hopeful enterprise; and the danger and difficulty of retreat against Cyrus' will were all too evident. Clearchus' deception here is on a level with Odysseus' white lies, which the goddess Athena commended with amusement, even admiration.[13] He was not committing perjury, as Tissaphernes would soon do.

Less admirable was Clearchus' attack on Menon. He was surely exceeding his authority when he sentenced one of Menon's soldiers to be flogged. Seriously though Clearchus was then provoked, narrowly escaping death from an axe blow and flung stones, and detestable though Menon was in Xenophon's eyes, he leaves us in no doubt that Clearchus was wrong to lead his Thracian troops against Menon's men, and that Proxenus and Cyrus were right to prevent a fight, whereupon Clearchus 'came to himself'. His response had been one of those fits of rage which he would come to regret. By contrast, his answer to Cyrus that Orontes 'should be got out of the way as soon as possible' was calmly deliberate: no hint of Xenophon's disapproval.[14]

What of Clearchus' tactics in the battle of Cunaxa? Cyrus shouted to him to lead his force against the enemy's centre where the King was, far beyond the Greek left. Clearchus 'was unwilling to tear away his right wing from the river, because he was afraid he would be outflanked on both sides, and replied to Cyrus that he would see to it that all went well', Plutarch concluded from Xenophon's narrative that Clearchus was to blame for Cyrus' defeat and death,

> for one who pursues safety at all costs, whose priority it is not to suffer, would have done best to stay at home. But having gone tens of thousands of stades from the sea in arms, not under compulsion but to put Cyrus on

12. The mildness of Agesilaus: *Ages.* 6.4, 11.5. The contribution of the Hellespontine cities: *Anab.* 1.1.9. Clearchus' reminder at Tarsus: *Anab.* 1.3.4. The stoning: *Anab.* 1.3.1–2. Greeks preferred to barbarians: *Anab.* 1.3.6.
13. Hom. *Od.* 13.287–97.
14. The fracas with Menon's men: *Anab.* 1.5.12–17. The proposed removal of Orontes: *Anab.* 1.6.9.

the royal throne, and then to look round and select a position not to preserve his leader and paymaster, but to engage safely and peacefully, resembles the behaviour of one who through fear of present dangers has abandoned the purpose of his actions, and betrayed his expedition's aim. For none of those arrayed round the King could have stood the shock of the Greek charge.

This is armchair, or rather, dinner-couch strategy. Cyrus' army had been caught unprepared by the King's steady advance; the Greek army 'was being formed in order from the men still coming up'; Clearchus was responsible for its safety as well as that of Cyrus. He had no time to confer with the other Greek generals, who were not under his command.[15] A hastily improvised slantways charge against advancing spearmen and scythed chariots would have been disastrous. Lions were not led by donkeys in those days; and Clearchus was an experienced predator, Cyrus a wildcat striker.[16]

As an undergraduate at Balliol College, Oxford, I found out more about the predator when Russell Meiggs, our magnificent Ancient History tutor, introduced us to the work of Diodorus Siculus. We learned that it was '(alas!) of importance'[17] and, in the absence of other narrative, inescapable, summarizing as it does the lost work of Ephorus for the period between the Persian Wars and the middle of the fourth century. Only for Italian and Sicilian history, and (possibly) for Cyrus' expedition once it had started, does Diodorus look elsewhere.[18] At first we had little respect for that flat-footed compiler. 'Diodorus Siculus / made himself ridiculous' was a catchphrase. And following Gomme, we took Ephorus to have been 'superficial in the extreme, and his historical judgment of the poorest'.[19]

In due course, we learned to qualify our condemnation by listening to Professor Tony Andrewes' lectures in New College Hall on 'Thucydides and his continuators'.[20] From the abrupt end of Thucydides' narrative in 411 down

---

15. J. K. Anderson, *Xenophon* (London, 1974), pp. 104–5.
16. Clearchus' tactics at Cunaxa: *Anab.* 1.8.13–14. Plutarch's comment: Plut. *Artax.* 8.4–5.
17. *Historical Commentary on Thucydides*, vol. 1, ed. A. W. Gomme (Oxford, 1945), pp. 52–3.
18. This was proved by C. A. Volquardsen, *Untersuchungen über die Quellen der griechischen und sicilischen Geschichte bei Diodor xi–xvi* (1868). Tony Andrewes' copy in his study at New College was the only one in Oxford. He was happy to lend it, there being no photocopying machines before 1962.
19. Gomme, *HCT*, vol. 1, p. 45.
20. Those lectures were worth attending if only to savour the Professor's pronunciation of 'Thucydides'. Opinion was divided about whether you could make out what he said with less difficulty from the front or the back of the hall. Once you had done so, you

Xenophon's Dangerous Liaisons

to at least 394, Ephorus was shown to have been using the *Hellenica Oxyrhynchia*, the unexciting but sober and well-informed work of an as yet unidentified writer, evidently contemporary with the events he describes. Portions of it had come to light in Andrewes' lifetime: the London papyrus in 1908, the Florentine in 1949. The Cairene was to follow in 1975–6. By collating the evidence of the *Hellenica Oxyrhynchia* with that of other writers who drew on Ephorus, Andrewes demonstrated that Diodorus' accounts of the battles of Notium (407) and Cyzicus (410) are in important respects sounder than Xenophon's.[21]

Now, the *Hellenica Oxyrhynchia* goes beyond battle descriptions: it explains Athenian politics, the Boeotian constitution, the causes of Theban prosperity during the Peloponnesian War, and the niggardliness of Persian satraps in paying their Greek allies.[22] So what Diodorus writes about Clearchus' activities before he joined the Asian expedition probably goes back through Ephorus to that excellent history. Surprisingly for a reader of Xenophon, it turns out to be the story of a trusted, capable officer turned terrorist warlord.

Other information sets it in context. Clearchus was the son of Rhamphias, one of Sparta's ambassadors to Athens in 431, who had led an army into Thessaly in 422. In 411, aged twenty-nine, Clearchus was entrusted with command in the Hellespont. Despatched north with forty Peloponnesian ships to collect pay from the Persian satrap of Hellespontine Phrygia, Pharnabazus, and enable Byzantium to revolt from Athens, he was turned back by a storm, returned to the Spartan base at Miletus, and proceeded to the Hellespont by

    found it bafflingly elliptic. His high courtesy prevented him from assuming any ignorance on the part of his audience. The best plan was to write everything down, and after overcoming your ignorance by independent reading, to return to your notes, which would then prove wonderfully lucid and helpful. There could have been no better way of learning.

21. He published his conclusions, thirty-two years after their 'remote genesis' in 'Notion and Kyzikos: the sources compared', *JHS* 102 (1982), pp. 15–25. We now recognize the value of what the judicious Busolt had called 'a worthless piece of Ephorean fantasy' (*Griechische Geschichte*, vol. 3 (1904) p. 1527 n. 2). In this context it is worth noting that Polybius (12.25.2–3 = *FGH* 70 T 20) praised Ephorus for his accounts of the naval battles of the Persian admirals against the Cypriot king Evagoras (after 390) and of Cnidus (394), though he was contemptuous of Ephorus' accounts of the land battles of Leuctra (371) and Mantinea (362), to which the *Hellenica Oxyrhynchia* will not have extended. This discriminating judgement, by an historian who insisted on topographical knowledge and military experience, deserves respect: it is not an instance of 'the great decline in intelligent criticism and scientific thought in general after the third century B.C.' to which Gomme attributed Ephorus' undue influence on later writers (Gomme, *HCT*, vol. 1, p. 45).

22. Athenian politics: *Hell. Oxy.* 6.2–3. The Boeotian constitution: *Hell. Oxy.* 16.2. Theban prosperity: *Hell. Oxy.* 17.3–4. The stinginess of satraps: *Hell. Oxy.* 19.2.

land; but ten of his ships made good their passage meanwhile and effected the Byzantine revolt.[23]

In 410 Clearchus led the obstinate Peloponnesian resistance at the sea battle of Cyzicus, and survived the defeat. Presumably he found his way back to Sparta, where he functioned as Byzantium's *proxenos* (honorary consul). In 409, to stop the grain ships from the Black Sea sailing past Byzantium to provide for Athens, he was sent back to Byzantium with fifteen troopships. All but three escaped the Athenian patrols. As governor in 408, with a raggle-taggle force, he defended Byzantium against a massive Athenian siege. When he had unsuspectingly crossed the Straits to get more pay from Pharnabazus and raise more ships, conspirators opened the city's gates to the Athenians. Alcibiades' proclamation that the Byzantines would suffer no harm caused them to change sides. Outnumbered, Clearchus' lieutenants eventually surrendered. One of the conspirators, Anaxilaus, was afterwards tried for treason at Sparta, but successfully pleaded that he was not a Spartan national, and that Clearchus had given all the food in the city to his soldiers while women and children were starving.[24]

How far a commander should favour his own troops is a matter of degree. Baden-Powell, long idolized as the hero of the siege of Mafeking in 1899–1900, and immortal as the founder of the Boy Scouts, is today excoriated for giving the besieged Africans shorter rations than the British. But this partiality did not at the time diminish the loyal enthusiasm of Plaatje, one of South Africa's most distinguished black spokesmen. From Anaxilaus' acquittal, and the promptitude with which Athens readmitted the Byzantines into alliance, we may conjecture that Clearchus' behaviour was worse than Baden-Powell's. He was not given another command. Though the Spartan High Admiral Callicratidas designated him as his successor before his death in the battle of Arginusae in 406, the post seems to have passed to Eteonicus. When, after the Athenian disaster at Aegospotami in 405, Byzantium reverted to Sparta, its governorship was assigned to Sthenelaus.[25]

23. Rhamphias' embassy: Thuc. 1.139. The raid on Thessaly: Thuc. 5.12–13. Clearchus' command in the Hellespont: Thuc. 8.8.2. The revolt of Byzantium: Thuc. 8.80.
24. William Joyce (Lord Haw-Haw), the notorious pro-Nazi broadcaster from Berlin during the Second World War, was similarly to plead at his treason trial that he was an Irish, not a British national. His plea failed because he had once held a British passport. The defeat at Cyzicus: Diod. 13.51. The escape from the Athenian patrols: *Hell.* 1.1.36. The charge of preferential food distribution: *Hell.* 1.3.15–22, Diod. 13.66.5–67.7.
25. Callicratidas' decision: Diod. 13.98.2. The command of Eteonicus: *Hell.* 1.6.35–8 and Diod. 13.100.5, with H. G. U. Kahrstedt, *Forschungen zur Geschichte des ausgehenden fünften und des vierten Jahrhunderts* (Berlin, 1910), pp. 178–9. The governorship of Sthenelaus: *Hell.* 2.2.2.

Clearchus' next chance did not come until 403, during Lysander's ascendancy. It was no Scout's Honour that he then displayed.

The Byzantines were in a bad way because of civil strife and war against the neighbouring Thracians. Unable to solve their internal quarrels, they asked Sparta for a general. So the Spartiates sent Clearchus to settle the city's affairs; and he, entrusted with overall command, collected many mercenaries, and became not champion but tyrant. First he invited the magistrates to a sacrifice and killed them. Then, there being no government in the city, he arrested thirty Byzantines of note, put a cord round them and strangled them. After appropriating the property of all those he had put to death, he picked out the wealthy among the rest, and by launching false accusations killed some and exiled others. So, having the mastery of a great fortune and having collected a crowd of mercenaries, he made his power secure.'[26]

His ruthless use of that power was noised abroad; and the Spartan government sent ambassadors to persuade him to lay it down. He paid no attention. Sparta then despatched an army against him. On its approach, Clearchus transferred his treasure and troops to nearby Selymbria, knowing that the Byzantines would side against him. In a battle against his countrymen, who fought splendidly, his forces were destroyed. Besieged with a few companions in Selymbria, he grew fearful and slipped over to Ionia, where he associated with Cyrus, who was already plotting to lead an army against his brother. This was how he came to be granted the sum with which he raised another mercenary army in the Hellespont.[27]

In Polyaenus' collection of *Stratagems*, which draws freely upon Ephorus, six belong either to Clearchus' Byzantine tyranny in 408 or to his return, with Cyrus' money, to the Hellespont in 402/1. Five are contrivances to plunder the Thracians. There is no suggestion here that he was waging a patriotic war against them. The Hellespontine colonies on the European coast had a long history of intermittent warfare with their Thracian neighbours, but also of alliances and interaction. Miltiades I had led the first Athenian settlers to the Dardanelles in response to an appeal by one Thracian tribe against another; his kinsman Miltiades, victor of Marathon, married a Thracian princess, as the Athenian general Iphicrates was to do in 386. That the Hellespontine cities needed help to defend their lands is doubtless true; but Clearchus' campaigns were hardly a Hellenic crusade against ethnic cleansing. In 405, the Thracian

26. Diod. 14.12.2–3.
27. Diod. 14.12.4–9.

kings Medocus and Seuthes had offered to furnish Alcibiades with an army against the Spartan forces in the region. Though Athens had rejected the offer, the war of 403 will have been a sequel. Xenophon, with other survivors of the Ten Thousand, was to have no qualms about entering the Thracian king Seuthes' service in winter 400/399.[28]

The tricks recorded by Polyaenus are rather dirty tricks; but for Greeks, as for ourselves, few holds are barred in war. 'How is one to overcome one's enemies?' asks the youthful Cyrus the Great in Xenophon's romance. 'By being a plotter,' his father replies, 'crafty, tricky, a cheat, a thief, and a brigand, overreaching the enemy at every turn.' The ingenuous boy bursts out laughing. Is this not plain contrary to his having been taught to be just and law-abiding? 'Yes, to your friends and fellow-citizens. But don't you remember being taught to do all possible harm to your enemies?' One trick, against friends, not Thracians, must date to 402/1. Clearchus, having 'under penalty from the ephors sailed with four ships to Lampsacus', received an appeal from the Byzantines against Thracian besiegers. He sailed to Byzantium, persuaded the assembly to put their cavalrymen and hoplites on board as if to attack the Thracians, and enticed their two generals into a tavern, where he had them isolated under guard and murdered. He enjoined strict silence on the tavern-keeper, and used the unsuspecting troops to retake the city.[29]

Clearchus was following a pattern. Class conflict had long poisoned the life of many Greek cities. After the collapse of their empire, it beset even the Athenians, previously so cohesive. The Three Thousand, upper-class cavalry and hoplites, for a time uneasily ranged themselves, at the bidding of the iniquitous 'Thirty Tyrants', against the common people. Yet the boundaries of class conflict kept shifting. Evaluations had been constantly misapplied.[30] The democratic Many did not everywhere outnumber the oligarchic Few, whom poor men might find it profitable to support. In Samos, the champions of the Many had seized power in 412, only to transform themselves into the Few in the following year, and turn on their own people.[31] The anti-democratic juntas

---

28. Clearchus' stratagems: Polyaenus *Strat.* 2.2.5–6, 8–10. Athens' rejection of Thracian help: Diod. 13.105.3–4.
29. Cyrus' conversation with his father: *Cyrop.* 1.27–9. The tricking of the Byzantines: Polyaenus *Strat.* 2.2.7.
30. Thuc. 3.82.4. Not that the words themselves changed their meanings: see J. Wilson, '"The customary meanings of words were changed" – or were they? A note on Thucydides 3.82.4', *CQ* 32 (1982), pp. 18–20.
31. Thuc. 8.21, 73.

installed in Athens and elsewhere after the Athenian defeat in 404 did not, as Theramenes had hoped, set up governments of property-owners, but plundered the rich.

Looking again, in the light of his known past, at Xenophon's account of Clearchus' role during Cyrus' expedition, we find no difficulty in believing that he was not the man to retire with his winnings, that he was brave, loyal to his paymaster and concerned for his men. But what warlord or gangster is not? Perhaps, if forced to choose, he really would have preferred danger with his men to safety with Cyrus; no doubt there was sincerity in his rough morality of doing good to friends and harming enemies. But it is hard to dissociate it from mere brutal opportunism. He is reported to have advised the execution of Orontes not out of revulsion against his disloyalty, but because it would be too much trouble to keep him under guard. He trusted in the oaths made in the name of the Great King only because he did not think it was worth the King's while to break them. Tissaphernes had Clearchus' measure. He enticed Clearchus into the death tent with a broad hint that he was worth cultivating because he might be bidding for the kingship himself. What, then, was the value of Clearchus' promise to do the King all possible good if he would let his men go home peacefully?

Cyrus the Younger

Xenophon's obituary of Cyrus[32] is, unlike that of Clearchus, unqualified in its praise. I never quite swallowed it, even as a schoolboy. My generation had seen too many millions misled by leaders whom right-minded people found repulsive; and I knew and regretted that genuine charm combined with power was almost irresistible. Even the prosaic Mr Attlee was impressed by the gallant, debonair Marshal Tito, who had had so many of his countrymen shot.

Cyrus the Younger, says Xenophon, was the kingliest and most worthy to rule of all Persians since Cyrus the Great. He was brought up at the King's portals, like all the noblest Persians, to *sōphrosynē*, that quality, often translated as temperance, which lies at the heart of Greek morality and embodies moderation, modesty, discretion and wisdom: it is the theme of Plato's *Charmides*. Cyrus learned to rule and be ruled, to be obedient to his elders, and to excel in horsemanship, archery and javelin-throwing, eager to learn and

32. *Anab.* 1.9.

to practise. He loved hunting and once, thrown off his horse, grappled single-handed with a bear.[33]

Sent by his royal father to govern western Asia Minor and muster the forces there, he was, according to Xenophon, faithful to every undertaking and treaty, never telling a lie. That was why 'all the Greek states' took his side against Tissaphernes, except for Miletus, whose exiled citizens he refused to abandon. He never let down his friends, however much reduced in number and fortune. He was said to pray for life long enough to out-trump all those who had helped or injured him. No one man ever had so many friends so eager to devote their cities, money, and persons to him.[34]

He was tough on crime. Men deprived of a hand, foot, or eye were often to be seen on the highways. So everyone, Greek or barbarian, could travel safely.[35]

He personally observed those who were brave on campaign, and rewarded them with rule of the lands he subdued. In consequence, he was never short of volunteers. He was glad to enrich anyone distinguished for *dicaeosynē*, justice, and practised justice himself, so that generals and officers crossed the sea to serve him. He rewarded just administrators who improved the lands they ruled and created revenues; he showed no jealousy of anyone's wealth.[36]

Xenophon commends his generosity. He would send his friends well-chosen gifts and personal adornments, half-flagons of wine, half-loaves of bread, and half-eaten geese from his table, and in times of scarcity, fodder for their horses.[37]

And so no one, Greek or barbarian, was better loved. Except for Orontes, no one deserted him for the King, though many a vassal of the King went over to Cyrus. Nearly all his bodyguard fell with him in battle.[38]

Xenophon did not, in his other writings, depart from his eulogy. In the *Oeconomicus* he has Socrates repeat the substance of the foregoing paragraphs. If Cyrus had lived, Socrates declares, he would have been the best of rulers, as is shown by the loyalty he commanded. He quotes Cyrus' claim that he was justified in collecting revenue from a countryside which he had taken such care to equip and protect; and he repeats Cyrus' words when he showed Lysander his 'paradise': the park at Sardis which he had planned and even to some extent

33. *Anab.* 1.9.1–6.
34. *Anab.* 1.9.9–12.
35. *Anab.* 1.9.13.
36. *Anab.* 1.9.14–15.
37. *Anab.* 1.9.16–28.
38. *Anab.* 1.9.28–31.

planted with his own hands. 'I swear by Mithras that when I am in health I never take supper without having sweated at deeds of war or agriculture or some honourable pursuit.' Lysander seized Cyrus by the hand and said that his excellence gave him the right to be happy.[39]

Yet the eulogy has sinister undertones. Let us take its points one by one.

Cyrus' education follows the ideal which Xenophon expounds at the beginning of his *Cyropaedia*, the most attractive part of that once widely read novel. The Greeks put *sōphrosynē* and *enkrateia*, self-control, above all other virtues, perhaps because they did not come naturally to their temperament. Compassion and forbearance, our own priorities, came some way behind. That was why so many of them admired Sparta, the least compassionate of Greek states: it was the paramount example of self-control on a national scale. *Sōphrosynē* in Xenophon's *Symposium* is the shining virtue of young Autolycus; in the *Memorabilia*, he never tires of telling how old Socrates practised and preached *enkrateia*. Yet compassion and forbearance are by no means absent from Greek popular morality. In the catalogue of Cyrus' virtues, they are conspicuous by their absence. Now Xenophon, to quote an eminent xenophontologist, 'was a man of uncommon reserve. It would be a grave error to suppose that what he did not mention he did not know about. His silences speak loud.'[40] In a eulogy, they are deafening.

Xenophon speaks as a keen huntsman himself when he commends Cyrus' prowess. In his *Cynegeticus*, he extols hunting as a divine invention, which promotes soldierly, intellectual, and moral virtues, in sharp contrast to the verbal manipulativeness of sophists and the man-hunting ways of self-seeking politicians. Unlike the Persians, who rode to hounds, Xenophon's huntsmen, in a countryside unsuitable for riding, took them out on foot, against hares, deer, boar, feral cats, and, best of all, wild beasts hostile to mankind. Who will disagree with his view that hunting induces strenuous courage and knowledge of terrain? We note with interest that he did not, in principle, exclude women from the sport, and thought the hunting of foxes a disaster.[41]

But are lovers of hunting always excellent without exception, accompanied by *sōphrosynē*, conspicuous for piety, good to parents, city, friends, and fellow

---

39. *Oec.* 4.15–25.
40. The virtue of Autolycus: *Symp.* 1.8. Socrates and *enkrateia*: *Mem.* 1.5.1–6, 2.1.1–7. Compassion among the Greeks: Dover, *Greek Popular Morality*, pp. 195–205. The reserve of Xenophon: G. L. Cawkwell, introduction to *Xenophon: A History of my Times* (Harmondsworth, 1979), p. 33. Cf. also Cawkwell, chapter 1 in this volume.
41. Women hunters: *Cyn.* 13.8. Foxhunting: *Cyn.* 6.3.

citizens? We cannot blame him for not foreseeing how many Bad Kings, such as William Rufus, were to be keen huntsmen; but we may raise an eyebrow at his outburst, in concluding the *Cyropaedia*, against Artaxerxes II and his court for neglecting to hunt under the influence of drink. The *Cyropaedia* dates from after 362/1, since it refers to the satraps' revolt, when Artaxerxes was either eighty-four or ninety-two years old.[42]

Truthfulness was the cornerstone of Persian morality, as we know from Darius I's Behistun Inscription and the Zoroastrian scriptures, ever inveighing against followers of the Lie. Herodotus wrote of the archetypal education of young Persians in horsemanship, archery, and truth-telling.[43] But if Cyrus was indeed truthful when he first came to his western province, he was following a tactic that was, in medieval times, to be enunciated by another Persian in his advice to his son: 'Strive after a reputation for truthfulness. You will find it useful when you need to tell lies.'

For the story of Cyrus' expedition is one of elaborate deception. He long deceived his royal brother by paying him deference and sending him tribute, while camouflaging his war preparations. He kept deceiving the Ten Thousand, at first telling them that their expedition was against the Pisidians, and at Tarsus fobbing them off with an alleged campaign against Abrocomas on the Upper Euphrates. This was not the deception of national enemies that the *Cyropaedia* allows. At the outset of his governorship, he had cemented friendship with the Spartan High Admiral Lysander by a gift of ten thousand gold darics, the same amount that he was later to give to Clearchus; but this was no friendship between lovers of truth. Lysander's maxim was to cheat boys with knucklebone dice and men with oaths.[44]

Why did the Greek states nearly all take Cyrus' side against Tissaphernes? To say that a Greek state takes sides means that its dominant faction does, as is evident from Thucydides' history. From the moment that Lysander reached Ephesus from Sparta in 407, and formed a strong link with Cyrus as friend and paymaster, he set up *hetairaiai*, conspiratorial groups, with a view to their seizing control of their cities as soon as they could get rid of the Athenian-imposed democracies. He promoted his friends to great honours and generalships, and to gratify their covetousness joined in their

42. The tirade against Artaxerxes: *Cyrop.* 8.8.12. The revolt of the satraps: *Cyrop.* 8.8.4; cf. Diod. 15.92, Anderson, *Xenophon*, p. 152 n. 1. The age of Artaxerxes: Lucian *Macr.* 15, Plut. *Artax.* 30.9.
43. Hdt. 1.136.
44. Cyrus' gift to Lysander: Plut. *Lys.* 4. Lysander's maxim: Plut. *Lys.* 8.5.

injustice and wrongdoing. Many in consequence sought to ingratiate themselves with him.[45]

After the Athenian collapse in 405, Lysander sailed round the cities, suppressing democracies 'and other constitutions', and imposing rule by decarchies (boards of ten) drawn from the conspirators. He gave them absolute power of reward and punishment, and was complicit in the massacres and expulsions they perpetrated. These self-seeking juntas were not even representative of the oligarchic Few: they were chosen neither *aristindēn*, by birth, nor *ploutindēn*, by wealth. It would appear that the victorious Spartan forces then departed from Asia, on the understanding, perhaps agreed in 407, that its Greek cities would be autonomous but tributary to the King, and that Cyrus continued at Sardis as ruler of Lydia and Greater Phrygia, and Tissaphernes as satrap of Caria, where he was to have his residence in 397. The two rivals were thus in competition for Ionia, not strictly within either province; and the King was for the moment content to leave them at variance, provided he received his tribute.[46]

So it was not entirely Cyrus' nobility of soul that attracted the loyalty of the 'Greek states'. And who were those Milesian 'friends' whom Cyrus backed against Tissaphernes and vowed never to desert? Once again, there is an account in Diodorus which may well derive from the *Hellenica Oxyrhynchia* through Ephorus, though Diodorus has, alas, disfigured it by what is, even for him, an unduly silly measure of simplification: he writes 'Pharnabazus' for 'Tissaphernes', as he does throughout his narrative until Cunaxa.[47] In 405,

---

45. 'The Chiots', he tells us, planned a rebellion from Athens in 413, and with Tissaphernes' support invited help from Sparta. When the contingent duly arrived in 412, 'the Many were amazed and dumbfounded; the Few had arranged for the Council to meet', and by disingenuously reporting that many more ships were on the way, persuaded them to revolt (Thuc. 8.5.4–5, 14.1–2). So 'the Chiots' prove to have been only the Few. Presently the Few, with Spartan help, imposed an oligarchy on the unwilling island, having executed the party of Tydeus son of Ion, no plebeian but most likely the son of the rich and well-connected pro-Athenian Ion of Chios, dramatist, elegiac poet, and writer of memoirs (Thuc. 8.38.3, Gomme, Andrewes, and Dover, *HCT*, ad loc.). The behaviour of Lysander: Plut. *Lys.* 5.5–6.
46. I am happy to follow the meticulous though admittedly tentative reconstruction by Lewis, *Sparta and Persia*, pp. 122–3, and do not share the misgivings of Donald Kagan, *CW* 74 (1980), pp. 42–3. Selection by neither birth nor wealth: Plut. *Lys.* 13.5–7. The understanding between Sparta and Persia: *Hell.* 3.2.12.
47. When Thucydides breaks off, Tissaphernes is on his way to make excuses to the Spartan fleet, which has sailed to the Hellespont, exasperated by his failure to bring them pay and the help of the Persian navy (Thuc. 8.109). Thucydides, speculating on the reason for that failure, guesses that Tissaphernes wanted to wear down both sides (Thuc. 8.87). Diodorus transmogrifies the satrap that summons and then sends back the Persian

certain people in Miletus, aiming at oligarchy, put an end to the democracy with Spartan connivance. First, during the Festival of the Dionysia, they seized their chief opponents in their homes and slaughtered some forty of them. Then, when the market-place was full, they picked out three hundred of the richest and killed them. The most upper-class [*chariestatoi*] of those who favoured the democratic cause, not fewer than a thousand, fearing the situation, fled to the satrap 'Pharnabazus' [viz. Tissaphernes].

He received them kindly, gave each of them a gold coin, and settled them in 'Klauda, a fort of Lydia', which I venture to emend to Klaunda, a fort of Lycia, i.e. Calynda on the Carian–Lycian border.[48] Tissaphernes must have succeeded in restoring the democrats to Miletus after the Spartan withdrawal. That slippery satrap had for some time found that it suited him to take the democratic side in Greek politics. He had moved closer to the Athenians after 411. In their decree in honour of Evagoras (408/7?) they named Tissaphernes, evidently as an ally;[49] and they chose him as their spokesman in 407, before he and Cyrus fell out, in the vain hope that he would weaken Cyrus' Persian support for Sparta. Cyrus' siege and blockade of Miletus was to secure the comeback of anti-democratic murderers.

navy, into Pharnabazus (Diod. 13.37). But the excuses he presently has 'Pharnabazus' make – that the King had to give priority to a threat from Egypt (Diod. 13.46.6) – are true. What Thucydides did not know was explained by David Lewis in 1959 when, by collating the evidence of two Aramaic correspondence dossiers, he found that in 411 there had been a revolt in both Upper and Lower Egypt (D. M. Lewis, 'The Phoenician fleet in 411', *Historia* 7 (1959), pp. 392–7). Here is confirmation that the second-rate Diodorus was using a first-rate source.

48. Diod. 13.104.5–6. See A. Andrewes, 'Two notes on Lysander', *Phoenix* 25 (1971), pp. 213–14 n. 15. The friendly satrap was certainly Tissaphernes, for Pharnabazus' province of Hellespontine Phrygia was a long way to the north. *Klauda* is unknown. The Loeb text prints Wesseling's emendation *Blauda*. But *Blaudos* (Steph. Byz. 171.19–20) or *Blaudon* (Strabo 12.5.2, 567, Xylander for MS *Blauron*) will not do, for the name never ends in -a; and Blaudos/Blaudon was remote from Tissaphernes' protection, being deep inland in Cyrus' province, seventy miles east of Sardis; moreover, it was in Phrygia, though close to the Lydian border. Andrewes notes Barbara Levick's suggestion of *Clanudda* (Peutinger Table 9.4), which ends with -a, is on the Lydian side of the border, and has been identified with Hacet Kalesi, where there are ancient remains and walls of squared stone (Karl Bürchner, *RE* 11 (1922), p. 547). But being a little to the north of Blaudos, it was even further away from Tissaphernes' province. In 1961 Andrewes encouraged me to 'publish in some trade journal or other' my emendation of *Klauda phrourion ti tēs Lydias* to *Klaunda phrourion ti tēs Lykias*. I do so now, with apologies for the delay. The people of *Calynda*, a Carian town on the Lycian border (Hdt. 1.172) and therefore safely under Tissaphernes in 405, are spelt [K]*laundioi*, [K]*laundēs* on the Athenian Quota Lists.
49. *IG* I^3 113.39.

The atrocities committed by Clearchus and Cyrus' friends cannot be dismissed as partisan fiction, for they closely resemble the well-documented crimes of the 'Thirty Tyrants', whom Lysander installed at Athens in 404. Socrates' liaisons with Critias, who 'during the oligarchy proved the most rapacious and violent of all', and with Critias' crony Charicles, were to prove lethal. Xenophon's *Memorabilia* provides a convincing posthumous defence against Socrates' death sentence. It was not he who had corrupted any of that grisly gang. As long as they were associating with Socrates, they practised *sōphrosynē*; they abandoned his precepts when they fled abroad – Critias when he began to consort with lawless villains in Thessaly.[50]

In power, Critias nursed hatred for Socrates in consequence of a personal reprimand. He and Charicles framed a law to prevent him from teaching, tried but failed to browbeat him in an interview and afterwards had no more to do with him. Xenophon, so far as we know, resembled Socrates in keeping his own honour untarnished. But Socrates' association with Critias and Charicles had preceded their bloodthirsty misdeeds. Clearchus and Cyrus were already stained with political crime when Xenophon followed them, turning a blind eye.[51]

No Greek state in Xenophon's time practised judicial mutilation. Elsewhere and at other times, physical punishment to fit the crime has been devised with gusto. During the early republic, Roman soldiers convicted of theft had their right hands cut off in the presence of their comrades. In the later Empire, Constantine prescribed the lopping of the foot of a slave who went over to the enemy.[52]

In the Orient, judicial mutilation, never abolished in Saudi Arabia, may yet become more widespread. Afghanistan, in its present lawless plight, has reason to look back on the reign of Amir Abd ar-Rahman (1880–1901) as a golden age, for that monster of cruelty, who chopped the hands off thieves, blinded rebels, and unhesitatingly ordered executions, prided himself on his success in repressing crime. The modern West cannot pride itself on success, and though more squeamish, is not all that more humane. While the millennial fight against crime continues, with no victory in sight, we should not censure too sweepingly Xenophon's praise of Cyrus' methods. It is perhaps comparable to

50. The crimes of the Thirty: *Hell.* 2.3–4, Lys. 12, 13. Their *sōphrosynē* while with Socrates: *Mem.* 1.2.18. Critias' associates in Thessaly: *Mem.* 1.2.24.
51. Critias' resentment of Socrates' rebuke: *Mem.* 1.2.29–31. The attempt to browbeat Socrates: *Mem.* 1.2.31–8. The breaking-off of contact: *Mem.* 1.2.47.
52. Republican hand-lopping: Marcus Cato ap. Frontin. *Str.* 4.1.42. Imperial foot-lopping: *Cod.* 6.1.3.

a sermon of Bishop Latimer's, delivered in the presence of Edward VI, which commended King Cambyses for covering a Persian judge's seat with thongs made out of the skin of the judge's father who had been flayed for taking bribes to give an unjust sentence. Latimer was expressing hatred of injustice and corruption, not seriously urging his sovereign to introduce Cambysean upholstery into the law-courts.[53]

Before and after Cambyses, Persian rulers had, with no less gruesome humour, devised exemplary punishments of hideous cruelty, beside which the lopping of thieves' hands was positively mild. Darius I informed all his subjects that he had cut off the nose, ears, and tongue of the Median rebel Phraortes, put out one of his eyes, and kept him bound at his palace entrance for all the people to see before impaling him. Queen Parysatis secured the execution of a personal enemy 'in boats', a revolting method that took seventeen agonizing days.[54]

Xenophon does not attribute any such abominations to Cyrus the Younger, but says nothing to suggest that he refrained from what under Achaemenid rule were cruel but not unusual punishments. Had he done so, Xenophon

---

53. Note Abd ar-Rahman's conversation with Lord Curzon in 1894: 'Is there a city in your country called Birmingham? . . . Is it well governed?' . . . Lord Curzon: 'I believe that it prides itself on its municipal administration.' . . . (Producing a small piece of newspaper from a fold in his robe): 'Here is an extract from the *Standard* . . . which says that in Birmingham last year there were ——— murders . . . Is that true?' 'If the *Standard* is quoting official statistics, I have no doubt that it is true.' (Turning to his courtiers . . .): 'What is the population of my country?' 'Your Majesty rules over eight million of people.' 'Ah, and how many murders were committed in the whole of Afghanistan last year?' 'Under Your Majesty's just and benevolent rule . . . only six murders were committed in the entire country, and the guilty were caught and condemned to immediate execution.' (Turning to Curzon): 'And this is the country and these are the people whom I am accused in England of not knowing how to rule, and am taunted with being barbarous and bloody and cruel!' . . . 'I own', writes Lord Curzon, 'that I found it a little difficult to pursue, with dialectical advantage, this strain of conversation.' Marquess Curzon of Kedleston, *Tales of Travel* (London, 1923), pp. 71–3. Under English law, convicted thieves were not mutilated, but intermittently hanged between the thirteenth century and the 1820s. They now form part of Britain's 73,000 prisoners, among whom there is a rising suicide rate. The fight against crime in the United States is currently imprisoning two million Americans – seven thousand of them for life under California's 'three strikes' law, four thousand of these for non-violent offences. The flaying of the judge: Hdt. 5.25. 'It is a great while ago since I read the history . . . Surely it was a goodly sign, a goodly monument, the sign of the judge's skin. I pray God we may once see the sign of the skin in England!' H. Latimer, *Sermons*, introd. Canon Beeching (London, 1906), p. 125.
54. Phraortes: Behistun Inscription (DB) §31 2.70–8. R. G. Kent, *Old Persian Grammar, Texts, Lexicon*, 2nd rev. edn (New Haven, 1953), p. 124. Parysatis' revenge: Plut. *Artax.* 16.

would have told us, for the Greeks in principle if not always in practice repudiated cruelty and applauded those who gave no pain to others. At the conclusion of his *Memorabilia* Xenophon tells us that Socrates was 'so just as not to harm anyone in any way however small'. However implausibly for a politician and general, Pericles on his deathbed claimed as his finest and greatest achievement that no citizen through his means had ever worn mourning. Cyrus for his part will have followed pitilessly, regardless of mourning, the injunction of his great-great-grandfather Darius I: 'The man who co-operated with my House, him I rewarded well; whoever did injury, him I punished well. Darius the King says: you who shall be king hereafter, if a man should be a Lie-follower or a doer of wrong, do not be a friend to those; punish them well.'[55]

Darius' successors fulfilled their royal mission by allotting preposterous rewards as well as atrocious punishments. Xerxes doubtless believed that he was acting as a true son of Darius in first rewarding the hospitality of Pythius the Lydian by making up his fortune to four million gold darics, and then, when Pythius asked for one of his five sons to be spared military service, having his eldest cut in two halves so that the army should pass between them. 'Gratitude, laid up in the Royal House' was a Persian king's traditional response for a good deed. Artaxerxes II gave a gold bowl and a thousand gold darics to a peasant as a reward for a drink of river water. The King's subjects will have been pleased rather than shocked by such profligacy; we may guess it to have been as popular as the modern British state lottery.[56]

So the generosity of Cyrus the Younger was in keeping with family tradition; but he lacked the King's means, though he was not, at first, kept as short of money as were other satraps. He arrived in his province with a fund of five hundred talents from his royal father, in addition to his own fortune. That fund was equal to a year's tribute from Lydia in Darius I's time; but Cyrus' province embraced not only Lydia but also Greater Phrygia and Cappadocia. His war subsidies of thirty-three and a third talents to Lysander, and later to Clearchus, were modest by comparison with the huge Athenian outlay at the

---

55. The repudiation of cruelty among the Greeks: Dover, *Greek Popular Morality*, pp. 195–205. The justice of Socrates: *Mem.* 4.8.11. The deathbed claim of Pericles: Plut. *Per.* 38.4. The injunction of Darius: DB §63–4 4.65–9, Kent, *Old Persian Grammar, Texts, Lexicon*, p. 132.
56. The treatment of Pythius: Hdt. 7.27–9, 38–9. The gratitude of the King: Hdt. 8.85.3, Thuc. 1.129.3, ML 12.15–17, *Esther* 6: 1–2. Artaxerxes and the peasant: Plut. *Artax.* 5.1.

beginning of the Peloponnesian War: two thousand talents for the siege of Potidaea alone.[57]

The five hundred talents cannot have lasted long. Cyrus could more easily afford grandiloquent promises. He promised to pay Lysander out of his own money if his father's failed, and if all else were lacking, to turn into coin the gold and silver of his throne. He is reported to have written to the Spartans in early 401 for troops, promising horses to foot-soldiers, carriages to horsemen, villages to owners of fields, cities to owners of villages, and pay not by count but by measure. The Ten Thousand entered his service for a daric a month, equivalent to some twenty-two Attic drachmae. This was about as much as the four obols (two-thirds of a drachma) a day which Lysander had secured for his men in 407, but less than the drachma a day which Athens had paid to hoplites and sailors in good years.[58]

But when they reached Tarsus, Cyrus had not paid his Greek mercenaries for three months. He was only rescued from his dilemma by a present from the Cilician king's wife, with whom he was rumoured to have slept. When he induced the troops to advance to the Euphrates under pretext of fighting Abrocomas, he promised a rise from a daric a month to a daric and a half. Upon revealing that the advance was to be upon Babylon, he upped his promise to a lump sum of five minae (five hundred drachmae) plus full pay until their safe return to Ionia. Finally, when Artaxerxes II's advance was imminent, Cyrus declared: 'my fear is not that I shall not have enough to give my friends, but that I shall not have enough friends to give to. To each of you Greeks I will give a crown of gold.' Pies in the sky, castles in the air![59]

Xenophon says that Cyrus was vexed when unable to pay, for 'it was not his way to withold payment when he had money'. If true, this was Mr Micawber's predicament exactly. But was it entirely true? Among Cyrus' Greek mercenaries, Xenophon's bugbear Menon and the encouraging soothsayer Silanus did get paid, the latter on the eve of Cunaxa with three thousand darics down, equivalent to ten talents. That sum could have supplied each of ten thousand deluded men with ten days' basic pay.[60]

---

57. The fund of five hundred talents: *Hell.* 1.5.3. The tribute from Lydia in the time of Darius: Hdt. 3.90. The size of Cyrus' province: *Anab.* 1.9.7. Athenian outlay for the siege of Potidaea: Thuc. 2.70.2.
58. The promise to Lysander: Plut. *Lys.* 9.1. The letter to the Spartans: Plut. *Artax.* 6.1.
59. The rise from a daric to a daric and a half: *Anab.* 1.3.21. The promise of a lump sum and full pay until the return to Ionia: *Anab.* 1.4.13. A crown of gold apiece: *Anab.* 1.7.7.
60. Cyrus' profession of frustration: *Anab.* 1.2.11. Silanus' pay: *Anab.* 1.7.18.

In the *Memorabilia*, Xenophon stresses the importance of provisioning troops. He even has Socrates defend the election to the Athenian generalship of a public-spirited businessman without military experience, because a sound manager of supplies can be expected to take every precaution against defeat, and strenuously provide what is needed for victory. Cyrus is never blamed by Xenophon for neglecting his commissariat; but he should have known what to expect in the desert lands along the Upper Euphrates, where baggage animals perished of hunger, grain failed the army, and no food was to be got for money except at high prices in the Asian troops' market.[61]

That his previous travels to and from the King's headquarters had been by the Royal Road, running through less barren land, is no excuse. Artaxerxes III was to make no such mistake when invading Egypt through the Sinai Desert in 343, with 'baggage animals beyond number, victims fattened for slaughter, many bushels of spices, many bags and sacks and vessels of root vegetables and all other necessities, and so much salted meat of all kinds in such big piles that those approaching from a distance took them to be ridges and hills'. Cyrus at the last advanced with insufficient caution. When his unprepared troops learned of the King's advance, there was wild confusion. That the Greeks fought so well, when they had not had time to complete their formation, was due to courage and competent command. Cyrus died bravely but as an incompetent commander.[62]

One small touch is telling. When wagons stuck in the mire during the long march beside the Euphrates, Cyrus gave some Asian troops the task of extricating them. They were slow about it; so he angrily ordered his entourage of Persian nobles to lend a hand. They did so, willingly and well, regardless of their costly tunics, embroidered trousers, necklaces, and bracelets. Xenophon extolled this model of good discipline. Years later, in *c.* 385, Artaxerxes II, no longer young, campaigned against the Cadusian mountaineers near the Caspian. In emergencies, he did not stand and watch like Cyrus, but shared his men's hardships like Clearchus.

> He let neither his gold nor his robe nor the royal ornaments, worth two thousand talents, that were always about his person, prevent him from labouring and toiling like anyone it might be. With his quiver at his side and holding his shield he himself led the way over craggy and precipitous ways,

---

61. Socrates on military elections: *Mem.* 3.4. The dearth beside the Euphrates: *Anab.* 1.5.5–6.
62. The invasion of Artaxerxes III: Theopompus *FGH* 115 F263 ap. [Longinus] 43.2. Confusion at the King's advance: *Anab.* 1.8.1–2.

leaving his horse, and so gave wings to the others and lightened their burden when they saw his enthusiasm and strength.

When they reached a wonderful royal park in bare, treeless country, it being cold, he told his soldiers to cut the trees for firewood, sparing neither pine nor cypress; and when they hesitated, wishing to save them because of their size and beauty, he took an axe and chopped down the largest and best of them himself. We are left with the impression that Cyrus' brother, far from being a pampered coward, had better qualities of leadership, though he sullied his record by heavy losses on campaign, and reprisals against many nobles afterwards.[63]

What won Xenophon and others over was Cyrus' courteous affability, an attractive quality when combined with power, for power all too often tends not only to corrupt, but also to induce arrogance. Yet Artaxerxes II's mildness and graciousness were attractive too, and Cyrus was not always affable. As an adolescent ruler he had in 406 kept Callicratidas, Lysander's successor as High Admiral, hanging about at his gates two days for an audience. Callicratidas, who had come to Sardis to collect his sailors' pay from funds which Lysander had handed back to Cyrus, was told that Cyrus was busy drinking.[64] He left in disgust. Cyrus subsequently sent him money along with *xenia*, presents in token of friendship. Callicratidas took the money but returned the presents. Cyrus made a display of magnanimity when refusing to send warships from the Syrian port of Myriandrus to pursue the mini-deserters Xenias the Arcadian and Pasion the Megarian; but this gesture he could afford. It would have been a different matter if the main body of Greek troops had deserted at Tarsus. He might then, as Clearchus warned, have turned dangerously hostile.[65]

Cyrus' final speech to his Greek generals and officers shows a wonderful understanding of Greek mentality: 'Men of Hellas, it is not for lack of barbarian allies that I lead you; I recruited you because I think you better and stronger than many barbarians. So be worthy of the freedom you possess and for which I count you fortunate. You know that I would choose freedom instead of all I have and much else.' The Greek world had in the past resisted the Persians in the name of freedom, as Xenophon was to remind them after

---

63. Cyrus and the wagons: *Anab.* 1.5.8. Artaxerxes on campaign: Plut. *Artax.* 24.20–25.1–2.
64. Such behaviour is derided in the *Cyropaedia* (1.3.11).
65. The affability of Artaxerxes: Plut. *Artax.* 24.20–25.1–2. Callicratidas' refusal of *xenia*: *Hell.* 1.6.6, 10, 18; Plut. *Apophth. Lac*, Callicratidas 1–4 = *Mor.* 222 B–E. Clearchus' warning: *Anab.* 1.3.12.

Tissaphernes' betrayal; Greeks continued to match their freedom against barbarian enslavement.[66] Yet Cyrus' words in praise of Greek freedom, if truly his and not Xenophon's, attest not to sincerity but to skill in following and improving upon the Achaemenids' practice of ministering, with the help of local advisers, to their subjects' predilections.

This went back to the beginnings of their empire. Cyrus the Great, though by no means a lenient conqueror, provided for records in verse and prose of his re-establishment of the cult of Marduk at Babylon which the last Babylonian king, Nabuna'id, had neglected. He also repatriated the leading Jews from their Babylonish captivity, and summoned them to rebuild the Temple in Jerusalem.[67]

Cambyses, contrary to what Herodotus tells us, did not kill the Apis bull whom the Egyptians worshipped, but respected Egyptian cults; he sacrificed to the goddess Neith at Saïs on the advice of Udjahorrosne, admiral of the Pharaohs, whom Cambyses retained under the title of chief physician. Darius I favoured the sacred gardeners of Apollo at Magnesia on the Maeander; his general Datis learned to speak Greek, however imperfectly, sacrificed to Apollo at Delos and invoked Greek mythical genealogy in an attempt to win over the Athenians before the battle of Marathon.[68]

Xerxes used the same technique, with more success, to keep Argos neutral; well informed about Greek preconceptions, he went out of his way to sacrifice at Troy before crossing over to Europe. Xerxes' temple-burning during his

---

66. 'Men of Hellas': *Anab.* 1.7.2–4. Freedom vs. slavery: K. Raaflaub, *Zum Freiheitsbegriff der Griechen* (Berlin, 1981), pp. 212–15, 314–16. Xenophon's reminder: *Anab.* 3.2.13.
67. 'A Persian verse account of Nabonidus', in *Babylonian Historical Texts relating to the Capture and Downfall of Babylon*, trans. Sidney Smith (London, 1924), ch. 3, pp. 27–97 and pl. 4–9. The Nabonidus Chronicle: A. K. Grayson, *Assyrian and Babylonian Chronicles* (New York, 1970), introd. pp. 21–2, text pp. 104–11. The Cyrus Cylinder: P.-R. Berger, 'Der Kyros-Zylinder mit dem Zusatzfragment BIN II Nr.32 und die akkadischen Personennamen im Danielbuch', *Zeitschrift für Assyriologie* 64 (1975), pp. 193–203, A. Kuhrt, 'The Cyrus Cylinder and Achaemenid imperial policy', *Journal for the Study of the Old Testament* 25 (1983), pp. 83–94. The rebuilding of the Temple: 2 *Chronicles* 36: 22–3, *Ezra* 1: 1–11, cf. *Isaiah* 44:28, 45:1–7.
68. The claim that Cambyses killed an Apis bull: Hdt. 3.29. From a tomb inscription we know that an Apis bull died in 524, when Cambyses was campaigning in Ethiopia; another was born on 29 May 525, shortly before Cambyses entered Memphis, and lived through Cambyses' reign to 31 August 518, the fourth year of Darius I: G. Posener, *La Première Domination perse en Égypte* (Cairo, 1936), Inscriptions 3–5, pp. 30–41. The sacrifice to Neith is attested by inscriptions on two statuettes of Udjahorrosne: Posener, *La première domination perse en Égypte*, Inscriptions 1, 2, pp. 1–29. The sacred gardeners at Magnesia: *ML* 12. Datis' imperfect Greek: Ar. *Pax* 289. His sacrifice at Delos: Hdt. 6.97. His attempt to win over the Athenians: Diod. 2.27.

invasion was attributed by the Greeks not to zeal for his own aniconic religion, but to a desire to avenge the burning of the temple to Cybele at Sardis by the Athenians and Ionians. He dented but did not reverse the imperial tradition of coming to terms with the traditions of subject peoples.[69]

Graeco-Persian interaction in western Asia Minor gathered strength during the fifth century.[70] Cyrus' welcome of 'Zeus Saviour and Victory' as the Greeks' watchword at Cunaxa was no more remarkable than Tissaphernes' sacrifice to Artemis of Ephesus in 411. Cyrus' philhellenic outlook, then, was no innovation, and it had its limits. For all that he had two Greek mistresses, he employed, as did Tissaphernes, an interpreter. This man, Pigres the Carian, was at Cyrus' side on the battlefield of Cunaxa.[71]

Cyrus' conduct in his province towards his Persian subordinates, rewarding courage and refusing to envy anyone's wealth, contrasts with the all too frequent tendency of rulers to promote the unworthy and despoil the deserving. His gifts of half-eaten geese and half-loaves of bread were comradely. He still stood in a dynastic tradition of comradeship. Darius I's Achaemenid relatives and descendants, together with those of the Six Persians who had helped him to power in 522, had with their retainers fought as a loyal band of brothers in the Great Persian War of 490/79. But subsequent internecine feuds, murders, and rebellions had left their mark. Cyrus had Megaphernes, a wearer of the royal purple, executed for no known cause, destroyed the palace and park of Belesys, governor of Syria, and declared his intention of attacking Abrocomas,

---

69. Argos' neutrality procured: Hdt. 7.150. The sacrifice at Troy: Hdt. 7.41. Xerxes' temple-burning: Hdt. 5.99. The discovery in 1935 of Xerxes' inscription recording his destruction of a sanctuary 'where the *daivā* [false gods] were worshipped' (XPh, Kent, *Old Persian Grammar, Texts, Lexicon*, pp. 150–2) revealed him as a religious fanatic; but this fanaticism must have been confined to Iran. So far was Xerxes, or any other Persian king, from forcing his own religion on the Greeks that no reference to their supreme god Ahuramazda is found in Greek literature before the mid fourth century (Pl. *Alc. I* 122a). The Persians were known not to worship images (Hdt. 1.131); but before Cicero (*Rep.* 3.9, 14; *Leg.* 2.10, 26; *Nat. D.* 1.41, 115) we know of no one who attributed Xerxes' temple-burning to iconoclasm. Fifth-century Greeks spoke of it as impiety (Oath before Plataea, Lycurg. *Leoc.* 81, Diod. 11.29.3). The burning was in any case selective. Xerxes left the temple of Artemis at Ephesus inviolate. He spared the Oracle at Delphi, which had expected him to win (Hdt. 7.140.1); after he lost, a very tall story was needed to explain Delphi's survival (Hdt. 8.35–9). His policy is reassessed by J. Wiesehöfer, *Ancient Persia from 550 BC to 650 AD* (London, 1996), pp. 51–5, with a bibliographical essay pp. 260–3.
70. M. C. Miller, *Athens and Persia in the Fifth Century BC* (Cambridge, 1997), pp. 89–133.
71. The watchword at Cunaxa: *Anab.* 1.8.16–17. Tissaphernes' sacrifice to Artemis: Thuc. 8.109. Cyrus' interpreter: *Anab.* 1.2.11, 8.12.

governor of Phoenicia. His spite against personal enemies must be set against his affability to comrades. Affability, in any case, is not a cardinal virtue. Villains, out of self-interest, can display it too.[72]

Most commendable of all is Cyrus' pride as governor in protecting and equipping the countryside. The expression *kataskeuazein chōran* applies in the *Hellenica Oxyrhynchia* to farm buildings. In the hinterland of Asia Minor, which supplied Miletus' woollen industry, the emphasis must also have been on stock. The Pisidians, 'who gave trouble to Cyrus' own *chōra*', will not have spared its herds. It will have been the need to protect his subjects' flocks that motivated Cyrus' campaign against them, not just the wish to round off Persia's conquests. Here, too, he was following Achaemenid precedent, exemplified by the claim of Darius I after seizing power in 522: 'I restored to the people the pastures and the herds, the household slaves and the houses which Gautama the Magian took away from them. I established the people on its foundation, both Persia and Media and the other provinces.'[73]

That is not to say that if Cyrus had won, the Greek cities of Asia would have found him a Good King. They would have continued to suffer under his 'friends' the decarchs, gorged with ill-gotten wealth that he did not envy. These were removed in the first instance by Tissaphernes. By the time the Spartans re-entered Asia Minor to fight the Persians in 400, the ephors had turned against decarchies in favour of *patrioi politeiai*, traditional constitutions. In 398 the Spartan commander Dercyllidas found the Asian cities in happy case. They were afflicted by political disturbances soon after; but the Spartan king

---

72. Compare with Cyrus' bounty the less unappetising, but more condescending, whole hams and haunches of venison which might be sent by an English nobleman to a protégé, and the gifts of country produce that a protégé might send to his patron, e.g. Sydney Smith to Lord Holland. The execution of Megaphernes: *Anab.* 1.2.20. The destruction of Belesys' property: *Anab.* 1.4.10. The intention to attack Abrocomas: *Anab.* 1.3.20, 4.3, 5, 18, 7.12. All shrewd rulers ingratiate themselves with their bodyguard; Caligula and Mrs Gandhi paid with their lives for not doing so. The nastiest of twentieth-century tyrants have, in the absence of chattel slavery, been affable to their staff. Stalin was kind to his cleaning lady, who liked him but was puzzled by his lack of reverence for icons. Hitler was considerate to his catering manager, as I know from his daughter (the catering manager's, I mean, not Hitler's). My father remembered an Irish landlady telling him how, as cook in Germany's London embassy, she had been considerately treated by Herr and Frau Ribbentrop. 'Then there must have been some good in them,' I observed. 'Nonsense,' replied my father. 'It was pure self-interest. She was an excellent cook.'
73. Cyrus' pride as governor: *Oec.* 4.16. *Kataskeuazein chōran*: *Hell. Oxy.* 20.8. The ravages of the Pisidians: *Anab.* 1.1.11. Darius' claim: DB I §14 1.64–71, Kent, *Old Persian Grammar, Texts, Lexicon*, p. 120.

Agesilaus presently pacified them, and Lysander's plan to restore decarchies in 396 failed.[74]

The reintroduction of Persian rule, confirmed by the Peace of Antalcidas in 386, seems to have left the traditional constitutions in being, and ushered in a benign half-century of indirect rule during which the historian Ephorus of Cyme was left free to write as patriotically as he pleased about past Greek victories against Persia. The aged Isocrates, still fulminating Polonius-like in 346 against Persian rule over Greeks, wrote to Philip of Macedon that Clearchus and his followers found the Greeks 'intensely hostile because of the decarchies which the Spartans had set up. For they thought that if Cyrus and Clearchus succeeded, they would be enslaved all the more, but that if the King conquered they would be rid of their present evils; and that is just what did happen to them.'[75]

How just was Cyrus' cause? There is reason to believe that it was his wrongdoing that began the quarrel with Artaxerxes II. In the text of Xenophon's *Hellenica* 2.1.8–9 we find an account of how Cyrus, towards the end of Darius II's life, put to death two first cousins 'because when they met him they failed to push their hands through the *korē* – a gesture that is made only in the presence of the King. The *korē* is a kind of long sleeve, longer than the *cheiris*.' This act of arrogant violence was reported to Darius, who summoned Cyrus to court, feigning illness. The detailed knowledge of Persian customs and the spelling *Dareiaios*, closer than Xenophon's *Dareios* to the Persian *Dārayavauš*, almost certainly prove this passage to be an interpolation from Ctesias of Cnidus, Artaxerxes II's Greek physician, whose eye-witness account was cited by Xenophon for how Cyrus wounded his brother in battle and was killed himself. Ctesias' *Persica* in twenty-three books, composed after his return home, survives in quotations and a lengthy Byzantine epitome. The ugly story of Cyrus' execution of his cousins can hardly have been inserted into the *Hellenica* by Xenophon himself, but must be a scribal interpolation.[76]

The story rings true, though we cannot be quite sure of it, because Ctesias, despite professed admiration of the Spartans and Clearchus, had as an

---

74. *Patrioi politeiai*: *Hell.* 3.4.2. Cf. A. Andrewes, 'Two notes on Lysander', pp. 206–26. Happy state of Asia in 398: *Hell.* 3.2.9. Political disturbances thereafter: *Hell.* 3.4.7. Pacification by Agesilaus: *Ages.* 1.37. Lysander's plan of 396: *Hell.* 3.4.2.
75. Isoc. 5.95.
76. Xenophon's citation of Ctesias: *FGH* 688 F20–1 ap. *Anab.* 1.8.23–7, Plut. *Artax.* 11. The epitome of Ctesias is conveniently printed with a French translation by R. Henry, *Ctésias, la Perse, l'Inde. Les sommaires de Photius* (Brussels, 1947). Scribal interpolation: Cawkwell, introduction to *Xenophon: A History of my Times*, ad loc.

adherent of Artaxerxes II a motive for discrediting Cyrus. And Ctesias was a monumental liar. He wrote, for instance, of the *martichōra* (a correctly formed Persian word meaning 'man-eater'), a creature as big as a lion, with two or three rows of teeth in each jaw, a lion's claws, a man's face and ears, the voice of a trumpet and speed of a deer; it shot stings a foot long from its tail, and ate men. An honest historian might believe all that from hearsay, but not claim, as Ctesias did, that he had seen one himself in Persia, sent to the King as a present from India.[77]

Modern scholars look to Ctesias, all the same, for information on the court life he witnessed personally, believing with Plutarch that here he could not help getting some details right. His is a case similar to that of the mendacious publicist Frank Harris. 'Had Frank Harris ever been known to tell the truth?' Max Beerbohm was asked. 'Sometimes, don't you know – when his invention flagged.' But even when writing of events he had witnessed, Ctesias told lies to magnify his role in them. Plutarch caught him out in one.[78]

Another suspect item, almost certainly from Ctesias, is Cyrus' alleged vaunt, in his recruiting letter to the Spartan state of early 401, that he was 'stouter-hearted than his brother, a better philosopher and a better Magian, and could drink and hold more wine, whereas his brother through cowardice and softness could not keep his seat on his horse when hunting, or on his throne when in danger'. The ethnic colouring looks convincing; but on reflection, we can hardly suppose that one who so well understood the mind of the Greeks would have boasted to them of his Magian learning, still less that he would have revealed in a letter to Sparta, at the beginning of his expedition, the hostility to his brother that he was keeping secret from his own mercenaries. What Cyrus must really have written emerges from Diodorus, who writes that his campaign purported to be against Cilicia as well as Pisidia. By this must be meant the intractable mountain territory of Cilicia Tracheia, 'Rough Cilicia', that was to be the Tora Bora of late Roman republican times until Pompey's victory of 66 BC. There was always a danger of brigands swooping down from their mountain fastnesses into the fertile Cilician plain, Cilicia Pedias, with whose king Syennesis Cyrus was presently to exchange gifts. That, as well as the wish to prevent Syennesis from hampering Cyrus, will explain the despatch of thirty-five Peloponnesian ships, with a Spartan admiral on board, to Issus

---

77. *Ctésias, la Perse, l'Inde*, trans. Henry, pp. 65–6 = *FGH* 688 F45 (15); F45d.
78. Frank Harris: S. N. Behrman, *Conversations with Max* (London, 1960), p. 101. Plutarch on Ctesias: Plut. *Artax.* 1.4, 13; *FGH* 688 F13.

in 401. They must have sailed home again when Cyrus sprang the surprise of marching inland towards Babylon.[79]

Xenophon relates that Cyrus went up from his province, accompanied by Tissaphernes, to the deathbed of his father Darius II, and that after the old King had died, Tissaphernes falsely accused Cyrus of plotting against the new King his brother, but was begged off by their mother, Parysatis. Plutarch tells the same story in colourful detail: Artaxerxes II had travelled to Pasargadae to be initiated into royalty 'by the priests among the Persians'. For this, he had to enter 'a temple of a warrior goddess whom one might compare to Athena' (viz. Anahita), disrobe, put on the garments which Cyrus the Great had worn before becoming king, eat from a cake of figs, taste the fruit of the turpentine tree, and drink a cup of sour milk; whatever else he may have done was known only to the initiated. Just before the ceremony, he was met by Tissaphernes together with one of the priests, who had been the younger Cyrus' Magian instructor and was a plausible informant because of his supposed grief at his pupil's not becoming King. This priest told Artaxerxes that Cyrus intended to conceal himself in the temple and murder him when he undressed. 'Some say Cyrus was arrested because of this accusation; others, that he actually entered the temple and was betrayed in his hiding-place by the priest.' Parysatis then flung her arms round Cyrus and won his pardon with her tears.[80]

It is a fair guess that Ctesias was among those who wrote of Cyrus' plot as genuine. Once again, we may disbelieve him. But whether the plot was genuine or a fabrication of Tissaphernes, Artaxerxes acted with generous forbearance in sending Cyrus back west as governor once again, and was basely rewarded by Cyrus' collecting an army against him in secrecy so as to take him unawares.[81]

Cyrus' ingratitude was surely worse than that of Orontes, whom he sentenced to death after twice forgiving his rebellions, for Orontes had only deserted the expedition with a view to joining Artaxerxes II, and had not tried to kill Cyrus personally. Moreover, Artaxerxes was his lawful sovereign. A Persian King clearly had in principle the right to choose his successor within the Achaemenid family, while taking into account the claims of primogeniture.[82] Darius II's choice was unobjectionable.

---

79. Cyrus' alleged boast: Plut. *Artax.* 6.4. The campaign against Cilicia: Diod. 14.19.3, 6. The dispatch to Issus: *Anab.* 1.4.2.
80. Plut. *Artax.* 2–3.
81. *Anab.* 1.1.1–6.
82. Orontes: *Anab.* 1.6.6–11. The right of regal selection is still true of some oriental dynasties, as evidenced by the recent unexpected accession of King Abdullah II of Jordan

Plutarch attributes to Queen Parysatis the unavailing argument that Cyrus should succeed because she had borne him when his father was already King, as Atossa had borne Xerxes, designated as crown prince by Darius I on the advice of the exiled Spartan king Damaratus, who invoked Spartan practice. It is, however, unlikely that any Persian king would have been interested in copying what was done at Sparta. Xerxes had indeed been a younger son, but was preferable to the older ones because he was Cyrus the Great's grandson.[83] Since both Artaxerxes and Cyrus were sons of Darius II by Parysatis, Cyrus had no comparable claim.

Plutarch knows a story of Cyrus being aggrieved because Artaxerxes did not provide him with enough for his daily dinner. It is not as silly a story as Plutarch thinks, for we know from the nature of the royal grants to Themistocles, and from a fragment of Heraclides of Cyme, that rations were distributed to high officials on a massive scale, to provide for their courts and garrisons. The publication of the Persepolis Fortification Tablets in 1969 has furnished further examples: in 500, for example, Pharnaces, the royal kinsman in charge of Persepolis, was receiving two sheep, 90 quarts of wine, and 180 quarts of flour daily. But Plutarch is right to protest that Cyrus could draw on his mother's wealth and could afford to recruit the Ten Thousand; and Xenophon gives no hint of Cyrus being stinted after his brother's accession.[84]

Stretch your credulity, and try to believe that Cyrus did not put to death his two cousins, never plotted against his brother at Pasargadae, was snubbed in the matter of rations, and was truly the better man for the Persian throne. Does that justify fratricide? Cyrus spoke as though he were engaged on some chivalrous joust. 'Do you think your brother will fight you?' Clearchus asked him. 'By God, if he is a son of Darius and Parysatis, and my brother, I shall not win the prize without a battle.' If we are to believe Ctesias, as Xenophon did, he caught sight of his royal brother in the battle, could not contain himself – no *enkrateia* here – and made straight at him with the cry 'I see the man!' and wounded him before he was himself cut down.[85]

instead of the Crown Prince, and by the Bhopal Succession Case of 1925, argued in detail before the Viceroy: *Rufus Isaacs, First Marquess of Reading, 1914–1935*, by his son the Marquess of Reading (London, 1945), pp. 321–3.
83. Cyrus and Xerxes: Plut. *Artax.* 2, Hdt. 7.2–4. The superior claim of Xerxes: J. M. Cook, *The Persian Empire* (London, 1983), pp. 74–5.
84. Cyrus' dinner money: Plut. *Artax.* 4.1. The grants to Themistocles: Thuc. 1.138.5, Plut. *Them.* 29.11. The fragment of Heraclides: *FGH* 689 F2, ap. Athen. 4.26, 145a–146a. The allotment to Pharnaces: R. T. Hallock, *Persepolis Fortification Tablets* (Chicago, 1969), pp. 654–69; D. M. Lewis, *Sparta and Persia*, p. 5; cf. Wiesehöfer, *Ancient Persia*, pp. 66–75.
85. The conversation with Clearchus: *Anab.* 1.7.9. The wounding of Artaxerxes: *Anab.* 1.8.26.

To kill him would have been no end of a coup. A Roman general who personally killed the enemy chieftain in battle was entitled to the *spolia opima*, the rarest of honours; there were only three instances of such a feat in Roman history, the last in the event unrewarded, the first, by Romulus, mythical. Yet Romulus received no honour for killing his brother Remus because of 'that ancestral evil, the desire for kingship'. The curse of the crime of fratricide, *scelus fraternae necis*, was thought to have pursued the Romans with relentless fatality, leading eventually to the civil wars that cost them their freedom. Fratricide was the biblical Curse of Cain: 'Behold, thy brother's blood crieth unto me from the ground.' All civilizations regard it with horror.[86]

Or are oriental monarchies an exception? The Ottoman Law of Fratricide allowed an incoming sultan to execute his brothers. Mehmet III, on succeeding Murad III in 1566, made use of it to strangle all nineteen of his. That law, however, was framed to offset any danger of an attack like that of Cyrus, from which even the Turks recoiled. If Artaxerxes II had acted like Mehmet III, he would have saved many lives. (As it was, he was kind to all his brothers and also to his wife, though somewhat too indulgent towards his mother, who got away with many atrocities, and somewhat too fond of his daughter, whom he married.) Darius I did not approve of Cambyses' secret killing of his full brother. There was nothing in the Zoroastrian scriptures to condone the internecine crimes of the Achaemenids, any more than there was in the Christian gospels to condone Henry I's imprisonment of his brother Robert, or King John's feud against his brother Richard I. The Greeks recorded with fascination the differing customs of the barbarians, whom they did not invent; but they did not exempt them from the unwritten moral laws which, Xenophon writes, have all come together from the ends of the earth, for men who are not all of one speech, and were made by the gods who are everywhere worshipped.[87]

Xenophon, even more than his fellow Greeks, evinces a wide spectrum of attitudes towards the Persians. Where he is at his most hostile, after the arrest of Clearchus and the other generals, it is because Persians had impiously broken oaths which were as binding on them as on the rest of mankind. The homily he put into Socrates' mouth in favour of brotherly love, even of the most disagreeable of brothers, did not, we may be sure, apply to Greeks alone.

---

86. 'Ancestral evil': Livy 1.6.4. *Scelus fraternae necis*: Hor. *Epod.* 7.17–18. The Curse of Cain: Genesis 4: 20.
87. Darius' disapproval: DB §10 1.26–35, Kent, *Old Persian Grammar, Texts, Lexicon*, p. 119. Barbarian customs contrasted with Greek: Hdt. 3.38. Xenophon on the moral laws: *Mem.* 4.4.19.

He professed himself shocked by Artaxerxes II nailing up the head and hand of the dead Cyrus – his own brother, son of the same parents! In the *Cyropaedia*, he portrays as blameless the behaviour to his family of the model king Cyrus the Great, who, fortunately for the story, was an only son, though Justin attests a sister. Xenophon's blind eye towards Cyrus the Younger's attempted fratricide was due not to double standards but to partial vision.[88]

'Fortune', Diodorus writes about Cyrus' duel with his brother, 'brought the fraternal strife for hegemony to single combat, as if in imitation of the ancient desperate fight between Eteocles and Polynices, celebrated in tragedy.' Tragedy tells us something about the Greek attitude to fratricide. Aeschylus' *Seven against Thebes* shows Eteocles as protagonist of Thebes against the surrounding Argive invaders called in by his brother Polynices. Eteocles determinedly marshals the defence of each of Thebes' seven gates against its opposing champion. It must be this part of the play that, according to an Aristophanic line, 'made every man fall in love with bravery'.[89]

But the anguished prayers of the women of Thebes turn to horror when they learn that Eteocles means to fight his brother himself and kill him. 'This death of two brothers, one slain by the other, is a pollution that can never grow old.' 'The dark curse of the race of Oedipus has reached its completion.'[90]

Each brother fought with better justification than Cyrus. Eteocles saved his native city from invaders and merited honourable burial. Euripides puts Polynices' point of view: 'I call the gods to witness that I am doing everything with justice, being unjustly deprived of my country in the most unholy manner.' Yet for Euripides the brothers' killing each other was a dreadful misfortune, the cause of their mother Jocasta's suicide. The Phoenician women of the chorus lament it with barbarian cries but with dismay indistinguishable from that of Greeks: 'woe is me, Thebes! Your strife is no strife, but murder upon murder has brought to fulfilment the destruction of the house of Oedipus, with terrible bloodshed, grievous bloodshed.' Pindar, in a victory ode for an Aeginetan Aeacid, touches on the murder of Aeacus' son Phocus by his

88. On Xenophon's attitudes to the Persians, S. W. Hirsch, *The Friendship of the Barbarians: Xenophon and the Persian Empire* (Hanover, New Haven, and London, 1985), provides an admirably thoughtful discussion. Persian oath-breaking: *Anab*. 3.1. Socrates on brotherly love: *Mem*. 1.3. The nailing-up of Cyrus' head and hand: *Anab*. 3.1.17.
89. The analogy with the sons of Oedipus: Diod. 14.23.6. Diodorus makes no reference to tragedy in his earlier, matter-of-fact account of that conflict (Diod. 4.64–65.3). So the comparison probably derives not from him but from his unidentifiable source. Aristophanes on the *Seven*: Ar. *Ran*. 1021–2.
90. Aesch. *Sept*. 681–2, 832–4. For this pollution, see R. Parker, *Miasma* (Oxford, 1983), p. 137.

half-brothers Telamon and Peleus; but this legend is so painful that he immediately turns away: 'I am ashamed to speak of a big deed not hazarded with justice.' We need to refer to Pausanias' work of over six centuries later for the details which Pindar suppressed.[91]

Plato in his *Laws* proposed that fratricide committed in self-defence should be accounted 'pure' – for instance in civil war. Civil war was, as we have seen, endemic. The German refugees who joined the British forces to free their country from Hitler ran a similar risk, though much smaller in view of the huge numbers involved in twentieth-century war. Anyone who killed a brother in anger should, Plato suggested, be punished with three years' exile and the dissolution of family bonds. Anyone who killed a brother in cold blood should be put to death and his corpse cast out naked to a crossroads outside the city, where every man was to make public expiation by hurling a stone at its head. The remains were then to be cast out unburied beyond the frontier.[92]

Not long after Xenophon's time, Timoleon, the future liberator of Sicily, was involved in the assassination of his brother Timophanes at Corinth. Diodorus dates it to 346/5. He writes that Timoleon tried but failed to reason with his brother, who with his band of ruffians was hell-bent on tyranny. Then he put him to death while walking in the market-place. Civil strife ensued 'because of the enormity of the deed' and Timoleon was prosecuted before the Council of Elders. During the trial the appeal from Syracuse arrived. The court decided that if he ruled Syracuse well he would be judged a tyrannicide, otherwise a fratricide. He chose to rule well. Plutarch, who puts the assassination in 365, writes that Timoleon's brother, whose life he had saved, had secured a bodyguard and become tyrant by dint of getting many opponents put to death without trial. After failing to dissuade him, Timoleon called on him again with two friends, only to be jeered at. Then, while Timoleon stood aside to weep with his face covered, the two friends killed Timophanes. Though applauded by the democrats, Timoleon found himself reviled for this 'impious and abominable act'; his mother refused even to see him again; and he grieved for twenty years before answering the call from Syracuse. Nepos gives yet another version: Timophanes had made himself tyrant, and Timoleon refused the offer of sharing in his power, but to free his country contrived the tyrant's death with

---

91. Eteocles' justification: Eur. *Phoen.* 491–3. The dismay of the Phoenician women: *Phoen.* 1493–6. Pindar's horror: Pind. *Nem.* 5.14. Pausanias' details: Paus. 2.29.2, 9–10, 10.30.4.
92. The feelings of the German refugees are expressed in the autobiography of Keith Spalding, formerly Karl Spalt: *33 – alles umsteigen, eine Autobiographie* (Lübeck, 1992). Plato on punishment for fratricide: Pl. *Leg.* 9.868e, 869c–d, 873a–b.

the help of a soothsayer and his brother-in-law. Not wishing to lay hands on his brother himself or look on his blood, he stayed at a distance while the deed was being done – but kept guard.[93]

We need not here decide between these variants. They all show how dreadful fratricide, even for the highest motives, was in Greek eyes. Cyrus did not attempt fratricide for the highest motives. The words that Ctesias put into the mouth of the Cadusian chieftain Artagerses may be fictitious, but are consonant with Greek morality and that of all good men of all nations: 'You who disgrace the most noble name of Cyrus among the Persians, most unjust and senseless of men, are coming here leading base Greeks on a base journey to plunder the good things of the Persians, hoping to do away with your lord and brother, who has ten thousand times ten thousand servants better than you.'[94]

In following Clearchus and Cyrus and writing about them, Xenophon was true to the crude principle enunciated so often throughout his works, of being loyal to friends and doing harm to enemies. This was inconsistent with the higher morality that he admired in Socrates, of doing no harm to anyone whatsoever; but this inconsistency is universal, and Christians continue to live with it today, two thousand years after their redemption. 'The Sermon on the Mount is the last word in Christian ethics,' wrote Churchill. 'Everyone respects the Quakers. Still, it is not on these terms that Ministers assume their responsibilities of guiding states.'[95]

It is not on the highest principles, either, that we can expect ordinary people invariably to govern their lives. But if loyalty to their friends is to be their guiding light, we may reasonably expect them to choose virtuous friends.[96] Xenophon was aware of this. 'Association with worthy people', he wrote, 'is a training in virtue; with the base, it is its dissolution. To this the poet is a witness: "From the good you will learn goodness; but if you mingle with the bad, you will lose what sense you have now".'[97]

93. Diod. 16.65.3–9; Plut. *Tim.* 5–6; Nep. 20.1.3–4.
94. FGH 688 F19 ap. Plut. *Artax.* 9.2.
95. W. S. Churchill, *The Second World War*, vol. 1: *The Gathering Storm* (London, 1948), p. 251.
96. Failure to do this was the undoing of the land of my birth. Since the French Revolution, *Deutsche Treue*, German loyalty, had been its maxim. The Germans, true to their traditional rulers, however limited and unintelligent, sent no innocent victims on tumbrils to the guillotine. In subsequent wars, millions gave their lives in the spirit of German loyalty. Disaster came when German loyalty was unthinkingly rendered to a leader who was utterly unworthy of it. The dilemma of those who refused to do so was as grave as that which faced Timoleon: see C. Sykes, *Troubled Loyalty: A Biography of Adam von Trott* (London, 1969).
97. *Mem.* 1.2.20. The quotation is from Theognis 35–6.

'Good' and 'bad' were, for the Greeks, loaded terms; they spoke of the rich and well-born as 'good', and of social inferiors as 'bad'. But 'badness', as Hesiod said, 'can be acquired easily and in shoals: the road to her is smooth, and she lives very near.' The aristocratic Cypselids acquired badness when they assumed the tyranny of Corinth and failed to help Corinth's traditional allies in Euboea. Xenophon's blindness to the badness acquired by Clearchus through tyranny, and by Cyrus through attempted fratricide, is understandable in a gentleman adventurer who, without sharing directly in their misdeeds, had faithfully followed them in the hope of making his fortune. No one likes to admit he has been in the wrong. But that modern scholars have also turned a blind eye to those misdeeds makes one gasp and stretch both one's own.[98]

---

98. For 'good' and 'bad' as terms of social standing, cf. e.g. Solon fr. 34.9 West. Hesiod on badness: Hes. *Op.* 287–8. The badness of the Cypselids: Theognis 891–4.

4 One Man's Piety:
The Religious Dimension of the Anabasis

ROBERT PARKER

When the distinguished student of Hellenistic and late antique religion, Father Festugière, delivered his Sather lectures on the subject of *Personal Religion among the Greeks* in 1954, he was hard pressed to find any. By page 37 of the book based on the lectures he had already reached 'The Hellenistic mood and the influence of Plato'; of the previous 36 pages, half had been devoted to Euripides' Hippolytus, a character in a play, and one portrayed as having abnormal religious attitudes. Xenophon is completely absent from the book. We need not agonize over the question whether the concept of personal religion is a useful one to use in relation to ancient Greek religion; but if one wants to bring individuals into that study at all, it is very odd to omit Xenophon.[1] He offers what is in an ancient Greek context a unique opportunity to observe religion in a life, to track the religious activities of an individual (or at least a selection of them) over a period of time, that covered by the *Anabasis*. And, though there is nothing unique about the religion of Xenophon, which is in outline that of all other Greeks, one can observe characteristic emphases and priorities, a distinctive inflection.

A useful introit might be through a speech of Hermogenes in Xenophon's *Symposium*. The participants in the banquet are stating in turn what they are most proud of, and Hermogenes claims that he piques himself most on 'the virtue and power of my friends, and the fact that such figures take care of me'.[2] When asked who these powerful and caring friends are, he reveals that they are the gods, and illustrates their care for him as follows:

---

1. For a proper appreciation of Xenophon's evidence, see M. P. Nilsson, *Geschichte der griechischen Religion*, 3rd edn, vol. I (Munich, 1967), pp. 787–91. See too H. Bowden, 'Xenophon and the scientific study of religion', in C. J. Tuplin (ed.), *Xenophon and his World* (Stuttgart, 2004). I am grateful to Robin Lane Fox for the invitation to participate in the original *Anabasis* seminar, to him and other participants, especially Teresa Morgan, for stimulating observations, and to Tim Rood and Christopher Tuplin for extremely helpful written comments on a draft.
2. *Symp.* 3.14.

> The gods, whose knowledge and power are absolute, are such friends to me that, because they take care of me, they notice all my doings by both night and day – where I am about to go, what I am about to do; and because they know how every one of these acts will turn out, they give me signs, sending as messengers sayings and dreams and omens [literally 'birds'], about what I ought to do and what not. When I obey them I never regret it; but sometimes I have disobeyed and been punished.[3]

It is true that Xenophon himself is not the speaker here, and that there is an element of sport and paradox, appropriate to a symposium, in Hermogenes' claim. But many other explicit statements by Xenophon, or by characters treated by him as exemplary, justify us in seeing this as an extreme and playful formulation of what he regards as a proper religious attitude. He often compares the relation between man and god to that between man and man; gods, for instance, like friends, must be cultivated in good times as well as in bad. A restrained friendship (*philia*) between man and god is possible:[4] Xenophon's gods are, in fact, rather like a good general, efficient, fair-minded, dignified, but not inaccessible.

As a first slogan to characterize Xenophon's religious attitude one might therefore take 'healthy-mindedness', in the sense in which it was used by William James in *The Varieties of Religious Experience* to characterize an optimistic worldview and the optimistic views about the divine that go with it. According to F. H. Newman as cited by James, healthy-minded believers read the character of god, 'not in the disordered world of man, but in romantic and harmonious nature'. Xenophon did in the main think that he could read the character of god even in the world of man – justice catches up with the wicked – but he was certainly also one of the first Greeks to read the character of god in harmonious (if not romantic) nature. Though he did not invent the momentous 'argument from design' for the existence of god, he seized upon it eagerly and elaborated it; his Socrates argues in two crucially important passages of the *Memorabilia* that the physical structure of this world was designed by the gods specifically for the benefit of man, and such is his persuasiveness that his interlocutor is reduced to wondering whether 'the gods

---

3. *Symp.* 4.48.
4. 'Treat gods like men': *Cyrop.* 1.6.3; for other instances of the principle see *Cyrop.* 1.6.6, 7.2.17, *Mem.* 1.4.18. *Philia* between man and god: *Cyrop.* 1.6.4; *Mem.* 1.4.18.

have nothing else to do than serve [*therapeuō*, a verb normally used of mortals' service to gods] us men'.[5]

Religious optimism is not unique to Xenophon among Greeks, a form of it being in fact built into civic piety. Nor is his optimism unmitigated; in the *Hellenica*, when brute facts of history have to be confronted, the gods sometimes become grimmer and harder to understand.[6] Nonetheless, one can reasonably cite Xenophon as providing the clearest and fullest illustration of the Jamesian healthy-mindedness of all Greeks known to us before the philosophers.

A second characteristic trait emerges from the same passage of the *Symposium*. The first and indeed the only benefit that Hermogenes claims to receive from the gods is guidance through a variety of forms of sign and omen. The prominence of divination in Xenophon is an entirely obvious point; what may deserve emphasis is the way in which, in explicit statements, divination is repeatedly singled out, as by Hermogenes, among the greatest benefits conferred on mortals by the gods. For Xenophon, one might say, Greek religion is above all a religion of divination. Naturally then he is concerned to defend it against sceptical attacks.[7]

A third distinctive trait is Xenophon's rationalism, or what he sees as such. For Xenophon it makes sense to honour the gods: it is the reasonable, the

5. 'The religion of healthy-mindedness': William James, *The Varieties of Religious Experience* (London, 1902), lectures 4 and 5. The citation of Newman, which appears on p. 81, is said to come from *The Soul, its Sorrows and Aspirations*, 3rd edn (1852), pp. 89, 91. The 'argument from design' in the *Memorabilia*: *Mem.* 4.3.1–17 – the phrase quoted is from 4.3.9 – and 1.4.2–19 (For *therapeuō* used of the cultivation of gods by men, see e.g. 1.4.18). On these passages and their antecedents, see R. Parker, 'The origins of Pronoia: a mystery', in *Apodosis: Essays Presented to Dr W. W. Cruickshank* (St Paul's School, London, 1992), pp. 84–94. I do not think that there is much authentic Socrates in these chapters; but even if there were, Socrates' thought on this topic became Xenophon's.
6. For religious optimism and civic piety, see R. Parker, 'Gods cruel and kind: tragic and civic theology', in C. B. R. Pelling (ed.), *Greek Tragedy and the Historian* (Oxford, 1997), pp. 143–60. For the outlook in the *Hellenica*, see K. Joël, *Der echte und der Xenophontische Socrates I* (Berlin, 1893), pp. 108–14 (the whole treatment of Xenophon's religious outlook, pp. 69–170, is valuable); J. Dillery, *Xenophon and the History of his Times* (London, 1995), pp. 179–94. In *Hellenica* note 6.4.3, where something like the old *atē* or god-sent madness seizes the Spartan populace; 6.4.23, an amoral conception of the gods 'rejoicing' in exalting the low and humbling the mighty; 7.4.3, where a paradoxical twist of events is seen in Herodotean fashion as especially 'divine' (*daimonion*); 7.5.13, where divine control of events is asserted but not explained. Where in other texts the apparent arbitrariness of divine favours is noted, it is not stressed or condemned (*Oec.* 11.8; *Cyrop.* 1.6.46).
7. Divination as a benefit: *Mem.* 1.4.14–16, 4.3.12; *Eq. Mag.* 9.8–9; *Cyrop.* 1.6.46, 8.7.3. Defence from sceptical attacks: *Cyrop.* 1.6.46, which responds to a simpler form of criticisms such as that aired in Eur. *Hel.* 744–57.

natural thing to do. He would never dream of professing to 'believe because it is absurd'. His gods are reasonable beings, who make no impossible demands in the cult they expect from mortals. The advice they offer through omens will always turn out to make perfect sense, once the full picture is visible. The following two turns of thought in the *Anabasis* are characteristic, though Xenophon himself is not the speaker in either case: 'When I sacrificed to march against the king I failed to get the omens. And with good reason [*eikotōs*], as now appears. For, as I now learn, between us and the king lies a navigable river, the Tigris'; and 'It's not surprising [*eikotōs ara*] we aren't getting the omens [to march away], because news has just arrived that Cleander is on his way to bring supplies to us in ships.'[8]

To rely on divine guidance on matters within the scope of human understanding is quite wrong, and unproductive. But in situations impermeable to human intelligence, the only rational thing to do is to seek such guidance. By turning to divination one is not surrendering use of one's intelligence, but merely acknowledging its limits.[9] Not to use divination in these circumstances would be for Xenophon the true irrationality.

Is this religious optimist and rationalist beginning to sound, his penchant for divination aside, a rather modern figure? An incident from the Corinthian war in 392 from the *Hellenica* can serve to remind us that Xenophon is not a nineteenth-century unitarian. An Argive force finds itself disastrously hemmed in by the Spartans against one of the Corinthian long walls.

> The Spartans had no shortage of people to kill. For the god granted them on that day an achievement such as they would not even have prayed for. A host of the enemy put in their power in a state of terror, shock, their unarmed sides exposed, no individual turning to fight, every man of them doing everything possible to secure their own destruction: how could one not consider that divine [*theion*]? So many fell in a small area that, instead of the heaps which men are used to seeing, of corn or logs or stones, they saw heaps of corpses.[10]

---

8. Reasonableness of the gods: *Mem.* 4.3.16–17. 'When I sacrificed . . .'; *Anab.* 2.2.3. 'It's not surprising . . .': *Anab.* 6.4.18.
9. *Mem.* 1.1.6–9; *Cyrop.* 1.6.23; 1.6.44–6; *Eq. Mag.* 9.8–9; for the simple point that the gods only help those who help themselves also *Cyrop.* 1.6. 5–6; *Oec.* 8.16, 11.8. 'Divination does not require a suspension of disbelief, but the intellectual ability to make sense of the signs,' writes Bowden: 'Xenophon and the scientific study of religion'.
10. *Hell.* 4.4.12.

This will have been divine justice, in Xenophon's view,[11] but certainly no gentle justice.

I turn now more specifically to the *Anabasis*. Cawkwell's essay in this volume is a useful reminder of the need to be suspicious of Xenophon's text, not to be lured by the famed simplicity and charm of his Greek into taking it for a reliable and unproblematic record of reality. Cawkwell's Xenophon, like so many a modern politician sinking into obscure retirement, has a conscious purpose to set the record straight and provide proper illumination of his own achievements. But we must also be wary of distortions that are due to the way in which the mind of a pious Greek reconfigures remembered experience. Every reader of Herodotus knows that his *Histories* are full of stories that point a religious moral. Whether it was Herodotus himself or his sources who gave such material its religious shape, it is usually impossible to translate such stories back out of this religious code into the secular code of what we might suppose actually to have happened. Similar stories are found in Xenophon, but are harder to detect. Consider for instance the famous incident of the army's delay at Calpes Limen in book 6,[12] when, though eager to march away, it was held up for three days by failure to get good omens, and during this period suffered extreme discomfort from lack of supplies.

This incident is very regularly cited to illustrate the willingness of some Greek generals to neglect, in obedience to omens, what ordinary human calculation would judge the best policy. It is one of the two stock examples of this phenomenon, Nicias' disastrous delay at Syracuse in 413 in response to an eclipse of the moon being the other. What needs also to be noted is the way in which this whole section of narrative is designed to be exemplary, if not in quite the way it has become. Questions of divination dominate it, and a clear moral emerges. Xenophon stands firm against the protests of the hungry men: he refuses to lead the army out until good omens are secured. Another general, Neon, leads a sortie nonetheless, and it ends in the death of five hundred men. Xenophon rescues the survivors, but not without first performing an improvised sacrifice (of propitiation? The case is singular, and unclear).[13]

11. For the impiety of the Corinthians and Argives see *Hell.* 4.4.1–3.
12. *Anab.* 6.4.12–5.2.
13. The delay at Syracuse: Thuc. 7.50. The improvised sacrifice: *Anab.* 6.4.23–5; on Xenophon's *sphagion* sacrifice here see M. H. Jameson, 'Sacrifice before battle', in V. D. Hanson (ed.), *Hoplites: The Classical Greek Battle Experience* (London, 1991), pp. 197–227, at p. 205.

Xenophon's firmness is vindicated in the end; no harm results from the long delay, and when the army finally secures good omens and marches out, it wins a brilliant victory. There is a similar narrative in the *Hellenica* using similar motifs: Dercyllidas, though chafing against adverse omens, obeys them and succeeds, whereas Athenadas, who makes a rash attack in defiance of them, destroys his company. We regard exemplary stories of this type when told by Herodotus as just that, exemplary stories. Similar stories told by Xenophon we sometimes believe, perhaps through failing to notice that they are exemplary.[14] The claim is not or need not be that Xenophon is a liar, but that piety selects and distorts in order to create illustrations of what it believes to be truths; we cannot neglect the narrative shaping that has made these stories what they are, and treat them as simple data directly illuminating Greek behaviour.

It was not necessarily Xenophon who did the shaping. Such stories are created by believers talking to believers, not believers in isolation. There are two agreed miracles in the *Anabasis*, moments when it seemed to most or all bystanders that normal natural processes had been altered by religious factors. The uniquely low level of the River Euphrates allowed Cyrus and his army to cross on foot, and 'it seemed that this was divine [*theion*], and that the river had clearly drawn back before Cyrus because he was to be king'; during a storm a slaughter sacrifice was performed to the wind, and 'everyone felt that the violence of the wind had diminished noticeably.' In the first of these cases, events proved the 'miracle' illusory; the Euphrates withdrew before Cyrus as before one destined to be king, which he never became.[15] That shows that the supposed bending of the laws of nature was not imagined by Xenophon long after the event, but detected by the army at the time.

14. Dercyllidas vs. Athenadas: *Hell.* 3.1.17–19. L. Robin, *La Pensée hellénique des origines à Épicure* (Paris, 1942), p. 101, speaks of 'une technique en exemples, technique morale, religieuse, militaire'.
15. *Anab.* 1.4.18, 4.5.4. For the special relation between the Great King and water see C. J. Tuplin, 'Xenophon's *Cyropaedia*: education and fiction', in A. H. Sommerstein and C. Atherton (eds), *Education in Greek Fiction* (Bari, 1996), pp. 65–162, at n. 54. Divine intervention in the *Anabasis* can also be seen (in this case explicitly by the author) in an entirely natural event that happens at a peculiarly significant moment: at *Anab.* 5.2.24–5 a chance event, the torching of a house by an individual, suggests to Xenophon the tactic of burning other houses and is acclaimed by him (in an iambic trimeter) as a 'means of salvation' sent by 'one of the gods'. On the various modalities of divine intervention in Herodotus see T. Harrison, *Divinity and History* (Oxford, 2000), ch. 3, 'Miracles and the miraculous'. Comparable to the unsuccessful sequel to the 'miracle' of the Euphrates' behaviour is Cyrus' failed though initially plausible attempt to treat the password 'Zeus the Saviour and Victory' as an auspicious omen (*Anab.* 1.8.17).

And what of that more conscious distortion by Xenophon which many detect? Xenophon had much to explain and much to justify in the *Anabasis*, and it is very possible that this apologetic purpose also affects his presentation of religion. Controversial policies become less easy to attack if they have been followed in obedience to divine commands. Already in 1893 Felix Dürrbach claimed that: 'whenever Xenophon's attitude is embarrassed, suspect, or questionable, a sacrifice, an omen, a dream substitutes for adequate explanation and diverts the untimely curiosity of the reader.'[16] According to Dürrbach, large tracts of the work are little better than self-serving fiction. But to secure whatever apologetic aims he may have had, Xenophon must surely have needed to be at least plausible. So his text offers evidence for the kind of uses a public figure might credibly have made of (for instance) divination, even if not of the uses that the historical Xenophon in fact made.

There is religion on every page, as it were, of the *Anabasis*. The Greek generals and the Persian Ariaeus and his followers, for instance, swore alliance, extraordinarily, by sacrifice of 'bull, and wolf, and wild boar, and ram' into a shield, if we accept the reading of the majority of manuscripts at 2.2.9.[17] I will mention one or two of the most striking passages before investigating certain themes more systematically.

Xenophon's account of the estate at Skillous near Olympia which he bought for Artemis of Ephesus was apparently already a favourite in antiquity; the 'sacred law' (quoted in his text) which he wrote for the sanctuary was copied

---

16. 'à chaque fois que l'attitude de Xénophon est embarrassée, suspecte ou douteuse, un sacrifice, un présage, un songe tient lieu d'explications satisfaisantes et détourne la curiosité indiscrète du lecteur. Citons, outre cet exemple, le songe, III, 1, 1 sqq., le sacrifice avant l'élection du général en chef, VI, 1, 22–4, les sacrifices renouvelés, VI, 4, *passim*, celui qu'il offre avant d'aller trouver Seuthès, VII, 2, 15, puis devant le devin Euclide de Phlionte, VII, 8, 3': F. Dürrbach, 'L'apologie de Xénophon dans l'Anabase', *REG* 6 (1893), pp. 343–86, at p. 377 n. 1.

17. The wolf is omitted by the important MS C in its uncorrected state and thence by Marchant in the OCT. This gives a more normal number of victims, but the addition of the wolf by a scribe has no obvious motive, and the longer text is accepted by Hude in the Teubner. The use of a wild animal (after capture by netting, presumably) for sacrifice is an anomaly, but one which also applies in the case of 'wild boar', unless with V. Manfredi, *La Strada dei Diecimila* (Milan, 1986), p. 144, we suppose that ordinary pig was in fact used (the habitat being impossible for boar). Christopher Tuplin points out to me that, in Plut. *De Is. et Os.* 46, 369e, wolf's blood is used in Persian offerings to 'Areimanios'. He also comments that the form of oath ceremony described here is apparently not of a standard Greek type. Dipping of hands or spear in the victims' blood is paralleled in Greek sources only in the heroic Aesch. *Sept.* 43–4 (and the parody of it in Ar. *Lys.* 185–6); dipping of a spear in blood (the swearer's own, which is then drunk) is ascribed to the Scythians at Hdt. 4.70.

on stone on the island of Ithaca in the Roman imperial period. The estate was bought from money promised to Ephesian Artemis as a tithe from the sale of captives taken during the march. Xenophon describes punctiliously the punctilious care he took in paying off both this tithe and a similar one owed to Apollo of Delphi. The site to be bought was chosen with oracular guidance; doubtless Xenophon chose and the god merely approved, but Xenophon characteristically speaks as if the whole decision were the god's. There was, he notes carefully, a river Selinous traversing the estate at Skillous, just like the Selinous which flowed past the temple of Artemis at Ephesus. And what is more, there were fish and shellfish in both![18] The temple and the cult statue too were designed as miniature replicas of those at Ephesus. And here was held an annual festival attended by all the local residents with their wives, to whom 'the goddess' provided rich hospitality.[19]

The intense but this-worldly piety that pervades Xenophon's description is a marvel. But the institutional arrangements that underlie the lovely description are puzzling.[20] The estate is very sizeable, and Xenophon himself appears to have the usufruct of it, while paying dues to the goddess. What exactly has happened? Has Xenophon leased out to himself (and on what terms?) the estate bought for the goddess? Will his heirs inherit the lease? It looks as if Xenophon may have profited, not financially perhaps but in terms of the social standing deriving from patronage of a popular cult, in a way he could not have done at home in Athens.

The *Anabasis* also offers an example of a topic dear to contemporary scholarship, the argument from *syngeneia*, mythical kinship. The use of such arguments illustrates, in a general way, the continuing relevance of the world of myth to the reality of the fifth and fourth centuries; but this particular instance is set in a striking and revealing context. Xenophon and the minor Thracian king Seuthes are meeting for the first time. The intention is that Xenophon's

18. 'There is a river in Macedon, and there is also moreover a river at Monmouth . . . and there is salmon in both': Fluellen, in *Henry V*.
19. The account of the estate at Skillous: *Anab.* 5.3.4–13. The copy of the 'sacred law' on Ithaca: F. Sokolowski, *Lois sacrées des cités grecques* (Paris, 1969), no. 86.
20. Cf. O. Lendle, *Kommentar zu Xenophons Anabasis* (Darmstadt, 1995), pp. 321–2. The whole Skillous digression is a defence against a charge of appropriation of sacred funds, according to Dürrbach, 'L'apologie de Xénophon dans l'Anabase', p. 362 n. 3; an unsuccessful defence, according to Robin, *La Pensée hellénique*, pp. 95 n. 1, 96, 106 n. 1. I am very grateful to C. J. Tuplin for showing me a draft of a penetrating study of the whole incident; he also, inter alia, asks why Xenophon chose, precisely, the Artemis of Ephesus, and studies the implications, and limits, of Xenophon's re-creation of the Anatolian cult in the Peloponnese.

One Man's Piety 139

force is to serve with Seuthes, but there is great mutual mistrust between the two men; Xenophon evokes the atmosphere crackling with suspicion in which the first meeting is conducted. Xenophon makes an elaborately defensive speech to prove his honesty in his dealings with Seuthes so far; he then calls in some of the other leaders, ordering them to leave their weapons outside. 'Seuthes on hearing this answered that he would never mistrust any Athenians. For he knew that they were his kinsfolk, and he regarded them as friends well-disposed to him.' The reference, which does not need to be spelt out, is to the marriage of the mythical Thracian king Tereus to the Athenian princess Procne. Paul Veyne has discussed the role of appeals to mythology as a form of 'langue de bois', an untranslatable expression indicating the elaborate and meaningless courtesies uttered on ceremonial occasions. This claim to ancient kinship and friendship between two parties who were completely uncertain whether they were safe in each other's company is an elegant illustration. This is not the whole truth about *syngeneia*, but it is an important part of it.[21]

I turn now to themes which occur more regularly in the work. The place of religion within the daily routines and life of this wandering and heterogeneous city is an alluring topic. When the army found itself for once in a well-supplied village in Armenia, Xenophon notes that 'Here they had every kind of good provisions, sacrificial victims [*hiereia*], wheat, fragrant old wines, raisins, pulses of all sorts.' What is desirable about the sacrificial victims in this context is obviously not that they permit communication with the divine but that they are made of meat; but in order to eat meat one had also to communicate with the divine, and Xenophon's little phrase is a lovely illustration of the rule that meat other than game did not reach the table except by way of sacrifice. The Ten Thousand will all have sacrificed whenever they could.[22]

References occasionally occur to the different customs of different ethnic components in the force. Early on, the army paused for three days at Peltae while the Arcadian commander Xenias 'sacrificed the Lycaea and held a competition. The prizes were gold crowns.' The Arcadians were the largest ethnic

21. The meeting with Seuthes: *Anab.* 7.2.31. For the Procne connection, cf. Thuc. 2.29.3, and now K. Zacharia, '"The rock of the nightingale": kinship diplomacy and Sophocles' Tereus', in F. Budelmann and P. Michelakis (eds), *Homer, Tragedy and Beyond: Essays in Honour of P. E. Easterling* (London, 2001), pp. 91–112. *Syngeneia* in contemporary scholarship: O. Curty, *Les Parentés légendaires entre cités grecques* (Geneva, 1995); S. Hornblower, *A Commentary on Thucydides, Volume II: Books IV–V.24* (Oxford, 1996), pp. 61–80; C. P. Jones, *Kinship Diplomacy in the Ancient World* (Harvard, 1999). 'Langue de bois': P. Veyne, *Les Grecs ont-ils cru à leurs mythes?* (Paris, 1983), pp. 89–104.
22. The village in Armenia: *Anab.* 4.4.9. Meat and sacrifice: cf. G. Berthiaume, *Les Rôles du Mágeiros* (Leiden, 1982), pp. 62–70. For sacrificing wherever possible: cf. e.g. *Anab.* 6.1.4.

group among the Ten Thousand, and the Lycaea was easily the most important pan-Arcadian festival.[23]

No second instance can be quoted, perhaps because conditions subsequently were usually so hard; but during the stay of forty-five days at Cotyora the Greeks 'held processions in their tribal groups'. And, at a banquet held by the Greeks for the Paphlagonian king Corylas and his followers, both sides put on dancing displays, with the Ainianes, the Magnesians, and 'the Mantineans and some other Arcadians' performing regional specialities on the Greek side.[24]

But, all in all, there is less material on this subject than might have been hoped. Still more disappointing is the depiction of the distinctive religious behaviour of non-Greeks.[25] I turn to a richer theme, that of religion and morale.

Probably the greatest crisis of the expedition and the moment of lowest morale came with the treacherous capture of the Greek generals by Tissaphernes at the end of book 2. This is the moment when Xenophon first comes to the fore in his own narrative, and one may well suspect him of retrospective image-building. But if this is a representation of how an ideal commander would have behaved in these circumstances, it is in a sense all the better for our purposes. Xenophon credits himself with a long speech which he supposedly made to the whole army. His first argument is a hackneyed one: they are oath-breakers, we are pious, and in consequence they will have the gods as enemies while we can have high hopes of safety (*sōtēria*). In times of crisis, says Thucydides, orators are not ashamed to trot out the old arguments (*archaiologein*); evidently the pious cliché was not discredited to the point where to use it would have been actually counterproductive.[26]

23. The pause at Peltae: *Anab.* 1.2.10. The 'competition' of the Lycaea was traditional, but the prizes in Arcadia were supposedly the less portable bronze tripods (Polemon ap. Schol. Pind. *Ol.* 7.153d). Xenias surely offered 'gold crowns', not 'gold strigils', though the Greek word *stlengis* can mean either. Is Xenophon's preference for the rarer word (in lieu of *stephanoi*) influenced by Arcadian usage? See T. H. Nielsen, 'The concept of Arkadia – the people, their land and their organisation,' in T. H. Nielsen and J. Roy (eds), *Defining Ancient Arcadia: Acts of the Copenhagen Polis Centre*, vol. 6 (Copenhagen, 1999), pp. 16–79, at pp. 27–8, 45.
24. Processions in tribal groups: *Anab.* 5.5.5. The tentative suggestion at Lendle, *Kommentar zu Xenophons Anabasis*, p. 334, that this ritual is a kind of 'Olympics away from home' is unpersuasive not least because of this stress on ethnic differentiation. Dancing displays: *Anab.* 6.1.1–13.
25. As Christopher Tuplin observes to me. See only *Anab.* 1.4.9 on Syrian reverence for fish; the Armeno-Persian background to the 'horse sacred to the sun' in 4.5.35 is not explained, any more than the nature of the dealings of Cyrus and Orontas with 'Artemis' in 1.6.7.
26. Xenophon and oath-breakers: *Anab.* 3.2.10; similarly 2.5.7, 3.1.21. Thucydides on cliché: Thuc. 7.69.2.

More interesting is an incident during the speech. Just as Xenophon pronounced the phrase 'high hopes of safety', somebody sneezed, and all the soldiers with one accord 'paid reverence to the god'.[27] Xenophon's response was masterly, at least as recorded in retrospect:

'Men, since an omen of Zeus the Saviour occurred while I was speaking about safety, I propose that we vow to make "safety offerings" to this god in whatever friendly territory we first come to, and vow too to sacrifice to the other gods as best we can. All who agree raise their hands!' They all raised their hands. After this they made their vows and sung a paean.

As a description of the exact circumstances in which a military vow was made this is perhaps unique.[28] The situation is appropriately dramatic, and the whole army is involved; whether this last detail is typical, or the product of a happy improvisation by Xenophon, is impossible to say.

The fulfilment of the vow on arrival in Trapezus is duly recorded, and the ensuing athletic competition is given a page of description. A further vow is perhaps recorded later. The Ten Thousand are faced with a single last hard fight against the Colchians before reaching a Greek city, Trapezus. 'We must eat these people raw, if we only can,' says Xenophon. The generals marshal their troops, and then pass the word to the troops to 'pray/make a vow [*euchesthai*]'; 'and after praying/making a vow and singing the paean they marched ahead.' 'After making a vow' is very probably a better rendering than 'after praying'. Greek religion is based on gifts; a simple prayer is not a gift, and establishes no claim to divine favour, whereas a vow that promises a gift may. Perhaps this was a kind of recharging of the original vow.[29]

In both these cases the pronouncing of the vow is followed by singing of the paean; often too in the *Anabasis* the troops sing a paean while advancing into battle, and then raise a cry (*elelizō, alalazō*) to Enyalios. Such hearty communal singing just before the onset of the terror is the easiest of all

---

27. For prophetic sneezes, see the note of A. S. F. Gow in his commentary on Theoc. *Id.* 7.96.
28. On the military vow see W. K. Pritchett, *The Greek State at War*, vol. 3 (Berkeley, 1979), pp. 230–9.
29. Fulfilment of the vow in Trapezus: *Anab.* 4.8.25. The athletic competition is given no specific motivation. Pritchett, *The Greek State at War*, vol. 3, p. 155 n. 3, writes 'Given an assemblage of Greeks under practically any circumstances, it would be almost inevitable that games of some kinds would be started.' Christopher Tuplin suggests to me rather that the games added extra weight to the vow-fulfilling sacrifice. The two views can perhaps be combined. 'We must eat these people ... they marched ahead': *Anab.* 4.8.14–16. 'Recharging' the vow: so Lendle, *Kommentar zu Xenophons Anabasis*, p. 286.

illustrations of the morale-building role of religion. Omens too have an obvious relation to morale: 'men, the sacrificial omens are fair and the bird omens are favourable and the slaughter-sacrifice omens are ideal: forward against them!'[30]

A correlate to this bracing influence of religion in times of crisis is its celebratory and tension-releasing role once success has been achieved. Alongside the setting up of trophies and the performance of processions and games we can take as exemplary here the spontaneous erection of a cairn by the troops on Mount Thekes at the spot where they first sighted the sea.[31]

A final incident bearing on the theme of morale occurs in book 5. The Greeks are back on the southern coast of the Black Sea, but it is a time of discontent, divided counsels, suspicion, and complaints against the generals, Xenophon above all. Xenophon fears mutiny, and even lynching. He summons a formal assembly in order to defend himself, and launches a counter-attack against the growing indiscipline in the army. He denounces in particular a war crime committed by a small splinter division of the army. It is agreed that the guilty parties should be punished, and on Xenophon's suggestion (and with the support of the seers) a purification of the whole army is performed.[32]

This is a lovely example of the role of ritual in reinforcing group solidarity. But the ritual act alone does not restore harmony. It is also decided that the generals should 'stand trial' (such is the language used, though we might prefer to speak of 'submit to audit') for their past conduct. Some are fined, but Xenophon, as he records, clears his name with brilliant eloquence, and that particular narrative sequence comes to an end.[33] So two processes designed to 'clear the slate' operate in tandem: the troops are purified, the generals submit to trial.

I turn now, inescapably, to divination. It is irresistible to start with the Theban Coiratadas who makes a memorable brief appearance in book 7 at

30. Paean and cry: *Anab.* 1.8.17–18; 4.3.19; 5.2.14; 6.5.27; paean alone: *Anab.* 1.10.10; 4.3.29, 31. See W. K. Pritchett, *Ancient Greek Military Practices*, vol. 1 (Berkeley, 1971; later called *The Greek State at War*, vol. 1), pp. 105–8; R. Lonis, *Guerre et religion en Grèce à l'époque classique* (Paris, 1979), pp. 117–28. 'Men, the sacrificial omens . . .': *Anab.* 6.5.21; cf. 1.8.15. For the confidence engendered in troops by the belief that their commander respects omens see *Eq. Mag.* 6.6.
31. Setting-up of trophies: *Anab.* 4.6.27; 6.5.32. Processions and games: *Anab.* 4.8.25; 5.5.5. Erection of a cairn: *Anab.* 4.7.25–6 – not however a formal ritual: see C. J. Tuplin (to whom I owe these points too), 'On the track of the Ten Thousand', *REA* 101 (1999), pp. 331–66, at pp. 361–4.
32. Fear of lynching: *Anab.* 5.7.2. Denunciation of war crime: *Anab.* 5.7.5–33. Purification of the whole army: *Anab.* 5.7.34–5.
33. *Anab.* 5.8.

Byzantium, a man who roamed abroad 'not in exile from Greece but eager to serve as a general and offering his services should any city or tribe need a general'. Lured by his promises, the troops briefly engaged him, and he arranged to present himself the next day with sacrificial victims, a seer, and food and drink for the army. He duly arrived with victims and a seer but only trivial quantities of food; on that day he failed to secure good omens, and made no distribution of food. On the second day he was about to sacrifice when three of the existing generals told him to desist unless he could provide rations for the troops. When it emerged that he could not produce even enough for a day per man, 'he took his victims and went away, renouncing the generalship'. So departed this character from Evelyn Waugh who had strayed into the pages of the *Anabasis*.[34] He stands as a comic illustration of the general's need for sacrificial victims and a seer.

The *Anabasis* is full of evidence for military divination in the narrow sense, for sacrifice before battle, before marching through dangerous territory and so on. The topic has been much discussed of late, and I will speak only of broad issues. There exist two extreme positions: for some, military divination is all a sham, a set of mechanisms deployed by generals to improve morale when they choose to attack, and to provide an excuse when they choose not to. As an early representative of this tradition of scholarship we can cite William Mitford, commenting early in the nineteenth century on the famous delay at Calpes Limen mentioned earlier: 'Xenophon recurred to his usual resource, the power of superstition over Greek minds'; or again, with regard to the omens that prevented an attack on the hospitable Tibereni, 'if ever deceit, for preventing evil, might be allowed, it would do credit to the scholar of Socrates, in the business of the Tibarenes.' Suspicions that Xenophon was manipulating divination to his own ends are in fact mentioned in the *Anabasis*, and elsewhere he accuses other people of similar fraud. But it is a long established anthropological truth that faith in diviners and incredulity about diviners go hand in hand: societies that abuse seers are also those that believe in them, and vice versa.[35] The second

---

34. *Anab.* 7.1.33–41. That this experienced figure (see *Hell.* 1.3.15–22; probably *Hell. Oxy.* 20.1) was in truth the buffoon Xenophon portrays him as is highly implausible. C. J. Tuplin in 'Boeotians and the *Anabasis*', due to appear in *Proceedings of the 4th International Conference on Boeotian Studies* (Athens, forthcoming), points out that Coiratadas' intervention removed the Ten Thousand from Byzantium and led to stasis among them, so serving Spartan interests very effectively.
35. For recent discussions of military divination, see above all Jameson, 'Sacrifice before battle'; also R. Parker, 'Sacrifice and battle', in H. van Wees (ed.), *War and Violence in Ancient Greece* (London, 2000), pp. 299–314. Mitford's comments: *History of Greece* (5

extreme position is that of those who credit the Greeks or some Greeks with a genuine willingness to suspend their rational sense of their own advantage, and to entrust themselves more or less blindly to divine guidance.

A middle way is perhaps available.[36] It can be argued that enough flexibility was built into the sacrificial system to allow one both to be a more or less sincere believer, and to act most of the time more or less as one felt to be sensible in secular terms: the only projects which a general really abandoned because of bad omens were ones which he genuinely suspected might not be advisable. There must often have been ambiguity as to whether particular omens were good or bad; there existed, above all, the possibility of repeating sacrifices, the 'if at first you don't succeed' principle.

These considerations are very plausible in general terms, but it must be acknowledged that they are not always easy to apply to particular incidents of the *Anabasis*. The 'if at first you don't succeed' principle proves defective, because instances are found of omens refusing to come right even at the third try. (There was perhaps a convention of making three successive attempts only.) The extreme case is the delay at Calpes Limen, when the army was held up for three days during which the omens were taken unsuccessfully eight or more times. Initially the intention was 'to march away', and it was already muttered on the first day of the delay that 'Xenophon wants to establish a colony and has persuaded the seer to say that omens for marching off cannot be secured'. Xenophon claims that he rebutted the rumour by inviting any interested persons, including seers, to witness subsequent performances of the sacrifices – yet they still failed to secure good omens. (But some moderns still suspect Xenophon of deviousness, both in his behaviour at the time and in his subsequent description of it.)[37]

vols, London, 1808–18), vol. 3, pp. 179–80 and 192; I owe these references to Tim Rood. Accusations of fraud: *Anab.* 6.4.14; cf. *Hell.* 4.2.18. Abuse and belief: E. Evans-Pritchard, *Witchcraft, Oracles and Magic among the Azande* (Oxford, 1937).

36. I argue this in Parker, 'Sacrifice and battle'. As I now see, a very similar case was already very effectively presented in a work that has been lost from the literature, A. Zucker, *Xenophon und die Opfermantik in der Anabasis* (Nürnberg, 1900) (on which see further n. 40 below).

37. Failure even after three tries: *Anab.* 5.5.3; 6.6.35–6. Calpes Limen: *Anab.* 6.4.12–5.2; as described, the eight attempts consisted of two single attempts (I accept Schneider's *boun* for MSS *bous* at 6.4.22), and two where three victims were sacrificed in a row, to no avail. 'Xenophon wants to establish . . .': *Anab.* 6.4.14. The case for Xenophontic deviousness: F. Dürrbach, 'L'apologie de Xénophon dans l'Anabase', pp. 379–80; E. Meyer, *Geschichte des Altertums*, vol. 5 (Stuttgart and Berlin, 1902), pp. 190–1. Meyer writes: 'Seine Darstellung der Vorgänge in Kalpe ist offiziell gewiss richtig; aber offenbar hat er es verstanden, die Opferzeichen halb gläubig, halb sich selbst betrügend so

After two days, a rumour that a ship was on the way bearing supplies convinced the troops that the gods had had their interests at heart in discouraging departure (note the vindication even at this stage of Xenophon's firmness). The goal therefore changed to a sortie to secure food in the interim; but this too the gods barred for a day. If a plausible emendation is accepted, at this stage Xenophon once asked a different general, Cleanor the Arcadian, to 'initiate the sacrifice' (*prothuesthai*[38]) in search of better omens, but to no avail. During all this period the troops suffered considerable discomfort through lack of supplies. If the system was as flexible as was suggested above, why did the army delay so long?

It was in part in an attempt to pre-empt that kind of question that I stressed earlier that this incident is making an exemplary point, and for that reason the details cannot be trusted. But let us suspend disbelief and look at it as if it constituted a reliable record. A central uncertainty here is our ignorance of exactly how 'good' and 'bad' omens were determined. Whatever the answer to that question may be, it is very hard to believe that eight victims in a row might have been deemed to share whatever characteristic constituted a 'don't do it' sign, if the generals had been genuinely keen to march out. The situation was in reality a very dangerous one, as is clear from Neon's disastrous sortie and the difficult battle that ensued when the army did eventually move. The troops initially resisted Xenophon's tentative (and revealing) suggestion that the omens might improve if they were willing to establish a secure base on an impregnable peninsula; they feared it as the presumptive site of his projected colony. Only after the peninsula was secured did the omens come right.[39]

Some tension between generals and troops is very likely expressed in the recurrent search before that moment for good omens and its recurrent failure. To reduce the situation to one of cautious (or ambitious) generals tricking their impetuous troops by seercraft might be extreme.[40] But generals nervous

---

einzurichten, wie er sie wünschte.' (For the strength of the belief that Xenophon still had colonial plans see *Anab.* 6.4.7, 6.6.3–4.) H. Popp, 'Die Einwirkung von Vorzeichen, Opfern und Festen auf die Kriegführung der Griechen', Diss., Erlangen, 1957, p. 67 n. 86, dissents.

38. Bornemann (and C. G. Krüger, in his edition of 1826) for MSS *prothumeisthai* in *Anab.* 6.4.22.

39. *Anab.* 6.4.21 with 6.5.1–2. This paragraph derives from Zucker, *Xenophon und die Opfermantik*, pp. 42–51.

40. Such is the conclusion of Zucker, *Xenophon und die Opfermantik*, pp. 42–51, in relation to this and a few further incidents. His starting point had been different (n. 36 above). That believers in divination can also manipulate it is, of course, true (n. 35 above), so his position is not fatally inconsistent.

about the wisdom of an advance would inevitably have sensitized their seers to the smallest defect in a victim's liver.

Another striking instance of action debarred by omens is the 'business of the Tibarenes' mentioned by Mitford.

> From there they came to the Tibareni. The land of the Tibareni was much flatter and had less well fortified settlements on the coast. The generals wanted to attack the settlements and let the army get some benefit, and they did not accept the gifts of friendship that came from the Tibareni but told them to wait until they had considered the matter, and began to sacrifice. Many victims were sacrificed, and the seers eventually all stated their opinion that the gods did not at all approve of the war. And so they accepted the gifts of friendship . . .[41]

Omens therefore force the commanders to abandon a policy on which they were supposedly resolved. Some suppose that the commanders had feigned to adopt that policy only in the knowledge that the troops would anyway press for the licence to loot; but, moral men, the commanders welcomed, and indeed provoked, the adverse omens debarring aggression against a friendly people.[42]

On such a view, the deception practised by Xenophon and the other commanders against their followers was perpetuated (for what reason?) by Xenophon against his readers; for the account just given is certainly not that which lies on the surface of the text. Perhaps the commanders were genuinely of divided mind about the proposed raid. On such matters we can scarcely hope to advance beyond possibilities.[43]

I turn now to broader contexts in which Xenophon reports divine guidance which he received during the expedition. At the point in book 3 where he is about to present his own first significant intervention, Xenophon steps back and explains how he first came to be involved. He had received a letter from his guest-friend Proxenus inviting him to come and serve with Cyrus:

---

41. *Anab.* 5.5.1–2.
42. So e.g. Zucker, *Xenophon und die Opfermantik*, pp. 41–2, and Mitford, *History of Greece*, vol. 3, pp. 179–80, 192.
43. At *Anab.* 6.6.33–6 Cleander the Spartan is offered and accepts command of the force, but then resigns it after failing to secure marching omens for three days. For Zucker, *Xenophon und die Opfermantik*, pp. 39–41, Cleander had never been seriously interested. Perhaps one should rather say that the offer of leadership, though attractive, was not irresistibly so.

> On reading the letter Xenophon consulted Socrates the Athenian about the journey. Socrates suspected that he might incur blame from the city for becoming a companion of Cyrus ... and advised him to go to Delphi and consult the god about the journey. Xenophon went and asked Apollo what god he should sacrifice and pray to in order to perform the journey which he had in mind best and most successfully, and after achieving success get home safely. Apollo told him the gods to whom he should sacrifice. When he got back, he reported the prophecy to Socrates. On hearing it, Socrates criticised him that he did not first ask whether it was better for him to go or to stay, but decided on his own account that he should go, and just asked how he could make the journey most successfully. 'But since you asked as you did,' he said 'you must do as the god told you.' Xenophon sacrificed as instructed by the god, and sailed off ....[44]

This is instructive in several different ways. Xenophon 'consults' Socrates, and Socrates advises him to 'consult' (a form of the same verb, *anakoinousthai*, is used) Apollo; oracular consultation can be seen as just one amid a variety of different ways of seeking advice. The question 'about a journey' is of a type constantly posed to oracles, and Xenophon's formulation of the question finds many parallels, even the secretive 'journey which he has in mind'.[45] But it was because of a specific anxiety, not the general risks of travel, that Socrates counselled Xenophon to undertake the trouble and expense of a trip to Delphi.

Xenophon, as he so candidly reveals, both followed and ignored the philosopher's advice. And this enabled him to follow the god's advice while not jeopardizing what was evidently his fixed resolve to run the risk of involvement with Cyrus. The story is exemplary of the stratagems by which believers avoid surrendering their autonomy of action even when consulting gods whose mandates they believe themselves unconditionally willing to obey.[46] Yet, narrow though the limits were that Xenophon set to Apollo's advice, it was evidently in its own way still worth having.

44. *Anab.* 3.1.4–8.
45. For the term *symboulē* in this context, see B. Haussoullier, 'Inscriptions de Didymes', *Rev. Phil.* 44 (1929), pp. 248–77, at pp. 272–4. For journey questions, see e.g. H. W. Parke, *The Oracles of Zeus* (Oxford, 1967), pp. 268–71, nos 19, 22–4 (examples from Dodona: there are many more); 'which he has in mind': see *Bulletin Épigraphique* (1959), no. 299 (there are also many instances from Dodona).
46. See Evans-Pritchard, *Witchcraft, Oracles and Magic*, p. 350: 'A Zande does not readily accept an oracular verdict which conflicts seriously with his interests ... A man takes advantage of every loop-hole the oracle allows him ... He uses the authority of the oracle to excuse his conduct or compel others to accept it.'

Xenophon describes a further divine message which narrowly preceded his first crucial intervention. After the treacherous murder of the existing Greek generals, despair seized the whole camp.

> The situation was desperate, and Xenophon was as miserable as everybody and could not sleep. But he fell asleep briefly and had a dream. He dreamt that there was a thunderclap, and a lightning bolt fell into his parental home, and the whole house was lit up by it. He woke up at once in terror, and decided that the dream was in one respect a good one, because in a situation of trouble and danger he had dreamt that he had seen a light from Zeus. But in another regard he was afraid: since he thought that the dream came from Zeus the King, and the fire burned around in a circle, perhaps he might be unable to escape from the territory of the king, but be shut in by difficulties on every side. One can tell what it means to dream a dream such as this from what happened subsequently...[47]

Xenophon does not claim that the dream influenced his action on the following day, so this is not an instance of divine guidance in the normal sense. It is more a confidence shared with the reader, an anticipation of the shape that the story of the *Anabasis* will really have, both immediately (in Xenophon's success at the following day's assembly) and in the longer term. But omens invite multiple interpretations, and the reader may wonder whether the one to which the author explicitly commits himself is the only possible one or even the most likely. Places struck by lightning are abandoned, says Artemidorus in his *Dream-Interpreter*.[48] might not the fire from heaven in Xenophon's ancestral home have hinted at his exile?

Xenophon's next reported dream again comes in a desperate situation. The army urgently needs to cross the River Centrites, which is deep and guarded on both sides. An attempt to wade across has proved vain.

> For that day and night they stayed where they were, completely at a loss. But Xenophon had a dream. He dreamt that he was bound in chains, and these fell off him spontaneously, so that he was freed and could move as much as

---

47. *Anab.* 3.1.11–13.
48. The dream as foreshadowing success at the assembly: so Dillery, *Xenophon and the History of his Times*, p. 73. Places struck by lightning: Artemidorus: Artem. 2.9. p. 110.20–2 Pack. Christopher Tuplin also adduces the diverse interpretations of Pyrrhus' thunderbolt dream in Plut. *Pyrrh.* 29.3.

he wanted. Just before dawn he went to Chirisophus and told him that he thought all would be well, and described his dream. Chirisophus was delighted, and as soon as dawn broke all the generals assembled and sacrificed. And the omens proved fair with the first victim.[49]

And, lo and behold, a piece of serendipidity at once revealed a safe way to get across the river. The story is an example of that divine care for humans, as manifested through prophetic signs, of which Xenophon so often speaks. It is significant too that the gods have chosen Xenophon as their messenger. Important dreams only come to important people,[50] and in imparting this dream – he had kept the previous one to himself – Xenophon was relying on his enhanced prestige at this stage of the campaign.

These dreams raised morale (of Xenophon or others) but did not in other respects change the course of events. I turn now to a series of cases where Xenophon portrays divination as central to a decision-making process. I begin with a list of instances.

1 Xenophon forms the plan of establishing a colony at Cotyora on the south shore of the Black Sea. 'He thought it would become a great city ... and he sacrificed about this plan, summoning Silanus the Ambraciot who had been Cyrus' seer, before mentioning it to any of the troops.'[51]
2 Xenophon has come under pressure to seek sole command of the expedition, and is completely uncertain how to respond. 'In his inability to make up his mind he decided it was best to consult [*anakoinōsai*] the gods. He brought two victims and sacrificed them to Zeus the King, who had been recommended to him by Delphi ... When he sacrificed the god gave him clear indications that he should not seek the command nor accept it if they chose him.'[52]
3 The Arcadians and Achaeans have formed themselves into a breakaway contingent. Xenophon believes that the rest of the army should stay together, but Neon urges him to join him in sailing off with his own men. 'Xenophon initially set about (*epecheirēsen*) leaving the army and sailing away. But when he sacrificed to Heracles the Leader and consulted him [*koinousthai*] as to whether it was better and preferable to continue the

---

49. *Anab.* 4.3.8–9.
50. Hom. *Il.* 2.79–83; cf. R. Parker, *Miasma* (Oxford, 1983), p. 266 n. 48.
51. *Anab.* 5.6.16, to be read with 5.6.26–9, which is discussed later in the text.
52. *Anab.* 6.1.19–24.

campaign with the remaining troops or to depart, the god indicated through the sacrifice that he should campaign with them.'[53]

4   All other options being excluded, Xenophon 'sacrificed to see if the gods permitted him to lead the army to Seuthes' (a policy he had hitherto resisted strongly). The sacrifices seemed to indicate that he and the army 'could safely go to Seuthes'; and they did so.[54]

5   Seuthes has proved a poor paymaster, and the army wish to depart. 'Taking two victims Xenophon sacrificed to Zeus the King as to whether it was better and preferable to stay with Seuthes on the terms proposed by Seuthes or to depart with the army. He responded [*anairei*] that he should depart.'[55]

In all these cases, we observe, divination by sacrifice is an exact substitute for Xenophon for consultation of an oracle. The language of 'consulting' (*anakoinousthai* or variant) a god, the question formulae ('is it better and preferable?' often followed by alternatives, 'to do x or y'), and even the verb once used of the 'response' (*anairei*) are too familiar from the practice of Delphi and other oracles for it even to be necessary to quote parallels. The hotline to Zeus is always open; the commander has his mobile as long as he can find a sheep to sacrifice.[56]

Or two sheep, perhaps one should say; for Xenophon twice specifies that he brought a pair of victims to the altar. Why so? Commentators, if they discuss the point at all, say that the second victim was a reserve in case good omens were not secured with the first. But this cannot be correct, because the cases that concern us are not like those where the 'if at first you don't succeed' principle applied: Xenophon is not seeking divine approval prior (say) to marching out, but posing a question. Nor does the theory explain Xenophon's insistence, in these cases alone, on the presence of more than one victim, but two, not three, as the other explanation would require. Probably we are dealing with some form of checking, whereby for instance victim one was asked 'is it

---

53. *Anab.* 6.2.13–16. Here and in Pl. *Prt.* 310c (well cited by C. G. Krüger in his commentary ad loc.) there is a temptation to weaken *epecheirēsen* to 'planned'. But I do not know that it can have this meaning.
54. Xenophon's resistance to approaching Seuthes: *Anab.* 7.2.10. The decision to approach the King: *Anab.* 7.2.15–17. 'The omens seemed': Zucker, *Xenophon und die Opfermantik*, p. 19, detects in this verb (*edokei*) a hint of the ambiguity and interpretability of omens.
55. *Anab.* 7.6.44.
56. But for an example of similar sacrificial divination performed by a settled community see Sokolowski, *Lois sacrées des cités grecques*, no. 118 (questions on religious topics posed by the Clytidae of Chios).

better and preferable to stay with Seuthes?' and victim two 'is it better and preferable to depart with the army?' and only the sequence 'yes–no' or 'no–yes' would count as a reliable answer.[57]

In each case the enquiry is addressed to a specific god, though Xenophon does not always identify him. He gives an extended explanation of his decision to put his dilemma about accepting sole command of the expedition to Zeus Basileus (case 2 above). When he first consulted Delphi about the expedition, Apollo had advised him to sacrifice to this god. The dream he dreamt when about to succeed to one of the murdered generals had come from him, he thought. And earlier, on his departure from Ephesus, he had seen an omen involving an eagle (the bird of Zeus); it betokened greatness and glory, but also toil and financial straits.[58]

Xenophon, then, was very close to Zeus Basileus. And the god did not let him down. The sole leadership which he reluctantly chose not to seek went instead to Chirisophus – and ended in great ignominy ten days later.[59] There is self-glorification and self-congratulation in all this, no doubt; but also a picture of one sense in which a Greek could feel himself especially close to a particular god.

The enquiries relate to Xenophon's own inclinations in a variety of ways. (The caveat must be repeated that Xenophon here is 'the Xenophon in the text', a figure who must, however, have been meant to be credible.) In case 2 he explains the factors pulling him in both directions, and represents himself as genuinely undecided. In the other cases he has or may have a preference for one of the two courses of action, but one presumably that he is willing to see overridden. In cases 4, 5, and 1 the gods support the policy that he favours or may favour. But in case 3 the response of Heracles causes him to abandon a course of action he has embarked on.[60]

Some decision-making among the Ten Thousand was collective. But Xenophon's consultations were in the main made in relation to decisions that he would take himself, even though they might also affect the fate of his whole contingent. Whether he spoke of the gods' responses to the troops, or merely

---

57. Such checking by varied questioning was normal in consultation of the Azande poison oracle: see Evans-Pritchard, *Witchcraft, Oracles and Magic*.
58. *Anab.* 6.1.19–24.
59. *Anab.* 6.2.12.
60. The potentially apologetic function of this last case has often been noted (e.g. by Lendle, *Kommentar zu Xenophons Anabasis*, p. 376): but for divine guidance, Xenophon would not have stayed with the expedition and become entangled with Thibron and Agesilaus.

issued orders in consequence of them, is not revealed; the only such consultation to which he refers back in a speech is his enquiry about assuming sole command of the expedition,[61] and this was an issue on which the power to decide was manifestly his alone.

Had the points at issue been ones on which the army's assembly insisted on its own right to decide, Xenophon would presumably not have been free to consult the gods of his own accord. We see this from the scandal created by consultation 1 above. The seer Silanus treacherously told the troops about it, and eventually Xenophon was denounced in an open assembly: 'it is outrageous for Xenophon to be urging people to settle and be sacrificing about settling, while saying nothing about it in public'. Xenophon had consulted the gods before consulting the people, whereas the principle in a democracy or even a broad oligarchy was that, where matters of collective concern were at issue, the decision to consult the gods was itself collective; otherwise the decision might be pre-empted. Xenophon responded with the not wholly convincing claim that he had merely asked 'whether it was advisable to make a start on speaking before you and acting on this plan, or not to embark on it at all'.[62]

Can any general conclusions be drawn from Xenophon's five reported consultations during the campaign? About his real motives perhaps none. But the simple point remains that he portrays the gods' advice as having a decisive influence on the decisions he made, and hopes to be believed.

I conclude with two final scenes of mantic life. Xenophon is planning to kidnap the immensely rich Persian Asidates in his stronghold. He sacrifices before setting out, and is promised success by the Elean seer Basias. The raid is a failure; half the Greeks are wounded, and the next day Xenophon plans to cut and run with his troops. But Asidates also turns to flight, and by ill chance stumbles upon Xenophon's force and is captured with all his property. 'And thus were the earlier omens fulfilled,' remarks Xenophon.[63] Seers were bound to flourish if even their signal failures were interpreted as brilliant successes in this way.

---

61. For collective decision-making, see Hornblower, chapter 8 in this volume. Mention of an enquiry in a speech: *Anab.* 6.1.31. Even here Xenophon mentions the divine advice only when a different argument against his assuming sole leadership, the supposed need for a Spartan commander, has been criticized. Neither in *Anab.* 7.3.3–6 nor in 7.6.13–14 is the consultation of 7.2.15 mentioned.
62. *Anab.* 5.6.28.
63. *Anab.* 7.8.9–23.

A little earlier, at Lampsacus, Xenophon has met a seer known to him from his life in Greece, Euclid of Phleious. On learning that Xenophon is impoverished, Euclid declares both that he is his own worst enemy (there is a hint of apologetics here, against the charge that Xenophon grew rich by profiteering during the expedition)[64] and that Zeus Meilichios is the 'obstacle' (*empodios*). 'Have you sacrificed to him of late, just as I used to sacrifice and make burnt offerings to him for your family at home?' When Xenophon replies that he has not sacrificed 'to this god' since his departure from Greece, Euclid urges him to do so immediately; he does, and on the very same day receives an expensive present, and a few days later captures Asidates and is rich for good.

The incident is famous among students of Greek religion for the way in which it splits Zeus in two: Xenophon's many sacrifices to Zeus Basileus have not prevented the neglected Zeus Meilichios becoming an 'obstacle' to him. One always needed advice – from Delphi, from seers – on exactly the right god to propitiate. But the incident also illustrates the theme of relations with seers. Four named seers appear at different points in the Anabasis (Silanus the Ambraciot, Arexion of Arcadia, Basius of Elis, and Euclid), and there are also nameless 'seers' accompanying the Ten Thousand.[65]

They turn out to be of very different character: a type of the very bad seer is Silanus, who leaks confidential information against his employer and later 'runs away'.[66] Quite different is Euclid, the old family friend: 'are you in funds, Xenophon? Tut, you bring it all on yourself. Have you kept up the sacrifices to Zeus Meilichios?' This is the seer as, so to speak, the best type of family doctor, solicitous for Xenophon's financial well-being. I end deliberately with this mundane and bathetic image. The reason why Father Festugière neglected Xenophon was perhaps at bottom that he could find in him nothing that he recognized as spiritual aspiration. Religion for Xenophon is not a *mysterium tremendum*, an encounter with the absolutely other; the gods are reasonable if slightly remote figures with whom one can do business, rather like the better sort of Spartan. But this really is personal religion *à la grecque*.

---

64. Dürrbach, 'L'apologie de Xénophon dans l'Anabase', p. 362.
65. *Anab.* 4.3.17, 4.5.4, 5.2.9, 5.5.3, 5.7.35, 6.4.15.
66. *Anab.* 5.6.17–18, 5.6.28–9, 6.4.13.

5   The Persian Empire

CHRISTOPHER TUPLIN

Introduction

The last generation has seen a renaissance of Xenophontic studies and one important contribution to the renaissance has been the emergence of the Achaemenid Empire as a discipline in its own right rather than a sideshow to Greek or Jewish history or postscript to Assyriology and Egyptology.[1] Xenophon's two works set in Asia, the *Anabasis* and the *Cyropaedia*, have benefited, but in neither case does there exist an account of the whole range of material that their text contributes to our knowledge of the Empire.

While considering the *Anabasis* from this angle, I shall often be posing questions, because this is what Xenophon does – a characteristic combination of selection and silence. On the one hand Xenophon writes as participant eyewitness. This viewpoint can produce vivid moments: when Artaxerxes' approaching army at Cunaxa emerges from the dust cloud like a *melania*, the image is drawn from skin disease. It is even more arresting than an otherwise comparable passage in Winston Churchill's description of Omdurman.[2]

---

1. For recent work on Xenophon, see C. J. Tuplin (ed.), *Xenophon and his World* (Stuttgart, 2004), listing some forty monographs and commentaries since Breitenbach's 1967 Pauly-Wissowa article ('Xenophon', *RE* IX A2). For a sense of the transformation in Achaemenid studies, and access to its results, see P. Briant, *Histoire de l'Empire perse. De Cyrus à Alexandre* (Paris, 1996), worth consultation on almost everything that follows, not just where cited explicitly; the bibliographical updates in P. Briant, 'Bulletin d'histoire achéménide (I)', *Topoi* suppl. 1 (1997), pp. 7–127, and *Bulletin d'histoire achéménide* II (Paris, 2001), and other material accessible via www.achemenet.com.
2. *Anab.* 1.8.8. *Melania* is normally the quality of being black. For more concrete meanings LSJ cites three texts: (a) Polyb. 1.81.7 (below); (b) Theophr. *Hist. pl.* 5.3.1: the blackness of ebony-trees is in the tree's core; (c) the present passage, where *melania* is translated 'black cloud'. *Melania* can apply to rain-clouds (Arist. *Mete.* 375A, Anaxim. 12 A23 = Aët. 3.3.1, Anaxag. 59 A84 = Aët. 3.3.4), but *hōsper melania tis* is not a new comparison for *koniortos*, replacing *hōsper nephelē leukē*, but a new element – the long dark line, soon revealed as the ranks of an army. The only certain concrete use refers to a skin complaint (Polyb. 1.81.7, and several passages in Galen); the first sight of the enemy is as of a diseased patch on the whiteness of the dust cloud. Churchill's description of Omdurman: see F. Wood, *Young Winston's Wars* (London, 1972), p. 100.

On the other hand, the vividly evocative eyewitness often yields to someone who apparently failed to ponder what he saw. For example, Xenophon uses differing language to describe the settlements of the Drilae and Mossynoeci (*chōria* doubling as *poleis*) and the Chalybes (*ochura* doubling as *polismata*), or those of the Taochi (*chōrion*, no *polis*, and no houses) and those of the Carduchi (villages and houses only).[3] But he offers little or nothing to explain why these differences existed.

A final prefatory observation concerns Xenophon's engagement, not with what he saw, but with what he read. I have in mind two citations of Ctesias in the *Anabasis*, on Artaxerxes' chest wound and the number of his entourage who died in the mêlée. That Xenophon cites Ctesias for the wound is reasonable (Ctesias is a privileged source), but did he have to cite him for the second point? Perhaps there were already versions circulating in which Artaxerxes was said to have been unwounded and Cyrus to have inflicted no damage,[4] but I wonder whether Xenophon (unconsciously?) wanted to draw attention to Ctesias, as not just a source on Cunaxa but as a treatment of 'Persian matters' with which his own *Anabasis* might be contrasted. Since the *Anabasis* is formally unprecedented, such questions are at least worth asking.

The imperial landscape

The Persian Empire is the *archē* of the King, or *archē patroia*. It is bounded by habitability. This description is not a Persian conceit; it is perhaps Greek interpretation of the 'universal rule' claimed in Persian royal inscriptions, just as passages in the *Cyropaedia* use a Greek version of the definition-by-marches formula.[5]

---

3. Drilae and Mossynoeci: *Anab.* 5.2.3ff.; 5.4.2ff. Chalybes: *Anab.* 4.7.16f. Taochi: *Anab.* 4.7.1–2. Carduchi: Anab. 4.1.8–3.2.
4. Ctesias in the *Anabasis*: *Anab.* 1.8.26. Other versions: Dinon, *FGH* 690 F17 (Plut. *Artax.* 10), with R. B. Stevenson, 'Lies and invention in Deinon's *Persika*', *AchHist* II (1987), pp. 27–35, at p. 30, and *Persica: Greek Writing about Persia in the Fourth Century BC* (Edinburgh, 1997), pp. 87f.
5. The *archē* of the King: *Anab.* 1.5.9. *Archē patroia*: *Anab.* 1.7.6. 'The King's *chōra*' appears in the interpolated *Anab.* 7.8.25 (where it apparently stretches to European Thrace). Neither *archē* nor *chōra* nor *ethnos* can safely be regarded as reflecting any conscious understanding of Achaemenid terms of reference; cf. P. Briant, *Bulletin d'histoire achéménide* II, pp. 30f. In particular if the *dahyava* which constitute the empire are 'lands' (as reaffirmed by R. Schmitt, 'Zur Bedeutung von alters. /*dahyu*/', in P. Anreiter and E. Jerem (eds), *Studia Celtica et Indogermanica. Festschrift für W. Meid* (Budapest, 1999), pp. 443–52), not 'peoples', armies brigaded *kata ethnē* are not being described in strictly

Within this universe the King's power makes even his brother a slave – the ultimate example of a familiar Greek construction of the relations between the Persian King and others, even those of highest rank. The King's power can also (Greeks supposed) be exercised in odd ways: Xenophon appears to imply that Artaxerxes did not really mind about the war between Cyrus and Tissaphernes or the army's willingness to pretend that attack on Abrocomas might not represent insurrection.[6]

This empire is a *Persian* empire, but the 'Medes and Persians', familiar in *Esther* and *Daniel*, do appear: dallying with the beautiful and tall wives and *parthenoi* of the 'Medes and Persians' is cited as a likely consequence of Greek settlement in Mesopotamia. The usage of 'Medes and Persians' is uncommon in classical Greek, and belongs with military conflict. It represents a triumphalist cliché rather than any special view of the distribution of power and status between those two peoples within the Empire. (The women are *megalai*, not because they are fat as in Greco-Persian representations nor by transfer from a typical Greek perception about Persian males, but because height is a mark of beauty and of presence appropriate to an imperial people.)[7]

Persian terms. Habitability: *Anab.* 1.7.6, *Cyrop.* 8.6.21. Universal rule: royal titulary regularly speaks of being king in the earth (*bumi*). There is also comment on the number and variety of men over whom he rules. See C. Herrenschmidt, 'Désignations de l'Empire et concepts politiques de Darius Ier d'après ses inscriptions en vieux-perse', *StIran* 5 (1976), pp. 33–65. Definition-by-marches: *Cyrop.* 8.6.21, 8.1. *Cyrop.* 1.1.4 offers an aberrant equivalent to the Lists of Lands which are another way of describing the Empire in royal texts; cf. C. J. Tuplin, 'The Persian decor of Xenophon's *Cyropaedia*', *AchHist* V (1990), pp. 17–30, at pp. 17 and 19.

6. The attitude of Artaxerxes: *Anab.* 1.1.8. Interpretation of the attack on Abrocomas: *Anab.* 1.3.20. Persians as the King's slaves: *Anab.* 1.9.29, 2.5.38. Cf., e.g., *Hell.* 4.1.36, 6.1.12, Dem. 15.15, 23, Andoc. 3.29, Diod. 9.31, 15.8; and Ael. *VH* 12.43, Plut. *Mor.* 326e, 337e, 340b (with Briant, *Histoire de l'Empire perse*, pp. 791–2) on the 'slave' who became Darius III. Cyrus' and Pharnabazus' desire for 'freedom' (*Anab.* 1.7.3, *Hell.* 4.1.36) reflect this Greek perception, as do *Anab.* 1.9.15 (the less successful become slaves of the more successful) and perhaps 3.2.3 (Mithradates defecting 'with all his servants'). Nor is it only Greek; Elamite and Akkadian use comparable terms to represent *bandaka*, the Old Persian word applied to tributary imperial subjects (DB §7) and satraps/generals (DB §§ 25, 26, 29, 33, 38, 41, 45, 50, 71). Elamite *libar* and Akkadian *qallu* may not match the semantics of *doulos* exactly, but do designate servants (including servile ones). See A. Missiou, '*Doulos tou basileōs*: the politics of translation', *CQ* n.s. 43 (1993), pp. 377–91, at pp. 385f.; M. A. Dandamaev, *Slavery in Babylonia* (DeKalb, 1984), pp. 81–102, esp. pp. 90ff.

7. 'Medes and Persians': *Anab.* 3.2.25; cf. *Esther* 1.3, 14, 18, 19, 10.2; *Daniel* 5.28, 6.8, 12, 15. Other Greek parallels: Simon. 90D = ML 24, Thuc. 1.104.2, Adesp. Eleg. 58 West = *P. Oxy.* 2327 f.27 ii. The 'Persian and Median army' in DB §§ 25, 33, 41 is not a true parallel: see C. J. Tuplin, 'Xenophon in Media', in G. Lanfranchi, M. Roaf and R. Rollinger (eds), *Continuity of Empire: Assyria, Media, Persia*, History of the Ancient Near East: Monographs Series (Padua, 2003), pp. 352–5. On Greek use of 'Mede' as a substitute for 'Persian', cf. C. J. Tuplin, 'Persians as Medes', *AchHist* VIII (1994), pp. 235–56. Greco-Persian rep-

At the Empire's heart is the King and his family. Here we encounter some novelties. First of all, the King's bastard brother is important enough to command an army.[8] Xenophon is the only evidence that Darius II fathered children with anyone except his queen, Parysatis, who allegedly bore thirteen. But eleven of the children post-dated Darius' accession, while the others may have been born some time before. Perhaps Parysatis' role in the accession transformed her status; and the bastard son could appropriately be assigned to her too and given a birth-date back in the early 420s or 430s.

Second, Xenophon refers to the brother of the King's wife, a person who is not just unknown, but impossible if we believe Ctesias' claim that all the siblings of Artaxerxes' wife Stateira were eliminated after the Teritouchmes affair.[9] Perhaps Xenophon meant the King's sister's husband (assuming Artaxerxes had an otherwise unknown sister, since the known sister married Teritouchmes), or perhaps he (or his informant) simply got it wrong – or perhaps Ctesias did.

It is rather odd that both of these individuals (like the brothers of Ariaeus and Tissaphernes) are anonymous. It seems unlikely that Xenophon's ultimate informant knew their relationship to the King but not their names, so Xenophon had evidently decided that the information was not worth remembering or recalling. He provides few personal names (outside the Greek army), but one might have thought these cases exceptional.[10] Perhaps a preoccupation with Tissaphernes after Cunaxa caused him to forget or discard other names. (Orontes' name survived because he accompanied Tissaphernes for some weeks and the Greeks later entered his territory, having outsmarted his forces.)

The anonymity of the King's daughter (Orontes' wife) initially seems less surprising, but only because we are used to Greek unease about naming respectable women. This reticence, however, is hardly relevant to a barbarian princess. In fact we know her name (Rhodogune) from Plutarch and later inscriptions. Orontes' union with her reveals his importance, but Xenophon

---

resentations of women: cf. e.g. J. Boardman, *Greek Finger Rings and Gems* (London, 1970), nos 854, 876, 879–80, 891–2, 903. Greek perception of Persian males: T. Hölscher, 'Ein Kelchkrater mit Perserkampf', *AK* 17 (1974), pp. 78–85, citing Hdt. 7.117, 9.25, 83, 96, Curt. 4.13.5, 7.4.6, Just. 11.13.

8. Bastard brother's command: *Anab.* 2.4.25, 3.4.13. The King is occasionally described as 'Great': *Anab.* 1.2.8, 4.11, 7.2,13; and cf. 2.5.10.
9. Brother of the King's wife: *Anab.* 2.3.17. The Teritouchmes affair: *FGH* 688 F15 [56].
10. The brothers of Ariaeus and Tissaphernes: *Anab.* 2.4.1, 5.35. The anonymity of 'one of Tissaphernes' *oikeioi*' (*Anab.* 3.3.4) is a different matter.

(though providing a date) lacks the knowledge (or interest) to note the royal marriages of other grandees who are encountered in the *Anabasis*.[11]

Xenophon's lack of references to other children of Darius and Parysatis at the very beginning obviously has a literary component: it preserves the simple clarity of his famously unadorned opening sentence. However, did Xenophon not know that Darius and Parysatis were half-siblings?[12] In the background to fraternal strife this fact has a piquancy which might have entitled it to a mention.

Apart from these silences about royal family detail, there are distinctive points about the King and the upper classes for which the *Anabasis* is important evidence. What about courtiers and functionaries? In book 1 Cyrus executes Megaphernes, a royal *phoinikistes*. In my view he is a 'secretary', not a 'wearer of the purple', and he is comparable to the royal *grammateus* of a hyparch in Herodotus. He is described with a word no late fifth-century Athenian would naturally use in place of *grammateus*. Its appearance does not indicate that Megaphernes worked in a foreign language or alphabet. Rather, I suspect, Xenophon received the description from an East Greek informant (even a Greek-speaking Persian?) for whom the words *phoinikistes* and *phoinikeia grammata* (Greek letters) were perhaps still ordinary language.[13]

Another unusual (indeed, unrecorded) functionary is Tiribazus, the man whose unique right it was to assist the King to mount his horse. This observation recalls Dinon's remarks on Cunaxa: when Artaxerxes' horse was wounded, Tiribazus remounted him, saying, 'Remember this day, O King, for it does not deserve to be forgotten.' Lendle infers that the right was newly conferred on Tiribazus. If it was, it still had no effect on Xenophon's narrative of the battle. But another possibility is that the privilege had no connection with Cunaxa before Dinon chose to invent one.[14]

11. Rhodogune: Plut. *Artax.* 27; *OGIS* 391–2. The marriages of other grandees: Tissaphernes (Diod. 14.26.4), Pharnabazus (*Hell.* 5.1.28), and Tiribazus (Plut. *Artax.* 27).
12. *FGH* 688 F15 [47].
13. Megaphernes: *Anab.* 1.2.21. *Grammateus*: Hdt. 3.128.4b. 'Phoenician' is inappropriate; one expects *Assyria / Syria grammata* for Aramaic (Thuc. 4.50, Diod. 19.23.3, 96.1, Polyaenus *Strat.* 4.8.3) or cuneiform (*FGH* 688 F1 [13.2], Hdt. 4.87, *FGH* 139 F9, *Cyrop.* 7.3.15). Xenophon is aware of language issues: the *Anabasis* mentions interpreters and translation often. *Phoinikeia grammata* as an Ionian description of Greek writing: Hdt. 5.58.2; cf. Teian curse-inscriptions (*ML* 30.37; P. Herrmann, 'Teos und Abdera im 5 Jh.v.C', *Chiron* 11 (1981), pp. 1–30, at p. 8 (d). 19 = *SEG* 31.985). The same appears in Crete: L. H. Jeffery and A. Morpurgo Davies, '*poinikistes* and *poinikizein*: BM 1969.4–2.1. A new archaic inscription from Crete', *Kadmos* 9 (1970), pp. 118–54. This evidence well pre-dates the incident at Dana.
14. Tiribazus and the horse: *Anab.* 4.4.4. Stevenson, 'Lies and invention in Deinon's *Persika*', p. 30, and *Persica*, p. 93, sees this passage as confirming Dinon's story, but says nothing

Cyrus also has staff-bearers, or *skēptouchoi*, a category which is found in the King's entourage and in that of Panthea in the *Cyropaedia* but not elsewhere. However, Calmeyer has adduced the staff-carrying figures who introduce delegations to the King on the Apadana frieze. An association of this role with eunuchs in the *Cyropaedia* might imply knowledge that some *skēptouchoi* were only 'titular' eunuchs, as perhaps were (some) Assyrian *ša resi*. But the Achaemenid role of eunuchs interested Xenophon, and so one might expect him to display awareness of pseudo-eunuchs explicitly if they were at issue here.[15]

Eunuchs belong in palaces and (some said) they contributed to the education of Persian princes. The *Anabasis* provides information on two of these elements, reporting that Cyrus, like all children of 'the noblest Persians', was educated 'at the King's Gates'. Persian education is addressed by several Greek sources with a complex pattern of overlap and difference of detail. The picture here broadly matches the one in the *Cyropaedia* (the *Anabasis*' failure to stress *dicaeosynē* is a notable deviation) and that found elsewhere, though other Greek texts which include *mageia* or *philosophia* in the curriculum do take us further afield.[16]

Greek authors are liable to see the topic through a Hellenic moral prism: even Herodotus is making a point about the 'old-fashioned' simplicity of

> on the privilege. Tiribazus is also a 'Friend of the King': cf. Hdt. 7.39, Plut. *Them.* 29, *Artax.* 11, 24; Diod. 15.10.3, 11.2, 16.50.7, 52.1, 17.35.2, *FGH* 472 F6. Of similar status are Cyrus' *homotrapezoi* (*Anab.* 1.8.26) = *suntrapezoi* (1.9.31): cf. Hdt. 3.132, *FGH* 688 F14 (43), Chariton 7.2.5 (*homotrapezoi*), Hdt.5.24 (*sussitoi*), 7.119 (*homositoi*), a privileged subgroup of the *sundeipnoi* (*FGH* 689 F2). Did Xenophon see Cyrus' passion for making everyone his friend and debtor (*Anab.* 1.9.7ff.) as transcending the principle of constructing the court in terms of affective social relationships?
> 15. *Skēptouchoi*: *Cyrop.* 7.3.15 (often deleted), 8.1.38, 3.15f., 4.2. Aesch. *Pers.* 297 seems different; so too Hellenistic *skēptouchiai* (Strabo 11.2.13, 18). Association with eunuchs: *Cyrop.* 3.15, 8.4.2, transferred to *Anab.* 1.8.28 by Ael. *VH* 6.25, with no known independent justification. Briant, *Histoire de l'Empire perse*, pp. 285–8, 945, has argued this case, but the equation of *ša resi* and actual eunuchs has been reasserted. Xenophontic interest in eunuchs: *Cyrop.* 7.5.60f. 'Real' Assyrian eunuchs: H. Tadmor, 'Was the biblical *sarys* a eunuch?', in J. E. Coleson and V. H. Matthews (eds), *'Go to the Land I will Show You': Studies in Honour of D. Young* (Winona Lake, 1995), pp. 317–25; A. K. Grayson, 'Eunuchs in power', in M. Dietrich and O. Loretz (eds), *Vom Alten Orient zum Alten Testament* (Neukirchen-Vluyn, 1995), pp. 85–98.
> 16. Eunuchs and education: Pl. *Leg.* 695A, *Alc. I* 121Dff. (cf. C. J. Tuplin, *Achaemenid Studies* (Stuttgart, 1996), p. 163). The turn of phrase 'at the gates' in this sort of context is also used at *Cyrop.* 1.2.11, 2.1.8, 2.4.4, 2.5.31, 6.5.23. Genuinely oriental (DB §§ 32, 33; VS 6.128; CT 22.101; *Esther* 2.19, 21, 3.2, 3, 4.2, 6, 5.9, 13, 6.10; further Akkadian material in *CAD* s.v. *bābu* A1b2′, 1c4′, 1d3′), it appears in other Greek texts, e.g. Diod. 9.31, 14.25, Hdt. 3.117, 119, 120, 140, Plut. *Them.* 26, 29. Other Greek texts dealing with the curriculum: Hdt. 1.136.2 (riding, shooting, telling the truth); *CEG* 2.888; *FGH* 688 F15 (55); Nic. Dam. 90 F67, F103x; Strabo 733C; Plut. *Artax.* 2,3; Arr. *Anab.* 5.4.5.

Persian upbringing. Xenophon is prone to do the same, and so the narrative at *Anab.* 1.9.2f. (the only account of the education of a historical individual) cannot claim special authority. Indeed, the absence in Xenophon's account of a counterpart to Persian *arta* (represented in other Greek sources by 'truth', 'justice', or *aretē*) may actually make it *un*authoritative.[17]

A familiar proposition about the King is that he alone may wear his *tiara* upright. Xenophon is not the first to mention this, but his context is unusual. Tissaphernes says to Clearchus: 'the *tiara* on the head only the King may have upright, but the *tiara* in the heart someone else as well could perhaps, with your support, easily have [upright]' – a colourful, but veiled, response to Clearchus' hint that by employing the Ten Thousand, Tissaphernes could turn himself into a semi-autonomous ruler.[18]

This response lulls Clearchus into a false sense of security, but the striking image of the *tiara*-crowned heart casts no decisive light on the *Realien* of actual *tiara*-wearing on the head. There are various associated problems – why are there three technical terms for the object (*tiara, kitaris, kurbasia*), what did the headgear look like, how does it fit extant iconographical evidence? I note Xenophon's evidence about the gorgeous apparel of high-ranking Persians (memorably embedded in the scene where Cyrus' Persian companions rush to dislodge wagons stuck in the mud). He also refers to the clothing, jewellery, and gold objects which constitute 'customary gifts of honour from the King'. This passage alludes to a central feature of Achaemenid kingship, the giving and receiving of gifts, and contributes to Xenophon's characterization of Cyrus as the generous prince.[19]

17. Cf. C. J. Tuplin, 'Xenophon's *Cyropaedia*: education and fiction', in A. H. Sommerstein and C. Atherton (eds), *Education in Greek Fiction* (Bari, 1996), pp. 65–162, at pp. 135ff., suggesting that Xenophon got more information after writing *Anab.* 1.9.2f. *Cyrop.* 1.6.33 makes learning Justice – a keynote in that work's picture of Persian education – involve insistence on truth-telling and outlaw deception. The stress on veracity and trustworthiness in *Anab.* 1.9.7f. (and their apparent absence in Tissaphernes' behaviour in book 2) do not gloss the formal account of education in a similar way.

18. Tissaphernes and the *tiara*: *Anab.* 2.5.23. Other sources: *Cyrop.* 8.3.13; Arr. *Anab.* 3.5.23; *FGH* 81 F22, 137 F5; Plut. *Mor.* 488D; Luc. *Pisc.* 35; Dio. Chrys. 13.24 (*tiara*); Plut. *Artax.* 26, 28, *Mor.* 340C; Arr. *Anab.* 6.29.3; Plut. *Them.* 29 (*kidaris*); Sch. Pl. *Rep.* 553C (*kurbasia*). Only some texts explicitly affirm the King's unique right, but it is surely implicit throughout. See C. J. Tuplin, 'Treacherous hearts and upright tiaras', in L. Llewellyn-Jones and M. Harlow (eds), *The Clothed Body in Antiquity* (Oxford, forthcoming), which also discusses Tissaphernes' remark in more detail.

19. Companions in the mud: *Anab.* 1.5.8. 'Customary gifts of honour from the King': *Anab.* 1.2.27. Cf. also *Cyrop.* 8.2.8: 'what gifts are so easily recognized as those which the King gives . . . things which no one there may have unless given them by the King?' Did Xenophon think Cyrus' gift to Syennesis *ultra vires*? Gift-giving and Achaemenid king-

Besides the dress code, paying 'obeisance' or *proskynēsis* is another familiar feature of protocol. The traitor Orontes still receives *proskynēsis* on his way to execution, a vignette which brings home vividly its importance. So does the remark that just before his death Cyrus was 'receiving *proskynēsis* already as King from those around him' – though one wishes Xenophon had identified what distinguished *proskynēsis* to a King from that to a mere son or brother of a King and how this obeisance could be paid in mid-battle.[20]

Later Xenophon provides a statement of the proper Greek attitude about *proskunesis* – Greeks perform it to no human *despotes* but only the gods. This commonplace is closely preceded by a scene in which soldiers do *proskunesis* in response to a well-omened sneeze. The response is not a neutral matter, as Greek *proskunesis* was commonly a female gesture: by doing it, the army marks its vulnerability.[21] That is why Xenophon almost immediately afterwards ends an argument drawn from victory in the Persian Wars by adducing the freedom enjoyed by Greek cities and glossing 'freedom' as a situation in which *proskunesis* is reserved for the gods. A parallel interplay between *eleutheria*, *proskynēsis*, and *despotēs* occurs in Agesilaus' discussion with Pharnabazus in the *Hellenica*: it is as if the satrap will become an honorary Greek, albeit a rich a powerful one. These passages do not show that Xenophon thought Persians regarded their King as divine. They did not, but in an appropriate rhetorical context he was as capable as Isocrates of associating *proskynēsis* with a presumed claim to divine honours.[22]

We also need to consider Xenophon's evidence for the Persian Empire itself. The Empire in the *Anabasis* contains satraps and other types of ruler;[23] comparatively extensive regions; cities; smaller settlements or focal points; long-distance routes; systems for extracting tributary or other profit; and a

---

ship: Briant, *Histoire de l'Empire perse*, pp. 78ff., 314ff., 406ff., 474ff., and more generally Index Général s.vv. Don royal, Dons faits au roi. Cyrus as generous prince: *Anab.* 1.2.11, 27, 1.4.8, 1.7.6f., 1.9.14ff.

20. *Proskynēsis* to Orontes: *Anab.* 1.6.10. *Proskynēsis* to Cyrus: *Anab.* 1.8.21.
21. *Anab.* 3.2.13, 3.2.9. *Proskynēsis* as a female gesture: F. T. van Straten, 'Did the Greeks kneel before their gods?', *BABesch* 49 (1974), pp. 159–89.
22. Agesilaus and Pharnabazus: *Hell.* 4.1.35–6. *Proskynēsis* and divine honours: *Ages.* 1.34. Agesilaus caused Greeks who previously had to perform *proskynēsis* to be honoured by those who had insulted them, and forced those who claimed divine honours (*proskynēsis*) to be unable to look a Greek in the face. Cf. Isoc. 4.150; neither passage attributes to Persians actual belief in a divine king.
23. The interpolator constructs territory traversed by the army as a series of *archai* or autonomous regions (*Anab.* 7.8.25); his terminology differs slightly from Xenophon's. Cyrus divides the universal empire into satrapies: *Anab.* 1.7.6.

military structure. There are also regions of recalcitrance or even (apparent) total detachment.

Among satraps, most unusual is Cyrus. He is satrap of Lydia, Great Phrygia, and Cappadocia (other sources ignore the second two) and the general or *karanos* of those who assemble at Castolupedium. This occurs in Xenophon's *Hellenica* and is a precise title; other sources speak simply of 'controlling the seaboard'.[24]

Two observations are in place. In the *Anabasis*, Xenophon did not find the title *karanos* important enough to mention, nor does it recur in his other allusions to military 'assembly'. Secondly, some believe that Cyrus did not displace existing satraps of Lydia, Phrygia, and Cappadocia: he superimposed a different sort of satrap on top of them.[25] Satrap (*xšacapavan*, 'protector of the realm') *is* intrinsically a fluid term, so a hierarchy of coexisting but unequal satraps is theoretically possible.

We also need to consider Tiribazus, Orontes, and Belesys. Tiribazus and Orontes controlled Western Armenia and Armenia respectively. The division recurs in the sources for Alexander's march, and could be seen as fitting a model of a satrapal system with several tiers.[26] Both men were destined for exciting (and interconnected) futures, partly within Greek horizons (they are involved in events in Western Anatolia and Cyprus) and so potentially within Xenophon's knowledge at the time of writing.

---

24. *Karanos*: *Anab.* 1.9.7. Contrast Just. 5.5.1; Plut. *Artax.* 2; Diod. 14.12.5, 19.2, 26.4. On *karanos* (etymology and significance) see C. Haebler, 'Karanos: eine sprachwissenschaftliche Betrachtung zu Xen. Hell.I 4.3', in J. Tischler (ed.), *Serta Indogermanica* (Innsbruck, 1982), pp. 81–90; T. Petit, 'Étude d'une fonction militaire sous la dynastie achéménide', *LEC* 51 (1983), pp. 35–45; N. Sekunda, 'Achaemenid military terminology', *AMI* 21 (1988), pp. 69–77, at p.74; D. Testen, '*karanos = kurios*', *Glotta* 69 (1991), pp. 173–4; A. G. Keen, 'Persian *karanoi* and their relationship to the satrapal system', in T. W. Hillard et al. (eds), *Ancient History in a Modern University* (Grand Rapids and Cambridge, 1998), pp. 88–95.
25. So J. M. Balcer, 'The ancient Persian satrapies and satraps in Western Anatolia', *AMI* 26 (1993), pp. 1–90, at p. 88, and Keen, 'Persian *karanoi*'. For the usual view cf., e.g., D. M. Lewis, *Sparta and Persia* (Leiden, 1977). My comments are a consciously peremptory incursion into a contentious area (as is also true in other parts of this paper): see P. Debord, *L'Asie Mineure au IVe siècle* (Bordeaux, 1999), pp. 124f., for recent discussion. Military 'assembly': *Cyr.* 2.1.5, 6.2.11, *Oec.* 4.5f.
26. Western Armenia: *Anab.* 4.4.4. Armenia: *Anab.* 3.5.17. 'Greater' and 'lesser': cf. B. Jacobs, *Die Satrapienverwaltung im Perserreich zur Zeit Darius' III* (Wiesbaden, 1994). Xenophon consistently treats *hyparchos* as designating a subordinate position: *Anab.* 1.2.20, 8.5; *Hell.* 3.1.12 , 6.1.7 (non-Persian). Occasional Greek application of the term to high-level satraps simply reflects everyone's subordination to the King.

There is, however, no reflection of this future in the *Anabasis*.[27] Tiribazus simply has status as Friend of the King and enjoys the privilege of helping the King mount his horse, while Orontes marries the King's daughter. These honours mark them as imperial high-fliers, but they can have been known to Xenophon in 401.

Belesys (Belšunu) is remarkable: a non-Iranian (Babylonian) elevated to a major satrapy, who is also known from an extensive business archive.[28] From this evidence we discover that he left office between 16 January 401 and Cyrus' arrival in Syria in summer 401, perhaps to be replaced by Abrocomas. He still appears in business contexts in 401/0, so he did not die in harness, but Xenophon records no gossip about what was surely no coincidental change in such a strategic area. He does not explain Cyrus' destruction of Belesys' *paradeisos* and palace. Nor does he show awareness of his non-Iranian origins.

The *Anabasis* also exemplifies non-satrapal authorities, both substantial and modest. In the first category are Corylas in Paphlagonia and Syennesis in Cilicia – of whom Xenophon says too little to make clear what he was up to.[29] It is often assumed that Syennesis (and his dynasty, or the native rule he represented) were eliminated shortly after 401, but this inference may ascribe to him more importance than he deserves.[30]

On a much smaller scale the army encounters a Persian-speaking *kōmarch* who is responsible for a group of Armenian villages. He is a unique example of the local implications (including tribute) of imperial rule. The 'Persian' that he speaks is what the village women speak; he has relatives locally and is not an official individually intruded from outside. Whether or why they were

27. Tiribazus was prominent in the process behind the King's Peace (*Hell.* 4.8.12–17, 5.1.6, 25–31). He and Orontes then fought Evagoras and successively lost the King's favour (Diod. 15.2, 8–11, *FGH* 115 F103). Orontes' treachery in the Satraps' Revolt potentially had indirect ramifications for Greek observers.
28. For Belesys, see M. W. Stolper, 'Belšunu the satrap', in F. Rochberg-Halton (ed.), *Language. Literature and History* (New Haven, 1987), pp. 389–402.
29. *FGH* 688 F16 [63] and Diod. 14.20.3 reckon he tried to be on both sides. Differing reactions (*Anab.* 1.2.22) to Cyrus among Tarsians and those further west are seen by Debord, *L'Asie Mineure au IVe siècle*, p. 332, as reflecting differing degrees to which people had a stake in the imperial system. Or was it just that Tarsus was bound to be most at risk militarily?
30. O. Casabonne, 'Local powers and the Persian model in Achaemenid Cilicia: a reassessment', *Olba* 2 (1999), pp. 57–66, at pp. 59f., argues for continuation of a native Cilician dynasty into the earlier fourth century.

speaking 'Persian' is more debatable. It might be a result of earlier strategic Persian settlement in the area – not inconceivable if these (fortified) villages lay on a major east–west route from Media to Anatolia, or perhaps Iranophone people had spread through this region since pre-Achaemenid times. If the latter explanation is right, the 'Persian'-speaking 'village ruler' is typical of outposts in peasant-based empires – something we might postulate anyway but which it is captivating to have so circumstantially attested.[31]

The most interesting other local rulers are the Demaratids and Gongylids of Aeolis. Two points merit notice. First, Procles the Demaratid was in Cyrus' expeditionary force. He was not part of the Ten Thousand, but must have been present as a subordinate ruler within Cyrus' province (thus placing the Caicus valley within the Lydian satrapy in 401?). If he was accompanied by a military contingent, we face the possibility that there were Greek troops at Cunaxa other than Cyrus' mercenaries. Certainly Procles returned with Tissaphernes and other elements of Cyrus' Anatolian army.[32]

Second, there is good evidence of Demaratid–Gongylid intermarriage, but the idea has also spread that Hellas was not only Gongylus' wife, but a daughter or granddaughter of Themistocles or named after a postulated Hellas daughter of Themistocles.[33] This view is exciting, but would a Themistoclean daughter called Hellas have escaped notice by the sources that record his other daughters as Sybaris, Italia, and Asia? A Themistoclean granddaughter remains possible, but would Xenophon have been unaware or silent about such a thing?

If we turn to the regions of the Empire, Xenophon's nomenclature is mostly unproblematic. Paphlagonia does stretch unusually far east in his story, but it

---

31. The *kōmarch*: *Anab.* 4.5.10. Possible location on a Media–Anatolia route: V. Manfredi, *La Strada dei Diecimila* (Milan, 1986), pp. 207f. Pre-Achaemenid Iranophones: H.-P. Drögemüller, 'Der kurdisch-armenisch Raum', *Gymnasium* 94 (1987), pp. 385–420, at p. 413. 'Village ruler' in a peasant-based empire: S. Hornblower, 'Persia', in *Cambridge Ancient History*[2], vol. 6 (Cambridge, 1994), pp. 45–96, at p. 51. But that the army automatically negotiates with the *kōmarch* and not the satrap does not, pace Hornblower, reveal much: the Greeks did not want to get involved with the satrap.
32. Procles in Cyrus' force: *Anab.* 2.1.3. The Demaratids and Gongylids: *Anab.* 7.8.8f., 16f.; *Hell* 3.1.6; Hdt. 6.70; Paus. 3.7.8; Ath. 29F. M. L. Whitby, 'An international symposium? Ion of Chios fr. 27 and the margins of the Delian League', in E. Dabrowa (ed.), *Ancient Iran and the Mediterranean World* (Krakow, 1998), pp. 207–24, enticingly locates Ion fr. 27 (= Ath. 463 BC) at a symposium in the Aeolian home of Demaratus or his son. The return of Procles: *Hell.* 3.1.6. Debord, *L'Asie Mineure au IVe siècle*, pp. 190f., 239, sees Procles, Gongylus, and Gorgion as hostile to the Greeks at *Anab.* 7.8.17.
33. A. Wiedersich, 'Hellas', *RE* suppl. 4 (1924), pp. 728–9, col. 728; J. P. Stronk, *The Ten Thousand in Thrace: An Archaeological and Historical Commentary on Xenophon's Anabasis Books VI.iii–vi VII* (Amsterdam, 1995), p. 292; O. Lendle, *Kommentar zu Xenophons Anabasis* (Darmstadt, 1995), p. 480; Debord, *L'Asie Mineure au IVe siècle*, p. 190.

does not pose insurmountable problems. His 'Arabia' east of the Euphrates is also susceptible of explanation.[34]

However, another case is harder. After crossing the Physcus at Opis (two highly controversial toponyms) the army entered 'Media'. Since they were in the Tigris basin, this topography is odd, given that Media is usually an area in the north-western Iranian plateau and adjacent parts of the Zagros. I am confident that Xenophon's perception here of the eastern Tigris basin as a part of Media interrelates with his conception of Media in the *Cyropaedia* (where Media lies between Assyria – including Babylon – and Persia). It is also, I believe, consistent with his notion of Nimrud and Nineveh as Median cities which fell to the Persians.[35]

I am less sure whose name it was for this region in 401 (if anyone's) or why. But I do note a comparable oddity in Herodotus' use of 'Matiene', a term otherwise proper to a Zagros region, for a large zone on both banks of the Tigris. Plutarch has Tiribazus advise Artaxerxes not to retreat from 'Media, Babylon, and Susa' to Persis.[36] In context, this advice is also consistent with the view that Media was outside the Zagros.

Not only in this instance, Xenophon's categories of thought were not perfect for what he saw. However, even with named *poleis* all is not straightforward. Susa and Ecbatana appear as the conjoint destination or source of a road which reaches the Tigris from the east. In the first case the King's brother arrives thence with reinforcements and encounters the Greeks somewhere around the Tigris–Diyala confluence and on the edge of Xenophon's lowland 'Media'. In the second case a route from the northern Tigris plain (beyond or at the edge of 'Media') leads to Susa and Ecbatana. Xenophon had never seen a map, and would have been unable to make accurate sense of figures given in Herodotus' description of the Royal Road; he perhaps imagined Susa well north of its true position and on the direct road from Mesopotamia to the Persian heartland.

---

34. *Anab.* 5.5.6 implies that Paphlagonia starts close to Cotyora (modern Ordu) whereas other ancient views (W. Ruge and K. Bittel, 'Paphlagonia', *RE* 18 (1949), cols 2486–550, at cols 2489ff.) find the edge at Amisus, the Halys, or just west of Sinope. Ruge and Bittel, 'Paphlagonia', regard Xenophon's position as valid ethnographically (for its date). His treatment of land east of Cotyora is also distinctive but not clearly due to simple error. 'Arabia': cf. J. Retsö, 'Xenophon in Arabia', in S. Teodorsson (ed.), *Greek and Latin Studies in Memory of C. Fabricius* (Göteborg, 1990), pp. 122–31; C. J. Tuplin, 'Modern and ancient travellers in the Achaemenid Empire', *AchHist* VII (1991), pp. 37–57, against F. Donner, 'Xenophon's Arabia', *Iraq* 48 (1986), pp. 1–14.
35. Physcus and Opis: cf. Tuplin, 'Modern and ancient travellers', pp. 51f. Entry to 'Media': *Anab.* 2.4.27. Nimrud and Nineveh: *Anab.* 3.4.7–12.
36. Hdt. 5.52; Plut. *Artax.* 7.

As for Ecbatana, it was 'where the King spends the summer',[37] and Xenophon (who experienced a Mesopotamian summer) may have deduced a mountain location.

Cities he *had* seen receive scant description. Celaenae has palaces, a *paradeisos*, the River Maeander, and the story of Marsyas; Tarsus has a palace and the River Cydnus; Issus is 'on the sea'; Myriandus, also 'on the sea', is an *emporion* with many merchant ships in harbour; Corsote is encircled by the Mascas; Sittace, fifteen stades from the Tigris, has a *paradeisos* nearby; Opis is on the Physcus; Ceramon Agora, Iconium, and Issus are frontier towns. Ironically it is only the 'dead' cities of Larisa and Mespila which provoke reference to architectural features and precise (if inaccurate) estimates of size. Perhaps the interplay of emptiness and extent at these two sites was exceptional.[38] Elsewhere the sentences about Celaenae come closest to an evocation of place, and yet history and mythology bulk as large in it as accurate depiction. In general, however, cities did not feature in an essentially military narrative.

One description he does apply to cities is *oikoumenē*, but its significance remains unclear. It is not just that they are not deserted. This clarification would be superfluous when (as often) he also calls them 'large and flourishing'. Nor is it that they have a genuine political organization – for how did he know that Iconium, Charmande, and Sittace did not, whereas Keramon Agora, Thymbrion, Opis, and Caenae did? There is a lack of consistency in his use of terms which makes one wonder if his descriptive tags deserve serious regard.[39]

The tendency not to describe recurs with smaller places. Palaces (*basileia*) are never evoked as architectural objects. At Celaenae we hear about the relation of Xerxes' palace to river sources and the acropolis. Elsewhere we hear only about the *paradeisoi* or villages associated with palaces.[40] It is a pity no

---

37. Susa and Ecbatana: *Anab.* 2.4.25 and 3.5.15. 'Where the King spends the summer': see C. J. Tuplin, 'The seasonal migration of Achaemenid Kings: a report on old and new evidence', in M. Brosius and A. Kuhrt (eds), *Studies in Persian History: Essays in Memory of David M. Lewis* (Leiden, 1998), pp. 63–114.
38. *Anab.* 1.2.7–9 (Celaenae); 1.2.23 (Tarsus); 1.4.1 (Issus); 1.4.6 (Myriandus); 1.5.4 (Corsote); 2.4.13–14 (Sittace); 2.4.25 (Opis); 1.2.11, 19, 1.4.1 (frontier towns); 3.4.7–12 (Larisa and Mespila).
39. Cf. C. J. Tuplin, 'On the track of the Ten Thousand', *REA* 101 (1999), pp. 331–66, at pp. 334f.
40. Paradeisoi: *Anab.* 1.2.7, 1.4.10. Villages: *Anab.* 3.4.24, 4.4.2, 4.4.7. Debord, *L'Asie Mineure au IVe siècle*, p. 47, identifies *Anab.* 4.4.2 as one of the Armenian satrapal capitals. *Anab.* 4.4.7 is a comparable spot; that the *basileion* here is not specifically 'for the satrap' does not mean it lacks official status, but at most that it belongs to the hyparch of W. Armenia, whereas the other belonged to the (higher-ranking) satrap of Armenia.

palace was ever attacked: we might then have got the (still modest) sort of information which is provided about Asidates' *tursis* at the end of the expedition – high and extensive, with *promacheōnas* (battlements?) and a wall eight bricks thick.

However, one description of fortifications which we *are* given is the one of the Cilico–Syrian Gates. They have two walls enclosing a river and blocking the road between the sea and 'beetling cliffs'. It gives us a rare sight of a permanent (though abandoned) Achaemenid garrison location, in a place which is mentioned in later sources but without precise details.[41] Tiresomely, however, it has been referred to at least two distinct locations near Jonah's Pillar, and the exact site is still uncertain.

A similar misfortune means that on the two occasions on which the army passes the property of a queen we are in a topographically obscure stretch of narrative. We are thus denied the satisfaction of securely identifying somewhere on the ground as part of Queen Parysatis' estates.[42] The same goes for the *paradeisoi*, none of which receives more than a baldly formulaic description.

Nonetheless, Xenophon is the first surviving Greek author to mention *paradeisoi* – perhaps a feature of Persian landscape which particularly struck him. I have cautioned elsewhere against inferring that his Skillous estate imported the idea of the paradise-park into Greece. L'Allier has now independently argued the contrary, maintaining that Artemis is associated with the goddess Anahita and the goddess Anahita with *paradeisoi*. In his view, the lack of a hunting enclosure reflects Xenophon's criticism elsewhere of hunting enclosed animals, and Skillous, then, is an improved sort of *paradeisos*, one which is better for promoting military skills and more respectful of the natural world.[43]

However, the latter two points mean that Skillous is *not* a *paradeisos* – and certainly not a hunting *paradeisos* in any useful sense. The first point may be

---

41. *Anab.* 1.4.4. Later mentions: *FGH* 124 F25; Strabo 14.5.3, 14.5.19, 16.2.33; Arr. *Anab.* 2.6.1, 2.8.1–2; Dio Cass. 75.7; Curt. 3.8.13. For other material (a little from the *Anabasis*) on Achaemenid garrisons see C. J. Tuplin, 'Xenophon and the garrisons of the Achaemenid Empire', *AMI* n. f. 20 (1987), pp. 167–246. On the Homeric resonance of 'beetling cliffs', see C. J. Tuplin, 'Heroes in Xenophon's *Anabasis*', in G. Zecchini and C. Bearzot (eds), *Modelli eroici dell'anthichità alla cultura europea* (Rome, 2003). Locations: Manfredi, *Strada dei Diecimila*, pp. 91f., N. G. L. Hammond, 'One or two passes at the Cilicia–Syria border?', *AncW* 25 (1994), pp. 15–26.
42. Location of Parysatis' estates: east of the Beilan Pass (*Anab.* 1.4.9) and east of the Tigris (2.4.27).
43. The Skillous estate: *Anab.* 5.3.7–13. On the importation or otherwise of the paradise-park, see Tuplin, *Achaemenid Studies*, pp. 113f.; contra, L. L'Allier, 'Le domaine de Scillonte: Xénophon et l'exemple perse', *Phoenix* 52 (1998), pp. 1–14.

true, but the association of the park with Artemis reflected the *army*'s reservation of booty for Apollo and Artemis, so it is hard to demonstrate that much follows. The goddess Artemis certainly fitted the hunting aspects of Xenophon's Scillus, without need of a Persian explanation. Any temple would happily have cultivated land among its possessions.[44]

What about tribute and exploitation in general? Cyrus insists on a maximization of profit, from which individual *oikonomoi* would also profit personally. This ideally fits in with a general understanding (partly based on Xenophontic evidence) that fostering agricultural productivity was a fiscal and ideological good in the Persian Empire.[45]

Xenophon also indicates that individual Greek cities constitute tributary units, and that the duty to transmit tribute was personal to the relevant satrap. Cyrus thus sent tribute from cities of Tissaphernes which were de facto under his control; the implication is that, since they had not been given him by the King, he need not have done so. The tribute is not a bureaucratic obligation from city to King which someone has to administer. It is a debt from satrap to King which relates to the extent of authority granted personally to the satrap by the King.[46]

In Armenia we see at the local level a phenomenon otherwise known on a larger scale, the provision of horses as tribute (*dasmos*). Actually, the link with other sources is tricky. We hear elsewhere of horse-tribute in Cappadocia, Cilicia and Aspendus, whereas for Armenia we encounter annual despatch of 20,000 animals for sacrifice at the Persian festival of the Mithrakana.[47] In the *Anabasis* Xenophon surrenders for sacrifice a horse that he has heard is sacred to the Sun, and takes instead one of the tributary foals. Some, but not all, evidence favours assimilation of the Sun and Mithras, the god who is the dedicatee of the *Mithrakana*.[48] Should we then assume the foals were actually collected

---

44. For a fuller discussion see C. J. Tuplin, 'Xenophon, Artemis and Scillus', in T. Figueira (ed.), *Spartan Society* (London, forthcoming).
45. Cyrus and profit: *Anab.* 1.9.9. P. Briant, *État et pasteurs au Moyen-Orient ancien* (Paris, 1982), pp. 431–73; 'Guerre, tribut et forces productives dans l'Empire achéménide', *DHA* 12 (1986), pp. 33–48; Briant, *Histoire de l'Empire perse*, pp. 244ff.
46. Cities as tributary units: *Anab.* 1.1.8. Cf. C. J. Tuplin, 'The administration of the Achaemenid Empire', in I. Carradice (ed.), *Coinage and Administration in the Athenian and Persian Empires* (Oxford, 1987), pp. 109–66, at pp. 147f.
47. Horses as tribute: *Anab.* 4.5.24. Cappadocia: Strabo 11.13.8. Cilicia: Hdt. 3.90. Aspendus: Arr. *Anab.* 1.26.3. Armenia: Strabo 11.14.9.
48. Xenophon's horse: *Anab.* 4.5.35. Sun and Mithras: Strabo 15.3.13, Hesychius and the Suda say that Persians identified them (cf. M. Boyce, *A History of Zoroastrianism* vol. 2, (Leiden, 1982), p. 110); other evidence is equivocal and occasionally (e.g. Curt. 4.13.12)

for sacrifice to Mithra-Helios? Or should we insist on the letter of Xenophon's text – and even question whether the Mithrakana existed in 401, Mithra being an only modestly attested divinity who acquired a higher profile during Artaxerxes II's reign? The word *dasmos* – strongly associated with (Persian) imperial tribute – is not intrinsically inappropriate to the apportionment of sacrificial animals. But the links between 'tribute words' like *baziš* or *bazikara* and animals in the texts from Persepolis itself also appear resolutely secular.[49]

This passage is one of the few in the *Anabasis* which raise the question of Achaemenid-period Persian religion. Three other items come to hand. One is the miraculous crossing of the Euphrates: it conforms to a pattern associating Iranian rulers with water,[50] but Xenophon displays no awareness of it and without other evidence we should happily see the comment simply as a commonplace Greek judgement.

The other two are Orontes' renewal of loyalty oaths at Artemis' altar (*Anab.* 1.6.7) and the Greco-Persian oath scene at 2.2.9. The latter is problematic (especially given a textual uncertainty), while the former recalls Tissaphernes' sacrifice to Artemis at Ephesus – indeed, as Orontes' altar may have been that of Ephesian Artemis in Sardis.[51] Neither episode says anything about Persian deities or practices, but both may confirm the impression of texts in the Fortification Archive (and Greek sources) that the religious environment within which the Persian elite operated could be comparatively inclusive. We do not have to imagine that Orontes simply identified Artemis with Anahita. It was

    hostile. B. Jacobs, 'Der Sonnengott im Pantheon der Achämeniden', in J. Kellens (ed.), *La Religion iranienne à l'époque achéménide* (Gent, 1991), pp. 49–80, reviews the evidence about Persian sun worship.
49. The earliest certain source for Mithra is *FGH* 76 F5. Though represented in personal onomastics, Mithra (like Anahita) only appears in royal inscriptions (alongside Ahuramazda) in Artaxerxes II's reign. See Briant, *Histoire de l'Empire perse*, pp. 262f., 695f., 1024f. *Dasmos* and imperial tribute: cf. O. Murray, '"*ho archaios dasmos*"', *Historia* 15 (1966), pp. 142–56, D. Whitehead, '*Ho neos dasmos*: "tribute" in classical Athens', *Hermes* 126 (1998), pp. 173–88. *Baziš* and *bazikara*: Briant, *Histoire de l'Empire perse*, pp. 452f., G. Aperghis, 'The Persepolis fortification tablets – another look', in Brosius and Kuhrt, *Studies in Persian History*, pp. 35–62.
50. *Anab.* 1.4.18. Iranian kings: T. Nöldeke, 'Geschichte des Ardašir i Papakan', *BIGF* 4 (1878), pp. 22–69 at pp. 48 and 53; Tuplin, 'Xenophon's *Cyropaedia*: education and fiction', p. 125.
51. Loyalty oaths: *Anab.* 1.6.7, 2.2.9. The three victims have Greek parallels in various contexts (but see below), whereas dipping spear-points in the blood recalls Scythian practice and a scene in Aeschylus' *Persae* whose oddness is underlined by Ar. *Lys.* 185f. Some MSS add a wolf to the victims – not very Greek, but Plut. *Mor.* 369F alleges Persian use of wolf's blood in sacrifices to Areimanius. The Artemisium in Sardis: Thuc. 8.108. Xenophon also (*Anab.* 5.3.7) mentions without comment the *neokoros* of the Ephesian Artemisium.

obviously possible in principle for Persians to exchange loyalty oaths without having recourse to non-Iranian deities, and I cannot believe it was impossible to do so in late fifth-century Sardis. There was simply no point in picking the altar of a Greco-Anatolian deity and then pretending it was 'really' sacred to an Iranian one. The venue reflects a real acknowledgement of the authority of a local, very high-status deity.

What can we infer about ways of exploiting resources? The Fortification Archive discloses an imperial landscape worked with forced labour (Cappadocians or Ionians working in Persis must qualify for that term). There is a complex system of collection, storage, and distribution of food commodities.[52] Is there any sign of this in the *Anabasis*?

In book 2, Tissaphernes permits the Greeks to loot villages belonging to Cyrus' mother Parysatis *plēn andrapodōn* – i.e. to take anything except human booty.[53] (The term describes their future fate, without defining their existing status.) Briant has suggested that Tissaphernes makes this exception because the people had a protected status (they were perhaps worker inhabitants of a donated estate) and so their removal would destroy Parysatis' advantage in possessing (the usufruct of) the villages. He does not explain why Tissaphernes' ill-feeling was limited by such legalistic nicety.

But if the produce alone had been assigned to Parysatis (and Xenophon does not say that), the workers may not have been her property. They might even be the King's, and we may be looking at people whom Elamite or Aramaic texts would call *kurtaš* or *gardu*. But perhaps Tissaphernes' motives in exempting them were pragmatic – human booty would simply mean more mouths to feed.[54]

Another group of *andrapoda* do appear in Aeolis, those around Asidates' *tursis* who decamp when the Greeks attack. Two hundred fail to evade capture,

52. R. T. Hallock, 'The evidence of the Persepolis tablets', in *Cambridge History of Iran* II (Cambridge, 1985), pp. 588–609; D. M. Lewis, 'The Persepolis fortification texts', AchHist IV (1990), pp. 1–6, and 'The Persepolis tablets: speech, seal and script', in A. K. Bowman and G. Woolf (eds), *Literacy and Power in the Ancient World* (Cambridge, 1994), pp. 17–32; Briant, *Histoire de l'Empire perse*, pp. 434–87; Aperghis, 'The Persepolis fortification tablets – another look'.
53. *Anab.* 2.4.27.
54. These villages' relation to Parysatis differed from that of the Syrian ones given for 'girdle money' (*Anab.* 1.4.10), the latter being donated to fund a particular need or for a special reason; cf. G. Cardascia, 'La ceinture de Parysatis: une *Morgengabe* chez les Achéménides?', in D. Charpin and F. Joannès (eds), *Marchands, diplomates et empereurs. Études sur la civilisation mésopotamienne offertes à P. Garelli* (Paris, 1990), pp. 363–9. For the terminology cf. Pl. *Alc. I* 123B, Ath. 33F, Cic. *Verr.* 2.3.76. Xenophon's failure to comment on it is notable. On donated villages and linking of estates to provision of specified commodities see Briant, *Histoire de l'Empire perse*, pp. 475f.

but one can draw no firm conclusion about their status. In a region of military colonization[55] it is conceivable that they were an artificially organized labour force.

From time to time the army encountered extra-urban places (generally 'villages') which contained significant amounts of food. Perhaps these places exceeded storage for normal subsistence against bad times, and imply a more organized system. But it is hard to be sure. Descat has claimed that the verb *episitizdesthai* alludes specifically to the drawing of supplies from official store-places. This suggestion is part of a thesis about mercenary-contracts which I have questioned elsewhere, but *episitizdesthai* is used in various contexts and seems intrinsically neutral as to the nature of the food sources. It can certainly allude both to purchase and loot, and when it implicitly refers to Tissaphernes' permission to take supplies from the land, there is no need to detect any bureaucratic overtones.[56]

However, denying any sign of the system being used does not mean denying that some of what was used had been intended for such purposes. The army finds itself at villages associated with a *basileion* where there are supplies of wine and cereal-products 'collected for the satrap of the region'. Briant infers they were a royal depot on the road following the Tigris left bank, and Lendle discerns a Herodotean royal staging post or meeting place. I doubt the troops are on *the* Royal Road here, but where there is a 'palace' there must be a locally significant road network. A traveller with correct documentation would doubtless have been able to draw on official resources. Xenophon, of course, is much more interested in the fact that the food is there and that he can take it than in why it had been accumulated. The same is true earlier where villages which contain 'much corn' also supply sinews and lead from which the Greeks make slings and slingshot. Briant infers an arms depot and presumably an official food-store, but it is a little worrying that we have just been told that Persian slingers use large stones, not metal shot, and I suspect there are simpler (agricultural) explanations of what the Greeks found. Earlier still, I see no reason to identify the 'conspiracy' at Dana as a quarrel about Cyrus' access to official food-stores – this at a place which was inside his *archē*.[57]

---

55. *Anab.* 7.8.14–15, with Tuplin, 'Xenophon and the garrisons', pp. 197f., 213, and Debord, *L'Asie Mineure au IVe siècle*, p. 194 and n. 7. N. Sekunda, 'Achaemenid colonization in Lydia', *REA* 87 (1985), pp. 7–30 (esp. pp. 11f., 26) sees things differently, identifying the troops as recent arrivals or locally hired mercenaries.
56. Mercenary contracts: cf. Tuplin, 'On the track of the Ten Thousand', pp. 342f. Purchase: *Anab.* 7.1.7. Loot: *Anab.* 6.2.4. Permission: *Anab.* 2.3.26.
57. Satrap's supplies: *Anab.* 3.4.31. Corn, sinews, lead: *Anab.* 3.4.17f. Dana: *Anab.* 1.2.20.

What about the measures in which such stores were calculated? Xenophon does cite an exorbitant cereal price in a Persian measure, the kapithe, which is said to equal two Attic choinikes. That measure sounds straightforward, but other Greek texts provide two different conversion rates, viz. a choinix and a half-choinix, and the truth has been much discussed.[58]

The situation is complicated by a newly discovered fact. The kapithe recurs in an Egyptian form as kp*d*, and is attested on a cosmetic jar bearing Xerxes' name, as well as in Hellenistic papyri.[59] Since the jar epigraph reads '12 kp*d*' and its capacity is 1,200 ml, 1 kp*d* = 10 centilitres (0.1 litres), i.e. about one-tenth of a choinix! We thus have a fourth, radically different but authentically Achaemenid-period valuation. In short, Xenophon's firm statement on an objective matter about which he ought to be well informed cannot be validated.

Can we be more exact about roads and routes? Focal places are joined by roads, but the *Anabasis* says little about them. Looking across the River Centrites into Armenia the Greeks see a 'hand-made' road – but Xenophon spoils things by saying it was 'as if it was hand-made'. Was it really *not* artificial at all? By the time the troops use it, the issue has disappeared from the author's mind: we discover only that there were no villages near the river because of Carduchan attacks.[60]

Elsewhere, in less disturbed regions, we encounter rivers which were crossed on boat-bridges. It is nice to have direct attestation of an everyday version of the famous bridges which Darius and Xerxes built over the Bosporus and the

---

58. 1 kapithe = 2 choinikes: *Anab.* 1.5.6. Hesychius s.v.: 1 kapithe = 2 kotylai (i.e. a half-choinix). Polyaenus *Strat.* 4.3.32: a kapetis or kapezis = 1 choinix. A. D. Bivar, 'Achaemenid coins, weights and measures', in *Cambridge History of Iran* II, pp. 610–39, concludes that 10 kapithai = 1 maris = 1 Elamite marriš = 9.28 litres. This would mean that Polyaenus is right and Xenophon wrong – which is worrying: the circumstances might suggest that Xenophon is right or exaggerating, but his figure produces a *less* extravagant (if still exorbitant) price than Polyaenus'. Perhaps Xenophon absorbed the situation in drachmae-per-choinix and translated back into sigloi-per-kapithe, getting relatively familiar sigloi roughly right but misremembering the size of a kapithe – a confusion possibly assisted by disagreement about how many choinikes constituted a day's ration. But an alternative view is that Polyaenus' figure, though embedded in a documentary source, is only a gloss, and therefore not authoritative.
59. The Xerxes jar: Yale BC 2123 = G. Posener, *La Première Domination perse en Égypte* (Paris, 1936), no. 53, with R. K. Rittner, 'The earliest attestation of the kp*d*-measure', in P. der Manuelian (ed.), *Studies in Honor of W. K. Simpson* II (Boston, 1996), pp. 683–8. Posener missed the demotic epigraph when publishing the Xerxes text. Hellenistic papyri: Pap. BM 10225, Pap. Cairo 30791, Pap. Vienna 6257 and unpublished BM papyri (including Pap. BM 10399).
60. 'Hand-made': *Anab.* 4.3.5. No villages near the river: *Anab.* 4.4.1.

Hellespont, but one would gladly hear more about the roads themselves.[61] Two other matters call for comment.

Xenophon seems unaware of Herodotus' Royal Road. How startling this is depends on whether his route ever coincided with the Road, a matter which cannot be explored here. Any coincidence was confined to the journey's start, but it is certain the Greeks crossed such a road in northern Assyria, a crossing which occurs without allusion to Herodotus. There were, of course, other 'royal roads' but this merely increases the chance that the army used one – and with it, our irritation at the characterlessness of Xenophon's record.[62]

Of course, the royal staging-posts may in fact have been too modest to matter to a large army. Something similar may apply to ordinary surveillance and security measures; these are implicit in the unique report that Cyrus guaranteed safe travel by displaying maimed criminals along major routes. Outside that passage we hear little about non-military travellers, perhaps only Epyaxa in her *harmamaxa*, who is a marginal case, as she was on a diplomatic mission about military activity, and the Euphrates valley inhabitants who sell millstones in Babylon.[63]

One famous feature Xenophon's journeys often have is a measurement in parasangs. Examination of the phenomenon suggests the possibility that there were indeed 'milestones' along the road, but this topic remains controversial. I add only two points. First, one possible explanation of the topographical problems presented by Xenophon's journey between Myriandus and the Euphrates is that he got his record confused by misinterpreting the termini to which a milestone figure referred.[64]

---

61. Boat-bridges: *Anab.* 1.2.5, 2.4.13, 24. Not at Thapsacus (*Anab.* 1.4.18), where the contrast between *ploiois* and *pezēi* and comparison with 2.2.3, 5.4.9 suggest ferry boats. Darius and Xerxes: Hdt. 4.83f., 7.33f., with N. G. L. Hammond and L. J. Roseman, 'The construction of Xerxes' bridge over the Hellespont', *JHS* 116 (1996), pp. 88–107.
62. Northern Assyria: *Anab.* 3.5.15. Xenophon's flourish (*Anab.* 3.2.24) about the King building a road fit for four-horse chariots to facilitate Mysian departure conceivably trades on the idea of royal roads.
63. Maimed criminals: *Anab.* 1.9.13. The association of Persians with physical cruelty has little other resonance in the *Anabasis*. The imputation of torture at *Anab.* 3.1.29 is contradicted by 2.6.29, except in the case of Menon (who, Xenophon seems to think, deserved it). Contrast Braun, chapter 3 in this volume. Epyaxa: *Anab.* 1.2.16. Sellers of millstones: *Anab.* 1.5.5.
64. Xenophon has sixty-five parasangs (twelve days) for Myriandus to Thapsacus, i.e. *c.* 325 km, about twice the airline distance to Zeugma or Carchemish (and little better to Meskheneh), and substantially more than 'obvious' routes, e.g. Iskenderun–Aleppo–Jeraklus (265 km) or Iskenderun–Afrin–Kilis–Gaziantep–Birecik (275). So

Second, a recent discussion of Herodotus' Royal Road has identified a route which matches Herodotus' parasang figures with exactitude. It suggests that 'the Achaemenid administration may possibly have erected stones... intended... officially to indicate the distances along the road.' Unfortunately, although the route may be correctly identified, it is not the one which Herodotus' text describes. For the only likely alternative route Herodotus' text gives a distance nine or ten parasangs too short. So the question is still unsolved and there is no immediate prospect of proving anything about publication of parasang figures. [65]

What do we learn about the Persian armies which we would not know already from the sources? An exhaustive account would cover such things as the first literary reference to protective armour for a cavalryman's legs, the first uncontestedly historical scythed chariots, front-line royal participation in battle (imposed by fraternal civil war?) and the principle of royal command from the middle of the battle-line. There is also the question of Xenophon's *gerrophoroi*, the Persian with an 'Amazon-like *sagaris* [or axe]', the performance of Persian and Greek ballistic missiles, the whipping of troops into action even in conditions of tactical advantage.[66] As it is, I draw attention to just three military matters.

The Greek propensity to grotesque estimates of Persian armies is well known. It is startling to find Xenophon guilty. Not only does he report the annihilation of 120,000 men by the Carduchi, but his figures for both armies

---

Cyrus' route was indirect. Manfredi, *La Strada dei Diecimila*, pp. 95ff., provides a reasonable route, but its first stage is too short. Perhaps Xenophon took his distance Myriandus–Chalus from a stone which actually measured the distance from somewhere else and gave a result five parasangs too high.

65. D. H. French, 'The Persian Royal Road', *Iran* 36 (1998), pp. 15–43. A fuller discussion of this will appear in C. J. Tuplin, 'Medes in Anatolia', *Ancient West & East* (forthcoming).
66. Protective leg armour: *Anab.* 1.8.6. Scythed chariots: *Anab.* 1.7.10f., 8.10f. Ctesias ascribed them to Semiramis and Ninus (Diod. 2.5.4); Xenophon has them invented by Cyrus the Great (*Cyrop.* 6.1.29, 2.17, etc.). See A. K. Nefedkin, *Boevye Kolesnitsy i Kolesnichie Drevnikh Grekov* (St Petersburg, 2000), pp. 271ff., 517, and 'On the origin of the scythed chariot', *Historia* (forthcoming). Command from the middle of the battle-line: *Anab.* 1.8.22. Gerrophoroi: *Anab.* 1.8.9, 2.1.4; *Oec.* 4.5; *Cyrop.* 4.5.58, 5.1.2, 7.1.33–4, 8.5.11. Cf. Tuplin, 'Xenophon and the garrisons', p. 221 n. 177. They correspond to the standard Persian infantry of the *Cyropaedia*, not carriers of the large rectilinear shields used at Plataea and Mycale to form protective walls. Sagaris: *Anab.* 4.4.16. The only other foreign-named weapon (the *akinakes*: *Anab.* 1.2.27, 8.29) appears as a gift-of-honour (though also a means of suicide). Ballistic missiles: *Anab.* 3.3.6, 3.4.16f. Whipping troops: *Anab.* 3.4.26; in Hdt. 7.56, 103, 223 (or indeed 7.22 [workers]) reluctance to perform is more predictable.

at Cunaxa are vast, and exceed those in Ctesias and Diodorus.[67] Perhaps the fact that even a militarily literate eye-witness could exaggerate so much casts light upon the urge Greeks felt to surround barbarian armies with fantasy. We are denied a chance to impose a reliable scale upon Persian military resources; and Xenophon's complete neglect of Cyrus' non-Greek forces is particularly vexing.

Numbers aside, one observes that in about six months Artaxerxes assembled an army capable of confronting forces from three Anatolian satrapies and more than 10,000 Greek mercenaries. This achievement is a useful reminder that the King did not always take ages to prepare for war. Debate reported in non-Xenophontic sources about where to face Cyrus (Mesopotamia or Iran) reflects royal psychology and genuine strategic choices, not problems of rapid mobilization. Abrocomas' late arrival is a result of tactical circumstances and (perhaps) indecision on his part, and the even later appearance of troops from Susa and Ecbatana presumably means that they had originated far to the east of those places.[68] The troops that *were* at Cunaxa are only summarily described and the terms of the description are paralleled in other Xenophontic texts. What exactly transpired is obscure; but the impression that only some of Artaxerxes' army engaged (or was expected to) is not alien to other accounts of Achaemenid battles.

Cyrus' employment of Greek mercenaries moves into a different league from *known* precedents, certainly in terms of their assemblage into a single element in a field army and perhaps too in terms of the numbers employed at one time in Western Anatolia. However, the determination to employ Greek

---

67. The massacre by the Carduchi: *Anab.* 3.5.16. Numbers for Cunaxa: Cyrus, 100,000 barbarians, 12,900 Greeks; Artaxerxes: 900,000 (cf. Plut. *Artax.* 7.3) and 150 chariots. Diod. 14.19.7, 22.2 gives Cyrus 70,000 barbarians and 13,000 Greeks, Artaxerxes 400,000 (14.22.2, explicitly quoting Ephorus). There is no preserved Ctesian figure for Cyrus, but the King again has 400,000 (*FGH* 688 F22).
68. Debate about where to face Cyrus: Plut. *Artax.* 7, from Deinon (Stevenson, *Persica*, p. 28). The arrival of Abrocomas: *Anab.* 1.7.12. Calculations show that Abrocomas' journey exceeded Cyrus' in length by anything from 0 to *c.* 165 miles (one combination of data *could* make it shorter), that its excess in time (5 + x days) might have been great enough to accommodate the greatest difference in length without Abrocomas needing to travel more quickly than Cyrus (this would effectively require $x = 5$), and that the chances are good that he was actually travelling more slowly. If the distance they covered was the same and if $x = 1$ (the minimum), then Cyrus travelled about 15 per cent faster. Is that enough to make Abrocomas' behaviour culpable or suspicious? Troops from Susa and Ecbatana: *Anab.* 2.4.25. Briant, *Histoire de l'Empire perse*, p. 648, conjectures that some came from as far as the Indus Valley.

mercenaries remains a feature (not necessarily a weakness) of Persian military planning in the Aegean and East Mediterranean, and one sees something of it after Cunaxa. Behind the slightly indecisive treatment of the Ten Thousand lies a disinclination to liquidate an unparalleled military resource. At the same time one should remember that in Xenophon's Persian Empire not all 'mercenaries' are Greek or (perhaps) in identical contractual relationships.[69]

Finally, some questions about the boundaries of Persian authority and Xenophon's view of its limitations. Briant has suggested that the intermittent periods of satrapal truce and reciprocal relations with the Carduchi are analogous to the King's special 'gift relationship' with Uxians, Cossaeans, Elymians, and Mardians. If so, Xenophon's words are an odd way of putting it, but the situation is equally reminiscent of upland Mysia, Pisidia or (in other sources) Cadusia. However, unlike Mysians, Cadusians and other non-subject people, or indeed the Mardians and Cossaeans, the Carduchi never appear in Persian service, even as mercenaries, as the Cardakes in the fourth century military establishment are not Carduchi. They appear genuinely odd, and one wonders whether there were other Zagros peoples of a similar sort.[70]

In north-eastern Anatolia, too, there is no sign of Persian authority after Armenia. Unfortunately geographical interpretation of the narrative in the relevant part of the text is troublesome – and there *could* be serious disruption of the record. But Chalybians and Taochians are certainly non-subject, though not necessarily hostile (some serve as *misthophoroi*). People further north seem to be more detached, but Xenophon offers no systematic classification: that was left to the interpolator, who designated Macronians, Colchians, Mossynoecans, Coetans, and Tibarenians as 'autonomous' (but ignored Greek cities).[71]

One point may be noted: the guide who showed the Greeks the sea was given 'Persian equipment'. If this means a set of clothing, then a man from Gymnias

69. See J. Roy, 'The mercenaries of Cyrus', *Historia* 16 (1967), pp. 292–323 (esp. pp. 321f.) and chapter 9 in this volume; Stronk, *The Ten Thousand in Thrace*, pp. 37f. There were Greeks in the Levant too: *Anab.* 1.4.3 (Abrocomas). The *Anabasis* uniquely reveals two striking peripheral aspects of the process in the figure of Phalinus, valued expert in *hoplomachia* (*Anab.* 2.1.7), and the availability of families as hostages for a mercenary's good behaviour (1.4.8). Non-Greek mercenaries and those under odd contracts: *Anab.* 4.3.4, 4.4.18, 7.8.15. See Tuplin, 'Xenophon and the garrisons', pp. 222ff.
70. Carduchi: *Anab.* 3.5.16. Uxians, Cossaeans, Elymians, and Mardians: Arr. *Ind.* 40, Strab.11.13.6, Arr. *Anab.* 3.17, Strabo 15.3.4, Diod. 17.91, 19.19, with P. Briant, *Rois, tributs et paysans* (Paris, 1982) and *Histoire de l'Empire perse*, pp. 726ff. Cadusia: *Hell.* 2.1.13; Nic. Dam. 90 F66 (11–16); Diod. 15.8,10, 17.6; Pomp. Trog. *Prol.* 10; Plut. *Artax.* 24; Just. 10.3.70.
71. Disruption of the record: cf. Manfredi, *La Strada dei Diecimila*, pp. 207ff. I have sometimes wondered if there might be a textual lacuna somewhere around *Anab.* 4.6.4–5.Chalybians and Taochi: *Anab.* 5.5.17. Interpolation: *Anab.* 7.8.25.

The Persian Empire 177

saw no problem in wearing costume evocative of Persian power, since costume was a common gift object of high-status Persians, and perhaps to be worn by non-Persians only as a specially conferred right.[72] This fact suggests an autonomous but easy relationship with the Empire.

Along the coast of the Black Sea we find both Greeks and non-Greeks. Once again, however, a direct Persian presence is elusive. The Bithynians invoke Pharnabazus' assistance, but relations with him were often strained and the clear implication of the *Anabasis* is that the region north-east of the Sea of Marmara was not directly controlled imperial territory.[73]

Paphlagonia is particularly interesting. It is technically subject to Persian authority, and the Paphlagonians serving with Cyrus suggest that there was an obligation to serve in satrapal forces. A Paphlagonian satrap supplied Alcibiades with a safe-conduct in *c.* 404; Louis Robert envisaged a satrapal capital at Gangra-*Cankiri* and another has now been posited around Merzifon.[74]

But Alcibiades initially sought safe-conduct from the Dascyleium satrap, and in 334 the Paphlagonians at the Granicus river battle were under Arsites, and Alexander subjected them to Arsites' successor. So any Paphlagonian 'satrap' was surely of a subordinate type. The conjunction of a subordinate position with the large geographical extent of Paphlagonia presumably reflects the coexistence of native rule and the region's marginality from a central or southern Anatolian perspective.[75]

72. 'Persian equipment': *Anab.* 4.7.27. Costume as explicitly Persian/Median gift object: Ael. *VH* 1.22, 32; *Cyrop.* 8.3.1–3, Hdt. 3.84, 7.116, *Esther* 6.6f. (clothing the King had worn, given to a non-Iranian). Implicit: Hdt. 3.20, *I Esdr.* 3.6, *Cyrop.* 1.3.3, Lucian *Hist. conscr.* 39. Iranian clothes and a horse on the Nereid Monument may represent a gift from satrap (in the King's name) to local dynast (W. P. Childs and P. Demargne, *Fouilles de Xanthos* VIII (Paris, 1989), p. 282). Persian clothing as a specially conferred right: cf. Plut. *Alex.* 31.
73. Assistance: *Anab.* 6.4.24, 5.30. The interpolator's designation of Pharnabazus as ruler of the Bithynians (and as nothing else) is a false inference from these passages. Bad relations: *Hell.* 3.2.2.
74. Paphlagonia subject to Persia: *Anab.* 5.6.8. Paphlagonians serving with Cyrus: *Anab.* 1.8.5. This logic presupposes that the region was included in Cyrus' *archē*, presumably via Hellespontine Phrygia (cf. below), which was subject to Cyrus as *karanos*. Safe-conduct: Diod. 14.11. Gangra-*Cankiri*: L. Robert, *A travers l'Asie Mineure* (Paris, 1980), pp. 203f., 265ff. Merzifon: S. Durugönül, 'The sculpture of a lion in the Amasya museum', *AnSt* 44 (1994), pp. 149–52.
75. Safe-conduct: Diod. 14.11.3; Plut. *Alc.* 38. Cavalry: Diod. 17.19.4; Arr. *Anab.* 2.4.1f. (Arsites was satrap of Hellespontine Phrygia). The region or some of it had been non-tributary immediately beforehand: Curt. 3.1.23. Despite the region's marginality, material evidence contains Persian traces. Rock-tombs: H. Von Gall, *Die paphlagonische Felsgräber* (Istanbul, 1966), and 'Medische Felsgräber', *AA* (1966), pp. 19–43, at pp. 40ff., and a lecture summary in *AA* (1967), pp. 585–95. 'Greco-Persian' relief carving: P. Doncel-

Xenophon's evidence is confined to native rule. Corylas' rejection of Persian authority recalls his evidence in the *Hellenica* about Agesilaus and Gyes in 395/4 and the contumacy of Thuys in the 380s. Corylas was encountered around the eastern borders of Paphlagonia (though he also had designs on Sinope), whereas Otys was much further west. It is conceivable they were both regional, not national, rulers: the contexts in which we meet them are ones where misrepresentation is possible, and any assumption that 'Paphlagonia' was united under first Corylas and then Otys contrasts Plutarch's life of Pericles, where territory near Sinope – certainly Paphlagonian – contained 'kings' in the 430s. Alternatively, of course, the emergence of a single Paphlagonian ruler may be what had made rejection of Persian authority possible.[76]

In book 7, Xenophon contrasts the Ten Thousand's temporary seizure of Byzantium ('the first Greek city we have come to') with its failure to seize any 'barbarian *polis*'. Some infer that Xenophon counts Greek cities in northern Anatolia as 'barbarian' – i.e. 'within the Persian Empire'. Xenophon certainly does imply that only when at Byzantium is one back in Greece, but we cannot infer that what is not 'in Greece' is simply in the Persian Empire. At no point does Xenophon hint that Persian authority might be an issue in a Pontic Greek city – unless (doubtfully) in the fact that he uses *dasmos* of the tribute levied by Sinope on local subject cities; but he also calls it *phoros*. Information about Heraclea and Sinope is thin between the Athenian interventions in the 430s/420s and events substantially after 401, and nothing certain is known which links them to Achaemenid rule in this period.[77] The smaller places here

---

Voute, 'Un banquet funeraire perse en Paphlagonie', in R. Doncel and M. Lebrun (eds), *Archéologie et religions de l'Anatolie ancienne (Mélanges en l'honneur du Prof. P. Naster)* (Louvain, 1984), pp. 101–18. Merzifon lion: Durugönül, 'The sculpture of a lion', pp. 149–52. Sinope: silver phiale, oinochoe, alabastron, bowl, cup and spoon (E. Akurgal, 'Vaiselle d'argent de l'époque achéménide', *AE* 2 (1953–4), pp. 11–19); silver phiale (*AK* 6 [1963] 72f.); amphora-rhyton (P. Amandry, 'Toreutique achéménide', *AK* 1 (1958), pp. 38–56). Amisos: two ibex-decorated handles (Amandry, 'Toreutique achéménide', pp. 50f., 54, pl. 26.2, 27.2–3, 28.4); terracotta fragments showing horses with Achaemenid saddle-cloths (P. Amandry, 'Fragments de figurines en terre cuite de style phrygien récent', *RA* (1976), pp. 195–204); mirror and phiale (P. S. Moorey, *Cemeteries of the First Millennium BC at Deve Hüyük* (Oxford, 1980), p. 139).

76. Corylas: *Anab.* 5.6.8. Gyes/Otys/Cotys: *Hell. Oxy.* 21.2; *Hell.* 4.1.1ff. Thuys: Nep. *Dat.* 2–3; *FGH* 115 F179. For Otys, our most easterly reference point is Gordium: *Hell. Oxy.* 22[17].1f. 'Kings' in Paphlagonia in the 430s: Plut. *Per.* 20; cf. Debord, *L'Asie Mineure au IVe siècle*, pp. 110–15, for a recent general treatment.

77. Seizure of Byzantium: *Anab.* 7.1.29. Sinopean *dasmos*: *Anab.* 5.5.10. *Phoros*: *Anab.* 5.5.7. The location of an extensive, high-rank Persian estate in Mariandynian territory by A. B. Bosworth and P. Wheatley, 'The origins of the Pontic house', *JHS* 118 (1998), pp. 155–64, is part of an admittedly speculative construction.

The Persian Empire 179

are even more obscure. Athenian tribute was claimed hereabouts in 425; the end of the Peloponnesian War must be a watershed, but there is no sign that anything actually happened. Relations between army and cities were awkward; I see no reason why Xenophon should have suppressed an awareness that they were technically Persian subjects.

Readers of the *Anabasis* do, however, encounter three Anatolian regions which challenge the authority and interests of the Achaemenid state: Mysia, Pisidia, and Lycaonia. Cyrus had fought the first two, and initially claimed to be targeting Pisidia again in 401. All three appear in a further speech: 'we know the Mysians inhabit many prosperous and large cities in the king's land against the king's wishes, we know the same goes for the Pisidians, and we saw for ourselves that the Lycaonians have seized strong places in the plains and exploit [*karpountai*] their [Persians] land.' This is why, as they traversed Lycaonia, Cyrus let them loot the land as if it were enemy territory.[78]

What Xenophon says about Mysia is odd: 'independent' Mysia should be the upland area which Agesilaus crossed in 395/4, a region lacking *poleis*, let alone large and prosperous ones, until the late Hellenistic era. The remarks about the King building roads in order to encourage Mysian emigration confirm that Xenophon refers to this comparatively inaccessible region, not to lowland Mysia (where small *poleis* were to be found).[79]

The mention of 'large and prosperous cities' of the Mysians is therefore rhetorical overstatement. By contrast, what he says about Lycaonia is quite distinctive. These are not people locked away in a mountain fastness: they have *erumna* (strongholds), but in the plains, and the Lycaonians use them, not to loot Persian land on an occasional basis, but to take over its exploitation – almost as if by internal colonization.[80]

What sense can we make of this? Lycaonia (as usually defined) does include a mountain section immediately west and south of Konya, but the land east of that city through which the army passed is flat. In current conditions this

---

78. Pisidia: *Anab.* 1.1.11, 2.1, 9.14, 2.5.13, 3.2.23; *Hell.* 3.1.13; *Mem.* 3.5.26. Mysia: *Anab.* 1.6.7, 1.9.14, 2.5.13, 3.2.23; *Hell.* 3.1.13; *Mem.* 3.5.26. Pisidia as initial target in 401: *Anab.* 1.1.11, 2.1; Diod. 14.19.6. 'We know the Mysians . . .' *Anab.* 3.2.23. Looting Lycaonia as if it were enemy territory: *Anab.* 1.2.19. I stress this, because here too Briant thinks Cyrus was having trouble with official storage-and-distribution sites.
79. Agesilaus: *Hell. Oxy.* 21(16).1f. General character: T. Wiegand, 'Reisen in Mysien', *AM* 29 (1904), pp. 254–339; L. Robert, *Études anatoliennes* (Paris, 1937), pp. 188, 191f., 267, 379f., 399f. Road-building: *Anab.* 3.2.23.
80. Contrast Debord's picture (*L'Asie Mineure au IVe siècle*, p. 164) of bandits in the upland parts of Lycaonia/Isauria (based on Diod. 18.22 and Strabo 12.6.1f.) – a picture complementary but not identical to Xenophon's.

area is partly cultivated, partly desolate. A century or less ago, conditions were different, and the situation may have varied often over time.[81]

Survey work in the western sector (particularly the Carsamba delta) is revealing that there was extensive Iron Age settlement, with a peak which may fall in the Achaemenid period. French has discussed the pattern of roads through the sector; he is non-committal on fifth-century conditions, but what he identifies as a first-century route passes close to Türkmenhüyük, where there is a particularly large Iron Age site; perhaps this route could have been an established one in Xenophon's time. A more southerly route has been postulated, partly to explain Xenophon's parasang figures, partly in the belief that this was necessary to get water supplies.[82]

However, the Carsamba survey (and doubts that past conditions can be inferred from current ones[83]) suggests the latter point is not cogent. In any event, the army's route traversed 'plains' (Xenophon's term) at least until the vicinity of Ayranci. But, although the landscape is generally open and very flat, there is one big exception, a range of volcanic hills (Karadağ) which lie north of Karaman and dominate the region. The army had to pass fairly close to this range (whether north or south), and I suggest that this is where (at least some of) Xenophon's Lycaonian *erumna* 'in the plains' were located. It is this distinctive geography (a zone of high mountain in the middle of a huge, dead flat plain) that provokes Xenophon's distinctive (if sketchy) picture.

Why was the Lycaonian plain 'enemy territory'? The case differs from Mysia and Pisidia, which were entirely mountainous areas; an additional oddity is that Iconium, 'the last city of Phrygia', is physically in the Lycaonian plain, and so the boundary of control is not prima facie geographical.[84] Perhaps, then, the real boundary was between cultivated land around Iconium (including the Carsamba delta) and open steppe further east on either side of Karadağ, where exploitation by the Lycaonians was predominantly pastoralist.

---

81. K. Belke, 'Lykaonien', *Neue Pauly* 7 (1999), cols 555–6, at col. 555, locates Lycaonia between Tuz Gölü (north), Kara Dag (east), the Taurus (south) and Beyshehir Gölü (west). The evidence (aside from geographical parameters) is mostly Roman; apart from the Taurus, none of the limits need be precisely accurate for Xenophon's context. I am indebted to Geoff Summers and Doug Baird for further information in this paragraph. Strabo 12.6.1f. regarded the Lycaonian plain as a sheep-run.
82. Road pattern: D. H. French, 'The Site of Barata and Routes in the Konya Plain', *EA* 27 (1996), pp. 93–114. Southerly route: Manfredi, *La Strada dei Diecimila*, pp. 65f., Lendle, *Kommentar zu Xenophons Anabasis*, p. 24.
83. In which land near the mountain rim to the south does look much greener than that along the Konya–Karaman highway.
84. 'Enemy territory': *Anab.* 1.2.19. Iconium: *Anab.* 1.2.19.

1. The springs of the Marsyas River in southern Phrygia, 'where Apollo is said to have hung the flayed skin of Marsyas in a cave' (*Anab.* 1.2.8).

2. The Cilician Gates, 'where the entrance was by a waggon-road, mightily sheer and very hard for an army to enter' (*Anab.* 1.2.21).

3. One of the tells near the River Chalus in Syria, on or near the 'villages of Parysatis' (*Anab.* 1.4.9).

4. 'A big settlement named Corsote', near Bashirie by the Euphrates River, 'where they remained three days and provisioned the army' (*Anab.* 1.5.4).

5. The probable site of the Battle of Cunaxa.

6. Ancient Nimrud, probably the 'big deserted city, whose name was Larisa' (*Anab.* 3.4.7).

7. The ford at the Centrites River, the crossing place where 'they saw an old man, a woman and some little girls depositing what looked like bags of clothes under a rock' (*Anab.* 4.3.11).

8. In ancient Armenia they found rich supplies, the first snowfall and 'many fires visible by night' (*Anab.* 4.4.9).

9. 'The Sea! The Sea!': The army would have seen the sea directly above Boztepe, here on the horizon at far right. (*Anab.* 4.8.24).

10. The peninsula of Calpe on the southwest coast of the Black Sea (*Anab.* 6.4.3).

11. Rhododendron luteum in early June in the Pontic woodlands. The source of 'mad honey'.

12. The Great Bustard (*Otis tarda*), 'which flies only a short way, like a partridge, and soon tires. Its flesh was very delicious' (*Anab.* 1.4.2).

facing page

13. A girl dancing the pyrrhiche (*Anab.* 6.1.13), from an Athenian red-figure lekythos (oil vase). Helmeted and armed with shield and spear, she dances wearing short 'boxer trunks'. In the field is a feminine tag 'kalē' with the name Zephyria. Mid fifth century BC.

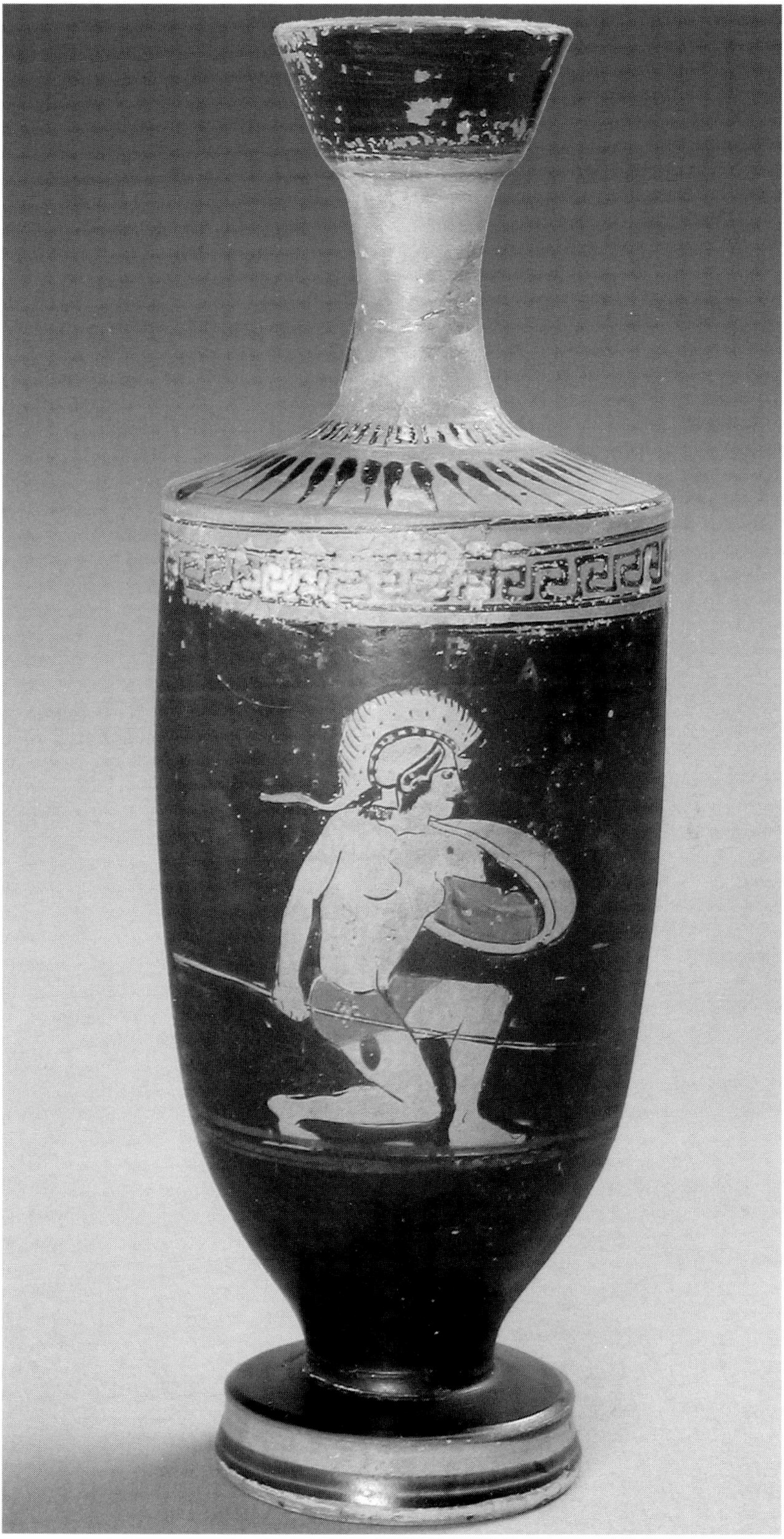

14. A mounted Persian attacking a Greek hoplite soldier on a rolling from a late fifth-century cylinder seal of the Greco-Persian class. Blue chalcedony, height 29mm.

If we are at the interface between two types of land use, does this fact illuminate Persian failure to assert control over one of them? Perhaps it might happen by default (open steppe is harder to control than cultivated land). The area was marginal in macro-geographic terms. Direct land routes between Cilicia and the west were of low strategic (and political) priority because of the Cilician Gates.[85]

Also, the Royal Road either did not run from Dinar to Kayseri through the northern extension of the steppe or was regarded as securely insulated from (Xenophon's) Lycaonia by distance (the Road's route lies *c*. 100 km north of Karada). Furthermore, the impression of aggressive independence may be misleading. Xenophon was glad to categorize Lycaonia as hostile but his excuse was Cyrus' treatment of it as 'enemy territory' – and Cyrus' attitude in the unusual circumstances of 401 may have subverted the normal pattern of life.[86]

Xenophon cites Lycaonia (and Mysia and Pisidia) to show that Achaemenid power has limits. I end, therefore, with some remarks on the question of whether the *Anabasis* expresses a view about the defeatability of the Persian Empire.

There *is* one plain-speaking passage, about the Empire being vulnerable because of size (an idea also found in Isocrates). There are also various more or less implicit allusions to a strategy of Greek conquest or settlement, while the possibility of exploitable Babylonian dissidence seems taken for granted. It is conceivable that Xenophon's allusions to *oikoumenai poleis* were meant to suggest Asia was not wholly inhospitable to urban existence.[87]

The effect of the Ten Thousand's story in Greece is explicitly broached on two occasions and we know it formed part of Panhellenist argument. Also, there is a possible echo of Gorgias' *Olympikos logos*, another hint, perhaps, at this agenda. Evocations of the Persian Wars of 480 are also appropriate.[88] But there are things to be said on the other side.

There is an evident ambiguity about 'Hellenism', about supposed Greek 'superiority', practically or morally. It appears in many guises, not least in the

---

85. Cf. *Anab.* 1.2.21. For a radically different view of how Cyrus (and others?) crossed the Taurus, cf. F. Williams, 'Xenophon's Dana and the passage of Cyrus' army over the Taurus Mountains', *Historia* 45 (1996), pp. 284–314.
86. The interpolator (*Anab.* 7.8.25) conjoins Lycaonia with Cappadocia as the province of Mithradates.
87. Plain-speaking: *Anab.* 1.5.9; cf. Isoc. 4.141. On the significance of *oikoumenai poleis*, cf. Tuplin, 'On the track of the Ten Thousand', p. 335: I feel less confident about this now.
88. Gorgias: *Anab.* 3.2.12; cf. Gorg. 82 A1. Cf. also *Ages.* 1.7f.: the contest is to be about Asia, not Greece. Persian Wars: *Anab.* 1.2.9f., 3.2.11.

environs of the episodes about founding a colony in books 5 and 6. They disclose Greek unwillingness to settle and include examples of strikingly unpleasant Greek behaviour. The remark in book 1 about Persian vulnerability to attack is followed instantly by an episode in which Greeks fight among themselves. As for the attractions of life in Asia, the lack of olives at Calpes Limen or the sickness-inducing palm-'brains' of Mesopotamia show that even places apparently attractive for settlement present problems for Greek visitors.[89]

As presented in the *Anabasis*, mercenaries are apt to be disorderly and ill-suited to a Panhellenist agenda involving colonial settlement. John Dillery has recently seen the *Anabasis* as a Panhellenist text, but as one which propounds a different Panhellenism from the Athenocentric or Isocratean variety or a simple scheme of plunder-and-return. Myself, I wonder if it is a Panhellenist text at all. At any rate, any inclination to assume that Xenophon has a straightforward view about the topic should be discarded. As a general rule of thumb, beyond an irreducible core of moral and technical principles, Xenophon found much to be uncertain about. This attitude is a respectable one and is not proved inapplicable in this context by the later success of a pathologically self-confident Macedonian prince, Alexander the Great.

The *Anabasis*, then, provides material on a wide range of topics connected with the Achaemenid Empire. What it offers is sometimes similar to what we find elsewhere, except that it relates to a different time or place or is the earliest surviving record. But on other occasions, although the content is not wholly novel, the context is remarkable for one reason or another and adds some colour or circumstantiality to what would otherwise be a bald record. In some cases we find information which is genuinely distinctive or prompts a new understanding of other evidence. The material touches major topics briefly and tangentially: the *Anabasis* does not exist to offer a systematic account of the Achaemenid Empire or Persian political and social customs;[90] Xenophon not only neglects landscape in a Romantic sense but also evinces little positive awareness of an imperial landscape as such. But how much such awareness does Thucydides promote of the Athenian imperial landscape? We had better not draw hasty inferences about the 'invisibility' of Persian rule.

---

89. *Anab.* 5.6.15–34 (the debates at Cotyora), 6.4.1–6.38 (Calpes Limen). Bad behaviour: *Anab.* 5.7.13–33, 6.6.5–34. Olive dearth: *Anab.* 6.6.1. Nauseous palms: *Anab.* 2.3.16.
90. A rare hint at personal social behaviour is *Anab.* 2.6.28: Menon was a close associate of Ariaeus because the latter 'took pleasure in handsome youths'. We need not infer Ariaeus was unusual among Persians in this (cf. Hdt. 1.135: Persians learned from Greeks to have sex with boys); in context it is Menon whom Xenophon wishes to present as aberrant.

Although there are all sorts of things about which we should like more data, it is quite hard to identify broad aspects which are wholly untouched.[91] Making sense of the Persian material in the *Anabasis* requires the context which is provided by all the information in other sources covering over two hundred years of Achaemenid history. But the experiences of some Greek mercenaries during two years of that long history do have a good deal to offer in return.

---

91. Despite Tamos' ships (*Anab.* 1.2.21, 4.2), the naval arm of the Achaemenid military system is a possible example.

6 Sex, Gender and the Other in Xenophon's Anabasis

ROBIN LANE FOX

It seemed to me that I had landed at Cerasus from the Argo and had wandered up from the coast into those woods and had eaten myself full of ripe cherries and of azalea honey so that I lay in a swoon, pretending to be dead ... and I saw that the Mossynoici did not change at all for they were still having intercourse with women in public as they lay about the woods and I thought, this would never do if it was Hyde Park. I wondered which of the Argo heroes I was ... and I do not know if I was a hero or one of their mistresses ... since the mistresses of heroes used to go everywhere about the world with them and we do not really hear enough of their doings as they are taken for granted in histories. They went on the Crusades ... and they marched with Xenophon's Ten Thousand and must have got drunk on the Trebizond honey and they marched all about France with our army during the Hundred Years' War and with Wellington's army about the Peninsula, where the Spanish and the Portuguese soldiers liked them very much, and with the Royalist troops during our own Civil Wars, where Cromwell did not like them at all, so he had them massacred. Yes, I thought, women have been everywhere with armies, making themselves useful, because soldiers need love, but now the women who go with armies are not encouraged to be so useful to them, they are called ATs and Wrens and WRACs and are kept behind the battle lines and are only a small consolation to the troops, though soldiers still need love.

Rose Macaulay, *The Towers of Trebizond*

I

In winter 401, the Ten Thousand's retreat took them into the territory of the Carduchi, people who are still claimed as direct ancestors by the local Kurds. They appear to have marched up the valley of the river Bohtan Su and to have reached the lower slopes of Herakol Dag. Their main road ahead was blocked by a strong local force and a bypass was badly needed. So they turned to two local guides whom Xenophon had prudently ambushed for the purpose.[1]

1. *Anab.* 4.1.23–4.

The guides' reaction is a grim reminder of local expectations of an army's passage. Each one was questioned separately. The first one denied that he knew any other route except the one which was held by the army. Even when 'a great many threats were applied to him', he held to his story. He was then slaughtered in front of the other guide. The second guide then explained the reason for the first man's denial. He had a married daughter living in the neighbourhood, and, although there was a passable route nearby, he had denied it.

This incident rightly impressed the Victorian novelist George Gissing.[2] Not only did the guide give his life for the sake of his daughter. He reminds us of fears which other Greek narratives gloss over. Was he afraid that the husband would be killed and his daughter widowed? Surely he was also afraid that she would be captured and raped. Rape by foreign soldiers is a widespread modern war crime, but it is rarely reported as a Greek practice in the Greek historians.[3] There is, however, a reason. After a victory, an enemy's womenfolk would become captive slaves and would be at the sexual whim of their captors: the details of such slavery did not need spelling out. The Ten Thousand were in non-Greek territory and they continued to take slaves as they went.

Nonetheless, the troops were not simply brutes. At other times they showed courtesy, a combination which Xenophon appreciates in all his writings. Outside an Armenian village, a few days later, the Spartan Chirisophus met 'women and girls' by the water spring, that regular point of female contact with strangers in the ancient world. Chirisophus had an interpreter with him who spoke 'Persian'.[4] If Xenophon is being precise about the language, in Armenia even the girls understood Persian. They duly escorted Chirisophus and his men inside the village, young Nausicaas in a foreign land.

---

2. G. Gissing, *The Private Papers of Henry Ryecroft* (London, 1903), ch. 9: 'it would not be easy to express more pathos than is conveyed in these few words. Xenophon himself, one may be sure, did not feel it quite as we do, but he preserved the incident for its own sake and there in a line or two shines something of human love and sacrifice, significant for all time.'
3. Valuable evidence and caution in W. K. Pritchett, *The Greek State at War: Part V* (Berkeley, 1991), pp. 238–42 and for the continuous enslaving, 401–399 BC, the invaluable table on pp. 516–18; Alexander is a good exception (Plut. *Alex.* 22.4).
4. *Anab.* 4.5.10; for the language, see especially P. Bernard, 'Les Origines thessaliennes de l'Arménie', in *Topoi Supplément 1. Recherches récentes sur l'empire achéménide* (1997), pp. 131–216, at pp. 143–61; R. Schmitt, 'Iranisches Lehngut in Armenien', *REArm* 17 (1983), pp. 51–72.

If read closely, Xenophon's *Anabasis* is extremely rewarding for historians of gender relations. So far, it has not been exploited in this way:[5] I wish to bring out some of the evidence, much of which is for relationships, not rape. There are relationships between men and women, but there are also those between men and men. There is an imbalance to most of them which Xenophon does not dwell on. We need to be alert where he inclines us to see something fine or really rather sporting.

After considering these 'dependent liaisons', I will turn to the Greeks' more general perceptions of 'others'. Here, Xenophon has been accused of 'ethnocentric ethnography', as if he tells us more about Greek perceptions than about foreign realities, or even as if he views other cultures within a very limited framework, or code.[6] Here too, the *Anabasis* is richer and more suggestive than many texts written by soldiers about their exploits.

With both these questions before us, we need to ask first what behaviour is distinctively masculine in the *Anabasis* and how much of it is distinctively Greek? The Ten Thousand's masculinity is clearly marked. It is they alone who fight: they make all the speeches and hold the meetings. Greek women were present on the march, but only as slaves. The one exception occurs at the end of the march, the meeting with the expatriate Greek female, Hellas. Evidently she spoke out and initiated actions: she 'entertained' the Greek generals and she directed them to a military target. Yet she was an amazing anomaly, the descendant, surely (though some dispute it) of the great Themistocles, who would be in her mid-sixties or more, and the surviving widow of the Greek Gongylus, an arch-Medizer, the very same one (in my view) who had received an estate in Persian-ruled Asia Minor in the 470s.[7] By birth and marriage, old Hellas had local property and power, while sharing the Ten Thousand's Greek language. She was resoundingly Greek by name, but not by social position: she is a great exception, who does not invalidate the rule.

In the Ten Thousand's culture, prominent male behaviour also included drinking, hunting, and athletic sports. Together with fighting, meeting, and public speaking, this culture went back to the male aristocracies of archaic

---

5. In other works by Xenophon, cf. P. A. Cartledge, 'Xenophon's women: a touch of the other', *Liverpool Class. Papers* 3 (1993), pp. 5–14.
6. P. A. Cartledge, *The Greeks* (Oxford, 1993), p. 44: 'how travel narrows the mind, a classic piece of ethnocentric ethnography.'
7. *Anab.* 7.8.8–9, with J. P. Stronk, *The Ten Thousand in Thrace* (Amsterdam, 1995), pp. 291–2, for the family tree I prefer: as Themistocles did not reach Asia until 465, Hellas as his daughter would be in her sixties (not seventies) in 399. Contrast C. J. Tuplin in this volume, p. 164 n. 33.

Greece. It had already been in place for Homer's Greek heroes and while some of the niceties developed, it filtered downwards socially among other Greek males after the eighth century. How much of it was distinctive to Greek males only?

Of course non-Greek males made speeches too, but they tended to be proclamations by a king or leader. Naturally, no non-Greek could deploy rhetoric: Persian nobles, like other barbarians on the march, were illiterate and had never had a teacher in the arts of speaking (unlike Menon and Proxenus, two pupils of the great Gorgias). Nor is there any record of long debates among participants on the Persian side, let alone of 'free speech'. When the wife of the ruler of Cilicia, Epyaxa, meets Cyrus, she does converse with him privately: the Greek troops' gossip was that Cyrus was having sex with her.[8] Only Greek males ever voted after a debate, and in due course they did so by holding up their hands individually. No non-Greek, of course, ever did such a thing. Spartan members of the army would have had to learn to join in too, since a show of individual hands was not Spartan practice at home, either.[9]

What about warfare? Obviously, Asia's men fight too but in Xenophon's *Hellenica* we have the superb sketch of the female Mania, 'woman-as-satrap', who succeeded to her husband's command, not least by the necessary art of gift-giving.[10] During her rule, she took several towns but not even she would fight in person: she would watch from her Oriental wagon (like Epyaxa the Cilician in the *Anabasis*) while her Greek mercenaries fought on her behalf. Inland in Asia, however, the Ten Thousand did entertain the possibility of finding Eastern women as warriors. Like Alexander the Great and his army, they were open to a sighting of Amazons. Whereas Alexander's troops did actually see foreign women on horseback and interpreted them as Amazons (they were assumed to be likely to rape them, too), the Ten Thousand saw only a suggestive type of weapon. They captured an 'axe' (or *sagaris*) in southern Armenia which looked like one of the axes carried typically by Amazons. Plainly they knew the paintings on walls and pottery which defined Amazons back in Greece. Actually, the axe turned out to belong to a Persian-speaking man, another proof of a Persian's 'womanish' side.[11]

8. *Anab.* 1.2.12 (*elegeto* is surely army gossip).
9. *Anab.* 5.6.33: G. E. M. de Ste Croix, *Origins of the Peloponnesian War* (1972), pp. 348–9.
10. *Hell.* 3.1.10–28; E. Baragwanath, 'Xenophon's foreign wives', *Prudentia* 34 (2002), pp. 125–58.
11. *Anab.* 4.4.16; Arr. *Anab.* 7.13 with E. Baynham, 'Alexander and the Amazons', *CQ* 51 (2001), esp. pp. 120–1, though I cannot accept her suggestion of 'prostitutes who had been taught to ride and who were playing out a contrived fantasy', nor that Alexander

Like warfare, hunting was not predominantly Greek either, but everywhere it was a sport for men only. If the *Anabasis* had described Persians at ease they would certainly have been hunting vigorously in the parks, or *paradeisoi*, which Xenophon mentions on the march up-country. Was it during the Ten Thousand's quick passage through Syria that Xenophon learned of the locals' unsporting habits, as they put poisoned bait down for bigger game on the hillsides?[12] This journey, after all, was his only visit to the area. In Armenia, he is explicit. He troubles to mention that the son of a village chieftain was away hunting hares, although he had only been married for eight days. Here was a young man, one feels, who was after Xenophon's own heart.[13] When the Greeks on the march tried and failed to catch ostriches, they might, by contrast, seem rather amateurish. The right answer is to get on the outside of the bird and turn it and then hunt it with hounds on horseback, as the noble Greek Synesius exemplified in Libya with greater panache some eight hundred years later, probably lassoing his prey.[14]

Both Greeks and non-Greeks, then, shared a keen hunting culture. But between Greeks and Persians there was a slight difference in its scope. Xenophon is not merely being picturesque when he recalls how some of the Greek soldiers once chased the unpopular market supervisor Zelarchus during their time at Cerasus. Someone 'viewed' him and then 'holloaed' aloud, whereupon more of the soldiers chased after him 'as if a wild boar or stag had appeared'.[15] If something animal moved, the Ten Thousand would have had a go at it. In Persian armies, soldiers were more likely to leave the first shot to a noble or a King. They were used to a formal and socially stratified practice of hunting which centred on kings and nobles in their special coverts. Spartans or Arcadians would simply hunt when their individual fancy took them.[16]

What about drinking parties? Among the Greeks, these parties were male occasions, their symposia after dinner: the only females present would be

sent them away 'because he wished to maintain exclusive rights'. For later 'sightings', Plut. *Pomp.* 35.3; Strabo 11.5.1 (Theophanes); App. *Mith.* 103, and R. Lane Fox, *Alexander the Great* (London, 1973), p. 545.
12. *Cyneg.* 11.1.
13. *Anab.* 4.5.24.
14. *Anab.* 1.5.3: Synesius *Epist.* 5 with D. Roques, *Synésios de Cyrène et la Cyrénaique de Bas Empire* (Paris, 1987), pp. 413–14; F. Joannès, 'L'Itineraire des Dix-Mille en Mésopotamie', in P. Briant (ed.), *Dans les pas des Dix-Mille*, [*Pallas* 43] (Toulouse, 1995), pp. 187–8, on ostrich hunts here in the eleventh–ninth centuries BC.
15. *Anab.* 5.7.24.
16. R. Lane Fox, 'Ancient hunting from Homer to Polybius', in G. Shipley and J. Salmon (eds), *Human Landscapes in Classical Antiquity* (London, 1996), pp. 119–53, esp. pp. 139–41.

slaves, for sex, music, or both. Far from home, Greek males still liked to respect the proprieties to which they had been brought up. In Armenia, some of the troops 'went native' and sucked the sweet, strong barley-wine which they found in underground houses by drawing it up with a straw, not with a cup. All sorts of meat accompanied their drinking. But over in Chirisophus' company, there was no such crude 'mess practice'.[17] Memorably, we read of his men wearing improvised party wreaths of dry hay (a Greek party guest needed a wreath) and indicating to young Armenian boys in sign language, 'as if to the deaf and dumb', what proper waiters were required to do. It is particularly relevant that Chirisophus' men were Spartans. In their dinner messes at home, Spartans expected Spartan boys to wait on them and pour their wine. In their absence they used local boys instead, keeping up Spartan standards with the only 'dumb waiters' available.[18]

Near Cotyora leading Greeks held a similar all-male party for those Paphlagonians who were showing signs of being philhellene.[19] Again, they improvised a familiar sort of etiquette. Reclining at a drinking party was the Greek fashion, but the usual couches (*clinai*) were unavailable. So they used *stibades* (mattresses) and reclined on the floor instead. Once again, their guests were males only. Drinking cups were also usual for Greeks participants, and during the march precious 'cups' had been acquired as booty: the 'cups' in Asia were always a treasure which Greeks recognized, one well worth taking. Here, however, there was scope to make a concession to the guests' non-Greek habits. They used drinking-horns, which were much more amusing. Perhaps they were hollowed-out horns of real animals, prototypes of the *rhytons* of precious metal which appear (not always with known provenance) in modern collections.[20]

Among Greeks, drinking was social, and parties were for men only. When the exceptional old lady, Hellas, 'entertained' the remains of the army, did she herself appear for any drinking party which took place? It is most unlikely, because even in barbarian company, the Greeks found that drinking parties

---

17. *Anab.* 4.5.30–3.
18. Plut. *Lycurg.* 12; Xen. *Lac. Pol.* 3.5 and 5; Athen. 4.139D (absence of *stephanoi* at the Hyacinthia is seen as exceptional); J. N. Bremmer, 'Adolescents, symposion and pederasty', in O. Murray (ed.), *Sympotica* (Oxford, 1990), pp. 135–49; N. R. E. Fisher, 'Drink, *hybris*, and the promotion of harmony', in A. Powell (ed.), *Classical Sparta: Techniques behind the Success* (London, 1989), pp. 26–50, at pp. 33–4.
19. *Anab.* 6.1.1–13.
20. George Ortiz, *In Pursuit of the Absolute: Art of the Ancient World* (1996), nos 152–4: 'allegedly from the region of the Black Sea'.

were for men only. The classic instance is at Seuthes' court in Thrace. Xenophon's fine description is aware, of course, of the hearty departures from Greek etiquette. There were big drinking-horns here too and after drinking a toast the proposer sprinkled the man whom he toasted with the remaining drops of wine, an un-Greek bit of behaviour.[21] The guests all had to sit on chairs and it was an honour to be one of the 'chair-men' (*endiphrioi*). Since Homer, this sort of seating had been long lost in Greece; in Macedonia little iron replicas of dining chairs and tables attest it there archaeologically *c.* 500, but by King Archelaus' day the fashion had changed.[22] In Seuthes' non-Greek common room, the eating and drinking were merged into a single barbarian whole. Little three-legged tables with food on them were set before each seated guest. The king had a most un-Greek habit: he threw bits of bread across the room to his guests and then did the same with bits of meat. Bun-throwing is hilariously barbarian, but it was such fun that almost all the guests, including Greeks, joined in. As dinner ended, trumpeters then blew on ox-hide horns: Seuthes' court was a fine place for hornblowers. But here, too, drinking had its etiquette and again it was strictly for men only, even though Seuthes did have a wife. Xenophon has no reason to make the point, but we should picture Alcibiades, 'friend of Seuthes', in a similar setting about five years earlier while he was away from Athens in disgrace.[23] No doubt he was sprinkled with wine drops, too, and bombarded with bits of bread and meat.

Drinking parties were also important for Persian satraps, and Alcibiades could have told us much more about them than the Greek generals who stayed on Xenophon's march. In Armenia, they did capture the satrap Tiribazus' tent with its cups and silver-footed couches.[24] But the satrap was not there to entertain them and we hear no more about these spoils: did the couches make it with the Greeks all the way to the Black Sea coast? Clearly, satraps did keep up a dining culture in the provinces, even in Armenia. At dinners they were also used to dancers, as Bagoas the eunuch later showed Alexander the Great. Greek males were very capable dancers too, as their Paphlagonian guests witnessed. But the art was not unique to them: expertise was shown by other barbarian males, Mysians as well as some very adept Thracians. One of the best snapshots on the entire expedition is the Thracian Seuthes, well tanked up but not

---

21. *Anab.* 7.3.22 and 32.
22. R. A. Tomlinson, 'Furniture in the Macedonian tombs', in *Ancient Macedonia* vol. 3 (Thessaloniki, 1993), pp. 1495–9, citing the Sindos graves.
23. Diod. Sic. 13.105.3. Compare Dercyllidas, also a guest of Seuthes in 398 BC: *Hell.* 3.2.9.
24. *Anab.* 4.4.21; compare the silver couches for Alexander's guests in 324, Chares *FGH* 125 F4.

Sex, Gender and the Other in Xenophon's Anabasis

actually drunk and fumbling, standing up from his chair, shouting a war-cry and jumping to one side 'very nimbly, as if avoiding a missile'.[25]

The Greek males had a war-cry too, but what most amazed their Paphlagonian guests was that all the dancers at their party performed while carrying weapons.[26] Thereupon, one of the barbarian dancers, a Mysian, had a word with one of the Arcadians (the Mysian, then, could speak some Greek). The Arcadian owned a dancing girl as a slave, and was persuaded to allow her to be brought in and dressed up 'as finely as possible' (like the preceding Arcadian dancers). With a light shield, she danced a Greek war dance, the *pyrrichē*, 'gracefully'.

This slave girl raises some fascinating questions. Had she followed the army throughout, despite the repeated attempts to diminish its baggage? Or had she been acquired more recently, perhaps from an owner of dancing girls in one of the Greek cities by the Black Sea? She might, perhaps, have learned the war dance by watching her male captors, but if she had been with her owner throughout the march, she had probably learned the dance earlier in her Greek career at home. For we have Greek vase paintings (from *c.* 440–400, especially) which show women dancing this war dance and carrying a shield or weaponry.[27] We might suspect a joke in these pictures or an element of fantasy, but the Arcadian's dancing girl was so accomplished and the war dance was plainly one of her existing female skills. She was not told to 'try it on' as an improvised joke for the occasion. To judge from vase paintings, her costume would have been see-through, at most. The Mysian, plainly, had seen her perform this dance already, and so he sent for her in order to bemuse the Paphlagonians even more. After the applause, they duly asked the Greeks in all seriousness if their women fought together with them. The Greeks told them yes, 'these are the very women who routed the Persian king from his camp'. The display then ended in a gender joke which made fun of 'womanish' Persians: the Greeks liked to wind their barbarian visitors up.

In each of these spheres, Greek and non-Greek males shared a similar masculine culture, although the etiquettes varied. But Greeks had two peculiarities: competitive athletics and theatrical drama. Near Trapezus, they celebrated their return with athletic games, on the Spartan Dracontius' stony choice of

25. *Anab.* 7.3.33.
26. *Anab.* 6.1.11.
27. J.-C. Poursat, 'Les Représentations de danse armée dans la céramique attique', *Bulletin de correspondance hellénique* 13 (1968), pp. 560–615, esp. pp. 586–615, and P. Ceccarelli, *La pirrica nell'antichita greco-romana* (Pisa, 1998), esp. pp. 58–80. I owe this to Robert Parker.

hillside. They organized events which they knew from their famous Games back home, although they omitted chariot-racing (they lacked the equipment and terrain) and the lengthy pentathlon.[28] The long-distance race was monopolized by Cretans, 'more than sixty of them', a great sight, as Cretans were such specialists in this field.[29] There was boxing and wrestling, too, events which were surely for Greeks only, and then there were the horse-races, which were slowed up amusingly by the hilly ground. Back in Greece, there would be boys' athletic events as well as men's, but where were boys to be found in an army up at Trapezus? A few had followed the camp, but 'most' of the boy entrants were 'captives, taken by the spear'.[30] In the interests of a varied Greek programme, barbarian slave boys were allowed to compete. In Greece, races were usually for free persons only, but the Greeks on Dracontius' hillside would surely not agree with a modern judgement that there was 'something subversive in the spectacle... very remarkable... an eccentric and little-noticed competition'.[31] To enjoy the usual Greek variety, they had simply wanted a boys' race and what other boys were available? The boys' race was the short *stadion*, about two hundred metres, the sort of distance which boys might attempt the world over. But the long-distance race was for Greeks, the real experts.

The next Greek conquerors in Asia, Alexander's men, also enjoyed this same combination: horse-racing and an athletic contest, a *hippikos kai gymnikos agōn*. This entertainment was put on at Alexander's command, but at points which were also remote and significant. Our sources mention one on the River Jaxartes, the furthest ever Greek racing known to us, others at the Indus and at Taxila and another (most significantly) after the decision to turn back at the Hyphasis. The Jaxartes (Alexander wrongly believed) marked the border between Asia and Europe, while the Indus and Taxila were the first big stops in India and the Hyphasis was the last stop on the march east. But Alexander also put on drama for his followers all across Asia, and personally sent home for texts by Aeschylus, Sophocles, and Euripides.[32] Among Xenophon's men, Leon of Thurii is said (correctly?) to have expressed his wish to float homewards like Homer's Odysseus on his back.[33] Otherwise, nobody is said to have

---

28. *Anab.* 4.8.27.
29. H. Bengtson, 'Aus der Lebensgeschichte eines griechischen Distanzlaüfers', Symb. Osl. XXXII (1956), pp. 35–9.
30. *Anab.* 4.8.27; Pritchett, *The Greek State at War: Part V*, p. 169 on *aichmalotoi*.
31. M. Golden, *Sport and Society in Ancient Greece* (London, 1998), pp. 1–4.
32. Arr. 4.4.1, 5.3.6, 5.8.3, 5.29.2 on games and horse-races; on drama, Plut. *Alex.* 29.1–6; B. Snell, *Scenes from Greek Drama* (Berkeley, 1964), pp. 129–38; Plut. *Alex.* 8.3.
33. *Anab.* 5.1.1.

sung or referred to a poem or chanted any words from a dramatic chorus, even though Athenians were present and by the 390s a theatre could be found in quite a humble town in Arcadia.[34] When the troops reached Cotyora, they stopped for six and a half weeks and held religious processions 'people by people' (Arcadians, Argives, and so forth). This fine 'performance archive' of Greek religion is unfortunately lost to us, though it would have included hymns to the gods. But of drama, even of pantomime, there is not a whisper, not even in the Greek cities to which the soldiers returned. Were the Ten Thousand so totally untheatrical, or is this impression due to 'colonel' Xenophon himself, rather than being shared with him? For Xenophon is the Greek author who shows next to no interest in the theatre or in the Athenian dramas around him.[35]

II

In this general context of male behaviour, there is the particular sphere of sexual relations. Xenophon had heard and admired Socrates and throughout the *Anabasis* it is a nice question how far he conforms to Socrates' (probable) teachings. On the matter of sex, the Socratic ideal, at least, is clear. Love between men is fine, but not if it is physically focused and consummated. One aim of Xenophon's remarkable *Symposium* is to emphasize this Socratic principle in the most controversial company, among Athenian high society, including the very grand Callias and the much discussed Autolycus, a boy at the time. Autolycus had even been the object of an entire Attic comedy in his youth, so there was plenty of scandal, no doubt, for Xenophon to counter and explain away.[36] There was plenty, too, to explain away in Sparta. In his *Constitution of the Spartans*, Xenophon answers the case that Spartan soldiers have sex together by denying that they sink below spiritual love and admiration. In the *Symposium*, 'gays in the army' are acknowledged as a fact in a few Greek communities (Boeotia and Elis). However, male lovers are placed together here in battle (he tells us) so that each will fight harder 'out of respect' (*aidōs*). Among Athenians, says Xenophon, this practice is the object of reproach.[37]

34. Diod. Sic. 15.40.2.
35. P. J. Wilson reminds me of *Oec.* 8.18–20 where 'Ischomachus praises household pots when arranged tidily like a chorus' (probably a dithyrambic one).
36. By Eupolis in 421/0, with K. J. Dover, *Greek Homosexuality* (London 1978), p. 147.
37. Xen. *Lac. Pol.* 2.12–13; *Symp.* 8.32–3; compare Plat. *Symp.* 182 A–B.

When he turns to history, these Socratic and 'Spartan' ideals are not in evidence. Outside his idealized *Constitution*, the real Spartans whom he describes are predictably carnal. They were conditioned by their male upbringing, with its inevitable pederasty, and outside Sparta they ran true to form. In 377/6, on Euboea, the Spartan commander Alcetas took time off to busy himself with a boy from Oreus, a fine and noble one, who was attending him: his Theban prisoners there took military advantage of his absence 'on other business'.[38] In Asia, Xenophon's hero, King Agesilaus, fell for the son of Spithridates, putting a more tangible interpretation on what Sir William Tarn would later idealize as the 'brotherhood of man'. In his panegyric of Agesilaus, Xenophon had to insist on Agesilaus' self control here after just one kiss.[39] As for the *Anabasis*, the cardinal examples are two Spartans who dealt with the Ten Thousand after their return to the Hellespont. At Byzantium, the Spartan admiral Anaxibius was most unwelcoming to the troops in accordance with Spartan policy at the time. Ten years later, in 389/8, this same Anaxibius contrived to return to a command in the area but was ambushed by the Athenian general, Iphicrates. He was killed together with his sex-boy, or *paidika*, who died bravely beside him. Presumably the boy was a local boy whom Anaxibius had acquired on campaign. No doubt he had had others before, at the time when Xenophon and the Greeks bargained with him at Byzantium.[40]

There is also the indelicate question of Thibron, the Spartan commander who recruited the remaining Greek troops at the expedition's end. The question of 'male love' in Xenophon and his texts has been very well studied recently by Clifford Hindley, but in this case he presses the explicit meaning, I think, too far.[41] Eight years after recruiting the Ten Thousand, Thibron met his own death in Asia Minor. According to Xenophon in the *Hellenica*, he was busy 'after breakfast' with Thersander the *aulos*-player (oboist). As Hindley has excellently observed, the manuscripts do not support the modern emendation that Thibron was busy 'throwing the discus' (*diskeuōn*). Rather, he was 'camping apart' (*diaskēnōn*). Xenophon explains that this *aulos*-player, Thersander, 'laid claim to physical strength, seeing that he was a laconizer'. Hindley interprets this 'laconizing' as an explicit taste for sodomy. This sense

---

38. *Hell.* 5.4.56–7.
39. *Hell. Oxy.* 21.4; C. Hindley, 'Eros and military command in Xenophon', *CQ* 44 (1994), pp. 347–66, esp. pp. 363–5.
40. *Hell.* 4.8.39.
41. Hindley, 'Eros and military command', pp. 351–60; *Hell.* 4.8.18; C. Hindley, 'Xenophon on male love', *CQ* 49 (1999), pp. 74–99.

of the word is indeed attested in later lexicographers who had evidently found it in Athenian comedy. But Xenophon is never so blatant about sexual tastes and comedy's usage is not his here. Nonetheless, Hindley's general point, I think, is right: a sexual reference is implicit, but rather in the words 'strength' (*alkē*) and 'camping apart' (*diaskēnōn*). Thibron took a chunky *aulos*-player and went off for an after-breakfast tussle in a tent. The Persians, Xenophon tells us, seized their chance and the first to be killed were Thibron and his partner while much busied 'under canvas'. As so often, Xenophon does not need to be more explicit. He is not entirely critical of Thibron (he goes on to describe him as 'attractive', *euschēmōn*), but he does conclude that he was ruled by 'pleasures of the body' and was not 'pulled together' as a general.

There is a certain poetic justice in the final recruiting of the Ten Thousand by a man who went on to die because of his taste for sodomy. For what Xenophon's *Hellenica* reveals about individual Spartans abroad is amplified by his *Anabasis* and extended to Greeks from other cities in the 'third Greece' (outside Athens and Sparta). From northern Greece, we meet Episthenes of Olynthus who had no time whatsoever for Athenian-style 'reproaches' or the spiritual 'Socratic' ideal. Xenophon describes him quite openly as a pederast, a man who had 'once assembled a squadron, considering nothing else except whether the men were handsome'.[42] This same Episthenes then interceded to save a lovely local young boy who was about to be executed on the march. Unfortunately, there is an uncertainty in the manuscripts: this 'saving' Episthenes is perhaps distinct from another possible 'Episthenes' or 'Pleisthenes', a man from Amphipolis, who was entrusted with the young son of a village chief in Armenia.[43] This local boy was 'just reaching his prime' and when his father deserted, his Greek guardian fell in love with him, brought him home and found him utterly faithful (so unlike a spoilt, fickle Greek boy, we are to conclude). As Agesilaus had found, the doe-eyed boys of Asia could be irresistible. Since the march, Xenophon had plainly continued to hear good news of the two of them. During all their years of good faith, it is hard to imagine that this man from Amphipolis was keeping a wife as well.

Not that pederasty was confined to northern Greeks. When Xenophon defends himself against the charge of hitting a fellow soldier, he presents himself as asking why he would ever have done so. 'Was it that I was asking

---

42. *Anab.* 7.4.8.
43. *Anab.* 4.6.1 with O. Lendle, *Kommentar zu Xenophons Anabasis* (Darmstadt, 1995), ad loc.: the meliores read 'Pleisthenes', the deteriores 'Episthenes'.

you for something which you would not give back? Was I fighting over a boy? Was I drunk?'[44] From such things, typical Greek quarrels began, though neither Herodotus nor Thucydides ever mentions male sex as a factor in Greek armies. Among the Ten Thousand, it was very tenacious. Among the Carduchi, the Greek generals agreed and announced a 'baggage limitation'. Luggage had become a recurring problem (as it was for Alexander's army too) and this order was already the second attempt to thin it out.[45] To enforce it, the generals then stood by the narrow road and checked the troops' baggage. Whatever had been banned had to be surrendered, and the troops obeyed 'except if one of them smuggled something, for example because he was keen on a boy or one of the good-looking women'. Objects of desire, both male and female, were thus disguised from the authorities: did the Arcadian hide his dancing girl?

What was the status of these non-negotiable treasures? The Amphipolitan's Armenian boy was perhaps not seen as an outright slave. If he returned to Amphipolis, however, he can hardly have been granted citizenship and his status would have been metic at best. Most of the 'comfort boys' and girls would simply be captives, like the boy whom Episthenes later rescued, and therefore they were slaves. Apparently, members of the Ten Thousand had arrived at Sardis with a slave already in tow, the usual Greek soldier's practice.[46] In Cilicia they were already capturing more slaves. To encourage the troops after Cunaxa, Xenophon urged them that as victors, they would be able to regard their enemies as 'baggage carriers', slave-Xanthiases for the expedition.[47] Surplus baggage, he proposed, should be burned meanwhile (including all the tents, although winter would soon be with them). But the 'crowd' of followers, the *ochlos*, was left intact.

Up among the Carduchi, the limitation was more stringent: this time, all the captive slaves were to be abandoned too. Together with other camp-followers, there were so many that they more or less doubled the army's numbers. They were truly the 'other Ten Thousand'. Would the local Carduchi capture them or would they simply starve? We do not know how newly taken slaves or prisoners had been allotted to individual Greek soldiers (presumably, they bought them), but the 'boys and lovely girls' were evidently slaves from

44. *Anab.* 5.8.4.
45. *Anab.* 4.1.14; compare Q. C. 6.6.15–16 and Plut. *Alex.* 57.1–2 with D. Engels, *Alexander the Great and the Logistics of the Macedonian Army* (Berkeley, 1979), p. 86 n. 76.
46. W. K. Pritchett, *The Greek State at War: Part I* (California, 1971), pp. 49–51; P. Ducrey, *Le Traitement des prisonniers de guerre dans la Grèce antique*, 2nd edn (Paris, 1999), pp. 155–9, with *skeuophoroi* at *Anab.* 1.10.5.
47. *Anab.* 3.2.29.

among their number. Xenophon surely mentions the smuggling by their desirous owners because he thought it fine, and rather jolly.

One modern view is that it mattered little for most Greek males whether the slave to be penetrated was male or female: desire was simply desire. It would, however, be good to know which soldiers smuggled boys, which girls, and why. It is also worth remembering the balance of force. Xenophon remarks on these signs of pederasty as if they are ever so jolly, but they are not the result of a courtship with gifts (including animals, dead and alive) such as we see on Attic pottery. They were not conducted between free citizens, one older, one younger, 'ephebophilia' as the Catholic Church has now designated it. On the *Anabasis* one partner was simply a captive, a slave. A man like Episthenes was also an officer with military authority. Who would have dared say 'no' to him or to the harsh Clearchus if he had taken a Laconian fancy to a handsome youth in his ranks? It is to Roman anecdotes, not Greek, that we have to look for tales of 'military harassment' by superiors and brave resistance by a younger reluctant party.[48] Xenophon tells none. The Greek word for a 'sex-boy', *paidika*, is revealingly neuter, impersonal and not individual. What, then, of Xenophon himself, the committed proponent of 'Socratic love' in his other writings? During his *Memorabilia*, when his Socrates rebukes the young Critobulus for physically desiring another male, Xenophon admits that he, Xenophon, might also commit a similar lapse.[49] Did he, then, smuggle a boy through the baggage check? Surely not, but he did bring a '*pais*' with him to Seuthes' dinner party where another guest also gave a *pais* to the King. Hindley suggests that Xenophon's *pais* here is a sex-boy: in context, he reads like a slave (not a *paidika*) and we should perhaps credit 'Socratic' Xenophon with observing the very fine line between male slave and sex object.[50]

How distinctively Greek are Episthenes and those others who approximated to his *tropos* ('manner', perhaps not 'orientation')? According to Herodotus, it was the Greeks who taught the Persians to 'have sex with boys'.[51] Certainly, Greeks had a culture of it and perhaps (like modern New Yorkers) they really did encourage foreigners to be bolder and more overt. Xenophon endorses this view in his idealized fiction, the *Cyropaedia*. From observation Greeks knew that Persian males had the un-Greek habit of kissing each other when they

---

48. Plut. *Marius* 14.4–9; Val. Max. 6.1.12; Cic. *Mil.* 49; F. Dupont, T. Éloi, *L'Érotisme masculin dans la Rome antique* (Paris, 2001), pp. 18–25.
49. *Mem.* 1.3.9–10.
50. *Anab.* 7.3.20; Hindley, 'Xenophon on male love', pp. 81–2.
51. Hdt. 1.135.

met: they kissed on the lips, even, if they were social equals. In the *Cyropaedia*, however, the noble Artabazus keeps on wanting a real kiss from Cyrus the Great, not just one of these social kisses for good form. Cyrus fends him off, even promising him a kiss in thirty years' time: Greek readers would enjoy this play on the two people's 'gender gap'.[52] At Cyrus the Great's dinners, the gap is then clearly brought out. Whereas a dinner with Socrates provoked discussion (according to Xenophon) of spiritual love between men, dinner with Cyrus provokes discussion of men's love for women only.[53] However, one Persian dinner among Xenophon's many imagined parties does bring a man, Sambaulas, to recline beside Cyrus. Significantly, he had brought an extraordinarily ugly male friend. Cyrus asks him why he is taking a 'boy' around with him when he is himself he is handsome 'in keeping with the Greek fashion'. Sambaulas explains that sex does not come into the matter, because the boy is so horribly hairy and hideous and, as he himself demonstrates, it would be an awful ordeal to kiss him. In Persian company, even this apparent example of 'Greek taste', Xenophon playfully tells us, is an exception which proves the non-Greek rule.[54]

What, though, was the barbarian reality? Pederasty is nowhere described among the barbarian peoples whom the Ten Thousand met. Even the outlandish Mossynoecians were feared only as a sexual threat to women: there were no Asmats or Matrinds, sodomizing peoples of New Guinea, waiting to be found in the Asian hinterland.[55] The one non-Greek pederast to be singled out is the Persian Ariaeus, but the context for this mention is notoriously polemical, the obituary of Menon the Thessalian.[56] Xenophon delivers three blows here. First he implies that Menon owed his command of mercenaries to his sexual appeal (Menon had been given it by Aristippus, a most nobly named Thessalian, while still 'in the bloom of youth'). Secondly, he then became 'most intimate' with Ariaeus 'who was a barbarian': Menon was also still 'in the bloom of youth' and Ariaeus 'used to take pleasure in beautiful boys'. By implication, it was even worse to submit to a barbarian than to a Greek. Thirdly, Menon himself had a boy lover, the 'bearded' Tharypas, although he himself was still unbearded. The ages of these two men reversed the Greek norm, worst of all, and Xenophon claims to know who was the active partner.

52. Hdt. 1.134; *Cyrop.* 8.4.27 with 1.4.27–8.
53. D. L. Gera, *Xenophon's Cyropaedia* (Oxford, 1993), pp. 133–6.
54. *Cyrop.* 2.2.28–31.
55. *Anab.* 5.4.33; contrast T. Schneebaum, *Where the Spirits Dwell* (London, 1988).
56. *Anab.* 2.6.29.

This ascending trio, a 'triple whammy', is unique in Xenophon's sexual allusions. It is so intriguing because its object is the same young Menon whom Plato immortalized in his dialogue of that name. Plato's Menon was a boy of seventeen or eighteen, surrounded at Athens by many slaves. He was impetuous in his reactions and responses to Socrates' questioning.[57] A true young nobleman, Plato's Menon believed in doing the maximum good to his friends, the maximum harm to his enemies. He was beloved by Aristippus, just as Xenophon says: self-evidently, says Socrates, young Menon still has male lovers, penetrating partners, as he is a handsome young man, imperious and rather spoilt. For young Menon, it was proper for a woman 'to manage the house well, to look after what is inside it and to be subject to her husband'.[58] Plato's dialogue is set just before the *Anabasis* began, in the Athens of 402: Plato wrote it before Xenophon wrote his *Anabasis*, but did he already know how the petulant young Menon had turned out in Asia so soon after his skirmish with Socrates?[59] Possibly he did, but did Xenophon also intensify his attack on Menon because he knew how Plato had represented him as a fine young nobleman, no patient arguer but a pupil of Gorgias and his rhetoric? Xenophon mentions that Proxenus, his own friend and a fellow commander, had indeed studied with Gorgias but he says nothing about Menon's similar studies, although it was surely a bond between him and Proxenus. It is hard to know where, if anywhere, conscious 'intertextuality' exists here: I suspect that it does not.

On the *Anabasis*, nonetheless, boys were only one class of supernumerary. Soon after the baggage limitation, the army went on to the fiercely fought crossing of the river Centrites and here, in Armenia, we suddenly learn that there were 'many *hetairai*' (prostitutes) in the camp. They even added their howls to the war-cry (alalalai!) which the Greek males raised while attempting the river crossing.[60] Were these 'many' *hetairai* 'the lovely women' whom the troops had recently smuggled past the authorities? Some of them surely were, but the majority are more likely to have joined the troops after that recent thinning-out. Twice, during the fight to escape the Carduchi, the army had found itself in well-supplied villages. Xenophon first mentions the many fine houses and the 'abundant wine' (always one of his particular memories) which was stored in the residents' cisterns. Next, he recalls the general comfort, the

57. R. W. Sharples (ed.), *Plato: Meno* (Warminster, 1985), p. 18, for supporting texts.
58. Plat. *Men.* 71E.
59. T. S. Brown, 'Menon of Thessaly', *Historia* 35 (1986), pp. 387–404, esp. p. 400.
60. *Anab.* 4.3.19.

soldiers' swapping of stories and the fact that the troops 'slept sweetly'.[61] Additional sweeteners, surely, were local girls, acquired by the troops on their approach to the river. The ban on superfluous baggage had been very short-lived in the face of sex.

Nowhere in Thucydides do we find a mention of *hetairai* with an army: in Herodotus, they are mentioned as a presence only in the Persians' camp.[62] What is the novelty, then, about the *Anabasis*: is it that Xenophon mentions *hetairai*, or is it that *hetairai* were present for such a long time? I suggest that the latter is correct. In taking *hetairai* with them, the Ten Thousand are, for us, 'Hellenistic' some eighty years too soon. For Alexander's officers hired the top Athenian tarts and his army took concubines along on their march (Asian ones supposedly from 330 onwards): 10,000 Asian women had certainly been 'taken on' by the troops when they reached Susa in 324.[63] In Hellenistic armies women continue to surface and jolt our imaginations. In 317/16, Antigonus' army, chasing Eumenes in Iran, is suddenly revealed to have women with it, wives even and children, or 'wives, children, concubines, slaves, gold, and silver'.[64] Like those who survived the Gedrosian desert with Alexander, they had marched for miles through Iran in extreme heat. Already for the Ten Thousand, 'women' were an important part of the baggage, just as they were to be in Hellenistic parlance later. The Greek soldiers were living like nomads, with their riches and their concubines (but probably not 'wives') accompanying them on the move. When the girls were at risk, they dropped back, even, to defend them. From Trapezus, they sent home '*paides*' (presumably slaves, not their bastards) and '*gynaikes*' (women, whatever their status).

On the Persian side, such a presence was already quite conventional: Persian army commanders travelled in style, with women, cooks, and butlers too. Famously, Cyrus the Younger brought not one Greek concubine but two on the march, a Phocaean and a Milesian.[65] Artaxerxes took the Phocaean girl as plunder at Cunaxa, but the Milesian escaped, 'naked', to the Greeks. Xenophon names no names, but he does comment that the Phocaean was 'said to be clever [*sophē*] and beautiful'. From other Greek sources, we know her very well as Aspasia, daughter of Hermotimus. The longest praise of her survives in

61. *Anab.* 4.2.22 (cf. 4.4.9; 4.5.29 on wines); 4.3.2.
62. Hdt. 9.76.
63. Athen. 13.576D–E, 13.594D–595D; Arr. 7.4.8; Justin *Epit.* 12.4.1. Compare Appian, *Hisp.* 85.367, for a Scipionic expulsion of *hetairai* from the camp in Spain.
64. Polyaen. *Strat.* 4.6.13.
65. *Anab.* 1.10.2–3.

Aelian's *Miscellaneous History*, in the early third century AD, where he describes her golden curls, her skin like roses, and her extreme self-control when Cyrus first groped her and fondled her breasts. To Aelian, their relationship was 'almost one of equal honour which did not fall short of the concord and restraint of a Greek marriage', but these are the morals of his later era. Xenophon refers to her 'reputed cleverness and beauty': was it hearsay, or had he read reports of Aspasia's 'reputed cleverness', presumably in Ctesias? Ctesias may underlie Aelian and even, perhaps, the story that Aspasia was made to wear the dark robe of Artaxerxes' best-beloved eunuch, after the eunuch's death.[66] King Artaxerxes liked to see Aspasia dressed in it, the most macabre result of Cyrus' march.

Like this Aspasia, the *hetairai* of Ionia were famous and while waiting to be summoned to Cyrus, the Greek mercenaries had no doubt made use of them. Up at Abydus, near Clearchus' mercenary base, there were the recent stories of Alcibiades' sexual experiments with a local Greek tart: she and her fellow professionals would have been irresistible.[67] At the other end of the march the Ten Thousand's 'concubines', including non-Greeks, made the journey right on to the Black Sea: we know of them, because there were fears there that the Mossynoecians would have sex with them in public.[68] There must already have been many bastards as a result of their months in the camp, the Ten Thousand's ignored legacy to Asia. What were their relationships like? For a sense of such troopers and their aspirations, we have capital evidence, but not in Xenophon or his lifetime. *Hetairai* and Greek mercenaries (who have returned from abroad) are stock items in Athenian comedies in the years after Alexander. Their stereotypes are larger than life, but they are firmly based on it. In 1951, Marcel Launey devoted superb pages to these 'typical' soldiers' mentality, and conjured up real soldiers, too, behind the comic casting.[69] They saw themselves, he reasoned, as 'les coqueluches des dames' (women's sweethearts), disagreeable lovers (in Launey's view), however, who were coarse, jealous, boastful, and stupid. Their conversation was 'killingly dull and nauseating', 'ce qu'une femme un peu délicate supporte mal'.

Here, too, the Ten Thousand had already lived out a Hellenistic stereotype (though Launey omitted them). No doubt they had boasted, as they

66. Aelian *V. H.* 12.1, a 'sex and gender' classic.
67. Lysias ap. Athen. 12.535A; 13.574E.
68. *Anab.* 5.4.33.
69. M. Launey, *Recherches sur les armées hellénistiques*, 2nd edn (Paris, 1987), vol. 2, pp. 802–3.

remembered and recounted their recent stories; they had surely competed for girls (and for the boys whom these sanitized Athenian comedies omitted); they were no doubt pretty thick. But were they really so ghastly? Most of the concubines in the camp would be non-Greeks (unlike the *hetairai* of New Comedy), but in the Greek soldiers' eyes the women of Asia (like the boys) were highly attractive. They were *megalai*, tall (not fat), unlike the short-legged Greek women at home.[70] Any who served them and followed them would be maintained, although they would not be regarded, surely, as women of free status. For evidence, we can look ahead to Ptolemy II's edict of 260, applying to Syria and Phoenicia: obscure though much of its scope and purpose is, it plainly assumes that the 'native women' whom soldiers have 'taken on' might be thought to be of servile status, needing to be exempted, therefore, from the proposed registration of slaves.[71]

Yet perhaps the Greek soldiers, too, were not always as Launey (and Athenian comic poets) implied. The most tantalizing evidence is their 'sports day' near Trapezus, on Dracontius' choice of hillside. It was heavily subscribed by male competitors 'and the spectacle', writes Xenophon, 'was a fine one'. Many entered the contests and as '*tōn hetairōn*' were watching, there was great rivalry.[72] Who are '*tōn hetairōn*': should they be given a Greek accent which makes them male ('their companions') or one which makes them female ('their *hetairai*', or concubines)? The manuscripts cannot decide the accentuation, but Xenophon's usage is more helpful. Nowhere does he call fellow soldiers unqualifiedly '*hoi hetairoi*', 'the companions': it is never his word for the Ten Thousand. Without an adjective, the plain '*tōn hetairōn*' surely refers here to the '*hetairōn*' whom we have already met in the narrative: '*hetairai*', or females. There was 'great rivalry', then, because 'the girls' were watching. Presumably, the men ran naked, the usual Greek practice, but *hetairai* were no inhibition, being more than familiar with men in the nude.

70. *Anab.* 3.2.25; a different explanation, which I do not accept, in C. J. Tuplin, chapter 5, p. 156 above.
71. S. B. 8008, with M. M. Austin, *The Hellenistic World* (Cambridge, 1981), no. 275 B, lines 15–18; interpretations vary, but the 'native women' cohabiting with soldiers are at least 'akin' to slaves, and hence exempted by the edict. M. Rostovtzeff, *Social and Economic History of the Hellenistic World* (Oxford, 1941), pp. 341–4; W. Westermann, 'Enslaved persons who are free', *AJP* 59 (1938), pp. 7–8; C. Préaux, *L'Économie royale des Lagides* (Brussels, 1939), pp. 313–15, and especially I. Biezunska-Malowist, *L'Esclavage dans l'Égypte gréco-romaine I* (Warsaw, 1976), p. 24.
72. *Anab.* 4.8.21–8, also discussed, with earlier bibliography, in Golden, *Sport and Society in Ancient Greece*, pp. 1–4.

The Ten Thousand are remembered nowadays for anything from their male shout of 'Thalatta' (The Sea!) to their celebrations with the locals' wine in Armenia or the Black Sea's potent azalea honey. But they have another distinction, not one for 'une femme un peu délicate', but the women concerned were their slaves and captives, and were not so delicate, either. They are the first known beneficiaries of female cheer-leaders in the history of athletic sport.

III

As Cyrus considered that there must be sufficient guards for Babylon, he appointed adequate Guards there and he ordered that the people of Babylon should pay wages to them, wanting the people of Babylon to be as helpless as possible, so that they might be very humbled and very easy to hold down. This Guard about his own person and the one established in Babylon persists in the same way, still, even now.'

Xenophon *Cyropaedia* 7.5.69–70

Our history books forget them, but Xenophon gives us glimpses of this 'other Ten Thousand', with slave girls and pretty boys to the fore. It is worth bringing out the Ten Thousand's non-Christian Greekness by contrasting them, here, with those other military raiders in the Near East, the first Crusaders.[73] The Crusaders, too, kept concubines and attracted prostitutes: they founded and supported brothels in their camps and in urbanized territory, especially Antioch. Some of them also had sex with boys, especially Greek boys in the brothels of the Byzantine Empire. Yet their leaders were Christians, not hardened Arcadians or Spartans. So, unmarried women who became pregnant in their camp were atrociously tortured, as were their pimps. Women in camp were also encouraged to pray for victory, while defeats were blamed by Christian chroniclers on the male soldiers' sexual sins. There was no such rhetoric among the Ten Thousand. Like Xenophon's men, Crusaders did praise the charms of Eastern women: better a Byzantine girl than a dowdy old Frank at home. But Christian opinion objected on religious grounds, as

---

73. I draw on J. A. Brundage, 'Prostitution, miscegenation and sexual purity in the First Crusade', in P. W. Edbury (ed.), *Crusade and Settlement* (Cardiff, 1985), pp. 57–65, esp. p. 63 n. 16 and p. 64 n. 48.

Xenophon never did. These Eastern women were Muslims. Turks and other Muslim males were also extremely lascivious: heaven help those Christian women who slept with them.

A whole range of perceptions was thus absent from the Ten Thousand and their historian, although the Crusaders' actual sexual conduct was often so similar to theirs. In more general terms, how did Xenophon and his fellow soldiers regard strangers whom they met? Religion never complicated the encounters: as polytheists, Greeks and Persians would accept the power and reality of whatever local gods they met. Yet even among the Greeks themselves, there were sharply perceived differences, between Spartans and Athenians, between Arcadians and the rest. The sharpness is well brought out in the affair of Apollonides. After the defeat at Cunaxa, the difficulties of the situation were stressed by this man who 'spoke in Boeotian dialect'. An Arcadian, Agasias, then saw him off. He had no connection with Boeotia, Agasias argued, nor with Greece 'whatsoever': he had pierced ears, Agasias had noticed, 'like a Lydian'. So they drove Apollonides out.[74]

Yet Apollonides had a Greek name and there is more here than the brisk Arcadian realized. His 'Boeotian dialect', surely, was Aeolic Greek and as an Aeolic speaker, Apollonides, I suggest, was a man from Lesbos or the Troad.[75] Apollonides spoke with 'oi' for 'ou' and used dative plurals which sounded Boeotian to mainland Greeks. Tough mercenary soldiers had no patience with earrings or pierced ears, but back on Lesbos other Greeks may have been more flexible. 'Lydian' fashions may well have continued in use there since Sappho's day: poor Apollonides may have been misclassified and wrongly expelled from the camp.

When perceptions between Greeks were so keen, what about Greeks' views of non-Greeks? Xenophon's own limits are clearest in the work of his advanced old age, the *Ways and Means*. He states here that it would be a 'benefit' to the Athenian community if Athenians no longer served as hoplite infantry together with 'Lydians and Phrygians and Syrians and every sort and kind of barbarian'.[76] Xenophon was such a natural in other ways for a future with Alexander the Great, but he would have had a truly Macedonian lack of sympathy, it seems, with the 'participation' and 'incorporation' of barbarians in the

---

74. *Anab.* 3.1.26 and 31.
75. For 'Lydian' style on Lesbos, L. Kurke, 'Crisis and decorum in sixth century Lesbos', *QUCC* 47 (1994), pp. 67–92, at least for the evidence. I owe the linguistic point to Dr J. B. Hainsworth.
76. Xen. *Poroi* 2.3–4.

army of Alexander's later years. Yet his prejudice varied with social class. The 'Lydians, Phrygians, and Syrians' whom he disdains would often be ex-slaves, Athenians' freedmen in the metic population. In the more prestigious circles of the Athenian cavalry, Xenophon could cheerfully contemplate a non-Athenian metic presence: by definition it would be classier.

A similar double vision runs through his writings about Asia. While idealizing 'the Greek' and classing the barbarian foes as 'dogs' he could eulogize fine individuals like Cyrus the Younger or his fictional Cyrus the Great and give the satrap Pharnabazus some noble words on honour in answer to Agesilaus, his esteemed Spartan king. There is a class basis here to his perceptions: Xenophon could find more in common with a barbarian nobleman than with the Greek lower classes, back in Athens. The *Anabasis* does not often focus on the trials and courage of ordinary individual soldiers.

Xenophon's likings are patchy, but is he also blind or incurious about the peoples he encounters? Real understanding would require that the Greeks could communicate with them. Here, Xenophon is exceptional among surviving Greek historians: he frequently notes the use of interpreters between Greeks and non-Greeks. This 'language problem' first appears in our surviving Greek literature in the Homeric *Hymn to Aphrodite* (*c.* 550): with the enigmatic *Periplus of Hanno*, Xenophon is its poet's true successor.[77] He may not have distinguished fully between what we class as Iranian dialects (hence the 'Persian' which was spoken, in his view, to those Armenian girls), but he does note Persians' own use of interpreters, both Cyrus' and Tissaphernes'. Cyrus even uses a Carian, Pigres, and an Egyptian, 'Glos, son of Tamos', two trilingual individuals, it seems, to communicate with the Greeks. Gaulites of Samos is another example, a bilingual Greek who had prospered linguistically in exile.[78]

For a similar emphasis on the language problems in a mixed mercenary army, we have to look right ahead to Polybius and his sources for the bitter mercenary war in north Africa in the 230s.[79] But Xenophon also dwells on the problems of communication with remote peoples his army met. He also

---

77. Hom. *Hymn Aphrodit.* 111–16; *Periplus of Hanno* 11 (Cathaginians, with local interpreters).
78. *Anab.* 1.2.17, 1.4.16, 1.8.12, but interpreters are not explicitly mentioned at, e.g., 1.7.6 or 1.8.16–17. For Tissaphernes, 2.3.18 (despite 2.5.16–23). Philinus is also surely bilingual (2.1.7), but not, I expect, Mithradates (despite 3.3.1–4).
79. Polyb. 1.67.3, 1.67.8 (very explicit), 1.67.9–10, 1.69.12, and esp. 1.80.5–6. Oddly, even F. W. Walbank does not comment. Compare Caesar, *BG* 1.19.3 and 1.47.4, which I owe to L. Pitcher.

explains how communication was possible with the remote Macronians: one of the Ten Thousand had been born there, before being brought to Athens in his youth as a slave. Seuthes' Greek, and its limits, are also well observed: uniquely, Xenophon is the Greek author who remarks on varying degrees of linguistic competence.[80] Seuthes, he notes, could understand some, but not all, of what was said in Greek. The point is also relevant to Cyrus and Tissaphernes. Cyrus had two Greek concubines and (according to Xenophon) spoke once to Xenophon personally. Yet he also addressed the Greek troops through interpreters.[81] Evidently, he knew some Greek but was not sufficiently confident to make an important speech in it.

What, though, about the Greeks themselves? Famously, Momigliano diagnosed the Greeks as monoglots, a 'fault of the Greeks' (in his view) which was not shared by other peoples (Romans, Jews, or Carthaginians) around the Mediterranean.[82] It is not such a grave fault of Xenophon's when we find him negotiating with the Carduchi through an interpreter: Athenians had never had dealings with them, though somebody here (his interpreter) could nonetheless speak both Greek and a local language. It is more glaring that Xenophon never learned any Persian, though he wrote at such length on Cyrus the Great. But not every Greek was a Xenophon. At Seuthes' Thracian court, the smooth coordinator of the gift-giving, Heraclides of Maronea, could surely converse with his superior Seuthes in Thracian as well as in Greek. On the Black Sea, we then meet Timesitheus of Trapezus who was the *proxenos* among the people of Trapezus for the outlandish Mossynoecians. Evidently he could speak and understand Mossynoecian. At such 'interfaces' between Greek and barbarian territories, all around the Greek world, there were surely similar Greek *proxenoi* who did not suffer at all from Momigliano's 'fault'.[83]

Do Xenophon's perceptions of 'others' vary with the possibility of intercommunication? We might well think so, but we must remember that he was writing up a march, not an ethnographic mission. Occasional, specific perceptions are exact, but as our one eye-witness record of whole chunks of the Persian Empire he is a disappointing source, much like the memoirs of modern plant-hunters, which show such blindness to the culture and social realities (but not to the plants) of western China. Where the Ten Thousand meet hostile warriors and are not said to have someone capable of communicating in a local

80. *Anab.* 4.8.4 and 7.6.8–9 (Seuthes).
81. *Anab.* 1.10.2, 1.8.15 and 1.8.12.
82. A. Momigliano, *Alien Wisdom: The Limits of Hellenization* (London, 1975).
83. *Anab.* 5.4.2–4.

language, Xenophon simply describes what he saw and survived: warriors armed with this or that. But the Macronians were friendly, and through the bilingual ex-slave were linguistically accessible. Together with the Greeks, they spent time hacking down trees and making a track, yet Xenophon shows next to no curiosity or knowledge about their social existence, apart from noting their gift of a 'barbaric spear' as a pledge of friendship.[84]

Lacking the languages, Xenophon and the men connect what they see to stories they know at home. At Celaenae, Xenophon remembers the flaying of the satyr Marsyas (he does not need to be echoing Herodotus here) and at Thymbrion he comments on the story of Midas and the satyr (the story is quite widely featured on Attic pottery, another possible source of his interest).[85] Up on the Black Sea he notes the descent to the underworld, used by Heracles at Heracleia. It remained a great curiosity, visited eight centuries later by the orator Libanius too.[86] Among these Greek connections, local names in Asia come out in Greek distortions: the '"far-sounding" river Teleboas' (arguably based on a Hittite local name, surviving in this former Hittite territory) or the ruins at 'Mespila' and 'Larissa', so often believed to be Nimrud and Nineveh. Plainly these two places were given Greek names from some local term of reference which the troops misunderstood.[87] The histories of the capture of each place are also wonderfully distorted, no doubt through stories passed on by non-Greek informants and transformed by Greek troopers. Like Roman legionaries, the Ten Thousand were at times their own worst historians.

From Josephus to Edward Said, the Greeks' giving of Greek names to places in Asia has been related to 'power' and 'empire'.[88] But it was also less dramatic

---

84. *Anab.* 4.8.1–9.
85. *Anab.* 1.2.8. Herodotus is certainly not the source for the story about Xerxes' buildings here; as for Marsyas, see the early poetic sources listed by J. E. Atkinson, *A Commentary on Q. Curtius Rufus' Historiae Alexandri Magni Books 3 and 4* (Amsterdam, 1980), p. 81.
86. *Anab.* 6.1.2 with the excellent study by W. Hoepfner, 'Topographische Forschungen: das Acherontale bei Herakleia Pontike', *Denkschriften Akad Wien* 106 (1972), pp. 40–6; L. Robert, *A travers l'Asie Mineure* (Paris, 1980), pp. 98–9 with pp. 5–6 on Ap. Rhod. 2.138–45; F. Vian and E. Delage's Budé edition of Apollonius (Paris, 1974), 1.276–7, cites a good letter from P. Faure on Apollonius' ice fantasy here. Add Libanius Oration 1.30 (*kai tēn anabasin eidon*).
87. V. Manfredi, *La Strada dei Diecimila* (Milan, 1986), pp. 192–5 (Teleboas), pp. 165–6 (Larisa and Mespila, which I accept). But Assyriologists still hesitate over the latter two: A. Kuhrt, 'The Assyrian heartland in the Achaemenid period', in Briant, *Dans les pas des Dix-Mille*, pp. 239–54, at p. 243.
88. Josephus *A. J.* 1.121; E. Said, *Culture and Imperialism* (London, 1994).

and at times it was just an inconsequential misunderstanding. The attempt to see others and their landscape in terms of one's own mythology is not necessarily an attempt to dominate them or keep them at a disdainful distance. It is also grounds for friendly relations (as we will see in Thrace) which the 'others' themselves can adopt and use, presenting themselves as the 'same'. The *Anabasis*' two most memorable encounters are with the Mossynoecians and with Seuthes' court in Thrace. Xenophon enlarges on the Mossynoecians because they really were the 'most barbarian' people the Greeks met. However, he certainly does not judge them to be so simply because of their non-Greek diet.[89] They arrive in hollowed canoes; they have a war dance which is positively Maori in its rhythmic pace; they live in tall towers; they claim that one such tower is their 'citadel' and is not to be dominated by one ruling group; they communicate between wooden towers by shouting; they show off the well-fed children of their well-off members who are white-skinned and amazingly obese, being almost as broad as they are tall. Their backs are tattooed with flower patterns. It is only one more oddity that Mossynoecians store up salted dolphin meat, the previous season's bread and masses of flat nuts. According to Xenophon, they also 'kept trying to have sex in public with the *hetairai* whom the Greeks were bringing with them: public sex was their custom'. We may well suspect a Greek stereotype here, which is already visible in Herodotus' account of really remote Indians.[90] But it may also be that Xenophon is correct. In his eyes there was a more general 'polarity': these people reversed what others did in public and in private. They would talk and dance and laugh by themselves. Here (as in Herodotus' Egypt), a pattern has probably got the better of accurate understanding, but even so, we cannot be sure that solipsistic dancing, muttering, or laughing was not a Mossynoecian practice at all.

For the Ten Thousand, these people were the 'most barbaric' on the march, but they were not (as we might think) a new Greek discovery. Hecataeus had already reported their name and location and according to Herodotus, Mossynoecians had actually served on Xerxes' march in 480: they were commanded by a satrap, the same Artayctes of Khwarezm who later misbehaved

---

89. *Anab.* 5.4; Cartledge, *The Greeks*, p. 44, thinks 'the main reason for this distinction was a matter of their food-habits': I disagree.
90. Hdt. 3.101; compare *Dissoi Logoi* 2.4; Plat. *Hipp. Maj.* 299A; Megasthenes ap. Strabo 15.1.56 (in 'the Caucasus'); note R. Sorabji, *Emotion and Peace of Mind* (Oxford, 2000), pp. 274 and 411–12.

near the Hellespont.[91] Mossynoecians had already been listed in a Persian tribute-paying district, but in 480 they were under Artayctes, a rather distant commander who was based far to the west at Sestos. According to Herodotus' army list they were equipped like 'the Moschoi', with wooden helmets, therefore, small shields, and small spears with long spear-heads. Xenophon, however, saw no wooden helmets. Leather ones, rather, were typical, while the Mossynoecian spears were six cubits long and their shields, like an ivy leaf, were most distinctive.[92] Herodotus' list has perhaps drawn on something found in Hecataeus, whereas Xenophon the eye-witness is surely correct. But we would never suspect from his encounter that Mossynoecians had once marched off into Greece.

Relations with Seuthes were more fraternal: the option of being his 'brothers' is stressed and in order to emphasize his own trust in Athenians, Seuthes himself recalls his 'kinship' with them. It was derived, we learn elsewhere, from the ill-fated marriage of the Athenian legendary princess, Procne, with the Thracian Tereus. Rebutted by an indignant Thucydides, this kinship had surely featured in diplomacy between Thracians and Athenians in 430.[93] Here, it is Seuthes, the 'other', who claims to be one of the same. C. P. Jones sees this episode as Xenophon's 'cool, amused portrait of the barbarian prince who professed implicit faith in the kinship in order to win over his Athenian interlocutor'.[94] But was it so 'cool'? The 'kinship' is not cited repeatedly, but after their merry dinner, the Greek guests and Seuthes announce the important army password. It is Athena, 'in accordance with their kinship': both sides, then, could entertain the kinship rather more seriously than Thucydides. It was not just 'professed' or 'regarded with cool amusement'.[95]

Values and behaviour at Seuthes' court are not Athenian, but (at times) they are decidedly Homeric. Dinner guests sit upright, like Homeric heroes; gifts are extremely prominent in social relations with the prince (though Seuthes, the host, receives, whereas Homeric hosts give); future reciprocity is an explicit part of the transaction; *charis*, gratitude, to friends and benefactors is repeatedly praised. Like some Homeric suitors, Seuthes offers to pay a bride-price

91. Hecataeus *FGH* 1 F204; Hdt. 7.78; and, in general, A. Peretti, *Il Periplo di Scilace* (Pisa, 1979), pp. 460–5.
92. Hdt. 7.78 and *Anab.* 5.4.12–13.
93. Thuc. 2.29; *Anab.* 7.2.31; R. Parker, *Athenian Religion: A History* (Oxford, 1996), p. 174 and n. 76.
94. C. P. Jones, *Kinship Diplomacy in the Ancient World* (Harvard, 1999), pp. 30–1 n. 14.
95. *Anab.* 7.3.39.

for any marriageable daughter Xenophon may have (a most interesting misjudgement, surely, of Xenophon's age at the time of their meeting).[96] When Seuthes talks of his life as an exiled orphan, he tells of his resentment at 'living with his eye turned toward another's alien table': to escape, he implored his host as a suppliant by a classic act of *hiketeia*. So, too, Homer's Andromache had predicted expulsion from table-society for her orphaned son, Astyanax: we can imagine Astyanax, too, in such exile with his eye 'turned' likewise towards another's table-company.[97] Above all, speeches between Xenophon, Seuthes, and a high-ranking Thracian invoke precisely the values of 'honour' and 'shame' which have been upheld as central to Homeric heroes' mentality. Xenophon reproaches Seuthes for 'not being ashamed before the gods nor this man here', an important Odrysian envoy. The Odrysian then says that he 'sinks beneath the earth with shame when he hears these things'. In due course, Seuthes assures Xenophon that he will not be less honoured (*atimoteros*) among the Greek troops on his, Seuthes', account. Xenophon concludes by assuring Seuthes that any honour for himself, granted anywhere, will be honour for Seuthes too.[98]

There are no explicit echoes of Homer in Xenophon's language here, no deliberate 'intertextuality'. Nonetheless, has Xenophon, reared on Homer, misunderstood his encounters with a Thracian prince by seeing them through a Homeric haze? 'Shame' is not confined to scenes in Thrace: from time to time, even the Greek leaders' motives on the march are presented with touches of 'shame culture'.[99] But the simple view is here the most convincing, that Xenophon really has recalled correctly one side of Thracian values, speech, and practice. In 1922, Marcel Mauss picked on the gift-giving in this episode and the obligation, so he believed, for recipients to offer a counter-gift: he detected an institution of gift and contract here in Thrace, a flicker of the famous potlatch 'qui existe un peu partout'.[100] Concisely, Thucydides had already observed that Thracian kings 'took, rather than gave' and that not to give, when requested, was 'shameful'.[101] 'It was impossible to achieve anything if one did

---

96. *Anab.* 7.3.21 with Athen. 1.11F ff. and the superb note of E. Fraenkel, *Aeschylus: Agamemnon* (Oxford, 1950), vol. 3, pp. 754–5; on gifts, *Anab.* 7.3.15–19 and 31–6; 7.7.23. 7.2.38 is hard to square with a Xenophon born (we guess) in the early 420s.
97. *Anab.* 7.2.32–3; Hom. *Il.* 22.496–7.
98. *Anab.* 7.7.9; 7.7.11; 7.7.46, 52.
99. e.g., *Anab.* 1.3.10; 2.3.22; 2.6.19.
100. M. Mauss, 'Une Forme ancienne de contrat chez les Thraces', *REG* 34 (1921), pp. 388–97, esp. p. 390. I am grateful to S. C. Humphreys for reminding me of this article.
101. Thuc. 2.97.4.

not give gifts.' At Seuthes' court, there was only the promise of a greater favour in return, a promise duly belied, whereas the 'gifts' were artfully coaxed from the guests.

In 1954, Moses Finley's penetrating study of *The World of Odysseus* threw Homeric gift-giving into sharper focus by citing comparative studies by Malinowski (on the Trobriand Islanders) and Marc Bloch (on Tacitus' Germans). His discussion upheld the reality of this aspect of Homeric society by reference to Malinowski's 'primitive peoples' and to his own 'flat rule of both primitive and archaic society that no one ever gave anything... without proper recompense, real or wishful, immediate or years away...'.[102] In 1985, Homeric reality was made even more immediate when the entire Trojan War itself was 'relocated', by absurd criteria, to the very river plains outside Cambridge, within direct reach of M. I. Finley himself.[103] More pertinently, Finley's insight into Homeric reality never cited the evidence of Xenophon (or Herodotus and Thucydides) though this evidence was internal to the Greek world and to its own 'anthropology'. In 1954 Mauss's book on *Le Don* was not even cited by Finley (it had not been translated when he first wrote) and as late as 1977, Finley was still under the impression that Mauss's work on gifts extended only to this book and was 'strangely without reference to the Greeks'.[104] In fact, Mauss had seen in 1922 that the gift-world of Odysseus could be validly compared with Thrace as observed in Xenophon's *Anabasis*. Neither Finley nor Mauss went on to observe how much more of a 'Homeric' flavour was alive and historically flourishing in the Thrace which Xenophon described for us. Xenophon's account of Thracian 'others' is a cardinal analogy for those who continue to debate the reality, or lack of it, in the Homeric world. But unlike a Homeric hero, Xenophon also tells his Thracian host to put a proposal to his people for a democratic vote: the Thracian brusquely refuses.[105]

---

102. M. I. Finley, *The World of Odysseus* (New York, 1954), p. 68.
103. I. J. Wilkens, *Troy in England* (Century Press, 1990), with the website www.troy-in-england.co.uk.
104. I differ, then, from S. Hornblower (a Finley pupil, however) whose *A Commentary on Thucydides* (Oxford, 1991), vol. 1, p. 373, sees Mauss's book as 'a work which influenced M. I. Finley's *World of Odysseus* (London, 1956)'. The first edition of Finley shows no sign of it at all. M. I. Finley, *The World of Odysseus* (London, 1956 edition), p. 168, does refer to the 'recent correction' of the long-standing lack of a systematic account in English by the translation of *Essai sur le don*. This edition, p. 176 n. 43, does quote (one!) secondary foreign source (in German). But M. I. Finley, *The World of Odysseus* (1977 edition), p. 183, still believes that Mauss's work had been 'strangely without references to the Greeks'.
105. *Anab.* 7.7.18.

What, finally, about Xenophon's view of Persians? The main contrasts here have been abundantly studied, the stereotype of Persian 'effeminacy', but also the praises of Cyrus' generosity and valour (he even bore marks of a bear-bite, from a day's hunting) and the observation that Persian noblemen were really tough and muscular on those occasions when they took off their finery and put their shoulders to the wheel.[106] Here, I wish only to relate Xenophon's observations to his subsequent, idealizing work, the *Cyropaedia*. For, throughout that work (but especially in the first two books and the last two) Xenophon relates Persian customs in his story to the present day, observing that they 'still persist, even now'. At those points, he is claiming knowledge of contemporary Persian practice, and the source for that knowledge is not the reports of recent Greek ambassadors or generals in Persian service. It is his own remembered experience when serving first with Cyrus, then with Spartan generals, in Persian company and Persian Asia Minor from 401 until the later 390s.[107]

What Xenophon points out about 'even now', then, carries historical weight, though it is embedded in the surrounding romance. In these passages, especially, the *Cyropaedia* gives us the ethnographic details about Persians which the *Anabasis*, a different genre, omits. There may be exaggeration in them, but there is also first-hand evidence. The gift-giving, the hunting, the presents given by the King to Persian women on visiting the district of Persia: these and other persisting customs we can back up from independent sources.[108] According to Xenophon, an army would circulate round a region of the King's empire with a general, a son, or a brother of the King, checking and inspecting that all was being properly done: should we not believe him here too? There is even a possible instance in the *Anabasis* and another, perhaps, in Arrian's *History of Alexander*.[109]

Sometimes, we can trace such details exactly to Xenophon's own previous experience. In the *Anabasis* he had passed through Armenia, the Chalybes, and the 'Median' territory, about which he cites details in the *Cyropaedia* persisting 'even now'.[110] In Asia Minor, he personally had encountered Egyptian

106. *Anab.* 1.9.6 (a she-bear, moreover); 1.5.8–9; C. J. Tuplin, 'Xenophon's *Cyropaedia*: education and fiction', in A. H. Sommerstein and C. Atherton (eds), *Education in Greek Fiction* (Bari, 1996), pp. 65–162; C. J. Tuplin, 'Modern and ancient travellers in the Achaemenid Empire', *Ach. Hist.* VII (1991), pp. 37–57.
107. *Eti kai nun* passages are listed in B. Due, *The Cyropaedia* (Aarhus, 1989), pp. 31–8, and Gera, *Xenophon's Cyropaedia*, pp. 298–9.
108. e.g., *Cyrop.* 8.2.7–9, 8.1.24 and 8.5.21 (with Plut. *Alex.* 69.1–2 and Ctesias ap. Plut. *Mor.* 246A–B, Nic. Dam. *FGH* 90 F66 and Polyaen. *Strat.* 7.45.2).
109. *Cyrop.* 8.6.16; *Anab.* 2.4.25 may be related and perhaps Arr. *Anab.* 3.19.4–5.
110. *Cyrop.* 3.2.24.

colonists, settled at 'Larissa', a settlement which he then, in the *Cyropaedia*, traces back to Cyrus the Great's ancient gift.[111] Importantly, the *Cyropaedia* dwells on the Hyrcanians and their honoured service and their skill as cavalrymen. In 399, as the *Anabasis* ended, he had encountered exactly such Hyrcanians, colonists who were sent up to defend Asidates' 'tower' against Xenophon's raid. They were cavalrymen, no less. Their prominence in *Cyropaedia* book 4 is thus rooted in his own eye-witness memories of them in Asia Minor in 399.[112]

In the opening books, observations on the Persian practice of kissing and the luxurious dress, cosmetics, and ushers of the Medes underpin whole sections of the *Cyropaedia*'s fiction.[113] It is not, I suggest, that Xenophon simply dropped passing remarks about 'even now' into this very lengthy work of invention. Parts of it actually developed in his mind as aetiology, not history; he transferred to the distant Cyrus the Great living facts which he had seen, heard, and remembered for himself. This 'origin' helped to explain them and also to shape and fill out his invented picture of Cyrus.

Aetiology, or 'origins', is a widespread category in Greek invention, but it has not been sufficiently considered as one origin of Xenophon's own 'Persian' fiction. The origin of this particular interest in 'origins' was the Anabasis-march and its aftermath. He did not retell it with any stress on 'origins' in his narrative. There is a fine contrast here with the next noble horse-rider and author in Asia, the aristocratic Medeius of Larissa. When this Thessalian wrote a text of what he saw on Alexander's march, he described how Armenia and Media had a most exciting 'origin': their people were kinsmen of the Thessalians and shared a common Thessalian ancestry. Dress and religion, languages, place names and even the geology of the two countries' river plains proved their common origins.[114] When Xenophon takes us through Armenia, there is not a hint of speculation about any people's or place's kinship with anyone in Greece. But 'aetiology' surfaced, elsewhere, for Xenophon, the upper-class military man, a Medeius in Socrates' Athens. His fictional

---

111. *Cyrop.* 7.1.45 with *Hell.* 3.1.7; E. Delebecque, *Essai sur la vie de Xénophon* (Klincksieck, 1957), pp. 396–402, saw a connection too, but explained it differently.
112. *Cyrop.* 4.2, esp. 4.2.8 with *Anab.* 7.8.15 and Diod. Sic. 17.19.4 with L. Robert, *Hellenica* VI 19; Lane Fox, *Alexander the Great*, pp. 141 and 517, to which add the reference to von Domaszewski, adduced by S. Hornblower, *Mausolus* (Oxford, 1982), p. 143 n. 49, of which I was unaware in 1973. N. Sekunda, 'Achaemenid colonization in Lydia', *REA* 87 (1985), pp. 7–30, presses Xenophon's *misthophoroi* at *Anab.* 7.8.15 more precisely than I do.
113. *Cyrop.* 1.3.2; 1.4.27.
114. Strabo 11.4 and 11.14 with Bernard, 'Les Origines thessaliennes'.

Cyropaedia gives the aetiologies of customs and places which he had personally confronted on his Anabasis-march.

Memories, then, of the 'others' he had seen on his march had not been short-lived. It is apt for the main subject of this essay that Xenophon remarks in the *Cyropaedia* how the 'Medes and Hyrcanians' followed up a victory with Cyrus by rounding up the enemies' carriages full of the 'finest women, some of them wives, some of them concubines who were brought along because of their beauty'. 'Still, even to this day,' he comments, 'those who campaign in Asia go on campaign with what they value most. They say that they fight even more if what is dearest to them is present too.' Xenophon himself is unsure: 'but perhaps they do so, gratifying their own pleasure'.[115] Here, too, what he had seen on his Anabasis, both under Cyrus and among his fellow Greeks, gave him well-grounded reasons for his suspicions.

---

115. *Cyrop.* 4.3.2.

7 Xenophon's Ten Thousand as a Fighting Force
MICHAEL WHITBY

Introduction

The third day was difficult and the north wind blew into their faces, slicing through absolutely everything and freezing the men. Then one of the seers said that they should sacrifice to the wind, which they did, and everyone indeed thought that the severity of the wind eased. The depth of the snow was six feet, with the result that many of the animals and slaves perished and 30 of the soldiers... Next, for the whole of the following day they marched through the snow... The rest of the soldiers, those who were unable to complete the march, passed the night foodless and without fires; as a result some of the soldiers perished. Some of the enemy had formed groups and attacked, seizing the weaker of the baggage animals and squabbling amongst themselves about them. Those soldiers whose eyes had been affected by the snow or whose toes had fallen off because of the frost were left behind. It was a help to the eyes if one held something black in front of the eyes while marching, and for the feet if one kept moving and never stood still and undid one's shoes at night; but for those who slept with their shoes on, the straps sunk into their feet and the soles froze to them.[1]

This memorable description by an eye-witness, Xenophon, portrays the acute sufferings of the Ten Thousand and their many camp-followers, slaves, and animals as they struggled across the mountains of what is now eastern Turkey. These physical hardships are the setting for the military achievements which I wish to discuss: how capable were the Greek soldiers and their leaders? In winter 400 they were in territory which no Greek is likely to have crossed before, on a journey which no army of such a size had previously attempted,

---

1. *Anab.* 4.5.3–14. Translations of the *Anabasis* are adapted from Rex Warner (trans.), *Xenophon: The Persian Expedition* (Harmondsworth, 1972).

least of all in the winter months. In such conditions they had to confront a variety of enemies whose hostility was often intensified by the competition for precious food resources.

In Greek history Xenophon's account of the expedition deserves the attention of military historians for several reasons. One, of course, is the extraordinary achievement of the Ten Thousand in escaping from Persia and surviving an Armenian winter.[2] Another, less often emphasized, is that the *Anabasis* stands out as our fullest account of an extended campaign by a Greek army. Although warfare was a common activity in the Greek world, and the predominant concern for Greek historians, we are surprisingly ill-informed about detailed procedures. Authors assumed that everything was too familiar to need to be described in full,[3] and the earliest historians established the practice. Herodotus, for all his concern with the outcome of great battles, gathered information over a generation after the Persian Wars, and preferred the unusual detail to the ordinary practicalities of military action. Thucydides was far better informed and is responsible for our best accounts of battles in the classical period, the Delium campaign and Mantinea, but he constructed his narrative paradigmatically,[4] and many encounters are recorded more perfunctorily. Against this background, Xenophon's account deserves serious study for its information on Greek military practices and the general fighting capabilities of Greek troops, primarily hoplites, as well as the specific achievements of the Ten Thousand in coping with diverse challenges and conditions.

Preliminary considerations

For military historians, Xenophon's own role as participant–author needs to be clarified. On several grounds he has been accused of self-justification and bias in the *Anabasis*,[5] and military matters are part of them. It would not be

---

2. By way of comparison, in 36 the army of Antony lost 8,000 men, perhaps 20 per cent of his force, while crossing the same region in winter (Plut. *Ant.* 51.1). In April 628 AD Emperor Heraclius sent back to Constantinople a long message in which he referred to the good fortune of his army in reaching the shelter of the Persian royal capital of Canzacon (Takht-i Suleiman in north-western Iran), since shortly after he had crossed the Zagros mountains severe storms had blocked the passes (*Chronicon Paschale*, pp. 731–2).
3. P. Cartledge, 'Hoplites and heroes: Sparta's contribution to the technique of ancient warfare', *JHS* 97 (1977), pp. 11–27, at p. 12.
4. S. Hornblower, *Thucydides* (London, 1987), p. 43.
5. G. L. Cawkwell, introduction to *Xenophon: The Persian Expedition* (Harmondsworth, 1972), pp. 17–26, and cf. Azoulay, chapter 10 in this volume.

surprising if Xenophon enhanced his own contribution to proceedings, and blamed others for whatever acts of indiscipline became associated with the Ten Thousand. He is suspiciously prominent as the man who extricated the expedition from a series of difficulties through morale-boosting speeches and clever tactical solutions; others are given credit when a proposal is not implemented, for example the anonymous Rhodian for the plan to cross the Tigris. He may also have wanted to underline the contrast between the collective successes of the Ten Thousand during their march north (e.g. co-ordinated operations in Carduchia) and their subsequent disruptive behaviour as his own influence waned (e.g. the fragmented actions along the Black Sea).[6]

It is, however, unlikely that Xenophon invented military incidents, the evidence on which my assessment of the army is based. Here his accounts are certainly plausible, and the successful passage of the Ten Thousand through Carduchia and Armenia suggests that the positive sides of their actions have not been overstated. Xenophon is a reasonable guide for examining how the Ten Thousand functioned as a military unit and what they achieved.

A second basic issue is the composition of the army. The Ten Thousand was a mixed force, predominantly hoplite but with an important element of peltasts: according to Xenophon, the ratio of hoplite to peltast was between 5:1 and 4:1 in the early stages of the expedition, and there was also a contingent of two hundred Cretan archers. As the march progressed, the Greeks improvised other supporting units, most significantly a small unit of cavalry who were mounted on baggage animals and a contingent of slingers recruited from among the Rhodians in the company, developments for which Xenophon claimed credit and which proved to be the turning point of the march.[7]

It is assumed that these Rhodians were recruited from the mercenaries, which is certainly possible, but Xenophon merely says that there were Rhodians in the army, *en tōi strateumati*, in the same way as he says that there were horses in the army capable of being adapted for cavalry service. These men, who already happened to have a sling in their possession or who were skilled in its use, may have been recruited from the servants and other camp-

---

6. The plan to cross the Tigris: *Anab.* 3.5.7–12. Coordination in Carduchia: *Anab.* 4.2.25–6. Fragmented action along the Black Sea: *Anab.* 5.4.16; 6.5.26. J. Dillery, *Xenophon and the History of his Times* (London, 1995), suggested that Xenophon structured the *Anabasis* around four distinct phases in the development of the Ten Thousand: units with individual loyalties down to Cunaxa; a community struggling for survival from Cunaxa to the Black Sea; a proto-*polis* full of hopes and dissent as it returned towards Europe; the dissolution of the collective in the Thracian campaigns.
7. Hoplite: peltast ratios: 5:1 (*Anab.* 1.2.9), 4:1 (*Anab.* 1.7.10). The Cretan archers: *Anab.* 1.2.9. The Rhodian slingers: *Anab.* 3.3.16–18.

followers: this would at least explain why Xenophon contemplated offering privileges to attract volunteers.[8]

The composition of the Ten Thousand raises an important question, relevant to modern scholarship on the development of Greek heavy infantry: how far had the hoplites evolved from the traditional heavy-armoured Greek infantryman towards the lighter phalangite of the fourth century? The standard view is that the Ten Thousand already represented a more lightly equipped and mobile type of hoplite. The crucial passage is the description of the parade at Tyriaeum, when Cyrus inspected all his troops in order to impress the Queen of Cilicia. The Greeks wore bronze helmets, scarlet cloaks (*chitōnas*), and greaves, with their shields uncovered; breastplates are not mentioned, and so it is assumed that these troops no longer wore such protection.[9]

Other passages appear to lend support. The improvised cavalry unit was provided with jerkins (*spolades*) and breastplates; when Xenophon dismounted during an assault uphill in response to grumblings from a Sicyonian soldier, he found it difficult to keep up with a company of peltasts and picked hoplites while carrying the Sicyonian's shield, since he was also equipped with a cavalry breastplate, but he could do so without the shield. Finally the Spartan Leonymus died when an arrow penetrated his shield and jerkin (*spolados*).[10]

This evidence is less conclusive than is assumed. Leonymus was killed during a desperate uphill march through a storm; he might have decided not to wear his full equipment, although Xenophon presumably mentioned that the arrow had pierced the jerkin because he regarded it as a moderately effective barrier. Xenophon's uphill struggle occurred while he was attempting to

8. *en tōi strateumati*: *Anab.* 3.3.16. Horses for cavalry service: *Anab.* 3.3.19. A. M. Snodgrass, *Arms and Armour of the Greeks* (London, 1967), p. 107; L. Rawlings, 'Alternative agonies: hoplite martial and combat experiences beyond the phalanx', in H. van Wees (ed.), *War and Violence in Ancient Greece* (London, 2000), pp. 233–59, at p. 240, used this development to argue for the flexibility and versatility of Greek hoplites, but the evidence may well not be relevant.
9. The parade at Tyriaeum: *Anab.* 1.2.16. Snodgrass, *Arms and Armour of the Greeks*, p. 109; followed by S. Perlman, 'The Ten Thousand: a chapter in the military, social and economic history of the fourth century', *Rivista Storica dell'Antichità* 6–7 (1976–7), pp. 241–84, at p. 267, and J. K. Anderson, *Military Theory and Practice in the Age of Xenophon* (Berkeley, 1970), pp. 26–8; V. D. Hanson, *The Western Way of War: Infantry Battle in Classical Greece* (New York, 1989), pp. 57–8. E. Jarva, *Archaiologia on Archaic Greek Body Armour* (Rovaniemi, 1993), pp. 17–43, 63, 111–17, argued that phalanx members had never all worn heavy metal armour and that chest protection of leather and other materials was common in the Archaic period.
10. *Thōrakes*: *Anab.* 3.3.20. Xenophon and the Sicyonian's shield: *Anab.* 3.4.43–9. The death of Leonymus: *Anab.* 4.1.18.

keep pace with the most agile of the expedition's hoplites, those capable of operating alongside peltasts; the fact that he specified that he was wearing 'a cavalry breastplate' may indicate that the cavalry version of this item was heavier than the equivalent infantry item, not that the breastplate was restricted to the cavalry. Xenophon, as one of the wealthier members of the expedition, might also have had particularly robust and heavy items.[11]

The defensive equipment provided for the scratch cavalry force is similarly inconclusive. If the riders were former infantrymen,[12] whether peltasts or hoplites, they were now being given the extra protection which the abandonment of their shields required. If, however, they were drawn, at least in part, from the grooms and any other camp-followers that were experienced in horse-riding, they were now being kitted out for the first time. Neither possibility demonstrates that the hoplites on the expedition did not have breastplates.

For the parade ground scene, the first point to establish is the meaning of *chitōn*, which is rendered as 'cloak' above but as 'tunic' in standard translations. A *chitōn* could be worn over a breastplate, as is shown by Herodotus' account of the death of the Persian Masistius at Plataea: after being thrown from his wounded horse he managed to survive Athenian attacks for a time since he had a breastplate (*thōrax*) made of golden scales underneath his scarlet cloak (*chitōn*); the implication is that the breastplate was hidden, which explained why the Athenians took some time to realize that he was actually wearing defensive body armour. In the parade scene, Xenophon was concerned with the collective visual impact of the Greeks, and so mentioned their red cloaks along with those items which the cloak would not conceal, namely helmets, greaves, and shields; he chose not to record what the Greeks were wearing underneath, whether that was jerkins or breastplates. Among the Ten Thousand, equipment may have differed between units, or according to the

---

11. L. Iapichino, 'I Diecimila di Senofonte: techniche di combattimento, equipaggiamento militare e approvvigionamento degli strumenti di guerra', *Rivista Storica dell'Antichità* 29 (1999), pp. 91–105, at p. 99, suggests that the hoplites with whom Xenophon was struggling to keep pace might not have been wearing their full kit, but it is equally significant that they were in any case the fastest movers in the army. For the increasing weight of cavalry armour, see Snodgrass, *Arms and Armour of the Greeks*, p. 104, followed by I. G. Spence, *The Cavalry of Classical Greece: A Social and Military History* (Oxford, 1993), p. 61. There is in fact little evidence for the development, though Diod. 14.22.6 indicates that the quality of Greek equipment was recognized by outsiders.
12. As Anderson, *Military Theory and Practice*, p. 27, assumed; but the need to issue jerkins as well as breastplates might suggest that some of the new troopers had not previously been fighting men of any category.

wealth of the individual, and by the end of the march some infantry seem to have worn breastplates;[13] this may always have been the case, and there would certainly have been differences between what peltasts and hoplites wore under their cloaks. Xenophon focused on the homogeneous appearance of the Greek contingent provided by their cloaks.[14]

The final preliminary issue springs from the second, and concerns the nature of 'standard' hoplite warfare, or at least scholarly views on this. This is a contested topic, but needs to be considered briefly so that the performance of the Ten Thousand can be examined in an appropriate context. The traditional view of the hoplite is dominated by his inflexibility both as an individual soldier and collectively in the phalanx: the defensive equipment which gave security to each soldier rendered him clumsy and vulnerable unless protected in a group; as a result hoplites could only operate effectively in specific geographical conditions, where small plains permitting easy deployment were flanked by mountains that prevented encirclement and offered refuge in flight. The inappropriateness of this form of warfare for the predominantly mountainous Greek landscape is regarded as one of the paradoxes of the hoplite phenomenon.[15]

The Greek approach to warfare was held up to ridicule by the Persian Mardonius, on the grounds that they had to agree to fight their conventional battles but could not conceive of agreeing alternatives to such a costly form of combat. Although Mardonius' exaggerations and the irony of his deprecation of the soldiers who would repulse Xerxes' invasion are recognized, elements of his characterization of hoplite combat still hold sway. Hoplites are seen as being good at fighting other hoplites, but vulnerable to forces which did not observe their rules.[16]

13. *Anab.* 7.4.16.
14. *Chitōn* is translated as 'tunic' in Warner (above, n. 1), p. 61; as too in the Loeb and Budé translations: C. L. Brownson, *Xenophon, Hellenica Books VI and VII, Anabasis Books I–III* (Cambridge, Mass., 1921), p. 259; P. Masqueray, *Xenophon, Anabase I (livres I–III)* (Paris, 1949), p. 53. Masistius: Hdt. 9.22. Anderson, *Military Theory and Practice*, p. 26, rejects the interpretation advanced above on the grounds that body armour, whether jerkin or breastplate, is always displayed over a tunic in paintings and sculpture: this assumption is contradicted by his plate 11, a late fifth century Athenian depiction of a trophy which shows a cloak pinned at the shoulder and covering a breastplate. Iapichino, 'I Diecimila di Senofonte', p. 99, has also rejected the standard inferences from this passage, though on the grounds that the parade was a special occasion and so irrelevant to the mercenaries' normal equipment.
15. e.g. Cartledge, 'Hoplites and heroes', p. 18.
16. The jibe of Mardonius: Hdt. 7.9. Vulnerability of hoplites to those playing outside the rules: V. D. Hanson, *The Other Greeks* (New York, 1995), p. 332.

It is now becoming fashionable to query the predominance of primarily hoplite conflict in the totality of Greek warfare. Scholars emphasize the gradual and piecemeal adoption of classic hoplite equipment and tactics, with the process only being complete shortly before the Persian Wars. Alternatively, they point to the emergence of new forms of fighting in the mid fifth century so that by the Peloponnesian War purely hoplite war was an outmoded and parochial practice confined to a few inland states.[17]

At its most radical, this revisionist approach questions the notion of inflexibility, and instead characterizes hoplites as all-rounders whose training gave them the ability to undertake a variety of military tasks. The hoplite mode of combat might seem in danger of disappearing completely, but its efficiency as a means of resolving a particular campaign was still recognized, as at Delium in 424 or Leuctra in 371. Even after Demosthenes in the 340s drew a contrast between the good old days of the customary open hoplite campaigns waged by the Spartans during their supremacy and the contemporary professionalism of Philip's new Macedonian army, the Athenians still focused their attention on improving their hoplites through better training, and it was a primarily hoplite army which confronted Philip at Chaeronea. For Demosthenes enumerating the elements in Philip's army, as much as for Xenophon envisaging a hypothetical force, hoplites naturally headed the list.[18]

The inappropriateness of attempting to categorize the varied Greek military practices in a single way should be recognized. The combination of geographical and agrarian conditions with specific socio-political factors is particularly relevant to the practice of hoplite tactics in the central and southern Greek peninsula, but in the broader Greek world conflict had always been necessary against opponents who had no reason to accept the conventions of hoplite capabilities, and over terrain which did not provide the tactical advantages of the Greek homeland. In the wider world of what might be termed 'colonial' warfare, since much of the fighting involved forces from the colonial diffusion of Greeks, whether in Asia Minor, the Black Sea, Thrace, or

17. Gradual adoption of hoplite tactics: H. van Wees, 'The development of the hoplite phalanx: iconography and reality in the seventh century', in van Wees, *War and Violence*, pp. 125–66. Hoplite war as outmoded and parochial: V. D. Hanson, 'Hoplite battle as ancient Greek warfare: when, where, why?', in van Wees, *War and Violence*, pp. 201–32, at p. 216.
18. Hoplites as all-rounders: L. Rawlings, 'Alternative agonies: hoplite martial and combat experiences beyond the phalanx', in van Wees, *War and Violence*, pp. 233–59. Efficiency at Delium and Leuctra: Hanson, 'Hoplite battle as ancient Greek warfare', p. 222. Demosthenes on Philip's Macedonian army: Dem. 9.48–50. Xenophon's hypothetical force: *Oec.* 8.6.

southern Italy and Sicily, hoplites constituted the backbone of Greek infantry and retained their reputation in a variety of conditions. There may have been disasters, such as the failure of Dorieus' adventures in the West, or the elimination of the Athenian colony at Ennea Hodoi, when the inability of traditional hoplites to cope with different types of fighting may have played a part, but no details are known, and the incidents did not persuade states to reduce their reliance on hoplites. Most of this 'colonial' fighting is completely unknown to us. Indeed, we have very little information about the conditions of 'pure' hoplite warfare before Thucydides, since the engagements of the Persian Wars recounted by Herodotus were not fought against hoplite opponents, while no battle between Greek armies in the Archaic Age is described in any detail.[19]

Xenophon's *Anabasis* is exceptional for both the quality and quantity of its information about the even less well recorded 'colonial' warfare. What is apparent is that although the tight phalanx formation was suited to hoplites, especially the part-time soldiers of many Greek *poleis*, hoplites were also capable, with the appropriate training, of operating much more flexibly. Personal skills did matter, and the lives of hoplites who had to advance uphill in column formation or participate in disorganized combat during the capture of a stronghold might depend on such abilities.[20]

Integration and training

The Ten Thousand began as a disparate group, created from the various contingents whose preparation and subsequent arrival at Cyrus' camp are described by Xenophon. Although most of the troops had ultimately been financed by Cyrus, the soldiers were still primarily attached to their particular captain and there was no single leader for the Greek contingent before Cunaxa. This is clear both from the account of Clearchus' attempts to calm the mercenaries' mutiny in Cilicia, when his professed respect for his men's wishes induced two thousand men from the contingents of Xenias and Pasion to transfer themselves to his leadership, and then from the confrontation

---

19. On the geographical and socio-political factors behind hoplite tactics: cf. Hanson, 'Hoplite battle as ancient Greek warfare', p. 211. Dorieus' failure: Hdt. 5.42–7. Ennea Hodoi: Thuc. 1.100.3.
20. Cf. Pl. *La.* 181e–182b for training in fighting in armour which is said to be useful in battle and especially after the formation is disrupted.

during the Euphrates march between Clearchus' and Menon's men after Clearchus had ordered a beating for one of the latter's soldiers.[21]

Unity was forged in the crisis after Cunaxa, unsurprisingly though not inevitably, but the continuing importance of the different elements within the expedition became apparent after the safety of the Black Sea was reached. Alternative views now emerged about the advisability of ravaging expeditions, the advantages of attempting to establish a permanent settlement on the Black Sea coast, and the attractions of a rapid return home. At Heraclea, divisions eventually led to fragmentation when the army split into three: the largest group, more than four thousand Arcadian and Achaean hoplites, represented a national element which had been latent in the expedition throughout; Chirisophus the Spartiate led the 700 Thracian peltasts who had originally been hired by Clearchus, and many of his 1,400 hoplites had probably also started out under Clearchus; Xenophon led the remainder, 1,700 hoplites, 300 peltasts, and the small cavalry squadron in whose creation he had been involved and which had been commanded by the Athenian Lycius. This physical separation soon proved unfortunate for the purely hoplite contingent of Arcadians and Achaeans, who were severely mauled by light-armed Thracian troops. Rivalry between units, however, had advantages if competition stimulated men to greater endeavour, as can be seen in the competition between various Arcadian captains to capture a hilltop village.[22]

The individual contingents were well-trained professionals before they combined in Cyrus' expedition, as the display which they put on for the Queen of Cilicia revealed: 'The generals passed on the order to the soldiers, the trumpet sounded and, with spears at the ready, they moved forward. Then as the soldiers advanced more quickly, shouted and automatically came to be running towards the tents, the barbarians were in a great panic...' The effects of the performance anticipate Alexander's demonstration of Macedonian drill in the Balkan mountains, an incident often cited to illustrate the superior quality of Macedonian discipline.[23]

---

21. Preparation and arrival at the camp of Cyrus: *Anab.* 1.1.6–11; 2.1–6. Transfer to the command of Clearchus: *Anab.* 1.3.7 Altercation during the Euphrates march: *Anab.* 1.5.11–14.
22. Division of army: *Anab.* 6.2.16. Mauling by Thracian troops: *Anab.* 6.3.1–9. Competition to capture the village: *Anab.* 4.7.8–12; cf. also 5.2.11, and Sall. *Cat.* 7, for the principle in operation at Rome.
23. The display for the Queen: *Anab.* 1.2.17–18. Alexander's display in the Balkans: Arr. *Anab.* 1.6.1–4.

After Cunaxa, an orderly march past was used to impress watching Persians as well as boost Greek confidence. The disciplined stance of Clearchus' hoplites in their confrontation with Menon's men, when they 'held their position with shields resting against their knees', presages the tactic which brought fame for Chabrias when his mercenaries awaited the approach of Agesilaus' Spartans with a show of contempt, shields leant against knees and spears upraised; Agesilaus was sufficiently impressed by that disciplined performance to abandon his attempt to force his way past them. At Cunaxa, the hoplite contingent showed that it could cope, perhaps instinctively, with the almost inevitable disruptions of a massed advance: when a surge threatened to leave part of the phalanx behind, the slower element advanced at the double to re-establish unity, before everyone raised the battle cry and charged.[24]

The traditional view that hoplites needed no skills other than bravery and fitness was outmoded, if indeed it had ever applied outside the most amateur of *polis* forces. Throughout the march north the constant threat of attack will have ensured that the military effectiveness of the expedition remained high. After the pressure relaxed and overall cohesion began to deteriorate along the Black Sea coast, the desire for booty came to the fore, though desperation also drove some of the independent raids for booty.[25]

Even when supplies were available in a market, an interest in continued pillaging suggests that not all soldiers had resources to exchange, or that some at least preferred to attempt to preserve their gains for the return home. When properly led, these raids were successful: this is the message of the concluding incident in the *Anabasis*, the raid conducted by Xenophon himself for the benefit of his friends and closest followers, when tight discipline and good leadership rescued the raiders from a Persian counter-attack.[26] On those occasions that disaster struck, as when the Thracians mauled the Arcadian

---

24. The march past at Cunaxa: *Anab.* 2.4.26. The stance of Clearchus' men: *Anab.* 1.5.13. Chabrias and Agesilaus: Diod. 15.32.5. The charge at Cunaxa: *Anab.* 1.8.18. G. Wylie, 'Cunaxa and Xenophon', *L'Antiquité Classique* 61 (1992), pp. 119–34, at p. 125, slightly misrepresents Xenophon's account of the sequence of events.
25. The traditional view of the hoplite: *Cyrop.* 2.3.9–11. The desire for booty: *Anab.* 6.1.17. Desperation as a motive for looting: *Anab.* 6.4.23.
26. Interest in continued pillaging even with a market available: *Anab.* 6.1.1; cf. G. Hutchinson, *Xenophon and the Art of Command* (London, 2000), p. 57. The choice of Xenophon's raid as the story with which to end the *Anabasis* has occasioned some surprise (ibid., p. 92), since it appears to show Xenophon indulging in the type of freebooting which earned the Ten Thousand their bad name. But Xenophon's target was suitable: a rich pro-Persian, he received the support of a respectable expatriate, Hellas wife of Gongylus, and the expedition was a display of effective tactics. See also Azoulay, chapter 10 in this volume.

contingent or Pharnabazus' cavalry killed a quarter of a large ravaging party, the fault seems to have been inadequate leadership, which failed to foresee and respond to threats, rather than a failing of the soldiers.[27]

Military performance: Cunaxa

The military achievement of the Ten Thousand became a powerful argument for the practicality of a Panhellenic campaign against Persia. Xenophon has Jason of Pherae, as quoted by Polydamas of Pharsalus, assert that the Persian king had been reduced to dire straits by the relatively small forces which had marched with Cyrus and Agesilaus.[28] Isocrates, when advocating Philip of Macedon as the leader of his projected expedition, also focused on Cunaxa:

> I am, however, not going to encourage you on the basis of such occasions, but of men who were regarded as failures – I mean those who campaigned with Cyrus and Clearchus. For it is agreed that they were as victorious when fighting the king's whole power as if they had encountered their womenfolk, but that when they already appeared to be in control of affairs they failed because of the impetuosity of Cyrus... For they would clearly have mastered the king's affairs if it had not been for Cyrus. But for you it is easy...[29]

There is, unsurprisingly, considerable distortion in this survey, which belittles the quality of the Ten Thousand but maximizes their impact. Cyrus may have come close to victory at Cunaxa, but that was mainly because he personally wounded Artaxerxes in the chest; the contribution of the Greek contingent was disputed in antiquity and different views are still held. Xenophon made the most of the Greek charge, which terrified the opposing Persians into fleeing even before they came to grips: Persian chariots failed to disrupt the Greeks, and may have caused more trouble in their own ranks, while the Greeks managed to maintain their formation even during the pursuit, and only suffered one casualty. In the confused manoeuvres after Cyrus' death, the Greeks again charged Artaxerxes' troops and drove them from the field.[30]

27. Arcadians: *Anab.* 6.3.1–9. The run-in with Pharnabazus' cavalry: *Anab.* 4.23–4.
28. *Hell.* 6.1.12.
29. Isoc. 5.90–2.
30. *Anab.* 1.8.17–20; 1.10–11.

Xenophon, however, later reveals, when explaining how Tissaphernes reached the Greek camp, that the first charge was not quite so conclusive since Tissaphernes, far from being driven to flight, had advanced on the peltasts near the river; the peltasts opened their ranks to let him through, and apparently harassed the Persians sufficiently as they passed to dissuade them from returning for another encounter, although the prospect of booty in Cyrus' camp may have been as strong a reason for them to press ahead. At any rate the Greeks had permitted a strong contingent of the enemy to reach a dangerous position behind their ranks. In Xenophon Clearchus' first charge received full justification since he made Cyrus endorse their conduct: 'Cyrus was pleased when he saw the Greeks defeating and pursuing those opposite them, and he was already being saluted as king by his entourage.' Xenophon had no way of knowing Cyrus' views, but by recording this reaction he deterred his audience from considering the possibility that the Greek pursuit had left Cyrus exposed. Instead Cyrus' death was blamed on the failure of his own entourage to maintain cohesion after routing Artaxerxes' guards.[31]

What happened at Cunaxa is unclear, but the glorious Greek charge may only have secured limited advantage for Cyrus; indeed, as Xenophon almost admits, they had laid themselves open to an attack in the flank or rear from the main Persian army, a danger which led Cyrus to his fatal attack on Artaxerxes.[32] The other accounts of the battle, in Plutarch and Diodorus, do not provide significantly different material about the Greek actions even though they preserve extra details and some alternative information on the wounding of Artaxerxes and Cyrus' death.[33] Plutarch, however, made the Greeks responsible for Cyrus' failure since as the armies converged Cyrus exhorted Clearchus to advance against the enemy's centre where Artaxerxes was stationed, a request which was met with an equivocal response, as

31. Tissaphernes' advance: *Anab.* 1.10.7. Cyrus' praise for the Greek conduct: *Anab.* 1.8.21. Cyrus' entourage blamed: *Anab.* 1.8.25.
32. Limited effect of the charge: Wylie, 'Cunaxa and Xenophon'. Cyrus' fatal attack on Artaxerxes: *Anab.* 1.8.24.
33. For discussion of sources, see R. B. Stevenson, *Persica: Greek Writing about Persia in the Fourth Century BC* (Edinburgh, 1997), pp. 86–93: Plutarch cited discrepant information from Ctesias (whose account Xenophon knew) and Deinon, while Diodorus, via Ephorus, might ultimately have preserved some material from Deinon. By contrast Wylie, 'Cunaxa and Xenophon,' claimed that Xenophon was Diodorus' main source, whereas H. D. Westlake, 'Diodorus and the expedition of Cyrus', *Phoenix* 41 (1987), pp. 241–54, argued that Diodorus drew supplementary information from Xenophon, but did not depend on him for his main account (for this Westlake proposed, implausibly, the *Hellenica Oxyrhynchia*, via Ephorus). For detailed discussion, see Stylianou, chapter 2 in this volume.

Xenophon also conceded;[34] instead Clearchus stuck to his station beside the Euphrates, with the river protecting the right of his formation, and drove from the battlefield opponents whose fate was irrelevant to the eventual outcome. Thereby Cyrus was deprived of the services of the unit in which he had placed particular faith.

Plutarch's criticism of the Greek action seems reasonable at first sight, but it is unjustified. Cyrus knew that Artaxerxes would be in the centre of his formation, since this was standard Persian practice, and he himself followed this in his own deployment. Although Cyrus had allowed his army to advance with less caution after crossing the ditch which he had expected Artaxerxes to defend, and the announcement of Artaxerxes' approach initially caused confusion, he had already allocated positions to his various contingents, with Clearchus in command of the Greeks on the right wing. Cyrus intended to attack the King himself with his best Persian troops, who were preceded by a heavily armoured contingent of cavalry, not with his Greek troops, whether because it was thought improper for a Persian royal competition to be decided by foreigners or because of the implausibility of an infantry charge being able to scatter the elite mounted guards around the King.[35]

On seeing the size of Artaxerxes' army, Cyrus did attempt to adapt his battle plan by urging Clearchus to advance diagonally leftwards, but the significance of this operation is obscured by the uncertainty over how Artaxerxes' location related to Cyrus' dispositions. Xenophon states that Artaxerxes, placed in the middle of his line, was beyond Cyrus' left wing, which suggests that he had an enormous numerical superiority. For Diodorus it was Cyrus' left wing under the command of Ariaeus which was in danger of being outflanked and encircled, whereas Cyrus himself had no problem in charging at Artaxerxes.[36]

---

34. Greeks responsible for Cyrus' failure: Plut. *Artax.* 8.3–7. Plut. *Artax.* 8.7 converts the order to advance against the centre into instructions to Clearchus to take up his own position in the centre, an unjustified extrapolation. The equivocal response: *Anab.* 1.8.12–13.
35. Plutarch's criticisms underpin the negative reconstruction of the battle in Wylie, 'Cunaxa and Xenophon.' The central position of Artaxerxes: *Anab.* 1.8.21–2. Lack of caution after the ditch: *Anab.* 1.7.19–20. Confusion at the approach of Artaxerxes: *Anab.* 1.8.2. Allocation of positions to the various contingents: *Anab.* 1.8.3–4. Cyrus' contingent of cavalry: Diod. 14.22.5–6; his information on the deployment is quite clear.
36. Persian practice: *Anab.* 1.8.13. In this case Cyrus asked Clearchus to launch a diagonal advance across the full frontage of his own army; cf. Cawkwell, introduction to *Xenophon: The Persian Expedition*, pp. 37–8. Wylie, 'Cunaxa and Xenophon', pp. 124–6, concluded that this implausible move indicated Cyrus' desperation caused by his own poor planning. Diodorus' version: Diod. 14.24.1.

Diodorus' version makes more sense than Xenophon's, although this does not guarantee that it is more accurate. On Diodorus' dispositions Cyrus was trying to make a reasonable and relatively minor adjustment to his battle plan whereby all his contingents would have advanced on a slight diagonal so that his own station in the centre became roughly opposite that of Artaxerxes and the risk of outflanking on his left was reduced. Clearchus would have been instructed to adjust his charge somewhat towards the King, but not actually to engage the King since this had never been the role envisaged for the hoplites.[37] Plutarch misunderstood his information about the battle.

Overall it would be unsurprising if Greek writers had not exaggerated the Greek achievements at Cunaxa. The relative confidence, however, which the Greeks displayed after the battle even in their desperate position suggests that their performance had given them reason to trust their own abilities. Ctesias, for his own reasons, may have chosen to denigrate the overall impact of the Greeks' contribution even though he could not challenge their ability to rout oriental troops. Whatever the truth about the battle, the effectiveness of the Greek charge is only one aspect, and perhaps the most predictable one, of the military achievement of the Ten Thousand.

Military performance: the march

Before Isocrates latched on to Philip as the saviour of Greece, when he was still canvassing a Persian campaign under the joint leadership of Athens and Sparta, he had set aside the success on the battlefield at Cunaxa and highlighted instead the mercenaries' ability to withdraw safely from the king's territory:

> And indeed there is no reason to fear the army which wanders around with the King nor the courage of the Persians, for they were clearly revealed by those who marched up country with Cyrus to be no better than those near the sea. I omit all the other battles in which they were defeated and I grant that they were split by civil strife and were not willing to endanger themselves too enthusiastically against the king's brother. But after Cyrus' death when all who inhabit Asia came together, in these conditions they cam-

---

37. Clearchus may even have carried out the order, at least partially, since the fact that Tissaphernes' cavalry contingent, which must have been substantially larger in terms of frontage than the Greek peltasts opposite it, escaped the effects of the charge and maintained its station on the banks of the Euphrates is a plausible consequence of an oblique advance leftwards by Clearchus.

paigned so shamelessly ... For they had to deal with 6,000 Greeks, men not picked for valour but who were incapable of living in their own lands because of impoverishment, who did not know the country, who were deserted by their allies ... then as they set out he sent Tissaphernes and the cavalry with them; although they were plotted against by them throughout the entire journey, they accomplished their march as if under escort, being especially afraid of the uninhabited part of the country and considering it the greatest of benefits if they encountered as many enemy as possible.[38]

Again there is considerable distortion, both of the Greek numbers and the intensity and duration of Persian pressure, but there is less doubt about the reality of what the Greeks achieved: the vast majority of the Greek soldiers, together with a considerable train of camp-followers, baggage and booty, managed to escape from the centre of the Persian Empire across extremely formidable and quite unknown terrain. Even if they were only under direct Persian attack, and that not always whole-hearted, for a small part of the route, they had thereafter to force their way past different tribes whose natural hostility will have been sharpened by the competition for valuable food resources which the Ten Thousand provided during an Armenian winter.

The difficulties which might have overwhelmed the Greeks can be seen from two unsuccessful fighting retreats.[39] In AD 363 Emperor Julian's grand invasion of Persia was harassed so effectively by the Persians under Shapur II in the territory which the Ten Thousand had managed to cross that it was only able to extricate itself, after Julian's mortal wounding in a skirmish, by humiliating surrender and the transfer of considerable territory in Mesopotamia to the Persians. Our main source, Ammianus, participated in the expedition and described the increasing frustration as the large Roman army ground to a halt under the incessant attacks. Even before Julian's death shattered morale, Persian attacks seriously threatened the safety of the rearguard and restricted the column to an advance of seventy stades (about eight miles) in a day. After Julian's death the army only struggled forward thirty stades (almost four miles)

---

38. Isoc. 4.145–9.
39. A third, less disastrous, example is offered by Antony's fighting retreat across northwestern Iran in 36 after he was forced to abandon the siege of the Median capital of Phraata (or Phraaspa), located somewhere to the south of Tabriz. Antony knew his Xenophon and used similar tactics to the Ten Thousand (e.g. Plut. *Ant.* 41.4–5) to fight his way north to the Araxes, a journey of twenty-seven days, but lost about one-third of his massive army in the process (*Ant.* 50.1). In the African campaigns of the Roman Civil Wars in 46 Caesar twice had to extricate his troops from severe harassment by Numidian cavalry and light infantry: Caes. *B Afr.* 12–18, 69–70.

on the last day it managed to move, and the persistence of Persian attacks then tied it down at Dura for four days, after which negotiations were opened.[40]

The Athenian retreat from Syracuse in 413 was even less successful: on the three days for which Thucydides recorded the distance covered by the Athenians, they managed to advance between four and thirty-six stades, between half a mile and four and a half; on one day they were forced to return to their starting point. The Athenians did force one defended river crossing at the Anapus, but repeated attempts to break through a fortified pass were repulsed, and the contingent under Nicias was finally overwhelmed at the crossing of the Assinarus. The Athenians adopted a hollow square formation with the hoplites on the outside and the other survivors of the expedition and the baggage in the middle, but they failed to devise an effective response to attacks by Syracusan cavalry and light-armed troops.[41]

What could be achieved by well-trained and determined troops under good leadership is illustrated by Thucydides' description of Brasidas' retreat from Lyncestis after he had been abandoned by King Perdiccas.[42] Brasidas too drew up his forces in a square with the hoplites, who numbered about 3,000, on the outside with the light-armed inside, but he also made provision for counter-attacks by the youngest soldiers and had 300 picked troops to bring up the rear. Thucydides allocated Brasidas a speech to boost his men's morale and underline the importance of resisting initial attacks to dissuade the enemy from pressing home subsequent assaults.

The Athenians at Syracuse were certainly hampered by the sheer size of their column, as perhaps was Julian's army, although this was a better balanced force than either of the Greek armies since it contained significant cavalry and missile units.[43] The Ten Thousand was a large body which required good discipline and leadership if it was to survive, but it may also, fortuitously, have been close to the optimum military size to permit both effective fighting and reasonable progress.[44]

40. Seventy stades/day: Amm. Marc. 25.1.5, 10. Grinding to a halt at Dura: Amm. Marc. 25.6.9, 11.
41. Distance covered by the Athenians: Thuc. 7.78, 80; in Africa, Caesar's harassed forces managed to cover only a hundred yards in four hours (Caes. *B Afr.* 70.1). Repeated failure at the fortified pass: Thuc. 7.78–9. The crossing of the Assinarus: Thuc. 7.84–5.
42. Thuc. 4.125–8.
43. Also true for Caesar's and Antony's armies.
44. In discussion of Byzantine warfare, J. Haldon, *Warfare, State and Society in the Byzantine World 565–1204* (London, 1999), p. 291, suggested that 'armies substantially larger than this [10,000] would rapidly lose in flexibility and speed'.

The task of escaping from Mesopotamia was made much easier by the fact that the Greeks had already come about 250 miles from Cunaxa, across the Tigris and Lesser Zab as well as small rivers and canals, all under watchful Persian escort, and only had about a hundred miles to traverse after Persian attacks began before reaching the different challenges of the mountains. Success was certainly not guaranteed, however, as the reverses suffered by the independent Arcadian contingent in Bithynia show:[45] first the local Thracians annihilated two of the Arcadian contingents, each probably numbering about 400 hoplites, of which one was routed when crossing a watercourse; the remaining Arcadians, probably about 3,000 strong, were confined to a hillock and so harassed by missile attacks that they opened negotiations to surrender. A single day would, therefore, have been enough to bring disaster on the Ten Thousand in Mesopotamia.

The march north from the River Zab demonstrated that the Ten Thousand, under perceptive leadership, matched Brasidas' men in fighting ability and flexibility. The Greeks had, on Xenophon's advice, formed up in a hollow square, but on the first day fared no better than the retreating Athenians, advancing only two and a half miles.[46] Mithradates with only 200 cavalry and 400 archers proved a most effective restraint, since Xenophon's rearguard could not get to grips with or shake off the Persians and the day's march had ended in despondency.

The Ten Thousand had failed Brasidas' first test, of denting the enemy's enthusiasm, since Mithradates returned on the next day with 1,000 cavalry and 4,000 archers and slingers, full of confidence that he could now overwhelm his demoralized opponents. The Greeks, however, again at Xenophon's suggestion, had learned from their troubles and overnight improvised sufficient cavalry and missile troops to thwart the Persians. The combination of effective slingers, charging horsemen, and close support from combined hoplites and peltasts rectified the previous day's reverses; although the cavalry and light-armed were the new element in the equation, it is also clear that their impact depended on the stability afforded by the close support of heavy infantry.[47]

At the second attempt the Ten Thousand imposed the essential respect on the Persians, a message underlined by the mutilation of Persian corpses: after

---

45. *Anab.* 6.3.1–9.
46. Hollow square: *Anab.* 3.2.36; 3.3.6. Two and a half miles on the first day: *Anab.* 3.3.11.
47. For the importance of denting enemy enthusiasm, cf. Plut. *Ant.* 44.1: after four days of successful fighting retreat, an ill-judged action by the Roman rearguard (*Ant.* 42) fully restored Parthian morale. The return of Mithradates: *Anab.* 3.4.2. Greek success in the sequel: *Anab.* 3.4.3–5.

an unchallenged day on which the Greeks managed eighteen miles, the Persians approached them again under Tissaphernes' command but were too wary to come close and were soon persuaded to stay out of range of the Rhodian slingers.[48] Antony's retreat in Media, roughly parallel to but about a hundred miles to the east of the Ten Thousand's route, used the same tactics: 'he led his army in a hollow square after covering not only his rear but also both flanks with numerous javelin men and slingers, and he told his cavalry to rout the enemy when they attacked but not to pursue them further once they were routed'; on this occasion too, however, it was the heavy armour which provided protection for everyone in the most difficult places.[49]

A hollow square provided reasonable protection while marching across open ground, and gave structure to a fighting retreat, as Xenophon noted when describing his private expedition for booty at the end of the *Anabasis*.[50] The formation demonstrated the Greeks' determination to fight their way out of trouble, and prevented their assailants gaining confidence by recapturing the booty easily. But success required excellent discipline, resolute morale, and good leadership.

The Roman disaster at Carrhae in 53 illustrates the consequences when these were lacking. Crassus' light-armed troops could not drive off the Parthian mounted archers and instead caused confusion by retreating into the main square. A counter-attack led by Crassus' son and accompanied by a strong cavalry force allowed itself to be lured too far from the main army and was destroyed, and the Parthians then managed to compress the main square and impede the ability of the Romans to defend themselves.[51]

The Ten Thousand were superior to Crassus' expedition on all counts, but still found that their formation could run into danger at more constricted points since bunching might create confusion as the road narrowed and gaps could appear if the sides of the square did not fill out quickly when the road opened out again; these disruptions might be exploited by an enemy who, while lacking the confidence to press attacks from the flanks, was tagging along

---

48. Eighteen-mile Greek advance: *Anab.* 3.4.10. Wariness of the Persians: *Anab.* 3.4.14–15.
49. 'He led his army . . .': Plut. *Ant.* 42.1. For the importance of not initiating ill-disciplined pursuit, cf. Plut. *Ant.* 41.4–5 and Caes. *B Afr.* 15 (no advance more than four feet from the standards). The importance of heavy armour: Plut. *Ant.* 45.2; cf. also Plut. *Crass.* 24.4.
50. *Anab.* 7.8.16–18.
51. Plut. *Crass.* 24.4, 25, 27.1–2. By contrast, Caesar's resourcefulness and composure were instrumental in extricating his troops from bouts of prolonged harassment: Caes. *B Afr.* 15, 17, 69–70.

behind in case an opportunity arose. The Ten Thousand devised a solution to these problems, by identifying six companies of a hundred men each who would drop behind the square whenever the flanks were compressed and then fill up any size of gap which might appear as the formation spread out.[52]

Once into the rough mountainous country of Carduchia, the modern Hakkari region in south-east Turkey, there was rarely space for the formation to open out, and the Ten Thousand proceeded in column, with Chirisophus in the van and Xenophon in charge of the rearguard. Their achievement in forcing a way across this region can be gauged by the Persian king Khusro I's unhappy retreat from Melitene in AD 576, when it was necessary to create a route by felling trees and cutting rocks. Khusro ended the campaign in complete despair.[53]

In this section it was essential for the army to push ahead as rapidly as possible while still ensuring that the front and rear of the column maintained contact. Marching by night was always problematic: it was during the last desperate night retreat towards the sea by the Athenian remnants in 413 that the divisions of Nicias and Demosthenes became separated, to be picked off separately over the next three days. Once the Ten Thousand had reached Thrace, Xenophon explained to Seuthes that the Greeks had a method of retaining cohesion on night marches, by putting the slowest units in the front. Even when there was a need for speed this principle seems to have been observed: when moving towards a crucial summit in Carduchia the Greeks advanced across a plain during the latter part of the night, but on reaching the start of the ascent at dawn all the peltasts were transferred to the front since speed was essential and there was now little danger of attack from behind. The line of march had constantly to be adapted to the conditions: a race to secure a crucial hilltop was won by the peltasts and 300 picked hoplites from Chirisophus' vanguard, all placed under Xenophon's command; the select group recalls that of Brasidas in Thrace.[54]

Xenophon only recorded one occasion when the column became separated, during a difficult march over narrow passes through a storm: Xenophon's rearguard, under constant harassment, was frequently forced to stop to repel their

52. Difficulties of the formation: *Anab.* 3.4.19–20. The solution: *Anab.* 3.4.21–3.
53. John of Ephesus 6.9. For the historical context, see L. M Whitby, *The Emperor Maurice and his Historian: Theophylact Simocatta on Persian and Balkan Warfare* (Oxford, 1988), pp. 262–8.
54. The Athenian retreat to the sea: Thuc. 7.80–4. Xenophon's explanation of night marches: *Anab.* 7.3.37. The advance in Carduchia: *Anab.* 4.1.5–6; contrast 3.4.38–40. Speedy select group under Xenophon's command: *Anab.* 3.4.42–9.

assailants and Chirisophus would halt the vanguard as soon as word was passed forward; eventually, however, Chirisophus did not wait but pressed on fast, passing the word back that the rearguard should follow as quickly as possible, with the result that their 'progress came to resemble flight'. The Spartan Leonymus and Baias the Arcadian were killed during this phase and their bodies had to be abandoned, as Xenophon angrily pointed out to Chirisophus when he eventually reached the site for the night's camp; Chirisophus' explanation was that he had hoped to be able to reach a pass on the only apparent route through the region before it was occupied by the enemy. In spite of the loss of two brave men, and presumably unnamed others, the Ten Thousand had escaped relatively lightly from this crisis and thereafter there appears to have been closer integration between vanguard and rearguard in clearing blockages in front of the column and driving off attacks on the rear: as required, Chirisophus or Xenophon would lead their men towards higher ground than that occupied by the enemy threatening their advance, 'And so they were constantly assisting each other and supporting each other strongly.'[55]

The crossing of a river or ravine was always a point of danger when the army might fall into confusion, as the Athenians did at the Assinarus. The Ten Thousand did not always succeed. One Arcadian hoplite contingent was annihilated in Bithynia, and Xenophon's rearguard was prevented from crossing a watercourse in Carduchia by a barrage of boulders rolled down on them.[56]

Alexander the Great's campaigns provide the best ancient examples of both attacking across a defended river and retreating when under attack. At the Jaxartes in 329 artillery mounted on ships was used to drive back Saca horsemen mounted on the northern bank, just as archers might have been used on the Danube crossing in 335. When Alexander was almost trapped by Glaucias in the Balkan mountains in 335, he extricated his army across a river by deploying his best missile troops, the Agrianian javelin men and the archers, to cover the narrow crossing while the phalanx battalions crossed in column, with orders to deploy as soon as they were safely across; when Glaucias threatened the rearguard, Alexander brought up the Agrianians and archers to shoot from midstream, ordered the phalanx to threaten to recross the stream to

55. Halting of the vanguard when the rearguard was harassed: *Anab.* 4.1.15–16. 'Progress came to resemble flight': *Anab.* 4.1.17. The disagreement between Xenophon and Chirisophus which follows should be added to what Xenophon claimed as the 'only occasion' when he had disagreed with Chirisophus on the march (*Anab.* 4.6.3). Closer integration between vanguard and rear: *Anab.* 4.2.25–6.
56. Annihilation in Bithynia: *Anab.* 6.3.5. The barrage of boulders: *Anab.* 4.2.3–4.

attack, and used his artillery shooting at maximum range to disrupt the attack in a demonstration of the flexibility as well as discipline of these troops and of his own abilities as commander.[57]

Xenophon's attention to the details of river crossings is shown by the fact that he recorded a plan that was not put into action and a complicated but ultimately uneventful crossing. At the borders of Carduchia, when the Greeks were contemplating crossing the Tigris to avoid the march through the mountains to the north, a Rhodian came forward with a plan to construct a floating bridge: 2,000 animal skins would be needed which, when inflated, would be anchored by heavy stones attached to ropes; wooden planks and earth were to be laid on top, and the whole would permit the transit of 4,000 hoplites at a time. The scheme does not sound robust enough to withstand the force of the Tigris's current at this point, but it was never put to the test, since the generals thought that there were too many Persian cavalry on the west bank to permit the Greeks even to secure a bridgehead there. Later in Bithynia, immediately after Neon's men had been mauled by Pharnabazus' cavalry, Xenophon narrated the crossing of a substantial wooded gully: at first the army halted in uncertainty about how to proceed and it was only after Xenophon himself had ridden up from the rearguard and convinced his colleagues that the crossing could be made safely that the army advanced. Xenophon decided that it was safer for the army to cross on a broad front, with each man advancing from his current position, rather than to squeeze everyone across the single bridge. The plan worked and the Greeks emerged on the further side in good formation to attack the Bithynians. Even though the crossing turned out to be relatively simple, Xenophon chose to underline the incident, and his own contribution to resolving the problem, by according himself two speeches.[58]

On the other hand, not every major crossing is described: Xenophon did not say how the Ten Thousand got over the Greater Zab and omitted to mention the Lesser Zab completely. The Ten Thousand were lucky to approach these rivers in October, when their flow is lowest; the Lesser Zab would have been fordable at the major route through this part of Mesopotamia; the

---

57. Alexander at the Jaxartes: Curt. 7.9.2–9. See A. B. Bosworth, *A Historical Commentary on Arrian's History of Alexander II* (Oxford, 1995), pp. 28–9, for reasons for preferring this account to Arrian (*Anab.* 4.2.2–6), who says that the artillery were stationed on the southern bank; it makes no difference to the principle of using missiles to clear a landing space. The Danube crossing in 335: Arr. *Anab.* 1.3.3. The attack by Glaucias: Arr. *Anab.* 1.6.6–8.
58. The plan to cross the Tigris: *Anab.* 3.5.7–12. The successful crossing in Bithynia: *Anab.* 6.5.12–25.

Greater Zab is only fordable in drier autumns, and otherwise a ferry was probably used.[59] It was only after the Ten Thousand had passed the Greater Zab that Mithradates began the harassment which would have complicated matters, or even rendered that crossing impossible, while the Lesser Zab must have been passed a week or more earlier when relations with the Persians were still reasonable.

The most complicated river crossing undertaken by the Ten Thousand was at the Centrites, the modern Bohtan Su, a substantial tributary of the Tigris whose width Xenophon records as 200 feet. The north bank was guarded by Persian cavalry with good quality mercenary infantry stationed in support on a terrace three or four hundred feet further back. To make matters worse, the Carduchi, through whose territory the Ten Thousand had just fought their way, began to assemble on the high ground in their rear. The chance discovery of a partially screened ford slightly upstream from the main ford helped the Greeks, since Chirisophus was able to cross with half the army, including the peltasts and archers, while Xenophon distracted the Persians by threatening to return to the main crossing; the Persian cavalry retired to safer ground, soon to be followed by the infantry. However, as the Greek baggage and non-combatants began to cross, the Carduchi rushed down from the hills to cut off the weakened rearguard, but Xenophon promptly drew up his hoplites in opposition, while Chirisophus sent back the peltasts and other missile troops in support; Xenophon ordered these to station themselves part way across the river on either side of the ford and provide covering fire from there, while the hoplites were to charge the Carduchi as soon as sling shots rattled on their shields but then, when the trumpeter sounded the attack, they were all to race back to the river and cross as they came to it to avoid bunching and delay.[60] The plan worked well, even though some of the enemy quickly saw through the trick of the fake trumpet call for attack and the Greek missile troops advanced further into the river than Xenophon had intended and so came within range of the pursuing Carduchi. Alexander never had to attempt such a challenging crossing with enemies on both banks and, even by his high standards, the Ten Thousand performed their complicated manoeuvres in exceptional fashion, especially considering that the field artillery on which

---

59. The omission of the Lesser Zab: Cawkwell, *Xenophon: The Persian Expedition*, p. 123 n. 7, and cf. also his contribution to this volume, chapter 1. For the approaches to these rivers in October, see Admiralty War Staff, Intelligence Division, *Handbook of Mesopotamia III* (1917), on the routes to the east of the Tigris.
60. *Anab.* 4.3.1–8, 20–34.

Alexander depended for long-range protection had not yet been developed and that they had a much smaller number of missile troops to protect their passage.

The Ten Thousand repeatedly had to undertake attacks uphill, to clear their route through Carduchia and Armenia and secure supplies from hilltop refuges. Although hoplites are traditionally believed to be ill-equipped to succeed in such conditions, the Greeks had initially welcomed their approach to the mountains because they promised relief from harassment by Tissaphernes' cavalry; while they did experience problems, they quickly learned to cope with these and overall were very successful in maintaining their advance – much more so than the demoralized Athenians withdrawing from Syracuse. Initially the Ten Thousand found themselves hard-pressed since their light-armed troops were driven back inside the hollow square, while the hoplites could not move uphill quickly enough to catch the enemy but found themselves exposed to counter-attack when retiring downhill. The solution was, once the Greeks had secured a high point, to deploy a flank guard of peltasts in a position to threaten any possible attackers during the Greek descent.[61]

In the mountains of Carduchia this process of manoeuvring to secure the local high ground could become complicated. After the incident in which Chirisophus' unsuccessful rush to occupy a summit had led to the separation of Xenophon's rearguard, the Greeks found themselves in danger of being trapped. However, a way to dislodge some of the blockaders was revealed and Xenophon engineered a diversion with the rearguard to distract attention from the ascent of a flanking force; at dawn this dislodged the enemy, and then the infantry under Chirisophus at the front of the column were able to climb up by rough tracks, being pulled up by their spears at the steepest points. The baggage and rearguard under Xenophon were still in danger, and had to dislodge some Carduchi from a commanding ridge, which they managed to do by advancing with their companies in column. Xenophon found that he had to secure three hills in succession to protect the passage of the baggage, and the detachment holding the first hill was evicted from its covering position before the difficult section of the route was completely negotiated.[62]

61. The promise of relief from harassment in the mountains: *Anab.* 3.4.24. For the breach of the hollow square, cf. the Roman position at Carrhae (above, p. 232, with n. 51). Counter-attack while retiring downhill: *Anab.* 3.4.26–9; cf. Plut. *Ant.* 45.2, for problems on a steep descent.
62. *Anab.* 4.1.20–1, 4.2.2–12, 17. There is a comparable, though simpler, incident during the passage over the Pontic Alps: *Anab.* 4.6.20–6.

On Xenophon's push uphill, speed, which was vital when persistent harassment had to be neutralized, was less important than physical occupation of the ground dominating the line of march, and hoplites were well suited to this task: while moving uphill the columns ensured that the smallest frontage was exposed to enemy attack, and hoplite armour provided reasonable protection from missiles, especially if the columns advanced obliquely with their shield arms to the fore. The advantages of an advance in column are spelled out by Xenophon in a speech to the generals when they were debating how to drive the Colchians from a superior position on the last significant barrier before the Black Sea coast. An advance in line of battle would run three distinct risks: if it advanced on a broad front, to match that of the Colchians, it would lose cohesion as it moved over uneven terrain (the traditional problem for hoplites); if the line formed up more deeply cohesion might be preserved, but the enemy would easily outflank it; a thinner line would be broken by an enemy attack and the whole formation endangered. Xenophon therefore proposed an advance with companies formed into columns which would be spaced out to overlap the full extent of the enemy line: the bravest Greeks would be in the lead of each column and could choose the best way up for their followers, while the enemy would be threatened by attacks on the flanks but could not run the risk of advancing between the columns to attack their sides; it would be difficult to break through the individual columns. The hoplites were divided into eighty companies, each with about a hundred men, while the peltasts and archers were split into three larger units to be located on each wing and in the centre.[63] The plan worked since the Colchians felt obliged to counter the danger of being outflanked and so removed troops from the centre, but this permitted the peltasts in the Arcadian division to charge uphill; the Arcadian hoplites followed closely and drove the remaining enemy from their positions.

The peltasts played a minor part in this success and the engagement demonstrated that well-trained hoplites under good leadership could operate on adverse terrain, securing a position even if they did not catch enemy troops. For hoplites, going uphill under fire was in fact probably easier than retiring downhill: they were well protected to the front, but when withdrawing their shields might be more hindrance than protection, and the enemy might dare to come to closer quarters since they knew that the hoplites would have to turn around before attempting a pursuit. As noted above, this was what happened to the hoplites who attempted to drive off the Persian hillmen, and in

---

63. *Anab.* 4.8.10–15.

Carduchia Xenophon's rearguard came under severest pressure when withdrawing from the hills it had occupied.[64]

The plundering expedition against the Drilae illustrates that problems of withdrawal were not confined to hoplites, since here it was the peltasts who had advanced towards a hilltop settlement across a ravine only to find that they could neither retreat nor assail the defences. The arrival of the hoplites provided the stability and solidity for an attack on the pallisade, which was supported by missiles from the archers, peltasts, and slingers; Xenophon then deliberately held back as many hoplites as possible while the lighter troops pillaged the settlement, to be ready for the appearance of fresh enemy troops. The hoplites were again needed when the pillagers came under pressure and the possibility of attacking the citadel emerged. The Greeks' eventual retreat across the ravine outside the settlement was covered by a few picked troops who distracted the enemy by setting fire to the houses nearest the gates. The following day, as the Greeks attempted to remove their booty to safety, Xenophon delayed the enemy with a fake ambush and then used his Cretan archers to hold the enemy back while the ambushers escaped.[65]

The attack on the Drilae's settlement underlines the key factor in the military performance of the Ten Thousand, namely the integrated operation of the different elements in the expedition. Another demonstration of this is provided by the capture of the metropolis of the Mossynoeci: an initial attack by some friendly Mossynoeci, in which numerous Greeks participated without orders in the hope of plunder, was repulsed, but on the next day the Greeks formed the hoplites into columns with the archers and peltasts as a screen to deal with stone throwers and advanced successfully uphill; the Mossynoeci were prepared to engage the peltasts, but retreated when the hoplites came up, and they again withdrew from the outer parts of their metropolis when the Greek troops came to close quarters.[66]

Conclusion

Each element in the Ten Thousand had its advantages and limitations. Hoplites could not respond effectively to harassment at long range and lacked

---

64. The attack on the Persian hillmen: *Anab.* 3.4.28. The withdrawal in Carduchia: *Anab.* 4.2.20.
65. *Anab.* 5.2.4–7, 11–19, 26–32.
66. Repulse of the initial attack: *Anab.* 5.4.14–16. Successful advance the next day: *Anab.* 5.4.22–6.

mobility on slopes and broken terrain. Peltasts could not deliver the weight of charge of a hoplite unit, and might be routed by a formation which hoplites could repel, such as Persian cavalry and Bithynian infantry.[67] Missile troops needed the protection of a hoplite formation when under serious attack.

The Ten Thousand was never a balanced unit. The men had been recruited for their special military skills, primarily hoplites but also a modest number of peltasts and a small contingent of archers: they had no cavalry, as they despondently reflected after the arrest of their generals, since Cyrus knew that he could recruit much better cavalry in Asia and missile troops were also available in abundance. Xenophon rhetorically disparaged the significance of the diverse non-Greek troops and cavalry when attempting to bolster the morale of the Ten Thousand – men did not often die from being kicked by a horse, and the position of a hoplite on the ground might seem more secure than that of a cavalryman up in the air – but Xenophon also presented himself as the Greek who recognized the need for diversity and saw how to create it. The Ten Thousand could never achieve the flexibility of a planned expeditionary force such as Alexander the Great's, and, as a result, the minor units in the army had to work hard for coordinated tactics to succeed, as the crossing of the Bohtan river showed. At Cunaxa, the Greek hoplites' achievement deserves respect, in contrast to the disparagement in Plutarch, and on other occasions their presence was required to overawe opponents by lending weight to peltasts or light-armed troops. The hoplites would never have survived by themselves, as the mauling of the Arcadian contingent in Bithynia shows, but the march is, overall, testament to their qualities and potential.[68]

The Ten Thousand were highly trained professionals, but it was not their individual prowess and tactical flexibility which ensured their survival so much as the skill with which they were used. Good leadership was what enabled the Ten Thousand to demonstrate the versatility of Greek troops. Thus Xenophon advocated the use of reserves, which was unusual in contemporary warfare.[69]

For Xenophon tactics were only part of the business of generalship, as he has Socrates complain after hearing of the tuition provided to a young friend

---

67. *Anab.* 6.5.26.
68. Reflections on the lack of cavalry: *Anab.* 3.1.2. Disparagement of the non-Greek troops: *Anab.* 3.2.17–20. Xenophon and the need for diversity: *Anab.* 3.3.12–20. The mauling in Bithynia: see above n. 67.
69. On the professionalism of the Ten Thousand, cf. Perlman, 'The Ten Thousand', p. 269. The use of reserves: *Anab.* 6.5.9.

by Dionysidorus. Tactics and formation were subordinate to soldiers' confidence and enthusiasm, or their absence, as factors which influenced success, and skilful deployment of tactics could be most significant because of the impact on morale, as with Epaminondas' manoeuvres at Mantinea.[70] In the *Anabasis*, Xenophon shows that he paid particular attention to swings of mood, partly because this highlighted his own contribution to the expedition since he was often the person (at least in his own account) whose rhetoric or suggestions revived spirits among his companions, but also because it mattered: in comparable circumstances the armies of the Athenians in Sicily and the Romans at Carrhae lost the determination and discipline to fight their way out of trouble, in part because of the behaviour of Nicias and Crassus. Antony in Media only just saved his troops from despair.

In addition to their human enemies, the Ten Thousand had to cope with extreme weather conditions, and it is worth returning to this aspect of the expedition. Xenophon, in command of the rearguard, was best placed to observe the suffering and casualties caused by the severe winter. He also had the moral responsibility to attempt to prevent the men from dropping out or abandoning wounded comrades, tasks which fully tested his abilities as a leader; it also led to some complaints later about his harshness, although Xenophon's justification of his methods won over the men. Keeping the army moving in itself was an achievement: when campaigning in AD 114, in the same area but probably to the east of Lake Van, Bruttius Praesens found that his army could not advance because of snow falls up to sixteen feet deep; local inhabitants had to instruct the Romans how to construct snow shoes. When a heavy snowfall buried men and animals, Xenophon himself set the example by rousing himself from the insulating warmth of the snow and starting to split logs. After soldiers suffering from frostbite sat down on a patch of thawed ground and refused to advance, in spite of the proximity of hostile pursuit, Xenophon improvised a counter-attack to drive off the enemy and then arranged for the stricken men to be sent up the column to where the vanguard was encamped. Xenophon sustained the morale of his men under the most

---

70. Socrates and generalship: *Mem.* 3.1; cf. *Cyrop.* 1.6.12–14. For exhaustive discussion of Xenophon's views of command, see Hutchinson, *Xenophon and the Art of Command*. Confidence and enthusiasm as the main factors in success: *Anab.* 3.1.39–42. Epaminondas at Mantinea: *Hell.* 7.5.20–4, with J. E. Lendon, 'Rhetoric of combat: Greek military theory and Roman culture in Julius Caesar's battle descriptions', *Classical Antiquity* 18 (1999), pp. 273–329, at pp. 291–2, on how Xenophon's 'grammar of battle' might have shaped his presentation of events.

extreme conditions as effectively as Alexander the Great.[71] If the men of the Ten Thousand deserve credit for their professionalism and tactical flexibility, their leaders, and Xenophon in particular, can take their place alongside the military innovators of the fourth century, Iphicrates of Athens, Epaminondas of Thebes, and ultimately Philip and Alexander of Macedon.

71. Xenophon's apologia for harshness: *Anab.* 5.8. The ordeal of Bruttius Praesens: Arr. *Parth. FGH* 156 fr. 153 (*FGH* IIB 876). Xenophon's example: *Anab.* 4.4.11–12. Care for the frostbitten: *Anab.* 4.5.15–22. For the comparison with Alexander, cf. Curt. 7.3.12–18 and 8.4.5–17, two cases where the army was struck by snow storms in Bactria, and Alexander's personal intervention and example were instrumental in rescuing his men.

8 *'This was Decided'* (edoxe tauta): The Army as polis *in Xenophon's* Anabasis – *and Elsewhere*[1]

SIMON HORNBLOWER

A soldier's job is to obey orders. This simple proposition might seem hard to argue with. In recent times it has been challenged only when offered as a defence in trials for atrocities perpetrated in war. My concern is not, however, with such ethically extreme situations. My chapter looks at those interesting historical episodes and even entire periods where armies seem on occasion to do the leading, and to exercise voting pressure on their commanders, rather than being unquestioningly led by those commanders. The classic example is from ancient Greece, and is described in the *Anabasis* of Xenophon, the subject of the present book. But was the behaviour described by Xenophon exceptional? I shall argue that on the contrary it was not unique, but rather an extension of a tendency found in other Greek (but not Roman) armies, especially in classical democratic Athenian armies, coalition armies, or both. The Athenian expeditionary force in Sicily in 415–413, described in detail by Thucydides, is a particularly rewarding comparative case study: it was not purely Athenian but Athenian-led and was thus a coalition army. That was just a decade and a half earlier than the army of the Ten Thousand. But I shall also glance for comparison at revolutionary armies in some other and very different periods in history.

But first, the *Anabasis*. Edward Gibbon, in the *Decline and Fall of the Roman Empire*, makes a celebrated comparison between Xenophon's *Anabasis* and his *Cyropaedia*. It is contained – like so many of Gibbon's best remarks – in a footnote: 'the *Cyropaedia* is vague and languid, the *Anabasis* circumstantial and animated. Such is the eternal difference between fiction and truth.' I am not however primarily concerned in this chapter with the literary qualities or rhetorical artfulness of the work. The theme of my paper can be adequately

---

1. I am grateful to Robin Lane Fox for the invitation to speak in his seminar and to contribute to this book, and for valuable written comments after the delivery of my paper. I thank also various members of the original audience for their comments at the time and afterwards. These are acknowledged in the notes below.

introduced by the sentence of Gibbon's text to which the footnote I have just quoted belongs. In the second volume of the *Decline and Fall*, the historian contrasts the disgraceful retreat of the Emperor Jovian with the glorious conduct of Xenophon's Ten Thousand: 'instead', says Gibbon, 'of tamely resigning themselves to the secret deliberations and private views of a single person, the united councils of the Greeks were inspired by the generous enthusiasm of a popular assembly'. It is that phenomenon, the 'generous enthusiasm of the popular assembly' in a tight military spot, which I want to explore.[2]

I shall not spend much space and time in establishing the point that the army of the Ten Thousand in some senses behaves like a political entity, like a *polis* in fact. In 1992 Andrew Dalby, in a perceptive article, qualified this by saying that it behaved less like a *settled* polis and more like a colonizing expedition or like the army in the *Iliad*, particularly in the way it provisions itself and hands out booty. But the basic *polis* point was elegantly made long ago by K. W. Krüger in his nineteenth-century commentary on a key passage in the *Anabasis*, where he noted that Xenophon invites a show of hands, just as in an Athenian political assembly. And we can add, bearing in mind that the law-courts were as important an element of Athenian democracy as was the *ekklēsia*, that the army easily accommodates notions of military hierarchy to the mentality of the law-courts: at one point the captains (*lochagoi*) are appointed as the dikasts (jurors) at a trial of malefactors. The Greek title of my chapter, *edoxe tauta*, is intended to make the point in two short words; those words, first found near the beginning of the whole work, and then several times in book 5, are a formula of participatory approval. I do not say 'democratic' approval, because that would beg certain questions. After all, even oligarchies, or at any rate some kinds of broad-based oligarchies, had mechanisms for gauging majority opinion among what was usually defined as the hoplite or heavy-armed infantry class – which is after all what most of the Ten Thousand belonged to. Thus the Spartan Chirisophus, soon after Xenophon's invitation just mentioned, finds it equally natural to invite a show of hands. I hope I do not need to prove that the Ten Thousand behave up to a point like a kind of *polis*. On the contrary I take that as my axiom or starting point. Qualifications such as 'up to a point' are necessary because in actual battle Xenophon reports his own orders to his men as just that, orders which he expects to be obeyed, He uses the verb *parangellō* on one occasion for this ordering, where the form of the orders is closely paralleled by the regular form

---

2. E. Gibbon, *The Decline and Fall of the Roman Empire*, ed. J. B. Bury (London, 1896), vol. 2, p. 523 and n. 119.

of those reported by Arrian and Ptolemy as given by Alexander, a royal commander. And we hear of 'the generals' meeting to decide on a plan of attack. But it is the element of grass-roots discussion and the implied possibility of rejection that interests me today. How unusual was it among Greek armies?[3]

There is in the modern literature a tendency to treat the Ten Thousand as being, in G. B. Nussbaum's words, 'unusual if not unique as an army in having an independent self-contained organisation like that of any normal society'. My quotation is from the introduction to what remains the standard and very useful monograph on the social organization of the Ten Thousand, published in 1967. Disconcertingly, Nussbaum goes on, two pages later, to say that he does not seek to 'apply the results obtained', as he puts it, or to 'exploit the *Anabasis* as a document of its own time'. In a footnote he briefly mentions, only to disclaim treatment of them for lack of space, other comparable armies such as the Athenian armament at Syracuse, the fleet at Samos in 411 and Alexander's army. And those are the only mentions of those overseas armies in the whole of Nussbaum's book. (There are to be fair a couple of allusions to Thucydides thereafter, but they are insignificant.) This is surely a strange procedure. If the army of the Ten Thousand was unusual and even unique, then why mention the other armies? But if those other armies are relevant, then surely we need to know at every stage whether a piece of behaviour attested for the Ten Thousand really is unusual military behaviour or whether on the contrary it is standard, or rather whether something like it is attested in, for instance, the Sicily of 415–413. In a word, we have a problem of what modern historians call exceptionalism. Nussbaum does in his text suggest also that there are similarities between the decision-making procedures of the Ten Thousand and Spartan civil practice. But he does not develop this parallel, which might have led him into some interesting if uncomfortable directions, uncomfortable I mean for his uniqueness thesis. But my main point is the need to look at other armies. Even Dalby has little to say about armies other than that in the *Iliad*.[4]

3. A. Dalby, 'Greeks abroad: social organisation and food among the Ten Thousand', *JHS* 112 (1992), pp. 16–30; see also L. P. Marinoviç, *Le mercenariat grec au IVe siècle av. n.è. et la crise de la polis* (Paris, 1988), esp. p. 193. C. G. (K. W.) Krüger (ed.), *Xenophon Anabasis* (Halle, 1826), pp. 154–5, note on *Anab.* 3.2.9; for show of hands cf. also Chirisophus at *Anab.* 3.2.33. *Lochagoi* as dikasts: *Anab.* 5.7.34. First use of *edoxe tauta*: *Anab.* 1.3.20, and several times thereafter, e.g. 3.2.38, and a notable clustering in 5.1. For hoplites see *Anab.* 1.2.3, the enumeration of the force by military categories. Xenophon gives straightforward orders: *Anab.* 4.3.29, with L. Pearson, *Lost Histories of Alexander the Great* (Philadelphia, 1960), p. 206 and n. 74. Meeting of generals: *Anab.* 4.8.9.
4. G. B. Nussbaum, *The Ten Thousand: A Study in Social Organization and Action in Xenophon's Anabasis* (Leiden, 1967), pp. 9, 11.

Mention of Sicily and 415 leads us to an important passage in Thucydides book 7. Halfway through that book we are told that the Athenian commander Nicias 'did not want the option of retreat or withdrawal from Sicily to be openly voted on among many'. On the meaning of the slightly unusual expression *meta pollōn* I follow Hobbes, who renders it 'with the votes of many'.[5] What do the words, so translated, actually imply? Their politically wide scope is startling: they seem to suggest that all, most, or many of the ordinary troops, not just generals or even senior officers (*taxiarchoi*) and *triērarchoi*, ship commanders, were going to be voting. That is, they would be casting real literal pebbles, *psēphoi*, or more likely exercising *cheirotonia*, 'holding up of hands' as in the *Anabasis*, on this basic question of retreat. (The Athenians at home were capable of using strictly inaccurate *psēphos* formations such as *psēphismata*, 'decrees', *psēphizesthai*, 'I vote', to describe most kinds of assembly voting, which actually took place not by ballot or pebbles but by show of hands. This, it is thought, is evidence that the assembly originally used pebbles.)[6]

The standard full-length commentaries on Thucydides toy with the idea that by the words 'with many' Thucydides meant nothing larger than a meeting of the generals augmented by *taxiarchoi*, as at a meeting described twelve chapters later, which we may note results in a decision introduced by *edoxe tauta*, the Xenophontic motto of my title. I concede that Thucydides' words *meta pollōn* do not have quite the same implication as *meta pantōn* ('with everybody') would have had. But 'voting with many' surely implies a body considerably larger than generals plus taxiarchs, in fact the mixed or perhaps just Athenian rank-and-file troops. I argue this not just from the words themselves, which as we have seen are difficult, but from what he goes on to say

---

5. The passage is Thuc. 7.48.1: *outí emphanōs sphas psēphizomenous meta pollōn tēn anachōrēsin* (cf. Thuc. 7.50.3). The only way of avoiding Hobbes's rendering is to take *meta* ('with') to refer to a vote taken by a few but in the midst, i.e. the presence, of many. But this would mean that Thucydides said the same thing twice in different words, because then *emphanōs* and *meta pollōn* would both mean something like 'publicly' or 'openly' and Thucydides is not a redundant writer. This is not the place for detailed textual or other discussion, which I reserve for my forthcoming commentary on Thucydides books 6 and 7. (I follow most editors in accepting the soundness of the text, though Krüger tried to delete *meta pollōn*.) We have already (Thuc. 7.47.1) been told that the soldiers are fed up with the delay.
6. For the verb *psēphizesthai* in the context of a military gathering see e.g. *Anab.* 1.4.15 and 5.6.11. *Cheirotonia* in the *Anabasis*: 3.2.9 and 38. Assembly and pebbles: M. H. Hansen, *The Athenian Assembly in the Age of Demosthenes* (Oxford, 1987). Cf. Eur. *Heracl.* line 141 with J. Wilkins's commentary (Oxford, 1993), p. 69, for vague use of *psēphos* in tragedy; see also P. Easterling, 'Anachronism in Greek tragedy', *JHS* 115 (1985), pp. 1–10, at p. 3 n. 10, for good remarks on this topic.

very plainly at the end of the same chapter, to the cynical effect that many or most of the ordinary soldiers, who were now so vociferous for withdrawal, would no doubt change their minds when they got back to Athens. If this is right, 'with many' are rather surprising words to use of an army which, and this is important, has not yet disintegrated as a fighting force; contrast the situation after the final sea battle where the utterly disheartened sailors refuse to re-embark. But normally a general who is about to send his troops into attack or is faced by an enemy onslaught does not, for elementary practical reasons, say to the mass of his men, 'hands up who think we should fight; those in favour? those against? abstentions? Sorry, I think I missed a few people at the back' and so on. The Thucydides passage raises a problem too little discussed in the voluminous literature about Athenian democracy, namely how did the *psēphos*-minded Athenians adapt to the concepts of taking orders on the battlefield, and of chains of command? I am not forgetting, and I shall return to this point, that the army in Sicily in 413 was far from being solely Athenian. But I do wonder how not just Athenians in particular but Greeks in general reconciled their normal and cherished voting habits with the necessities of army discipline. Xenophon's *Anabasis* is the prime text, but before we can use the *Anabasis* and the Ten Thousand, we need to be clear about the extent to which that army's procedures were abnormal. I shall be looking not only at other ancient Greek armies but at armies in other periods of history.[7]

Most of my material will be from the Peloponnesian War period (431–404) or later. I cannot go back systematically to cover earlier periods of Greek history or earlier literary texts such as the Homeric poems. I restrict myself to two pre-Thucydidean passages. The *dēmos* as army was a notion familiar to Pindar. In an ode written in about 470 BC for Hieron of Syracuse, he has what is undoubtedly the first statement of the constitutional triad of monarchy, oligarchy, and democracy, made famous in a much later document, the constitutional debate in Herodotus. For my purposes the *noun* is the relevant part, because Pindar uses for democracy one standard Greek word for 'host' or army,

---

7. *Historical Commentary on Thucydides*, vol. 4, ed. Dover (Oxford, 1970), p. 425; see also J. Classen and J. Steup, *Thukydides 7* (Berlin, 1908), p. 121. For the later meeting see Thuc. 7.60.2, with which compare the early meeting at *Anab.* 1.7.2 where Cyrus addresses only the generals and *lochagoi*. For *edoxe tauta* after this meeting see Thuc. 7.60.3, cf. 7.74.1. All armies, even the Achaemenid Persian, have such meetings of senior officers (see the final item at n. 2 above). For the idea that the soldiers might change their minds when they got home see Thuc. 7.48.4. The situation after the final sea battle: Thuc. 7.72.3 (but B. Jordan, 'The Sicilian expedition was a Potemkin fleet', *CQ* 50 (2000), pp. 63–79, at p. 74, observes that the fleet mutinied, the army did not).

namely *stratos*. Conversely, there is a nice example of an army (or rather navy) turning itself at short notice into a voting *dēmos* in Herodotus' account of Samian history in the sixth century BC. A large contingent of Samian malcontents (enough to fill forty triremes, therefore as many as 8,000 men) was sent off to Egypt by Polykrates. But en route they 'decided not to continue with their voyage': *sphi hadein to mē prosōterō mēketi plein*. What sort of assembly does this indicate, and how was it organized? The answer might provide us with a naval analogue to the Ten Thousand, more than a century earlier.[8]

I shall start my detailed classical discussion not at the obvious place, namely Athens, but at Sparta and Syracuse. The Athenian Thucydides comments that the Spartans have this thing called a chain of command; he speaks as if it were something remarkable and unexpected, the king hands down orders to the polemarchs, the polemarchs to the *lochagoi*, and so on down the line. It has always amused me that Thucydides thinks this worth commenting on as a peculiarity; you would think any decent army would have to operate on some such lines and that if the Athenian set-up was very different the results would be comically ineffective. But the passage is perhaps part of a rather conventional rhetorical polarization and forms a pair with Pericles' contrast in the funeral oration between relaxed Athenian military arrangements and the arduous exertion of the Spartans. This is surely overdone, though to say why would take me too far afield. The implication of both passages is of rigidity, discipline, and hierarchy in the Spartan army, not an atmosphere in which dissenting votes and voices, and criticism of commanders, might be expected to flourish. The truth I believe to be slightly different.[9]

Spartans and Argives differed in their treatment of generals who they thought had let them down. The Spartans in 418, cheated of a hoped-for confrontation with a hostile coalition, preserve discipline for the moment, but they punish their king Agis and place limits on his freedom when they get home. On the same occasion the Argives, by contrast, set about lynching their commander Thrasyllus by stoning him on their return. I think Thucydides disapproves of the Argives here and elsewhere, but characteristically he does not spell out this disapproval. Though Spartans may on occasion Say it with Sticks

---

8. Pind. *Pyth.* 2.87, cf. *Pyth.* 10.8. Constitutional debate: Hdt. 3.80–2. The Samians: Hdt. 3.45, a passage appositely cited by Thomas Braun in the discussion after the delivery of this paper in Oxford in 2001 and which I now gratefully incorporate.
9. Chain of command: Thuc. 5.66.3–4. Funeral oration: Thuc. 2.39. For Greek (in)discipline see W. K. Pritchett, *The Greek State at War*, vol. 2 (Berkeley, 1974), pp. 232–45.

they do not on the whole Say it with Stones; stoning is the paradigm of the undisciplined collective act. Or rather, as I have pointed out elsewhere, one unusual Spartan does, namely Amompharetus, who in Herodotus drops a huge rock at the feet of the Spartan regent Pausanias before the battle of Plataea in 479 and says 'there is my vote [pebble] against retreat.' This sort of Spartan *parrhēsia* or outspokenness can be paralleled from Thucydides; again in 418, an old soldier shouts out to King Agis that he is curing one ill with another, a proverbial expression, by his excessive eagerness to fight. This rather Herodotean-sounding anecdote is followed by an equally Herodotean comment: 'whether because of the shout or for some other reason', Agis acted on it. We would like to know more: did the old man's shout get him into trouble? Obviously not, one would think, but if not, it is worth reflecting that no such military anecdote has come down to us from supposedly open democratic Athens.[10]

Still staying with Thucydides, there is a very revealing and impressive story early in book 7. Gylippus, recently arrived in Sicily from Sparta, leads his troops straight into a disastrous attack involving loss of life because the terrain was unsuitable for the operation of the Syracusan cavalry. He promptly does what very few people do in any walk of life, then or now: he apologizes and takes all the blame himself. It is worth reflecting what a risk Gylippus took here by admitting having caused friendly deaths, given the chronic Spartan jealousy of their leading men, as commented on by Thucydides in connection with an earlier leader, Brasidas. Gylippus risked getting into trouble back home among the enemies he surely had. Thucydides I think admired the brave way Gylippus restored morale by taking responsibility and addressing the troops under him as if they were equals with a right to complain. This shows at the very least a flexible attitude to military command and we would say it shows Gylippus to be a very good general indeed. How typical he was is hard to say. Did Thucydides single this out because it was paradigmatic and illustrative, or because it was abnormal (just as he remarks that Brasidas was not bad at speaking 'for a Spartan', where surely we are meant to understand

---

10. Thrasyllus: Thuc. 5.60; cf. Eur. 1A, 1349–52. Amompharetus: Hdt. 9.55 with M. A. Flower and J. Marincola, *Herodotus Book IX* (Cambridge, 2002), p. 205. See S. Hornblower, 'Sticks, stones and Spartans: the sociology of Spartan violence', in H. van Wees (ed.), *War and Violence in Ancient Greece* (London, 2000), pp. 57–82, at p. 74. The old Spartan soldier: Thuc. 5.65.2–3; cf., for the proverbial expression, Hdt. 3.53.4. For such *parrhēsia* (a licence granted to the old?) compare Hom. *Od.* 7.155 (Echenous to Alcinous).

abnormality)? But I would be surprised if Gylippus behaved in a totally different and better way just because he was abroad; on the contrary, the view more usually found in Thucydides is that Spartans abroad behaved conspicuously badly.[11]

The mixed character of Gylippus' troops is, however, relevant to my topic. The nature of Gylippus' relationship to the local Syracusan command structure is a difficult problem, well discussed by Kenneth Dover, who plausibly concludes that Gylippus initially had some sort of overall authority which however dwindled as the Syracusan position strengthened. But it is clear that in such an anomalous and diplomatically delicate situation, persuasion, and a civilian willingness to accept blame, were more appropriate than they would have been for a Spartan general of a purely Spartan army. Even in the Spartan-led Peloponnesian League, allies needed persuading: we recall from Herodotus the speech of Soclees the Corinthian, who in the late sixth century protests at chatty length against the Spartan plan to restore the Athenian tyranny. Allies who could think of no better reason for refusing service could always invoke a venerable Peloponnesian League clause about providing military help 'unless prevented by gods or heroes'. I shall return later to the subject of mixed armies.[12]

Let us with all this in mind broaden things out and ask what sort of armies tend historically towards indiscipline, and the debating and questioning of orders. There is a good story of the Duke of Wellington's first cabinet meeting as prime minister in 1828, after which he is supposed to have remarked, 'I gave them their orders, but they wanted to stay behind and discuss them.' This anecdote cannot be quite true, given that he had for many years been a cabinet minister in Lord Liverpool's administration, but it indicates the relevant aspect of the civilian–military divide quite neatly. So what sort of soldiers want to debate orders and reject normal hierarchical habits?

First, there are (as I have hinted already) those armies which have disintegrated as fighting forces. In a way they are no exception to the norm because in a way they are by definition no longer armies. I am not thinking of the

---

11. Gylippus takes the blame: Thuc. 7.5.3. Xenophon makes an apology at *Anab.* 3.3.12 but then goes on to offer a partial self-justification. Spartan jealousy of their leading men: Thuc. 4.108.7. Brasidas' ability at speaking: Thuc. 4.84.2. Spartans abroad behave badly: Thuc. 1.77.6, said by an anonymous Corinthian speaker.
12. See *Historical Commentary on Thucydides*, vol. 4, ed. Dover, pp. 367 and esp. 380–82, discussing Thuc. 6.93.2 and 7.2.1. Soclees: Hdt. 5.92. 'Prevention of gods or heroes': Thuc. 5.30.3.

situation whereby, say, everyone in a trench has been killed by a shell and the senior man present assumes command. All armies must have mechanisms of this sort; the Roman system of suffects must have grown out of some such notion. A decapitated army which still forms a military entity needs to grow a new head or heads, and that is what happens with the Ten Thousand; Xenophon tells his colleagues that the enemy expect them to disintegrate because leaderless, and suggests how they should deal with the problem, including voting (*psēphizesthai*) to deal collectively with indiscipline, something he implies had been a problem hitherto. Near the other end of the *Anabasis* the organization of the Ten Thousand temporarily but badly breaks down; but unity is soon restored, by consensus decision (the Greek word is *dogma*). In any case, it is important to remember that we hear of army *ekklēsiai* or assemblies in the Greek army described by Xenophon long before Cyrus and the other generals have been killed.[13]

By disintegration, I am thinking more of, say, Crete in 1941, where in the retreat to the south of the island parts of the British, Australian and New Zealand forces became totally leaderless and undisciplined. To take another example from modern Greek history, the Greek army in its headlong retreat to Smyrna in August 1922 lost discipline pretty completely with the exception of one unit which forced its way to the sea and got away in good order, taking a group of civilians with it. This sort of irreversible breakdown does not however seem to have happened by the time of the meeting 'with many' envisaged by Nicias, because at this point in the narrative the decisive sea battle is still some way in the future; and in any case Nicias and Demosthenes continue to lead and maintain authority over their troops right to the very end. On the other hand it is reasonable to guess that in Sicily the command structure crumbled gradually over time, that is, that rank-and-file views and protests became more vocal and permissible, and were taken more into account, as the expedition neared its catastrophic close. Thus Thucydides says that because of the eclipse 'most of the Athenians urged the generals to wait'. The word for urged is *ekeleuon*, from a verb which can mean 'I order' but can also (as here) mean something milder such as 'invite'. Hobbes nicely translates this passage 'the greatest part of the Athenians *called upon* the generals to stay'. Whatever verbal

---

13. The first military meeting: *Anab.* 1.3.2, where it is called an *ekklēsia*; but at 5.6.1, when the generals summon a meeting of the army, the verb is *xunelegen*, the verbal form of *syllogos*. For the noun see J. Christensen and M. H. Hansen, 'What is *syllogos* at Thukydides 2.22.1?', *C & M* 34 (1983), pp. 17–31 = Hansen, *The Athenian Ekklesia* II (1989), pp. 195–211; R. M. Errington, '*Ekklesia kuria* at Athens', *Chiron* 24 (1994), pp. 135–60.

expression we choose, the impression is of gatherings and knots, something like the Roman *contio* perhaps.[14]

In parenthesis, I suggest that, as a general rule in Greek history, the feelings of the common soldiery were more vocal and were taken more seriously when religious obstructions were in question. The reason was perhaps that the troops feel they have god on their side and he outranks the top brass. Thus near the beginning of Plutarch's *Alexander* we hear of the Macedonians' doubts before the battle of the River Granicus. 'Most of them', says Plutarch (without specifying further) were afraid of the depth of the river and some thought they ought to respect the custom by which Macedonian kings did not take the field in the month Daisios. Alexander ignores the first objection but does something about the second, by the Gordian-knot solution of renaming the month as another Artemisios. The standard English translations say 'most' and then 'some' of '*the Macedonian officers*'. But the Greek does not say 'officers'; the words are quite unspecific.[15]

Second there are what we might call irregular armies, those whose members have an anarchic tendency to want to debate things and question authority. This can produce friction when such troops have to cooperate with regular forces. There is a good example from Greece of a later period, well discussed by Mark Mazower in his excellent book *Inside Hitler's Greece*. He is describing the *andartes* (partisans, guerrillas) of occupied wartime Greece:

> As members of a revolutionary army, the *andartes* had no time for the conventional forms of military hierarchy. They greeted each other proudly as 'Fellow-combatant'. Professional soldiers had trouble getting used to their ways. A British NCO who tried to stop his charges falling out of line before they had been given permission was reminded angrily by one that 'in ELAS every soldier has his rights!' They talked back to their superior officers, demanding explanations for orders, and wasting time to demonstrate their independence. What was the *andarte* fighting for if not freedom?

But as Mazower shrewdly adds on the next page, 'accusations of ill-discipline need to be examined carefully, especially as the *andartes* have to be judged by

---

14. Xenophon says the enemy thought the Greeks would all perish from indiscipline: *Anab.* 3.2.29. Unity restored: *Anab.* 6.4.11. Crete in 1941: A. Clark, *The Fall of Crete* (London, 1962), p. 158. Retreat from Smyrna: M. Llewellyn-Smith, *Ionian Vision: Greece in Asia Minor 1919–22* (London, 1998), pp. 295–6 and 299. Reactions to the Sicilian eclipse: Thuc. 7.50.4.
15. Plut. *Alex.* 16.

the standards of an irregular force rather than that of a professional army, as American and British officers tended to do'.[16]

Third, there are revolutionary or extreme left-wing armies, at least in the early phases of a revolutionary movement. The *andartes* Mazower is thinking of fall into this category too, because he is talking about the workings of ELAS, the military branch of EAM, the resistance arm of KKE, the Greek communist party. Or there is the French revolutionary army in its first *levée en masse* phase. Simon Schama describes an initial proposal to have officers elected for short periods from the rank and file and then for commissions to rotate; soldiers wore liberty caps in military council meetings, and when they wrote to superior officers they began '*salut et fraternité* from your equal in rights'. But Schama also shows that this did not last long; St-Just had a few delinquents shot publicly in the old-fashioned way and normal hierarchy and discipline was restored.[17]

Might we want to say that the armies of radical democratic Athens also belong to this authority-questioning type? Specific evidence for Athenian attitudes and practice is curiously hard to come by; the most concrete passage I know actually points the other way. The Athenian fleet at Samos are complaining that the government back home are not even providing 'good counsel, for the sake of which a city rules over armies'. This implies a very modern conceptual divorce between the state and the armies which act in its name, and carries the equally modern implication that in normal times the army was subordinate to the state. True, the passage is rhetorically slanted and comes from a most exceptional period, the year 411 when the democracy was briefly replaced by the oligarchy of the so-called Four Hundred. But it remains the most explicit counter to the usual and often correct view, what we might call the 'men are the city' view found from Alcaeus to Thucydides' Nicias, which conceived of a Greek *polis* as the totality of male hoplites, a principle that certainly facilitated the procedures we encounter in Xenophon's *Anabasis*. The Thucydides book 8 passage I have cited makes it at first sight odd that Nussbaum (above, p. 245) cites Samos in 411 as a *parallel* to the situation of the Ten Thousand. What he presumably means is that the fleet at Samos does in fact operate in general as a kind of city in exile; indeed for several years after 411 there was a de facto separation between the city of Athens and one set of its commanders overseas, the generals at the Hellespont. But I am not sure how

---

16. M. Mazower, *Inside Hitler's Greece* (New Haven, 1995), pp. 315f.
17. S. Schama, *Citizens* (London, 1989), p. 764.

far we can push 411. It was perhaps a bit like the revolutionary situation in Turkey after the First World War, when legitimacy gradually seeped away from the moribund Ottoman regime to Atatürk and his army. The fleet at Samos began as a dissident group from the controlling regime but in the end symbolized and imposed a return to legitimacy. A better example is Thucydides' remark that in 415, at the time of the profanation of the Eleusinian Mysteries, Alcibiades' enemies feared that 'the army' (*strateuma*) might be favourable to him and that 'the people' (*ho dēmos*) might be lenient. This, as Dover remarks, is a 'striking exception' to the normal position in a Greek state, whose nature 'normally precluded a difference of allegiance between "civilians" and "the army"'.[18]

What was the more normal situation in Athens? One way into the problem is via military discipline. Pritchett's collection of the evidence makes it clear that most of the evidence was Spartan; there is very little from Athens. True, there was an offence of 'leaving the ranks', *lipotaxion*, which we find in the orators. There was also an offence of *astrateia*, not appearing for military service when called on to do so. But though there was a word *ataxia*, indiscipline, it did not as far as I can find constitute grounds for an indictment. There must however have been procedures for dealing with military insubordination and indiscipline in the armies of classical Athens; my point is that the precise mechanisms are elusive and do not seem to have included corporal punishment. The Aristotelian treatise known as the *Constitution of the Athenians* says that generals have full power to arrest for insubordination or to cashier or inflict a fine, but that is all. Famously, the Athenians used Scythians (barbarians from the north) for police purposes, part of the democratic ideology. As Virginia Hunter puts it, 'the whip was considered too demeaning a punishment to be used against the free'. Her book does not specifically consider military policing at Athens except for a couple of pages on patrolling duties by young trainee soldiers, the so-called *ephebes*. Pritchett concludes his general section on Greek military discipline with a section on the *Anabasis* and remarks 'we gain the impression that discipline was very lax even in a mercen-

---

18. The fleet at Samos: Thuc. 8.76.6. For 'men are the city' (*andres gar polis*) see most memorably Thuc. 7.77.7 (Nicias speaks), but see already Alc. frag. 112. Behind both texts lie perhaps the stirring words of Ajax at Hom. *Il.* 15.733. For the generals at the Hellespont between 410 and 407 see A. Andrewes, 'The generals in the Hellespont, 410–407 BC', *JHS* 73 (1953), pp. 2–9. For 415 see Thuc. 6.29.3 with Dover, *HCT*, vol. 4, p. 290. In fact both 'army' and 'people' are suspected of being pro-Alcibiades, but it remains curious that Thucydides should distinguish the two. Note also the distinctions made between the various interest groups at Thuc. 6.24.

ary army.' When the Athenian Xenophon in the *Anabasis* punishes individuals physically, he might have justified himself by reference to an earlier collective agreement by the troops concerned. Actually his rhetoric is splendidly antipolitical: 'you had swords in your hands, not voting pebbles, and you could have come to their help if you had wanted'. What he really did, I suggest, was behave more like a Spartan than an Athenian: it is noticeable, as I have said already, that most of Pritchett's material about Greek military discipline is Spartan. (One episode has been cited to show that Athenian generals could inflict the death penalty. We learn from the orator Lysias that Lamachus, one of the Athenian generals on the Sicilian expedition, put to death a soldier who had been caught signalling to the enemy; but Pritchett thinks, presumably from the silence of the *Athenian Constitution*, that by the fourth century, generals had lost this power.) To sum up, democratic Athens does seem for ideological reasons to have been laxer about military discipline than some other states, conspicuously Sparta: Pritchett quotes with approval Gilbert's comment about Athens, 'the punishments for insubordination were light'. This is true even after allowing for on the one hand a rhetorical tendency to exaggerate the contrast between Athens and Sparta, and on the other hand for the phenomenon I have already noticed, namely Spartan *parrhēsia* as anecdotally exemplified by Amompharetus and by the angry old Spartan man who shouts at King Agis sixty years later.[19] But the Athenian situation is anyway only partially relevant because neither the expeditionary force in Sicily nor the Ten Thousand were purely Athenian. They were mixed armies and this brings me to my next head.

The fourth sort of army which is hard to control because it is argumentative is the ethnically mixed army, a topic I have already considered in connection with Gylippus. The higher up the command structure the mix goes, the harder the control. Thus in the last phase of the Second World War the friction between Eisenhower and Montgomery was notorious, and more recent post-Cold War coalitions have shown similar strains. This sort of army is very relevant to the two cases we have been considering, the Ten Thousand and the army before Syracuse. Nussbaum talks of the 'Athenian armament before Syracuse' but this is inaccurate. Just how the integration was achieved in Sicily

---

19. *lipotaxion*: Dem. 21, 103, for instance, with MacDowell's note. For Pritchett see above n. 9. Powers of generals: Arist. [*Ath. pol.*] 61.2. Scythians: V. Hunter, *Policing Athens: Social Control in the Attic Lawsuits 420–320 BC* (Princeton, 1994), p. 181. Xenophon on physical discipline: *Anab.* 3.2.30–1. Swords not voting pebbles: *Anab.* 5.8.21. Lamachus: Lys. 13.65.

at the level of detail is an interesting but insoluble problem. For instance, Dover addresses but cannot answer the question, how the ten-tribe Athenian system was adapted in military contexts to accommodate allies whose communities were still organized on the old four-tribe Ionian model, or were even three-tribe Dorian communities.[20]

I mentioned above stresses and insubordination in coalition armies. That was one reason for the tensions I discussed in my 'sticks and stones' paper, though it was not an aspect I was particularly concerned with there. The Spartan Astyochus threatens some Thurian and Syracusan sailors with his *baktēria* or staff, and they get very angry and try to rush him so that he flees to an altar. Thucydides stresses that they were angry because they were free men. Evidently they did not recognize Spartan authority. It was no good trying to impose authority by violence like Astyochus; you needed the tact of a Gylippus or the charisma of an Alexander, or if you did use force you needed to know how to justify it afterwards like a Xenophon.[21]

The fifth factor making (in antiquity at least) for unusual and self-directing if not actually undisciplined armies is that of great distance from home. To be sure, the temporary breakdown in the organization of the Ten Thousand takes place at by no means the furthest point from home, but the troops are still very far from their own Greek *poleis*. It is relevant to this distance-point that the only successful mutiny against Alexander took place at the point furthest from the Greco-Macedonian homeland, on the River Beas. Distance and consequent problems of communication are easily forgotten by us. Their consequences for the development of Roman imperialism have been explored by J. S. Richardson in his 1986 book *Hispaniae*, where he makes fruitful use of D. K. Fieldhouse's concept of 'peripheral imperialism' in the nineteenth century. That is, untrammelled and far-reaching decisions made by the military leaders on the spot. This is self-directed military action not in the sense that the troops have rejected the authority of their commanders or think they can do without it (sense A), but in the sense that there is no control from the home government over an army whose internal command structure may well be perfectly intact (sense B). Sometimes absence of policy can be explained in this way. The British prime minister Lord Salisbury a century ago always took the sensible view that it was no use even discussing what happened in Afghanistan because it was simply too far away and inaccessible for routine

---

20. On the tribal problem see Dover, *HCT*, vol. 4, p. 372, on Thuc. 6.98.4.
21. For Astyochus see Thuc. 8.84.2 and Hornblower, 'Sticks, stones and Spartans'.

intervention. In classical Greek history there is at first sight an instructive Spartan example of something like peripheral imperialism, the initiatives taken by Brasidas in north Greece. But I have argued elsewhere that for essentially literary reasons Thucydides has masked the degree to which the Spartan decision-making elite back home approved and directed his activities. In any case Brasidas maintained tight discipline even in the remotest section of his retreat, proving that distance from home control need not erode local authority. Or, as I put it just now, self-directing in sense B does not necessarily imply undisciplined, though it may do.

Now Sicily was not Greece, but it was not quite Afghanistan either. Unlike the Ten Thousand, who were answerable to no single governing group back in Greece, and unlike Alexander's army, whose ultimate source of authority is the king himself, who leads the campaign in person, the army in Sicily never quite forgets the authority of the assembly in the Pnyx, which however it is not realistic to consult. On the one hand the generals debate whether to withdraw, on the other hand both Nicias and Demosthenes refer to the political risks of withdrawing without a vote of the Athenians in Athens. Nor is the distinction betwen Athenians at Athens and Athenians in Sicily a sharp one. Nicias makes that point for me neatly. He says, in a sentence I have already mentioned, 'of the soldiers now present in Sicily, many, indeed the majority, who were now saying loudly what a desperate plight they were in, would on their return say equally loudly that their generals had been bribed to withdraw'. At this point, we may think, the two senses of 'self-directed' began to run together: the absence of clear guidelines, as we would now say, from home is tending to erode the authority of the commanders on the spot, and the situation is further complicated by the dual status of the troops themselves. That is, they are subordinates for the moment but may end up sitting in judgement on their commanding officers. This, it should be emphasized, is not a peculiarly Athenian and democratic paradox because the Spartan Agis was in an exactly parallel situation in 418 BC.[22]

Sixth and finally, there is the obvious point that mercenary soldiers are likely to be more outspoken than citizen hoplites. This needs to be qualified a little; the citizen–mercenary distinction is not always clear-cut in classical Greek warfare, and the fluid vocabulary reflects this. In any case, military service involved pay for all concerned. And mixed or coalition armies sometimes

22. Spain: J. S. Richardson, *Hispaniae: Spain and the Development of Roman Imperialism 218–82 BC* (Cambridge, 1986), p. 177. Demosthenes: Thuc. 7.49.2: it is impossible to withdraw the army from Sicily 'without a vote of the Athenians'. Nicias: Thuc. 7.48.4.

behave very like mercenary ones. Early in the *Anabasis* the troops initially refuse to go further when they realize the real object of the expedition is the Persian king, but this can be paralleled in Herodotus by the Corinthian refusal over a century earlier to take part in an attack on Athens when they realized what the object of that expedition was. We may also recall that the expedition of Cyrus did at least initially have Spartan backing; and that thereafter the Spartan attitude to the Ten Thousand is curiously ambiguous. It is not quite safe to treat them as a mercenary force in the sense of a body with no state ties whatsoever. When the question of the supreme command comes up at a late stage of the expedition, Xenophon hints plainly that the Spartans will have an interest in the outcome and will be less than pleased if a non-Spartan is appointed.[23]

To conclude a long discussion, the expeditionary army in 413, at the stage reached when Nicias is said not to want a general meeting, does seem to show signs of being self-directing in sense A. That is, it shows a tendency to take or at least influence decisions at a level which in 415, when the expedition set out, would I suspect have been above it. To that extent it behaves like a *polis*. The reasons are a combination of some of my six factors. The army is not mercenary, though pay was as always an incentive: Thucydides remarks on the ordinary soldier's hopes of eternal pay, *aidios misthophora*, in his paragraph about the motives of the various Athenian social groups on the confident morning of the Sicilian expedition. It has not yet disintegrated by the middle of book 7, but the imminence of danger and possible defeat may have made a difference. The army is not an irregular army, so that factor is irrelevant. Nor is it wholly Athenian, but it does manifest some of the Athenian laxity of discipline, which makes it a sort of distant relative of the anti-hierarchical revolutionary armies of other periods of history. (We should not forget that it was on the Sicilian expedition that Lamachus ordered the death penalty for a traitor, an item which has come down to us from an orator, not Thucydides. But Lamachus was dead by the end of book 6.) The army was mixed, and this may have encouraged the sort of freedom of expression I have noted in such armies; though Thucydides makes Nicias dwell on purely Athenian sentiments. Thus, though in his final pre-battle speech he will be including metics and other foreigners in his exhortation, he is, in the earlier chapter of Thucydides I am concerned with (note 6 above), worried only about what *most of the*

23. The Persian King the real target: *Anab*. 1.3.1. Corinthian refusal: Hdt. 5.92. Xenophon on the idea of a non-Spartan commander for the Ten Thousand: *Anab*. 6.1.26–8; see also on this passage Cawkwell, chapter 1 in this volume.

Athenians are thinking and about political reprisals from them when they are once again voters on the Pnyx back in Athens.

Finally the army is far from home and home control and this may have made a difference. In this connection we can add that the theme of the Sicilian expedition as an intended and super-ambitious act of colonization is very marked in Thucydides' account of 415–413. Now Nicias says very early on, and indeed when he is still at Athens, 'you must think of yourselves as going there to found a city in alien and hostile territory'. That is, he is already making the city–army equation and this helps prepare us for the idea of the army as a participatory body in book 7. In the same way it is natural that the army of the Ten Thousand also turn to thoughts of founding a colony by the time we get to book 6 of the *Anabasis*. Well and good, but one could turn that point upside down and say that most Greek colonies were military enterprises, and that the role of the oikist was rather more powerful and untrammelled than that of a political leader of a peaceful metropolis. We have seen already that Andrew Dalby rightly insisted on the differences between settled city and colonies and thus on the differences between the Ten Thousand and a regular *polis*. One of his points was that oikists have single rule, just as authority over the Ten Thousand 'for the time being rested with Xenophon and those whom he chose to consult'. For several weeks the ordinary soldiers are not consulted formally, as opposed to being told that it was all right to talk to Xenophon when he was eating or even to wake him up in his sleeping-bag, which is not quite the same thing as a democratic mechanism of decision.[24]

The transition from Athenian *polis*-mindedness and criticism of superiors, to Macedonian individual military *parrhēsia* is nicely effected for us by Euripides, an Athenian poet, but one who left his bones in Macedon, as Thucydides put it in his epigram for him, and whose tragedies were evidently familiar to Macedonian officers of Alexander's time. The particular passage I have in mind is that from the *Andromache*. It was quoted, as Plutarch tells us, by a furious Clitus, moments before his violent death at Alexander's hands. Clitus' criticism of Alexander took the form of a one-line quotation from Peleus' speech against Menelaus, 'Alas what a bad custom is in Greece', inoffensive enough on its own but everyone present knew how it went on: 'when

24. 'Eternal pay': Thuc. 6.24.3. Nicias addresses metics: Thuc. 7.63.3. For the colonization theme see H. C. Avery, 'Themes in Thucydides' account of the Sicilian expedition', *Hermes* 101 (1973), pp. 1–13, esp. pp. 8–13f. Key texts on this are Nicias at Thuc. 6.23.2 and 7.77.4; Hermocrates' alleged reflections at 7.73.1; and the authorial Thucydides at 7.75.5. Everyone knew it was all right to wake Xenophon: *Anab.* 4.3.10. See Dalby, 'Greeks abroad', p. 22, and cf. Cawkwell, chapter 1 in this volume.

an army sets up a trophy, it isn't the hard-working troops who get the credit, it is the general, though he was only one spear among many'. So the line was enough to 'push Alexander to murder' (in the title of André Aymard's brilliant discussion of the Euripidean verse). Interestingly, the sentiments and language of the Euripidean Peleus are exactly echoed in Xenophon's *Anabasis* when the dissident Arcadian elements in the army grumble about the recent choice of a Spartan commander. Euripides may be in Xenophon's mind here. So the *Andromache* neatly connects three armies discussed in my paper: those of democratic Athens, the Ten Thousand of Xenophon, and the Macedonian army of Alexander.[25]

I must deal briefly with Alexander's army as a collective; it too occasionally behaved like a voting community. It was not an irregular, a revolutionary, or a disintegrating army, but it was an ethnically mixed one. Before the battle of Issus in 333, Alexander makes some concession to this by including the 'leaders of the allies' alongside the generals and ilarchs in what has been called a council, although it is not much more than a one-sided speech of exhortation. His army did also, for much of the time, operate a long way from its domestic base, although as I have observed already, when Alexander was alive it took its ultimate source of authority with it, in the person of the king and his close advisers. But just how much the Macedonian army assembly could and could not do is an endlessly and not always very intelligently debated constitutional question. I have mentioned the Beas mutiny already, but mutinies are by definition a suspension of normality. Otherwise we hear of the army's role at moments of crisis like trials of prominent alleged traitors or conspirators such as Philotas in Alexander's lifetime, and after his death the army reject his so-called Last Plans. One curious incident takes place in remote Sogdiana: the Macedonians come across descendants of the Branchidae of Greek Miletus, deported in the Persian Wars a century and a half earlier. They are now bilingual though they have not forgotten their ancestral customs completely. Alexander leaves their fate to be settled by the Milesians in his army, but when their opinions varied he told them that he would himself decide. Their destruction was ruthless and total.[26]

We need to distinguish between Alexander and his Successors. The closest similarities with the Ten Thousand actually arise in the narrative of

---

25. On Eur. *Andr.* lines 693ff. and Plut. *Alex.* 51 see A. Aymard, 'Sur quelques vers d'Euripide qui poussèrent Alexandre au meurtre', in his *Études d'histoire ancienne* (Paris, 1967), pp. 51–72. For the possible Xenophontic echo see *Anab.* 6.2.10.
26. 'Council' before Issus: Arr. *Anab.* 2.7.3. Trial of Philotas: Curt. 6.11. Last Plans: Diod. 18.6. Branchidae (a story doubted by some modern scholars): Curt. 7.5.28–35.

Hieronymus of Cardia, that is, in the eastern sections of Diodorus books 18–20. Diodorus uses the very Xenophontic image, 'like a democratically run city', *hoion dēmokratoumenē polis*, about the army of Hieronymus' uncle Eumenes, and Plutarch's near-identical expression guarantees Hieronyman origin. Perhaps Eumenes' Greekness is relevant to his affable and democratic attitudes. So too there is a definite flavour of the *Anabasis* about the lifelike camp vignette which Hieronymus records under the year 317, where Eumenes tells the Macedonian *plēthos* (massed crowd) the Aesop fable about the lion who pulled out his own claws and teeth to ingratiate himself with the father of the girl he had fallen in love with, only to be clubbed to death by the man. When Eumenes had finished, the crowd shouted 'right!' and he then dismissed the assembly; the word is *ekklēsia*. Notoriously, this was an unusual period of military history when armies are found bargaining with the lives and persons of their commanders, such as Eumenes himself. We could hardly ask for a more spectacular inversion of the usual pyramid of command than this, and there is a distant but definite parallel with Nicias' fear that he will one day find himself politically at the mercy of his own troops. More generally, the writings of Xenophon were influential in the early successor period at the level of both historiography and of military practice; we ought therefore not to consider the similarities between the Ten Thousand and the early Successor period as a purely historical question but as a historiographical one. Xenophon's *Anabasis* may have influenced Hieronymus' literary presentation and also the actual conduct of some of the real-life generals he was writing about. After all, Arrian reports that Alexander himself, in his speech of encouragement before the battle of Issus, is said, *legetai*, to have recalled in some detail the exploits of Xenophon and the Ten Thousand. Of this Brunt remarks, 'not necessarily false. Al[exander] is likely to have read Xenophon.' Xenophon could have known not only of the real-life Sicilian expedition of 415–413 but of Thucydides' handling of it. This is not quite impossible on the composition dates, but the fate of that expedition was not such as to encourage imitation.[27]

27. 'Like a democratically run city': Diod. 19.15.4 with J. Hornblower, *Hieronymus of Cardia* (Oxford, 1981), p. 188 and n. 22 (of Eumenes of Cardia's successful proposal for daily council meetings to be attended by 'all the satraps and generals who had been chosen by the mass of the army'). Cf. Plut. *Eum.* 13.5 and 15.3. Eumenes was a Greek, but the Macedonians among the Successors also knew that it could be politic to consult their troops, see Diod. 18.33: Ptolemy was popular because he permitted *parrhēsia* to his commanders, unlike Perdiccas; cf. also Diod. 19.61 for an important common assembly, *koinē ekklēsia*, of the soldiers called by Antigonus (note the language used, *dogma*, *epsēphisato*, *epsēphisanto*). For Hieronymus and Xenophon see Hornblower, *Hieronymus of Cardia*, ch. 5 generally. The Aesop fable of the lion: Diod. 19.25 with Hornblower,

We have spent a long time away from Xenophon's *Anabasis*, to which we can now return. I conclude that, so far from being unusual or unique, the Ten Thousand resemble in some ways the mixed expeditionary force of 415–413 and perhaps other mixed or Athenian armies too. There are obvious enough differences from 413: the Athenian assembly retains a control which is not forgotten by the generals on the spot in Sicily even when it can no longer be consulted. And those generals are appointees of the assembly back home, not elected by the troops. But I have tried to suggest that Thucydides' reference to 'voting with many' is up to a point comparable to the Ten Thousand, and may indicate similar behaviour in the army whose conduct is best known to us in detail after the Ten Thousand, namely the expeditionary force of 415–413 in Sicily. I argued finally that there are also interesting parallels not just with 413 but with the armies of the early Successor period, though here we must reckon with knowledge of the Ten Thousand and of Xenophon's *Anabasis* on somebody's part. To the objection that Nicias' army was itself unusual in being mixed I would say No, many of the classical armies we hear of were also mixed or coalition armies; one need think only of the general Demosthenes' army in north-west Greece which included some Doric-speaking Messenians, the battle of Delium, both battles of Mantinea, the battles of the Corinthian War, that of Leuctra, and the Greek force at Chaeronea, although I am not forgetting that all of these armies stayed together for far shorter periods than did the army in Sicily. Coalition commanders did not of course expect to consult the rank and file of their allies, only their commanders. But stories like that of Astyochos and his *baktēria*, used against ordinary Syracusan and Thurian troops (above, p. 256), show that ordinary discipline was harder to exercise against nationals of other states. I have conceded that it is significant that we hear about soldiers voting in Thucydides book 7 but not in book 6. I do however wonder if dialogue between commanders and ordinary troops, and *parrhēsia* by the latter, may have been commoner than we tend to think.

> p. 19. Eumenes' troops trade him for their 'baggage': Diod. 19.43.8 with M. Holleaux, ' "Ceux qui sont dans le baggage" ', in *Études d'épigraphie et d'histoire grecques*, vol. 3 (Paris, 1968), pp. 15–26. Alexander before Issus: Arr. *Anab*. 2.7.8 with P. Brunt, Loeb edn of Arr. *Anab*., vol. 1 (Harvard, 1976), p. 147 n. 4. Space forbids me to go into another relevant category of Hellenistic evidence, epigraphically attested honorary decrees by a segment of the armed forces for their commanders; I am grateful to Robert Parker for raising this in correspondence after the delivery of my paper. For Rhamnous in Attica, where the groups doing the honouring are a wonderfully varied mix of soldiers and non-soldiers see R. Osborne, 'The *demos* and its divisions in classical Athens', in O. Murray and S. Price (eds), *The Greek City from Homer to Aristotle* (Oxford, 1990), pp. 265–93, at pp. 277–93.

Pericles in 431 'summoned no assembly or *syllogos*', where the reference in *syllogos* is to a military meeting. And *that* suggestion, namely that rank-and-file *parrhēsia* and participation in Greek and even Macedonian military discussions was greater than is normally assumed, not just in Athens but especially there, is the main thesis of this paper.

The question then arises, how with such informal and even anarchic attitudes did Greek armies fight, let alone win battles, even against each other? The answer would require another paper altogether. It would have to do with civically generated cohesiveness and determination not to let one's fellow fighters down, as attested by the Athenian ephebic oath and other evidence, not just Athenian but Spartan too, and Greek generally. The laxer discipline of Greek, especially Athenian and Ionian, armies and navies compared to the Persian lash or head-through-the-porthole punishments found in Herodotus, or to Roman harshness as described in Polybius book 6, needs in fact a political explanation, and it will not quite do to shunt off the Ten Thousand into the 'unusual if not unique' category. I hope I shall not be taken to be arguing something more than I am in fact doing. I am not saying that what the Ten Thousand were doing was standard military practice. I contend that it is interesting because extreme, but that it was an extreme version of something which has left traces in the behaviour of earlier and later armies as well. That is perhaps why the Ten Thousand adapted so easily to behaving like a sort of *polis*.[28]

---

28. In connection with Delium, note that Pagondas needs to *persuade* the Boeotians, a federal and so in a way a mixed army, to fight (Thuc. 4.91 and 93.1). Pericles in 431: Thuc. 2.22.1 with the modern works cited at n. 12 above. Ephebic oath: M. N. Tod, *Greek Historical Inscriptions*, vol. 2 (Oxford, 1948), no. 204. Persian harshness: Hdt. 5.33.2, the degrading punishment of Scylax of Myndos. The Romans: Polyb. 6.37.

9 *The Ambitions of a Mercenary*[1]

JAMES ROY

Mercenary service was an important and lasting feature of classical Greek society, and large numbers of men left home to earn a living as mercenaries in the service of Greek and non-Greek employers. Amid the generally anecdotal evidence for Greek mercenary service in the fifth and fourth centuries Xenophon's *Anabasis* provides an unparalleled wealth of information. Precisely because the *Anabasis* is unique, it is not a straightforward matter to decide to what extent the conditions of mercenary service which it shows are representative of its time. Coupled with that difficulty is of course the question of how far Xenophon's view of the life of a mercenary in the *Anabasis* is peculiarly personal, coloured by his own interests. This chapter nonetheless seeks to examine what the mercenaries of the *Anabasis* expected or hoped to find, and what we can suppose that they actually did find. It will concentrate mainly on the ordinary hoplites who made up the greater part of Cyrus' Greek troops, recognizing that other Greeks with Cyrus may have had different ambitions.

Recent work on the *Anabasis*, and on the other writings of Xenophon, has explored his literary sophistication, and it clearly cannot be supposed that what Xenophon says in the *Anabasis* is merely a simple chronicle of events. Yet often enough Xenophon does seem to offer a straightforward report. In the *Anabasis*, for instance, the standard wage for an ordinary mercenary soldier is consistently the equivalent of five obols per day (one daric or one cyzicene per month): it seems extremely unlikely that Xenophon systematically presented a biased and distorted view of mercenary wages, while leaving the rate within the range that we should expect. In what follows, comment on how literary

---

1. I am grateful for the comments offered when this piece was presented to the Oxford seminar on the *Anabasis*. Since I last wrote about the mercenaries of the *Anabasis* in 'The mercenaries of Cyrus', a great deal of fresh work has appeared, on some points correcting what I then wrote, and on some points my own views have changed. Changed views on points of importance are noted in what follows.

aims, or indeed other factors, may have coloured Xenophon's account is offered only when it is particularly necessary for the argument, but that approach to the *Anabasis* is not meant to suggest that literary analysis of the *Anabasis* is not needed for a full understanding of the text as historical evidence. Indeed, analysis of the speeches is extremely illuminating, as Rood shows in chapter 11 of this volume.[2]

In order to understand the mercenaries' ambitions, it is worthwhile to consider their situation before they joined Cyrus. The main relevant evidence comes in what Xenophon says about recruitment for Cyrus. Cyrus told all his garrison commanders in Ionia to recruit Peloponnesians in the greatest possible numbers and of the best quality. This eventually produced 4,000 hoplites under the command of Xenias. It is likely, in view of Cyrus' clear preference for Peloponnesians, that the mercenaries in the garrisons which he left in the Ionian cities when he marched against his brother were also Peloponnesian. In addition, for a siege of Miletus, which Tissaphernes controlled, Cyrus recruited a force of 300 hoplites and 300 peltasts commanded by Pasion: since Cyrus kept the wife and children of Pasion, like those of Xenias, under guard at Tralles, it is likely that Pasion had served Cyrus for some time as a mercenary commander in Ionia, and that Pasion's men were also recruited in Ionia.[3]

For that same campaign at Miletus, Socrates recruited 500 hoplites and Sophaenetus 1,000. These troops too were probably recruited in Ionia. Cyrus also raised 4,000 men and sent them to Aristippus in Thessaly, presumably recruiting them in Asia Minor: of these Menon brought back to Cyrus 1,000 hoplites, with 500 Dolopian, Aenianian, and Olynthian peltasts who, given their origins near Thessaly, may well have been recruited in their homelands. There was thus a large pool of potential mercenaries, predominantly Peloponnesian, available in Ionia when Cyrus began to recruit, in addition to those – probably also several thousand – already employed in his garrisons. It is of course possible that some men, hearing that Cyrus was recruiting mercenaries, travelled to Ionia in the hope of enlisting with him.[4]

2. On wages see J. A. Krasilnikoff, 'The regular pay of Aegean mercenaries in the classical period', *C & M* 44 (1993), pp. 77–95. For another approach to the question of speeches in Xenophon see P. Pontier, 'Place et fonction du discours dans l'oeuvre de Xénophon', *REA* 103 (2001), pp. 395–408.
3. Peloponnesians in the greatest possible numbers: *Anab*. 1.1.6. 4,000 hoplites under Xenias: *Anab*. 1.2.3. The mercenaries in the garrisons: *Anab*. 1.2.1. 300 hoplites and 300 peltasts under Pasion: *Anab*. 1.1.6–7, 11. Dependent hostages: *Anab*. 1.4.7–8.
4. Further recruiting for the Miletus campaign: *Anab*. 1.2.3. 4,000 men sent to Aristippus: *Anab*. 1.1.10. Hoplites and peltasts brought back by Menon: *Anab*. 1.2.6; cf. 1.2.1. On

Xenophon says that a force was gathered for Cyrus by Clearchus in the Thracian Chersonese opposite Abydus. Best suggested that Clearchus in fact recruited in Asia Minor, and it is at any rate possible that some of the men who joined him moved from Asia Minor to the Chersonese. On either reckoning there was a significant number of men available in the area, since Clearchus eventually had 1,000 hoplites, 800 peltasts, and 200 Cretan archers. The Thracians were presumably recruited near the Chersonese.[5]

Proxenus gathered 1,500 hoplites and 500 peltasts for Cyrus, probably in mainland Greece; 300 hoplites were also recruited by Sosis, but it is not known where. Lastly the Spartan Chirisophus brought 700 hoplites in response to Cyrus' request for help from Sparta: while Xenophon in the *Anabasis* is admittedly very reticent about Sparta's relations with Cyrus, he says nothing to suggest that these 700 men were different from other Greeks in Cyrus' army, and they were probably mercenaries from mainland Greece, whatever the role of their commander.[6]

Peltasts seem to have been recruited differently from hoplites, since many of them apparently enlisted directly from their home and served in an ethnically defined body. The main examples are Menon's Dolopians, Aenianians, and Olynthians, and Clearchus' Thracians. In addition the Milesian exiles who came to join Cyrus were also clearly a special case, if they did indeed march with Cyrus: they never appear again in the *Anabasis*, and do not appear to figure in Xenophon's numbers for Cyrus' forces.[7]

What emerges from this survey of recruitment for Cyrus is that towards the end of the fifth century there were in Ionia thousands of Greeks, including many Peloponnesians, available for service as mercenary hoplites, in addition

---

recruitment by or for Cyrus see J. Roy, 'The mercenaries of Cyrus', *Historia* 16 (1967), pp. 292–323, at pp. 296–309; that account overlooked the likelihood that Socrates and Sophaenetus recruited in Ionia. Xenophon speaks of men sailing to join Cyrus: the passage *Anab*. 1.19.7 refers explicitly to *lochagoi* and *stratēgoi*, while 6.4.8, apparently couched in more general terms, has – as will be argued below – particular reference to officers. Xenophon's views may have been coloured by the fact that he himself travelled to Asia Minor to join Cyrus' expedition.

5. Clearchus' force: *Anab*. 1.1.9. Cf. J. G. P. Best, *Thracian Peltasts and their Influence on Greek Warfare* (Groningen, 1969), p. 52 n. 92. On Xenophon's tendentious and somewhat incomplete account of Clearchus' career see S. R Bassett, 'The enigma of Clearchus the Spartan', *AHB* 15.1–2 (2001), pp. 1–13, and Braun, chapter 3 in this volume.
6. On Proxenus' recruiting (*Anab*. 1.2.3): Roy, 'The mercenaries of Cyrus', p. 301. On Chirisophus at *Anab*. 1.4.2, cf. *Hell*. 3.1.1, Diod. 14.19.2: D. M. Lewis, *Sparta and Persia* (Leiden, 1977), pp. 138–9, 151–2.
7. Milesian exiles: *Anab*. 1.2.2. The category 'peltasts' is a loose one, and Best, *Thracian Peltasts*, pp. 36–47, draws attention to Xenophon's willingness to use the term for troops equipped in various different ways.

to the mercenaries already in employment and to those available for recruitment elsewhere. It is reasonable to assume that the men in Asia Minor were looking for employment as mercenaries, since there is no other obvious reason for Peloponnesians to gather there. It seems safe to assume that it was known among Peloponnesians, and in particular among Arcadians, who – as will be seen – formed a large part of the Ten Thousand, that employment as mercenaries could be found in western Asia Minor. It is also likely that, whenever demand for mercenaries became more intensive than usual, word would reach the Peloponnese. There remain, however, questions about how so many Peloponnesians came to be in Ionia when Cyrus began recruiting.

In describing the battle of Cunaxa Diodorus says that the Greeks were much more experienced than the barbarians opposed to them because they had continually been engaged in battles throughout the Peloponnesian War. Many modern scholars have accepted the implication of this statement that at least the later stages of the Peloponnesian War had made many Greeks accustomed to a life of more or less professional soldiering, whether actually as mercenaries or as citizen troops mobilized for long periods, so that after the war they looked for a mercenary career. While the Peloponnesian War may have had that effect on some men, it is difficult to believe that it is the main, or even a main, explanation for the number of men available to be recruited by Cyrus. The numbers of mercenary infantry employed by either side even in the later Peloponnesian War were limited, to judge by the surviving evidence. (Paid rowers might be a different matter.) Already in 1933 Parke wrote that 'It could not be argued, however, that the hired hoplite contributed much strength to either side during the Peloponnesian War', and a recent study by Bettali came to a broadly similar conclusion. As for lengthy foreign service as citizen hoplites, it should not have fallen disproportionately on Sparta's Arcadian allies. For these reasons it seems doubtful that Cyrus's hoplites were mainly veterans of the Peloponnesian War.[8]

8. The experience of the Greeks at Cunaxa: Diod. 14.23.4. On Diodorus' account of Cyrus' expedition see H. D. Westlake, 'Diodorus and the expedition of Cyrus', *Phoenix* 41 (1987), pp. 241–54, G. Wylie, 'Cunaxa and Xenophon', *L'Antiquité Classique* 61 (1992), pp. 119–34, and Stylianou, chapter 2 in this volume. The view that the Peloponnesian War led men to mercenary service is found in, e.g., L. P. Marinoviç, *Le Mercenariat grec au IVe siècle av. n.è. et la crise de la polis* (Paris, 1988), p. 136 n. 8, and, recently, A. Tourraix, 'Les mercenaires grecs au service des Achéménides', in P. Brun (ed.), *Guerres et sociétés dans les mondes grecs (490–322)* (Paris, 1999), pp. 201–16, at p. 205. The quotation is from H. W. Parke, *Greek Mercenary Soldiers from Earliest Times to the Battle of Ipsus* (Oxford, 1933), p. 17; see also M. Bettali, *I mercenari nel mondo greco*, vol. 1: *Dalle origini alla fine del V. sec. a. C.* (Pisa, 1995), p. 141, and 'La guerre du Péloponnèse', in P. Brulé and J. Oulhen (eds), *La Guerre en Grèce à l'époque classique* (Rennes, 1999), p. 349.

On the other hand there seems to be no doubt that mercenary service was well developed by the end of the fifth century, and that certain basic patterns had been established. There was a recognized structure of command, with *stratēgoi* in charge and *lochagoi* under them, and this structure was used among Cyrus' hoplite force even though it meant that it remained a series of parallel contingents rather than a united force. There was also an established rate of pay: all employers or potential employers in the *Anabasis* offer either a daric or a cyzicene per month to the ordinary soldier, double to a *lochagos*, and quadruple to a *stratēgos*. At one point the rates for *lochagoi* and *stratēgoi* are described as 'the usual'. One area in which we know that there was enough mercenary service to allow such patterns to develop is the western provinces of the Achaemenid Empire, where Greek mercenaries had often been employed since the middle of the fifth century. So far as is known the individual units were not large, the biggest attested being the 700 mercenaries provided for Samians by the satrap Pissuthnes in 440. Nonetheless a number of such units could clearly provide employment for some thousands of men, and we know that Cyrus, for instance, had garrisons in several Ionian cities before he began recruiting for the campaign against his brother. The fact that there were many potential mercenaries available in Ionia when Cyrus was recruiting also suggests that the area was known to Greeks as offering opportunities for mercenary service.[9]

A large majority of the men recruited by Cyrus served under him as hoplites. It is worth considering whether they were already experienced hoplites when he enlisted them, since that would throw some light on the social background from which they came. The question has been raised in recent studies whether typically they came from families of hoplite status or from a significantly poorer background, but it has not received a clear answer. One way to look for an answer would be to consider whether the men provided their own arms and armour or received them from the employer. That question has recently been debated in print by Whitehead and McKechnie: the debate showed clearly

---

9. Structure of command: G. B. Nussbaum, *The Ten Thousand: A Study in Social Organization and Action in Xenophon's Anabasis* (Leiden, 1967), and J. W. I. Lee, 'The lochos in Xenophon's *Anabasis*', Liverpool Xenophon conference, 1999. Separate contingents of mercenaries in Cyrus' army: Roy, 'The mercenaries of Cyrus', pp. 287–96, 320–1. 'The usual rates': *Anab.* 7.3.10. Rates of pay: Krasilnikoff, 'The regular pay of Aegean mercenaries', pp. 82–8. Mercenaries in Persian service before the *Anabasis*: G. F. Seibt, *Griechische Söldner im Achaimenidenreich* (Bonn, 1977), pp. 219–20, and Tourraix, 'Les mercenaires grecs', pp. 203–5. The 700 Samian mercenaries: Thuc. 1.115.4. On garrisons, *Anab.* 1.1.6, 2.1: on Persian garrisons generally see C. J. Tuplin, 'Xenophon and the garrisons of the Achaemenid Empire', *AMI* n.f. 20 (1987), pp. 167–246.

that on some occasions the men provided their own equipment, and on others the employer, but it is much less clear whether one of these two practices was commoner than the other.[10]

Another indication of the men's social standing might be the demonstration by Krasilnikoff that mercenaries in the classical period were expected to buy their own food out of their wages, rather than receiving food from their employer in addition to the wage. (Using information taken from passages of Plutarch and not found in Xenophon, Descat argues that – exceptionally – Cyrus may have provided food under the revised terms of service agreed at Thapsacus.) The apparently standard wage offered in the *Anabasis* is the equivalent of five obols per day, which is not a large sum and would be even more modest once food had been paid for. It could be argued that men willing to serve for such a sum would not be prosperous. It should however be noted that the wage was paid for every day of service, whereas many Greeks working for payment in money would not earn every day, and mercenaries may also have hoped for booty or for bonuses paid by the employer (discussed below). It also appears that some at least of the men serving with Cyrus had a slave attendant, which suggests that they were not particularly poor and that their need to earn money did not prevent them from feeding a slave as well as themselves from their wages. Xenophon's account of how Persian cavalry killed Greeks both free and slave just after Clearchus and other generals had been seized certainly suggests that there was a significant number of slaves with the army even before the troops began to take captives on the march home; and, when in the territory of the Carduchi the army decided that it must reduce its baggage-train and the number of its followers, that was done by giving up the recently captured slaves, which suggests that the troops were allowed to retain slaves whom they had owned for longer. On balance such evidence, while

10. On the social origins of mercenaries see P. McKechnie, 'Greek mercenary troops and their equipment', *Historia* 43 (1994), pp. 297–305, at pp. 297–8, and M. F. Trundle, 'Identity and community among Greek mercenaries in the classical world: 700–322 BCE', *AHB* 13 (1999), pp. 28–38, at p. 33: P. McKechnie, *Outsiders in the Greek Cities in the Fourth Century BC* (London and New York, 1989), p. 80, broadly accepted the views expressed by Xenophon in *Anab.* 6.4.8, to the effect that the Greeks did not take service with Cyrus from poverty, but that passage from the *Anabasis* is far from clear as evidence (see below). On who supplied equipment see the debate between D. Whitehead, 'Who equipped mercenary troops in classical Greece?', *Historia* 40 (1991), pp. 105–13, and McKechnie, 'Greek mercenary troops and their equipment': without adding any major new argument L. Iapichino, 'I Diecimila di Senofonte: tecniche di combattimento, equipaggiamento militare e approvvigionamento degli strumenti di guerra', *Rivista Storica dell'Antichità* 29 (1999), pp. 91–105, favours Whitehead's view that the mercenaries typically provided their own equipment.

hardly clear-cut, at least suggests that not all mercenaries were driven to mercenary service by poverty.[11]

The language used by Xenophon in his obituary of Clearchus[12] about men who followed Clearchus 'because they had been ordered by a polis or from need [*tou deisthai*] or from some other necessity' is odd as a description of mercenaries alone and may refer not only to the men who served under Clearchus in Cyrus' forces but also to those who had served with him in various capacities in Thrace: it is at any rate unclear what kind of need is meant, and consequently the phrase does not necessarily point to men driven to mercenary service by poverty, though there would be nothing surprising about finding some men driven to mercenary service by want.

There is also however the question of how and when the men were trained as hoplites. If they were of hoplite status, they would presumably have been trained in their home communities and have come to mercenary service as experienced hoplites. That must presumably be the view of those who believe that Cyrus' hoplites were veterans of the Peloponnesian War. Perlman, for instance, wrote 'both in its [*sic*] tactical and military ability, the Ten Thousand – mostly veterans of the Peloponnesian War – were already a well-drilled mercenary army' and 'It seems that the Ten Thousand are a very professional mercenary army already at the beginning of the campaign . . .' Even if – as argued above – it was not the case that most of Cyrus' hoplites had gained their hoplite experience in the Peloponnesian War, it remains true that they appear to have been experienced when recruited. Recently Hutchinson has noted that 'Training does not arise as an issue in the *Anabasis*'.[13]

According to Xenophon, Cyrus told his garrison commanders in Ionia to recruit Peloponnesians, as many and as good as possible (*andras Peloponnēsíous hoti pleistous kai beltistous*). The term *beltistous* would naturally refer not simply

11. Slaughter of free Greeks and slaves by the Persian cavalry: *Anab.* 2.5.32. Wages and terms of service: Krasilnikoff, 'The regular pay of Aegean mercenaries'. Agreement at Thapsacus: R. Descat, 'Marché et tribut: l'approvisionnement des Dix-Mille', in P. Briant (ed.), *Dans les pas des Dix-Mille* (Toulouse, 1995), pp. 99–108, at pp. 103–4. On attendants A. Dalby, 'Greeks abroad: social organisation and food among the Ten Thousand', *JHS* 112 (1992), pp. 16–30, at p. 18, citing *Anab.* 2.5.32 and 4.1.12, argues persuasively against Roy, 'The mercenaries of Cyrus', p. 310, that numerous soldiers had servants even before the army started taking captives on the march home. R. J. Bonner, 'Xenophon's comrades in arms', *Classical Journal* 10 (1914–15), pp. 195–205, gives examples of mercenaries from different social backgrounds.
12. *Anab.* 2.6.13.
13. S. Perlman, 'The Ten Thousand: a chapter in the military, social and economic history of the fourth century', *Rivista Storica dell'Antichità* 6–7 (1976–7), pp. 241–84, at pp. 267–8: G. Hutchinson, *Xenophon and the Art of Command* (London, 2000), p. 61.

to good physical specimens but to competent soldiers, and in fact the language in this passage is very similar to another in the *Hellenica* where it certainly refers to military competence. In 394 Agesilaus was recruiting men, both allies and mercenaries, to take back to Greece and wanted to take with him men as good and as many as possible (*boulomenos hōs beltistous kai pleistous agein meth' heautou*): in order to get such troops he offered prizes for the best both to the cities sending allied forces and to the *lochagoi* recruiting mercenaries, and it is clear that he wanted trained men. (The passage also says that Agesilaus offered a prize for the *lochagos* who served with him with the best-armed *lochos*, but that is not evidence that hoplites provided their own weapons since the mercenaries in question may already have been serving with Agesilaus in Asia Minor: the same passage of Xenophon shows that Agesilaus had difficulty in persuading many of the men he already had to follow him to Greece.) Lee has provided an illuminating analysis of the manoeuvrability of the mercenary *lochos* as seen in the *Anabasis*, and has rightly pointed out that mercenaries on garrison duty might be called upon to operate in a variety of ways, and would need the skill to manoeuvre in small formations as well as in a regular phalanx. Another recent study by Rawlings has however shown that citizen hoplites possessed a range of skills and were adaptable: it follows therefore that experienced citizen hoplites would not need special training to adapt to the duties of a mercenary. On balance it appears likely that Cyrus recruited experienced hoplites, which in turn suggests that many of his men had come originally from at least modestly prosperous backgrounds.[14]

Cyrus' mercenaries varied in age: the youngest identified was a trumpeter of eighteen, who would have been about sixteen when he first joined the army, while there were a number of men over forty-five years old. It was common to select the younger men for more demanding duties, and the group selected is sometimes identified as being under thirty years old and sometimes as being the most agile; these two categories are at one point explicitly equated. On one passage Stronk noted that the men under thirty were 'sufficient . . . to perform a special duty'.[15]

14. 'As many and as good as possible': *Anab.* 1.1.6. Lee, 'The lochos in Xenophon's *Anabasis*'; L. Rawlings, 'Alternative agonies: hoplite martial and combat experiences beyond the phalanx', in H. van Wees (ed.), *War and Violence in Ancient Greece* (London, 2000), pp. 233–59.
15. Eighteen-year-old trumpeter: *Anab.* 7.4.16. Men over forty-five: *Anab.* 6.5.4. More demanding duties: *Anab.* 4.1.27; 4.2.16; 4.5.21; 7.4.6. Under thirty: *Anab.* 2.3.12. Most agile: *Anab.* 4.3.20; 4.5.24. Equation of agility and youth: *Anab.* 7.3.46. 'A special duty': *Anab.* 6.5.4.

Conversely, while the rest of the army marched from Trapezus to Cerasus, the men over forty were permitted to sail along with the sick, the women, and the children: as Lendle (ad loc.) notes, they cannot have been very numerous. At one point Neon's men were left to guard the army's camp while the others went out to find and bury the men killed in a disastrous sortie by Neon the day before, but, since most of his officers and men were too ashamed to remain in camp, finally only the men over forty-five remained on guard. The latter cannot have been numerous, but it may in any case have been normal – as Stronk suggests – for the older men to remain in camp as a guard.[16]

It is curious that, although the younger men were clearly regarded as better suited to a wide range of duties, older men were also recruited and apparently paid at the same rate: the older men may have been valued for their experience. It may be noted that of the generals who were seized by the Persians Clearchus was about fifty, Proxenus about thirty, and Agias and Socrates both about thirty-five. It is likely that any men in the army under thirty years of age, particularly any who were several years under thirty, would have left home before marrying because, although we are not well informed about the age at which men (and women) typically married even in classical Athens, it is commonly supposed that men there usually married when between twenty-five and thirty. In a surprising phrase Xenophon also mentions mercenaries who had 'run away' from their fathers and mothers: presumably young unmarried men are meant.[17]

Among Cyrus' hoplites was a large number of Arcadians. Xenophon states that, when the Arcadians and Achaeans in the army eventually decided to go off on their own, they numbered more than half the army, and gives figures for the rest of the army which add up to 4,140 (including 3,100 hoplites) while saying simply that the Arcadians and Achaeans numbered more than 4,000.[18] If one assumes that the Arcadians and Achaeans were at that time at least 4,200, and further assumes that up to that point the Arcadian and Achaean hoplites had suffered more or less the same rate of loss as the others, then it is

---

16. Men over forty sailing: *Anab.* 5.3.1. Neon's men: *Anab.* 6.5.4; cf. 6.4.23–7 for the disastrous raid.
17. Ages of the generals: *Anab.* 2.6.15 (Clearchus); 2.6.20 (Proxenus); 2.6.30 (Agias and Socrates). 'Runaway' mercenaries: *Anab.* 6.4.8. The quotation is from J. P. Stronk, *The Ten Thousand in Thrace: An Archaeological and Historical Commentary on Xenophon's Anabasis Books VI.iii–vi VII* (Amsterdam, 1995): see also his notes on *Anab.* 6.5.4 and 7.4.16. Age at marriage: J. Roy, '*Polis* and *oikos* in classical Athens', *Greece and Rome* 46 (1999), pp. 1–18, at p. 6.
18. Anab. 6.2.10; 6.2.16.

possible to divide the original total of hoplites in the same proportion that prevailed at their departure. At this point there were at least 4,200 Arcadian and Achaean hoplites and 3,100 others: divided in the same proportion the original 10,400 hoplites would give c. 6,000 Arcadians and Achaeans and 4,400 others.

Various arguments suggest that there might have been about twice as many Arcadians as Achaeans with Cyrus. In the breakaway group of Arcadians and Achaeans, it is clear that the Arcadians predominated: in his account of their separate venture Xenophon almost always refers to the whole group simply as Arcadians. Moreover, of the individuals named in the *Anabasis* whose origin is known, fourteen are Arcadian and seven are Achaean. Under the reform of the Peloponnesian League forces in 377 Arcadia contributed two army divisions while Achaea contributed only one. Finally, the area of Arcadia was calculated by Beloch to be roughly twice that of Achaea. Therefore there may well have been originally c. 4,000 Arcadian hoplites and c. 2,000 Achaean with Cyrus. These calculations involve some assumptions and are very rough and ready, but at least give an order of size for the Arcadian contribution to Cyrus' forces.[19]

It is worth evaluating the Arcadian component in Cyrus' army because it is commonly argued – e.g. recently by both Tourraix and Fields – that Arcadians were driven to mercenary service by poverty. If that is right and a significant part of Cyrus' hoplite force was motivated by poverty, then it could be argued that in all probability many of his other hoplites were similarly driven by want. It should be noted that, given Cyrus' known preference for Peloponnesians, and apparently for Arcadians, we must suppose that there would be yet other Arcadians in the garrisons which Cyrus left in the cities of Ionia. A large number of Arcadian mercenaries in the late fifth century fits well enough with the reputation, already established in the fifth century, of Arcadians for taking up mercenary service. We do not have reliable figures for the population of Arcadia in the classical period, but it probably lay between 100,000 and 200,000, and quite possibly in the lower part of that range. Two hundred thousand is therefore a high estimate of the total Arcadian population, and – using the ancient belief that adult males were roughly one-quarter

---

19. Reference to 'Arcadians' alone: *Anab.* 6.2.17–3.26 and 6.4.9–10, with a single exception at 6.3.24. The Arcadian contribution in 377: Diod. 15.31. The calculations set out in this paragraph appeared originally in Roy, 'The mercenaries of Cyrus', pp. 308–9. On the area of Arcadia see K. J. Beloch, *Die Bevölkerung der griechisch-römischen Welt* (Leipzig, 1886), pp. 112, 124, 129.

of a population – we can arrive at 50,000 as a high estimate of the adult male Arcadians. In that case more than 8 per cent of the entire Arcadian adult male population was in Cyrus' service. Clearly, if we assume an adult male population of 35–40,000 (which may well be nearer the truth) and suppose that there were one or two thousand Arcadians left in Cyrus' Ionian garrisons, the proportion of the Arcadian male population serving with Cyrus rises even higher.[20]

It is implausible that several thousand Arcadians suddenly turned to mercenary service because of the opportunity offered by Cyrus, though he may of course have attracted somewhat more than usual. Since the reputation of the Arcadian mercenary is already clear in Hermippus no later than 424,[21] it seems much more likely that significant numbers of Arcadians had been serving as mercenaries for some time before the *Anabasis*. Given the known opportunities for mercenaries, many of them must have been in Persian service, and indeed we have to suppose something of the kind in order to explain Cyrus' preference for Peloponnesians.

Possibly some of these men eventually returned to Arcadia, but few of those serving with Cyrus can have gone home, and generally mercenary service must have caused a loss of manpower to Arcadia. The situation evidently continued long after Cyrus' march since still in the 360s Xenophon makes the Arcadian leader Lycomedes boast that Arcadian mercenaries were preferred to any others. For generations, therefore, Arcadian families were producing sons in the knowledge that a significant number would go off on mercenary service, and producing daughters not all of whom would find husbands. While it might have been dangerous for Arcadian households deliberately to limit their reproductivity, it would be surprising if such a demographic pattern were maintained for generations unless it offered some advantage to Arcadians. One possible advantage is that, in a world where many children did not survive to adulthood, families could rear several sons: if all, or most, survived, then those for whom the family's resources did not suffice could go abroad as mercenaries. The situation could also have been eased by offering sons for adoption to families which lacked them, and possibly also by exposing girl children to

20. Arcadian mercenaries driven by poverty: Tourraix, 'Les mercenaires grecs', p. 206, and N. Fields, 'Et ex Arcadia ego', *AHB* 15.3 (2001), pp. 102–30. Arcadians' reputation as mercenaries: the evidence is set out by Fields, 'Et ex Arcadia ego', pp. 116–20, and is briefly reviewed by Roy, 'The Arkadian economies', in T. H. Nielsen and J. Roy (eds), *Defining Ancient Arkadia* (Copenhagen, 1999), pp. 320–81, at p. 347. Population of Arcadia: Roy, 'The Arkadian economies', pp. 340–1, 348.
21. Hermippus fr. 63 (Kassel-Austin).

redress the imbalance of the sexes. There is no direct evidence for such demographic patterns in classical Arcadia, but, unless we suppose something of the kind, it is hard to understand why Arcadia persisted in producing an excess of manpower.[22]

There is also the question of whether these Arcadians came from families of hoplite status. It must first be admitted that we do not know how the hoplite census was measured in classical Arcadian communities, and it may have been relatively lower than in Athens. Arcadia was considered one of the poorer regions of classical Greece, e.g. by Thucydides,[23] who included among the best land in Greece most of the Peloponnese except Arcadia.

It is however misleading simply to describe Arcadia as poor. The resources of Arcadia, though certainly limited, were real. While much of Arcadia is mountain, the valleys and basins within the mountains are fertile, and the region was famous for its flocks of sheep and goats. It is clear that some Arcadians were wealthy, and the general level of prosperity in Arcadia would depend on the size of the population which the region had to support. The calculations made by the Hodkinsons in their study of Mantinean territory suggest that around 400 'pressure on the agricultural resources of Mantinike will have been quite severe'. The conclusion to be drawn seems to be that Arcadia could offer a modest but reasonable living for its inhabitants, and a rich living for some, provided that its population did not grow too large. Emigration, temporary or permanent, provided a means of limiting population, as it often has done in upland areas. It does not necessarily follow that it was the poorest who emigrated, and families with land may well have been anxious to ensure that it was not asked to support too many sons. The mention of men who ran away from their fathers and mothers to become mercenaries suggests that in some cases there was a family disagreement: a dispute about shares of the family's resources would be a likely cause of such a quarrel. It is conceivable that those Arcadians who went off to become mercenaries were predominantly from peasant families of hoplite status. Sparta might well be happy enough to see a steady outflow of hoplites from the Arcadian communities which it dominated, since the loss of manpower would make the Arcadians easier to control. If Cyrus' Arcadians were in large part from a hoplite background, they may well have been trained as hoplites at home, and have supplied their own equipment when they became mercenaries. They would thus

22. The boast of Lycomedes: *Hell.* 7.1.23. Few men returned home: Roy, 'The mercenaries of Cyrus', p. 320, and below.
23. Thuc. 1.2.3.

cease to be evidence that a significant part of Cyrus' hoplites were driven to mercenary service by poverty.[24]

There may have been various ways for men from an upland community like Arcadia to seek a living elsewhere. One possibility is the building trade. In modern pre-industrial Arcadia men from some villages regularly left home to take work as builders, but the scanty evidence does not allow us to judge whether that happened often in the classical period. Presumably the widespread Greek distaste for banausic activities and for accepting paid employment made some occupations unattractive. Mercenary service however, although undertaken for a wage, seems to have been regarded as an acceptable way of earning a living. Xenophon unsurprisingly is anxious in the *Anabasis* to present it in that light, but critical views of mercenary service are of course found in classical Greek literature, and Isocrates notoriously attacked the Greeks who served with Cyrus as men who could not live in their own communities because of their worthlessness (*phaulotēs*). In the course of the fourth century Isocrates and others saw mercenaries as a danger to the *polis*. Mercenary service was not however condemned as inherently dishonourable as banausic occupations were, and the number of Arcadians, and others, who took it up suggests that it was widely regarded as at least a tolerable livelihood.[25]

So far this chapter has been concerned to argue that the hoplites who took service with Cyrus were in large part from the hoplite class in their own community, trained as hoplites at home and probably able to supply their own equipment. Such men, as citizen hoplites, would have been well equipped to play their part in the political activity within the army which is such a prominent feature of books 5 and 6. There remain, however, questions about what the men expected to gain by their military service. Obviously what in fact

24. Economic resources of Arcadia: Roy, 'The Arkadian economies', with references to wealthy men at pp. 340–1. Mantinea: S. Hodkinson and H. Hodkinson, 'Mantinea and the Mantinike: settlement and society in a Greek polis', *Annual of the British School at Athens* 76 (1981), pp. 239–96: the quotation is from p. 277. Previously (Roy, 'The mercenaries of Cyrus') I doubted that Arcadia could have provided Cyrus with c. 4,000 hoplites equipped with their own weapons; but on reflection it seems quite possible.

25. On Arcadians seeking work as builders see Roy, 'The Arkadian economies', pp. 326–7 (modern practice), 336–8 (ancient evidence). Mercenary service as an acceptable activity: e.g. *Anab.* 6.4.8. Isoc. *Paneg.* 146 on mercenaries: Isocrates' views on mercenary service are reviewed by Perlman, 'The Ten Thousand', pp. 252–4, while Parke, *Greek Mercenary Soldiers*, pp. 234–5, reviews the treatment of the mercenary in the New Comedy, where he is often ridiculed. Cf. also Azoulay, chapter 10 in this volume. Trundle, 'Identity and community', argues that mercenary service offered a reasonable livelihood, without discussing the point at length.

happened to the Ten Thousand was exceptional, much of it unique, but it is possible to draw conclusions from the *Anabasis* about more ordinary mercenary ambitions.

Whatever their ambitions and whatever their agreement with an employer, occasionally mercenaries might in fact have to settle for very little, such as food to live on. The employer did not normally supply food, but was expected to ensure that it was available. Exceptionally Cyrus may have provided food for the troops in the last stage of the march to Cunaxa, from Thapsacus onwards. That would explain Xenophon's report that Cyrus transported a stock of food to be given to the Greeks in case of shortage, though it was in fact captured by the King's forces at Cunaxa. The food was carried in wagons, according to rumour four hundred in number.[26] Arguments used to question the existence of these wagons have recently been refuted by Gabrielli, though Gabrielli does not explain why a large stock of supplies had not been distributed while the army crossed terrain where food was scarce and then faced a decisive battle. However, it was quite exceptional for the employer to give food to mercenaries.

Nonetheless the availability of food was of the highest importance, and the employer had to ensure that the men could find food, whether by purchase or by capture. When the soldiers had the prospect of leaving Seuthes to take service under the Spartans against Tissaphernes, there were complaints that Seuthes still owed them wages. In his very long response to these complaints, one of the points made by Xenophon is that at least the army had passed the winter with ample provisions taken from Seuthes' enemies in the area at no cost in money to the men.[27]

In addition to their pay, mercenaries could hope for booty, but whether they got any depended very much on circumstances. While Cyrus was alive, his mercenaries had few opportunities to loot, and when he allowed them to pillage Lycaonia as enemy territory it was an exceptional case. When Menon's men looted Tarsus without permission, Cyrus promised that if the slaves who

---

26. *Anab.* 1.10.18.
27. Complaints against Seuthes: *Anab.* 7.6.8–10. Xenophon's defence: *Anab*.7.6.31. Employer's responsibility with regard to food: Dalby, 'Greeks abroad', pp. 23–5, and Krasilnikoff, 'The regular pay of Aegean mercenaries'. Agreement at Thapsacus: Descat, 'Marché et tribut', pp. 103–4. M. Gabrielli, 'Transport et logistique militaire dans *l'Anabase*', in Briant, *Dans les pas des Dix-Mille*, pp. 109–22, at pp. 116–17, has refuted the arguments of Roy, 'The mercenaries of Cyrus', p. 311 n. 93, against the evidence of the wagons of *Anab.* 1.10.18, and has argued that the wagons would have been lightly loaded and could have kept up with the army.

had been taken were found, he would hand them back to their owners. When the men were serving with Seuthes, it was agreed that Seuthes would keep all booty and sell it to get money to pay the men's wages.[28]

When opportunity offered, however, the mercenaries were very ready to take booty, and that was a particular concern when they had no employer. They began looting on a major scale as they marched north out of Mesopotamia, though they had to abandon much of that booty in the territory of the Carduchi in order not to encumber their march through mountain country. Once the army reached the coast of the Black Sea the need to manage their relations with the Greek cities of the coast caused complications, but the desire to take booty grew pressing.[29]

Notoriously the last act before Thibron took command of the army was an assault led by Xenophon himself on the estate of the Persian Asidates: the raid was undertaken for booty, and Xenophon says that he invited friends among the *lochagoi* and, apparently, loyal soldiers to take part as a way of rewarding them. Xenophon had been advised to take three hundred men, but a further six hundred men took part against Xenophon's wishes. In any case Xenophon ultimately got a generous share of booty from the raid. He recounts this episode as entirely unexceptionable.[30]

Mercenaries could also hope for bonuses. Those who accompanied Cyrus to his father's court in 405 received such a bonus, but Cyrus seems to have given them only rarely to ordinary soldiers. Xenophon took a very favourable view of Cyrus and in his obituary stresses Cyrus' generosity, but – so far as mercenaries are concerned – his generosity benefited the officers rather than the ordinary mercenaries. *Stratēgoi* and *lochagoi* who sailed to take service with Cyrus to earn money found that good relations with Cyrus were more rewarding than a monthly wage. Shortly before the battle at Cunaxa Cyrus had assembled the *stratēgoi* and *lochagoi* and promised to reward them in the event of victory: the reward was to be a gold crown for each. When various individuals approached him after the meeting to enquire about their personal reward, he satisfied them all. It also seems significant that, when at the Euphrates Menon persuaded his men to cross the river while the rest of the

---

28. Pillaging Lycaonia: *Anab.* 1.2.19. Agreement with Seuthes: *Anab.* 7.3.10; 7.4.2; 7.5.2.
29. Booty abandoned among the Carduchi: *Anab.* 4.1.12–14. Pressing desire for booty: *Anab.* 6.1.17–18; 6.6.38.
30. The raid on Asidates: *Anab.* 7.8.11–23; there is some uncertainty about the reference to ordinary soldiers at 7.8.11. Advice to take three hundred men: *Anab.* 7.8.9. Cf. also Azoulay, chapter 10 in this volume.

Greeks were still deciding what to do, Cyrus simply sent congratulations to the men but – so it was said – gave generous gifts to their commander Menon.[31]

A bonus to the ordinary soldiers on the march is mentioned only as part of Cyrus' attempts to persuade the Greeks to march with him against the King. Originally a campaign against Pisidians was given as the reason for assembling the army. According to Xenophon, among the Greeks only Clearchus originally knew the real objective, while Diodorus says that the commanders knew: in any case it seems clear that the ordinary soldiers did not. When the army marched from Celaenae to Peltae it would have been possible to deduce that their route would not take them to Pisidia. At Peltae games were held in honour of Zeus Lycaeus, and as prizes gold *stlengides* were given.[32]

The games were organized by Xenias, who had clearly been in Cyrus' service for some time and commanded the troops recruited by Cyrus' garrison commanders, and there is little doubt that Xenias was here acting with Cyrus' approval. It is likely that Cyrus himself supplied the valuable prizes, as a way of maintaining the troops' morale when they might begin to have suspicions about where he was taking them. At Tarsus the Greeks refused to march any farther: 'For they already suspected that they were marching against the King, and they said that they had not been hired for that.'[33]

Cyrus now declared that his aim was to march against Abrocomas on the Euphrates, and after protracted negotiations the Greeks agreed to follow him in return for a 50 per cent increase in pay; some already suspected that they were being led against the King. At Thapsacus on the Euphrates Cyrus was finally obliged to reveal his true intentions, and the troops refused to march further unless they received a bonus like the Greek mercenaries who had accompanied Cyrus to Darius' court in 405, and Cyrus agreed to give them a bonus of five minae per man, to be paid at Babylon, and to pay their wages in

---

31. Bonuses in 405: *Anab.* 1.1.2 and 1.4.12. Cyrus' generosity: *Anab.* 1.9.1–31. Service more rewarding than a monthly wage: *Anab.* 1.9.17. A gold crown apiece: *Anab.* 1.7.4–8. Menon's reward: *Anab.* 1.4.13–17. The other person in the Greek army who is reported to have received a gift from Cyrus is the seer Silanus, to whom Cyrus gave 3,000 darics (*Anab.* 1.7.18). Cf. also Braun, chapter 3 in this volume.
32. Campaign against Pisidians, *Anab.* 1.1.11; 1.2.1: Diod. 14.19.3 asserts that the pretext for the march was a campaign against tyrants in Cilicia who were rebelling against the King, and then that Cyrus' army set out towards 'Cilicia and Pisidia' (14.19.6). Knowledge of the objective: *Anab.* 3.1.10; contrast Diod. 14.19.9. Celaenae to Peltae, *Anab.* 1.2.10: see O. Lendle, *Kommentar zu Xenophons Anabasis* (Darmstadt, 1995), ad loc. The games at Peltae: *Anab.* 1.2.10; cf. also Parker and Ma, chapters 4 and 12 in this volume.
33. Xenias' command, *Anab.* 1.2.1, 3: his wife and children were held under guard by Cyrus at Tralles (1.4.8). On Cyrus' likely part in the games at Tralles, see Roy, 'The mercenaries of Cyrus', p. 314. 'They already suspected': *Anab.* 1.3.1.

full back to Ionia. In the various negotiations to persuade the Greeks to keep marching with him Cyrus therefore only once offered a bonus, despite his evident desire to keep the Greeks with him and despite Xenophon's views on Cyrus' generosity. The bonus was of course never paid.[34]

Cyrus' mercenaries were clearly reluctant to follow him in his campaign against the King. The various real or alleged purposes for which they had been recruited were garrison duty in Ionia, a campaign against Miletus, and a campaign against Pisidians, apart from serving in the Thracian Chersonese and in Thessaly. The campaign against the Pisidians was then made the pretext for assembling the several contingents of Greeks.[35]

Xenophon joined Cyrus and his army while they were still at Sardis. He mentions no reluctance on the men's part to undertake the campaign against the Pisidians, and the terms in which he reports their protest at Tarsus when they realized that they were not marching against Pisidians and suspected that they might be marching against the King ('they said that they had not been hired for that') suggests that they regarded the Pisidian campaign as being within the terms of their contract with Cyrus. This gives some idea of how far they were willing to go from the Aegean. A similar indication is their agreement with Seuthes that while in his service they should not be required to go more than seven days' travel inland from the sea, though that stipulation may reflect what they had learnt from their experience with Cyrus. The mercenaries clearly wanted to remain near Hellas. Hellas was not precisely defined, but, as Xenophon conceived it in the *Anabasis*, evidently referred to the area of concentrated Greek settlement: at Harmene, the port of Sinope, with Trapezus, Cerasus, and Cotyora to the east of them, the Greeks were 'getting near Hellas', and near Calpes Limen, having passed more Greek settlements on the Black Sea coast, they were 'at the doors of Hellas'.[36]

The *Anabasis* also strongly suggests that the men wanted to be in Hellas. As Dillery puts it, 'In terms of long-range objectives, return to Greece is the soldiers' only goal.' Dillery also recognized, however, that 'Return is a complicated

---

34. Fifty per cent increase in pay: *Anab.* 1.3.1–19. At Thapsacus Cyrus may also have agreed to provide food for the troops at his expense: see Descat, 'Marché et tribut', pp. 103–4. Bonus to be paid at Babylon: *Anab.* 1.4.11–13.
35. Garrison duty in Ionia: *Anab.* 1.1.6. Campaign against Miletus: *Anab.* 1.1.7. Campaign against the Pisidians: *Anab.* 1.1.11. The Thracian Chersonese: *Anab.* 1.1.9. Thessaly: *Anab.* 1.1.10. Pretext for assembly of several contingents: *Anab.* 2.1.1.
36. Xenophon joins the march: *Anab.* 3.1.8. 'They said that they had not been hired for that': *Anab.* 1.3.1. The agreement with Seuthes: *Anab.* 7.3.12. 'Getting near Hellas': *Anab.* 6.1.17. 'The gates of Hellas': *Anab.* 6.5.23; cf. also Rood, chapter 11 in this volume.

matter.' Thus, despite repeated statements in the *Anabasis* that once Cyrus' death left the Greeks isolated, the men wanted to return to Hellas and to go 'home' (*oikade*) and to rejoin their families, where exactly the men really wanted to go is less clear. Xenophon also appears to assume consistently that any relationships which mercenaries had formed with women accompanying them during the march would be broken off once the army was back in Hellas in favour of the men's original families: this is a dubious assumption.[37]

As they approached Hellas the peculiar circumstances of the remnants of Cyrus' Greek mercenaries limited their options. They formed a large and dangerous army, and consequently posed a problem for the Greek cities in the area, and particularly for the Spartan commanders. They were also potentially a worry to the Persian authorities. It was not a solution for the mercenaries simply to split up; until they left the area the danger that they might reunite would remain, and those who felt threatened by them might attack small groups. Some men did nonetheless succeed in detaching themselves from the army. At Perinthus Neon left the army with 800 men; he evidently did so with the approval of the local Spartan authorities and was used soon afterwards by Aristarchus, the harmost in Byzantium, as an envoy to the main body of mercenaries. Neon, from Asine in Laconia, was originally *hypostratēgos* in Chirisophus' contingent and succeeded to the command of the contingent when Chirisophus died. Clearly the 800 men whom he took out of the army must have included many others besides the survivors of Chirisophus' original 700, but Neon, as the senior surviving officer of a force originally sent by Sparta to help Cyrus, was no doubt able to secure Spartan help.[38]

Xenophon also says that 'many' men left the army at Byzantium, some selling their weapons and sailing off as best they could, and others giving away their weapons and mingling with the population of local towns: in fact the number cannot have been greater than 500. Those who left apparently included most of the army's remaining peltasts, since afterwards the army no longer had an organized body of peltasts. On the other hand the harmost Aristarchus seized 400 men whom he found in Byzantium and sold them as slaves. In the circumstances it is not surprising that relatively few men left the

---

37. J. Dillery, *Xenophon and the History of his Times* (London, 1995), p. 68. Repeated references to a desire to return to Hellas and the continued presentation in the narrative of difficulties encountered in the attempt to return link the *Anabasis* to the theme of return (*nostos*) well known in Greek literature; cf. also Ma, chapter 12 in this volume. For relations with women, cf. Lane Fox, chapter 6 in this volume.
38. Neon's departure: *Anab.* 7.2.11. Aristarchus' envoy: *Anab.* 7.3.7. Neon as *hypostrategos*: *Anab.* 5.6.36. Chirisophus' original 700: *Anab.* 1.4.3.

army, and that it was still available as a body to take service first with Seuthes and then with Thibron. If the men wanted to go home to their families, few succeeded in the period covered by the *Anabasis*.[39]

How much the men wanted to go home is however hard to tell. The references to returning to Hellas and to going home occur mainly in speeches and have a clear emotional colouring. A rare exception is the simple statement that the seer Silanus wanted to reach Hellas as quickly as possible; the statement appears to be true since he did in fact hire a ship at Heraclea to take him.[40]

In some speeches the return to Hellas might simply mean a return to the area of concentrated Greek settlement, not necessarily a return to each man's home community. The first statement of a desire to return to Hellas, by a man primed by Clearchus in a meeting of Clearchus' troops,[41] can serve as an example. However, both return to Hellas and going home are several times linked with references to families and relatives, and therefore evidently mean a return not simply to the Greek world but to the individual's home community.

A classic example of this is the passage at the beginning of book 3 where Xenophon dwells on the misery of the Greeks after the loss of generals and other officers and men. The passage first offers a sequence of reasons for despair, each stated in bald terms: one is that they were no less than ten thousand stades from Hellas. It then describes in very obvious terms the effects of the despair – few ate, few lit a fire, and so on – and goes on to offer the supposed thoughts of the Greeks in terms of equal banality: they lay down where they happened to be but could not sleep for grief and desire for their native lands, their parents, their wives, their children, whom they thought they would never see again. The passage then introduces Xenophon, afflicted by the same despair but led by a dream to rouse the others.[42]

The sentimentality of this passage is obvious, but it is also clear that it links return to Hellas with return to homelands and families. Other passages make the same connection. In one passage Hellas is linked with children and wives,

---

39. Lack of peltasts: cf. *Anab*. 7.6.26. 400 enslaved by Aristarchus: *Anab*. 7.2.6. On the army's complicated relations with the local Spartan commanders see J. Roisman, 'Anaxibios and Xenophon's *Anabasis*', *AHB* 2 (1988), pp. 80–7, and Bassett, 'The enigma of Clearchus the Spartan'. Men leaving the army at Byzantium, *Anab*. 7.2.3, on which see Roy, 'The mercenaries of Cyrus', pp. 319–20.
40. *Anab*. 5.6.18; 6.4.13.
41. *Anab*. 1.3.14.
42. *Anab*. 3.1.2–15.

and in another return home (*oikade*) is connected with those at home (*tous oikoi*). Near Calpes Limen, the army was still not in Hellas, and Cleander offered to take them there, but from the time when they reached Byzantium, the references to returning to Hellas and to going home cease (apart from references to Xenophon's own return home).[43]

There is however a passage of interest in the speech in which Xenophon seeks to dissuade the troops when they propose to take over Byzantium under his leadership. Xenophon argues that the strength of Sparta makes such a plan impossible. With a clear reference to the allies of Sparta who would be mobilized against them, he says 'Let us not perish shamefully as enemies of our home communities and of our own friends and relatives', and then goes on very shortly afterwards to say, 'at least we must not be deprived of Hellas'. Even here the notion of home communities and those at home is associated with the notion of Hellas. All these references in the *Anabasis* to Hellas, to home, and to family are cast in very brief and general terms: it is not clear that they are founded on any hard evidence of sentiments actually found among the mercenaries. The one specific reference, the exception to all the others, concerns Xenophon himself: in a passage of narrative rather than a speech, it is said that Xenophon obviously was preparing to go home (*oikade*), and that the vote imposing exile had not yet been inflicted on him. It is clear that the passage refers to an intention by Xenophon to return to Athens. While Xenophon could write about his own intentions in specific terms, and could frequently represent return to home and family favourably in speeches in the *Anabasis*, it is not clear that the vague and often sentimental linking of return, homeland, and family truly represents the aspirations of most of the mercenaries, let alone what circumstances allowed them to achieve.[44]

There may have been a higher proportion of men who wanted to go home among the peltasts. Since many of them had been recruited in ethnic groups from their homelands, those who survived may have felt a stronger desire to go home, and have taken the opportunity to do so at Byzantium. When serving under Seuthes the army no longer had an organized body of peltasts. It is also true, however, that they suffered much heavier losses than the hoplites: whereas

---

43. Hellas, children, and wives: *Anab.* 3.4.46. Return home and those at home: *Anab.* 5.6.20; cf. also 3.2.26; 5.6.25; 7.1.29–30. Cleander's offer: *Anab.* 6.6.34. Xenophon's own return: *Anab.* 7.6.11, 7.6.33, 7.6.57.
44. 'Let us not perish shamefully...': *Anab.* 7.1.29–30. Xenophon's preparations to go home: *Anab.* 7.7.57.

among the original total of 12,900 men 2,500 had been peltasts, by the time the army reached Heracleia there were only 1,000 peltasts out of 8,340.[45]

A few special cases may be noted. The wives and children of Xenias and Pasion were kept under guard in Tralles by Cyrus,[46] and it is possible that the families of other senior officers were held similarly as hostages: these officers presumably hoped to rejoin their families in Ionia. On the other hand the apparently fairly numerous body of men under thirty years of age in the army may well have included a number who were not married, while even at that age many men would already have no parent alive. Such men may have had less motivation to go home, and the conventional references in speeches to wives, children, and parents would not fit their circumstances.

It is entirely likely that some men who had been engaged for some time in mercenary service in Ionia had wives and children in Ionia, as Xenias and Pasion clearly did. In speaking of going home, however, Xenophon does not appear to have in mind a return simply to Ionia. His speech concerning Byzantium, discussed above, links friends and relatives with home communities (*tais patrisi*). It is also notable that in the *Anabasis* Xenophon identifies any Arcadian whom he knows well not only with Arcadia but with the man's home community within Arcadia. 'Home' is not merely within Hellas but is the community from which a man originally came. Such a stereotypical notion of home ignores any households established by mercenaries in Ionia.[47]

Xenophon's own views about going home, as recounted in the *Anabasis*, fluctuated considerably. At one time he was anxious to leave the army and sail away, presumably to Athens, and did in fact leave the army, only to return at the request of Anaxibius. Later he was again getting ready to return to Athens.[48]

However he also considered various other possibilities. One was to found a city on the Black Sea coast, where he would presumably have remained. Another was to obtain from Seuthes an attractive refuge for himself and any children he might have: he evidently considered staying there for a lengthy period. Seuthes offered Xenophon his daughter in marriage, and as a residence Bisanthe on the coast, and later in addition to Bisanthe also offered Ganus and Neon Teichos; and these offers were subsequently renewed. While Xenophon

45. *Anab.* 6.2.16. On these numbers see Roy, 'The mercenaries of Cyrus', p. 319.
46. *Anab.* 1.4.8.
47. On Xenophon's reporting of Arcadians see J. Roy, 'Arcadian nationality as seen in Xenophon's *Anabasis*', *Mnemosyne* 25 (1972), pp. 129–36.
48. Anxiety to leave the army: *Anab.* 7.1.4; 7.1.38. Return at the behest of Anaxibius: *Anab.* 7.2.8–9. Later preparations to go back to Athens: *Anab.* 7.5.57.

The Ambitions of a Mercenary

ultimately declared that it was impossible to accept, he had taken enough interest to note that at one point Seuthes was no longer making the offer. Xenophon, writing with hindsight, clearly did not choose to suggest that he himself had clung single-mindedly to the notion of return to home and family. In fact the reader of the *Anabasis* knows that Xenophon was eventually exiled from Athens, and that he was settled by the Spartans on an estate at Scillus, but does not know how he got there.[49]

The various destinations to which Xenophon considered going when he left the army were not available to most of the soldiers, and it is questionable how far Xenophon understood what the ordinary soldiers wanted. In the *Anabasis* officers are very much more prominent than other ranks. In a recent study Dillery, with books 3 and 4 in mind, wrote: 'With the possible exception of one or two instances ... there are no examples of individual enterprise or bravery on the part of common soldiers, and this seems highly improbable. But a unified, very successful, and largely officer-grade army is what Xenophon wants us to see, an army of comrades united as an organic whole and aided by a significant but nonetheless supporting cast of anonymous troops.' Of the sixty-six individuals identified in the *Anabasis* all but ten are either officers or specialists (seers, trumpeter, herald).[50]

The ten ordinary soldiers are named for a variety of reasons. Only one is singled out for an act of bravery. Two were killed on the same occasion. Two men sent out as scouts are named, and it is noted that one had a reputation for accurate observation. A Macronian peltast, a former slave in Athens, is mentioned because he was able to converse with the natives when the army entered Macronian territory. The Spartiate exile Dracontius may have had some standing in the army even as an ordinary soldier: he was once chosen to organize games, and once sent with others as a spokesman for the army, where he is distinguished from *stratēgoi* and *lochagoi*. One man is named because he spoke up in a meeting. Finally two men are singled out for bad behaviour.[51]

---

49. Founding a city: *Anab.* 5.6.15–16. Refuge from Seuthes: *Anab.* 7.6.34. Bisanthe: *Anab.* 7.2.38. Ganus and Neon Teichos: *Anab.* 7.5.8. Renewal of these offers: Anab. 7.6.43; 7.7.50. Xenophon's refusal: *Anab.* 7.7.51. Seuthes' offer lapses: *Anab.* 7.5.8. Xenophon's exile: *Anab.* 7.7.57. Settlement at Skillous: *Anab.* 5.3.7–13.
50. Quotation from Dillery, *Xenophon and the History of his Times*, p. 77. Individuals named in the *Anabasis* are listed in Roy, 'The mercenaries of Cyrus', pp. 302–6.
51. Act of bravery: *Anab.* 5.2.29–32. Two killed together: *Anab.* 4.1.18. Two scouts: *Anab.* 1.10.14–15; 4.4.15–16. The Macronian peltast: *Anab.* 4.8.4–6; cf. also Ma, chapter 12 in this volume. Dracontius: *Anab.* 4.8.25–6, 6.6.30; cf. also Ma in this volume. The speaker in a meeting: *Anab.* 5.1.2. Bad behaviour: *Anab.* 3.4.47–9; 5.8.23–4.

Xenophon could clearly identify individuals when he wanted, but he did not choose to dwell on individual ordinary soldiers in the *Anabasis*. It is doubtful that he spent much time with them save for purely military purposes. He mentions that men could always approach him at mealtimes or even when he was asleep, if they had something to say on military matters,[52] but there is no reason to think that Xenophon mixed socially with the rank and file.

It was noted above that, in speaking of Cyrus' generosity, Xenophon relates it especially to the *stratēgoi* and *lochagoi*. The same concentration on the army's officers may well explain a well-known but controversial passage in which Xenophon considers the men's motives for taking service with Cyrus and their desire to return to Hellas:

> For of the soldiers most had sailed out for this mercenary service not from want of resources but hearing of Cyrus' merits, some also bringing men, others having spent money in addition, and others of them having run away from their fathers and mothers and some having left behind children in order to make money for them and come back, hearing also that the others, those with Cyrus, were doing very well. Being like this, they longed to return safely to Hellas.[53]

The passage refers to those who sailed out, and distinguishes them from those who were already with Cyrus. It is obviously concerned to argue against the view that the men were generally from a background of poverty, and it also links, like other passages of the *Anabasis*, return to Hellas and return to the family. An explanation is however needed for the words 'some also bringing men, others having spent money in addition'. 'Men' in the Greek is *andras*, which Parke translated as 'servants'. That is a very odd term for slave attendants, and would much more naturally refer to mercenaries. Both Proxenus and Menon brought contingents from mainland Greece to Cyrus, but the phrase can hardly refer only to two generals, and we would still need to explain why Proxenus and Menon 'spent money in addition'. There would obviously be expense, however met, in crossing from mainland Greece to Asia Minor, but to explain Xenophon's phrase there must in some circumstances have been greater expense than that. The words could be explained if some *lochagoi* recruited men in mainland Greece and took them to Asia Minor at least partly at their own expense. The only direct evidence in the *Anabasis* for recruiting

52. *Anab.* 4.3.10.
53. *Anab.* 6.4.8.

by a *lochagos* is where it is mentioned quite incidentally that the *lochagos* Episthenes, being gay, had once assembled a *lochos* chosen only for their handsome appearance. Lee has however pointed to the recruitment of mercenaries by Agesilaus in Asia Minor in 394: in order to get good men, Agesilaus offered a prize to the *lochagos* who brought the best-equipped *lochos*. Lee concludes, surely rightly, that *lochagoi* played a major part in recruiting mercenaries. If it had become known in Greece that Cyrus' garrison commanders were recruiting in Ionia, some men may well have travelled individually to enlist, presumably at their own expense, while *lochagoi* may have recruited others and paid at least part of the expense of their travel to Ionia in the expectation of securing a post as *lochagos* under Cyrus and possibly some further reward. Such a sequence of events would suit Xenophon's Greek, and also match his tendency to think primarily in terms of the officers rather than the men.[54]

However much Xenophon projected a return to home and family as the ambition of the ordinary soldiers in Cyrus' Greek force, it is clear that very few of the hoplites did return home within the period covered by the *Anabasis*, and one passage suggests that few of them wanted to. At Thapsacus, while the rest of the army was deciding whether to cross the Euphrates and march with Cyrus against the King, Menon persuaded his men to cross the river without waiting to see what the others decided. His argument was that if the rest of the army crossed the river, his men would earn Cyrus' gratitude for being the first to cross, while if the others did not cross, his men could cross back again and would still be rewarded by Cyrus for having shown their attachment to him. And in the latter case their reward would be that Cyrus would use them for garrisons and for posts as *lochagoi*.[55] That was probably the ambition of most of Cyrus' mercenary hoplites.

To conclude, the *Anabasis* is the story of the rare adventure of the Greek mercenaries who, not without reluctance, followed a rebel Persian prince into the heart of the Persian Empire. However, the background to the story is a well-established pattern of mercenary service in western Asia Minor, where Greeks manned garrisons for local governors. Individual garrisons required at most some hundreds of mercenaries, but in total there was employment for several thousands of men. This was work for experienced soldiers, often from

54. Parke's translation is at Parke, *Greek Mercenary Soldiers*, p. 29. McKechnie, 'Greek mercenary troops and their equipment', p. 93 n. 7, accepts Parke's translation, and accepts that the servants would be slaves, while admitting that 'andras' is an odd term for slaves. Episthenes: *Anab.* 7.4.8; cf. also Lane Fox, chapter 6 in this volume. On recruitment by *lochagoi* see Lee, 'The lochos in Xenophon's *Anabasis*', citing *Hell.* 4.2.5.
55. *Anab.* 1.4.15.

a background of hoplite status. Many of the Greeks were from outside the area, especially from the Peloponnese, and may have dreamt of going home some day, but a more immediate and pressing ambition for most of them was to stay in employment in or near Asia Minor.

10 Exchange as Entrapment: Mercenary Xenophon?

V. AZOULAY

Introduction

Xenophon's *Anabasis* is a work of apologetics, written in response to attacks against the author. The work answers two types of accusation concerning exchange and the right way to conduct exchange. The first accusation appears as the collective pressure from the rank and file of the Ten Thousand: Xenophon attempts to counter the forceful accusations of corruption levelled at him by the troops. Part of the *Anabasis* – especially book 7 – is devoted to refuting such accusations. But Xenophon also uses the *Anabasis* to respond to another type of accusation, produced much later by his aristocratic peers rather than the rank and file. The Athenian general seeks to put as much distance as possible between himself and the disgraceful shadow of the mercenary. He must erase anything that might portray him to his readership as a paid soldier, on the move for base financial reasons. For a Greek aristocrat keen to demonstrate his detachment from the purely monetary, such a mercenary's status was necessarily compromising, especially since two barbarians assembled the mercenary host in question: the Persian Cyrus, then a Thracian, the ambiguous character of Seuthes. The present chapter is offered as a reading of this double *exercice de style*.

Incorruptible Xenophon?

By the end of the fifth century, aristocratic networks were increasingly controlled by the community. Both inside and outside Athens, their very existence in the *polis* was tolerated only inasmuch as they could serve the *polis*.[1]

---

1. This is the central contribution of L. G. Mitchell, *Greeks Bearing Gifts: The Public Use of Private Relationships in the Greek World, 435–323 BC* (Cambridge, 1997), p. 106, in qualifying the sometimes too categorical views of G. Herman, *Ritualised Friendship and the*

Communal ideological control bore not only on exchanges between mass and elite (through the liturgical system), but also on the circulation of favours within the aristocratic sphere itself.

The effects of this long-term evolution were exacerbated by the impact of a momentous turn of events: the massive intrusion of Persian gold. The latter, in upsetting the old balances, alerted the citizens to the dangerous nature of aristocratic exchange: although it played a role in financing war, the King's gold mostly had a political impact – the seduction of local Greek elites.[2] In constructing, to disastrous effect, personal links between Persia and Greek aristocracies, Persian gold led to the discrediting of all such ties, especially when these were accompanied by gift exchange.[3]

The relationship of *xenia*, notably expressed by the reciprocal offer of hospitality gifts (a transaction which could designate the whole relationship by metonymy), encapsulates all the ambiguities and misunderstandings involved. As it sometimes included exchanges between unequal partners, *xenia* could awaken the *polis*' suspicion: receiving hospitality gifts might make a citizen end up as a pawn in the hands of foreign potentates, such as the Persian King or the King of Macedon.[4] *Xenia* and corruption intermingled; the mere existence of *xenia* ties might suffice to awaken the suspicion of corruption.

Greek City (Cambridge, 1987), pp. 156–61. In Athens and especially in Sparta, the *polis* could designate citizens as ambassadors or military officials on account of special relations established abroad: *xenia* was not rejected as such, but rechannelled to the profit of the community.

2. On Persian gold, see more generally D. M. Lewis, 'Persian gold in Greek international relations', in *L'Or perse et l'histoire grecque* [*REA* 91] (Bordeaux, 1989), pp. 227–36. This Persian bounty mostly showered down on Greece between 413 and 386. Fourth-century tradition spoke of 6,000 talents handed over to the Spartans by the Persians in 413 and 405 (e.g. *Hell.* 1.5.1–9). For the financing of war, witness the speedy reconstruction of the Athenian Long Walls in 393. For the seduction of elites, witness the abrupt recall of Agesilaus from Asia, as he was on the verge of driving deeper into the Persian Empire.
3. Occasionally, corruption involves Greeks among each other. In the *Anabasis*, the Sinopeans and the Heracleians try to corrupt some of the officers among the Ten Thousand, when they hear of Xenophon's colonizing projects: 'When the Sinopeans and Heracleians heard it, they sent to Timasion and urged him to take in charge, *for a fee*, the matter of getting the army to sail away' (*Anab.* 5.6.21: emphasis added). See also *Anab.* 5.6.26 and 35.
4. *Xenia* usually unfurls according to a codified protocol, starting with a solemn utterance, pursued by the exchange of gifts and oaths, and ending with a handshake (*dexiōsis*). On the age and permanence of the institution, A. W. Adkins, 'Friendship and self-sufficiency in Homer and Aristotle', *CQ* 13 (1963), pp. 30–45, at pp. 30–2, and P. Gauthier, *Symbola. Les Étrangers et la justice dans les cités grecques* (Nancy, 1972), pp. 22–3. For *polis* suspicion of *xenia* with potentates, cf. Dem. 18.284 and 19.195 and 314, pouring scorn on Aeschines for being a *xenos* of Philip of Macedon and hence a traitor in his employ. S. Perlman, 'On bribing Athenian ambassadors', *GRBS* 17 (1976), pp. 223–33, has shown how

The *Anabasis* shows the overlap, tending towards identity, between the two phenomena. When Hecatonymus, sent on embassy by the Sinopeans, advises the Ten Thousand to travel by sea rather than take the land route through Paphlagonian territory, his motives are immediately suspect: 'Some of his hearers were suspicious that he spoke as he did out of friendship for Corylas, for he was his official representative at Sinope; others imagined that he even had the idea of obtaining gifts on account of this advice; while still others suspected that the real purpose of his speech was to prevent the Greeks from going by land and so doing some harm to the territory of the Sinopeans.'[5]

Trapped in his *xenia* relationship with Seuthes, Xenophon also falls under the suspicion of having manipulated the army in order to receive gifts from the Thracian prince. The whole of book 7 can be read as an answer to this accusation, in a balancing act between the demands of aristocratic friendship and the necessities of responding to mass pressure. Even before the first interview with Seuthes occurs in the narrative, Xenophon the author carefully stages the incorruptibility of Xenophon the character. When an envoy from Seuthes asks that Xenophon bring the Ten Thousand into Seuthes' employ (the offer of presents remains implicit; but Seuthes also promises that in case of an agreement, Xenophon 'would not be sorry for it'), he answers, virtuously: 'Why, the army is going to cross over; so far as that is concerned, let not Seuthes pay anything either to me or to any one else.' Xenophon implicitly defends himself against any accusation that he led his men across the Straits into Europe in exchange for a bribe. Likewise, after his reintegration in the army, Xenophon declines Seuthes' offers, attractive as they might seem: '[Seuthes] begged him to bring the army to him, offering any promise whereby he imagined he could persuade him.'[6] The author's strategy is easily detectable: to dispel any suspicion of shady dealings with the Thracian dynast, even before their first encounter.

In this respect, Xenophon's description of his first meeting with Seuthes appears surprising, since it takes place under the sign of aristocratic entente. The two men meet at night, in secret. While the wine goes round, in the

the Persian (and later Macedonian) kings used hospitality gifts in diplomatic interaction. See also Mitchell, *Greeks Bearing Gifts*, p. 184; P. Briant, *Histoire de l'Empire perse. De Cyrus à Alexandre* (Paris, 1996), p. 688; and P. Brun, *L'orateur Démade. Essai d'histoire et d'historiographie* (Bordeaux, 2000), p. 163.
5. *Anab.* 5.6.11. On Corylas, governor of Paphlagonia, see *Anab.* 6.1.2.
6. Xenophon on the Straits: *Anab.* 7.1.5–6. In fact, Xenophon's intention at this point is to leave the Ten Thousand, in bitterness at the latter's ingratitude. Seuthes' later offer: *Anab.* 7.2.10.

Thracian fashion, they invoke the relation of kinship (*syngeneia*) between Athenians and Thracians, and the concomitant tie of *philia*.[7] This cordial atmosphere might suggest the establishment of closer, and more disreputable, links.

However, Xenophon carefully deploys practical, and rhetorical, devices, to fend off any subsequent accusations of impropriety. Xenophon reminds Seuthes of the latter's attempts to corrupt him and of his own very proper refusals to listen to such proposals; Xenophon has come to meet Seuthes only as a last resort, almost under compulsion. He has not given in to corruption, unlike those generals who tried to lead the Ten Thousand to the Thracian dynast well before there was any pressing need to do so: a few pages earlier, Xenophon mentions that 'Cleanor and Phryniscus wanted to lead the army to Seuthes, for he had been trying to persuade them to this course and had given one of them a horse and the other a woman'. In contrast, Xenophon emphasizes his own incorruptibility, which he particularly sets forth by underlining the richness of the gifts promised by Seuthes: not a mere horse or even a woman, but 'the places on the seacoast of which [he] holds possession'.[8]

After these first explanations, Xenophon takes care to create a practical set-up to ensure absolute transparency. Before starting any dealings with Seuthes, he brings in men chosen from every regiment, 'in whom each had confidence'. The troops thus participate in the negotiations, and the rankers – the military equivalent of the *dēmos* – can bear testimony of Xenophon's good faith. Negotiation does not occur in the occult context of improper transactions, but leads to a collective agreement which concerns the whole army: Seuthes promises 'to each soldier a Cyzicene, to the captains twice as much, and to the generals four times as much; furthermore, as much land as they might wish, yokes of oxen, and a fortified place upon the seacoast'.[9]

It is true that Seuthes also offers gifts to the leaders, on top of *misthos*; but these lavish presents are only a particular category within the broader rewards negotiated for the troops as a whole, and not a proof of improper dealings or treason. In order to illustrate the absolute blamelessness of his behaviour,

---

7. Circulation of the wine: *Anab.* 7.2.23. Invocation of *syngeneia*: *Anab.* 7.2.31.
8. Xenophon's reminder of his incorruptibility: *Anab.* 7.2.24–8. For the near compulsion of his present meeting with Seuthes, cf. *Anab.* 7.2.15. 'Cleanor and Phryniscus': *Anab.* 7.2.2. 'The places on the seacoast': *Anab.* 7.2.25.
9. 'In whom each had confidence': *Anab.* 7.2.17 (see also 7.2.29). Collective agreement concerning the whole army: *Anab.* 7.3.1; note that the two men grasp each other's right hand, establishing a personal tie of *xenia*, only after the collective negotiation. 'To each soldier a Cyzicene': *Anab.* 7.2.36.

Exchange as Entrapment 293

Xenophon details his final measure to make the whole procedure obvious: when Seuthes meets the army, Xenophon bids him come forward, 'in order that he might tell him within hearing of the greatest possible number what they had decided upon as advantageous'. The Thracian prince repeats his proposals before all, and these proposals are accepted by a unanimous mass vote.[10]

The point of all these precautions emerges in hindsight, at the end of the *Anabasis*, when after many events and useful service from the mercenaries, Seuthes, manipulated by his Greek adviser Heraclides, refuses to distribute the promised pay. The troops turn on Xenophon and formally accuse him. An Arcadian plays the role of Thersites, delivering a vigorous prosecutorial speech to demand that Xenophon be stoned to death. The argument is that Xenophon grew rich personally from his relation with Seuthes, while depriving the troops of their pay. Xenophon must defend himself in this improvised trial where his life hangs in the balance. He claims good faith, and attempts to involve the presumed corruptor: 'For it is clear that, if I have received anything from Seuthes, he will demand it back from me, and, moreover, he will demand it back with justice if I am failing to fulfil to him the undertaking for which I was accepting his gifts.'[11]

The accusation is quite precise, and Xenophon himself points out its seriousness. *Dōrodokia*, corruption, was generally punished by death.[12] By emphasizing the Thracian dynast's untrustworthiness, his own devotion to the army, and the latter's ingratitude, Xenophon managed to turn the Ten Thousand's opinion back in his favour.

10. Additional gifts to the generals: note that Xenophon is offered a very profitable marriage connection (*Anab.* 7.2.38). These perquisites for the generals are not mentioned in Seuthes' speech to the collective: he vaguely speaks of 'the customary pay' (*Anab.* 7.3.10). 'In order that he might tell him within hearing': *Anab.* 7.3.7.
11. The accusation of Xenophon: *Anab.* 7.6.8. The case for the prosecution: cf. *Anab.* 7.6.9–10 and Hom. *Il.* 2.212–44. 'For it is clear that': *Anab.* 7.6.16–17. Xenophon claims he has not even received 'what the other generals have received – nay, not even so much as some of the captains' (*Anab.* 7.6.19, referring back to 7.5.2–4).
12. On *dōrodokia*, see for the Athenian context F. D. Harvey, 'Dona ferentes: some aspects of bribery in Greek politics', in P. Cartledge et al. (eds), *Crux: Essays Presented to Ste Croix* (London, 1985), pp. 76–117; D. M. MacDowell, 'Athenian laws about bribery', *RIDA* 30 (1983), pp. 57–78; and O. de Bruyn, *Les Compétences judiciaires de l'Aréopage* (Stuttgart, 1995), pp. 63–73, esp. at p. 66: 'Le droit athénien faisait la distinction entre deux types de corruption, l'une, relativement bénigne, entraînait le payement d'une amende fixée au décuple de la somme reçue, l'autre, plus grave, entraînait la mort.' Various judiciary procedures were deployed against this protean evil (*graphē dōrōn, eisangelia, euthunai,* and *apocheirotonia*), whose exact workings are unknown before Ephialtes (pace O. de Bruyn). Though the scene in the *Anabasis* is hardly a full trial, the accusation is serious enough to entail an unmistakable death penalty.

All the same, the last conversation between Xenophon and Seuthes casts a very peculiar light on the nature of their ties. While Xenophon starts by recounting his constant refusal of Seuthes' presents, the thrust of his argument gradually changes during his speech:

> [the Ten Thousand] accused me before the Lacedaemonians of regarding you more highly than I did the Lacedaemonians, while on their own account they charged me with being more concerned that your affairs should be well than that their own should be; and they also said that I had received gifts [*dōra*] from you. And yet, touching these gifts [*ta dōra*], do you imagine it was because they had observed in me some ill-will toward you that they charged me with having received them from you, or because they perceived in me abundant goodwill for you? For my part, I presume that everybody believes he ought to show goodwill to the man from whom he receives gifts. You, however, before I had rendered you any service, welcomed me with a pleasure which you showed by your eyes, your voice, and your gifts of hospitality, and you could not make promises enough about all that should be done for me.[13]

In a spectacular volte-face, Xenophon finally admits that he has received many hospitality presents from Seuthes – not once, but many times. By a series of gradual shifts, he overturns his earlier viewpoint. He never received gifts; yet the soldiers believed he had received gifts; their reasons for believing this was that Xenophon's behaviour towards Seuthes was the behaviour of one who had accepted gifts; in actual fact, Seuthes did ply Xenophon with gifts . . .

In a few lines, Xenophon manages a virtuoso exercise in ideological gap-bridging, grounded in the ambiguity of *xenia*. His apparent duplicity reflects the implicit distinction, widely held in aristocratic circles, between hospitality presents, which are a legitimate part of *xenia*, and the *dōra* which embody the attempt and the temptation of corruption, and which must be eschewed at all costs. This distinction – always suspect in the eyes of third-party witnesses to transactions of exchange – allows Xenophon to enjoy the prestige of incor-

---

13. The last conversation between Xenophon and Seuthes: *Anab.* 7.7.39–47. Account of the constant refusal of Seuthes' presents: *Anab.* 7.7.39–40. '[The Ten Thousand] accused me': *Anab.* 7.7.44–6. *Xeniois* must be translated as 'hospitality gifts' and not 'hospitality' *tout court*; *dōra* might be translated as 'bribes', since these gifts are considered as corrupting.

ruptibility in the eyes of the soldiers, and the consequences of his devotion *qua* gift receiver in his relation to Seuthes.

Aristocrat and mercenary

Xenophon lies open to another accusation, not from his men, but from his fellow aristocrats, once the venture is over. Xenophon was not only attacked for having been a corrupt leader, but also for having been a mercenary. In the fight for pay and implicated in the logic of demand and supply, the mercenary embodies a deeply ambiguous and contested figure in fourth century Greece. The resort to paid fighters was occasionally represented as a necessary evil for whoever employed them; but mercenary service in itself was difficult to represent in any sort of positive light. While the recipient of gifts could be attacked as corrupt, the mercenary not only finds himself in the delicate position of recipient, but also spoils the relation by introducing the principle of service for cash: in the end, the mercenary is imagined as an excluded figure, without ties, lawless.[14]

Yet Xenophon at first sight seems completely outside the cash nexus of *misthos*. Throughout his works, he rails against mercenary exchange and its supposedly pernicious effects, partly as an heir to the old elitist views against coinage, partly under the influence of a double tradition, political and philosophical, opposed to money and trade in all its forms: the Socratic current, and philo-Laconism.[15] This staunch opposition to *misthos*, constantly expressed in his works, might well be a veil drawn over his own status as a mercenary in Cyrus' army.

In fact, Xenophon seems to have been the target of attacks about his status as a mercenary during the expedition. Among his more or less open

14. As P. Cartledge has pointed out (*Agesilaos and the Crisis of Sparta* (London, 1987), p. 323), all Spartan commanders in Asia used mercenaries against Artaxerxes II (as did the Athenians). By the mid fourth century, recourse to mercenaries has become normal, to the extent that Demosthenes recognizes the practice as necessary (albeit regrettable); he simply asks for 25 per cent at least of the relief expedition for Olynthus to be made up of citizens (*First Philippic* 19–21). On the detestable character of mercenaries, cf. Pl. *Leg*. 1.630b: mercenaries may be ready to die, but 'prove themselves reckless, unjust, violent, and pre-eminently foolish'.
15. I consider it unlikely that the Spartan hostility towards coinage is purely a Xenophontic construct, as suggested by O. Picard, 'Entre public et privé: le cas de la monnaie', *Ktèma* 23 (1998), p. 269; the contested monetarization of Spartan society may have entailed a hardening of positions, and hence the formalizing of what had earlier been a convention.

adversaries, Isocrates is probably the figure with whom Xenophon's relations are most ambiguous. They came from the same *deme*, shared many ideas, and their relations were cordial enough for Isocrates to write a laudation for Gryllus, Xenophon's son, fallen at the second battle of Mantinea. Nonetheless, apart from various disagreements on points of detail, their respective interpretations of the Ten Thousand's trek radically differ.[16]

For Isocrates, Cyrus had at his disposal 'only six thousand Hellenes – not picked troops, but men who, owing to stress of circumstances, were unable to live in their own cities'. The *Anabasis* should be read in relation to these accusations:[17] as an apologetic work, intended as an addition to an ongoing debate whose terms were hardly in Xenophon's favour. To defend himself, Xenophon resorts to a triple strategy: he points out that the mercenaries did not form a homogeneous body and that all did not follow Cyrus for the same, shameful reasons; he celebrates the nobility of the employer, the virtuous younger Cyrus; finally, he emphasizes his own lack of interest in the mercenary's *misthos*.

On the Black Sea, at a point which seems particularly appropriate to found a Greek colony, Xenophon classifies the reasons which compelled the mercenaries to leave:

16. For attacks on Xenophon, see É. Delebecque, *Essai sur la vie de Xénophon* (Paris, 1957), pp. 293–5 (hypothetical, if coherent); L. Canfora, *Histoire de la littérature grecque d'Homère à Aristote* (Paris, 1994), p. 383. Sophaenetus of Stymphalus is claimed to have written an *Anabasis* of his own – four paltry fragments survive – with Xenophon apparently appearing in a far less favourable light. See *FGH* 109 F1–4 and A. von Mess, 'Über die Anabasis des Sophainetos', *RhM* 61 (1906), pp. 360–90; A. Gwynn, 'Xenophon and Sophaenetus', *CQ* 23 (1929), pp. 38–9; J. Roy, 'Xenophon's evidence for the *Anabasis*', *Athenaeum* 46 (1968), pp. 37–46, at pp. 44–5; J. Dillery, *Xenophon and the History of his Times* (London, 1995), p. 63; and Cawkwell, chapter 1 in this volume. Isocrates and Gryllus: cf. Diog. Laert. 2.55, and see V. J. Gray, 'Xenophon and Isocrates', in C. Rowe et al., *The Cambridge History of Greek and Roman Political Thought* (Cambridge, 2000), pp. 142–54. Among disagreements between Isocrates and Xenophon, note their different attitudes to Timotheus, and indeed the elder Cyrus, whom Isocrates compares unfavourably to Evagoras (Isoc. 9.37–8). Isocrates considers the mercenaries as the principal cause of the fourth-century crisis of *polis*; this interpretation is followed, without much critical distance, by L. P. Marinoviç, *Le Mercenariat grec au IVe siècle av. n.è. et la crise de la polis* (Paris, 1988), pp. 237–69.

17. 'Only six thousand Hellenes': Isoc. *Paneg.* 145–6. This text was published in summer 380, that is, before Xenophon's *Anabasis*, which must be read as a response to Isocratean criticism, if one follows the dating proposed in Dillery, *Xenophon and the History of his Times*, p. 69, with earlier bibliography at p. 264 n. 1 (after Leuctra and the loss of the estate at Skillous). In any case, Xenophon did not need the stimulus of Isocrates' text to feel the need for self-exculpation. Contrast Cawkwell in this volume. Isocrates also goes so far as to call the mercenaries 'common enemies of mankind' (*On the Peace* 46). However, this attitude becomes more nuanced in his last works. In the *Philippus*, he claims that the potential conquest of the Persian Empire would be facilitated by the plentiful existence of mercenaries, easy to corrupt, whereas '[under Cyrus] in those days there was no body of professional soldiers . . .'

For most of the soldiers had sailed away from Greece to undertake this service for pay not because their means were scanty, but because they knew by report of the noble character of Cyrus; some brought other men with them, some had even spent money of their own on the enterprise, while still another class had abandoned fathers and mothers, or had left children behind with the idea of getting money to bring back to them, all because they heard that the other people who served with Cyrus enjoyed abundant good fortune. Being men of this sort, therefore, they longed to return in safety to Greece.[18]

Xenophon clearly distinguishes between two categories of Greeks. Some have followed Cyrus out of noble motives, and even recruited men out of their own means. On the other hand, many others have enrolled under Cyrus' banner only out of desire for profit. The Ten Thousand cannot be considered as a homogeneous group: those who followed Cyrus on account of his noble character are ready to found a *polis* on this welcoming coast and hence increase Hellas in Asia.[19]

The rank and file, on the other hand, along with some officers, would rather return to Greece laden with money. Symptomatically, the soldiers refuse Xenophon's colonial project, in favour of the financially attractive proposals put forward by another commander, Timasion, who promises good pay if they embark with him. Within the army, tensions separate the elite from the mass of rankers, but also introduce splits between members of the elite.[20]

18. *Anab.* 6.4.8; Xenophon repeats this passage at *Cyrop.* 4.2.10.
19. Greek aristocrats as recruiting sergeants: G. Nussbaum, 'The captains in the army of the Ten Thousand', *C & M* 20 (1959), pp. 16–29, at p. 19, and Marinoviç, *Le Mercenariat grec*, p. 141 n. 17. On Xenophon as failed oikist, see I. Malkin, *Religion and Colonization in Ancient Greece* (Leyde, 1987), pp. 102–4. This Panhellenic project (also found in Isoc. *Philippus* 120–1) could redeem the purely mercenary venture of the Ten Thousand. See especially Isoc. *Peace* 24, praising Athenodorus and Callistratus, the first a private individual, and the second an exile, but both city founders in Thrace: 'And those who claim the right to stand at the head of the Hellenes ought to become leaders of such enterprises [i.e. to found new *poleis*] much rather than of war and of hireling armies.'
20. On the greed of the rank and file, see Marinoviç, *Le Mercenariat grec*, pp. 141–2 (with references) and J. Roy, 'The mercenaries of Cyrus', *Historia* 16 (1967), pp. 292–323, at pp. 317–18, pointing out that the army contains 4,000 Arcadians and 2,000 Achaeans, from the poorest parts of Greece (cf. *Anab.* 6.2.10). See also J. Roy, 'Arcadian nationality as seen in Xenophon's *Anabasis*', *Mnemosyne* 25 (1972), pp. 129–36, and Dillery, *Xenophon and the History of his Times*, pp. 80–1 and 87–9, putting it elegantly: 'Greece and greed are somehow connected.' The enticements of Timasion: Anab. 5.6.23. Likewise, another fellow officer and rival of Xenophon's makes the same promise of pay: *Anab.* 5.6.56. Silanus the Ambraciot, Thorax of Boeotia and Timasion of Dardanus are singled out

A glance at the *Cyropaedia* will allow us to understand more closely these fracture lines, which, for Xenophon, are present in any army. The *Cyropaedia* also shows men leaving their fatherland under the command of a young, promising, foreign leader: when the elder Cyrus decides to continue waging war on the Assyrian Empire, after his first victories, many Medes elect to follow him. As in the *Anabasis*, some accompany him because they admire 'his ways'. Many enrol out of gratitude towards the Persian leader, 'grateful to him for freeing them, as they thought, from great impending danger', still others 'wished to requite him for some service he had done for them while he was growing up in Media'. But this framework of reciprocity is not operative for all: many follow Cyrus only 'when the report spread that [Cyrus] would lead them to rich plunder'.[21]

As in the *Anabasis*, Xenophon carefully distinguishes two groups within the Median army. The rank and file, on the one hand, are drawn by *misthoi* and the wealth they hope to win during the war of conquest.[22] On the other, there are those few good men who temporarily suspend their faithfulness towards their rightful ruler, out of gratitude towards the elder Cyrus.

The military elite among the Medes defines itself in a system where social dynamics are more operative than calculations of profit; Cyrus insists on this point in a speech to his 'staff officers': 'Men of Media and all here present, I am very sure that you came out with me, not because you desired to get money by it, nor because you thought that in this you were doing Cyaxares a service; but it was to me that you wished to do this favour, and it was out of regard for me that you were willing to make the night march and to brave dangers with me'.[23]

In the *Cyropaedia*, the best of the Medes join Cyrus' army to honour a relationship where mutual agreement and aristocratic distinction play the most

> as members of the elite who enrolled out of greed: e.g. *Anab.* 7.3.18, 7.3.27, 7.5.4 (Timasion); 6.4.14 (Silanus); 5.6.19 (Thorax).
> 21. *Cyrop.* 4.2.10. Xenophon adds that he had obtained favours from his grandfather for many of them, through his *philanthrōpia*. Cf. *Cyrop.* 4.2.11: men follow Cyrus 'not from compulsion but of their own free will and out of gratitude'.
> 22. Cf. *Anab.* 7.5.3–4, where *dōra* meant for the generals and *lochagoi* are opposed to the *misthoi* meant for the army.
> 23. *Cyrop.* 5.1.20–1; cf. *Cyrop.* 3.3.12 for the meaning of *epikairios*. Symptomatically, Cyrus thanks them for following them by declaring his gratitude: 'For this I am grateful to you – I should be in the wrong not to do so; but I do not think that I am as yet in a position to make you an adequate return, and this I am not ashamed to say.' By an extraordinary *retournement*, Cyrus' inability to requite past service becomes a claim on the allies' faithfulness: Cyrus wishes those who follow him to continue to do so, so that he may later show them gratitude.

important part. This is the angle which Xenophon uses to justify his own enrolment in the Ten Thousand. 'There was a man in the army named Xenophon, an Athenian, who was neither general nor captain nor private, but had accompanied the expedition because Proxenus, an old guest-friend of his, had sent him at his home an invitation to go with him.'[24]

By defining the exact process of his enrolment negatively, without assigning a precise status to himself, Xenophon avoids any embarrassing questions. Furthermore, the appearance of Xenophon as a character in the work is delayed until book 3, when Cyrus' expedition proper is over: this reflects the determination shown by Xenophon the author to avoid at all costs having to deal with his participation in a mercenary venture. Apparently, he ended up at Cunaxa out of the most aristocratic of reasons: far from being a paid mercenary, he tagged along with the troops because of his *xenia* ties with Proxenus of Boeotia. Likewise, Cyrus himself asked him personally to stay, in an attempt to retain him: just as the Medes leave Cyaxares, in the *Cyropaedia*, without denying their ties with him, Xenophon temporarily suspended his loyalty to his *polis* so as to honour his *philia* relationship with Proxenus, then Cyrus.[25]

Within this emphasis on interpersonal ties, the portrait of Cyrus is a potent element in Xenophon's apologetic strategy: the Persian prince's extraordinary virtues explain and legitimize Xenophon's rallying to him. Posthumous praise of Cyrus goes hand in hand with justification of the author. Cyrus' virtues appear numberless: the barbarian potentate knew how to create gratitude towards him, and hence the infrangible political loyalty of Greeks and Persians alike.[26]

---

24. *Anab.* 3.1.4. See Herman, *Ritualised Friendship and the Greek City*, p. 47.
25. In the first part of the tale, Xenophon as actor is perhaps to be detected under the rather self-important pseudonym Theopompus, 'god-sent' (*Anab.* 2.1.12–13). See O. Lendle, *Kommentar zu Xenophons Anabasis* (Darmstadt, 1995), p. 94, and L. Canfora, *Une Profession dangereuse. Les Penseurs grecs dans la cité* (Paris, 2001), pp. 36–7. All the same, Xenophon has already appeared, fleetingly, just before Cunaxa (*Anab.*1.8.15), allowing Xenophon the author to show that he knew Cyrus personally. Cyrus' personal request: *Anab.* 3.1.9. On *polis* loyalty, cf. Socrates' fear that Xenophon's friendship for Cyrus might be ill considered by the city (*Anab.* 1.3.5–7). In this passage, Xenophon the author condemns himself, as he frequently does in the *Memorabilia*. See V. J. Gray, *The Framing of Socrates: The Literary Interpretation of Xenophon's Memorabilia* (Stuttgart, 1998), pp. 98–9, analysing Xenophon's strategies for self-presentation, between blame and self-celebration. É. Delebecque, *Essai sur la vie de Xénophon* (Paris, 1957), pp. 90–2, holds that Xenophon followed Cyrus for financial reasons: perhaps, but Xenophon tried very hard to dispel any suspicion of such behaviour.
26. The virtues of Cyrus: *Anab.* 1.9. On the link between such praise and Xenophon's self-justification, see already F. Dürrbach, 'L'apologie de Xénophon dans l'Anabase', *REG* 6

Cyrus thus entraps aristocratic Greeks in a network of reciprocal ties, which works to his profit. When Xenophon explains their loyalty, he insists both on the close links between the Greeks themselves, and their shared feeling of obligation towards Cyrus: 'Then, although the Greeks were fearful of the journey and unwilling to go on, most of them did, nevertheless, out of shame before one another and before Cyrus, continue the march. And Xenophon was one of this number.' Here the author does not mention increase in pay, which he had earlier described to explain the rallying of the Greek rank and file. Xenophon merely writes of reasons drawn from the world of reciprocity: to forsake Cyrus would have been shameful and ungrateful, in one of those precise moments of danger which, in Xenophon's eyes, act as a touchstone of true friendship as opposed to pretence.[27]

In addition to presenting himself as an aristocrat entrapped in *philia* and *xenia*,[28] Xenophon emphasizes several times that he did not grow rich through mercenary status or service on the expedition. This angle helps understand the Skillous digression (as it is often called, rather clumsily, by readers of the *Anabasis*):

> There, also, they divided the money received from the sale of the booty. And the tithe, which they set apart for Apollo and for Artemis of the Ephesians, was distributed among the generals, each taking his portion to keep safely for the gods; and the portion that fell to Chirisophus was given to Neon the Asinaean. As for Xenophon, he caused a votive offering to be made out of Apollo's share of his portion and dedicated it in the treasury of the

---

(1893), pp. 343–86, at p. 348: 'En faisant le panégyrique [de Cyrus et de Cléarque], c'est sa propre cause qu'il plaidait.' Infrangible political loyalty: cf. *Oec.* 4.18: 'it is said that not a man deserted from Cyrus to the king.' M. Gabrielli, 'Transports et logistique militaire dans l'Anabase', in P. Briant (ed.), *Dans les pas des Dix-Mille* [Pallas 43] (Toulouse, 1995), pp. 109–22, shows that the actual situation was perhaps otherwise. In fact, Xenophon reveals the occurrence of unrest at Dana (Anab. 1.2.10), recounts the betrayal of Orontas in detail (*Anab.* 1.6.1–11), and mentions hostility to Cyrus in Lycaonia and Cilicia (see C. J. Tuplin, 'On the track of the Ten Thousand', *REA* 101 (1999), pp. 331–66, at p. 346, and Braun, chapter 3 in this volume).

27. 'Then, although the Greeks were fearful': *Anab.* 3.1.10. Cyrus increased the *misthos* in order to convince the Greeks to follow him against the King: *Anab.* 1.3.21 and especially 1.4.13. For his appeal to the weight of moral obligation, while exploiting any failings to this code, compare his conspicuous clemency to runaways at *Anab.* 1.4.9; the remainder continue 'with *greater satisfaction and eagerness*' (emphasis added). Cyrus plays on the whole repertory of reciprocity to bind the Greeks and their leaders to him. Danger as the touchstone of true friendship: *Mem.* 2.4.6.

28. Cyrus' army is founded on a network of *xenia* ties: see Herman, *Ritualised Friendship and the Greek City*, pp. 98–101, and Mitchell, *Greeks Bearing Gifts*, pp. 119–20.

Athenians at Delphi. He inscribed upon it his own name and that of Proxenus, who was killed with Clearchus; for Proxenus was his guest-friend. The share which belonged to Artemis of the Ephesians he left behind, at the time when he was returning from Asia with Agesilaus to take part in the campaign against Boeotia, in charge of Megabyzus, the sacristan of Artemis, for the reason that his own journey seemed likely to be a dangerous one; and his instructions were that in case he should escape with his life, the money was to be returned to him, but in case any ill should befall him, Megabyzus was to cause to be made and dedicated to Artemis whatever offering he thought would please the goddess. In the time of Xenophon's exile and while he was living at Skillous, near Olympia, where he had been established as a colonist by the Lacedaemonians, Megabyzus came to Olympia to attend the games and returned to him his deposit. Upon receiving it Xenophon bought a plot of ground for the goddess in a place which Apollo's oracle appointed.[29]

This is no excursus as foreign body in the narrative, but a 'digression' carefully contrived to give an image of Xenophon as disinterested actor. In a context where receiving money immediately creates suspicion, he takes care to account for money won during the expedition. First, it comes out of booty captured from the enemy, and not out of *misthos* begged for from a more powerful figure; it thus is a share of *timē* received legitimately by Xenophon *qua* military officer in the expedition. Furthermore, these riches are not used for personal profit, but immediately converted into dedications to the gods, and immobilized in a treasury; finally, part of the booty is used to celebrate the *xenia* ties between Xenophon and Proxenus, who has died after Cunaxa. Gains are thus deployed to create harmonious relationships with men and with gods.[30]

Xenophon as aristocrat refuses the salaried relation implied by mercenary service, and keeps shares of booty, gloriously won. Better still: he turns down

---

29. *Anab.* 5.3.4–7. On this 'digression', see further Parker and Ma, chapters 4 and 12 in this volume.
30. The donation to Artemis, as an act of 'gratification' (*charieisthai*), takes place in a horizon of reciprocity: in return, Xenophon expects the deity's protection over his life and property. Hence the inscription Xenophon ordered set up by the small shrine he built on his estate (*Anab.* 5.3.13): 'The place is sacred to Artemis. He who holds it and enjoys its fruits must offer the tithe every year in sacrifice, and from the remainder must keep the temple in repair. *If any one leaves these things undone, the goddess will look to it*' (emphasis added). In exchange for benefaction, the goddess herself can take the place of the owner, if the latter should be incapacitated.

any form of payment for services as leader of the expedition. When Seuthes finally decides to pay out the salary he has promised, Xenophon elects not to draw his pay. When he sees Charminus and Polynicus of Sparta, his reaction is to hand things over:

> 'This property has been saved for the army through you, and to you I turn it over; do you, then, dispose of it and make the distribution to the army.' They, accordingly, took it over, appointed booty-vendors, and proceeded to sell it; and they incurred a great deal of blame. As for Xenophon, he would not go near them but it was plain that he was making preparations for his homeward journey; . . . His friends in the camp, however, came to him and begged him not to depart until he should lead the army away and turn it over to Thibron.[31]

The author thus opposes his faithful companions with the fickle, ungrateful rank and file, which, like the carping *dēmos* in Athens, is concerned only with *misthoi*.

Xenophon refuses the *misthos* to which he has a right. He leaves the army poorer, hardly able to sacrifice or keep up the *xenia* exchange with guest-friends. When Euclid of Phleious asks him how much gold he has, he answers, under oath, 'that he would not have even enough money to pay his travelling expenses on the way home unless he should sell his horse and what he had about his person'.[32]

Nonetheless, thanks to a last razzia, Xenophon exits from this impoverished state, at the last moment. For this ultimate foray, Xenophon takes with him 'those captains who were his closest friends and others who had proved

---

31. Refusal of payment: *Anab.* 7.5.2–3. When Heraclides proposes that Xenophon take his share, the latter replies: 'Well, for my part I am content to get something at a later time; give rather to these generals and captains who have followed with me.' 'This property has been saved': *Anab.* 7.7.56–7; cf.. 7.5.3; 7.6.19. Xenophon has also just refused the silver talent's worth of compensation offered by Seuthes (*Anab.* 7.7.53–4). See Lendle, *Kommentar zu Xenophons Anabasis*, p. 476.
32. Xenophon's poverty on leaving the army: *Anab.* 7.8.5–6. When Bion and Nausiclides arrive 'with money to give to the army', they strike up a hospitality tie with Xenophon, buying back the horse Xenophon has been forced to sell off, 'and would not accept from him the price of it'. The *misthos* brought by the two Spartans only concerns the army, and does not preclude Xenophon's personal relationship of *xenia*, whence the issue of money has been evacuated. Xenophon's oath: *Anab.* 7.8.2. Xenophon offers a double religious guarantee, in the form of the oath and the reaction of the seer, for his truthfulness. On this passage, see also Parker, chapter 4 in this volume.

themselves trustworthy throughout, in order that he might do them a good turn'.[33] The project is conceived in a spirit of reciprocity and of distinction, unlike the purely contractual links Xenophon kept with the remainder of the Ten Thousand.

After the success of the foray, 'the Laconians, the captains, the other generals, and the soldiers joined in arranging matters so that he got the pick of horses and teams of oxen and all the rest; the result was, that he was now able even to do a kindness to another'. The *Anabasis* comes to its end, and the author can offer a picture of himself untainted by any considerations of salary. Unlike pay, booty is a highly positive mode of wealth acquisition, at least when it is not acquired off allies. In addition, this sudden enrichment is legitimizing in more ways than one: the Spartans allow Xenophon to dispose of the booty, and hence grant him recognition and honour, at an exceptional level.[34] Xenophon increases his fortune, without receiving any *misthos*; he avoids the fraught position of the recipient, stepping into the symbolical superiority of the giver of gifts, the initiator of the exchange of *charis*.

In his relations with the Ten Thousand, Xenophon claims to have behaved in a completely transparent manner. He insistently portrays himself as incorruptible, accused unjustly by an ungrateful, envious mob. This first rewriting of history is compounded by a second one, whose function is to write out Xenophon's status as mercenary. Xenophon followed a good man, his guest-friend, into a military campaign; he never really received any pay; he finally grew rich honourably – Xenophon writes his eastern venture as the trajectory of an aristocrat constantly privileging the ties of *philia* over the for-pay system of *misthos*. The issue of course is not to find the truthfulness of this portrait; our knowledge is definitely skewed by the many rhetorical strategies

---

33. *Anab.* 7.8.12. In addition, Xenophon points out that those who accompany him against his will are excluded from the distribution of booty: after leaving the army, Xenophon is no longer beholden to the fair distribution of a share of booty to everyone.
34. 'The Laconians, the captains': *Anab.* 7.8.23. Dillery, *Xenophon and the History of his Times*, p. 91, sees this final narrative as negative in its impact: 'While it is probably asking too much to believe that Xenophon intentionally portrayed himself negatively in this the final scene of the *Anabasis*, one cannot resist noting that the episode represents the very kind of independent action aimed at profit that he earlier so often deplored.' But this action does not mar the author's self-representation: Xenophon has left the army, and seizes, quite legitimately, booty in which he is granted the first share, as a signal token of honour. See Delebecque, *Essai sur la vie de Xénophon*, pp. 294–95, and Whitby, chapter 7 in this volume. For disposal of booty as a mark of status, cf. the absolute control allowed to Spartan commanders: *Hell.* 4.1.26–7.

and smoke screens deployed by the author. What matters is the defining processes applied in the early fourth century to the constitution of norms of legitimate exchange, at the intersection of both democratic and aristocratic pressure, between the spectre of corruption and the taint of relations based on salary.

11 Panhellenism and Self-Presentation: Xenophon's Speeches

TIM ROOD

When Romolo Amaseo published his Latin translation of the *Anabasis* in 1533, he wrote a dedicatory letter to a patron, Ludovicus, who had recently returned to Bologna with Emperor Charles V from an expedition driving the Turks back through Hungary. In this letter, Amaseo recalled a discussion he had had with Ludovicus about the ancient generals who had been victorious over Asia – the likes of Alexander, Themistocles, and Miltiades. Ludovicus had then asked him about the Greek expedition to Asia which Mark Antony praised so highly (he was alluding to Plutarch's story that Antony had gasped 'O, the Ten Thousand' in admiration during his own retreat from Parthia), and Amaseo had decided to enlighten him by publishing his translation. He proceeded to draw some explicit comparisons between the March of the Ten Thousand and Charles's recent expedition against the Turks: both had been victorious through virtue, not numbers; through counsel, not temerity; and through discipline, not rashness. He ended with the hope that Charles would wrest Constantinople from the hands of an impious enemy and lead his 'eagles' victorious into Asia.[1]

The terms in which Amaseo interpreted the Greeks' retreat through Asia have been used by many others since then. Edward Gibbon, for instance, wrote that the Ten Thousand surmounted every obstacle 'by their patience, courage, and military skill' and that their 'memorable retreat ... exposed and insulted the weakness of the Persian monarchy'. It is only fairly recently, indeed, that historians have started to show more reluctance to see Xenophon as a precursor of Alexander.[2]

The question I will be addressing is whether Xenophon himself meant to encourage the sort of expedition into Asia that Amasaeus was at least professing to hope that Charles V would undertake. Many scholars have argued that

---

1. R. Amaseo (Amasaeus) (trans.), *Xenophontis philosophi et historici clarissimi de Cyri minoris expeditione libri vii* (1536), pp. 5–7, alluding to Plut. *Ant.* 45.12.
2. E. Gibbon, *The History of the Decline and Fall of the Roman Empire*, vol. 1 (1994), pp. 951–2.

Xenophon's account of the expedition is marked by a strongly idealizing strand of Panhellenism: that is, Xenophon is thought to have written his account not just to promote a sense of a shared Greek identity and pride in a shared Greek achievement, but also with the more practical aim of encouraging a Greek attack on the Persian Empire. In the first part of this chapter, I will discuss the evidence for this alleged Panhellenic strand, and, more broadly, the presentation of Hellenic identity in the *Anabasis*. I will then consider, more briefly, Xenophon's self-presentation, and in particular the apologetic tendency that has often been noted in his text. Both Panhellenism and self-presentation are big topics which can best be illuminated through a discussion of some of the speeches that loom so large in Xenophon's text. More than a quarter of the whole *Anabasis* is formed of direct speech, and in some parts of the text (books 3, 5, and 7) the proportion of direct speech is close to half. My approach to the *Anabasis* will be broadly linear: my Panhellenic section will focus on some speeches in the first half of the text, my self-presentation section on some speeches in the second half. This decision is not arbitrary. It reflects the distribution and content of Xenophon's speeches, and this distribution of material will be central to my analysis of the work as a whole.

Support for the claim that Xenophon wrote the *Anabasis* to promote an attack on Persia can be sought in its ancient reception. Both before and after Alexander had conquered the Persian Empire, the Greeks' performance at Cunaxa and during the retreat could be used as a sign of the weakness of Persia. In his *Anabasis*, Arrian has Alexander appeal to the memory of the Ten Thousand, and the point was reinforced by the title of his work (no matter whether the title was given by Arrian himself or by a later editor). Polybius is the first historian we know of to make explicit a causal link between the retreat of the Ten Thousand and Alexander's conquest of the Persian Empire: the first cause of Alexander's expedition, he wrote, was 'the retreat of the Greeks under Xenophon from the upper satrapies, in which, though they traversed the whole of Asia, a hostile country, none of the barbarians ventured to face them'. But already Isocrates, the Athenian orator, had cited their example in his letter to Philip in 346: the Greeks who took the field with Cyrus 'won as complete a victory in battle over all the forces of the king as if they had come to blows with their womenfolk'. Isocrates also used their achievements as evidence of Persian weakness in his *Panegyricus*, composed in 380. Here he even slights the Greek mercenaries (they were not picked troops and there were only six thousand of them) so as to emphasize all the more the Persians' inability to deal with them: 'the Greeks continued their march to the end as confidently as if they had been under friendly escort, dreading most of all the uninhabited regions of that country, and deeming it the best possible fortune to fall in with as many of the enemy as possible.' This triumphalist tale is also exploited by characters in Xenophon's own *Hellenica* (c. 355): the ambitious Spartan Lysander, for instance, who, 'considering how the land force that had marched upcountry with Cyrus had got safely back', persuades the Spartan king Agesilaus to launch a new attack on the Persian Empire.[3]

That Xenophon attributes this reasoning to Lysander shows at least that he was aware that the retreat was open to exploitation by promoters of an attack on Persia. It also raises the question of the context of Xenophon's alleged support for such an attack. Scholars' arguments about the aim of the *Anabasis* tend to be connected with their views of its date and of the audience they think it was addressed to. Delebecque, for instance, thought that the first half of the work was written in the 380s and was addressed to the Spartans as a warning about the King's Peace, whereas the second half was written to defend tottering Spartan power (and Xenophon's own interests) at the time of the Second Athenian League (established in 378). More often, the *Anabasis* has been dated in the early 360s – at a time when Pelopidas was seeking to win Persian support for Thebes, a time of rapprochement between Athens and Sparta, a time, so it is claimed, when they could have conceivably turned their thoughts to Persia.[4]

After the discussions of the *Anabasis*' date elsewhere in this volume, it is enough to point out that arguments for the aim of the *Anabasis* based on its date are often circular. Scholars tend to twist the slender evidence for the date of the *Anabasis* to suit their idea of when Xenophon must have written it – if their own reading of the text's political context is to have any force.

Evidence that Xenophon aimed to show the feasibility of an expedition against Persia has been found in his presentation of the Persian Empire. In the *Anabasis*, he presents the battle of Cunaxa as a victory for the Greek hoplites, which was ruined by Cyrus' impulsiveness. And at one point he even makes an overt (if far from straightforward) claim of Persian weakness: 'it was possible for one who applied his mind to the king's empire to see that it is strong

---

3. Arr. *Anab.* 2.7.8–9; Polyb. 3.6.9–12; Isoc. 5.90, 4.148; *Hell.* 3.4.2 (cf. Jason of Pherae at 6.1.12). Cf. also Plut. *Artax.* 20.1–2.
4. Against the King's Peace: É. Delebecque, 'Xénophon, Athènes et Lacédémones: notes sur la composition de l'Anabase', *REG* 59–60 (1946–7), pp. 71–138, and *Essai sur la vie de Xénophon* (Paris, 1957), pp. 199–206, 288–300. Written in 360s: J. Morr, 'Xenophon und der Gedanke eines all-griechischen Eroberungszuges gegen Persien', *Wiener Studien* 45 (1926–7), pp. 186–201.

in extent of territory and number of inhabitants; but it is weak in length of roads and in the dispersal of its forces, if one were to attack with speed.'[5] All the stages and parasangs which are marked out carefully in Xenophon's account of the march up-country can also be taken as a sign of the feasibility of a Panhellenic expedition. Xenophon, it has been thought, was setting out an itinerary for a would-be conqueror of Persia.

Xenophon's account can also be interpreted as showing the desirability of an attack on Persia. In his account, the Persians' moral shortcomings are highlighted by their treacherous murder of the Greek generals. The material advantages to be won by conquering Persia are also well illustrated, notably by the satrap Tiribazus' luxurious tent, or by the Mesopotamian dates ('the sort which are to be seen in Greece were set aside for the servants, while the ones reserved for the masters were choice fruit, wonderfully big and good looking,' Xenophon remarks). Xenophon's account of the 'otherness' of the Persian Empire has also been seen as justifying its conquest. Xenophon seems to be most explicit, however, when he describes his plan to found a city on the shores of the Black Sea, 'thinking it would be a fine thing to found a city there and so gain more territory and more power for Greece'. John Dillery has recently argued that this plan aligns Xenophon with Panhellenic and utopian thinking.[6]

All the arguments which have been used to support claims that the *Anabasis* was designed to inspire an attack on Persia are linked by the large topic of Xenophon's presentation of Hellenic identity. 'The *Anabasis* is the story of the Greeks in miniature. Ten thousand men, fiercely independent by nature, in a situation where they were a law unto themselves, showed that they were pre-eminently able to work together and proved what miracles of achievement willing co-operation can bring to pass. The Greek state, at any rate the Athenian state, which we know best, showed the same.' These words are taken from Edith Hamilton's popular book *The Greek Way*. She concludes: 'What brought

---

5. *Anab.* 1.5.9.
6. Plan to found a city: *Anab.* 5.6.15–16; cf. J. Dillery, *Xenophon and the History of his Times* (London, 1995), p. 41; Morr, 'Xenophon', pp. 188–9. On *Anab.* 1.5.9, cf. S. Hornblower, 'Persia', in *Cambridge Ancient History*[2], vol. 6 (Cambridge, 1994), pp. 45–96, at pp. 52–3. Panhellenic parasangs: G. Cousin, *Kyros le jeune en Asie Mineure (printemps 408–juillet 401 avant Jésus-Christ)* (Paris, 1905), p. xxxix; J. Luccioni, *Les Idées politiques et sociales de Xénophon* (Paris, 1948), p. 39 n. 60. Luxury: Tent: *Anab.* 4.4.21. Dates: *Anab.* 2.3.15. Ethnography as justification of conquest: B. Tripodi, 'Il cibo dell'altro: regimi e codici alimentari nell' Anabasi di Senofonte', in P. Briant (ed.), *Dans les pas des Dix-Mille* [*Pallas* 43] (Toulouse, 1995), p. 54, and various other contributors to that same volume.

the Greeks safely back from Asia was precisely what made Athens great.' Such accounts are not just quaint relics of an earlier age of popular scholarship: compare the star appearance of the Ten Thousand in the opening pages of Victor Davis Hanson's recent bestseller, *Why the West has Won* – though the less sentimental Hanson entitles his section 'Enlightened thugs'.[7]

Readings of the *Anabasis* as a text encouraging conquest in the East have tended to make most of the frequent appeals to Greek identity made by Xenophon's speakers, including Xenophon himself. The problem is that the fairly simple clauses of Xenophon's speeches have tempted readers to imagine that they offer a privileged glimpse of the fairly simple mind of Xenophon himself. They have ignored not just the relation of these speeches to the narrative – which overturns many of the simplistic assumptions about Greeks and non-Greeks made in speeches – but also the complexities of the speeches themselves.[8]

The complexities of the speeches in the *Anabasis* are well illustrated by the speech delivered by Cyrus to the Greek generals and captains on the day when he expects to face the King's army. This speech is especially interesting because it offers a non-Greek perspective on the qualities of Greek and barbarian. As it is short, I will give the whole speech:

Men of Greece, I am not leading you as allies for lack of barbarian troops. I sought your help thinking that you were better and stronger than many barbarians. I want you, then, to show that you are men worthy of the freedom which you have won and which I think you happy in possessing. You can be sure that I would rather have that freedom than all I possess, and much more. But to give you knowledge also of the type of fighting into which you are going I will tell you about it from my own experience. The enemy's numbers are very great and they attack with a lot of shouting; but if you stand your ground against this, I really feel ashamed to say what sort of people in every other way you will find the men in this country to be. If you show yourselves men and if my fortunes turn out well, I shall see to it that those of you who want to return home will be envied by their friends

---

7. 'What made Athens great': E. Hamilton, *The Greek Way* (London, 1948), p. 162. 'Enlightened thugs': V. D. Hanson, *Why the West has Won: Carnage and Culture from Salamis to Vietnam* (London, 2001), pp. 1–5.
8. There are of course exceptions: B. Laforse, 'Xenophon, Callicratidas and Panhellenism', *AHB* 12 (1998), pp. 55–67, esp. pp. 57 n. 7, 58, 65 n. 40, has some good incidental remarks on Panhellenic appeals in the *Anabasis*.

when they get there, though I think I shall make many of you prefer what they will get from me here to what they will have at home.[9]

Recently, John Dillery has taken this speech as a sign of 'the panhellenic orientation of the work'. He argues that the attribution to a non-Greek of a perception of Greek superiority gives that perception 'an authority that surpasses that spoken by a Greek'. Many other writers, both modern and not so modern, have noted, or even been excited by, this Persian prince's paradoxical celebration of liberty. Gauthier argues that Xenophon thereby transforms the expedition into 'a crusade against the barbarian'; Delebecque has Xenophon presenting Cyrus as 'a champion of democracy'; and the loquacious early nineteenth-century translator N. S. Smith moralizes on how 'vice in every shape involuntarily pays homage to virtue'.[10]

It is, however, dangerous to attempt to infer from a mere speech why Xenophon wrote the *Anabasis*. All that Cyrus' commonplace contrast between disciplined Greeks and unruly barbarian hordes shows is that he has judged his audience well. The ensuing narrative, moreover, explicitly overturns one of Cyrus' remarks: 'Cyrus was wrong in what he said at the time when he called together the Greeks and told them to stand their ground against the shouting of the natives. So far from shouting, they came on as silently as they could, calmly, in a slow, steady march.' The Persian army in fact behaves rather like the Spartans in Thucydides' account of the first battle of Mantinea.[11]

What of Cyrus' stress on freedom? The association of Greeks and freedom is strengthened by the form of rhetoric Cyrus uses. In Greek historical narratives, commanders often call on their troops to be worthy of their country, or of the past deeds of their countrymen. Here freedom stands for Greece, and recalls the deeds which secured that freedom, the Greek victory in the Persian Wars (490–479). The Persian Wars may also be recalled by the opposition between barbarian *anthrōpoi* (lit. 'humans') and Greek *andres* ('[proper] men'). As was already noted by the eighteenth-century translator Edward

---

9. *Anab.* 1.7.3–4.
10. Cyrus' speech as Panhellenic 'autoethnography': Dillery, *Xenophon and the History of his Times*, pp. 60–1. Crusade: P. Gauthier, 'Xénophon et l'odyssée des "Dix-Mille"', *L'Histoire* 79 (1985), p. 21. Champion of democracy: Delebecque, 'Xénophon, Athènes et Lacédémones', p. 78, and *Essai sur la vie de Xénophon*, p. 201. In praise of liberty: N. S. Smith (trans.), *The Expedition of Cyrus into Persia, and the Retreat of the Ten Thousand Greeks* (London, 1824), p. 55.
11. Cyrus' error: *Anab.* 1.8.11. The Spartans at Mantinea: Thuc. 5.70.

Spelman, this opposition picks up Herodotus' description of the battle of Thermopylae – where the Persians' failure to break through the resilient Spartans shows that 'there are many *anthrōpoi*, but few *andres*'.[12]

These motifs drawn from the Persian Wars are reinforced by some Herodotean hints that have gone unnoticed. Various echoes of Herodotus' portrayal of the Persian Wars can be found in Xenophon's account of the first stages of the march: the use of the noun *stolos* to denote the expedition is common in Herodotus; an initial, admittedly underplayed, river crossing with a bridge of boats hints at a frequent (and often ominous) Herodotean motif; and, less obliquely, Xenophon mentions the palace built by Xerxes at Celaenae on his return from Greece – together with the fate of the unfortunate satyr Marsyas, where he seems to aim to improve on Herodotus' account.[13] Xenophon is evoking the rhythm of the large-scale Herodotus expedition. These hints also suggest that the Persians' propensity to launch grand expeditions can be turned against themselves – and that Cyrus is merely following in a line of similarly self-important Persian dynasts.

Yet when Cyrus states in his speech before Cunaxa that he values freedom over wealth, he seems to be separating himself from the Persian rulers portrayed by Herodotus. He is aligning himself rather with the Spartan king Agesilaus, who, in a famous scene in Xenophon's *Hellenica*, tells the Persian satrap Pharnabazus that 'to be free is worth all one's money' – though Agesilaus goes on to tell Pharnabazus that he has the chance to be both free and wealthy. Yet this parallel merely shows that Cyrus is being as manipulative as Agesilaus. (Indeed, the positive portrayal of Pharnabazus in the *Hellenica* shows that loyalty and honour are important as well as freedom – while, immediately before Agesilaus' speech, Spartan greed has alienated their Paphlagonian allies.) There is, moreover, a jarring note in Cyrus' speech. He ends with what is in effect a call to exchange freedom for wealth: 'I think I shall make many of you prefer what they will get from me here to what they will have at home.' He then makes another speech in response to a prearranged challenge to prove that he will be able to fulfil his promises. In this speech, he stresses the vastness of the Persian Empire, and says: 'if I win, I must make my own friends lords over all this'. Evidently he is offering his Greek companions some sort of role in his empire. And following this speech the generals and some

---

12. Hdt. 7.210.2. E. Spelman (trans.), *Xenophon: The Expedition of Cyrus*, vol. 1 (London, 1740–2), p. 74 n. 111.
13. *Stolos* and boat-bridge: *Anab.* 1.2.5. Xerxes and Marsyas: *Anab.* 1.2.7–9; cf. Hdt. 7.26.3.

others have private meetings with Cyrus, wanting to know what will be in it for them if they win. We are left to guess what they are offered.[14]

So Cyrus' lofty talk about liberty is followed by a seedy picture of Greek generals on the make, scrambling for their share of the booty that never came. Now, as Azoulay shows in chapter 10 of this volume, Xenophon did not think that there was anything especially wrong with seeking wealth – providing that the pursuit of wealth could be subsumed within or disguised by the traditional language of aristocratic guest-friendships, and separated from the cash nexus typified by the coin payments received by the mercenaries. Xenophon even closes the *Anabasis* by describing his own terrorist attack on a Persian grandee, Asidates – an attack which reaps enough booty for him to be in a position to do others a good turn (that is, to be a mini-Cyrus). While Xenophon tries to present this attack as the work of a select unit, it may still remind readers of the sort of private expedition that Xenophon criticizes earlier in the work, before the troops have signed up to work for the Spartans. And it was this desire for profit that created tensions both among the Ten Thousand themselves and between them and the Greeks living on the Black Sea coast. It cost some of them their lives – most strikingly, Aeneas of Stymphalus, who tries to grab hold of a finely clad man who was about to throw himself down from a mountain stronghold, but gets dragged down with him. And the first time in the retreat when any of the troops are routed is when some of them rush ahead against a Mossynoecan fort, 'not ordered by the generals, but for plunder', Xenophon explains.[15]

So Cyrus' rhetoric about freedom and wealth is undercut by actions which eventually follow. It is also strikingly echoed by Xenophon towards the end of the work. The Greek mercenaries have been hired by the Thracian Seuthes to recover his father's kingdom, yet even though they have helped him to achieve this, he has failed to pay them. At this point, Xenophon warns him: 'I am perfectly sure that you would have prayed for the achievement of all that has been accomplished for you rather than for many times the amount of money.'[16] Xenophon is telling Seuthes that he should be more like Cyrus had professed to be.

---

14. The Pharnabazus scene: *Hell.* 4.1.35; cf. V. J. Gray, *The Character of Xenophon's Hellenica* (London, 1989), pp. 52–6; C. J. Tuplin, *The Failings of Empire: A Reading of Xenophon Hellenica 2.3.11–7.5.27* (Stuttgart, 1993), pp. 58–9. Cyrus' speech and its sequel: *Anab.* 1.7.7–8.
15. The attack on Asidates: *Anab.* 7.8.8–23; cf. Whitby and Azoulay, chapters 7 and 10 in this volume. The end of Aeneas: *Anab.* 4.7.13. 'Not ordered by the generals': *Anab.* 5.4.16.
16. *Anab.* 7.7.27.

Yet what the Greeks have accomplished for him is 'enslaving' some Thracian tribes – behaviour which led the eighteenth-century historian William Mitford to comment that 'Xenophon, it appears, knew how to value freedom; but was not nicely scrupulous of supporting the cause of despotism.' Compare also how Xenophon had earlier acknowledged that they served Cyrus with the aim of making Artaxerxes a slave instead of a king. This does not of course invalidate Cyrus' praise of the Greeks' freedom: Greek sensitivities were not quite the same as Mitford's. But the parallel between Cyrus and Seuthes suggests that Cyrus, far from being a champion of democracy, was only concerned with the freedom of one man. So, too, what is at stake in Agesilaus' appeal to Pharnabazus to be free is the freedom of just one man, Pharnabazus himself.[17]

Cyrus' speech to the Greeks before the battle of Cunaxa cannot, it seems, simply be isolated from its context and read as straightforward Panhellenic propaganda. Since Cyrus died at Cunaxa, we cannot be sure how many of the Greek officers would have taken up his offer to stay and be wealthy – to exchange freedom for luxury. Xenophon leaves us with the pleasing image of them as wise advisers, telling Cyrus not to fight in the front ranks.

Soon after the battle of Cunaxa, Phalinus, a Greek in the Persians' service, came to the Greek army bearing Artaxerxes' demand that they hand over their weapons. This famous scene, whose impact has already been evoked in this volume by Braun, is worth discussing here because it takes further the text's use of motifs from the Persian Wars. Xenophon reports various responses to the Persian demands. A young Athenian Theopompus, for instance, says that 'the only things of value which we have at present are our arms and our excellence – so if we keep our arms we think we could use our excellence'. And finally Clearchus appeals to Phalinus to think how his advice will be perceived by the Greeks at home, and argues that 'if we must become friends with the king, we would be more valuable friends if we have our arms than if we hand them over to someone else; and if we must fight, we would fight better if we have our arms than if we hand them over to someone else'. So the Greeks refuse to hand over their arms – an inspiring assertion of their expectation that their courage and excellence (*aretē*) will triumph over Persian numbers.[18]

The link with the Persian Wars is made explicit in Diodorus' account of this scene. Diodorus says that 'each general made a reply much like that which

---

17. Enslaving Thracians: *Anab.* 7.4.24, 7.29, 32; cf. W. Mitford, *History of Greece*, vol. 3 (London, 1808–18), p. 215. The intended enslavement of Artaxerxes: *Anab.* 3.1.17.
18. Theopompus: *Anab.* 2.1.12. For Theopompus as a possible 'ringer' for Xenophon, see Azoulay in this volume. The appeal of Clearchus: *Anab.* 2.1.17, 20.

Leonidas made when he was guarding the pass of Thermopylae, and Xerxes sent messengers asking him to lay down his arms' – and then he has Leonidas give exactly the reply that Clearchus gives in Xenophon.[19] This echo of the Persian Wars is, however, rather problematic. Leonidas' reply is not mentioned in Herodotus. Nor is Xerxes' demand, for that matter. So it is not inconceivable that Ephorus (say) got the reply from Xenophon, whose account, as Stylianou has shown in chapter 2 of this volume, formed the basis for Ephorus' own narrative of Cyrus' expedition. And in that case we only have some pleasing evidence of how the *Anabasis* could be read.

Still, Xenophon's own scene is clearly promoting a vision of Greek excellence that could promote Panhellenic thinking. The opposition of Greek excellence (*aretē*) and Persian numbers is standard in presentations of the Persian Wars.[20] And it is worth noting that when Clearchus asks Phalinus what his advice would be, he tells him that his advice will become known in Greece and determine his future reputation. Evidently the Greeks' final response to the Persian ultimatum is also directed towards a Greek audience – as Xenophon's account itself guarantees. It is meant to be a paradigmatic display of their excellence.

The excellence of the Greeks also seems to be praised in the speeches Xenophon himself makes during the Greeks' night of sleepless despondency after the murder of their generals. He addresses three different groups in turn (Proxenus' men, the officers, and the army as a whole), using slightly different rhetoric for the different audiences. Some of that rhetoric is manifestly unpersuasive – notably his attempt to persuade the troops that they need not feel fear on account of their own lack of cavalry. Horsemen, he assures the soldiers, are just men: 'no one has ever died in battle through being bitten or kicked by a horse.'[21] They are also, he adds, less stable than infantry, because they are afraid of falling off their horses. Soon, of course, the Ten Thousand do suffer greatly from their lack of cavalry. We are not meant to think Xenophon was stupid. He was just doing his best. But it is a reminder of the obvious point that even claims that Xenophon himself makes in his speeches are determined by the needs of his immediate audience and cannot automatically be extrapolated from their context within the *Anabasis*.

Xenophon does make a number of remarks that have been taken as promoting an invasion of the Persian Empire. He says, for instance, that 'if we

---

19. Diod. 14.25.2–3; cf. 11.5.5 for Leonidas' reply (also Plut. *Mor*. 225d).
20. e.g. Andoc. 1.107.
21. *Anab*. 3.2.18–19.

relax and fall into the King's power, what sort of treatment can we expect from him . . . ? Would he not go to all possible lengths in trying to inflict on us every conceivable misery and so make all men afraid of ever marching against him again?' Since the King fails in his aim to punish the Greeks, does that mean that Xenophon is suggesting that the Greeks should not be afraid of marching against him? Once more Xenophon seems to hint at the paradigmatic force of his account. His remark picks up an earlier passage, when 'most of the Greeks' were displeased by Clearchus' negotiations with the Persians: 'Is it not clear', they are reported as saying, 'that the King would do anything to destroy us, so as to make the other Greeks afraid of marching against the Great King? . . . He will not consent, if he can possibly help it, to our going back to Greece and telling the story of how we, so few of us, were victorious over the King at his own palace gates, and then, making him an object of derision (*katagelasantes*), got safely home again.'[22]

The rhetoric here is more excited, and it is explicitly the Greeks whom the King wants to stop marching against him. Has Xenophon anachronistically introduced an issue that was more of a concern in the 360s (probably the time when he was writing) than in 401 (the time of which he was writing)? Not necessarily. Perhaps we are just faced with the common notion of punishment as a deterrent. And Greeks could in any case have been imagined marching against the King not to overthrow his empire for themselves, but in the service of another rebel.

A possible link with Isocrates, the arch advocate of a united Greek attack on Persia, must be mentioned. In his *Panegyricus* (written in 380), Isocrates claimed that 'the Persians made themselves objects of derision [*katagelastoi*] under the very palace of the king'. Compare those Greeks in Xenophon who talk of making the King 'an object of derision' (*katagelasantes*). Scholars have asked whether Isocrates was imitating Xenophon, or Xenophon imitating Isocrates. It is enough here to note that Isocrates' description of the mercenaries retreating as if they were being 'escorted' does not bear much relation to Xenophon's account – which highlights the difficulties faced by the Greeks during the retreat. Indeed, those difficulties lend a heavy irony to the word on which the Isocratean intertext turns – *katagelasantes*. Laughter and mockery, we may recall, are more often than not ironic in Greek historians.[23]

---

22. 'If we relax': *Anab.* 3.1.17–18. 'Is it not clear': *Anab.* 2.4.3–4.
23. *Katagelastoi*: Isoc. 4.149. Isocrates echoing Xenophon: Morr, 'Xenophon', pp. 198–9; Delebecque, 'Xénophon, Athènes et Lacédémones', p. 96.

Scholars arguing that the *Anabasis* was written to promote a Greek invasion of Asia have put most weight on a passage in Xenophon's speech to the whole army:

> I am afraid that, if we once learn to live a life of ease and luxury, enjoying the company of these fine great women, the wives and daughters of the Medes and Persians, we might be like the Lotus-eaters and forget our road home. I think that it is right and reasonable for us to make it our first endeavour to reach our own folk in Greece and to demonstrate to the Greeks that their poverty is of their own choosing, since they might see people who have a wretched life in their own countries grow rich by coming out here.[24]

This passage has been taken as an overt appeal to the Greeks at home to seek *Lebensraum* in the East. Yet Xenophon is in fact warning of the dangers of luxury – dangers familiar from Herodotus, and also from Xenophon's own *Cyropaedia* (written *c.* 360). In those works it is the Persians who succumb to luxury – though the warning is felt to apply to Greeks too. Xenophon is also suggesting that the very practicality of a Greek settlement in the luxurious East is another reason for returning home. To show that Greeks can resist the dangerous allure of Eastern luxuries is to suggest that Greeks are glad to be poor. Xenophon is not promoting a settlement in the East. He is giving two reasons why the Greeks should go home. Yet this passage cannot simply be taken as a protest against colonial Panhellenism: Xenophon mentions the possibility of staying in Mesopotamia precisely in order to reject it, because his comrades do not want to stay.[25]

Another passage in the same speech has also been taken as a sign of Xenophon's Panhellenic tendencies. We encountered earlier some rather indirect references to the Persian Wars. Now Xenophon appeals directly to the memory of that great Hellenic endeavour:

---

24. *Anab.* 3.2.25–6. For further discussion, see Ma, chapter 12 in this volume.
25. *Anab.* 3.2.25–6 as Panhellenic: G. L. Cawkwell, introduction to *Xenophon: The Persian Expedition* (Harmondsworth, 1972), pp. 23–4, and 'Agesilaus and Sparta', *CQ* 26 (1976), p. 65; P. G. van Soesbergen, 'Colonisation as a solution to social-economic problems: a confrontation of Isocrates with Xenophon', *AncSoc* 13–14 (1982–3), pp. 141–2. Warning: Dillery, *Xenophon and the History of his Times*, p. 62 (though this seems to be at odds with his general interpretation); contrast Tuplin, review of Dillery, *Histos* 1 (1997), noting that ordinary Panhellenism before the time of Alexander 'surely did not envisage *Lebensraum* in Mesopotamia' (that is, it only envisaged colonization in Anatolia). *Cyropaedia* as anti-Panhellenic: P. Carlier, 'L'idée de monarchie impériale dans la Cyropédie de Xénophon', *Ktema* 3 (1978), pp. 133–63.

The Persians and their friends came with an enormous army, thinking that they would wipe Athens off the face of the earth; but the Athenians had the courage to stand up to them by themselves, and they defeated them. On that occasion they had made a vow to Artemis that they would sacrifice to her a goat for every one of their enemies whom they killed, but since they could not get hold of enough goats, they decided to sacrifice five hundred every year, and they still now sacrifice them. Then, when Xerxes later on collected his innumerable army and came against Greece, there was another occasion when your fathers defeated the fathers of these people both on land and on sea. You can see proof of this in our trophies, but the greatest evidence for this is the freedom of the cities in which you have been born and brought up.[26]

Xenophon is telling the mercenaries that their achievements will be a replaying of the Persian Wars. And we see in due course that they do set up trophies over the barbarians – including, perhaps, the famous cairn on Mount Thekes, which has recently been interpreted as 'a monument to the Ten Thousand's triumph over all the barbarians they met ... the entire campaign is crowned as a Panhellenic venture'. That cairn is not in fact strictly a trophy, and it would be rash to take it as a sign of Xenophon's Panhellenic ambitions. But when Xenophon mentions the Athenians' sacrifice to Artemis, we should perhaps remember that he himself will set up a festival to Artemis.[27]

Other strands in Xenophon's rhetoric implicitly evoke rhetoric familiar from celebrations of the Persian Wars: the appeal to the Greeks to be *agathoi andres* ('brave men'), the use of words such as *agōn* ('struggle') and *aretē* ('excellence') and *kalliston ergon* ('finest deed') that are sprinkled through his speeches. Such language is also found at some points later in the march, for instance when the other Greeks go to the rescue of the Arcadian detachment: Xenophon appeals to the men 'to make a united effort to save ourselves', and to be resolved 'either to die with honour or perform a most noble deed in saving so many Greeks'. The defensive context here brings this Greek feeling to the fore.[28]

26. *Anab.* 3.2.11–13.
27. Trophies: *Anab.* 4.6.27, 6.5.32, 7.6.36 (speech). Cairn: 4.7.25; Dillery, *Xenophon and the History of his Times*, p. 77 (but contrast C. J. Tuplin, 'On the track of the Ten Thousand', *REA* 101 (1999), pp. 331–66, at pp. 361–4, who argues that it is not a trophy). Artemis: *Anab.* 5.3.9.
28. *Agathoi andres*: *Anab.* 3.1.44; 3.2.3, 11, 15, 39, 4.1.19. *Agōn*: *Anab.* 3.1.16, 21–2, 2.15, 4.6.8, 8.9. *Kalliston ergon*: *Anab.* 3.1.16, 24, 4.6.8, 8.9, 6.3.17. Rescuing Arcadians: *Anab.* 6.3.17.

Xenophon also frequently stresses that the Greeks have accomplished a deed worthy of praise and commemoration: hints, surely, that his own account is commemorative. He even reports how the city of Sinope sends envoys to praise the Ten Thousand that 'you, being Greeks, are victors over barbarians' – one of many appeals to fellow Greek identity in this section of the text.[29]

These appeals have been taken as another sign of the Panhellenic orientation of the *Anabasis*. But while the Persian Wars motifs seem to retain their shine, it is far more problematic to wrench from their context the appeals to shared Hellenic identity made during the army's passage along the Black Sea coast. There is a constant tension between these claims, made in speeches, and the surrounding narrative, which highlights the difficulties that arise between the army and the cities on the coast. Xenophon shows how the people of Trapezus exploit the Ten Thousand's presence against their hostile neighbours, the Drilae – an exploitation that Xenophon in a later speech masks with the language of reciprocity (they helped the people of Trapezus in return for the honours they had received from them).[30]

Note, too, that the embassy that the Sinopeans send to praise the Ten Thousand has been sent in an understandable fear that they will ravage the city and land of the Sinopean colony Cotyora. And the envoys proceed to utter threats: any harm done to their colony they will treat as harm done to Sinope; and if necessary they will ally with the Paphlagonian king Corylas against the Ten Thousand. In response to which the Ten Thousand make a counter-threat: they will ally with Corylas against Sinope. They subsequently ask them, 'Greeks to Greeks', for advice on the best route; and a Sinopean, Hecatonymus, apologizes for their earlier threat: what he had meant was that 'though it was possible for them to be friends of the barbarians, they will choose the Greeks'. Even after he has spoken, however, some of the Ten Thousand suspect that he has advised them to go by sea because of his friendship with the Paphlagonian Corylas, whose representative (*proxenos*) he was. The problems for the Greek cities along the coast do not just arise from the practicalities of dealing with such a large group of men and women. They are especially acute because the army becomes more and more undisciplined: during the army's stop at Cerasus, a section makes an unprovoked attack on a non-Greek village that was on good terms with Cerasus, and had sold supplies to the army; the envoys

---

29. Praise: e.g. *Anab.* 5.5.8, 6.4, 7.33 *bis*, 6.6.16. Commemoration: e.g. *Anab.* 6.5.24. Future reputation: *Anab.* 2.1.17.
30. Manipulation at Trapezus: *Anab.* 5.2.2. Later whitewash: *Anab.* 5.5.14.

that these people send to complain about the attack are murdered; and then some local market officials are attacked.[31]

It is instructive to contrast Xenophon's account with Diodorus'. Even though Diodorus' account at this point is, as Stylianou has shown, ultimately derived from Xenophon's, Diodorus neglects all of the tensions on which Xenophon dwells. He says, for instance, that the Ten Thousand are received hospitably by the Greeks on the coast; and when he has them defeat the Mossynoeci, he does not mention that they were helping one local faction against another. Xenophon, by contrast, makes much more of the appeals to Hellenic identity – while showing them up as opportunistic, at most a way of creating dialogue and mediating tensions.

But what of the allusions to the Persian Wars? I have implied that the *Anabasis* is a commemoration of an achievement that is seen as similar to the Greek victories against the Persian invaders – and to that extent Xenophon's text does have a Panhellenic resonance. But this is not the whole story. As the Ten Thousand approach Greece, they start to have dealings with the Spartans – who, Xenophon informs us, 'were at that time the rulers over all the Greeks'.[32] And it is at this point that the Peloponnesian War becomes more important.

When the army decides to choose a single leader, Xenophon advises that they choose a Spartan, so as not to alienate the Spartans: 'the Spartans did not stop making war on my own country until they had made the whole city admit that the Spartans had power over them too [viz. as well as the rest of Greece].' Later he warns them that they must submit to Spartan justice – even if it means injustice. And when the army, excluded from Byzantium, appeals to Xenophon to be a man and seize the city, he restrains them again with reference to the recent war: he mentions how, for all Athens's financial and naval strength, for all the cities they ruled – including Byzantium itself – they were defeated.[33]

What sort of story is Xenophon telling? The way he presents the dangers confronted by the Ten Thousand in the last three books of the *Anabasis* repeatedly suggests links between the army's experiences before and after their arrival at the sea. Thus, when the army arrives back at what Xenophon calls in a speech 'the gates of Greece' (6.5.3), it finds itself as much at a loss as when it was

---

31. Threats from the Sinopeans: *Anab*. 5.5.10, 12. Counter-threats from the Ten Thousand: *Anab*. 5.5.23. Advice on the best route: *Anab*. 5.6.2–3. Proxeny with Corylas: *Anab*. 5.6.11. Hellenic language: Morr, 'Xenophon', p. 195.
32. *Anab*. 6.6.9.
33. 'The Spartans did not stop making war': *Anab*. 6.1.27. Spartan (in)justice: *Anab*. 6.6.12–13. Xenophon on the defeat of Athens: *Anab*. 7.1.27.

marooned at 'the gates of the King'. The Spartans even plot against Xenophon, rather as the satrap Tissaphernes had plotted against the Greek generals after Cunaxa. Xenophon's hints were picked by William Mitford, as alert as ever to signs of the disturbed state of the non-monarchical Greek world: 'In the midst of flourishing Grecian settlements, and almost in Greece, the Cyreians, threatened on all sides, found themselves more at a loss which way to turn, than when first deserted by their Persian allies, thousands of miles from home, in the middle of the hostile Persian empire.' So perhaps the *Anabasis* is an escape story that subverts itself, a celebration of Greek achievement that becomes an analysis of Greek weakness. Xenophon's Greek mercenaries move from relative unity in the face of a common danger to disunity and squabbling, and allusions to the Persian Wars are replaced by references to the Peloponnesian War. The journey of the Ten Thousand begins to seem like a mirror of the experience of the Greeks at large over the previous few generations. 'What brought the Greeks safely back from Asia was precisely what made Athens great.' What brought the Greeks into disharmony and disrepute in their journey from Trapezus to Byzantium was precisely what destroyed Athens's greatness.[34]

How strong, then, are claims that Xenophon wrote the *Anabasis* to boost the prospects of an attack on Persia? Paradoxically, the more one stresses Xenophon's presentation of the Ten Thousand as in some sense a microcosm of the Greek world, the stronger the impulse to conclude that, if the *Anabasis* is to be read as a Panhellenic text, the Ten Thousand are in many ways a negative paradigm. To succeed, a Panhellenic force would have to be made of different stuff from these mercenaries, and have rather different ambitions. But there is in any case no real evidence that Xenophon was promoting a Panhellenic expedition. His account can easily be read as stressing the difficulty of such an expedition rather than its feasibility. And he does not address at all what was presumably the most pointed Panhellenic issue – the status of the Greek cities in Asia. That was his concern in the *Hellenica*. The most we can say is that Xenophon did at one point want to increase the power of Greece by founding a city on the Black Sea. But when he came to write up the ambitions he had had at that time, he used a verb, *prosktēsasthai*, associated in Herodotus with the pressures on Eastern kings to expand, and used in

---

34. The gates of Greece: *Anab.* 6.5.3. The gates of the King: *Anab.* 2.4.4, 3.1.2. 'In the midst of flourishing Grecian settlements': Mitford, *History of Greece*, vol. 3, p. 208.

Thucydides of Alcibiades' ambitions for Athenian expansion: not very propitious intertexts.

Even though Xenophon's portrayal of his colonizing plan in the Black Sea is charged with irony, other aspects of Xenophon's self-presentation can be related to the Panhellenic theme. It has been argued that Xenophon's portrayal of his cooperation with the Spartan general Chirisophus, and his negative portrayal of Arcadians and others, supports Athenian–Spartan cooperation under Spartan leadership in the early 360s – a time when the Arcadians were breaking away from their political submission to Sparta. One scholar even thought that Xenophon was advertising his services for a Panhellenic expedition, again in the 360s. The same argument had earlier been made with great eloquence by the French epigraphist and traveller Cousin, writing in 1905: 'The ideal Xenophon who in the *Anabasis* sees all, directs all, adapts his tactics to circumstances, accepts responsibilities, and wins the great victory that lies in not being defeated – this is not the real Xenophon of history; this name is the provisional name of the general who one day will, by a daring attack, make the worm-eaten empire of the Great King crumble. His true name will be Alexander.'[35]

More humbly, Xenophon's presentation of his own leadership can be related to his general ideas about leadership – ideas that run through his different works. There is also much of literary interest in the way Xenophon describes himself: the use of the third person, for instance, the delayed, and Homeric, introduction at the start of book 3 (or what seems like an introduction: Xenophon does in fact appear a couple of times in the first two books). It has also sometimes been claimed that Xenophon twice disguises himself in the earlier books – first as the philosophical 'Theopompus of Athens', and later as an unnamed 'young man' (some manuscripts even have the name 'Xenophon' instead of Theopompus). The grounds for these claims are not strong (why would he disguise himself on these two occasions, given that he does mention himself by name twice before the delayed 'introduction' at the start of book 3?). A different disguise, however, is very pertinent to the question of

---

35. Spartan and Athenian cooperation: A. Körte, 'Die Tendenz von Xenophons *Anabasis*', *Neue Jahrbücher für das Klassisches Altertum* 49 (1922), pp. 15–24. Would-be leader of expedition: F. Robert, 'Les intentions de Xénophon dans *l'Anabase*', *Information Littéraire* 2 (1950), pp. 55–9. 'His true name will be Alexander': Cousin, *Kyros le jeune en Asie Mineure*, p. xxxix.

Xenophon's self-presentation: the *Anabasis* itself may well have been published under the pseudonym of 'Themistogenes of Syracuse'.[36]

The various issues involved in Xenophon's self-presentation are tied together by a question that it is impossible to evade: did Xenophon write the *Anabasis* to defend himself? The pseudonym, and the use of the third person, were seen by Plutarch as a device for making Xenophon's self-presentation more acceptable. Modern scholars have seen them as a device for propaganda without personal risk. Xenophon has been seen as justifying himself before an Athenian audience, perhaps seeking to win release from his exile (that event which he treats so elusively in the *Anabasis* itself). Or else he has been seen as justifying himself before his fellow soldiers, or before the Spartans. It has also been claimed that Xenophon sought to promote his own interests by exaggerating the role he played in the retreat. Scholars point out that he is not mentioned in Diodorus' account of the retreat to the sea. They speculate that Diodorus' account derives ultimately from the account by Sophaenetus, one of the other generals during the retreat, and that Xenophon was writing in response to Sophaenetus.[37]

It is undeniable that Xenophon comes out well from the *Anabasis*. There is admittedly some irony at his own expense in his account of how he fails to heed Socrates' warnings – and goes off and asks the wrong question at Delphi. But his consultations of the gods later in the work show that he does learn to ask the right questions. And in general he shows himself a model leader: accessible, ready to learn from mistakes, good at speaking and planning. Doubtless he is too good to be true. But how much did he exaggerate his role? There seems to be a slight tension between the claim that Xenophon does exaggerate his influence and the claim that he is defending himself. If he was not an important figure, he would not have had so much to defend himself about. It has, moreover, been shown that Xenophon's prominence in his account to some extent stems from his adopting the perspective of the rearguard, where he was stationed himself, and that Xenophon does not stress his own role in books 3 and 4 at the expense of the other leader of the rearguard, Timasion. What of Diodorus' silence? Diodorus, it should be stressed, does not focus on

---

36. Xenophon as model of the ideal leader: e.g. B. Due, *The Cyropaedia: Xenophon's Aims and Methods* (Copenhagen, 1989), pp. 203–6. Introduction: *Anab*. 3.1.4 – yet 1.8.15–17, 2.5.37, 40–1. 'Theopompus', 'young man': *Anab*. 2.1.12–13, 4.19. Themistogenes: *Hell*. 3.1.2; Plut. *De glor. Ath.* 345e.
37. Self-justification: e.g. F. Dürrbach, 'L'apologie de Xénophon dans l'Anabase', *REG* 6 (1893), pp. 343–86. Response to Sophaenetus (*FGH* 109): Cawkwell, introduction to *Xenophon: The Persian Expedition*, pp. 18–19 and chapter 1 in this volume.

any other leaders during the retreat to the sea. And he does have Xenophon as leader of the expedition into Thrace.[38]

It is also hard to locate the precise audience to which Xenophon wished to address this positive self-portrayal. There are many elements in the *Anabasis* that are hard to reconcile with claims that Xenophon was trying to appease the Athenians or the Spartans or to defend the behaviour of the mercenaries. And as for claims that Xenophon was seeking to correct Sophaenetus' portrayal of the expedition, it seems dangerous to argue that a work about which we know a lot was written in response to a work about which we know nothing – especially if, as Stylianou has argued in this volume, Sophaenetus did not write an *Anabasis* at all.

There is still much within the *Anabasis* itself that seems to suggest that we should treat the text as Xenophon's self-justification. Some of the attacks against which Xenophon is thought to be defending himself were, if we believe his account, already brought against him during the march along the Black Sea coast and during the stay in Thrace. And the *Anabasis* itself re-enacts his self-defence, notably through some rather long speeches – speeches that have seemed boring to many readers and even an indication of persecution mania. An especially striking grouping of speeches is found when the Ten Thousand have reached Cotyora in their march along the Black Sea coast, and Xenophon has to defend himself against an accusation that he wants to lead the troops back to Phasis. Xenophon first gives a geographical lesson to show that he could not have hoped to deceive them into travelling back east. He then deflects that charge by lecturing them on their growing indiscipline, but finds himself forced to defend his leadership at some points earlier in the campaign. Someone complains that he was struck by Xenophon. Xenophon realizes that this was a man who had tried to bury alive an injured soldier. To the defence that the soldier died anyway, Xenophon rather finely responds: 'We shall all die: is that any reason why we should be buried alive?' – and his audience shout out that Xenophon had not hit him enough (*Anab.* 5.8.11–12).[39]

Later in the march along the coast, a fracas arises over whether some plunder is public or private property. Xenophon finds himself suspected of

---

38. Irony at own expense: W. E. Higgins, *Xenophon the Athenian* (Albany, 1977), pp. 83, 98. J. Roy, 'Xenophon's Anabasis: the command of the rearguard in books III and IV', *Phoenix* 22 (1968), pp. 158–9, and 'Xenophon's evidence for the *Anabasis*', *Athenaeum* 46 (1968), pp. 37–46. Xenophon as leader of the Thracian expedition: Diod. 14.37.1–4; Diodorus fails to note that he serves under Seuthes.
39. Persecution mania: Delebecque, 'Xénophon, Athènes et Lacédémones', p. 112, cf. *Essai sur la vie de Xénophon*, p. 293. Xenophon's self-defence: *Anab.* 5.7–8.

orchestrating an attack on the Spartan representative Dexippus. Here, the man who led the attack, Agasias, exculpates Xenophon – and is then allowed to present his own defence.[40]

Later still, Xenophon has to remove Spartan suspicions that he is a demagogue, a friend of the soldiers; and to remove some of the soldiers' suspicions that he has taken bribes from Seuthes while letting them go unpaid. Here Xenophon gives a four and a half page speech demonstrating that he has profited less than others, that he has in fact lost his good standing. So there is a fair amount of overt self-defence. And Xenophon also shows himself offering a defence of the army's plundering to an embassy from Sinope, and later to Seuthes.[41]

While these various speeches do seem to be offering a defence of Xenophon's leadership and of the army's conduct at some points in its retreat, they can be read in another way too. These speeches also bear on important ethical themes. The attacks on Xenophon are presented as unreasonable, a mark of ingratitude. Xenophon tells the troops that he is surprised 'that you remember it and do not keep silent if I offended any of you, but that no one remembers it if I helped you during the cold weather or kept off the enemy . . . nor do you remember the times when I praised a man for doing something well'. 'It is fine and just and upright and more pleasant', he concludes, 'to remember what is good rather than what is bad.'[42] Here we see a slightly didactic Xenophon.

An even more didactic Xenophon emerges in the long lecture he delivers to Seuthes – another speech that lasts for four and a half pages.[43] Here the word *didaxōn* ('teach', 'instruct') appears in the first sentence: 'I am here, Seuthes, not to ask for anything back, but to instruct you, if I can, that you were not right to be angry with me . . .' And Xenophon goes on to tell Seuthes that it is in a ruler's own interest to be perceived as trustworthy. The ethical, didactic, and political aspects of the work merge. Xenophon's experiences, we see, have enabled him to play the Socratic adviser – to grow into the author of a *Cyropaedia*. Xenophon's earlier defence of his leadership could also be seen as having a strong didactic element: the positive qualities of his leadership (his maintenance of discipline and morale, for instance) are not left to be inferred from the narrative, but are presented as such in a speech, and acknowledged by his internal audience.

40. *Anab.* 6.6.17–24.
41. Four and a half page speech: *Anab.* 7.6.11–38. Apologia to the Sinopeans: *Anab.* 5.5.13–23. Apologia to Seuthes: *Anab.* 7.7.4–10.
42. *Anab.* 5.8.25–6.
43. *Anab.* 7.7.20–47.

Xenophon's didacticism is combined with analysis of the workings of the army as a political unit. By presenting the troops with whom he has to deal as unruly, unreasonable, and even bestial, Xenophon is encouraging us to analyse how the political agility of the individual can deal with the heightened feelings of the crowd. At Trapezus, recognizing that the soldiers are foolishly refusing to accept the possibility that they will have to march further by land, Xenophon says that he did not put to the vote his proposal to persuade the locals to mend the roads. He simply went and persuaded them.[44] Here, Xenophon bypasses the democratic framework of this army that has often been described as a '*polis* on the march' – or at least the army which seems to become much more like a *polis* when it reaches the sea. Thucydides' Pericles sometimes acted similarly.

Later, the soldiers, angry that Xenophon is said to be planning to lead them back to Phasis, hold gatherings (*xullogoi*) and stand round in groups. Xenophon's description recalls Thucydides' account of the Athenians agitating for an attack on the Spartans in the first year of the Peloponnesian War – when, Thucydides remarks, Pericles did not hold an assembly for fear that the Athenians should reach a decision moved by passion rather than by reason.[45] All the more impressive, then, that Xenophon at once steps in and confronts this mob.

The speech Xenophon makes at Cotyora warning against the dangers of indiscipline is particularly important for understanding his political analysis. His analysis of the army's functioning as a political unit is underpinned by a startling instance of narrative displacement: Xenophon postpones until this speech mention of some incidents that happened earlier in the march (notably his hitting that man who had intended to bury a wounded comrade alive). An effect of Xenophon's disposition of material is to highlight the way his audience responds to his advice. He warns that a self-appointed general may arise who would be prepared to kill without trial officer and private soldier alike – that is, that a tyrant may arise from this disordered democracy (as Greek political theory demands). This warning does hit home, as the army decides to institute judicial procedures. But soon afterwards there is further trouble in the army. The soldiers decide to elect one general as supreme leader, since they think it will increase their profits if the generals do not have to discuss everything with each other. There are limits to what even a Xenophon can do with these troops.

44. *Anab.* 5.1.14.
45. *Anab.* 5.7.2; Thuc. 2.22.

Xenophon then describes how he ponders whether to seek election himself:

> In some ways he wanted to, as he reflected that his own honour would be greater among his friends, and his name would be greater at Athens, and he might perhaps be the cause of some good for the army. Such thoughts made him desire to be commander-in-chief. But when he reflected that it is unclear to everyone how the future will be, and that for this reason there was a risk of losing even the reputation he had won already, he was uncertain what to do.[46]

A sacrifice makes clear that Xenophon should not accept the command. So when his name is put forward, he refuses – on the grounds that the Spartans would resent the choice of a non-Spartan. When pressed further, Xenophon makes a second speech, in which he mentions what he implies is the real reason – the divine opposition. So a Spartan is chosen.

This episode shows once more the importance of interpreting speeches in their narrative context in the *Anabasis*. Xenophon allows his readers to see through his speech and recognize how he tries to manipulate his audience. He reverses a familiar move in modern rewritings of ancient history: he does not use religion as a cover for politics, but politics as a cover for religion. Yet the very openness with which he exposes his own deception of his fellow soldiers itself throws emphasis on the motive he rejects – the danger of alienating Sparta. And in due course Xenophon does fall under Spartan suspicions for being too friendly to the soldiers' interest – a demagogue even.[47]

Nowhere is Xenophon's speech-making more forcefully integrated with his political analysis than in his account of the army's troubles at Byzantium. After the Ten Thousand have been persuaded by a promise of pay to cross over the Hellespont into Europe, the Spartan admiral Anaxibius fails to give them the promised money and orders them out of Byzantium. The Greek mercenaries then launch an attack on the city, trying to cut down its gates and at the same time to enter it from the sea. There is panic in the city, and Anaxibius takes refuge in the citadel and sends for reinforcements, thinking that his own troops will not be able to control the mercenaries. At this point the Ten Thousand appeal to Xenophon 'to be a man': 'You have a city, you have triremes, you have money, you have all these men. Now, if you wanted, you could help us and we could make you great.' Earlier they had been unwilling to settle in a new city

46. *Anab.* 6.1.20–1.
47. *Anab.* 7.6.4.

on the Black Sea coast that would have increased the greatness of Greece. Now they want to make Xenophon great. How will Xenophon respond? 'You speak well,' he tells them, 'and I will do this. If you want this, form up in ranks as quickly as possible.' Has Xenophon – who has earlier presented himself as attracted by the thought of winning a great name – given in to these insubordinate troops? No: he at once adds that he said this 'wanting to calm them down'.[48] Here Xenophon makes explicit what was implicit in some of his earlier speeches. He is prepared to use cunning, and even deceit if necessary, to impose his will on the unruly troops.

When the soldiers have grounded arms and become calmer, Xenophon addresses them again. Now he is much more reflective. He starts by saying that he is not surprised at their anger – rather as Thucydides' Pericles told the disheartened Athenians that he expected their anger towards him and understood its causes. Xenophon goes on to insist that they look to the past to understand what it would mean to be pronounced the enemies of the Spartans and their allies. It is here that he conjures up the thought of the Peloponnesian War: the Athenians had ships, money, cities, and troops, but they were still crushed by the Spartans. His warning is the more forceful because it echoes a similar warning pronounced by Athenian envoys at Sparta before the start of the Peloponnesian War. Those envoys had also looked to the past – the Persian Wars in their case – in an attempt to deter the Spartans from making war on a city like Athens. Xenophon's strong warning wins the day: the Ten Thousand are now prepared to withdraw from Byzantium and endure the wrongs that have been done to them.[49]

Many readers of the *Anabasis* have greatly admired the speech through which Xenophon prevents the Ten Thousand from seizing and sacking Byzantium. The nineteenth-century historian George Grote, a great champion of Athenian democracy, wrote that 'no orator ever undertook a more difficult case, or achieved a fuller triumph over unpromising conditions', and 'never did his Athenian accomplishments . . . appear to greater advantage'. Elsewhere, too, in his account of the Ten Thousand Grote emphasized the Athenian qualities underlying Xenophon's great speeches. He compared Xenophon's speech rousing the Greek army after the seizure of the generals with Pericles' speech to the despondent Athenians; and he also praised Xenophon for showing the ability of Pericles and Demosthenes not 'to accommodate himself constantly

---

48. *Anab.* 7.1.21–2.
49. Pericles to the despondent Athenians: Thuc. 2.60.1. The envoys at Sparta: Thuc. 1.73.3.

to the prepossessions of his hearers' in his speech at Cotyora warning against the growth of indiscipline in the army.[50]

The Thucydidean parallels to which George Grote draws attention lie at the heart of Xenophon's self-presentation. Xenophon is at times Thucydides' Pericles, a model leader, inspiring the despondent – as in his speeches to the troops after the murder of their generals – and calming the overconfident – as when the troops are rioting at Byzantium. But the Thucydidean parallels do not always suggest so comfortable a picture. When Xenophon ponders whether to stand for the post of army supremo, he becomes more like some of Thucydides' more ambivalent characters. He veers between being a Brasidas or an Alcibiades and being a Nicias: he is like Brasidas and Alcibiades because he is attracted by a post that would boost his fame, while he is like Nicias because he is afraid of the uncertainties of the future.[51] Throughout, what Xenophon is doing is offering a thoughtful analysis of how the army works as a community, of how its leaders attempt to create order, of how some of its leaders in fact undermine the attempt to create order. As an analysis of the fragility of the attempt to create order, the *Anabasis* fits rather well the concerns of some of Xenophon's other works.

The *Anabasis*, it has emerged, is a work with ethical and didactic aspects, but also a powerfully analytical work – and a slightly ironic and pessimistic one. It is a neglected text for the study of anti-democratic discourse. But it is also a celebratory work. It was a great achievement to get back to Greece from the plains of Mesopotamia.

It is the celebratory aspect that most readers have admired. The *Anabasis* has become a sort of myth of liberation – of freedom for the Christians under the Ottomans, as in Romolo Amaseo's fanciful dedication; or of freedom for the Greeks (and by extension for all of us) at the time of their revolt against the Ottomans, as in Shelley's *Hellas*, which alludes briefly to the Ten Thousand's triumphant shout of 'The Sea, the Sea'. The myth of the *Anabasis* also lived on in the 'Anabasis' of the Czech Legion in Siberia at the end of the First World War – an army that had been fighting behind Russian lines against the Austro-Hungarian Empire, and then, when it found itself stranded after the treaty of Brest-Litovsk, refused a Russian command to disarm and set off towards Vladivostok with the plan of joining the newly formed Czech national

---

50. Athenian qualities: G. Grote, *A History of Greece* (London, 1904), vol. 7, pp. 328–9, 253, 310.
51. Attraction to a post that would boost his fame: cf. Thuc. 5.16.1, 6.15.2. Fear of the uncertainties of the future: cf. Thuc. 5.16.1.

army fighting on the Western Front. This Czech Anabasis even had some practical benefits: the achievement was used to promote the Czech claim for a nation-state. The myth of the *Anabasis* also lives on in the notion of the Long March itself. The march of the Ten Thousand has been used as a foil to the 'even more majestic achievement' of the Chinese Communists led by Chairman Mao: 'Alike, Greeks and Chinese ... climbed snow-covered mountains, ate roots, slept in the snow, marched, fought, and marched again. Alike, they reconciled internal disputes that threatened to tear them apart. Alike, they survived.'[52]

---

52. S. B. Griffith II, *The Chinese People's Liberation Army* (London, 1968), p. 47; cf. D. Wilson, *The Long March 1935: The Epic of Chinese Communism's Survival* (Harmondsworth and New York, 1977), pp. 15, 292.

12 You Can't Go Home Again: Displacement and Identity in Xenophon's Anabasis

JOHN MA

Introduction

Who I am, where I am. The relation between place and identity is brought into sharp relief by the tag which I made into this chapter's title: you can't go home again – a wistful middle-class American tag, about the impossibility of regaining the nest once flown, about the loss of childhood safety. The tag, 'you can't go home again' seemed to me appropriate because it encapsulated a major theme in the *Anabasis*: the relation between displacement and identity, as it appears in the ways in which change of place puts interesting stresses on individual and collective identities. I wish to read the *Anabasis* as a story of displacement and reintegration, attempted yet impossible, and try to relate this reading to a historical context, the fourth century, and to historical questions, the elaboration of identity in a context of displacement throughout Greek history, from the Archaic to the Hellenistic period.

Two moments drawn from Xenophon's narrative might make the theme clear. The first incident comes towards the end of the mercenaries' march towards the Black Sea, when they have reached the land of the Macronians.

> From there, the Greeks travelled through the land of the Macronians, for three days and ten parasangs. On the first day, they came to the river which separated the land of the Macronians and that of the Scytheni. They had on the right a position that looked very strong, and on the left another river, into which the river which formed the boundary flowed, the river which had to be crossed. This river was bordered with trees which were not thick, but close together. As the Greeks advanced, they cut down these trees, being eager to move away from the fortified position. The Macronians, who were equipped with wicker shields, lances, and hair tunics, had drawn themselves on the opposite side to the crossing point, and encouraged each other and threw stones into the river; these failed to reach their target and did no

harm. At this point there came to Xenophon one of the peltasts, who claimed he had been a slave at Athens, saying that he knew the language of these people. 'And I think', he said, 'that this is my fatherland. And if there is no objection, I want to speak to them.' 'There is no objection,' said Xenophon, 'speak to them and first find out who they are.' When the peltast had asked them, they said that they were Macronians. 'Ask then,' said Xenophon, 'why they are ranged against us and want to be our enemies.' They answered, 'Because you march against our land.' The generals ordered the peltast to say 'we do not come to harm you, but having fought against the king, we are returning to Greece, and we wish to reach the sea.' The Macronians asked if they would give pledges of this. The Greeks said they wanted to give and receive pledges. Then the Macronians gave a barbarian lance to the Greeks, and the Greeks gave them a Greek spear, since they had said these were the pledges; both called on the gods. Immediately after the exchange of pledges, the Macronians helped in cutting the trees and built the road, to make the Greeks pass through, mingling freely with the Greeks, and they provided a market for supplies as much as they could, and they led the Greeks on until in three days they had brought them to the frontiers of the Colchians.[1]

The geography is marked by obstacle, physical and human. Yet this landscape of physical and human obstacle soon turns to an arresting story of encounter and communication. Earlier, such communications were always imperfect. The Persians prove untrustworthy, from noble Cyrus to Tissaphernes. The Carduchi do not communicate, or only under duress; Armenians are lied to, or made to act as serving boys through gestures.[2]

Here, at last, the two parties communicate clearly, simply, through an interpreter. This particular individual is one of the rare slaves whose life story is known in any detail. Presumably, the Macronian was sold off as a boy by his kin, or captured in a raid. He ended up in classical Athens, that great consumer of slaves: the slave trade and its concomitant social impact (raiding, dislocation of local interaction) must have been one of democratic Athens's signal exports to lands on the margins of the classical world, and it is remarkable from how far to the east this particular victim came. I would guess that our Macronian slave ran off during the Deceleian War, somehow escaping

1. *Anab.* 4.8.1–8.
2. The uncommunicativeness of the Carduchi: *Anab.* 4.1. Dealings with the Armenians: *Anab.* 4.5.25–36.

re-enslavement by the Boeotians at Deceleia, or regaining his freedom.³ He perhaps fought as a peltast in Attica, on the Peloponnesian side, helping ravage the fields of his former owner's compatriots. After the end of the Peloponnesian War, he was recruited as a mercenary by Proxenus, marched with Cyrus to Babylonia, attended the battle at Cunaxa, marched on through the land of the Carduchi and Armenia, until one day he had the odd sensation of recognizing the language.

The story is astonishing enough in its details, as we can reconstruct them; but the careful description of the peltast's reaction is the most haunting feature of the incident, at least in our eyes. He has undergone social death: from identity to no identity. He has undergone enforced displacement from his homeland and from any social position he had, through being sold as a chattel slave. When he arrives back in the land of the Macronians, his reaction is curiously uncertain: I think this is my *patris*. There is no emotional recognition, or at least no way of expressing it, for our lost Odysseus: instead, a mixture of intellectual recognition and failed memory. What takes over is the military impulse to report to the commanding officer: the Macronian is now a peltast, and finds his identity in the military hierarchy which figures so importantly in the desired authoritarian politics of the *Anabasis*. No name is given for the peltast; how could there be? No indication is given on his fate: did he stay, did he go on? This absence of name and of final resolution are emblematic of the Macronian peltast's fate: on the move, he finds no identity, even when he returns home.⁴

The second incident occurs slightly later, when the Ten Thousand are celebrating athletic games near Trapezus, when they have reached the Black Sea.

> To take care of the racetrack and preside over the contest, they chose Dracontius, a Spartiate who had gone into exile in his boyhood because he had killed a boy accidentally by striking him with his whittling-knife [*xuēlē*]. And when the sacrifice had taken place, they handed over the hides to Dracontius, and they ordered him to lead them to where he had made the racetrack. But he showed the place where they were standing, and said, 'This

---

3. P. Hunt, *Slaves, Warfare and Ideology in the Greek Historian* (Cambridge, 1998), p. 169, also suggests manumission after Arginusae.
4. The Macronian certainly lost his native name once in Athens, to be called by a generic Greek name, or an ethnic name such as 'Paphlagonian' or 'Colchian' (see *ML* 79, line 44 for an example). On his role as translator, see D. Gera's paper on 'The figure of the translator in Xenophon's *Anabasis*' in the volume of proceedings from the conference at Liverpool in 2000, edited by C. Tuplin; Gera emphasizes Xenophon's lack of interest in the Macronian himself (as opposed to the instrumental usefulness as translator).

hill is best for running wherever one wishes.' 'But how', they said, 'will people be able to wrestle in a place so rough and overgrown?' He answered, 'Whoever falls will suffer the more.'[5]

Dracontius truly cannot go home again: he has been in exile, for decades, since his accidental killing of another boy, with the Spartan whittling-knife.[6] The incident recalls the competitive, ritualized Spartiate education; it acts as a reminder, to Dracontius, of the very specific and special place he has left forever. Dracontius' identity is frozen in a certain state of Spartiate life – the excessive harshness of the educative system, which in fact is only one point of the evolving identity of the Spartiate male, from the infant to the harshly treated boy to shining, manly, youthful hoplite hopeful of beautiful death to respected elder. Dracontius' self is frozen in the in-between space of boyhood, the transitory, reversed, deliberately harsh, *rite-de-passage* moment of boyhood.[7] Dracontius' Spartiate identity is an expatriate's parody, incomplete, misunderstood, within his own mythology of self, his own distorted version of his fatherland's practice. Living in his own private Sparta, did Dracontius wear a threadbare cloak in winter, sleep on a pallet of rushes, and steal his food? How did he relate to the other, real, Spartiates in the army, how did he meet their embarrassed or contemptuous eyes when their authenticity looked upon his made-upness? At least, he confidently enacts his Spartiateness before his companions, oblivious to their surprise, perhaps even their embarrassment, when they discover that in return for the privileges of *agōnothesia*, of superintending the games, he actually has done nothing, expecting the remembered tags of a Spartiate boyhood and his ostentatious Spartiate toughness to be enough, and perhaps even to excite admiration (as Spartiates are meant to do).

Recounting aporia, *experiencing déjà vu*

These stories about not going home fit into a broader text structured around the difficulty or impossibility of return. At first sight, the *Anabasis* is about

5. *Anab.* 4.8.26–7.
6. As T. Braun suggests to me, Dracontius presumably fled to Tegea, living there in exile. He may have been recruited by Sparta to join the not-so-secret military aid sent to Cyrus (*Anab.* 1.4.2–3; *Hell.* 3.1.) – with a promise of reinstatement in case of good service?
7. On all this, J.-P. Vernant, 'Between shame and glory: the identity of the young Spartan warrior', in F. Zeitlin (ed.), *Mortals and Immortals* (Princeton, 1991), ch. 13; also E. Kourinou-Pikoula, 'Mnama Geronteias', *HOROS* 10–12 (1992–8), pp. 259–76, for a recent epigraphical example.

going home: fighting, marching to sea, and back to the Greek cities: that is the shape in which the text is often remembered, and in fact Xenophon himself summarizes it thus when mentioning it as the account of 'Themistogenes of Syracuse'. But in fact, the *Anabasis* is much more complex: the protracted activity of 'going home' solves nothing; resolution and return are constantly deferred.[8]

From the start, going home was always going to be difficult. This even applies to Cyrus' attempted return to Persia, which leads him into a successor plot out of which he emerges with great trouble. Generally, the earlier part of the text is driven by Cyrus' relentless movement forward, through a disconcertingly changing landscape, in which the final goal is constantly deferred: the objective is the Pisidians, then the Lycaonians, then Abrocomas, and finally the Great King. The battle of Cunaxa itself is oddly disorienting: the enemies flee, the Greeks pursue into nothingness, a charge that settles nothing. This 'victory' leads to an unclear situation where the Greeks, on their way back, have to mount another charge, which again leads to no satisfactory, decisive resolution.[9]

This world of *aporia* is peopled by actors who are conscious of obstacles, and constantly speak of them. Very early on, in Cilicia, when Clearchus' men realize where they are going, they have to accept that there is no turning back, only *fuite en avant*: the realization is carefully, didactically set up by Clearchus. After Cunaxa, a whole series of speeches is devoted to the themes of distance and the impossibility of return.[10]

This awareness colours the Greeks' perception of the physical landscape, converting it to constant suspicion: rivers might be impassable; sluice gates are opened, trenches flooded. Once hostilities break out, this imagined landscape of hostility and obstruction turns all too real: the Greeks retreat in the face of Persian harassment, and they must deal with the obstacles posed by rivers and hills. The land of the Carduchi offers the threatening image of a place that is no place (*dyschōria*), where a whole Persian army once vanished.[11]

---

8. 'Themistogenes': *Hell.* 3.1.20. On the further narrative complexities of this volume, see also Rood, chapter 11 in this volume.
9. Cyrus' attempted return to Persia: *Anab.* 1.1.2–3. Lack of resolution at Cunaxa: *Anab.* 1.8; 1.10.4–7.
10. Realization in Cilicia: *Anab.* 1.3, esp. 1.3.16. Distance and the impossibility of return: *Anab.* 2.1.11; 2.4.5–7; 2.5.9.
11. Impassable rivers, flooded trenches: *Anab.* 2.3.10–13; 2.4.3. The land of the Carduchi: *Anab.* 3.5.36.

This image is realized in a geography of constant fighting, through passes and heights, a threatening geography of obstacle which the Greeks must overcome: they do so by the application of fluid, light infantry tactics, which unlock the passes and the heights, and turn these physical features into advantages against the human opponents who first exploited them. The Greeks' successes lead them to believe that they will emerge from the impassable landscape. The Colchians are presented as the last obstacle. Once the sea is reached, Leon of Thurii dreams of return, stretched out like Odysseus.[12]

But a curious déjà vu sets in: again we encounter speeches about obstacles, psychologies of distrust, and opacity in human interaction, starting with the dealings between the Ten Thousand and Hecatonymus of Sinope. The incidents on the march are about the same problems of geographical obstacles and entrapment by human opponents; both Paphlagonia and Bithynia prove to be places where one gets stuck, full of obstacles such as impassable gullies, and familiar-looking enemies, barbarians holding the passes and the high ground, and Persian cavalry (the horsemen of Pharnabazus); the Straits, once reached, become a human obstacle, as well as a geographical feature: Xenophon's dealings with Spartans are deeply murky, since they are ambivalent about whether the Ten Thousand should pass the Straits or not, and about where exactly they should go. The Spartans prove almost as treacherous and dangerous as the Persians in the earlier part of the work.[13] After creating an ideal, military community of Greeks, arrival among real Greeks leads to a much more complicated situation, and recreates, in ways often different, but with similar results, the cloud of uncertainty in human interaction which makes progress simultaneously the only solution and a very dubious proposition.

Xenophon himself tries to slip away to go home, on his own, only to be sent back from Parium to Byzantium; at the end, Xenophon, hoping to go home, embarks on a foray which leads to an odd mini-Anabasis, an expedition against an eminent Persian, with a messy fight, and, again, Greeks trapped by Persian forces. The abrupt, indeterminate ending of the whole work produces another effect of déjà vu – the survivors of Cyrus' expedition are in western Asia Minor, fighting against Tissaphernes, precisely back where they started.[14]

The whole story ends with no real escape, but only a starting over again. The *Anabasis* is about repetition: nested structures of obstacle and escape

12. The Colchians as the last obstacle: *Anab.* 4.8.14. Leon and Odysseus: *Anab.* 5.1.
13. Hecatonymus: *Anab.* 5.6.3. Impassable gullies: *Anab.* 6.4–5. Dealings with the Spartans: *Anab.* 6.6; 7.1.
14. Xenophon, Parium, and Byzantium: *Anab.* 7.1.40, 7.2.8. The 'mini-Anabasis': *Anab.* 7.7.

towards other obstacles. The gestures and narratives of sacrifice, divination and religion offer meaning and certainty. But the constant movement is corrosive of certainty; it subverts certainty about where one is going, except into a succession of trials where survival and loss are present in equal measure. In this context, we should return to Xenophon's dream of a thunderbolt setting on fire his paternal house. The first interpretation is suggested to us – Xenophon will escape this predicament. But in fact, once he achieves escape, Xenophon will find himself in exile – the paternal house is destroyed by fire, there is no going home. One escape from danger only leads to another situation where return is impossible; one exile leads to another.[15]

Displacement and identity: band of brothers?

As an introduction to this chapter, I looked at some cases where movement created dislocation of identity. Yet within the tale of impossible return, there also is a story of piecing together identities and creating, pragmatically, new ways of interacting with the self and the other, in constantly recreated contexts. The 'Odyssey' of the Ten Thousand is also the story of Odysseus-like experimentation with identity, under the pressures of survival and the constant changes in context and interaction brought about by movement. J. Dillery has shown how the *Anabasis* is about the creation of community. Staying alive entails staying together, creating a new form of community, which, in the march in Carduchia, takes on a new, rather non-*polis* or post-*polis* form: military, ordered, hierarchical, but collaborative, mobilized, and Hellenic: as P. Gauthier has shown, the Ten Thousand are never quite the '*polis* on the march' that they are sometimes said to be.[16]

The founding moment takes place in Babylon when, after the capture and murder of the generals, an ad hoc war council convenes in the murdered Menon's detachment. Apollonides' lack of resolution, his insistence on *aporiai*, and his view that safety only resides in petition to the King, endanger Xenophon's project to resist and to fight: all these traits are matched by his

---

15. On divination and religion, see Parker, chapter 4 in this volume. The dream of the thunderbolt: *Anab.* 3.1.11–13 (and cf. once more Parker). On dates and details of the exile, C. J. Tuplin, 'Xenophon's exile again', in Michael Whitby, Philip Hardie and Mary Whitby (eds), *Homo Viator: Classical Essays for John Bramble* (Bristol, 1987), pp. 59–69.
16. J. Dillery, *Xenophon and the History of his Times* (London, 1995), pp. 59–98. P. Gauthier, 'Xénophon et l'odyssée des "Dix-Mille"' in C. Mossé (ed.), *La Grèce ancienne* (Paris, 1986), pp. 237–69.

foreignness. He is opposed by Hagesias of Stymphalia, the tough Arcadian, an image of Hellenic authenticity (his plainness, bravery, *aretē* are a leitmotiv in the work): he duly detects Apollonides' foreignness – the latter is a soft, earring-wearing Lydian. This is no time for half measures, cultural interaction or curious exploration; the Other is driven out into the nowhere of *aporia* and danger, where his fate remains unknown and no matter of concern. We might wonder about Apollonides' story: whether he was indeed a Lydian who learned Aeolian Greek in Cyme or Phocaea, and hence sounded 'Boeotian', if not completely convincing, to mainland Greeks; or perhaps a Boeotian who had spent time (during the Ionian War?) in Lydia. If the former, Hellenism was brutally redefined as descent based, in terms of ethnic character; if the latter, then the members of the council that night invented a convenient Other out of one of their own comrades, and cast him out. The remaining Greeks, defined by solidarity, after this primal, scapegoating scene of Greekness, can later listen to a speech by Xenophon in which he proceeds to a localized reworking of Greek history, especially the Persian Wars, a privatized, instrumentalized 'invention de la Grèce', borrowing from Athenian rhetoric to create a community of Greeks from the mercenaries lost in Babylonia. The specifically Athenian elements are blurred, to enable the cooptation of the Persian Wars as a 'national past' by the diverse groups of mercenaries.[17]

For now, this new community becomes the only community. Clearchus had already said to his own contingent: I think that you are my *patris*, my *philoi*, my *summachoi*. At that time, the Greek mercenaries existed not as a group, but as several contingents with their leaders and their own solidarities: in a dispute between his men and Menon's, he decided the latter were the culprits, and struck a man in Menon's contingent, nearly leading to a pitched battle between the two bodies of mercenaries. Yet later, after Cunaxa, during the 'phony war' between Clearchus and Tissaphernes, and when the Greeks already exist as a single body, his fearsomeness has become accepted by all. As the Greeks struggle to cross muddy canals by bridging them with palm trunks, Clearchus rains blows with his Spartiate stick, but these are now recontextualized whacks: his Spartan traits of looking out for his men, and applying violence to subordinates, now produce the social goods of collaboration and hard work beyond

17. The war council at Babylon: *Anab.* 3.1.26–30. Xenophon's 'Invention de la Grèce': *Anab.* 3.2.10–12; the phrase refers to N. Loraux's study of Athenian self-fashioning in funerary rhetoric, *L'Invention d'Athènes*; Eng. trans. *The Invention of Athens: The Funeral Oration in the Classical City* (Cambridge, Mass., 1986). My attention was drawn to this passage in a paper by an undergraduate at Princeton, M. Poe.

one's duty: *suspeudein* is the word used. It also recalls a similar situation: Cyrus' order to his noblemen to help a chariot out of the mud – *suspeudein* is also used. Clearchus' violence now participates in a new project, the emergence of a disciplined, hierarchical military community, similar to Cyrus' entourage of mobilized and loyal Persians. Clearchus' Spartan bloody-mindedness and violence become good things; so do the Rhodians' skill with the sling, exploited to create an ad hoc body of slingers, or the Cretans' skill at light infantry warfare.[18]

The new Hellenic community picks and mixes pragmatically; identity and survival collaborate. Later, when the forward movement of the Ten Thousand has taken them forward to the Black Sea and its frustrating world of postwar politics and unhelpful Greek cities, older loyalties reassert themselves: the soldiers parade *kata ethnē*, by ethnic groups rather than the contingents which form the Ten Thousand's original, specific subdivisions; later, the Arcadians and Achaeans secede, driven by their own interests and their memories of their earlier, pre-expedition identities: 'it was shameful that an Athenian and a Spartan should command Peloponnesians, when neither had provided troops'.[19] The seceding body is all made up of hoplites, in contrast to the diverse, multi-tasking army of the Ten Thousand; the Arcadians get into serious trouble, and have to be rescued by the rest of the army, after which the army is reunited, passing a decree against any future proposal to split up, and reconstituting the original regiments which left with Cyrus the previous year: the formal corporate decision both embodies as well as imposes unity. Unthinking adherence to earlier identities is disastrous; in the new community, with its pragmatic identity-making, lies safety.

The Ten Thousand as community can create their own memories and culture. I earlier analysed Dracontius' rootless identity. But in the context of the Ten Thousand, it proves good enough for the there and then: it provides the opportunity for a good joke; more importantly, the contests turn out to be a splendid affair, *kalē thea*.[20] Slave boys race the *stadion*, no less than sixty Cretans run the double *stadion*, the oddly shaped race track makes for a gripping horse-race, complete with whoops and laughter and encouragement by the mercenaries' women. Out of the disparate elements at hand (slaves, exiles, camp-followers, mercenaries from different backgrounds), the occasion allows for the improvisation of community.

18. 'My *patris*, my *philoi*': *Anab.* 1.3.6. Clearchus' ferocity accepted: *Anab.* 2.3.11. Cyrus and the wagon in the mud: *Anab.* 1.5.7–8. The Rhodian slingers: *Anab.* 3.3.16.
19. Parade *kata ethnē*: *Anab.* 5.5.5. Secession of the Arcadians and Achaeans: *Anab.* 6.2.
20. *Anab.* 4.8.27–8.

Just as revealing is the scene of ethnic dancing. The dances, whatever their original context (symposiastic or festive), are used for a purpose, to entertain but also to intimidate the Paphlagonians, by giving an image of the prowess, the diversity but also the unity of the Ten Thousand: fencing, light infantry raiding and footwork, hoplitic square-bashing. (The Paphlagonians duly ask for alliance after these terrifying displays.) The dances also include an improvisation, now commemorating the Ten Thousand's own folklore: a female dancer performs the *pyrrichē*, and the Paphlagonians are told that the women not only fight, but drove off the King from the Greek camp (in reality, Xenophon tells us, Cyrus's mistresses were captured, though one of them, 'the Milesian, the younger one', slipped away naked). A dance is invented to cap traditional performances; the event captures a shared memory, refers to common achievement, and adds a private joke.[21]

For this ad hoc community, the temptation or the desire is to find place; to look at a landscape otherwise than as a sequence of battle scenes; to convert strategic and tactical space – the space of march and supplies, of battle terrain, of frontal assault and clever flanking moves, of ambushes and high ground, of tactical problems and hard fighting, the landscape of the Ten Thousand's war – into a place of one's own, where identity and community could exist fully.[22]

The temptation is there from the start, at least as a jibe or a joke. Xenophon professes fear that the Greeks might want to stay in Babylonia, comparing the Greeks to the Lotus-Eaters. The temptation to stay on is used rhetorically to transform the threatening landscape into a landscape where the Greeks are empowered to stay or leave; the same figure is used in Thucydides' portrayal of the Sicilian expedition.[23]

But rhetoric soon turns into desire: this mass of armed men which turns into a community evokes the possibility of settling down as a *polis*, the only move needed to convert this guild of warriors into a city-state, under the paternal leadership of Xenophon himself. Since the mass of armed men is one of the ways in which a *polis* likes to imagine itself, the reflex is to find a place to realize the potential. Calpes Limen is described at length, in a description which, for the first time, gives a sense of place, of possible syzygy between

21. Ethnic dancing: *Anab.* 6.1.7–12. The escape of Cyrus' mistress: *Anab.* 1.10.3.
22. On place as a lived, human reality, Y.-F. Tuan, 'Space and place: humanistic perspectives', *Progress in Geography* 6 (1974), pp. 211–46.
23. The Lotus-Eaters: Anab. 3.2.25. Compare Thuc. 7.70.8: Athenian generals ask shirkers if they find this most hostile of lands more familiar than the sea; cf. also Nicias' last speech, Thuc. 7.77.5, you are so powerful *qua* polis, that no city in Sicily could resist you or uproot you if you settled: fighting is like home. On the rhetoric of colonization and the army as *polis*, see also Hornblower, chapter 8 in this volume.

the community and a geographical setting. But it is only one of many locales mentioned as possible places to stay on: north-western Asia Minor and Chersonese are evoked, as well as Phasis, Byzantium, and the various places proposed by Seuthes to Xenophon himself.[24]

But this desire is constantly frustrated: the soldiers want to go home and hence condemn themselves to the move and to this identity without place. When soldiers are interested in settling in Byzantium, setting up Xenophon as a tyrant, he is terrified of the Spartan reaction. The common identity is centred on a common project: keep moving, get out of here; identity is not founded on 'being there', but precisely on an 'elsewhere': coming from elsewhere, going elsewhere. Contradiction lies in the shared project itself: it creates, but also destroys community.[25] In the end, the temptation is simply to slip away, as even Xenophon tries to do.

The other way in which finding a place figures in the *Anabasis* is the desire for social situatedness, for a place within a network of benefaction and *charis*. Clearchus' speech early on lays out this theme: he tells his soldiers, 'I think that I am *timios* [honoured] among you, because I can do good to people.' Xenophon insists that most people went not for profit or poverty but out of the honourable desire to increase social substance, by coming back richer and being able to help – starting with one's family, but presumably also one's friends; in other words, to gain honour.[26] Xenophon's own desire, visible at the end, is that of being able to do good, *eu poiēsai*, to his friends; to be someone in a network of reciprocity. Cyrus offered precisely this possibility; once Xenophon lost this best friend he never had, the same desire colours Xenophon's stay with the Thracian dynast Seuthes. There, too, the dream of social substantification through interaction with a potentate ended badly (though Xenophon finally did get rich thanks to the final *coup de main* on Asidates' estate).

Both these ways of being there, being someone – locally rooted community, and social context – come together in Xenophon's description of the sacred estate at Skillous. Xenophon finds an identity, but a constructed one: the reference is not Xenophon's Athens, but Ephesus, a reminder of places he has been to, and adventures he has experienced; cult, architecture and hydrography

24. Calpes Limen: *Anab.* 6.4.1–6. Other locales canvassed: *Anab.* 5.6.19–25; 5.6.36–7.9; 7.1.21; 7.2.38.
25. The desire for home: *Anab.* 6.4. Settling at Byzantium: *Anab.* 7.1.21–31. The contradictions of the shared project: Dillery, *Xenophon and the History of his Times*, pp. 59–98.
26. On *charis*, see Azoulay, chapter 10 in this volume. 'I think that I am *timios*': *Anab.* 1.3.6. Gaining honour: *Anab.* 6.4.8.

hark back to Ephesus, in a sort of personal myth of colonization gathering echoes meaningful to Xenophon in terms of his personal history. In this place, festival creates community, from local citizens, travellers (perhaps pilgrims on their way to Olympia), neighbours, women; hunting involves Xenophon's sons and all comers, *hoi boulomenoi*. The latter phrase is not a political expression as in Athens, but designates the festival community and its apolitical basis. At last, a place to be, where money has been used to create social relations and local meanings; at last, somewhere for Xenophon to develop his desire for place, over the years and thanks to collective religious experience. But there also is a twist: the play of tenses hints at a difference between the things that stay the same, in the present tense, and the imperfect, which might suggest loss, probably Xenophon's exile from Skillous after 371. The inscription is curiously impersonal and periphrastic, and already implies future absence: 'The place is sacred to Artemis. Let him who holds it and exploits it offer the tithe every year, and out of the remaining income repair the temple. If one does not do that, it will be the goddess's concern.' Even here, finding place is uncertain.[27]

Towards a history of Greek identities on the move

The fourth century, as everyone knows, started in 404 (just as the eighteenth ended in 1815 and the nineteenth in 1914): in this respect, the story of the *Anabasis* belongs to the fourth century. It is all the more justified to start by considering this text in a fourth-century context because it was written in the course of that century, and because its theme of displacement resonates in that great century of migration. The *Anabasis* itself is peopled with exiles (starting with Clearchus), as is Xenophon's *Hellenica*. The *Anabasis* also shows freebooting Greeks searching for military or court positions in non-Greek contexts, the fourth-century 'brawn drain': Phalinus the military instructor, Coeratadas the unsuccessful condottiere from Boeotia, Heraclides of Maronea at Seuthes' court.[28]

---

27. The estate at Skillous: *Anab*. 5.3.7–13 (present tense: 11–13). I owe the notion of 'festival community' to P. Martzavou.
28. Chronology of the *Anabasis*: cf. Cawkwell, chapter 1 in this volume. Exiles of the *Hellenica*: *Hell*. 5.2–3; 7.4.3. Note also *Mem*. 1.18, being deprived of one's city features among the unknowables in life, if you marry into a grand family; among the epigraphical references, *SEG* XXVI, no. 1282, Tod 141–2. On Coeratadas, see Parker, chapter

Should we read the *Anabasis* as a text about fourth-century free-floating *particules élémentaires*, indeed, as a text written by one of these free-floating elements? P. McKechnie, among others, has argued for the increasing importance of mobility and individuals in the fourth century, culminating (in his view) with the King's Friends of the Hellenistic age. Does the *Anabasis* show the fourth century to be an age of 'rootless individuals'? McKechnie himself warns us against any such facile assumption, in view of the evidence for the continued relevance of *polis* ideology and institutions; a recent collection of essays on the fourth century, edited by P. Carlier, shows the complexity of the period, and the persistence of *polis* identity into the Hellenistic period. How to read the *Anabasis* within its century?[29]

The *Anabasis* is precisely not a text about 'rootless individuals', but the relation between migration and the desire for identity. Identities are on the move, but also being made on the move, as in the case of the improvised, pragmatic community of the Ten Thousand. A striking example of identity on the move occurs early on in the *Anabasis*. The Arcadian mercenaries in Cyrus' guard celebrate an Arcadian festival, the Lycaea, under their officer, Xenias of Parrhasia, one of Cyrus' original Greek captains (he later deserts from the expedition, leaving his relatives behind as Cyrus' hostages). The Arcadians must have kept a calendar; on their march, they packed the gilt fillets for the victors. But what is the status of the festival when celebrated in Phrygia rather than south-west Arcadia? Is it a private version of the official festival? What is the status of the athletic victors? Is the celebration of a festival about time rather than place? Is it about those who celebrate? How unusual was this sort of phenomenon? What needs are being fulfilled by the gesture? All these and many other questions are raised by this celebration. These questions reflect our curiosity, but were already implied in 401, by the completion of ritual out of context; yet the ritualized nature of the occasion perhaps subordinated such questions ('just what are we doing?') to the creation of community feeling ('who are we?'), literally on the march: the Arcadian mercenaries reaffirmed their group identity by performing their local festival before their Persian employer and his court, non-Greek soldiers, and other Greeks. A later parallel may be found in the fragments of Callimachus: Pollis of Athens keeps the

---

4 in this volume. The 'brawn drain' (an expression I owe to E. Fantham): *Anab.* 2.1.7, 7.1.33–41, 7.3.16.

29. P. McKechnie, *Outsiders in the Greek Cities in the Fourth Century BC* (London and New York, 1989). P. Carlier, *Le IVe siècle av. J.-C. Approches historiographiques* (Paris, 1996); see especially the concluding essay by J. M. Bertrand, pp. 369–81.

Attic festival calendar in Alexandria, and celebrates the Feast of Cups with friends.[30]

And what if Xenophon had founded a city – the *polis* of the Calpitae, or the Limenitae? We might now know about its fortifications and its harbour, thanks to early modern and modern travellers and more recent (but still badly published) excavation. We could ponder its Arcadian onomastics, myths, cults and festivals, notably the Lycaea (alluded to on fine bronze and silver coinage). We would have found a *temenos*, probably for an *oikist*, in the agora, [..3–4..]phon son of Gryllus; we could meditate evidence for cultural exchange with nearby Persian elites, but also subordinate Paphlagonian villages. We would debate the city's economy, and especially the evidence for trade relations across the Black Sea and with the Aegean. Amphora stamps would tell us of imports: some wine, and much olive oil. Solid, old-fashioned historical geography would allow us to guess at probable resources, especially timber (we would examine nineteenth-century travellers and pore over twentieth-century Turkish maps). Hellenistic decrees would inform us of institutions, Panhellenic in inspiration and names; the local funerary *stelae* would show evidence of a surprisingly martial culture, throughout the fourth and third centuries. For this imaginary city of Xenophon's desire, I have of course been summarizing an imaginary article by L. Robert. What matters is that this virtual city of the very early fourth century can be imagined in Hellenistic or 'pre-Hellenistic' terms, and could have been treated with the same attention to invented identity, cultural politics and Hellenism which L. Robert devoted to the Hellenistic city at Ai Khanoum, founded in the very late fourth century or the early third.[31]

Both the Lycaea and the potential cultural history of Xenophon's intended city are 'pre-Hellenistic', in that they fall before the formal definition of the

30. The Lycaea: Anab. 1.2.10, and cf. also Parker in this volume. The Feast of Cups: Callim. frag. 178.
31. If need be, here are some imaginary references, drawn from the library of L. Robert's great unwritten books: see generally L. Robert, 'Cultes et onomastique de Calpè', in *La Bithynie*, vol. 1, pp. 27–118 (cf. *Hellenica* 14, pp. 279–83; *Paysages et gens d'Anatolie*, pp. 422–31 and plates 14–15 with captions, especially for travellers' accounts, abundantly quoted; *Noms indigènes de l'Asie Mineure*, vol. 2, 12 n. 5 and index s.v. Calpè, for the mix of Arcadian, Persian and Paphlagonian onomastics). To leave the realm of fictional scholarship: for Robert on Ai Khanoum, see 'De Delphes à l'Oxus. Incriptions grecques nouvelles de la Bactriane', *Comptes rendus de l'Académie des inscriptions et belles lettres* (1968), pp. 416–57, reprinted in *OMS* 5, pp. 510–51.

Hellenistic period, but show close similarity with the characteristics of the Hellenistic world. This similarity invites us to consider the phenomena of migration and identities on the move. For the Hellenistic period, mobility coexisted with strong *polis* identity, as can be seen in the institutions of peer polity interaction between *poleis* in this period: one striking example is the *syngeneia* politics between 'kindred' communities related by myth.[32]

But exile, *anastasis*, and emigration can also be seen in the archaic period: witness the Phocaeans' saga after their emigration when the Persian came; Arion striking it rich in Sicily, misguidedly wishing to entrust his person and his cash only to a good Corinthian ship; the astonishing trajectory of Democedes of Croton, who finally did manage to get home, where all his Persian-gained wealth allowed him to cut a dashing figure in his home town and contract a good marriage; and especially, the case of the Samian aristocrats, exiled by Polycrates, who went on an Aegean spree and founded Cydonia, in East Crete, where they lived happily before the Aeginetans intervened to destroy their *polis* and their corporate existence. All these incidents come from Herodotus; Thucydides provides equally striking instances for the fifth century: the Aeginetans in the Thyreatis, the Plataeans settled in Scione, the Delians in the Troad, during the Peloponnesian War.[33]

In all these periods, individual mobility and group identity, even community coexist. We are not dealing with floating individuals, but a complex relation between mobility and community. What matters is not the supposed existence of 'floating individuals', but the impact which the experience of floating had on the issues of identity and place: it resulted in a nexus of inventiveness and memory. The *Anabasis* is both a document about and an artefact produced by these processes. It points to a swathe of experience, shared by the individual exiles, as well as the groups waiting to go home, the fourth-century exiles which opened this section: the Thespians and Orchomenians who waited till 338 to go home, the Samians who waited till 323 until, to the Athenians' anger, they started swarming back to their island from the neighbouring cities which had sheltered them, and all those who never went

---

32. 'Pre-Hellenistic': F. Millar, 'The Phoenician cities: a case-study of Hellenisation', *PCPhS* 209 (1983), pp. 55–71. *Syngeneia* politics: O. Curty, *Les Parentés légendaires entre cités grecques* (Geneva, 1995); C. P. Jones, *Kinship Diplomacy in the Ancient World* (Harvard, 1999); see also Parker in this volume. I hope to return to Hellenistic 'peer polities'.
33. Herodotean examples: Hdt. 1.23; 3.129–37; 3.57–60. See also N. Purcell, 'Mobility and the *polis*', in O. Murray and S. Price (eds), *The Greek City from Homer to Alexander* (Oxford, 1990), pp. 29ff. Thucydidean examples: Thuc. 2.27.2, 5.32.1, 8.108.4.

You Can't Go Home Again 345

home – the Proconnesians who died in exile after Cyzicus took over their island, the scattered Olynthians after the capture of their city by Philip II.[34]

In this chapter, I tried to show that displacement takes its toll on identity, but also that it can prove a boon for it. Umberto Eco, in an essay on his *patris*, Alessandria (Piedmont), tells a small story about an immigrant which might balance the two Xenophontic stories at the opening of this paper. Aged twenty, Salvatore leaves his home town for Australia, where he spends forty long years working and saving. At sixty, Salvatore embarks on the long journey home. As the train finally brings him closer Salvatore's excitement grows. Will anyone still know him? Will he find his boyhood friends? Will they recognize him, ask for stories about kangaroos and Aborigines? At the deserted, sweltering station, Salvatore sees an old railway employee. In spite of the now worn face and sloping frame, he recognizes his old school mate, Giovanni. Salvatore walks towards Giovanni, pointing at his own face with a trembling finger: 'It's me, I'm back.' Giovanni turns towards Salvatore, and says, 'Hello Salvatore, are you leaving us?'[35]

---

34. Generally, McKechnie, *Outsiders in the Greek Cities*, pp. 34–51. Proconnessus: L. Robert, *Monnaies grecques* (Geneva and Paris, 1967), pp. 15–22, with L. Robert, *Hellenica*, vol. 2 (Paris, 1946), pp. 88–90. For a parallel, see G. Duby on the agglutinative tendencies ('société granuleuse') of the freebooting young men of the eleventh and twelfth centuries: G. Duby, *William Marshal: The Flower of Chivalry* (London, 1986). Mobility and associative tendencies precisely coexist.
35. Appropriately (or not), I only know this story from a French translation: U. Eco, *Comment voyager avec un saumon. Nouveaux pastiches et postiches* (Paris, 1997), p. 272. The Italian original can be found (I assume) in *Il secondo diario minimo* (1992) – *non vidi*.

Contributors

GEORGE CAWKWELL came to Oxford as a New Zealand Rhodes Scholar in 1946 and became the Ancient History Fellow at University College, Oxford in 1949. His writings include *Philip of Macedon* (1978), *Thucydides and the Peloponnesian War* (1997), and numerous articles on Greek history.

P. J. STYLIANOU is a Research Associate of the A. G. Leventis Foundation. Presently a Senior Visiting Research Fellow of the Centre for the Study of Ancient Documents at the University of Oxford, he is the author of *A Historical Commentary on Diodorus Siculus Book 15* (1998).

THOMAS BRAUN served as an Oxford University Lecturer in Ancient History from 1963 to 2002, a Tutorial Fellow of Merton College, Oxford from 1963 to 1999, and a Senior Research Fellow from 1999 to 2002. His publications include 'The Greeks and the Near East', in *The Cambridge Ancient History 2nd ed. III (3)* (1982).

ROBERT PARKER is Wykeham Professor of Ancient History in the University of Oxford. He has published *Miasma: Pollution and Purification in Early Greek Religion* (1983) and *Athenian Religion: A History* (1996); a sequel to the latter, *Polytheism and Society at Athens*, is forthcoming.

CHRISTOPHER TUPLIN is Professor of Ancient History at the University of Liverpool. His publications include *The Failings of Empire* (1993), *Achaemenid Studies* (1996), *Xenophon and his World* (ed., 2004), and numerous papers on Xenophon, the Achaemenid Empire, and classical Greek history.

ROBIN LANE FOX is a Fellow of New College and Reader in Ancient History at the University of Oxford. His publications include *Alexander the Great* (1975).

MICHAEL WHITBY is Professor of Classics and Ancient History at the University of Warwick. He is the co-editor of *The Cambridge History of Ancient*

Warfare (2004–5), and author of *The Emperor Maurice and his Historian: Theophylact Simocatta on Persian and Balkan Warfare* (1988).

SIMON HORNBLOWER is Professor of Classics and Ancient History at University College, London. He is writing a commentary on Thucydides (two volumes so far) and has published on Herodotus as well. He edited and contributed to *Greek Historiography* (1994). His latest book is *Thucydides and Pindar: Historical Narrative and the World of Epinikian Poetry* (2004).

JAMES ROY is Reader in Greek History at the University of Nottingham. He has written several articles on the *Anabasis*.

V. AZOULAY teaches Greek history at the University of Marne-la-Vallée. His works include several papers on Xenophon and a forthcoming book, *Xenophon et les Graces du pouvoir. De la charis au charisme*.

TIM ROOD is Fellow and Tutor in Classics at St Hugh's College, Oxford. He is the author of *Thucydides: Narrative and Explanation* (1998) and *The Sea! The Sea! The Shout of the Ten Thousand in the Modern Imagination* (2004), as well as several articles on Greek historiography.

JOHN MA is Fellow and Tutor in Ancient History at Corpus Christi College, Oxford. His publications include *Antiochos III and the Cities of Western Asia Minor* (1999).

Index

Abrocomas   15–16, 18, 50, 54, 110, 120, 156, 163, 279
Achaeans   85, 223, 272–3, 338
Aeneas Tacticus   30
Aeschylus   126
Agesilaus   65, 87, 100, 122, 161, 178, 194, 205, 224–5, 271, 287, 313
Alcibiades   18, 31, 82, 84, 104, 106, 177, 190, 321, 328
Alexander the Great   1, 10, 19, 22, 24, 26–7, 36, 44, 54–5, 57, 187, 190, 192, 200, 223, 233–4, 240, 242, 245, 252, 256, 259, 260–61, 306
Anabasis
    as apologia   21–2, 73, 137, 216–17, 289, 296, 299, 322
    date of composition of   47–50, 307
    MS tradition of   7–8
    'Pan-Hellenism' in   64–7, 181–3, 306–20
    reception of   2–4, 45–6, 185–6, 244, 306, 308–9, 313, 327–9
    speeches in   309–28
    use of notes in composition of   30, 51–9, 75–8
Antony, Mark   2, 232, 241, 305
Apollonides   204, 336–7
Arcadians   267, 272–88, 338, 342

Ariaeus   20, 77, 95, 137, 157, 198
Aristippus   16–17, 198–9, 265
Aristophanes   64
Arrian   1–2, 89, 212, 245
Artaxerxes II   1, 12–13, 15, 18–20, 92, 110, 115, 117–18, 122, 124, 126, 155–6, 169, 201
Asidates   9–10, 152, 167, 171, 213, 278, 312
athletics   191–2, 338

Belesys   120, 162–3
Bisitun inscription   20, 110, 114–15, 121
Brasidas   230–1, 233, 249, 257, 328

Cape Jason   28–9
Carduchia   11, 21, 79–80, 155, 172, 174–5, 185–6, 196, 199, 206, 233, 235–7
Carrhae   232, 241
Chirisophus   55, 60, 62, 86–7, 96, 185, 189, 223, 233, 236, 266
    Xenophon's attitude towards   63, 72–3, 321
Cilician–Syrian Gates   89, 167
Clearchus   4, 17, 20, 31, 51, 82–3, 85–6, 97–107, 112, 160, 222, 224, 225, 266, 272, 282, 313, 337, 340

Index

Coeratadas 10, 142–3
Constitution of the Spartans 193
Crusades 203–4
Ctesias 6, 19–20, 49–50, 53, 56, 69, 76, 90–95, 122–4, 129, 155, 157, 174, 228
Cunaxa 1, 5, 10, 19, 22, 34, 77, 87, 91–4, 101–2, 155, 174, 224–8, 240, 267, 307
Cyropaedia 48, 110, 126, 159, 165, 197–8, 203, 211–14, 244, 298, 316, 324
Cyrus (the Great) 106, 119, 126, 198
Cyrus (the Younger) 1, 12–20, 34, 66–7, 160, 162, 200, 206, 225, 227, 278–9, 299, 310
    death of 19–20
    Xenophon's attitude towards 49–50, 54, 107–30

Darius I 114–15, 119, 121, 125, 172
Deinon 20, 158
Diodorus Siculus 6, 50, 53, 60–61, 68–96, 102–3, 111, 122, 126, 174, 225, 227–8, 267, 279, 313, 319, 322
divination 133, 135, 141–6, 149–51
Dracontius 202, 333
dreams 148–9, 282, 335
drinking 188–9

Eco, Umberto 345
Ephorus 18, 31, 50, 61, 102, 122
    relationship to *Hell. Oxy.* 62, 82, 87, 103, 111
    relationship to Xenophon's *Anabasis* 61, 68–96, 314, 319
Episthenes 6, 195, 197
Euclid of Phleious 8, 153, 302

eunuchs 159–60
Euripides 259

gender issues 156, 193–203, 281
Gibbon, Edward 244, 305
gift-culture 210–11
Gorgias 181, 187, 199
Grote, George 327–8

Hamilton, William J. 40–2
Harpasus 23–4, 44
'healthy-mindedness' 132–3
Hecataeus 53, 57
Hellas 10, 32, 164, 186, 189
Hellenica 5, 12, 55, 58–9, 61, 83, 133–6, 161, 178, 307, 311
Herodotus 55–7, 64, 110, 135–6, 158–9, 165, 196–7, 200, 208–9, 216, 248, 250, 258, 311, 320
Homer 210–11
honey 9, 36–45, 79, 82
horses 10–11, 168
hunting 109, 186–7

Isocrates 64–5, 84, 122, 181, 225, 228–9, 276, 295, 306, 315

Julian 229–30

Karanos 162
Kinneir, John Macdonald 3, 23, 28, 43–4

languages 51, 53, 119–20, 158, 163, 185, 204–6, 260, 331–2
Larisa 51–3, 166, 207
Libanius 207
Lycaea 139–40, 342–3

Medeius   27, 213
'Media'   165
Memorabilia   197
Menon   20, 86, 101, 116, 187, 198–9, 224, 265, 277–9, 286–7, 337
Mespila   52–3, 166, 207–9
Mitford William   313, 320

Neon   60, 135, 145, 235, 272, 281

Parysatis   9, 12, 20, 51, 114, 124–5, 157, 167, 170
Persians
    Persian dress   160
    Persian gold   290
    Persian measures   172
    Persian 'truth-telling'   26, 110
    Persian women   156, 201
    Xenophon's attitude towards   212–14
Pharnabazus   14, 18, 33–4, 92, 104, 162, 177, 205, 235, 311, 313, 331
Phoinikistes   158
Pindar   126–7, 247–8
Plato   128
Plutarch   101–2, 225–8, 240, 267, 307
Polyaenus   31, 105–6
Polybius   306
Proxenus   51, 54, 77, 86–7, 101, 146–7, 187, 199, 268, 272, 286, 299

Rhodogune   157–8

Seuthes   21–2, 31–2, 47, 106, 138–9, 190–91, 206, 208–10, 277, 280, 283, 291–5, 312, 324, 340

Silanus   152, 282
Sinope   30, 178–9, 291, 318, 324
Skillous   47–8, 137–8, 167–8, 285, 300–01, 340–41
Socrates   10, 12, 20, 55, 108–9, 113, 115, 117, 126, 132–3, 147, 193, 197, 322
Sophaenetus   6, 50–51, 61–2, 69–74
Syennesis   90, 123, 163
Symposium   131–2, 133, 193
Syngeneia   138–9, 142f., 292
Syracuse, Athenian defeat at   230, 233, 237, 241, 244–5, 251, 257–9

'Ten Thousand', the
    ages of   271–2, 284
    command structure of   244–5, 262–3, 268
    desire for return of   280–84, 287, 333–4
    Hoplite warfare and   220–22, 239–41, 268–70, 276
    military composition of   217–19, 223, 266
    raiding activities of   224, 278, 302, 312, 335
    relations with Sparta of   16, 32–5, 83–4, 91, 94, 319, 335
Thalatta, Thalatta   1, 3, 11, 21–2, 35, 80–81
Theces, Mount   39, 79, 142, 317
'Themistogenes of Syracuse'   322, 334
Thibron   32, 35, 194–5, 278
Thucydides   196, 200, 216, 230, 245–6, 275, 310, 321, 324, 327–8
Timoleon   128–9
Tiribazus   26, 162–3, 165, 190, 308

Index

Tissaphernes 21, 35, 91, 93–5, 98–9, 107–8, 110–12, 119–21, 124, 149, 156–7, 160, 169–71, 206, 225, 320, 337

wages 116, 268, 292–3, 295–304
Wall of Media 20, 77
Ward, Frank Kingdom Ward 38
Ways and Means 204

Xenia 118, 290–91, 294–5, 299–300
Xenias 15, 118, 139, 265, 279, 284, 342

Xenophon
   as 'artful reporter' 5, 9, 98, 135, 264–5, 309
   evasiveness and silences of 17, 20, 23–31, 43–5, 51, 55, 58, 61, 72–3, 83, 109
   works: see under individual titles
Xerxes 119–20, 125, 172, 208, 311, 314

Zab, Greater 10–11, 55, 235
Zab, Lesser 55, 58, 231, 235–6